Marketing in Travel and Tourism

Marketing in Travel and Tourism

Fourth edition

Victor T. C. Middleton,
Alan Fyall and Michael Morgan,
with contributions from Ashok Ranchhod

LONDON AND NEW YORK

First published 1988 by Butterworth-Heinemann
Second edition 1994
Third edition 2001
Fourth edition 2009

Published 2013 by Routledge
2 Park Square, Milton Park, Abingdon, Oxon OX14 4RN
711 Third Avenue, New York, NY, 10017, USA

Routledge is an imprint of the Taylor & Francis Group, an informa business

British Library Cataloguing in Publication Data
A catalogue record for this book is available from the British Library.

Library of Congress Cataloging-in-Publication Data
Middleton, Victor T.C.
Marketing in travel and tourism / Victor T.C. Middleton; with Alan Fyall, Mike Morgan and Ashok Ranchhod. – 4th ed.
p.cm.
Includes bibliographical references and index.
ISBN 978-0-7506-8693-8
1. Tourism–Marketing. I. Fyall, Alan. II. Morgan, Michael. III. Ranchhod, Ashok. IV. Title.
G155.A1M475 2009
910.68'8–dc22
2008054448

ISBN 13: 978-0-750-68693-8 (pbk)
ISBN 13: 978-0-080-94295-7 (ebk)

Companion website: www.routledge.com/9780750686938

Dedication

This book is dedicated to the memory and contribution of Professor S. Medlik (1928 to 2007) who was influential in the production of the first edition of this book and took a keen interest in the subsequent editions, offering many helpful comments over the years. Rik was a pioneer of tourism studies in the UK and European mainland with highly regarded contributions to the field of tourism as a scholar, educator and consultant in many other countries over several decades.

Born in Czechoslovakia, Rik came to England as a refugee in 1948. A graduate in economics and commerce at the University of Durham, he became a lecturer at Battersea Polytechnic in the Department of Hotel, Catering and Institutional Management in 1955, becoming Head of Department of Hotel, Catering and Tourism Management at the University of Surrey from 1966–1977. He undertook an evaluation of the main tourism courses in Europe in 1966 before establishing the first short tourism course in the UK at Surrey in 1968, subsequently developing the first postgraduate course in England at Surrey in 1972.

With his colleague John Burkart, using a business analysis approach, Rik co-authored the first substantive textbook on tourism – *Tourism: Past Present and Future* published by Heinemann in 1974. Middleton acted as reader and commentator for that book in the draft stages.

In all, Rik published some 20 books with Heinemann, Butterworth-Heinemann and latterly Elsevier and acted for over two decades as a consultant author for the publisher's tourism titles. He was the right man in the right place at the right time as tourism studies developed. His wise influence in many countries around the world and on the lives of hundreds of students is unlikely to be equalled and this book celebrates his memory one year after his death.

About the principal authors

Professor Victor Middleton has had some forty years' international experience of marketing practice. Commencing his career with Procter & Gamble and Gillette he worked for the national tourist office in Great Britain before becoming a full time academic at the University of Surrey. He was one of the first in Europe to teach marketing in tourism to undergraduate and postgraduate students in the 1970s. He has been an independent management consultant, author and academic since the 1980s and has produced over one hundred articles, chapters and books during the last 30 years. He holds appointments as a visiting professor at two British universities and was awarded an OBE for services to tourism in 2005.

A founder fellow and former Chairman of the UK Tourism Society, apart from marketing, Victor Middleton's research interests encompass the measurement of tourism, the development of sustainable tourism, destination management and small businesses. He has worked for the European Commission, PATA, and national, regional and local governments in the UK and in many countries around the world.

By the same author in recent years

British Tourism: The Remarkable Story of Growth (2005 and 2007)

Marketing in Travel and Tourism (1988, 1994 and 2001)

Sustainable Tourism: A marketing perspective (with Rebecca Hawkins) (1998)

Measuring the Local Impact of Tourism (1996)

New Visions for Museums in the 21st Century (1998)

New Visions for Independent Museums in the UK (1989)

Review of Tourism Studies Degree Courses in the UK (1993)

Dr Alan Fyall is Deputy Dean, Research & Enterprise in the School of Services Management and Head of Enterprise, Centre for Research & Enterprise, Bournemouth University. His research interests lie in destination management and emerging destination management structures while he has published numerous books and peer-reviewed journal articles on all aspects of destination management and marketing, the management of heritage and visitor attractions, sport tourism, festivals and events and collaboration marketing. Alan is a former member of the Bournemouth Tourism Management Board while he is currently serving as an adviser to the Commonwealth Tourism Centre in Malaysia. Alan has undertaken contract research for major clients in many countries around the world including projects undertaken in the Caribbean, Southern Africa, Central Asia, Europe and the Far East.

Michael Morgan is Senior Lecturer in Tourism and Leisure Marketing at Bournemouth University and Leader of the MA European Tourism Management programme delivered in six European Universities. Coming to academic life after a career in travel and tour operations, he has written numerous articles and book chapters on tourism marketing and is currently conducting research into tourist experiences and experience management.

Foreword

Marketing grows ever more important for managers in the 21st century as companies seek to win the attention of their customers and stakeholders. All parts of the business are involved, from boardroom to front line staff. Marketing is just as relevant to not-for-profit organizations and government bodies that serve the public, as it is for multi-nationals, small businesses and sole traders in the private sector. Over the last decade in particular prosperity in business has reflected the ways in which companies:

- Organize their product design and delivery around customer interests – the customer centric approach reflects a world that has increasingly shifted the balance of power towards buyers.
- Establish core values that underpin strategic planning and decision-making at every level of the business, usually reflecting wider social and environmental values.
- Create and promote distinctive branding for product portfolios that promotes relationships with customers.
- Control, maintain and continuously improve product quality to match or exceed the offers of competitors.
- Sustain profitability in challenging times.

Marketing is fundamental to each of these five business processes. Each has to be developed and delivered continuously in a globally competitive context utilizing the remarkable developments of the Internet since the widespread availability of Broadband and the rapidly developing world of e-marketing.

The fourth edition of this well-established book addresses the meaning and application of marketing in what is commonly described as the Worlds 'largest industry'. It examines the principles of marketing in global services management, focussing on each of the main sectors in travel and tourism. It does so against an economic and political backdrop in 2008/2009 of what many now expect to be global economic recession more severe than any experienced in our current working lives.

I endorse the close attention that the authors pay throughout this book to explaining the cohesive thought processes through which marketing decisions are made. Vision, planning, implementation, research and the use of management information systems to monitor decisions are the fundamentals of all industries. But it is a far from perfect process and the big decisions invariably reflect judgement and foresight backed by experience and the best available evidence. Marketing is very much an evolving body of knowledge, still as much art as science, repaying continuous evaluation and development.

Above all, as this book stresses, marketing is a continuous learning process and an experience that daily redefines the leading edge of business practice in consumer centric organizations. This book reflects that and I am pleased to commend it to readers.

Alan Parker CBE
Chief Executive, Whitbread PLC

Contents

Dedication v
About the principal author vii
Foreword ix
Preface xiii
Acknowledgements xix
List of figures xxi
List of tables xxiii
List of mini-cases xxv

Part One The Meaning of Marketing in Travel and Tourism 1

CHAPTER 1 Introducing travel and tourism 2

CHAPTER 2 Introducing marketing: the systematic thought process 20

CHAPTER 3 The special characteristics of travel and tourism marketing 38

CHAPTER 4 The dynamic business environment: factors influencing demand for tourism 56

Part Two Understanding the Consumer and the Marketing Mix in Travel and Tourism 75

CHAPTER 5 Understanding the consumer: tourism motivations and buyer behaviour 76

CHAPTER 6 Market segmentation for travel and tourism markets 96

CHAPTER 7 Product formulation in travel and tourism 118

CHAPTER 8 The evolving marketing mix for tourism services 136

Part Three Planning for Marketing Strategy and Short-term Operational Objectives and Compaigns 159

CHAPTER 9 Marketing research in travel and tourism 160

CHAPTER 10 Planning marketing strategy 180

CHAPTER 11 Marketing planning: the process 204

CHAPTER 12 Planning marketing campaigns: budgeting and evaluating marketing performance 220

Part Four Communicating with and Influencing Consumers 239

CHAPTER 13 The growth and role of information and communications technology and the rise of the dominant consumer 240

CHAPTER 14 E-marketing: the effective use of ICT 258

CHAPTER 15 Distribution channels in travel and tourism: creating access 274

CHAPTER 16 Integrating the promotional and communications mix 292

CHAPTER 17 Brochures, print and other non-electronic information 316

Part Five Applying Marketing in the Main Sectors of Travel and Tourism 335

CHAPTER 18 Marketing tourism destinations 336

CHAPTER 19 Marketing accommodation 362

CHAPTER 20 Marketing passenger transport 382

CHAPTER 21 Marketing visitor attractions 404

CHAPTER 22 Marketing inclusive tours and product packages 426

Part Six Case Studies of Marketing Practice in Travel and Tourism 445

CASE 1 Tourism New Zealand 447

CASE 2 YOTEL 453

CASE 3 Agra – Indian World Heritage Site 459

CASE 4 Travelodge: 465

CASE 5 Alistair Sawday Guides 471

Epilogue: Prospects for travel and tourism marketing 477

References and select bibliography 487

Index 493

Preface

It is now some twenty years since the first edition of this book was published. As every author knows, any book is a leap in the dark. One can hope but one cannot know in advance how readers will receive it. In fact *Marketing in Travel and Tourism* has been sold internationally to tens of thousands of readers, translated into several different languages, endorsed as essential reading on hundreds of courses and reprinted almost every year to meet demand. For the fourth edition, encouraged by reviews and by many people in several countries, the book has been developed further to reflect the global marketing conditions of the twenty-first century. Alan Fyall, Mike Morgan and Ashok Ranchhod joined the principal author in the preparation of this edition and we share an enthusiasm for the subject of tourism marketing that we hope is transparent.

The information in each chapter has been updated and the content revised. We have retained the overall structure of the book and some of the core content because it clearly works for readers. New material has been added to all chapters, diagrams have been modified and up-to-date case studies of international practice included. In particular, the new edition reflects:

- The growing impact of globalization in demand for and supply of travel and tourism products
- The exponential growth and revolutionary impact of the Internet since the first pioneering B2C travel websites appeared in 1995
- The effects of a decade of real income growth in most developing countries on changing and sophisticating the consumer demand patterns of more experienced travellers
- The remarkable economic growth in China and India that underpins massive potential for expanding the markets for travel and tourism within, from and to those countries
- The continued worldwide growth of courses and books on every specific aspect of travel and tourism, which in our judgement increases the need for a cohesive holistic understanding of the subject of marketing that this book aims to provide
- The impact of international terrorism, already evident since the 1970s but massively influenced by 9/11 in 2001, the invasion of Iraq and subsequent events
- The perceived impact of global warming and climate change caused by world population expansion, rapid industrial growth and associated CO_2 pollution and the use of fossil fuels in particular for heating and transport. Sustainable development has risen substantially on the international political agenda and

international travel and tourism, especially air transport, is increasingly targeted for tighter regulation to limit growth

Nearly all these 21st century developments were reflected to some extent in the third edition published in 2001 but with the understanding and perceptions of the late 1990s. Thinking has moved on substantially in the years to 2008 and this edition reflects up-to-date evaluation of each of these key developments drawing on the perspective of new authors. The Epilogue has also been rewritten drawing on our current appreciation of key events affecting worldwide travel and tourism. As this book goes to press, the world financial markets are engulfed in crisis and predictions of severe economic recession are being made daily. If, as seems likely, the recession is deep, the impacts on travel and tourism will be very significant with business collapses certain. But these events will not undermine or change the arguments for better marketing made in this book.

Academic contributions have explored the subject of marketing on as many dimensions of travel and tourism as can be identified. Such development is a natural process appropriate to an expanding subject area. It is the case, however, that many such contributions have adopted a linguistic complexity that is often confusing to people working in the business and to students. The authors of this book are guided by the opposite view. We believe a textbook should aim to explain and illustrate the essential principles in a clear, unambiguous style – simplifying as far as possible and relating the principles within a carefully structured narrative and integrated framework supported by case studies drawn from current practice. What is difficult to read is hard to understand and its utility in the real world is marginalized. We wish this edition to be read and appreciated by students and practitioners of tourism marketing all over the world, as all its predecessors have been.

The book is presented as before in six parts. The structure is designed to follow a logical development of the subject although, as every manager knows, marketing is a circular rather than a linear process with many feedback loops. As far as possible, the parts are designed to be reasonably self-explanatory, with the intention that lecturers and students can fit the chapters into whatever pattern the logic of their courses suggests.

Part One defines travel and tourism and the component sectors of the visitor economy that are referred to throughout the book. The subject of marketing is introduced, especially for those who are coming new to the subject, and the special characteristics of travel and tourism to which marketing responds are explained. This part of the book also explains the factors in the external business environment that influence the development of market demand and supply.

Part Two explains the core tools in marketing that have not shifted greatly *in principle* in the last quarter of a century The chapters cover the meaning and marketing implications of buyer behaviour, market segmentation, product formulation and the evolving marketing mix for travel and tourism.

The major changes in tourism marketing of the last decade have reflected the development of far more sophisticated and demanding customers who are increasingly empowered to exercise better choices and become more involved in purchasing decisions through interaction with suppliers on the Internet. The Internet also has major supply side implications for business operations and it has revolutionized the way that the traditional marketing mix operated until the 1990s.

Part Three focuses on the tools of marketing research and what is involved in the processes for planning marketing strategies and short-term operational objectives and targets leading to actionable marketing programmes that have to respond to changing market conditions. Chapter 12 reviews the process for planning and monitoring marketing campaigns

Part Four examines the revolutionary impact that the Internet has had on travel and tourism marketing over the last decade since the first B2C sites were launched in the mid 1990s. Stressing the pivotal role of modern ICT and e-marketing this Part shows that the traditionally separate processes of the marketing mix are still widely practiced but can now be simultaneously combined through the medium of corporate web sites and associated Internet portals. Traditional and new methods co-exist in travel and tourism but the shift to e-marketing is inevitable. Integrated marketing communications are covered with a separate chapter on the role of brochures and other marketing print.

Part Five analyses the meaning and applications in practice of marketing in each of the five main sectors of travel and tourism using a broadly common approach.

Part Six contains five new case studies that illustrate the thrust of modern marketing as explained in the book.

The Epilogue draws together the principal trends emerging in the book and identifies seven key influences on marketing in travel and tourism for the coming decade.

Our approach to the subject

We base our approach to travel and tourism on the definition adopted by The UN World Tourism Organization – in its full range of day and staying visits for multiple purposes embracing business, social and recreational activity as well as holidays. We aim to be as relevant to domestic as to international tourism. We believe our approach to the subject and its complexities are relevant in all countries dealing with travel and tourism. In that broad context we believe that tourism and the visitor economy it supports is a structural or core element of all modern and developing societies. We consider that the marketing of tourism is still in a development phase that will influence the sectors of travel and tourism to an increasing extent in the globally competitive conditions of the twenty-first century. We see marketing as a dominant management philosophy or corporate culture, a systematic thought process and an integrated set of techniques focused on understanding and responding to customer needs and aspirations. Combined, the application of the thought process and techniques is used in marketing-orientated organizations to define their strategic options and goals. Marketing thinking guides the way businesses understand and influence their target markets, and respond to them in a rapidly changing business environment.

Marketing is equally relevant to both private and public sectors of travel and tourism, and to smaller businesses as well as to international corporations. It is a proactive management response to more demanding consumers, excess capacity of production and volatile market demand that are commonly found in international travel and tourism. The rapid growth of tourism demand around the world over the last two decades tended to cushion many organizations from the full effects of competition and delayed the full application of marketing in many travel and tourism businesses. But the easy days are over. A combination of information communications technology, global competition, climate change and international economic downturn will challenge and expose vulnerable destinations and sluggish businesses. Many will not survive.

Marketing is not viewed, however, as a goal or the only focus of business management. It does not determine the nature of an organization's values or its long-run goal or mission. Throughout the book the requirement of responding to customers' needs is balanced against the growing requirement of organizations to make the most sustainable as well as the most profitable use of existing assets and to achieve integration of management functions around customer-orientated objectives that respect sustainable goals. But marketing techniques are always essential inputs to specifying revenue-earning objectives that are precise, realistic, achievable and measurable in the markets or audiences in which an organization operates. In this sense the adoption of a marketing approach is as relevant to museums responsible to non-profit-making trusts, national parks for which the long-run goal is public access and a sustainable environment and to local government tourist offices, as it is to airlines, hotels or tour operators in the private sector.

Links to internationally accepted marketing theory

Marketing as a body of knowledge is international. Like travel and tourism it does not depend on geographical boundaries. While many of the principles and techniques were developed originally in North America and Europe for selling manufactured consumer goods in the first half of the twentieth century, they are now being practised and developed all around the world in the much larger sectors of modern service industries. For reasons that are set out in Chapter 3 we believe it is possible to construct an overall understanding of travel and tourism marketing based on three essential points: first, that the theories of consumer marketing are common to all its forms; second, that service industries display particular characteristics, which do not alter the principles but must be understood before marketing can successfully be applied in practice; third, that there are important common characteristics of travel and tourism service products that require particular forms of marketing response.

It is too much to claim that an internationally agreed theory of travel and tourism marketing yet exists. But the generic and common characteristics of travel and tourism services are leading to increasing consistencies of approach in marketing, adapted in the different sectors of travel and tourism to the opportunities and threats they perceive. These common approaches point to a coherent, systematic body of knowledge within the framework of services marketing that will be further developed in the coming decades.

The aim of the book and its intended audience

The book has three aims, which are to provide:

- Concepts and principles drawn from international marketing theory, balanced with illustrations of recent practice.
- A necessary companion volume for all concerned with travel and tourism marketing, but not a substitute for the many excellent texts that explain marketing theory in its overall and service product context.
- An easy to read and comprehensive text about what marketing means in the global travel and tourism industry.

On both sides of the Atlantic the better of the standard texts on marketing are now substantial volumes, many of them having developed over several editions. This book makes no attempt to replace them. It is intended, instead, to fit fully within a framework of internationally accepted marketing principles that have stood the test of time, and to develop these concepts in the specific context of travel and tourism. We believe that students in particular will profit from the breadth of understanding this conveys.

For students, the book is written to meet the needs of all on travel and tourism and hospitality courses and related leisure industry programmes. Marketing will be a very important influence in their careers, whether or not they are directly engaged in marketing practice. The material will be relevant to other courses in which service industries are an important element.

For those working in travel and tourism, the book recognizes that marketing is a very practical subject and it is aimed at the many managers in travel and tourism who have some responsibility for aspects of marketing but who have not formally studied the subject. Much of the contents have also been exposed to the critical reaction of managers in the industry over the years, and modified in the light of their responses.

Finally, this book contains no *golden rules.* But if people in the industry read the book with care and relate its principles to the particular circumstances their own organizations face, most should perceive useful insights and ways to improve the effectiveness of their marketing decisions. If they do not, the authors will have failed in their purpose.

Victor T.C. Middleton; Alan Fyall; Michael Morgan and Ashok Ranchhod
October 2008

Authors' note

Repeated use of 'he or she' or of 's/he' can be cumbersome in continuous text. For simplicity, therefore, only the male pronoun is used throughout the book. No bias is intended and, wherever 'he' or 'his' appears, it applies equally to 'she' or 'hers'.

Acknowledgements

All errors and omissions are the authors' sole responsibility but we have had much help in the preparation of this edition – so much that it is impossible to list all who influenced the book with their insights, encouragement and sometimes much needed prods to get on with it. The most important group is undoubtedly the hundreds of students on undergraduate and postgraduate courses in the UK and other countries who have been exposed to the initial thinking and helped to shape it with their feedback and their own ideas. Their reactions improved our own thought processes more than they knew.

We appreciate too the views and responses of the many managers on short, post-experience courses around the world to which we have variously contributed over the last two decades; they sharpened our appreciation of international marketing and attention on the practice that validates theory.

As principal author, Victor Middleton is especially grateful for the support of Alan Fyall and Michael Morgan who agreed to be joint authors for this edition. Thanks also to Ashok Ranchhod who contributed throughout the process with numerous inputs to the development of the chapters for the 4th edition.

For the Foreword we are most grateful to Alan Parker, Chief Executive of Whitbread PLC. For particular contributions to chapters in this book we wish to acknowledge in alphabetical order; Angus Bond, Head of Product and Commercial for USA and Caribbean at Virgin Holidays; Nick Cust, Joint Managing Director of Superbreak; and Derek Robbins and Thanasis Spyrisadis of Bournemouth University for their specific contributions to Chapter 20 and the updating of many figures and tables throughout the text. For the images used in this edition we acknowledge contributions from staff at Bournemouth University and the resources at Butterworth-Heinemann. Thanks also to Grahame Senior for his much appreciated support when the ideas for the 4th Edition were being developed. For providing and allowing us to use case material for Part Six we wish specifically to acknowledge, Gerard Greene and Jo Berrington of YOTEL, Guy Parsons of Travelodge, and Tourism New Zealand.

Finally our thanks are due to Sarah Long and the team at Butterworth-Heinemann/Elsevier for all their support in handling the publishing side of this edition.

For providing and agreeing the use of case material for part six we wish specifically to acknowledge, Gerard Greene and Jo Berrington of YOTEL, Guy Parsons of Travelodge and Tourism New Zealand.

Figures

1.1 The five main sectors in travel and tourism ... 11
1.2 The systematic links between demand and supply: the influence of marketing ... 12
2.1 The marketing system for service products ... 30
5.1 A stimulus response model of buyer behaviour ... 78
5.2 Implications for marketing of the Consumer Decision Process ... 90
7.1 The spectrum of emphasis between film-centric and consumer centric organizations ... 131
8.1 Examples of the marketing mix in travel and tourism ... 141
8.2 The core marketing mix in context of the overall marketing system ... 143
9.1 The process of developing tourism research in the Balearics ... 173
10.1 The key stages in developing marketing strategies ... 184
10.2 Corporate purpose, values, policies and positioning: the Ashridge Model ... 185
10.3 Elements and stages involved in a corporate business strategy: the hierarchy of objectives ... 193
10.4 Product – market growth strategies ... 196
10.5 A simplified concept of branding ... 198
11.1 Stages in the marketing planning process ... 207
11.2 Co-ordinating operational marketing objectives, targets with budgets and marketing mix programmes ... 215
12.1 A marketing budget campaign model for a tour operator ... 228
12.2 Variance of sales against targets for an airline ... 235
12.3 Variance of satisfaction over time for a tour operator ... 236
13.1 Multimedia convergence of content, processing and transmission ... 243
14.1 The impact of ICT on the marketing mix ... 260
14.2 Four uses of cyberspace for marketing ... 262
15.1 The distribution triangle for producers, distributors and customers ... 277
15.2 Distribution options in choosing channels for travel and tourism products ... 280
15.3 Distribution channels for international tourism ... 281
16.1 The Communications process ... 298
16.2 Filters in awareness and interact that blunt the communication process ... 299
18.1 The destination marketing process for NTOs ... 347
18.2 A market/product matrix model for NTO/DMO marketing planning ... 351
18.3 Tiscover multi-channel distribution ... 356
19.1 Principal serviced and non-serviced types of accommodation used in tourism, by market-segment ... 365

19.2 www.hotels.com: Visualiser website *367*
22.1 The logical sequence of putting together and marketing an air-inclusive tour programme *434*
22.2 Targeted vs actual bookings achieved in a normal year for a tour operator *440*
22.3 Targeted vs actual bookings achieved in a problematic year for a tour operator *441*

Tables

1.1 Recorded and projected growth in worldwide international tourist arrivals, 1950–2020 ... *6*
1.2 Changes in UNWTO world regional shares of international tourism arrivals, 1950–2020 ... *6*
2.1 Summary of the marketing system ... *32*
3.1 Generic characteristics distinguishing services from goods ... *47*
6.1 Segment/buyer behaviour/usage characteristics by sequence of purchase and product usage ... *107*
7.1 UK Post Office Holiday Costs Barometer, 2007 ... *125*
9.1 Six main categories of marketing research and their uses ... *164*
9.2 The marketing research menu or tool kit ... *168*
9.3 Basic requirements of client and agency in commissioning marketing research ... *174*
10.1 Revenue by market regions/segments for Thomas Cook Group ... *191*
10.2 Thomas Cook - International product portfolio ... *192*
12.1 The principal marketing campaign techniques used in travel and tourism ... *223*
15.1 Services provided by distribution channels ... *283*
15.2 New gateways for travel and tourism information and bookings ... *287*
16.1 Advertising options in the United Kingdom in 2006 – Advertising Association figures ... *297*
16.2 Types of public relations activity in travel and tourism ... *307*
16.3 Potential negative events requiring crisis management in travel and tourism ... *308*
18.1 Destination brand core values ... *346*
19.1 A typical market/product mix for an urban coastal hotel ... *372*
20.1 Principal passenger transport systems used in travel and tourism ... *384*
21.1 Ten main types of managed attractions open to the public ... *410*
21.2 A segmentation planning model for a large visitor attraction approximately 10 miles from London ... *416*
21.3 Sustainability: a marketing perspective for resource-based visitor attractions ... *418*

Mini Cases

5.1 Disneyland Paris ... *84*
6.1 Segmentation for Australia in the UK long-haul market – Self-Challenges ... *108*
7.1 Product options from Holiday Hypermarket ... *131*
8.1 Managing customer relationships ... *149*
9.1 The Balearics Tourism sector survey (2004) ... *170*
10.1 The Thomas Cook Group ... *189*
13.1 Collaborative e-marketing for small tour operators ... *253*
15.1 Opodo ... *288*
16.1 Film tourism and an example of a press release ... *309*
18.1 Tourism market recovery in the Maldives ... *340*
18.2 The devolution of tourism in England ... *349*
19.1 Small Luxury Hotels of the World ... *375*
20.1 Flybe.com ... *391*
20.2 Star Alliance ... *399*
21.1 Marketing Manchester United ... *408*
21.2 Managing seasonality ... *420*
22.1 Royal Caribbean – the ultimate holiday experiefnce ... *438*

The Meaning of Marketing in Travel and Tourism

Part One sets out the key definitions of travel and tourism and outlines the component sectors of the visitor economy that are referred to throughout the book. The subject of marketing is introduced, especially for those who are coming new to the subject, and the special characteristics of travel and tourism to which marketing responds are explained.

This part of the book also explains the main factors in the external business environment that influence tourism market demand and supply in all parts of the world.

'There are few regions of the world where tourism does not make an impact'
Kamila Pirowska c/r Bournemouth University.

CHAPTER 1

Introducing travel and tourism

Tourism comprises the activities of persons travelling to and staying in places outside their usual environment for not more than one consecutive year for leisure, business and other purposes.

(WTO, 1992: subsequently ratified by the UN Statistical Commission in 1994)

This chapter introduces and defines the subject matter of this book. First it identifies for practical marketing purposes the nature of travel and tourism and the sectors of the modern visitor economy it supports. Secondly it indicates the role of tourism in the global economy of the twenty-first century and its growth potential in the next decade.

After studying this chapter you should be able to understand:

- How travel and tourism is defined internationally.
- How to identify the main component parts of tourism.
- The limitations of the term *tourism industry* and the wider concept of *visitor economy*.
- The linkages between demand and supply in tourism.
- Trends in the global economy that have redefined the significance of tourism in modern societies and created what many now identify as the world's largest industry.

Although the niceties of definitions can be debated endlessly, the authors of this book believe that travel and tourism is best understood as a market. It is a market that reflects the demands of consumers for a very wide range of travel-related products and the supply of services by a wide array of commercial and public sector organizations. It is widely claimed that this total market is now serviced by the *world's largest industry*. In the twenty-first century increasing interest is being shown in many countries in the potential of global travel and tourism as an important contributor to economic development, measured in terms of investment, employment and balance of payments. In developed countries in particular there is also increasing interest in the potential environmental and cultural contributions of tourism to the social and cultural life of host communities and to the built and natural environments. Effectively managed, tourism can play an important role in more sustainable developments at visited destinations; tourism is also of interest because of its ubiquitous nature. There are very few regions of the modern world where tourism and the contribution of the visitor economy to residents' lives are not a relevant consideration and travel extends to all parts of most countries. As a result tourism sustains not only international organizations such as airlines, tour operators and hotels but also thousands of small and medium-sized enterprises (SMEs) that are vital elements in most economic systems.

Recognition of potential is, however, matched by growing concerns about the negative effects of travel and tourism in the conspicuous use of energy and water supplies, impact on CO_2 emissions, global warming and climate change, and damage to marine environments and the ecosystems of some destinations developed as major tourism resorts.

Marketing is a subject of vital concern in travel and tourism because, in practical terms, it harnesses the power of massive commercial forces as well as government and regulatory influences. As explained in Chapters 2 and 3, it is the principal management influence that can be used to shape the size and behaviour of a major, growing global market.

Within the total market there are many sub-markets or segments, and many products designed and provided by a wide range of organizations, which are categorized in Fig. 1.1 (p.11). As an overall market, travel and tourism is best understood in terms of demand and supply. Marketing is introduced in Chapter 2 as the vital linking mechanism between supply and demand focused on exchange transactions in which consumers exercise preferences and choices, and exchange their time and money in return for the supply of particular travel experiences or products. For reasons discussed subsequently, the principles and practice of marketing are also highly relevant to tourism resources for which no market price is charged, such as national parks and historic towns. Marketing is a vital role for national tourism organizations (NTOs) and other area organizations identified as destination management organizations (DMOs), most of which are not directly engaged in the sale of products although they are increasingly involved with commercial partners that are.

AN OVERVIEW OF TRAVEL AND TOURISM DEMAND

In defining travel and tourism for the purposes of this book it is useful to follow the basic classification system used in nearly all countries where measurement exists. This system is discussed in detail in most introductory texts and it is based on three overall categories of visitor demand with which any country is concerned; each is a different sector of the total market:

1. *International visitors*, who are residents of countries other than that being visited and travelling for tourism purposes (see below). Also known as *inbound tourism*.
2. *International visitors*, who are residents of a country visiting other countries and travelling for tourism purposes. Also known as *outbound tourism*.
3. *Residents* visiting destinations within their own country's boundaries and travelling for tourism purposes. Also known as *domestic tourism*.

Readers should note that it is the concept of *visiting* and the term *visitors* that underlie all definitions of travel and tourism. It is for this reason that the modern concept of *visitor economy* rather than the traditional *tourism industry* is addressed later in this chapter.

Defining travel and tourism is a primary responsibility of the UN World Tourism Organization (UNWTO), which undertook a major review of its definitions at an international conference on travel and tourism statistics in Ottawa in 1991. In 1994 revised definitions were adopted by the United Nations (UN) Statistical Commission. The following are the principal terms adopted then and used today:

- *Visitors* to describe all travellers who fall within agreed definitions of tourism.
- *Tourists* or staying visitors to describe visitors who stay overnight at a destination.
- *Same-day visitors*, or excursionists, to describe visitors who arrive and depart on the same day.

Same-day visitors are mostly people who leave home and return there on the same day, but may be tourists who make day visits to other destinations away from the places where they are staying overnight.

As outlined above, these three categories are easy to understand. In practice the technicalities and costs of achieving statistical precision in measuring both international and domestic visitor numbers are extremely complex. Despite agreed international guidelines, no uniformity yet exists in the measurement methods used around the world. Eurostat, for example, which publishes the statistics for tourism in Europe, issues guidelines for the collection of data but has to rely on the different methodologies used by individual countries to compile their data.

While the definition of travel and tourism outlined in this chapter will be adequate for the working purposes of those involved in marketing, this book does not set out to be a detailed study of the nature of tourism. Readers seeking further elaboration of concepts and measurement issues are referred to the reading suggestions noted at the end of the chapter. Marketing managers will, of course, require their own definitions of the market segments with which they are involved, and these will be far more detailed than the broadly indicative aggregate categories introduced here (see Chapter 6).

International tourism

Visitors who travel to and stay in countries other than their normal country of residence for less than a year are described as international tourists. They are usually treated by governments as the most important market sector of tourism because, compared with domestic tourists, they typically spend more, stay longer at the destination, use more expensive transport and accommodation, and bring in foreign currency which contributes to a destination country's international balance of payments. Because it crosses national borders, international tourism is usually easier to measure than domestic tourism and such visitors tend to be more recognizable as tourists in their form of dress and behaviour patterns at destinations.

Around the world, measured as *arrivals* or *trips*, the numbers of international tourists and their expenditure have grown strongly since the 1950s, notwithstanding temporary fluctuations caused by the major international energy and economic crises such as those of the early 1970s, 1980s and 1990s or political crises such as those

TABLE 1.1 Recorded and projected growth in worldwide international tourist arrivals, 1950–2020

Year	International arrivals (millions)	Index of growth for each decade
1950	25.3	–
1960	69.3	274
1970	165.8	239
1980	275.9	173
1990	436.1	160
2000	683.3	150
2005	803.4	–
2010[a]	1000.0	146
2020[a]	1600.0	160

Notes: These are arrivals as supplied by governments over the years to UNWTO, plus projections at 2008. Although their accuracy cannot be assured, they provide indicators that are widely used around the world.

Source: UNWTO Market Trends (2008).

[a] Projected figure.

occasioned by the war in the Gulf, 9/11 in 2001 and the Iraq invasion in 2003. The overall growth pattern is revealed in Tables 1.1 and 1.2, and the reasons for it are discussed in some detail in Chapters 4 and 5. For the purposes of this introduction it is sufficient to note the recent growth and current size of the international market, and to be aware of consistently confident projections that international tourism will continue to grow well into the twenty-first century, fuelled in large part by the growth in the global economy and the development of China and India in particular as major generators of tourism. Although annual fluctuations in volume reflecting economic and political events are certain and likely to be related to efforts to reverse global warming and climate change, current UNWTO projections are for annual growth of

TABLE 1.2 Changes in UNWTO world regional shares of international tourism arrivals, 1950–2020

	Shares of total arrivals at end of each decade [shown as (%)]		
Year	Europe	Americas	Asia Pacific
1950	66	30	0.8
1960	73	24	1.0
1970	71	23	3.0
1980	66	21	7.0
1990	62	20	13
2000	59	20	16
2010[a]	52	19	21
2020[a]	46	18	27

Notes: These are shares for the three main UNWTO regions only. The projected growth in the share of Asia Pacific arrivals since 1990 is the most significant trend.

Source: UNWTO, Tourism 2020 Vision (2007).

[a] Projected figure.

the order of some 4% per annum over the period to 2020 as a whole. The rapid growth in share of international arrivals projected for the Asia Pacific region (Table 1.2) has major implications for the future of world travel and tourism. (See also WTO, 2007.)

At present, reflecting the proximity of borders in Europe, it is common for well over half the adult population living in Northern Europe to have made one or more international tourist visits during the previous five years, mostly on vacation. Experience of international travel is very much less for Americans, reflecting the size of the USA and the distances most of them have to travel to make international trips. US inter-state tourism, e.g. between the North East and Florida, should perhaps be viewed as similar in principle to tourism between European countries over similar distances, especially as the latter develop the European Union with new member states, using its widely adopted currency, the euro.

Although not shown separately in Tables 1.1 and 1.2, international same-day visits are an important market sector in countries with common land frontiers, such as the USA and Canada, the Netherlands and Germany, and Malaysia and Singapore. Because of the speed and efficiency of cross-Channel ferries and the Channel Tunnel, same-day visits between Britain and France and Britain and Belgium are also important elements of the total market for tourism.

Domestic tourism and day visits

Visitors who travel and stay overnight within the boundaries of their own country are classified as domestic tourists. Domestic tourism has two important categories comprised of visitors who stay overnight and a very much larger number who take day visits from their homes. Estimates of the size of both these sectors of the market vary because in many countries domestic tourism is not adequately measured at present. As an indication, the UNWTO estimates that domestic tourism around the world outweighs international tourism by a factor of around 10:1. In the USA, where good measurement does exist, Americans take only one trip abroad for every 100 domestic trips defined as travel to places more than 100 miles distance from home. Even for longer visits of over ten nights' duration, international trips were no more than 3% of the US total visits. For the British, reflecting the shorter distances to travel abroad, international tourism is now much greater by value than domestic tourism although, allowing for day visits there were still some four domestic tourism visits for every visit abroad in 2005.

Evidence from surveys of the vacation market in Europe and North America in the 1990s indicates that, in most countries, between a half and three-quarters of the adult population took one or more holidays away from home in any twelve-month period of at least one night's duration. This includes international and domestic holidays, although the latter are the largest category by volume. Increasing numbers of people now take several vacation visits a year, a factor of great importance to marketing managers, for reasons discussed later.

Market research data analysing the complete tourism experience of the same individuals over periods of more than one year are rarely available although they exist, for example, for France and the Netherlands. But, excluding the very old, the sick, the severely disabled and those facing particular financial hardship, it is realistic to assume that recent and frequent experience of some form of staying and same-day tourism now extends to over nine out of ten people in most economically developed countries.

Within the total volume of domestic tourism, same-day visits are the most difficult to quantify. In most developed countries the frequency of day visits is already so great that it is not easily measured by traditional survey techniques, because people find it hard or impossible to remember the number of trips they have taken over a period of months or even weeks. There is, however, a rough but useful estimate for developed countries that there are at least twice as many domestic day visits for leisure purposes within a country, as there are tourist days or nights spent away from home for all purposes. Thus, for example, in the UK in 1998 an estimated 100 million domestic tourism visits for all purposes generated 350 million nights away from home. An additional 1000 million same-day visits of at least three hours duration from home for leisure purposes were made by the British in the same year (2000 data). This is equivalent to over eighteen visitor days per person for leisure purposes over a year. Very few countries have a measure of the number of day visits taken for business and non-leisure social purposes, although such visits are obviously a very large market especially for operators of transport, meetings and catering services.

To summarize, the total market for travel and tourism comprises three main elements: international visits inbound to a country; outbound international visits made by a country's residents; and domestic visits including day visits from home. The total market has grown rapidly in recent years and is now very large, encompassing the great majority of the population of economically developed countries. Frequent, repeat purchases of travel and tourism products in a year are already a normal experience for many people. Although the statistics are inevitably open to dispute, travel and tourism is now the largest sector of world trade and in developed countries typically contributes 5–10% of gross domestic product.

As the world's most populated countries, China and India, expand and develop their economies and tourism sectors in the coming decades they are projected to take dominant positions as destinations and generating countries in the global market. One may safely predict that marketing will be a subject of growing significance and interest in both countries. Adapting and developing in different socio-economic and political cultures what are essentially the sophisticated techniques of commercially oriented Western societies will ensure continuing interest in tourism marketing for decades to come. The Olympic Games in China in 2008 is a significant indication of what can be achieved.

A WORKING DEFINITION OF TRAVEL AND TOURISM

Before drawing the discussion of the main markets in travel and tourism into a working definition, it may be helpful to clarify one important potential source of confusion. What, if any, are the differences between *tourism* and *travel*, used on their own as single terms, and *travel and tourism* used as a combined term? What can a definition of tourism mean if it does not include travel? This book proceeds in the belief that an acceptable definition of tourism necessarily covers all relevant aspects of travel. In normal usage *tourism* and *travel and tourism* are terms that relate to exactly the same market and they are used interchangeably.

Travel and tourism tends to be the term used most often by managers, especially in North America, because it is convenient, practical and widely understood. Accordingly, this usage is adopted generally throughout the book. Where, for the sake of convenience, *tourism* is used alone, it also means travel and tourism; students should be aware that no conceptual difference is implied between the two expressions in this book. Similarly the words *visitor* and *tourist* tend to be used interchangeably in common use and in this book.

Although academics have debated conceptual definitions of tourism for several decades, and there were earlier international agreements on statistical definitions, it was not until 1992 that the WTO endorsed the definition at the head of this chapter, ratified in 1994 by the UN Statistical Commission. It serves as the working definition of the total market that is used throughout this book.

The UN definition pulls together the three main elements of travel and tourism:

1. Because of the stress on the words "outside the usual environment..." visitor activity is concerned only with aspects of life other than normal routines of work, sustenance and social commitments, and outside the locations of those normal daily routines. Although this is easy to state, it is very difficult to define what it means in practice and measure it in surveys.
2. The activity necessitates travel and, in nearly every case, some form of transport to the destination.
3. Specific destinations are the focus for a range of visitor activities, and a range of facilities required to support those activities. Such activities and facilities have a combination of economic, social and environmental impacts that are the basis for tourism policy and visitor management programmes as well as marketing.

Five important points are stressed in relation to the definition:

- There is nothing in it that restricts the total market to overnight stays; it includes same-day visits.
- There is nothing in it that restricts the total market to travel for leisure or pleasure. It includes visits for business, social, religious, educational, sports and most other purposes – provided that the destination of travel is outside the usual routines and places of residence and work.
- All tourism includes an element of travel but all travel is not tourism. The definition excludes all routine commuter travel and purely local travel, such as to neighbourhood shops, schools or hospitals.
- Travel and tourism absorbs large elements of individual leisure time and encompasses many recreational activities, but it is not synonymous with either because the bulk of all leisure and recreation takes place in or around the home.
- All travel and tourism visits are temporary movements; the bulk of the total market comprises trips of no more than a few hours' or nights' duration.

THE COMPONENT SECTORS OF TRAVEL AND TOURISM SUPPLY – THE VISITOR ECONOMY

At the beginning of this chapter travel and tourism was identified from the demand side as a total market comprising three main sectors: international tourism, domestic tourism and same-day visits. This section identifies the sectors of supply that have loosely become widely known in many countries as the *travel and tourism industry*. The term 'industry' has been positive in promoting better understanding of the significance of travel and tourism around the world and earlier editions of this book have used the concept without challenge. Further reflection in the twenty-first century, however, convinces us that while the concept of an 'industry' is still broadly relevant to describe the commercial sectors of travel and tourism it does not sensibly apply to the government and other public sector elements with primary responsibility for destination interests and destination management. 'Industry' is a concept suggesting similarity in production processes and broad unity of purpose but these do not and cannot exist either within or across the multiple commercial sectors supplying travel and tourism services. We therefore argue below that the component sectors supplying services to travel and tourism markets should be identified by a wider concept of the *visitor economy*.

The major difficulty in understanding and dealing with travel and tourism as an 'industry' is the sheer number and diversity of private and public sector enterprises involved in supplying services. Although a guest house, a taxi firm, a global airline, a major visitor attraction and a budget hotel are all in the private sector and all theoretically part of the 'tourism industry', they do not recognize themselves as industry partners; they share little or nothing in common in their business practices other than being part of the supply side of a major market. National, regional and municipal authorities around the world are necessarily key players in the destinations that support the visitor economy. They have responsibility for investment in the infrastructure such as airports that travel and tourism depends on; they are responsible for the development and redevelopment of cities and other destinations as well as duties for public spaces such as parks, gardens, heritage buildings, theatres, conference centres and so on. But their primary responsibility is to residents not visitors and they do not see themselves as part of an industry sector. Moreover, many of the bigger commercial operators see tourism as only a part of their total operations. For example, airlines, trains, buses, restaurants and hotels, all deal with a wide variety of market segments, many of which do not fall within the internationally agreed definition of travel and tourism. Hotels have local trade for bars and meals, and transport operators carry commuters. Many visitor attractions, such as museums, and most visitor information bureaux also provide a range of services to local residents. This mixture of products designed to serve both tourism and other markets has great significance for marketing decisions; it is discussed in Part Five of this book, which considers marketing applications in the component sectors of the visitor economy.

From Fig. 1.1 it is obvious that what has traditionally and conveniently been called an *industry* comprises the products or outputs of several different industry sectors as these are conventionally defined and measured in the standardized industrial classifications adopted by most countries. In practice, convenient though the concept has been for all working within it, travel and tourism is not an industry that is recognized as such by economists. In assessing the performance of industry sectors it is normal for economists and government statisticians to use standardized classifications of economic activity to measure separately the outputs of sectors such as transport, hotels and similar accommodation, restaurants and similar outlets, bars, and catering. Such classifications indicate activity but they cannot identify what proportion of each output is generated by visitor spending. Recent work on satellite accounting, pioneered in Canada and taken up by the UNWTO and the Organization for Economic Co-operation and Development (OECD), provides a methodology for assessing the economic contribution of visitors using a country's national accounts.

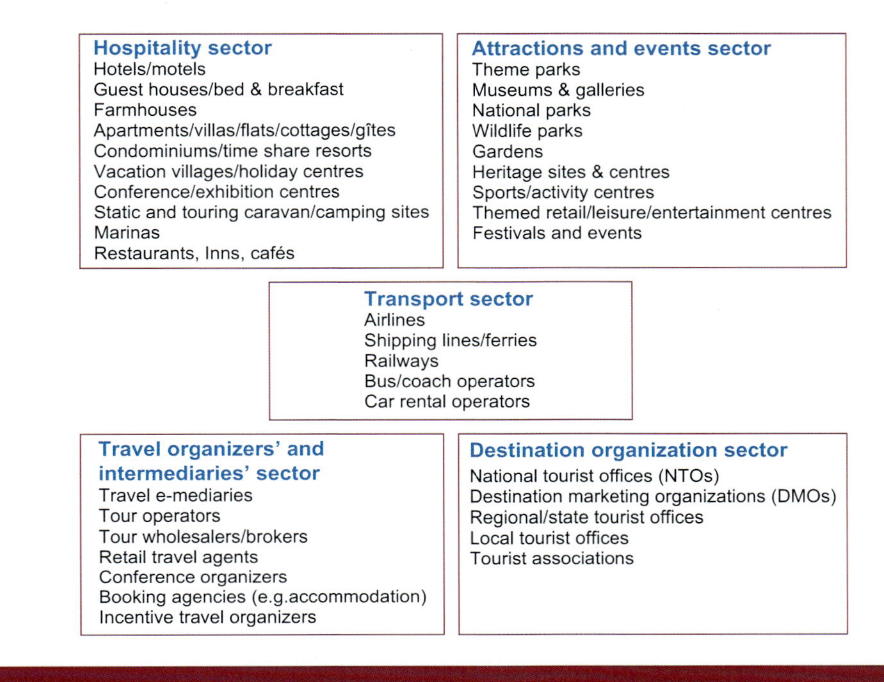

FIGURE 1.1 The five main sectors in travel and tourism

This methodology requires measurement of tourism volume and expenditure at a level of accuracy that few countries can provide and the process is fraught with technical statistical detail. Fortunately, this is not a matter of prime concern for marketing managers.

The five main component sectors in travel and tourism noted in Fig. 1.1 are reflected in the chapter headings and case studies included in Parts Five and Six of the book. Each of the sectors comprises several sub-sectors, all of which are increasingly concerned with marketing activities, both in the design of their products and the management of demand. The authors consider that the linking of sectors in Fig. 1.1 as the visitor economy is also justified by the existence within the sectors of certain common, integrating principles that underlie the modern practice of services marketing. Such principles (explained in Chapters 2 and 3) greatly facilitate the understanding of the subject and help to explain the common interests in marketing that practitioners in tourism recognize. Students may find it a useful exercise to extend the list in Fig. 1.1, using the same five sector headings and aiming to produce up to fifty sub-sectors involved altogether in the visitor economy.

It can be seen that some of the sub-sectors are fully commercial and operated for profit, some are operated as businesses for purposes other than profit and some are in the public sector for which cost effectiveness and provision of access to the public is the issue, not profit. This diversity of approach is another reason for preferring the term visitor economy to the superficially more homogeneous notion of an industry. To illustrate, in the first category are most hotels and airlines, in the second category many attractions, such as safari parks and heritage sites, and in the third category many state-owned national museums, national parks and most of the operations undertaken by national and area tourist offices. Internationally, growing recognition of the value of marketing in non-commercial operations in the second and third categories has been a remarkable feature of the last decade.

THE SYSTEMATIC LINKS BETWEEN DEMAND AND SUPPLY AND THE ROLE OF MARKETING

Figure 1.2 is provided to show vital linkages between demand and supply in travel and tourism that are fundamental to an understanding of the role of marketing. The figure shows the relationship between market demand, generated in the places in which visitors normally live (areas of origin), and product supply, mainly at visited destinations. In particular, it shows how the five main sectors of the visitor economy set out in Fig. 1.1 combine to manage visitors' demand through a range of marketing influences. Noted as the *marketing mix*, in the centre of the diagram, this important term is fully explained in Chapter 8.

Readers should note that the linkages in Fig. 1.2 focus on visitors in the left-hand box. A detailed knowledge of their customers' characteristics and buying behaviour is central to the activities of marketing managers in all sectors. Knowledge of the customer, and all that it implies for management decisions, is generally known as *consumer or marketing orientation*; a concept explained in the next chapter. Note also that there are two-way flows of information for each of the links shown.

It should be noted also that not all visits to a destination are influenced by marketing activity. For example, domestic visitors travelling by private car to stay with their friends and relatives may not be influenced by destination marketing in any way at all. On the other hand, first-time buyers in Europe or the USA of package tours to exotic destinations in the Pacific area may find that almost every aspect of their trip is influenced by the marketing decisions of the tour operator they choose. The operator selects the destinations to put into a brochure or on a Web site and

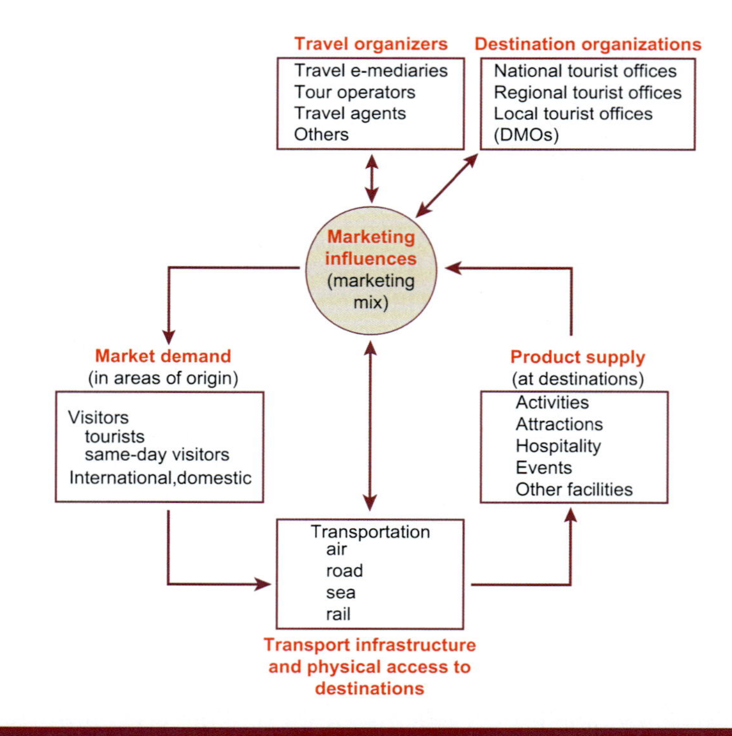

FIGURE 1.2 The systematic links between demand and supply: the influence of marketing.

selects the messages and images that communicate their attractions. Tour operators in this contest may select the accommodation, the range of excursions, the routes, the choice of airline and the prices. Somewhere in between these two examples a traveller on business selects his own destinations according to business requirements but may be influenced as to which hotel he selects. The range of influences, noted as the 'marketing mix', is obviously very wide, and it is varied according to visitors' interests and circumstances.

There are, of course, many other linkages between the five sectors of the visitor economy, for example, between national and regional tourist organizations and suppliers at the destination. These additional linkages are not drawn into Fig. 1.2 to avoid unnecessary confusion in this introduction. The linkages are, of course, identified subsequently in all parts of the book.

Link article available at www.routledge.com/9780750686938

(1) Farrell, B.H., Twining-Ward, L., 2004. Reconceptualizing Tourism. Annals of Tourism Research 31 (2), 274–295.

CHANGING PROSPECTS FOR TWENTY-FIRST CENTURY TOURISM

Looking back over the last thirty years it is easy to see the key economic and social trends that have transformed the former industrial economies in the developed world into post-industrial societies. On the one hand it is a story of severe economic decline, loss of employment and traditional community disintegration, hastened by the economic crises of the early 1970s, the early 1980s and the early 1990s. On the other hand it is a story of remarkable economic growth as new forms of economic activity, including travel and tourism, have emerged to replace those that have been lost. Developments of information and communications technology and of transport technology have unleashed powerful global economic forces, which have simultaneously speeded the decline of traditional industries in countries that developed them for over a century and facilitated the emergence of new forms of employment. It is in this crucible of change that most developed societies are being redefined, and it provides a fertile and volatile context for the trends that are influencing the future of tourism globally. (See also the Epilogue.)

As traditional areas of employment decline in the developed world, many of the industries involved are being re-established in the developing world using the latest technology combined with less costly labour and lower production costs. Such shifts inevitably arouse international ethical and environmental impact considerations but are expected to promote the economic growth of the developing world, and in turn promote further global tourism development.

The main areas of economic decline in developed economies can now be clearly seen with the benefit of hindsight:

- Iron and steel.
- Coal mining.
- Textiles.

- Manufacturing, especially of household goods and all forms of electronic goods.
- Shipbuilding.
- Traditional public transport [en] (with potential recovery to combat congestion and pollution).
- Docks and port facilities.
- Traditional paper-based clerical services.
- Agriculture and fisheries.
- Many small market towns.

The main areas of economic growth are equally clear:

- Information, communications and technology services – especially activity based on the Internet (see Part Four of the book).
- Financial services, such as banking, insurance, pensions and share trading.
- Media generally, broadcast media in particular, including websites, cable and satellite.
- Retailing – especially by branded chains concentrated in out of town/edge-of-town centres or alternatively in large regeneration developments in the centre of cities and towns.
- Education – further and higher education in particular and all forms of training.
- Air and rail transport and associated infrastructure; private cars and motorways; sophisticated road transport systems to service the growth sectors.
- Creative industries such as film, theatre, music and publication.
- The arts and culture generally including music, festivals, museums and art galleries.
- Leisure, recreation and sport and the products, facilities and infrastructure they support.
- Travel and tourism and its associated sectors of hospitality and catering, conferences, exhibitions, entertainment and visitor attractions

The forces in society promoting the growth of tourism are developed more analytically in Chapters 4 and 5. This introduction is intended only to underline the fact that world travel and tourism as defined in this chapter has shifted remarkably in a quarter of a century from what the *Economist* in the early 1990s was still assessing as a *Pleasure Principle* (*Economist*, March 1991) to an integral part of modern post-industrial society and a key element of the lifestyle and quality of life for all with discretionary income that takes them above subsistence level. Students will find it instructive to consider how all forms of tourism, international and domestic, day and stay, are involved in every one of the economic growth trends listed above. Tourism is no longer just the expression of leisure choices for an affluent minority but a core element in modern society, increasingly recognized as a primary economic driver in all countries. This trend also holds good for developing societies that are able effectively to harness some parts of the industrial manufacturing stage and bypass other parts to move straight into post-industrial economic forms as a result of global developments in communications and transport technology. The holding of the Olympic Games in China in 2008 fully demonstrates this point. It would not have been possible ten years earlier.

Changes as profound as those outlined above inevitably had major consequences for the places where millions of people live and work. Most industrial cities and towns in the traditional developed economies of the Western World suffered economically and environmentally since the 1970s as large sectors of their wealth creation based on traditional industries were rendered uneconomic through international competition, and were closed down. In response, supported in Europe by national governments and international funding through the European Commission, the drive to implement regeneration programmes radically altered urban structures in Europe in the last two decades with major development schemes focused on the new areas of economic growth. In nearly all these regeneration programmes the process of change embraced aspects of tourism, leisure and recreation, and forged a proactive climate for the arts, heritage and culture that underlies the development of many new tourism facilities in recent years. The visitor economy is an integral part of such change.

The old industrial economies of the twentieth century gave rise to concepts of mass production and mass consumption and hence *mass tourism*. But post-industrial societies everywhere and the emergence of the modern economy reflect the growth of more affluent, more mature, more culturally diverse, more educated, more demanding, more quality conscious, more cynical, more litigious and more sophisticated consumers in the early years of the new millennium. Such experienced customers are very far removed from the now outdated notions of 'mass tourism' commonly developed in the 1960s and 1970s, and still widely used in many tourism textbooks. These new consumers are able and determined to express their individuality; enabled by modern technology, they are no longer prepared to accept standardized product formats. They seek experiences that are meaningful to them and are prepared to participate in creating the product value they seek. This point is a major shift in the twenty-first century and is developed in Chapter 6 and Part Four of the book.

In post-industrial economies, the arts, heritage and culture are much more than just vibrant elements of the modern economy. They are also vital symbols for place and for a sustainable quality of life including education on which other parts of economic revival can build. The Guggenheim at Bilbao in Spain, the Brindley Centre in Birmingham and the Tate Modern in the UK, the Sydney Opera House and Darling Harbour in Australia, Baltimore and Boston in the USA are not just sites for urban regeneration and locations for museums and galleries. They are icons of local pride and phoenix symbols of determination to regenerate local economies from a lost industrial past into a more prosperous post-industrial future. They provide unique and comprehensible images that are so vital to communication in a modern world overwhelmed by information overload. It augurs well for future tourism that governments around the world are committed to urban and rural regeneration, and most support the role of culture and heritage and the ideas and concepts involved in the modern understanding of the visitor economy.

Courtesy of Dimitrios Buhalis.

Allowing for business and conference visits, and for day visits for many purposes including non-routine shopping, recreation and entertainment, the thrust of tourism development and the locus for tourism destinations is shifting in the early years of the new millennium. Impossible to quantify with available data, the pendulum has obviously swung away from traditional coastal resort locations and activities to new urban and rural locations and activities, many on the sites of former traditional industrial activity. The new forms of tourism are far more dispersed across virtually every community in developed countries. These changes have important environmental implications, both positive and negative as examined by Middleton and Hawkins (1998). Overall, we believe they augur well for sustainable growth and an exciting future for the world's largest industry.

CHAPTER SUMMARY

This chapter introduces travel and tourism as a nationally and internationally important market in which the natural focus of management activity is on exchange transactions between visitors (demand side) and the business sectors and destinations that compete to supply their needs (supply side). All the definitions are based on UNWTO endorsed principles that are valid for all countries, whether they are economically developed or not and whether their tourism industry is mature or just emerging. The chapter explains:

- The overall dimensions of the market.
- Key definitions in a form suitable for marketing purposes.

- The meaning of international tourists, domestic tourists and day visitors, stressing that holiday or vacation tourism is typically only a minority element in twenty-first century tourism.
- In line with the UNWTO definitions that focus on visits and visitors, we adopt the term visitor economy rather than travel and tourism industry to identify the five main sectors in the supply side of travel and tourism.
- Travel and tourism 'industry' is relevant to the commercial sectors of travel and tourism but it does not realistically define Government involvement nationally and at destinations. The five sectors of the visitor economy are outlined in Fig. 1.2, which traces the main linkages between supply and demand and, in particular, indicates how marketing influences all aspects of demand and supply.
- Visitor economy also reflects the shared nature of the supply of most facilities with the residents or 'hosts' of visited destination.

This chapter emphasizes that there are no conceptual differences intended between the use of the terms *tourism*, and *travel and tourism*, and they are used interchangeably throughout the book. The final part of the chapter looks at some growth implications for tourism and the visitor economy in the next decade. For those who wish to consider the definitions of travel and tourism in greater depth, although this is not necessary for marketing purposes, further readings are suggested.

QUESTIONS TO CONSIDER

1. What is the international definition of tourism?
2. List the three main categories and identify at least five different types of market demand under each category.
3. What is the difference between visitors and tourists?
4. Why is international tourism often seen as the most important market sector?
5. List the main growth sectors of the modern economy in developed countries.
6. Develop the list of sectors in Fig. 1.1 to identify up to fifty sub-sectors involved in the visitor economy.

REFERENCES AND FURTHER READING

Cooper, C., Fletcher, J., Fyall, A., Gilbert, D. and Wanhill, S. (2008). *Tourism principles and practice* (4th edn). FT Prentice Hall.

Evans, N., Campbell, D. and Stonehouse, G. (2003). *Strategic management for travel and tourism*. Elsevier Butterworth Heinemann.

Farrell, B.H. and Twining-Ward, L. (2004). Reconceptualizing tourism, *Annals of Tourism Research*, **31** (2), 274–295.

Holloway, J.C. and Taylor, N. (2006). *The business of tourism* (7th edn). Harlow, UK: Prentice Hall.

McIntosh, R.W. (1990). *Tourism: principles, practices, philosophies*. Chapters 1 and 3, Wiley.

Middleton, V.T.C. and Hawkins, R. (1998). *Sustainable tourism: A marketing perspective*. Butterworth-Heinemann.

Sharpley, R. (2006). *Travel and tourism*. Sage Publications.

Smith, S.L.J. (1995). *Tourism analysis: a handbook*. Chapter 2 (2nd edn). Longman.

Theobold, W. (ed.) (1994). *Global tourism: the next decade*. Chapter 1, Butterworth-Heinemann.

Now dated, the original conceptualization in Burkart and Medlik is still relevant: Burkart, A. J. and Medlik, S. (1981). Tourism: Past, Present, and Future. Chapters 4 and 7, 2nd edn, Heinemann.

American icon on the Las Vegas Boulevard 'The evidence of marketing activity surrounds us like the air we breathe'

CHAPTER 2

Introducing marketing: the systematic thought process

Marketing is the activity, set of institutions, and processes for creating, communicating, delivering and exchanging offerings that have value for customers, clients, partners and society at large.

(American Marketing Association, 2007)

This chapter explains the meaning of modern marketing as it is applied internationally to goods and increasingly to services of all types. It defines the essential characteristics common to all forms of marketing while Chapter 3 focuses on the special characteristics of services and travel and tourism marketing. Readers must appreciate that tourism marketing is not a separate discipline but an adaptation of basic principles that have been developed and practised for many decades across a wide spectrum of consumer products, and more recently developed for the public sector and for services provided by not-for-profit organizations.

The essential focus on the customer or user is common to all forms of marketing. But the nature and speed of development of the Internet and e-marketing, which is explained in Part Four of this book and referred to throughout, has delivered a seismic shift in the exchange process that has tilted the balance of power to the user/customer and away from the producer. We believe this to be the most important change in the marketing process over the last decade and the most significant development in marketing over the last 50 years. It has massive implications for the way in which all private and public sector firms and institutions have to respond to their customers or users in order to thrive and grow.

After studying this chapter you should be able to understand:

- Why marketing is an essential aspect of management in all types of commercial and public sector operations.
- The core idea of voluntary exchange between two parties, which underlies all marketing theories of the conduct of business.

- The shift of power within the voluntary exchanges towards users rather than producers.
- The meaning of marketing orientation that reflects management attitudes and approach to the conduct of business.
- The formal definitions of marketing, from which five key propositions are derived, the most important of which is that marketing is a system comprising a series of inter-linked stages, represented in an important diagram shown in Fig. 2.1.
- The combined effect of the five propositions and the growing significance of marketing in the twenty-first century.

While every aspect of this chapter is relevant to travel and tourism marketing, the intention is to introduce the subject as it applies to transactions generally for all types of goods and services.

In Chapter 1 we stated that 'marketing is a subject of vital concern in travel and tourism because in practical terms it harnesses the power of massive commercial forces as well as government and regulatory influences. It has become the principal management influence that can be used to shape the size and behaviour of a major, growing global market.'

To understand marketing it is first necessary to distinguish between the familiar word in everyday use and the concept as it is used professionally by marketing managers. Popular notions of marketing are probably more of a hindrance than a help to those studying the subject for the first time because, before reading any marketing texts, readers will be aware already of the continuous and competitive process of persuasion and inducements of every kind to which we are all routinely exposed in the conduct of our lives. All of us are daily the targets of massive and sustained marketing activity in a variety of forms, which range from advertising on television, radio, in the press and posters and increasingly for most of us on the Internet. Messages also appear on drink mats and bottles, through direct mail and promotional literature of all types, and through incentives, special offers and price reductions in retail stores. If we pause to think about it, the evidence of marketing activity surrounds us like the air we breathe and take for granted.

However imprecise their initial understanding of marketing, most people approach the subject with the view that it is important both commercially and socially. Many are suspicious about its potential influence on their lives and some have ethical concerns about its perceived negative effects upon society. What consumers see of promotion and persuasion, however, is only the visible tip of an extensive iceberg of marketing management activities, of which most people are completely unaware. Marketing as an approach to the conduct of modern business was developed in the early twentieth century in countries in the Western world with relatively free markets. But the concepts are now found increasingly in less developed countries. In the 1990s, following the remarkable collapse of old-style communist economies in Eastern Europe and the former USSR, there has been a deliberate stimulation of market-based organizations and marketing methods. For many decades, competition, profit and promotional activity were seen in the communist world as wasteful and against the public interest. Now, in the major growth economies of China and India, the need for speed of response to change in the global

Courtesy of McDonalds Corporation.

economy, competition and prospects for greater operational efficiency inherent (but not guaranteed) in marketing principles, are forcing the pace of radical rethinking of the traditional practices of centrally planned economies. Promoted by the global outsourcing of manufacturing to lower wage economies, marketing methods are now helping to generate as powerful a socioeconomic revolution as any we saw in the twentieth century.

MARKETING MEANS EXCHANGES

Chapter 1 explains that travel and tourism is best understood in terms of demand and supply within an overall market. At its simplest, marketing can be explained as the process of achieving voluntary exchanges between two parties. As indicated in the American Marketing Association (AMA) definition at the head of this chapter it is important at the outset to recognize that marketing is not restricted to products with prices. Not all products are exchanged for money and profit. For example, some visitor attractions such as museums may be available to visitors free of admission charges. Others, such as national parks may charge for admission or access by car but are operated on a not-for-profit basis. Governments and their agencies, and charities for example, are all involved in providing products or equivalent offerings to users who increasingly are targeted to achieve best value for money spent. Healthcare, community support services and much of cultural provisions are targeted as offerings to user groups. Provided users have an element of free choices as to which services they can use or buy, the central notion of exchange remains valid.

The two parties to marketing exchanges are

- Users or customers who choose to buy or use products or other services. *Users* include clients, user groups and partners.
- Producer organizations and other institutions, which design and supply products or other services to users.

In terms of users or buyers, marketing is concerned with understanding

- The needs and desires of existing and prospective users and any interaction they may seek with suppliers (including why they buy if a price to the user is involved).
- Which products or services they choose to use or buy (when, how much, at what price and how often).
- How they get information about products and other offers.
- Where they obtain or buy products from (direct or through a retail or other intermediary).
- What level of after sales or in use service is needed.
- How they feel after their purchase and consumption of products and services.

In terms of producer organizations, marketing focuses on

- Which products or services to provide and why; especially new products.
- How many products and other offers to produce (volume of supply).
- At what price or cost if price is not involved.
- How to communicate their offers and communicate with buyers, by which media.
- When, where and how to make them available/deliver to users or buyers.
- What level of pre/in use/and after sales or usage services has to be offered.

From this simple introduction it follows that all marketing involves a *management decision process* for producer organizations or institutions, focused on a buyer or *user decision process*, with the two sets of decisions coming together in an exchange transaction – money for products in the case of commercial operators. Assuming that customers have choices between different products, which is nearly always the case in travel and tourism, it is easy to see that producers have the strongest possible motivation to know their customers and prospective customers and to influence them to choose their products rather than those of a competitor.

Throughout this book, especially in dealing with exchange transactions based on services, it is convenient to refer to 'the conduct of business', 'business operations' or 'the management of operations'. In every case, exchange transactions based on the decision processes outlined above are the focus of activity.

MANAGEMENT ATTITUDES, CUSTOMER FOCUS AND THE EXTERNAL BUSINESS ENVIRONMENT

To understand the rationale for marketing it is helpful to focus first on the attitudes of managers in producer organizations. Whether or not a price and profit are involved, the spirit of marketing, its driving force and the reason that its professionals find the subject enormously stimulating, exciting and satisfying, lies in the way in which it is carried out in practice. Important though they are, marketing skills and techniques do not explain what the essence of marketing is. Attitudes do. In a few lines it is impossible to communicate the excitement, vitality and sheer energy surrounding successful marketing operations. Most managers will recognize the enthusiasm the subject inspires; students will have to take it on trust, though they should be aware that marketing has to be experienced 'live' before it can be fully understood. To students much of marketing must appear to be common sense. Only practice can demonstrate how difficult it is to achieve common sense in organizations run by a mix of different people all responding to their own particular perceptions and constraints.

Marketing orientation

Above all, marketing at a strategic level reflects a particular set of strongly held attitudes and a sense of commitment on the part of directors and senior managers – not just marketing managers – which are always found in marketing-led organizations. Combined, the guiding principles and attitudes that affect the whole of an organization are known as a 'management orientation' or 'corporate culture'. In the particular case of a *marketing orientation*, the commitment always means

- Recognition that the conduct of business operations must revolve around the long-run interests and satisfaction of customers or users rather than a focus on one-off exchanges. Where possible, the selective development of relationships with repeat or 'loyal' buyers or users is involved.

- Understanding that the achievement of profits and other organizational goals results from customer satisfaction and customer retention. Recognition that the development of the Internet over the last decade has revolutionized the traditional relationship between seller/provider and buyer/user by empowering customers in ways unknown to previous generations – apart from a small number of very wealthy people.

- A positive, outward looking, innovative and competitive attitude towards the conduct of exchange transactions (in commercial and non-commercial organizations).

- An outward looking, responsive attitude to events and conditions in the external business environment within which an organization operates, especially the actions of competitors.

- An understanding of the strategic or long-run sustainability balance to be achieved between the need to earn profits or maximize the use of existing assets and the equally important need to adapt an organization to achieve future profits, recognizing social and environmental resource constraints.

With these proactive attitudes integrated as the driving force in a management team, marketing techniques may be implemented with vigour and success, although it is never easy. Without the driving force, the most professional skills are unlikely to succeed because their practitioners will usually lose heart and seek more productive working environments. Management attitudes are partly learned and partly a necessary response to external circumstances, especially the current balance between the capacity of supply and the volume of demand in the markets that an organization serves. The next section considers some important effects of this changing balance or relation between supply and demand. The Epilogue discusses recent developments in the social and environmental constraints to which tourism marketing must respond.

A *marketing orientation* as described above is not the only choice for managers, especially those involved in not-for-profit institutions. At the risk of over-simplifying it is possible to comment on two other orientations, which at different times and in different market circumstances guide managers in the conduct of their businesses.

Product and production orientation

This term is often used to summarize the attitudes and responses of businesses whose products are typically in strong and rising demand, and profitable. Because demand does not present problems, there is a natural tendency for managers to focus their main attention on more pressing decisions, such as those concerning production capacity, quality and cost controls, finance for increasing production and maintaining the efficiency and profitability of operations generally. In the short run, where demand is buoyant and growing, an emphasis on production processes and financial controls appears both logical and sensible.

Consider the notional example of a small town with two hotels and one car rental operator. If the town's business community is prosperous and growing, the hotels and the car rental operation will probably be profitable businesses and their owners/managers very likely to be product and production orientated. Such demand conditions are quite commonly found in travel and tourism, even at the beginning of the twenty-first century. Readers should note that the focus of production orientation is *inward looking* towards product decisions and operational needs.

In non-commercial operations where a supplier, often a government or government-funded agency has an effective monopoly over the provision of public services, production orientation is an almost inevitable institutional response unless management attitudes are deliberately changed from the top down.

Sales orientation

This term is often used to summarize the attitudes and responses of businesses whose products are no longer enjoying steady growth in demand, or for which demand may be declining to levels that reduce profitability. Production is not now the main problem; surplus capacity is. The obvious first management reaction in these conditions is to shift the focus of attention to securing sales. Increased expenditure on advertising, distribution channels and on sales promotion or price discounting is a logical response in an attempt to secure a higher level of demand for available production capacity.

In the small-town example noted above, suppose a third hotel of similar size and better quality was built. The occupancy of the existing two would probably suffer an initial fall and a sales response from their managers would appear to be logical and sensible. Such changes in demand conditions are frequently met locally in travel and tourism. Readers should note that the focus of sales orientation is still essentially *inward looking* towards the needs of operations and shifting their surplus capacity. In this case additional sales and promotion costs and price discounting would further erode profit.

Contrast with marketing orientation

As noted earlier, the focus of marketing orientation is essentially *outward looking*. In the notional small-town example, suppose there were now five hotels of a similar standard for a current demand that will fill only three of them at profitable levels of room occupancy. In these conditions inward looking concerns with the production and operational efficiency will not make much impact on demand, especially if competitors' products are of a similar standard and price. Similarly, a strong sales drive with its emphasis on increased promotional expenditure will not increase demand significantly if competitors quickly follow suit with matching expenditure, and the increased expenditure will further undermine profitability. Reducing prices to increase demand will only cause further losses as competitors will have to follow suit.

In the strongly competitive business conditions noted above, which in fact are typical of those now faced by most businesses in the global economy, survival and future success lie in rethinking and adapting the business from the customer's standpoint – in order to secure and sustain an adequate *share* of the available demand and to develop growth in new markets. This always means applying the five marketing orientation principles outlined earlier and, because customers' needs and market conditions are nearly always in a state of constant change, adapting the organization as smoothly as possible and better or faster than competitors. This outward-looking approach and process of adaptation lend itself logically to the increasingly important balancing of long-run consumer interests with business interests and the growing twenty-first century concerns with sustainable development.

In not-for-profit services, the strategic principles of the marketing approach to business are exactly the same although mostly not, of course, the result of free-market competition. The principles have to be deliberately fostered, developed and constantly monitored by senior managers in order to maximize user benefits and satisfaction in the most cost efficient way that meets the longer run needs set out in the five propositions later in this chapter.

Link article available at www.routledge.com/9780750686938

(1) Tosun, C., Okumus, F., Fyall, A., 2008. Marketing philosophies: evidence from Turkey. Annals of Tourism Research 35 (1), 127–147.

DEFINING MARKETING FOR THE TWENTY-FIRST CENTURY

It would be highly convenient if there were just one standard definition of marketing. But, although the subject has now been studied and taught in academic courses for nearly a century (Bartels, 1976), it is still evolving and most consider it as much an art as a science. As any search of the Internet will reveal that there are thousands of definitions, although most of them are individual variations within a broad consensus that the marketing concept is exchange related; consumer led and value or profit orientated. It is important to stress, however, that consumer orientation does not always mean giving customers what they want, but it has to mean understanding their needs and wants in order to respond more efficiently in ways that make business sense for organizations – both in the short term of 6 months to a year, and especially in the longer run of several years.

The authors of this book have chosen to anchor their views on tourism marketing on the 2007 AMA definition quoted at the head of this chapter and that of Philip Kotler, the author familiar to most marketing students on both sides of the Atlantic. The essence of Kotler's definition is 'satisfying needs and wants through an exchange process.' Recognizing, however, the growing restraints on marketing imposed globally by pressures arising from the social, cultural and natural environments within which all institutions must operate, he developed the definition to add the words, *'in a way that preserves or enhances the customers' and the society's well being'* (Kotler, 1991: 26).

Both the AMA and Kotler definitions hold good for all forms of consumer and industrial product marketing, whether it is goods such as soap powders or pianos, or services such as banking, insurance, hotel rooms and airline travel. They are equally relevant to the marketing of people, ideas and places and to any exchange process where target markets and organizational goals exist. In the latter context they are clearly applicable to the products and offerings of government and other not-for-profit organizations. In a tourism context the word *services* is better than *offerings* although the latter includes services and is arguably more comprehensive in its scope.

FIVE MARKETING PROPOSITIONS

Both definitions noted above provide a basis for five important propositions, which are entirely relevant to travel and tourism marketing but not derived from it:

1. Marketing is a management orientation or philosophy.
2. Marketing comprises three main elements linked within a system of exchange transactions.
3. Marketing is concerned with the long term (strategy) and the short term (tactics).
4. Marketing is especially relevant to analysing and responding to twenty-first century market conditions and can make a major contribution to sustainable development.
5. Marketing facilitates the efficient and effective conduct of business.

Management orientation

The first proposition (management orientation) was discussed earlier. Each of the other four is developed below.

Three main elements in marketing exchanges

It is implicit in the AMA definition that marketing comprises the following core elements:

- The attitudes and decisions of target users or customers concerning the perceived utility and value of available goods and services, in terms of their needs, wants, interests and ability to pay.
- The attitudes and decisions of producers concerning production or provision of goods and services for sale, in the context of their long-term business objectives and the wider environment in which they operate.
- The ways in which producers communicate with consumers before, during and after the point of sale, and distribute or provide access to delivery of their products.

In other words, the key elements in any marketing system are the attitudes and thought processes of the two parties – buyers and sellers – or users and providers – in an exchange process.

It should be noted that there is no natural or automatic harmony between what consumers want and will pay for and what producers are able or willing to provide. In practice there is usually continuing tension between a producer's need for profit, the need to operate efficiently and sustainably with available assets and resources, and the customer's search for low cost, best available value and satisfaction in the experiences they seek. Marketing managers have to use judgement in balancing between these conflicting needs in the exchange process and to do so with imprecise knowledge about markets, distribution channels and their competitors' decisions. Their judgement is expressed primarily in the third element of the system, communicating, distributing and delivering products, on which the bulk of marketing expenditure is spent.

The better the balance between the interests in the exchange process, the smaller the marketing expenditure will need to be as a proportion of sales revenue and vice versa. For example, if a car manufacturer or a tour operator has accurately designed, priced and judged the capacity of its production process, distribution and sales will be achieved at a relatively low promotional cost. If, for whatever reason, the price is too high, the product design uncompetitive or the capacity excessive for the available demand, only massive promotional expenditure and discounting will bring supply and demand back into balance.

Linked within a marketing system

The three core elements in the marketing system are expressed in more detail in Fig. 2.1. This is an important diagram, which in addition to introducing all the main processes or stages involved in marketing also provides a framework for the contents of this book.

In Fig. 2.1 the logical flow and linkages between the main processes are shown as an integrated system that is relevant to all forms of service products. The process begins with a detailed analysis of the external business or operating environment, and works through marketing and campaign planning to produce business strategies and operational plans that specify the products to be offered and identify the marketing activities to be undertaken *(the marketing mix and budget)*. The research

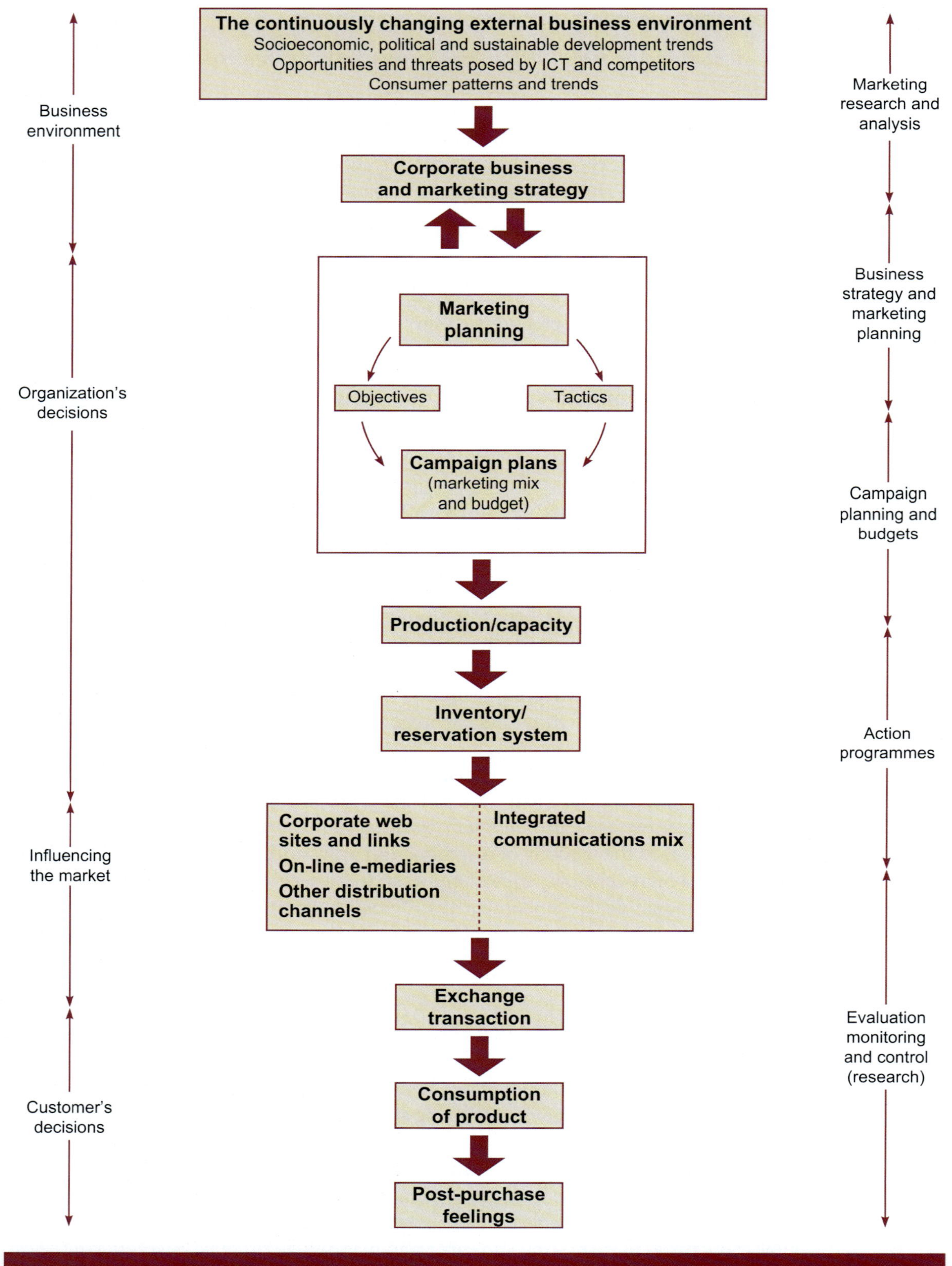

FIGURE 2.1 The marketing system for service products

and planning stages of the process incorporate all that an organization knows about its customers and potential customers, their attitudes and buying behaviour. Business strategies express an organization's attitudes and decisions over a specified time period. As the stages proceed, plans are turned into costed action programmes that express how an organization will communicate with and provide access for its potential customers, and delivery of its products. The development of the Internet, on-line e-mediaries and corporate websites over the last decade has revolutionized the communication and interaction process between buyers and sellers as explained in detail in Part Four of this book. The marketing process is completed with further research into customers' feelings about the quality of the experience they achieved, their satisfaction and the value for money they received from the purchases they made, and their attitude to further purchases. This may also involve direct Internet communication between a business and its customers.

To simplify the explanation, the marketing system in Fig. 2.1 is shown as a series of logical steps with an obvious beginning and end. In practice, as explained in subsequent chapters, the steps do not proceed in a straight line. They comprise a continuous cycle or rolling programme of decisions, actions and research, incorporating many feedback loops that are under constant management review.

Because this book is concerned with services rather than goods, production capacity is shown as being held within an inventory/reservation system. For an airline this would be a computerized reservations system for seats on flights; for a hotel, a reservation system for beds, bed banks and so on. For manufacturers of physical goods all the main stages in the marketing system are essentially the same, but transport, warehousing and related physical distribution systems would be the relevant considerations for inventory.

A summary of the marketing system is offered in Table 2.1. It should be read in tandem with Fig. 2.1 and it notes the main chapters in which each of the stages is explained and discussed in detail.

Concerned with the long term and the short term (strategy and tactics)

The meaning of strategy and tactics is discussed in Chapters 10 and 11, and in understanding marketing orientation it is always important to distinguish the timescale within which marketing decisions are taken. The short term (or short run) may be defined as the period of time in which an organization is able to make only marginal alterations to its product specifications, production capacity and published prices. In other words, in the short run an organization has no choice but to offer its goods or services for sale within the limits of a set of operational constraints that were established in part by its own earlier decision process. In the long run, according to its view of future markets and customers' requirements, an organization may decide to alter product specifications, production capacity, introduce new products or phase out old ones, alter its pricing strategy or change its position within a market. Mergers and business acquisitions or disposals provide other long-run options.

In the short run, organizations frequently find themselves unable to adapt their products quickly enough to meet changes in customers' needs or competitors' actions or other market circumstances such as economic recession. In order to survive, they have to stimulate the available demand through all the techniques of sales promotion, price discounting, merchandizing and advertising they can command. For example, if a rival airline gains permission to operate a route and reduces its competitor's seat occupancy (load factor) from, say, 64 to 54% in the first

TABLE 2.1 Summary of the marketing system

Process	Description	Main chapter reference
Marketing research and analysis	Continuous, detailed appreciation of past and projected trends in the external business environment (including sustainable issues)	4, 5 and 9
Business strategy and marketing planning	Developing research and analysis into overall business and marketing opportunities and devising strategies and operational plans	10 and 11
Campaign planning and budgeting	Producing costed operational programmes to integrate the four main elements in the marketing mix – the four Ps	8 and 12
Action programmes and implementation	Detailed programmes of daily/weekly/monthly activity for all elements in the marketing mix	14–17
Evaluation, monitoring and control	Monitoring and evaluating the results of marketing including all forms of market research and use of databases. Taking corrective action as appropriate	9 and 12

Note: Each of these processes is further illustrated in Parts Five and Six of this book. Each of the case studies is a demonstration of the marketing system at work.

6 months of a new service, the immediate task for the competitor's marketing is to fight for share and volume using aggressive sales tactics.

What always distinguishes the marketing-led organization in the short run is not the objectives of its tactics, but the speed and the way in which it uses and exploits its deep knowledge of customers to achieve its specified targets, while at the same time holding firm to its longer-term vision and strategy developed around long-run consumer orientation and satisfaction. Readers should note that most marketing definitions (including the AMA definition quoted in this chapter) are relevant primarily to the long run. In practice, however, most marketing decisions are made in the tactical context of the short run. The constraints imposed by marketing highly 'perishable' service products with a fixed capacity on any one day, make short-run marketing decisions especially important in travel and tourism, a point that is explained in the next chapter. They should also focus attention on the strategic vision that underlies the tactical options.

It is not possible to set a precise timescale for either short or long run, because it varies from sector to sector. Suffice it to say that the short run typically means 6 months to a year ahead, and the focus of decisions is on this year's and next year's operations and marketing campaign. The long run typically means not less than 2–3 years ahead, and the focus of decisions is strategic.

In the ideal world of textbooks, products and other services provisions are mostly designed to meet users' or customers' needs and they generate satisfaction and profit or other objectives of an organization. In the real world, products and services are mostly less than ideal in one or more respects and marketing managers have to live with the results of decisions that looked right when they were made some months or years previously but which have since been overtaken by unpredicted (and often unpredictable) events. In 2001, the unpredicted and massive impact on international travel and tourism markets of 9/11 in New York was an extreme illustration of circumstances that faced marketing managers. In 2008, the fall out of the international banking crisis that originated in the USA is being worked out as this book goes to print but it seems certain to radically alter the business conditions under which most services marketers planned to operate in 2009. All organizations are vulnerable to unpredicted events; sometimes they are overwhelming and business failures occur. Skilful marketing performs the only available compensating function for the gaps and mismatches between demand and supply that occur inevitably when markets do not move in the ways predicted by managers.

Especially relevant to twenty-first century market conditions

There is really nothing new in a marketing concept based simply on recognizing the need to satisfy customers, understand market trends and exploit demand efficiently. These essential characteristics of marketing have been practised by small businesses throughout history. No one survives long, especially in small service businesses, unless they understand their customers' needs and provide satisfactory service at competitive prices. What distinguishes markets in the twenty-first century from those in any previous era, is a combination of powerful trends outlined below:

- A relatively small number of large, still growing, highly competitive businesses with standardized products and internationally recognized brands that command a growing share of the markets they operate in. Such businesses operate on a national, international and, increasingly, a global scale. In travel and tourism as in other international markets for service products, large transnational corporations are increasingly able, through their marketing decisions and branding as well as economies of scale, to influence customers' expectations of products and prices. They also lead the way in the development of marketing skills. In this they are now able to command all the resources of modern Information and Communications Technology (ICT), which has revolutionized the speed and efficiency with which it is possible to manage and control large, multi-site operations – and communicate directly with customers.

- A special feature of travel and tourism, which differentiates the markets from most other major sectors of goods and services, is the massive number of small or micro-enterprises that dominate the sector numerically. Although impossible to count with any precision, there were estimated to be at least 2.7 million small and very small tourism firms in Europe at the end of the twentieth century – Middleton, 1998b). The significance of these small businesses is explained in Chapter 3.

- The revolutionary development of ICT that has simultaneously made possible the growth and management control of large corporations and offers a powerful networking collaborative route for small businesses to compete. (See Part Four of this book.)

- Capacity of supply considerably in excess of what markets can absorb naturally (without stimulation). Common across most sectors of the modern economy, competitive pressures derive from the number of businesses (large and small) competing for growing shares of available markets or competing to sustain the shares they already have. It is competitive pressures that do most to stimulate innovative marketing responses and product development.

- Growing numbers of consumers in developed countries with sufficient disposable income and leisure time to indulge in non-essential purchases, many of them choosing to engage in frequent travel for leisure purposes. With some notable setbacks in periods of international economic crisis, growing consumer affluence in most parts of the developed and developing world drives marketing developments. The growth of affluent middle classes in China and India is projected to expand significantly the demand for tourism over the next decade and beyond.
- Sustainable development requirements constraining business decisions that have flowed from the 1992 World Summit at Rio de Janeiro and subsequent inter-government meetings. These requirements, endorsed internationally by governments, are focusing in the twenty-first century on dealing with global climate change and the implications caused primarily by CO_2 emissions from the burning of fossil fuels. These developments have no parallel in the history of marketing and are now certain to dominate decision-making in commercial and not-for-profit organizations around the world. The requirements will increasingly have to be embraced and reflected in marketing decisions.

Facilitates the efficient and effective conduct of business through monitoring and control

A marketing orientation is no longer an option for large businesses in competitive markets. It has become a necessary condition for survival. But it is less clear from the definitions of marketing exactly how this orientation leads to the more efficient and effective conduct of business for profit or helps optimize cost/value calculations in the not-for-profit sector. In practice efficiency emerges from the systematic way that managers undertake the processes set out in Fig. 2.1; effectiveness emerges from skills in the business planning and targeting processes. But it is not the processes themselves that are characteristic of marketing orientation. All commercial organizations plan, promote and distribute products, and the processes are common to all larger organizations. What differentiates them is the corporate culture noted earlier and the way that marketing procedures are integrated and co-ordinated with other core business functions, especially the production and delivery or operational processes, human resource management and financial controls.

Marketing-orientated businesses are characterized by the systematic organization of their planning processes, their knowledge of the effects of their actions on their customers, the precision with which they state their targets and the speed at which they can act in relation to competitors. Identifying, responding and adapting to market changes ahead of competitors is the essence of the modern marketing approach.

Throughout this book it is stressed that efficiency and effectiveness in marketing are always based upon the specification of precise objectives and action programmes that can be closely monitored and evaluated. Precise marketing objectives also serve in practice as:

- An integrating and co-ordinating mechanism for the operational departments in a business.
- A control system for measuring actual performance against targets, overall and for specific business units.
- A means of evaluating tactical targets against strategic marketing objectives.
- A means of communicating the goals and achievements of the organization to employees and other stakeholders.

It is the thought processes involved in the specification of objectives and action programmes, combined with the close monitoring of results that make the modern marketing approach increasingly relevant to not-for-profit organizations.

CHAPTER SUMMARY

This chapter defines the meaning of modern marketing, first, as a *management orientation*, sometimes referred to as a management philosophy or corporate culture and, second, as a *systematic process* integrating the techniques used by marketing managers to influence demand. While the practice of marketing developed and is most easily understood in commercial operations, the orientation and the processes are increasingly applied to services provided by the public sector and in not-for-profit sectors also. The chapter stresses that

- To be effective in practice, the orientation and the process must be integrated and co-ordinated within the whole management team.
- Marketing is outward looking and proactive to the changing business environment, and to the needs, expectations and behaviour of customers or users.
- A marketing approach is a response to business conditions, especially competition, and that such conditions are increasingly common to all producers of consumer goods and services at the start of the twenty-first century.
- The particular conditions of fierce competition in markets dominated by large-scale, multi-site organizations, often with a considerable surplus of capacity of highly perishable products and seeking to influence available demand, are those that are now found frequently in travel and tourism markets in many parts of the world.
- Although larger international firms dominate modern markets the numbers of small businesses have a vital role to play in tourism marketing. The importance of small businesses practising the same marketing orientation and techniques without competing head-on in large volume markets is also stressed.
- ICT can be harnessed to work for the benefit of all sizes of operation.

- Figure 2.1 provides a step-by-step diagram of the modern marketing process applicable to all types of organization in the travel and tourism industry. It also serves as a framework for the contents of this book. The diagram is important and should repay careful consideration.

The authors believe that the twenty-first century conditions' trends noted in this chapter underlie the nature of modern international competition generally. They influence all sectors of the modern economy. In travel and tourism, the continuous need to fill thousands of under-utilized beds, seats and other supply components, provides the most powerful motivator now forcing the pace of modern marketing. There are no equivalent trends on a global scale in any previous period of history. These are the driving forces that explain the current and future importance of marketing orientation and the need for improved marketing techniques.

Above all, this chapter stresses that marketing is a proactive approach to business, conducted at best in a marvellously stimulating and positive spirit of competitive enthusiasm that no textbook can convey. The same spirit can also be developed in public sector and not-for-profit operations.

QUESTIONS TO CONSIDER

1. Explain the AMA definition of *offerings* in the context of travel and tourism.
2. What are the key strategic principles that together distinguish a modern marketing organization?
3. Choose a not-for-profit organization and explain how the key strategic principles are likely to work in practice.
4. Why might a commercial organization decide not to give its customers products that they say they want?
5. Explain the long and short run in marketing decisions and indicate some implications.
6. Why is marketing especially relevant to twenty-first century market conditions?

REFERENCES AND FURTHER READING

Baker, M.J. (1996). *Marketing: an Introductory Text*. Chapter 1 (6th edn). Macmillan.

Brassington, F. and Pettit, S. (2000). *Principles of Marketing* (3rd edn). FT Prentice-Hall.

Constantinides, E. (2006). The marketing mix revisited: towards the 21st century marketing, *Journal of Marketing Management*, **22**, pp. 407–438.

Cornelissen, J. (2002). Academic and practitioner theories of marketing, *Marketing Theory*, **2**(1), pp. 133–143.

Davidson, H. (1997). *Even more offensive marketing*. Chapters 1 and 2. Penguin.

Holland, C.P. and Naude, P. (2004). The metamorphosis of marketing into an information-handling problem, *Journal of Business and Industrial Marketing*, **19**(3), pp. 167–177.

Jobber, D. (2007). *Principles and practice of marketing* (5th edn). McGraw-Hill.

Kotler, P. and Armstrong, G. (1999). *Principles of marketing*. Chapter 1 (8th edn). Prentice-Hall.

Kotler, P., Wong, V., Saunders, J. and Armstrong, G. (2005). *Principles of marketing* (4th European edn). Pearson Prentice Hall.

McDonald, M. (2002). *Marketing plans* (5th edn). Butterworth Heinemann.

Tosun, C., Okumus, F. and Fyall, A. (2008). Marketing philosophies: evidence from Turkey, *Annals of Tourism Research*, **35**(1), pp. 127–147.

McDonald's restaurant in Shanghai, 'Major companies that have helped to shrink the globe'

Photo courtesy of McDonalds Corporation

CHAPTER 3

The special characteristics of travel and tourism marketing

Every textbook on marketing should be based upon services with a couple of chapters at the end on the 'special case of goods'.

(Bateson, 1995: vii)

Drawing on the contributions of widely recognized authors, Chapters 1 and 2 introduce the essential concepts of travel and tourism as a market, and of marketing as an approach to the conduct of modern business for commercial firms and other institutions in the not-for-profit sector. Organizations in travel and tourism are part of the *services sector* of the global economy, as distinguished by economists internationally from the manufacturing, construction and primary sectors. This chapter focuses on the special characteristics of the global travel and tourism industry as one of the major services sectors in the twenty-first century, highlighting the marketing responses required. Travel and tourism businesses are by no means unique in marketing terms but they do reflect some common structural patterns that determine marketing responses.

After studying this chapter you should be able to understand:

- The vital distinctions between the marketing of goods, from which much of the theory of marketing developed in the twentieth century, and the marketing of services that now dominate the economies of the developed countries.
- The significance of marketing for large-scale service operations.
- The differences between services provided by large organizations and the small and micro-businesses that dominate the visitor economy numerically around the world.

- The significance of the micro-businesses in most visitors' experiences, especially in leisure tourism.
- The special characteristics of the services products provided by travel and tourism organizations.
- The influence of those characteristics on the ways in which marketing decisions are made in practice in the sectors of the visitor economy noted in Chapter 1; especially the focus on influencing and managing customer demand.

MARKETING GOODS AND SERVICES

The origins of modern marketing theory are generally attributed to the USA in the first part of the twentieth century (Bartels, 1976). The early contributions to the study recognized the growing importance of sales and distribution functions for manufacturers of consumer goods. They reflected the opportunities provided at that time by rapid improvements in rail and road transport and telephone communication systems, and the consequent growth in the size of markets that businesses could reach with their products. For over 50 years the emerging theories focused almost exclusively on the marketing of physical goods, especially on the marketing of items manufactured on a mass-production basis for mass consumption by the general public.

Until the 1970s the significance of service industries and services marketing generally were largely ignored on both sides of the Atlantic. Or they were discussed in crude simplifications, which lumped together as one broad category personal services such as domestic cleaning and hairdressing, commercial services such as banking, transportation, restaurants and tour operation, professional services such as medical and legal services and public services such as education and health care. Yet in North America, Europe and Japan, for example, countries with developed economies, the proportion of the working population employed in all forms of services rose rapidly in the last half of the twentieth century to levels now approaching three-quarters of all employment.

It was the rapid growth in the 1960s, 1970s and 1980s of large-scale commercial service operations such as financial services, insurance and retail distribution, as well as transport, accommodation and catering, which prompted the shift of emphasis in marketing studies towards services. Even so, the first American Marketing Association Conference devoted specifically to service industries took place as recently as 1981. Since then there has been a massive output of articles and books on all aspects of services marketing. It is beyond the scope of this book to trace and analyse the growth of service industries and the recognition that the marketing of most goods also involves commitment to the provision of pre- and post-sales services. But the demand for services generally is related to economic growth, increasing levels of consumers' disposable income, the development of rapid transport communications within and between countries, the growth of telecommunications and the emergence of modern information and communications technology (ICT) for management information and control purposes.

Most importantly, associated with improved ICT and management control processes, the achievement of *economies of scale* in service operations, including marketing economies, has triggered much of the recent growth in the scale of services operations. Developments in franchising and management contracts for services, together with international mergers, acquisitions and alliances, have also facilitated the speed of growth in large commercial organizations in service industries, both nationally and internationally. In the last two decades, accelerated recently by the opportunities inherent in communications technology and e-commerce, major international service corporations have helped to shrink the globe with their international brands. Virgin, Ryanair, McDonald's, Holiday Inn, Accor, Hertz, Disney and American Express are just some examples.

LARGE-SCALE SERVICE OPERATIONS DOMINATE TRAVEL AND TOURISM MARKETING

It is not easy to define the point at which a service producer becomes a large-scale operator; it tends to vary in different sectors of industry according to the nature of their operations. Large-scale commercial operations in all parts of the world, however, usually display the following common characteristics, all of which have important implications for marketing:

1. Production, sale and distribution of purpose-designed, repeatable, quality-controlled service products – all operations managed and controlled using modern ICT.
2. Continuous production and availability throughout the year, typically in multiple sites. McDonald's, for example, operated some 24,500 restaurants in 2007.
3. Products typically heavily branded with advertising support and bearing standard prices (with frequent variations by place and time).
4. Products available on-line via corporate websites and typically also at multiple outlets. With its 24,500 restaurants around the world in 2007, McDonald's is a special case but multi-site operations for services delivery are common in travel and tourism.
5. Most marketing undertaken by corporate head offices, which control and direct the activities at individual production/delivery units.

These characteristics are common to most retail chains, fast-food chains, post offices, financial services providers, car rental and hotel corporations. They are not restricted to travel and tourism services.

Given the characteristics noted above, it should be appreciated that there are some strong similarities as well as differences between the operating needs of large-scale service organizations and manufacturers of goods produced and delivered on a continuous production basis. Levitt, for example, pushed this similarity to its logical conclusion in discussing the need to 'industrialize service production systems'. He explained that this could be achieved by reducing the level of discretion available to service staff through the use of standardized procedures, and the use of what he called *hard*, *soft* and *intermediate* technologies (Levitt, 1981: 37). Levitt cited the McDonald's Corporation as an excellent illustration of the successful blending of industrial processes in food production and distribution, with quality control over every aspect of standardized operations, including the motivation and performance of the staff who provide services in the restaurants. Most airlines, hotel groups, tour operators, retail travel agency chains and the larger tourist attractions are striving currently to organize, control and deliver their continuous production capacity in equivalent ways, for the same reasons. It is a global marketing issue for service providers.

During the last decade growing interest has been shown by service industries in systematic procedures for defining, regularly monitoring and providing certification for the quality of service products. Using a measurement process based on auditing tasks, producing manuals that specify all operations and regular assessments by external auditors, the international process is known as International Standard (ISO 9000), in Europe (EN 2900) and in the UK as British Standard (BS 5750). Closely related to benchmarking processes for evaluating service quality, such standards were first operated by some hotels, airlines and tour operators in the early 1990s. Quality monitoring poses considerable operational problems for multi-site service businesses but it is a vital development for marketing managers whose product promises have to be based on expectations of satisfactory delivery. Managing standards of service quality draws marketing managers and operation managers closer together, especially in measuring customer satisfaction and value for money.

Not to be confused with mass consumption

The recent developments in modern service industries noted above explain why the concept of services marketing set out in this book is primarily orientated around the marketing of large-scale, widely distributed, quality-controlled products. It has to be stressed, however, that production on a large scale no longer has to mean the mass production of undifferentiated products for mass markets. All the complexities of market segmentation and product differentiation are at least as relevant to service producers as they are to manufacturers of physical goods and there is also ample room for market niches to be tailored to particular groups in the market. As explained in Part Four, modern Internet communications are now opening new opportunities for businesses to interact with customers on a one-to-one basis that is shifting services marketing towards a more consumer centric rather than the traditional business centric approach. See also Chapter 7.

A primary reason for the growth of service organizations is the search for lower unit costs of production and delivery. From a cost-efficiency standpoint the essential requirement of continuous production on a large scale lies in effective product design and quality control of standardized operations. But once the technical problems of production have been solved, the ability to sustain production at efficient levels of utilization of premises and equipment forces management attention onto the systematic promotion of continuous consumption. In other words ensuring that there is a profitable balance between the volume of demand and the volume of supply. If sufficient demand cannot be generated, massive financial losses are inevitable. Recent examples are the financial losses sustained internationally in tourism sectors after 9/11 in 2001. As oil prices rise and the world economy stumbles over the international banking crisis of 2007/2008 international tourism demand seems certain to falter or decline between 2008 and 2010. The larger the operator, the more important it is to exert massive effort to secure and sustain a regular flow of customers to purchase the available capacity. This explains much of the modern focus on the role of marketing by these larger organizations.

It is interesting to speculate that the relative size of businesses is in fact more important in determining marketing responses than whether or not they are goods or services.

It is the fact of large-scale continuous production of many service products that provides the essential 'like with like' comparison with manufactured products. Of course, this characteristic has little if anything to do with most lawyers, undertakers, cobblers or beauticians. But then neither has it any relevance to basket weavers, jobbing potters, saddle makers or gunsmiths. A dentist and a street corner shoe shiner have more in common (in marketing terms) with each other and with bakers and candlestick makers, than any of them have in common with large scale producers of either goods or services. (Middleton, 1983)

PARADOXICALLY, THE VAST NUMBER OF SMALL BUSINESSES IS ALSO A DOMINATING CHARACTERISTIC OF SERVICE PROVIDERS IN THE VISITOR ECONOMY

At their best, small businesses reflect most of the features and characteristics that are unique to the tourism destinations in which they operate... The sector has vibrancy and originality and can play a vital leading edge role in delivering excellence with personality that big businesses cannot replicate.... At worst, however, small businesses make survival decisions that physically degrade the attractions of the local environment, damage the destination image and draw in the lowest spending clientele. (Middleton, INSIGHTS, 1997)

There is a broad consensus in Europe that small and medium-sized enterprises, commonly known as *SMEs*, play a vital part in the economic, social and environmental life of European Union (EU) member states. Their future role in providing employment and underpinning the economic and social life of local communities, especially in the tourism and recreation context, is well-recognized – at least in principle. In practice it is far from clear how best to recognize, measure, appreciate, support and regulate the sector with a light touch so that it may play its full potential role in achieving national and EU tourism objectives.

Within the SME sector (defined as businesses comprising less than 250 employees) it is the group representing the smallest employers (less than ten employees) that have unique characteristics that merit special attention. Identified as *micro-businesses* to distinguish them within the SME sector, the smallest employers are by far the largest numerically in the visitor economy, estimated at more than nine out of ten SMEs. In fact the majority of them employ less than five people and many comprise only the proprietor and immediate family. There were estimated to be over 2.5 million such enterprises actively trading within European tourism at the end of the 1990s (Middleton, 1998), although this may be a significant underestimate because of the problems of measurement. A more insightful way to put it is that for every large-scale national or international company operating in travel and tourism, there are at least 1000 micro-businesses.

Individually, micro-businesses are insignificant as players in international and domestic tourism and recreation. In practice they are often ignored in national and regional tourism policy developments. *Collectively*, however, they provide the bulk of the essentially local ambience and quality of visitor experiences at destinations on which the future growth of overseas and domestic visits depends. They also comprise a seed bed of entrepreneurial and enterprise 'culture' that is highly relevant for future destination marketing.

Major players in airlines, sea ferries and railways may provide the best of public transport. Global hotel groups may provide the highest standards of branded accommodation. But few visitors are motivated by the joys of transport to a destination, while most hotels and other forms of accommodation are often perceived as just a means to an end. In practice, on the ground, it is mostly small businesses that deliver the bulk of the visitor experiences that define a visitor's perception and enjoyment of a destination. It is likely that nine out of ten domestic and overseas leisure visitors will encounter micro-businesses at some point of time during their stay in a destination. Those encounters will influence their perception of sense of place, quality and value for money, and their wish to revisit – or recommend friends to visit.

Types of micro-business

Micro-businesses are found in all the industry sectors noted in Chapter 1. Operating in a very local context, many of them are motivated as much, or more, by a mix of personal, quality of life and community goals, as by the economic/commercial rationale that dominates big business. In Europe, for example, there are many semi-retired people who operate small accommodation businesses, not for profit but to support their lifestyle. Numbered in hundreds of thousands, micro-businesses are unique as individual enterprises and their service provision cannot be standardized – to attempt to do so would destroy their contribution. Unfortunately this makes them amorphous and difficult to measure and 'badge' as a coherent sector. It is often very difficult to influence the sector through any of the existing processes of tourism policy consultation. Many prefer to be left alone and they are not natural 'joiners' of trade organizations. The sector comprises

- Guesthouses and B&Bs
- Farmhouse accommodation
- Cafés, inns and restaurants
- Operators of sports activities and centres
- Taxi drivers
- Artists and others involved in cultural provision
- Self-catering in cottages/holiday parks
- Museums and other small attractions
- Coach operators
- Guides and interpreters
- Souvenir shops
- Small travel agencies

The importance of micro-businesses

Economically

- They make up some 95% of all the enterprises providing tourism services. Although the big players dominate tourism expenditure, the smallest players collectively generate perhaps a third of total tourism revenue, and much more locally.

- The money earned by micro-businesses tends to stay in the local community. They typically purchase locally and are part of the fabric of the local money circulation cycle.
- They are a vital part of new job creation – especially in areas of rural and urban regeneration. Even without new job creation they perform an important economic stability role in fragile areas.

In social terms

- Micro-businesses are part of the lifeblood of local communities – as local residents, neighbours, taxpayers and employers – even where they may be part of the unofficial or 'black' economy. Many micro-business proprietors are also found in local politics.
- To visitors they are often seen as the 'friendly locals'. As many large-scale businesses employ foreign labour for service delivery micro-businesses may represent all that most visitors will ever experience of real local character, knowledge and individuality at destinations – reflecting the special values of 'place' and 'host encounters'.
- Leading-edge small businesses are entrepreneurial role models of success and may inspire young people in their communities by example.

In environmental terms

- Micro-businesses typically express the local character of a destination through their operations, and in many ways also help to sustain that character and communicate it to visitors.
- They influence the perceived visual quality of the built and natural landscape by their actions and the buildings they use.
- Their operations impact daily upon local sustainability issues such as water usage, waste recycling and local purchasing of goods and services for use in their businesses.

Some marketing implications of micro-businesses

The sheer number of enterprises involved in all countries makes micro-businesses a core, not a peripheral part of the experience of most non-business visitors. The evidence suggests that such businesses are not scaled down versions of bigger businesses, however, and they cannot be treated in the same terms. At the leading edge, they embody the entrepreneurial spirit and vitality of places, and offer some of the best tourist experiences available anywhere. At the trailing edge, which may be a third or more of the total, many exist on the fringes of the visitor economy damaging the environment of the destinations in which they are located, reducing visitor satisfaction and the perceived quality of the overall visitor experience. Indeed, some of the worst visitor experiences will be found in this sector and they can undermine the other attractions and facilities, reducing the marketing potential of a destination.

Most micro-businesses have had no formal management education or training. Traditionally, most have had little engagement in marketing other than through the medium of print provided by local tourist boards and contacts with their own clients.

Only small minorities of them were ever involved in some form of co-operative marketing campaigns.

Business and consumer access to the Internet since 1995, however, have revolutionized opportunities for small businesses in the twenty-first century and radically shifted marketing power in their direction. This key issue is addressed in Part Four of this book.

Courtesy of Andrew Boer.

SERVICES AND THEIR CHARACTERISTICS

The essential difference between goods and services, as noted by Rathmell in one of the earlier contributions to the subject, is that 'Goods are produced. Services are performed' (Rathmell, 1974). This key difference holds good for enterprises of all sizes. Goods are products purchased through an exchange transaction conferring ownership of a physical item that may be used or consumed at the owner's choice of time and place. Services are products purchased through an exchange transaction that does not confer ownership but permits access to and use of a service, usually at a specified time in a specified place. Thus, for example, the buyer of a ready-to-wear suit takes it from the store and wears it when and where he pleases. The producer need have no further involvement unless the article is faulty.

The buyer of a hotel room agrees to arrive on a particular night or nights, and may forfeit a deposit or the full price if he fails to appear. Throughout his stay the traveller is closely involved with the hotel and its staff, and may participate directly in aspects of the service product by carrying his own bags, serving himself from a restaurant buffet, making his own tea and in other ways.

The manufacturer or retailer of suits can put his products into warehouses and shops, and it may not be a vital concern if 6 months or more elapse between the completion of production and sale to the customer. But, like newspapers, a hotel can perform its services once only on any given day. If customers are not available on that day, products are lost and cannot be held over for sale on the following day.

From this short introduction and the summary of the main generic characteristics that distinguish most goods from most services (see Table 3.1), the principal characteristics of service products may be summarized as follows:

- Inseparability, sometimes associated with intangibility and heterogeneity/variability.
- Perishability, associated with the inability to hold physical stocks of products for future sale.

Inseparability

This means that the act of providing a service and its consumption are simultaneous. The performance of the service requires the active participation of the producer and the consumer *together.* In the visitor economy it also means that production and consumption take place on the premises, or in the equipment (such as aircraft or hire cars) of the producer, and not in the consumer's home environment.

It means, too, that many of the staff of service companies have some 'front-of-house or front-line' contact with users and are seen by the customer to be an inseparable aspect of the service product. Factory workers, managers and many in the distribution chain for consumer goods do not usually meet customers; their attitudes and the way they look and behave in the factory are not necessarily relevant to product performance and customer satisfaction. Physical items can be tested and guaranteed, and precise product performance can be enforced by consumer protection laws. For services, by contrast, a wide range of product performance is determined by employees' attitudes and behaviour for which there can be none of the normal guarantees and mostly no prospect of legal enforcement. Staff can be encouraged and monitored but cannot be forced to smile at customers,

TABLE 3.1 Generic characteristics distinguishing services from goods

Goods	Services
Are manufactured	Are performed
Made in premises not normally open to customers (separable)	Performed on the producers' premises, often with full customer participation (inseparable)
Goods are delivered to places where customers live	Customers travel to places where the services are delivered
Purchase conveys ownership and right to use at own convenience	Purchase confers temporary right of access at a prearranged place and time
Goods possess tangible form at the point of sale and can be inspected prior to sale	Services are intangible at the point of sale; often cannot be inspected (other than 'virtually') although broadband Internet has transformed the options in the twenty-first century
Stocks of product can be created and held for future sale	Perishable; services can be inventoried but stocks of product cannot be held

Note: These characteristics are those that apply generally to most services and most goods. In practice, most physical goods are marketed with a strong service element attached.

for example. Inseparability of production and consumption is thus a vital concept in the marketing of services and it has special implications for management decisions on the services marketing mix. These decisions are developed in Chapters 7 and 8.

Two other characteristics that flow from inseparability are sometimes said to distinguish products based on services from those based on physical goods: one is *heterogeneity or variability* and the other is *intangibility* (see, for example, Stanton, 1981). Taken literally, heterogeneity means that every service performance is unique to each customer. Strictly, because human beings are not machines, this is true; services are intrinsically variable. But in practice it is a somewhat academic concept and it makes no sense to apply it to frequently used convenience service products such as those marketed by banks, retailers, transport operators, post offices, hotel chains and other large-scale service operators, all of which are committed to the specification and quality control of service performance. For all practical marketing management purposes frequently used 'convenience' services are no more heterogeneous than convenience goods such as groceries. For larger companies, it is a vital part of marketing controls to minimize the variability element.

Intangibility is an important characteristic of some, mostly the more expensive service products, in the sense that most services cannot easily be measured, touched or evaluated at the point of sale before performance. It follows that many service products are 'ideas' in the minds of prospective buyers. But many physical goods, such as motorcars, perfumes or expensive leisure wear and equipment, are also 'ideas' in customers' minds at the point of sale even though they can be inspected and guaranteed. On the other hand, bus services, fast-food restaurants and budget hotels and airlines are hardly less tangible to those who use them regularly than Marks & Spencer's socks or a washing powder. Accordingly, although the intangibility of travel and tourism products requires careful understanding by marketing managers and a particular response in the promotion and distribution of more expensive service products, it is not a generic difference between goods and services of the same order as inseparability and perishability.

Fortunately, inseparability does not mean that consumption and purchase cannot be separated. A primary aim of most services marketing is to create ways to distance the act of purchase from the act of consumption. That distance provides a scope for marketing initiatives that reduce the dependence on inseparability. A hotel, for example, which has only 20% of its capacity booked 12 hours before the scheduled performance of its particular services, becomes highly dependent upon passing traffic for last-minute purchases. Customers at the check-in desk may well negotiate prices that are half or less of published tariffs. The same hotel, if it is 85% pre-booked 3 months before the specified date of service production, is clearly in a much stronger position.

Perishability

Perishability is generally treated as a separate characteristic of services, although it follows logically from the fact of inseparability that service production is typically *fixed in time and space* and has a fixed maximum capacity on any day. This means that if service capacity or products are not sold on a particular day, the potential revenue they represent is lost and cannot be recovered. Service production therefore is better understood as a *capacity to produce*, not a quantity of products. Capacity is utilized only when customers are present on the producers' premises.

To illustrate the point, consider the example of a museum that has an effective visitor capacity (assessed as space in which to move in comfort around the exhibits and enjoy the experience) of, say, 500 visits per hour. This could mean around 2000 visits on a typical busy day making allowance for peak and slack times of the day. If the museum closes 1 day per week it has a nominal 'production' capacity of 313 days × 2000 visitors = 626,000 visits over 12 months. In practice such a museum is unlikely to exceed around 150,000 visits per annum but on around 10 days it may be overcrowded with 3000 visits per day, whereas on 100 days in the winter it may never exceed 200 per day. If 10,000 visitors want to visit the museum on a particular day, they cannot do so because the display space cannot be expanded, and the inevitable crowding and queues would destroy the experience causing most prospective visitors to go elsewhere. A would-be Sunday visitor is unlikely to be impressed by the fact that he could visit on Monday if he is going to be back at work on that day.

Hotels with a fixed number of rooms and transport operators with a fixed number of seats face identical problems of matching perishable supply to the available demand. Perishability is directly linked in the case of travel and tourism services with seasonality, which is discussed later in this chapter.

It follows from the characteristics of perishability that it is not possible for a service producer to create a stock of products to satisfy daily fluctuations in demand. By contrast, manufacturers of Christmas goods, for example, are able to manufacture their products around the year and create stocks, most of which are sold to customers in November and December. The process of stock creation and physical distribution between factories, warehouses and retailers is expensive, but it does create a relative stability and continuity in the production process that is not available to service producers.

Perishability and the impossibility of physical stockholding actually make the creation of inventory systems for forward selling a dominant marketing issue for all large-scale service products. As a result of modern ICT it has become ever easier to develop low cost computerized inventories for storing and marketing the daily details of each year's potential production capacity. From that standpoint there is no difference between selling stockholdings of physical goods and the inventories of services products. Modern marketing of service products reduces the impact of perishability to manageable proportions.

PARTICULAR CHARACTERISTICS OF TRAVEL AND TOURISM SERVICES

Associated with the basic or generic characteristics common to all services, there are at least three further features that are particularly relevant to marketing travel and tourism services. These are

- Seasonality and other major variations in the pattern of demand.
- The high fixed costs of operations, allied to fixed capacity at any point in time.
- The interdependence of tourism products.

Seasonality: peaks and troughs in demand

It is a characteristic of most leisure tourism markets that demand fluctuates greatly between seasons of the year. Residents of northern Europe and the northern states of the USA tend mostly to take their main holidays of the year in the summer months of June to September, because their winter months of November to March are generally cold, often wet and hours of daylight are short. While such climatic variations are not so relevant to many Mediterranean, Middle Eastern, Pacific or Caribbean tourism destinations, their main markets are still accustomed to think of summer and winter months. School and many business-year cycles reinforce such traditions. As a result, many tourism businesses dealing with holiday markets fluctuate from peaks of 90 to 100% capacity utilization for 16 weeks in a year, to troughs of 30% or less – and sometimes seasonal closure – for 20 or more weeks in the year.

On a weekly basis, city centre restaurants may fluctuate from 80% occupancy on Thursdays to 20% (if they open) at weekends. On a daily basis, seats on a scheduled air flight or train may be 95% full at 0800 hours, while seats on the following flight or journey at 1000 hours may be only 45% occupied. These demand variations are all the more acute because of the factor of perishability discussed previously and it is always a major preoccupation of marketing managers to generate as much demand to fill the troughs as market conditions permit.

High fixed costs of service operations

When the profit and loss accounts of service businesses in the travel and tourism industry are analysed, it is generally the case that they reveal relatively high fixed costs of operating the available (fixed) level of capacity, and relatively low variable costs. A *fixed cost* is one that has to be paid for in advance in order for a business to be open to receive customers; a *variable cost* is one that is incurred in relation to the number of customers received at any given time. What this means in practice may easily be understood in the case of an airline, which must fund the following main costs in order to be able to provide its flights.

- Fleet costs and premises (capital costs, debt repayments, leasing costs, rates and annual maintenance charges). Airport landing charges and crew costs if overnights are involved.
- Other equipment costs such as website and on-line services provision, other computer systems (including repairs, renewals and servicing).
- Fuel charges and other heating and lighting costs.
- Insurances.
- Wages and salaries and social provision for full time employees.
- Management overheads and administrative costs.
- The bulk of marketing costs.

The point to note is that these fixed costs are mostly committed ahead over a 12-month period and have to be met whether the flights offered achieve 30% or 100% seat occupancy. While variable costs arise in operating catering services, the variable cost of operating one additional seat on a flight is virtually nil. The same basic fact of operations is true for room sales in hotels, seats for all forms of visitor entertainment and admissions to visitor attractions.

To illustrate the point, consider an airline with a 160-seat airplane that operates a particular route for a seat price of say US$200 (average). Sales of 40 seats produce a basic gross revenue contribution of $8000. If 150 seats are sold, contribution is $30,000. If the fixed costs of operating the flight are $15,000, then 40 occupied seats produce a loss of $7000 and 150 occupied seats produce a surplus of $15,000. Breakeven (on gross revenue) occurs in this example with 75 seats sold. In practice seat prices will vary and some costs can be modified at the margin but the principal remains the same.

The facts of high fixed costs of operation in combination with seasonality fluctuations focus all service operators' attention on the need to generate extra demand. The need focuses especially on the additional, or marginal sales of which a very high proportion represents 'pure' revenue gain with little or no extra cost.

It is worth stressing that most large-scale businesses are obliged through competition to operate on a knife-edge of a very narrow margin between costs and revenue, with costs always under pressure. Plus or minus one percentage point in average load factors for airlines (seat occupancy) or room occupancy for hotels may not sound large, but over a year it may mean the difference between a substantial profit on assets employed or a significant loss. Imagine the atmosphere in boardrooms in the USA as travel companies sought to grapple with their marketing budgets in the short-run market downturn that followed 9/11 in 2001. Multiply that atmosphere to understand what has happened in boardrooms in the Autumn of 2008 as companies contemplate the consumer impact of the global credit crisis and the difficulty and cost of borrowing to cover short-run losses on operations. Falls of 25% and more are not unusual in travel and tourism markets in the after-math of economic and other crises. They powerfully demonstrate the meaning of high fixed costs and the inevitable impact on room rates and occupancy levels for hotels and fares and seat occupancy for airlines. Such conditions cause the collapse of previously profitable firms. The history of travel and tourism has many such examples and they impose very daunting tasks for marketing managers as the principal revenue generators.

Interdependence of tourism products: collaborative marketing

Most visitors need to combine several products in their travel decisions, not just one. A business visitor needs transport, accommodation, food and beverage, and maybe car rental and conference facilities. A vacationer chooses attractions at a destination together with the products of accommodation, transport and other facilities such as recreational activity and catering. Accommodation suppliers at a destination are therefore partly influenced by the marketing decisions of tour operators and travel agents, attractions, transport interests and tourist boards, which together or separately promote the destination and its activities and facilities. Over a period of years there is always a relationship underlying the capacity and quality of different travel and tourism products at a destination, and potential synergy to be achieved in their marketing decisions if the different suppliers and destination management interests can find ways to combine their respective efforts. There will normally be a range of opportunities for collaborative or joint marketing of the types discussed in Part Five of this book.

Often overlooked is the vital interdependence between commercial sector interests in tourism and the local government bodies that determine much of the quality of public spaces or *public realm* within which most of the important experiences associated with destination visits take place. Internationally this is a common characteristic of tourism. Apart from pubic realm, commercial developers and operators of tourism facilities and events mostly need planning and other regulatory permissions in order to operate. Airlines need permission to use airports, hotels need permission to build and expand and visitor attractions are also closely regulated in their development plans and operations. Their commercial decisions have impacts on residents of destinations that have to be recognized under all democratic systems.

Interdependence, if not natural synergy is, therefore, an inevitable process at destinations. It can best be understood when a new resort, e.g. a ski resort, is being planned. The basic concept for the resort is most likely to emerge from destination planners working within government planning guidelines – collaborating with prospective developers, investors and business partners. Capacity for the resort is calculated on the estimated number of skiers per peak hour who can be accommodated comfortably for a good experience on the slopes. With an estimate of skiers and non-skiers, and of day and staying visitors, it is possible to determine the optimum capacity of ski lifts, the number of beds needed, the required restaurant facilities, car parks, and so on. Collaboration is likely on architectural features and public spaces or public realm that respect and establish the image of the destination and its natural characteristics and establish the framework within which the resort will be branded. Each visitor facility in the resort is functionally related to other facilities and, even if they are all separately owned, their fortunes are certainly linked. This vital interdependence was designated *complementarity* by Krippendorf (1971). The same concept appears as 'partnership' in the USA (Morrison, 1989:175).

Partnership, collaborative marketing or co-branding provides opportunities to share destination management thinking and the costs of marketing; it typically also involves shared market intelligence and the costs of joint facilities such as Internet portals that facilitate collaborative approaches. It embraces both private and public sectors. See also Chapter 7.

Link article available at www.routledge.com/9780750686938

(1) Li, X., Petrick, J.F., 2008. Tourism marketing in an era of paradigm shift. Journal of Travel Research 46 (3), 235–44.

HOW DOES MARKETING IN TRAVEL AND TOURISM DIFFER FROM OTHER FORMS OF MARKETING?

Students of travel and tourism often find it difficult to be clear about the way marketing in travel and tourism differs from other forms of consumer marketing practice. It is common ground that the principles of the body of knowledge about marketing and its main theoretical elements hold good for all types of product. In other words the basic or core principles of marketing are relevant to all products, whether they are based on services or manufactured goods. Marketing managers at senior levels of responsibility can, and frequently do, switch between industries with little difficulty. This is only possible because the core principles of marketing can be applied in different sectors. In travel and tourism in particular, many marketing managers have been brought in from manufacturing and other service industries to bring their expertise to bear, as firms grow faster than the level of expertise available from within their own sector of business.

Against this evidence of common ground, however, experience convinces many in the industry, including the authors of this book, that the special characteristics of travel and tourism services are so dominant in their implications that the core marketing principles must be considerably adapted to ensure success in an operational context. This is clearly a very important consideration and it is based on the belief that marketing in travel and tourism reflects five aspects of demand and supply in the industry, which individually and combined give marketing practice its special approach and style. These special characteristics, outlined in this chapter, are developed and illustrated throughout Parts Five and Six of this book.

Marketing in travel and tourism is shaped and determined by the nature of the demand for tourism and the operating characteristics of supplying industries. The forms of promotion and distribution used for travel and tourism products have their own particular characteristics, which distinguish their use in comparison with other industries. These characteristics form the common ground on which marketing for travel and tourism is based.

CHAPTER SUMMARY

This chapter explains the characteristics of services production that influence marketing generally and notes the polarity between a small number of international and global service businesses at one end of the industry, and tens of thousands of micro-businesses at the other end. The main characteristics of travel and tourism operations are explained and the implications for constant preoccupation in the short run with managing demand around a fixed level of capacity are stressed. Effective short-run management of demand depends upon detailed knowledge of customers through effective market research.

In reviewing the distinctive characteristics of businesses in the services sector generally, and of travel and tourism in particular, this chapter has focused on five very important structural aspects of supply, summarized below. The first two apply to all service businesses; the others have a particular impact in travel and tourism:

- Inseparability and intangibility of services that are performed rather than produced.
- Perishability based on a fixed capacity in the short run and inability to create stocks of product that makes tourism businesses highly vulnerable to short-run fluctuations in demand.
- Seasonality.
- High fixed costs determining many of the short-run marketing methods used in travel and tourism to manage demand, especially the widespread use of price discounting to achieve last minute sales.
- Interdependence and collaborative marketing, including the public sector.

Apart from the sheer volume of micro-businesses, none of the aspects discussed are unique to travel and tourism but it is the combined effect of the characteristics that influences the conduct of marketing in the industry. Not least of the combined effects is the involvement of the public sector in destination planning, regulation and management, outlined as an aspect of interdependence and collaborative marketing.

All the characteristics together help to explain why much of travel and tourism is considered to be a high-risk business; a business in which entrepreneurs with a strong intuitive understanding of rapidly changing marketplace trends and a willingness to make the difficult adjustments in capacity faster than competitors, have so often thrived in the industry with spectacular success. The equally spectacular failures are usually traceable to the effects of high fixed costs and cash flow problems when demand fails in crisis conditions.

Students of marketing will be aware that the core distinctions drawn here between goods and services run some risk of oversimplification because many physical goods are now also marketed as experiences and require extensive service elements to support their sales and distribution – and vice versa. For the purposes of this book, however, the distinctions summarized in Table 3.1 should be helpful in clarifying differences that profoundly influence the nature of the marketing responses in travel and tourism. These differences hold good for the thousands of proprietor managed and marketed smaller enterprises that dominate the industry numerically, as well as for larger firms with marketing departments.

QUESTIONS TO CONSIDER

1. Outline three key attributes of service products that distinguish them from products based on manufactured goods.
2. What are the main operating characteristics that all large-scale operations (goods and services) have in common?
3. List the characteristics that make small or micro-businesses so important in travel and tourism.
4. What are the five key factors underlying the marketing of all travel and tourism products?
5. In your own words what does the interdependence of tourism products mean?
6. Why does collaborative marketing matter so much in marketing?

FURTHER READING AND REFERENCES

Appiah-Adu, K., Fyall, A. and Singh, S. (April 2000). Marketing culture and customer retention in the tourism industry, *The Service Industries Journal*, **20**(2), pp.95–113.

Baker, M.J. (1996). *Marketing: an introductory text.* Chapter 1 (6th edn). Macmillan.

Bateson, J.E.G. (1955). *Managing Services Marketing: Text and Readings.* Dryden Press.

Brassington, F. and Pettit, S. (2000). *Principles of marketing* (3rd edn). FT Prentice-Hall.

Jobber, D. (2007). *Principles and practice of marketing* (5th edn). McGraw-Hill.

Kotler, P. and Armstrong, G. (1999). *Principles of marketing*. Chapter 1 (8th edn). Prentice-Hall.

Kotler, P., Wong, V., Saunders, J. and Armstrong, G. (2005). *Principles of marketing* (4th European edn). Pearson Prentice Hall.

Leisen, B., Lilly, B. and Winsor, R.D. (2002). The effects of organizational culture and market orientation on the effects of strategic marketing alliances, *Journal of Services Marketing*, **16**(3), pp.201–222.

Li, X. and Petrick, J.F. (2008). Tourism marketing in an era of paradigm shift, *Journal of Travel Research*, **46**(3), pp.235–244.

Lovelock, C.H. and Wright, L. (1998). *Principles of services marketing and management*. Chapters 1 and 2. Prentice-Hall.

McDonald, M. (2002). *Marketing plans* (5th edn). Butterworth Heinemann.

Middleton, V.T.C. (1998). SMEs in European tourism: the context and a proposed framework for European action, *Revue de Tourisme* (4).

Palmer, A. (1998). *Principles of services marketing*. Chapter 1 (2nd edn). McGraw-Hill.

Pizam, A. and Mansfeld, Y. (2000). *Consumer behaviour in travel and tourism*. Haworth Press.

Zeithaml, V.A. and Bitner, M.J. (2000). *Services marketing: integrating customer focus across the firm*. Chapter 1. McGraw-Hill.

Modern Hong Kong with an old style sail ship: 'a rapidly growing middle class of professional and business people.. in China, India and other growing economies in the Asia/Pacific Region'

CHAPTER 4

The dynamic business environment: factors influencing demand for tourism

"Clearly anyone who has travelled since 9-11 is well aware that travel is not the same as it once was. Following on the heels of September 11, travel and tourism has had to face issues of food safety, health crises, natural disasters, and the rapid rise in petroleum prices resulting in major price increases for both land and air transportation."

(Peter Tarlow, 2008)

Chapter 2 explains that a marketing orientation is a particular form of business or corporate culture reflecting *outward-looking* (or *outside–in* as Kotler put it) management attitudes. Organized around a detailed knowledge of existing and prospective customers, outward looking also means being highly responsive and proactive to the constantly changing dynamics of the business environment within which any organization operates. It is widely recognized in the twenty-first century that the pace of change is accelerating around the world. External factors include the globalization of economies, growing competition among suppliers and an ever more pressing need to cope with world population growth, climate change and pressure on Earth's scarce resources such as food and oil. Governments alone cannot solve these problems; they are problems and opportunities requiring strategic business responses within which marketing will play a vital role.

It is the role of marketing managers to understand and seek to influence consumer or user demand in response to the dynamics of continuous change in the business environment in which they operate. Most marketing managers are not usually concerned directly to measure all the overall factors that influence total market movements. They are, however, invariably involved with interpreting such movements and deciding how best their organizations should respond. This chapter focuses on what Burkart and Medlik (1981: 50) identified as the 'determinants' of demand. These are the economic, technological, social, cultural and political factors at work in any society that combined together determine the volume and characteristics of a population's demand for travel and tourism. *Motivations*, explained in later chapters, are the internal factors at work within individuals, expressed as the needs, wants and desires that influence tourism choices.

After studying this chapter you should be able to understand:

- The reasons why more demanding consumers of travel-related products are now predominant in developed countries and emerging rapidly in the developing world.
- The ten key determinants of demand for travel and tourism that together reflect the external business environment for travel and tourism as it affects all countries.
- The characteristics (reflecting the determinants) of population sectors most likely and least likely to engage in travel and tourism.
- A summary of the implications of the determinants for marketing managers.

THE MORE DEMANDING CONSUMER OF TRAVEL AND TOURISM – A GLOBAL DEVELOPMENT

In all developed countries, reflecting economic growth over the last half-century and the more competitive business climate in the early years of the twenty-first century, businesses in travel and tourism and those responsible for destination management are having to respond to the expectations of more demanding customers. In particular they have to develop continuously the quality of the experience their services deliver. The reasons for this are summarized briefly below and developed in this chapter. Over the last two decades consumers have become, *on average*:

- More affluent, measured in disposable income per capita, ownership of property, household facilities and leisure and recreation equipment.
- Better educated and more interested and involved in continuing education and skills training.
- More healthy overall with many interested in more active pursuits.
- Older, as life expectancy rises, with a particular shift in the number and attitudes of the more active over 50s.
- More leisured in terms of agreed hours of work and holiday entitlement, although many at work are also experiencing greater pressure on their available leisure time.
- More travelled, for work and business as well as for holidays and leisure, with increasing numbers experiencing frequent international travel.
- More exposed to the media and information generally.

- More computer literate with access to the Internet still growing exponentially.
- More heterogeneous and individualistic in their demands and expectations.
- More culturally diverse in terms of ethnic origin and cultural background as well as in their range of lifestyle choices.

Developed countries are currently estimated by UN agencies to represent just one-fifth of the world's population and the same trends are expected to extend to at least the higher earning third of the populations in the developing world as their economies grow in the next quarter century. This basic expectation for the twenty-first century has massive implications for the future growth of travel and tourism around the world. More affluent and demanding customers are associated with a rapidly growing middle class of professional and business people, which is now evident in China, India and other growing economies in the Asia/Pacific region as well as in Russia and Brazil.

This all adds up to a global shift to more diverse, more experienced, more demanding, more quality conscious, better informed and generally more sophisticated consumers of travel and tourism around the world in the early years of this century.

We stress *on average* when indicating the changes to consumer demand above because, apart from global economic crises, there are clearly some twenty-first century countervailing trends that will change some of the optimistic expectations of growth in travel and tourism established over the previous half century. They include

- More time spent commuting in congested towns, cities and on motorways, eroding available free time and inhibiting day visit choices.
- The rising cost of housing, and in countries such as England, the charges for higher education making many younger people less rather than more affluent.
- More divorced people maintaining one or more families with associated care concern for sets of elderly parents.
- Obesity reducing life expectancy and limiting the activities of some.
- Failure of many people to make sufficient provision for retirement income needed to afford their lifestyles (including travel) – imposing added tax burdens on those in work.
- Taxes and other limitations intended to reduce growth in air transport and the use of private cars to reduce carbon emissions.
- Growing global concern for climate change shifting attitudes especially towards discretionary travel.

THE MAIN DETERMINANTS OF DEMAND

Fortunately for students and others wishing to understand the nature and potential of demand for travel and tourism, the underlying factors are common to all countries. Although the demand patterns generated for a particular region within any specific country are unique to that area, the same set of external demand determinants affects individual operators such as hotels, tour operators, airlines and attractions. The responses that marketing managers make as they keep the factors under continuous review and anticipate market shifts, differ according to their understanding and judgement of the factors at any point in time and their view of how best to achieve a competitive edge.

The main determinants of demand for travel and tourism are summarized under ten broad headings noted below and explained in this chapter:

1. Economic factors and comparative prices.
2. Demographic characteristics of tourism generating nations.
3. Geographic factors.
4. Socio-cultural attitudes to tourism.
5. Access to personal transport.
6. Government/regulatory 'infrastructure' surrounding travel and tourism.
7. Media communications.
8. Information and communications technology (ICT).
9. Environmental concerns and demand for more sustainable forms of tourism.
10. International political developments and terrorist actions.

SUPPLY ALSO AFFECTS DEMAND

The ten factors above cover demand side influences. But just as the building of a bridge or a new motorway tends to stimulate demand, tourism markets also respond to changes in the *supply* of products and the capacity of supply. For example, the significant growth in demand for long haul leisure travel from the USA and Europe to the Asia/Pacific region in recent years was not possible until a supply of products was available – based, in this case, on air transport technology capable of undertaking the necessary journeys at a speed and cost per passenger that the market could afford. New airports and resorts create tourism flows but would not be built unless there was a clear expectation of market demand. Demand and supply interact. The role of businesses making supply or product decisions in relation to their estimates of changes in the potential of demand is necessarily a constant theme throughout this marketing book. It is covered in most chapters and for this reason supply based determinants are not discussed separately here.

1. Economic factors and comparative prices

Wherever travel and tourism markets are studied, the economic variables in the countries or regions in which prospective tourists live are the most important group of factors influencing the volume of demand generated. For international tourism in the early part of the twenty-first century, 30 major countries of origin continued to account for over 90% of world travel spending. The top ten alone account for some two-thirds of spending and number of visits. The top 30 include USA, Japan and West Germany and other developed economies with the highest incomes per capita. By 2010 it is predicted that China will be among the top ten, reflecting its economic progress and the rise of consumer demand. See also Table 1.2 in Chapter 1.

The influence of economic variables in supporting tourism growth is especially obvious for leisure and holiday travel, but developed and growing economies also sustain large numbers of visits away from home for business purposes of all kinds. Meetings, attendance at conferences and exhibitions, travel on government business and social travel are all important segments of the travel and tourism industry. In 2005, for example, the UK received nearly 30 million overseas visits, of which only 32% were for holiday purposes, with business visits and visits to friends and relatives accounting for 27% and 29% of all visits, respectively (UK International Passenger Survey, 2007).

Using the published statistics of tourism and national economic trends, it is possible to trace the relationship over time between changes in real disposable income (measured in constant prices) and the volume of visits and expenditure away from home. In the short-term tourism markets are susceptible to economic events, such as the deep Pacific/Asia recession of the late 1990s, the dot.com market boom and bust at the turn of the century and most recently rising oil prices and the collapse of the sub-prime mortgage market in the USA. Wars and other political crises have the same effect. But for the bulk of the population in countries with developed economies, overall increases in real incomes over the last two decades have led to proportionately higher increases in expenditure on travel and tourism. This relationship between disposable incomes and expenditure on travel and tourism is known as *the income elasticity of demand*. For example, if the other determinants remain relatively unchanged and there is a greater than 1% increase in expenditure on travel and tourism by residents of a country in response to a 1% increase in real disposable income, the market is judged to be income elastic. If demand changes less than proportionately to income, the market is judged to be inelastic.

For over a quarter of a century, with some inevitable crisis downturns, demand for travel and tourism in developed countries was generally held to be highly income elastic. The evidence and projections noted in Chapter 1 indicate that future growth of demand in the relatively mature markets of the main generating countries is now more likely to change only in line with disposable income. Increasingly it is likely that travel and tourism expenditure in such countries will tend to rise and fall in line with the economic cycles of growth and recession that affect all countries. However, in the leading developing countries around the world, such as China and India, tourism markets are currently relatively small but are likely to develop very quickly responding to rapid economic growth. Such markets are likely to remain highly income elastic for many years to come.

Comparative prices

Price, which represents cost to customers in terms of money, time and effort, is relative to their spending power and reflects the economic determinants discussed above. But it is not a simple issue. There is convincing evidence in leisure tourism that, in the short run, the price of a firm's products, or the perceived price of a destination compared with those of competitors, is still the most important single determinant governing the volume of demand. For international tourism, price is complicated by the combined effects of comparative exchange rates between countries of origin and countries of destination, and by the comparative level of inflation in the destination area and the area where prospective visitors live. For Hong Kong, for example, one of the few Asia Pacific countries not to have devalued its currency at the end of 1998 following the economic crisis in that region, visits from Japanese tourists fell by some 50% in the period 1997/1998 (*Economist*, 28 November 1998). The global price of oil, which is especially important in all forms of air transport, adds a third variable to these price complications and it is also driven by the US dollar exchange rate in which oil prices are measured. As this book goes to print, oil prices would have doubled in a year and the impact of that is currently lowering growth expectations. It is easy to see why the effects of comparative prices are highly complex in practice. Prices have to be monitored constantly and it is impossible to predict them with precision. The following exchange rates for selected years tell a fairly dramatic story with big implications for prices paid by visitors:

	£1 = US$	£1 = Euros
1996	1.71	n.a.
2000	1.49	1.59
2001	1.45	1.63
2004	1.91	1.41
2007	1.99	1.36
2008	1.47	1.05

All rates taken at year end

It is also a new factor that consumers in developed countries have become highly price sensitive now that the Internet has opened up an easy process for price comparisons; products perceived by consumers as over priced cannot be sold.

2. Demographic factors

The term 'demographic factors' is used here broadly to identify the main population characteristics that influence demand for travel and tourism. Working much more slowly than the rapidly changing economic variations, the main characteristics determining tourism markets are population size, household size and composition, the effects of high levels of divorce and remarriage or new partnerships, the ageing of populations in developed countries and falling birth rates. Though not strictly an aspect of demography, the growing number of young people in further and higher education is also a powerful determinant of the level and type of tourism demand they generate. Higher education typically involves extensive travel to universities and colleges and an interest in worldwide gap year travel that is shared by many countries.

The biggest single issue in demography is the rising world population. At 6 billion persons in 1999, the number had doubled in less than 40 years. It is expected, on medium projections, to rise to over 7 billion by 2015 and nearly 9 billion by 2050 (UN, 1999, World Population Prospects). It is the combination of growing world population and their prospects for economic growth that is putting mounting pressure on finite resources, global warming and climate change as well as facilitating the growth of travel and tourism. There is a massive tension in all this, which will be played out over the coming decades.

In developed economies, one- and two-person households have grown much faster than those with young children. The proportion of households including couples and one or more children in the UK, for example, is now only a quarter of the total and the number of children under the age of 15 fell by over 2 million between 1971 and 1991. Such changes have obviously affected the many tourism businesses that targeted traditional family summer holidays, providing products based primarily around the needs and interests of children.

The increasing number of active, relatively affluent people over the age of 55 who are retired or nearing retirement is a vitally important population trend which will increasingly influence travel and tourism markets in the twenty-first century. In the USA there were some 39 million people over the age of 55 in 1970, 46 million in 1980 and over 67 million in 2007. In Western Europe it is estimated that one in four people were aged 55 or over by the year 2000. Apart from the size of the market, these retired and near-retired people have very different attitudes from any previous generation of senior citizens in the sense that most of them are far more active, fit and affluent than ever before. By 2010 many of them will have been brought up accustomed to high levels of personal mobility and most will have established patterns of leisure activities and holidays that many will be able to afford to continue into their 80s. Most will be computer literate and accustomed to using the Internet for travel decisions. The prospect that a large and growing proportion of the population will enjoy some 20 years of active travel and activity in retirement opens up marketing opportunities for which there is no historical parallel. Marketing managers around the world are studying ways to develop their shares of this expanding market and there are obvious profit prospects for those who design products that mature markets want to buy without the stigma of being patronized as old. The countervailing trend is that without radical change currently not in sight, a smaller population of younger people at work will have to bear the burden of paying in large measure for the pensions, health and other care needs of rapidly ageing populations around the world.

Economic growth has also shifted traditional socio-economic groupings in the populations of most developed countries. Traditional industrial manual labour employment has fallen and been replaced by post-industrial economic activities (see Chapter 1). The more recent service-industry employees have a social status and attitudes that are increasingly identified with what was the 'middle class'.

All these trends led logically in the last decade to greater segmentation and niche marketing of travel products. Examples are youth tour operators, short breaks marketed at young couples and 'empty nesters', coach tours for senior citizens, cruising and the separation of holiday village operations to cater for those with children and those without. There has also been an explosion of packaged recreational activity products from golf, to skiing, walking, sailing and travel arrangements reflecting an almost infinite range of sports, adventure and culture-related events that provide modern reasons for travel.

3. Geographic factors

Climate and scenic attractions accessible to large, relatively affluent urban centres are two of the principal 'pull' determinants of travel demand for leisure purposes that explains many destination choices. Related geographically is the 'push' determinant of the size and affluence of the communities in which populations live. For example, Spain and other Mediterranean countries offer the most accessible and scenic locations for warmth and sunshine for people living in Northern Europe. The Caribbean and Florida provide much the same attraction for many North Americans.

In the mid-to-late twentieth century the development of hundreds of Mediterranean resorts is explained by a combination of push and pull determinants in Northern Europe and the price of air transport journeys of up to around 1000 miles, which can be accomplished in around 2 hours' flying time from convenient regional airports.

Paradoxically in the last quarter century, large towns and cities, which were once the main generators of tourism to seasonal holiday destinations, have also become magnets for modern short break and day visit tourism. Year round interest in heritage, culture, sporting events and the arts, combined with developments in transport technology, has opened up virtually all the cities of Europe to receive as well as generate tourism flows. This trend has provided a massive economic boost for the visitor economy of the cities of Central and Eastern Europe, such as Prague, St Petersburg, Budapest and Cracow, especially when they were able to offer comparatively cheap prices.

Courtesy of Dimitrios Buhalis.

Geographic perceptions have changed dramatically over the last decade in Europe with the advent of budget airlines. Two hour flying distances, for example, are now substantially cheaper than train or car journeys making second home ownership in foreign countries an attractive option to tens of thousands of middle income groups in Northern Europe. By 2005 longer journeys of 6–12 hours were also becoming more affordable, giving market access to long distance destinations in all parts of the world. The demand for such long distances is clearly proven and potentially rising although it is not clear to what extent rising oil prices and governments seeking to reduce carbon emissions to limit climate change will curtail it in the future by increased regulation and taxation.

For accommodation suppliers and visitor attractions, the choice of geographic location for their businesses is usually the most important business decision to be made – or managed as access options change.

4. Socio-cultural attitudes affecting tourism

As noted earlier, the growing number of people with enough income, leisure time and mobility to generate and sustain market growth is a primary determinant for travel and tourism. An equally important consideration for marketing managers, because it shapes consumer expectations of products, is the general attitudes and behaviour of people towards holiday travel compared with other leisure products claiming their interest, time and money. This chapter deals only with generally held attitudes; Chapter 5 reviews the perceptions, motivations and behavioural factors that influence individual tourism choices that operate within the broader socio-cultural attitudes noted below.

Attitudes generally reflect the ideas, beliefs, aspirations and fears that people hold about their lives. Attitudes towards travel and tourism are subsets of wider views about peoples' desired quality of life and how to achieve it. They vary according to different national cultures, the places people live and they are reflected and stimulated by the popular media. They are developed in childhood and modified with experience of life. Attitudes can also be influenced by effective promotion and marketing is always most effective when it works with the grain of changing social attitudes to motivate and stimulate purchase. This section indicates just five such common current beliefs in North America and Europe that act as a form of 'received wisdom' for millions of tourists.

1. Most people in developed countries believe that holidays and leisure time are part of their 'rights' and necessities for quality of life and relieving the stress of modern living. Visits abroad for business or pleasure have become the outward symbols of economic and social status in society. Gap years involving extensive travel for university students and school leavers have become ever more popular at the youthful end of the lifetime travel scale and extensive travel following retirement is equally popular at the senior end.
2. In northern climates, millions of people hold the belief that there is a therapeutic value in warm sunshine and relaxing in beach resorts. Responding to such beliefs underlies much of the tourism destination capacity provided in beach resorts around the world. Recent concerns about global warming and the toxic effects of too much exposure to unfiltered sunlight may shift this deeply held attitude over the next decade, with negative effects on the future demand for the products of sunshine destinations.
3. The trend towards longer holiday entitlement in the late twentieth century, associated with rising personal income, has encouraged the remarkable development of consumer preference for taking several holidays and leisure/recreation breaks throughout the year. Multiple holiday taking has encouraged growth in the supply of 'additional' and short holiday products and made it possible for many leisure tourism businesses to extend their

traditional summer seasons, confident that there are sufficient people with the necessary leave entitlement and flexibility in their arrangements to travel outside what were once the peak summer months. The attitude to multiple travel is supported by growing numbers of retired people capable of travelling when they wish, the development of second home ownership in countries abroad and the growing ownership of recreation equipment such as boats and caravans that facilitate frequent travel. In countries such as the Netherlands, Sweden, Norway and Finland, national attitudes encourage large numbers of people to own second homes for weekend and summer use, perceiving them to be important attributes of a satisfactory lifestyle.

4. A relatively new attitude reflects growing international concern over what now appears to be inevitable climate change and the depletion of Earth's natural resources and biodiversity as a result of economic growth in developed and rapidly developing countries. A key aspect of that attitude is the still evolving expectation that travel-related products should be environmentally sustainable, or at least should observe minimum standards of environmental good practice. Not yet a major issue for suppliers, it appears likely to become much more important over the next decade.

   One may speculate that tourism, as the largest popular international witness of the environmental damage that has already occurred, will play an important role in shaping new attitudes to the natural and built environment. Visitors are well aware, for example, of the loss of coral reefs, erosion of glaciers and skiing areas and overdevelopment and destructive commercialization of many coastal areas and heritage cities, such as Venice, for large-scale tourism. As this attitude hardens in the next decade, more customers will reject the products of businesses that are unwilling to demonstrate sustainable credentials and turn away from polluted, overcrowded resorts and destinations. The influence on the marketing of all travel products of such a shift on a large scale will be profound.

5. Related to the emerging attitudes towards sustainability, recognizing the globally growing carbon footprint of airlines, is a probable attitude shift towards frequent flying. Promoted by budget airlines freed from traditional regulatory constraints since the 1990s, there was an explosion of demand for travel in Europe that followed lower prices and substantially changed the structure of tourism in all developed countries in little more than a decade. This demand and the products that supplied it are now challenged by rising oil prices as well as growing political recognition of the environmental damage caused by airport expansion and the associated demands and impacts on destinations. More government intervention to restrict air travel by imposing greater cost burdens seems inevitable.

5. Access to personal transport

Reflecting growth in disposable income and the broad socio-economic attitudes to travel noted above, the personal mobility provided by cars is a prime determinant of the volume and types of tourism, especially for domestic tourism. In the USA the private car has for years been the dominant holiday transport choice. Between European countries sharing land frontiers the car is also the preferred mode of transport for leisure tourism, and for much of business travel too. Car ownership is highest in the USA with over 600 cars per 1000 population but ownership and usage of cars have increased significantly in Europe over the last decade. As older generations of non-drivers die out in the new millennium, these figures will obviously rise further.

At the start of the twenty-first century most hotels, nearly all self-catering establishments, most tourist restaurants and the great majority of visitor attractions and entertainments in North America and Europe, are highly dependent on visitors arriving by car. Figures of 90% arrivals by car are common. Looking ahead, however, growing traffic congestion, CO_2 emissions and government fiscal and regulatory policies are likely to force restrictions on the usage of cars. The historic decision to restrict car access to Yosemite National Park in the USA in 1998 is one indicator of probable developments. But there is currently no reason to anticipate any lessening of the demand for personal mobility and the safety, comfort and sheer personal convenience it provides – especially for those with luggage and families. The growing experience of extensive road congestion will, however, cause changes to travel and tourism patterns. Leisure day visits from home at weekends or risking commuter congestion appear to be especially vulnerable to such changes. Traditional weekend leisure travel patterns of out on Friday evening, back on Sunday evening, are likely to be increasingly unattractive.

The use of surface public transport declined as car ownership increased. Although rising since the mid-1990s for the first time in decades, passenger miles by train were little more than 5% of all passenger miles in Europe at the end of the twentieth century. There remain, however, some important niche segments of the travel and tourism market that use public transport on longer journeys for economic reasons or through preference. Transport operators have developed and marketed a range of products to provide attractively priced choices for target market segments, such as those over 60, students still in full-time education and special interest groups. Coach and bus operators have found many niches to exploit, for international tourists as well as for the more traditional holidays based on coach tours. Such schemes are likely to develop further as traffic congestion grows and government regulations favour public transport. Scope for providing improved public transport options at destinations looks higher than the prospect of shifting people from cars for the journey from home to destination.

6. Government/regulatory factors

Governments and the armoury of regulation that they control are rather different in kind from the other determinants discussed in this chapter. They are, however, crucially important because they set and powerfully influence the national and international framework within which demand and supply evolves for travel and tourism. Regulation is the business of governments and their agencies and, because so much of tourism is an international business, it has to involve agreements between governments as well as decisions for their own countries. The subject of regulation, mostly incorporated into legal frameworks is vast and the subject of many books in its own right. For the purposes of explanation and illustration in this chapter, four aspects of the regulations are summarized below.

All democratic governments impose a wide network of laws and regulations to safeguard the health and safety and employment of their populations in all aspects of their lives and to control and plan the use of land and buildings, especially all forms of development. Such regulations are important but typically influence all forms of business activity and are not referred to in this section, which is specific to travel and tourism. Where they choose to intervene in markets, governments do so for four principal reasons that directly influence demand and supply and often have a particular impact on travel and tourism that marketing managers have to understand:

1. The first is regulation to ensure fair competition between suppliers and choice for consumers. This is usually intended to enforce safety in operations and prevent the formation of monopolies, cartels or oligopolies, which may otherwise be able to prevent new competition from entering their markets and/or control the capacity of supply and set prices in their favour, and not in their customers' interests. Until 1995, for example, air transport regulation did not permit the operation of budget airlines in Europe. After deregulation following earlier USA deregulation of the late 1970s the skies were opened up to massive competition that radically altered market prospects for travel and tourism in less than a decade.
2. The second is regulation to ensure that customers have choices and rights enforceable by law to products that are safe to buy and of proper merchantable quality necessary to meet the promises of producers and retailers. Such regulation cannot fully prevent but it does curtail with the support of the law attempts by unscrupulous businesses to exploit customers. The 1993 European Union Directive on package tours is one example. Statutory registration of visitor accommodation and classification and grading regulations operated in some countries provide another example that sets a framework for marketing decisions.
3. The third is to balance the requirements and costs to society in terms of noise, congestion and pollution against the needs and demands of specific developments. The most obvious illustration in travel and tourism lies in the planning controls that governments have over the location, size, development and access arrangements for new or expanded airports and other major development sites such as holiday villages.
4. The fourth, which is relatively new but expected to have a much greater future impact on travel and tourism, is regulation to ensure that existing business practices and proposed project developments operate in more sustainable, carbon neutral ways that do not damage the built and natural environment. Taxation on airline passengers, on landing fees and possible future fuel taxation have become a contentious political issue with global implications. Targets for carbon neutral operations with penalties for failure to comply will also affect hotels, restaurants and attractions. Around the world, rural, coastal and heritage environments attractive to visitors are increasingly targeted for special protection against unsustainable development. To date although environmental assessments are legal requirements in many countries for large new developments there are no formal requirements for businesses to

undertake a detailed environmental audit of their existing operations. Since the early 1990s, however, many larger organizations do. The World Travel and Tourism Council, a group of the world's largest companies in the business have been active in promoting more sustainable business operations.

7. Media communications

A major influence over demand for travel and tourism is the massive exposure to colour television and, more recently, the Internet now common to populations in all countries with developed economies. Television-watching emerges as the most popular leisure-time pursuit in many countries, with an estimated 35 hours a week per household in the USA and around 19 hours a week for the average adult in Britain (the figures are not directly comparable). No other leisure activity occupies more time than the number of hours spent at home in front of a TV or computer screen.

Over the last decade cable-based, space satellite transmitters and broadband access to the Internet have provided instantaneous international information and images of places and events, as well as a continuous stream of films identifying places and standards of living. They have helped to promote activities such as golf and tennis and patterns of behaviour, lifestyles and access to exotic resorts. The cumulative effect of television over the years in shaping travel and tourism images and expectations in the major demand-generating countries cannot be overestimated. Digitization of broadcasting is giving better pictures, multiplying by hundreds the number of specialist channels available, while the widespread extension of broadband Internet access indicates an even more influential role over the next decade, embracing mobile access from hand-held devices.

The cumulative impact of thousands of hours of television-watching, even before the full impact of new access to specialist channels and the Internet, has already had a major influence on travel demand. It influences strongly the social attitudes that are noted earlier in the chapter. The Internet is now a primary media for communicating many products in travel and tourism, and no previous generations ever had such massive, continuous exposure to events, people, places and influences outside their normal places of residence and work. Not least of the influences exerted by the mass communication media is the effect achieved by regular television travel programmes, which review and expose a wide range of tourism products on offer and provide critical evaluations of their quality and value for money. Such programmes achieve a level of authority and exposure that no individual organization's advertising budget could match.

At a lower level in terms of overall impact, the exposure of prospective travellers to books, films, newspapers, specialist magazines and radio, also contributes to awareness and attitudes. But the other media cannot reproduce the sense of colour and virtual interaction conveyed by television and the Internet, or command the same hours of attention.

The ability of modern media to expose and draw attention to the things that go wrong for visitors is also part of the effect on demand. It includes, for example, the global coverage given to deaths from terrorist actions or in airline crashes, the stories of murder, rape and muggings of tourists and the disasters to ferries. Such pictures and stories capture the imagination of people around the world. Where the majority of a population participates regularly in travel and tourism, the industry is of great interest to the media and is certain to generate stories the public wish to see and read.

The full effect on demand of continuous media coverage is still not well understood but there can be no doubt of its importance.

Link article available at www.routledge.com/9780750686938

(1) Hyde, K.F., July 2008. Information processing and touring planning theory. Annals of Tourism Research 35 (3), 712–731.

8. Information and communications technology

Developed later in Part Four of this book, this section simply flags up seven of the important influences over tourism demand exerted by the global revolution in ICT that is still in the relatively early stages of its global development. Some two-thirds of all households in the USA and in several countries in Europe now have Internet access in their homes and increasingly on the move. But these are averages and broadband access is already available to virtually all with a high propensity to engage in travel and tourism. The influences over tourism demand include

1. Increasing ability to promote and provide access to products on the Internet by both private sector businesses and destination marketing organizations, including online bookings and payment and the use of the Internet for vital last minute sales.
2. Growing availability of mobile phones and PDAs providing access to the Internet 24 hours a day in any place.
3. Reflecting the Internet options, the development of direct marketing (B2C and C2B) as the preferred form of choosing and booking, eroding the traditional role of traditional travel intermediaries such as high-street retail travel agents, while opening up a role for travel e-mediaries.
4. Customer database development following logically from direct C2B contacts and revolutionizing marketing information systems with the power to develop and communicate bespoke products with targeted customers.
5. Improved relationship marketing with repeat buyers and other stakeholders with whom it is now possible to have direct communication.
6. Creation of *virtual* enterprises for partners in the marketing of tourism-related products, for example short break holiday companies, in which ICT provides the network for collaboration and the linkages. Such networks have a special role in empowering the marketing initiatives of micro-businesses.
7. *Diagonal marketing* to generate new streams of business from existing customers and to create collaborative linkages with other businesses (as defined by Poon, 1993).

Taken together, the range of developments noted in this section were only possible by the wide scale commercial development of the Internet in the late 1990s. Collectively, they amount to the biggest changes in marketing since the first wave of large computers were developed over 50 years ago and have truly revolutionized marketing in travel and tourism. Part Four develops this theme.

9. Environmental concerns and the demand for more sustainable forms of tourism

Although not new, environmental concerns generally have risen rapidly up the political agenda in most countries in the first years of the new century. The emerging issues are traced in Middleton and Hawkins (1998). Concerns arise from a combination of:

- World population growth noted earlier in this chapter.
- Rapid economic development among previously undeveloped countries, exacerbating and at least doubling the impact of the population numbers noted above.
- Recognition that the earth's natural resources are not enough to satisfy the world population and its ambitions for rapid growth even at current population levels.
- Recognition that if existing use patterns of resources are not altered, climate change based on global warming will destroy biodiversity, cause flooding of coastal areas while creating desert conditions in many countries that will not be able to sustain production of the essential ingredients of life.
- The danger that the continuous daily movement of millions of people around the world brings increased exposure to the risk of rapidly mutating diseases that could turn into epidemics. The threats of SARS and Avian Flu in the first years of the new century and the risks of the transfer of infection to and between animals and humans could erupt at any time with dramatic consequences on international travel if emergency control measures have to be imposed.

Many argue that while the planet may survive the climate changes that now appear inevitable, there are growing concerns that millions of people around the world, especially in poorer countries, will face disaster and most will be denied access to the lifestyles or even the basics of food and water that people in developed countries currently take for granted. Such conditions are driving international migration to developed countries.

As one of the world's largest sectors of economic activity it is inevitable that travel and tourism will be targeted for government action. Reflecting the remarkable development of international debate if not consensus on how to deal with sustainable development and concerns for global warming, legislation, taxes and incentives designed to promote more sustainable growth now affects most sectors of the travel and tourism industry. Increasingly, large business can no longer ignore the need to reflect and communicate environmental concerns in their marketing strategies. Smaller businesses are likely to find good opportunities to promote their own products, stressing the local sourcing of the food and other materials used in their business.

Pressure on global resources has gained an awareness over the last 5 years that makes international government action inevitable. Action is also likely to be strongly supported by the development of indicators revealing the environmental impact of travel and tourism businesses, and the enforcement of the collection of such indicators on a frequent and regular basis.

10. International terrorist actions

In modern times, terrorist groups of various persuasions have targeted transport since the hijacking of a series of airplanes in the 1970s. The global conflicts stemming from the Middle East in general, and the wars in Iraq in particular, clearly heightened the determination of Islamic fundamentalists to attack targets in Western nations. Despite ever more elaborate security precautions, the generally easy access to public transport and to resorts frequented by tourists provides endless opportunities and the more recent development of suicide bombing has become ever harder to detect without radically altering the way that the great majority of people live their lives and travel for business and leisure in the twenty-first century. There is a terrible and lasting symbolism in the globally transmitted pictures of hijacked aircraft, icons of modern tourism, being flown into the twin towers of the World Trade Centre in New York in September 2001 with passengers using their mobile phones to inform their loved ones of their imminent fate. The Madrid train bombings in 2004, which injured and killed some 1800 people and the lesser but deadly destruction carried out on London buses and underground trains in 2005 followed the same transport theme. Transport is the essence of modern tourism and is clearly vulnerable to groups, reckless of their own lives, bent on destruction. Hotels, nightclubs and restaurants are equally and indiscriminately targeted around the world.

In the first decade of the twenty-first century, the impact on visitor markets following the major terrorist events has been evident in immediate falls in demand but so far such falls have had limited long-term impact – less, for example, than the influence of significant currency shifts affecting the cost to visit. Thus far tourism has always recovered from such acts after a delay of months or a very few years. As the world approaches the next decade it would be an optimist who believed that more such destruction will not occur and the easy assumptions about recovery in 1–2 years time may be challenged. Tourism provides terrorist groups with easy targets commanding global media attention. Exacerbated by understandable fears for personal safety and the disincentive of intrusive security checks and long miserable delays in transport systems, terrorism has already influenced international tourism patterns in particular. There is not much individual businesses can do about these events other than practice their own security and response procedures but as a risk factor in the external business environment, terrorism has become an important consideration.

THE RESPONSE OF MARKETING MANAGERS TO THE DETERMINANTS OF TOURISM

The role of marketing managers in response to the determinants of travel and tourism can be put simply. First, it is their business to monitor and as necessary to research and identify the opportunities and threats arising from external factors in the business environment that influence movements in the particular markets with which they are concerned (see also Chapter 9 on market research). Second, based on this knowledge, it is their business to forecast or make informed judgements about the direction and speed of change in the determinants and the implications of such forecasts for the travel patterns in their markets, taking action through strategic decisions (Chapter 10) and through the *marketing mix* decisions discussed in Chapter 8.

In both the long run and short run, investment and operating decisions in marketing-led organizations will always be based on their best understanding of a rapidly changing business environment. This is true in all circumstances, but especially true where markets are no longer growing rapidly, but are changing structurally and subject to increasing competition in conditions of economic downtown and recession.

Link article available at www.routledge.com/9780750686938

Hanlan, J., Fuller, D., Wilde, S., December 2006. Destination decision making: the need for a strategic planning and management approach. Tourism and Hospitality Planning and Development 3 (3), 209–221.

CHAPTER SUMMARY

This chapter focuses on the marketing implications of ten dynamic, external variables in the economic, political, social, cultural and technological environment within which all tourism businesses operate. It stresses that:

- These variables are common to all countries with developed or rapidly developing economies that currently generate the bulk of the world's tourism but they are not under the control of any one commercial organization and are only partly influenced by government decisions.
- Some of the determinants, such as income per capita, geographic factors and demographic shifts within a population have long-run implications for marketing. Such factors tend to produce fairly stable relationships with consumer demand and they are the basis of most of the forecasting models used to project tourism flows.
- Determinants such as socio-cultural attitudes – for example, in response to perceptions about climate change – have a longer term impact although developing with global media exposure they can shift some attitudes in months rather than decades.
- Other determinants, such as exchange rates, regulatory changes, energy prices, terrorist incidents and health scares, have a much more immediate, volatile and hard to predict effect on the volume of tourism demand and market patterns.
- Changes in consumer attitudes and the influence of unpredicted events are not included in econometric forecasting models because they cannot be measured. But their influence may be dominant in shifts of market behaviour over the coming decades. A lesson of the past decade has been the remarkable speed at which social attitudes can change and more such changes appear certain in the coming decade, fanned by media attention.

QUESTIONS TO CONSIDER

1. Why do more demanding consumers now tend to dominate developed tourism markets?
2. Why is the external business environment so important a concern for marketing managers?
3. Why do prices fluctuate so greatly in international travel and tourism?
4. In what ways are older people today so different from older people 50 years ago?
5. What evidence would you seek in deciding whether or not a tourism business is aiming to be more sustainable?

REFERENCES AND FURTHER READING

Baker, M.J. (1996). *Marketing: an introductory text.* Chapter 2 (6th edn). Macmillan.

Brassington, F. and Pettit, S. (2000). *Principles of marketing* (2nd edn). Prentice-Hall.

Castro, C.B., Armario, E.M. and Ruiz, D.M. (February 2007). The influence of market heterogeneity on the relationship between a destination's image and tourists' future behaviour, *Tourism Management*, **28**(1), pp. 175–187.

Decrop, A. and Snelders, D. (April 2005). A grounded typology of vacation decision-making, *Tourism Management*, **26**(2), pp. 121–132.

Hanlan, J., Fuller, D. and Wilde, S. (December 2006). Destination decision making: the need for a strategic planning and management approach, *Tourism and Hospitality Planning and Development*, **3**(3), pp. 209–221.

Hyde, K.F. (July 2008). Information processing and touring planning theory, *Annals of Tourism Research*, **35**(3), pp. 712–731.

Jobber, D. (2007). *Principles and practice of marketing* (5th edn). McGraw-Hill.

Kotler, P. and Armstrong, G. (1999). *Principles of marketing.* Chapter 1 (8th edn). Prentice-Hall.

Kotler, P., Wong, V., Saunders, J. and Armstrong, G. (2005). *Principles of marketing* (4th European edn). Pearson Prentice Hall.

Middleton, V.T.C. and Hawkins, R. (1998). *Sustainable tourism: a marketing perspective.* Chapters 1–4. Butterworth-Heinemann.

Pearce, D. and Schott, C. (2005). Tourism distribution channels: the visitors' perspective, *Journal of Travel Research*, **44**(1), pp. 50–63.

Riege, A.M. and Perry, C. (2000). National marketing strategies in international travel and tourism, *European Journal of Marketing*, **34**(11/12), pp. 1290–1305.

World Trade Organization (WTO) (1997). *Tourism: 20:20 Vision. Executive summary.* UNWTO.

UN (1999). World Population Prospects.

Understanding the Consumer and Marketing Mix in Travel and Tourism

Part Two explains the core tools in marketing that have not shifted greatly *in principle* in the last quarter of a century The chapters cover the meaning and marketing implications of buyer behaviour, market segmentation, product formulation and the evolving marketing mix for travel and tourism.

The major changes in tourism marketing of the last decade reflect the development of far more sophisticated and demanding customers who are increasingly empowered to exercise better choices and become more involved in purchasing decisions through interaction with suppliers on the Internet. The Internet also has major implications for product formulation and it has revolutionized the way that the traditional marketing mix operated until the 1990s.

Young couple looking the famous Machu Picchu
'Venturers (outer-directed, curious and confident travellers constantly seeking new experiences)'

CHAPTER 5

Understanding the consumer: tourism motivations and buyer behaviour

We are living in a desire economy: The majority of people have all the things they need. So you have to ensure consumers feel they want what you have. Emotional pull is central to brand attractiveness, rather than functional product performance.

(Tamar Kasriel, the Henley Centre 2003)

The previous chapter discussed the elements of the social, economic and political environment that are essentially external influences on individuals but collectively tend to determine the volume and patterns of travel and tourism generated within any country.

Propensities to participate in travel and tourism explain the overall level of demand generated in different countries but they do not explain the individual product choices that are made by different types of people. In the context established by the largely external determinants it is necessary for marketing managers to understand also how internal, psychological processes influence individuals to choose between different vacation destinations and particular types of product. That knowledge influences all the subsequent decisions in the marketing process.

Understanding the consumer is central to the marketing concept. Without a clear understanding of who your customers are and what they are buying from you, your marketing activities will be misdirected, wasteful and ineffective.

After studying this chapter you should be able to understand:

- How to deconstruct the process by which a consumer makes a decision to purchase a tourism product.
- The ways in which psychological, personal, social and cultural factors can influence the decision.

- How to evaluate the implications of these insights for marketing management.
- How contemporary marketing systems use data on consumer behaviour to develop and enhance customer relationships.

Marketing managers spend a large part of their budgets communicating with potential customers or users about their products and offers. To be effective, it is necessary for marketers to have the best understanding they can achieve of how that information is likely to be received and processed, and how the purchasing decision is made.

This chapter examines and 'deconstructs' the purchasing decision into its component parts. This analysis can be used to identify the information marketers need to obtain about their customers in order to make effective well-targeted marketing strategies and plans. The chapter draws on the insights of psychology and sociology that have been found useful by marketing academics and practitioners. In the space available it can only provide a brief outline of a number of complex concepts, which are the subject of continuing research and debate. For a fuller understanding, the readers should consult specialist consumer behaviour texts. Here, we focus on explaining their relevance to marketing planning.

A BUYER BEHAVIOUR MODEL FOR TRAVEL AND TOURISM

To help our deconstruction, the chapter uses the stimulus–response model shown in Fig. 5.1.

The stimulus–response model has three main components – stimulus, processing and response. In the centre, the buyer, the potential tourist, receives stimuli from the external environment. From this he absorbs information and forms an image of the products (e.g. destinations) available. Some of this is the result of marketing communications from organizations but much is formed over time through conversations with friends, or from the media through news reports, travel features or films. This information is processed by the buyer in ways influenced by social, personal and psychological factors, as a result of which a decision is made. The response in the right hand box is a particular set of choices, including which type of product, what brand, what price, at what time and through what distribution outlet.

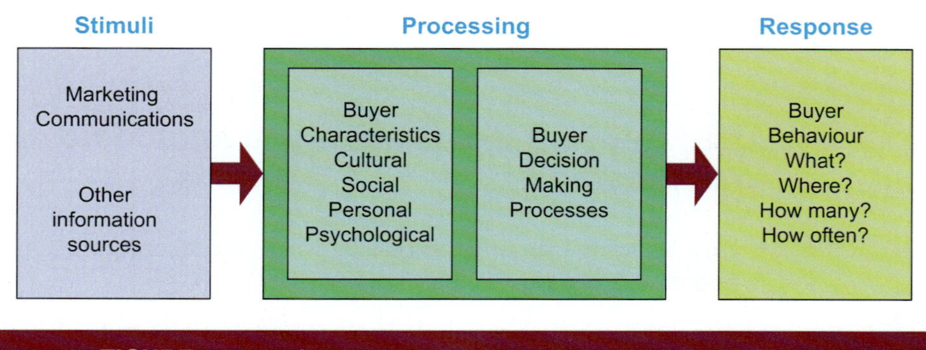

FIGURE 5.1 A stimulus response model of buyer behaviour

To understand the principles behind this model it may help to think of a computer. Both computers and the brains of consumers can only process information that has been fed into their decision systems at the right time, working within the limitations of their design and software (or personality constraints) and memory capacity. In other words, computers and buyers' minds receive information or *stimulus inputs*, which they process accordingly in their inbuilt capacities, and programmed 'states'. Both produce outputs that are a resolution of all the input variables. Obviously machines are totally predictable and consistent in their outputs, whereas people clearly are not. But the basic principle of inputs (stimulus), information-processing and outputs, is to be found at the heart of many models of buyer behaviour.

STIMULUS INPUTS: MARKETING COMMUNICATIONS AND OTHER SOURCES OF INFORMATION

Marketing communications covers all the elements of the marketing mix that are designed to motivate prospective customers. In any developed country there are dozens of tour operators offering holidays abroad to potential vacationers and dozens of domestic destinations and tourism businesses also seeking to attract the travellers' attention. A prospective tourist is faced by an almost infinite variety of choices, amounting to thousands of possibilities. He is only likely ever to be aware of a very few of the options.

Customers receive information and impressions of products in two ways. There are the formal communication channels or media, aimed at persuading prospective buyers through paid-for advertising, brochures, sales promotion techniques, public relations (PR) activity and the Internet. It is important that an organization integrates all of its communications to the customer, not only the promotional campaigns but also the other ways in which customers form an impression of a company. These include not only the physical evidence of printed materials, staff uniforms and signs on premises and vehicles, but also the prices charged and the quality of the service offered before, during and after the visit. Integrated Marketing Communications theory says that all these should convey the same message in a coherent way, consistent over time and each element complementing the rest (see Chapter 16).

There is also extensive information accessible to individuals informally through their family, friends and the groups of people with whom they interact at work and socially – known in the jargon as 'reference groups'. In other words the group of people whose approval or otherwise tends to influence large parts of our behaviour. Much research suggests that these informal channels of information, word of mouth, friends, and other reference groups are at least as influential on purchase decisions as the formal channels (Crotts, 1999).

Research into the images people hold of a tourist destination makes a distinction between the *organic* image created over time through these informal channels and the *induced* image that results from formal marketing communications (Gunn, 1972). These images are further modified by the *experiences* of visitors when they actually visit the destination. Marketing campaigns need to be based on the positive elements of the organic image, distilled in such a way as to induce a desire to visit. It is important, however, that the expectations raised by the campaign are realistic, as visitors are more likely to return or to recommend the destination to friends, if the experience lives up to their expectations.

BUYER CHARACTERISTICS INFLUENCING THE DECISION

How potential visitors receive and process the stimuli will depend on a range of personal and social factors. We will first consider individual motivation and then how this is affected by social and cultural influences.

Needs, desires and motives

One of the classic definitions of marketing is that it is the process of satisfying customer needs (UK Chartered Institute of Marketing). Psychological theory holds that the continuous churning of largely unconscious feelings of needs, wants and goals generates uncomfortable states of tension within individuals' minds and bodies. Such tension tends to build up and cannot be released until the needs are satisfied. States of tension, including hunger, fatigue and loneliness as well as the drive for self-development, are thus the *motivators* that trigger the actions that release tension states. Motivations are the dynamic process in buyer behaviour, bridging the gap between a felt need and the decision to act.

It is therefore necessary to distinguish between what Herzberg (1959) called *hygiene factors* (or dissatisfiers) – needs which cause dissatisfaction if they are not met but which are taken for granted if they are – and *motivators*, which are actively sought for their intrinsic satisfaction. In choosing a holiday, people will expect to have clean, comfortable premises and an efficient service, and if they do not get these they will complain and go elsewhere next time. However, what will make people choose one destination over another are the opportunities it offers for personally satisfying experiences achieved through activities, sightseeing and entertainment.

Maslow's (1970) well-known hierarchy states that there are basic human physiological needs such as food, drink, shelter and safety, but once these are satisfied they are replaced as motivators by higher needs or aspirations, first to belong to a group, then to gain status with the group and finally the inner-directed need for *self-development* (self-actualization in Maslow's terms). Self-development means an individual's striving for personal fulfilment of their potential.

It could be argued that in developed countries, these higher needs or aspirations are the main motivators. Pine and Gilmore (1999) argued that we are now living in an *Experience Economy*, where what we value most are not products or services but experiences. To them, the growth of the visitor economy is evidence of the added value people place on unique and memorable experiences. They go on to say that the most desired experiences are those that offer some kind of personal development or transformation, for example, adventure tourism, health spas, cultural tourism or activity holidays and learning new skills.

A number of writers have tried to classify the main types of tourist motivation. Iso-Ahola's (1982) view was that tourists are either escaping (from their everyday life) or seeking (new experiences). Their motives for doing so will be partly personal, psychological, in origin and partly interpersonal, i.e. socially influenced. A similar approach is found in Beard and Ragheb's (1983) *Leisure Motivation Scale*. This is based on four elements: *intellectual motivation* (to learn, explore, discover new things); *social motivation*, which is not only the desire to socialize but also to derive a sense of identity and belonging; the desire for *competence and mastery* of skills and abilities, usually through physically challenging activities *and stimulus-avoidance motivations* leading to the need to escape, seek solitude or relaxation.

Personality

Which of these motivations is dominant will depend very much on the psychographic profile or personality traits of the individual. Psychologists and marketing researchers measure individual's psychographic attributes, using dimensions such as confident or diffident, gregarious or loner, conscientious or happy-go-lucky, assertive or submissive, neurotic or well-balanced, tense or relaxed, adventurous or unadventurous, risk taker or risk avoider. These dimensions are widely used in product formulation and in promotional messages. A much-quoted example is Plog's (1972, 2001) personality scale that places tourists between the extremes of Venturers (outer-directed, curious and confident travellers constantly seeking new experiences) and Dependables (inward-looking, cautious people who prefer familiar places and faces). Venturers are the first to visit a new destination, which is then taken up by others until eventually it becomes a safe choice for the Dependables.

Courtesy of William Shaw c/r Bournemouth University.

Personal and economic circumstances

The individual's ability to turn their motivations into action will be constrained by the amount of leisure time and disposable income they have to devote to tourist activities. This will be determined by their occupation and income and by their age and family commitments. Young people of student age tend to be 'time rich and money poor'. Working people with young families tend to have higher incomes but also higher expenditure and less leisure time. From a tourism marketing viewpoint, the two most attractive segments are probably the young couples sometimes known as DINKYs (dual income, no kids yet) and those in their 50s and older whose children have left home and whose mortgages are lower in relative terms, the so-called empty-nesters. Gender and marital status will also affect the amount of time and money they have to devote to tourism.

Social and cultural influences

As noted, friends and family are an important source of information. Because we are all motivated by the need for belonging and status, their opinions will have a strong influence on the type of holiday destination and activities we choose. As well as these immediate reference groups, we are also influenced by the behaviour and opinions of those we admire and aspire to emulate. These 'aspirational reference groups' may include not only our superiors at work but also celebrities and others we see in the media. Marketers use celebrity endorsement of products to appeal to the aspirations of their target market.

Social influences cause new products and fashions to spread through a society. Roger's (1962) Adoption of Innovation curve shows how new products are first taken up by a small group he calls *Innovators*, who are then copied by *Early Adopters*, and so on until the fashion is adopted by the majority. Eventually, the Innovators and Early Adopters move on to something new while the product is finally taken up by a group of cautious conservatives he terms *Laggards*. Marketers need to know who are likely to be the innovators in their product field. Some trends are set by the rich and famous, others start with young people and 'street culture' before being commercialized. Some little known tourist destinations are first discovered by young backpackers, for example, while others start as the exclusive preserve of the wealthy.

The sum of the shared attitudes, values and behaviour of a social group is known as its culture. Culture is what unites the group and which divides or distinguishes them from others. It is the way in which the group has learned to live and work together by reducing the tensions that can arise from differences of opinion and behaviour. Cultures form over time due to the geographical, historical, religious, ethnic, economic and language differences that create separate groups of people. They express themselves not only through the arts, political and social institutions and sports allegiances, but also in the way that people behave towards each other in daily life. The values of the culture can influence the way people choose and experience a tourism product. The roles and influence of the family in decision-making also varies, for example, between the traditional English nuclear family and the Asian extended family.

HOFSTEDE'S RESEARCH INTO CULTURAL DIFFERENCES

Hofstede's (1980) research into IBM employees in 53 countries led him to identify four dimensions in which national cultures differ from each other in attitudes to work and organization.

Power distance

This measured the attitude of employees to their superiors, with the key question '*Would you be afraid to question your senior manager's decisions openly?* High power distance cultures developed hierarchical, authoritarian structures both in business organizations and within the family.

Uncertainty avoidance

Here the key questions were *Do you take risks, break rules to get things done? Or reduce risk by rules and rituals*?

It indicates to what extent a culture programmes its members to feel either uncomfortable or comfortable in unstructured situations, which are novel, unknown, surprising, and different from usual. Uncertainty avoiding cultures try to minimize the possibility of such situations by strict laws and rules, safety and security measures. High uncertainty avoidance cultures had bureaucratic organizations while low uncertainty avoidance cultures encouraged entrepreneurial and pragmatic approaches to business.

Individualism (as contrasted with collectivism)

Which is more important – belonging to the team, being an insider or looking after yourself, achieving personal goals?

In general, Catholic and Asian cultures rated lower on individualism than Protestant Northern European and American cultures.

Masculinity

Which values are dominant:

'Male' values of assertiveness, tangible signs of success, such as moneymaking and possessions?

'Feminine' values of more modest, nurturing relationships and the quality of life?

Hofstede found that while the overall results showed that these values divided on gender lines, in some cultures, such as Scandinavian, 'feminine' values were shared by the majority of both sexes, while in others, notably Latin American, 'masculine' values predominated.

For more on Hofstede see www.geert-hofstede.com.

While business cultures have converged towards the prevailing Western approach since the research was undertaken in the 1970s, the findings have been widely accepted as a guide to organizational culture and business behaviour. Though they were originally based on behaviour in the workplace, Hofstede and others (e.g. Reisinger and Turner, 2003) have claimed that they can also help an understanding of social and consumer behaviours. Uncertainty avoidance, the extent to which a culture takes risks or seeks to minimize them through rules and procedures, can be seen in traveller's preferences for the unknown or familiar. Tourists from high uncertainty avoidance cultures like the Japanese may prefer to eat familiar food and travel in organized itineraries (Pizam and Sussman, 1995). In individualist cultures such as Britain or the USA, it may be the norm for young people to go on adventure holidays or long backpacking trips, whereas more collective countries may prefer to travel in groups to 'culturally approved' attractions such as galleries and historical sites (Xu and Morgan, 2008). High power-distance cultures may attach greater importance to the status conferred by exotic holidays or first-class travel.

However, while these kinds of generalizations provide some help in explaining tourism behaviour, the stereotypes hide the complexity of individual human behaviour in any culture. What is important in visiting or doing business with another culture is to avoid the trap of ethnocentricity – expecting everyone to behave as they do in your own culture (as illustrated in the Disney mini case below). Learning to live and work in a culture is a continuous learning process that requires sensitivity and flexibility.

MINI CASE 5.1 DISNEYLAND PARIS

Walt Disney opened the original Disneyland in Anaheim California in 1951 with the aim of bringing to life for visitors the magic and fantasy of his cartoon films. By 1991 Disney's revenue from theme parks ($ 2.9bn) exceeded that from films and videos ($ 2.6bn). However, the US market for theme parks was becoming very competitive and Disney's California and Florida parks were battling for market share with both major 'destination parks' such as Universal Studios and Busch Gardens and also numerous smaller regional parks. Disney's films and merchandize already reached a global market and growing numbers of Europeans took their vacations in Florida in order to visit Disneyworld. It made sense for the company to exploit the potential demand for a Disney theme park in Europe.

A number of potential sites were considered in Germany, France, Spain and even the UK, but the ultimate choice was between the Paris region and a site south of Barcelona in Spain. Paris was chosen for a number of related reasons. It was in the centre of Western Europe rather than on the southern fringe, with 50m people within 4 hours drive, 300m within a short-haul flight. The transport infrastructure was already good, and Paris was already the world's premier tourist city, with 22m visitors a year.

Moreover, while other governments were ambivalent towards Disney, the French government offered an extremely attractive package of incentives to secure the prestige park and its economic and employment benefits for Paris. However, the project was not without its critics particularly from intellectuals who objected to this invasion of American culture into the heart of France, which was memorably described as the cultural equivalent of Chernobyl.

To comply with European and French law, a new company was set up, EuroDisney SCA, in which Disney had a 49% stake and European shareholders 51%; 95% of the cost of building was borrowed from banks and bondholders.

The Paris site included not only a theme park, the Magic Kingdom, but also a shopping and entertainment complex Festival Disney, seven hotels, a campsite, conference centre and a golf course. The total complex covered 1943 hectares, allegedly one-fifth the size of Paris.

Research into the European theme park market revealed a number of operators (e.g. Alton Towers, Parc Asterix, De Eftling) achieving between one and two million visitors with prices between £13 and £17 per adult. All closed down in the winter months. Based on their American experience, Disney was confident that the power of their brand would make possible a first full year target of 11 million visitors with a premium price of £28 per adult when the new resort attraction opened for business in April 1992.

This target was achieved in the first year but other aspects of the business plan were not realized. The premium price meant that visitors had less money to spend on food, drink and souvenirs, all of which were perceived as over-priced. As a result, secondary spend was 25% below budget. The concept of an all-inclusive resort proved hard to communicate to the European market, where theme parks were seen as day-visit attractions. The Disney hotels were seen as over-priced and isolated compared to the alternative of staying in Paris itself. Disney had budgeted for 70% occupancy but the reality was nearer 55%. These were the main factors accounting for a first year net loss of 5.3bn francs.

Courtesy of Dimitrios Buhalis.

In the press coverage of these results, a number of other criticisms were made of EuroDisney. There were not enough white-knuckle rides of the kind offered in European theme parks like Alton Towers. Disney specialized in lovingly detailed reconstructions of the world of the films, from Peter Pan to Pirates of the Caribbean, rather than pure adrenaline rides. The food outlets were designed with the American habit of grazing in mind – eating snacks when you are hungry throughout the day – and long queues developed at lunchtime. Not only did the French expect to eat at noon, they also expect to be able to have a bottle of wine with their meal. Disney banned alcohol from the park as being incompatible with the child-like fantasy atmosphere. Worse still, the English guests found there were no tea-making facilities in the hotel bedrooms.

More importantly perhaps, Disney assumed that most visitors would come as individuals by car or public transport. They failed to cater sufficiently for the needs of short-break and coach holiday operators. There were no group reductions, operators found Disney difficult to contact and unhelpful, group check-in facilities were painfully slow as each visitor had to be issued with an individual ticket, and there were no rest rooms or other facilities for coach drivers.

The staff were put through the same Disney University training scheme as used in America, but many visitors and journalists commented on the contrast between the enthusiastic 'have a nice day' attitude encountered in Florida and the more detached and less helpful demeanour of the largely French staff at the Paris site.

While EuroDisney had immediately established itself as Europe's most popular theme park and tourist attraction, the impression the media presented was that it was a financial failure, poorly conceived and managed, over-priced and poor value. This threatened to damage the overall global image of the brand.

QUESTIONS

Identify the significant differences between USA and European consumer behaviour revealed in this case study.
What changes could the Disneyland Paris management have made to their marketing mix to adjust to the local culture?

This case was compiled by Michael Morgan from a number of press reports during 1991–1993.

INFORMATION PROCESSING

Perception

An individual's motivations, personal circumstances, social and cultural influences will affect the way he responds to the marketing communications and other stimuli. As we are daily exposed to thousands of messages from advertising and the media, we are inevitably selective in which we pay attention to. Just as when sorting our email mailbox, the messages we give our attention to will be those which appear relevant to our current needs and interests, or those from known and trusted sources.

Perception is the term used to explain the way individuals select and organize the mass of information they are exposed to. Edward de Bono (1977) said that the mind is a pattern-making system: it is always trying to make new images and information fits into what it knows already. All the information and stimulus inputs, including the informal channels, pass through a perceptual 'sieve' or series of filters, which suppress much of the available information and highlight specific parts, often distorting it in the process.

Learning

Marketers can use this process to their advantage by selecting messages using familiar words and situations but including a surprising or puzzling twist. Because the brain has to work out the difference and fit it into its existing patterns, it is more likely to be retained in the memory than a straightforward statement would be. This is an example of what is termed *cognitive learning* or learning by elaboration.

Another type of learning exploited by advertising is learning by *classical conditioning.* Here the product is shown in a situation that evokes a pleasant emotional response, which then may become associated with the product.

Even more effective is learning from experience. Here, our experience of the product creates a set of positive or negative associations that influence subsequent decisions. This is known as *operant conditioning* or learning by reinforcement. A favourable experience reinforces our behaviour and encourages us to repeat it. For example, a good experience of an airline, with a punctual flight and friendly service, is highly likely to influence our future choices. A long delay, surly service or an overbooked flight can create tensions and frustrations that are likely to be recalled when we next have to choose an airline. Good marketing aims to achieve subsequent sales through harnessing product satisfaction as the most powerful means of influencing future buyer behaviour.

Attitudes

As a result of our experience and learning, we develop beliefs and *attitudes*. Attitudes are enduring favourable or unfavourable thoughts and feelings towards something. They develop slowly as the result of our own experience and the influence of our social reference groups and culture. The mind tries to reconcile new information with its existing pattern of attitudes towards the topic. If this is impossible, the individual experiences as uncomfortable feeling, known by psychologists as *cognitive dissonance* and may refuse to accept the information as correct or ignore it completely. Because long-held attitudes are difficult to change, it is always easier for a company to design products and marketing messages to appeal to people's existing attitudes than to try and change them.

THE CONSUMER DECISION-MAKING PROCESS

We next consider how a consumer uses the information available to make a decision to buy a particular product. One of the most widely used models of the consumer decision process is that of Engel et al. (1978). In the version used by Morgan (1996), it forms the acronym PIECE.

- Problem recognition
- Information search

- Evaluation of alternatives
- Choice of purchase
- Evaluation of post-purchase experience

Applying this 'PIECE Process' to the choice of a holiday, the first stage is for the customer to become aware that a holiday is the best solution to the tensions and desire for escape that he is feeling. In any year over 40% of British people still do not take a holiday of four or more nights away from home, although if the propensity to travel includes all types of travel of more than one or more nights, the proportion is very much higher. A tour operator selling overseas holidays must decide whether to concentrate on selling its brands to those who are already looking for a holiday or to try to expand the market by persuading others that they could indeed afford a holiday.

Once the need for a holiday is recognized and seen to be affordable, a customer will begin to look for information on what is available from formal and informal sources. He may simply seek the advice of friends or return to a company he has used before. The company needs to know where their target market normally look for information on their type of holiday, and make sure that their products are available there. The majority of people who take overseas package holidays still book through travel agents, though increasing they are first doing some initial research on destinations and prices on-line and growing numbers are booking on such sites (see Part Four of this book). For domestic or specialist holidays they are more likely to look for advertisements in the weekend press or magazines.

Websites and travel agencies have thousands of holiday products on sale but the customer is likely to make their choice from a very limited 'set' of alternatives. Kotler states that there is the *awareness set* – the brands the customer has heard of, which could be only a very small percentage of those available. Of these, he will only seriously study a smaller *consideration set* – the brands he used before, or has heard good reports of, or seen recent advertising or special offers. As he gathers information about these, only a few will exactly meet his requirements and become his *choice set*. The company needs to know where their brand stands in relation to these sets. Do they need to improve awareness through advertising, or should they concentrate on matching their product more closely to what the customers are looking for?

A customer then evaluates the alternatives offered. The consumer behaviour models suggest this is done by checking the features of the holiday against a mental list of *attributes*: for example, a scenic location, close to the beach, but in walking distance of the bars and night-clubs, within a certain price range, and so on. According to Fishbein (1963), the choice will depend not only on the relative importance of each attribute, but also whether he believes the particular brand or destination can provide it. Howard (1989) suggests that, in addition, the *confidence* the customer has in his beliefs about the company is also important and needs to be measured. The website and brochure may look wonderful but if the company is unfamiliar, he may feel safer remaining with a well-known brand. For larger companies, marketers commission market research to find out how potential customers rank in importance the attributes they expect from a holiday and how their company rates against competitors in delivering the key attributes. It then has the choice of either changing the attributes of its brand or of trying to change consumer perceptions.

Having made the *choice*, the customer returns to the travel agent or travel website to book it. It is by no means certain that he will come out with the holiday he intended to book. He may receive additional information, there may be a more attractive offer available or the holiday may simply be fully booked. In some sectors, 80% of consumer decisions are made at the point of sale, though in travel it is unlikely to be as high as, for example, in fashion. Nevertheless, it is important to make sure that the customer does not change their mind because of a hard-to-navigate website or a travel agency clerk trying to get the better rate of commission offered by a competitor.

If it's a summer package holiday, a customer typically pays a deposit in January and the balance in March for a holiday in July. At this stage all he has in exchange is a promise, contained in a brochure or an email confirmation. It is very likely therefore that he will experience what is know as *post-purchase dissonance*, an uneasy feeling of doubt about whether he has made the right choice. The company must seek to reassure him by sending out confirmation messages and tickets promptly. The professionalism and brand image of these communications will also help to reassure him that he has chosen a reputable, efficient and friendly organization. Otherwise, even if he does not cancel a booking, he may be critical and wary when he takes the holiday, more likely to find fault and complain.

Finally, the actual experience of consumption will strongly affect future attitudes towards a company. If the product exceeds expectations, the customer will learn to associate the brand with positive emotions and the prospects of establishing some form of continuing relationship with that customer are high. If the experience is disappointing, the opposite will occur and, depending on the importance of the purchase, the consumer may never buy that product again. Worse by far for marketing managers, such consumers will influence their circle of friends with negative stories about that product. Good after-sales service, reducing post-purchase dissonance, can save the company a lot of money on advertising for new business.

It is this recognition of business retention that has given rise to the concept of *Relationship Marketing*. Relationship Marketing sees the decision-making process not as an isolated event leading to a one-off transaction, but as just one episode in a developing relationship between the consumer and the company or destination. A positive experience this time will change the way in which marketing messages are received and evaluated next time. Most customers respond well to a sense of being treated as in some way special.

Figure 5.2 summarizes the implications for the company's marketing strategy of each stage in the consumer decision-making process and some examples of the decisions to be made after research.

What we have described here is known as an *extended problem solving process*, which assumes that the individual is what Gabbott and Hogg (1997) described as a rational mathematician, carefully weighing up alternatives and making a choice based on logic. In reality, of course, few human decisions are made in this way. Even when the purchase is an important and expensive one, emotion will still play a strong part and the consumer may be influenced by the image of the brand, his own self-image or the desire to impress others as well by purely functional and economic considerations. It is particularly important in tourism where the customer is not buying a product or a service but the expectation of an experience. As Holbrook and Hirschmann (1982) put it, an experience is a subjective emotional state full of symbolic significance. It is therefore important for marketers to carry out not only quantitative research into each stage of the decision-making process but also

Stage in Consumer Decision Process	Implications for Marketing Strategies	Options
Problem Recognition	Targeting of marketing campaign	Target existing customers or new ones?
Information Search	Distribution of publicity Website design, links and search engine position	Sell direct or through intermediaries? On-line or traditional channels?
Evaluation of Alternatives	Product design Promotional message	Adapt product to customer's criteria? Adapt the message?
Choice at Point of Sale	Marketing to retailers Easy-on-line booking	Ensure availability Incentives to sell
Evaluation of post-purchase experience	After Sales Service Relationship Management	Prompt and efficient service Good customer relations

FIGURE 5.2 Implications for marketing of the Consumer Decision Process (based on Morgan, 1996)

qualitative research exploring the emotions the consumer experiences during (and after) the process, and the meaning of the holiday in the wider context of their life.

It should also be recognized that these kind of extended problem-solving processes are only used when the purchase is important, expensive or carries a physical, financial or psychological risk. Such purchases are described as *high-involvement* decisions, involving the customer's full attention and powers of reasoning. Lower risk purchases are low-involvement decisions and can be made out of habit, routine, or on impulse, seeking variety and change for its own sake. Traditionally, holidays have been seen as major, high-involvement purchases, but as travel becomes easier and cheaper, many short breaks and day-trips are now taken on impulse without an extended information search or evaluation. This increases the importance of Relationship Marketing. If the customer already knows and trusts a company they are more likely to use it for additional impulse bookings, perhaps prompted by a carefully targeted persuasive email.

Link article available at www.routledge.com/9780750686938

(1) Sirakaya, E., Woodside, A., December 2005. Building and testing theories of decision making by travellers. Tourism Management 26 (6), 815–832.

RESPONSE: BUYER BEHAVIOUR

The range of psychological processes by which an individual chooses to buy a product are complex and hard to measure. The mind of the consumer has been described as a black box. You can observe what went in and what comes out, but what actually happens inside remains a mystery. For this reason, it is important that marketers make full use of the evidence provided by the resulting behaviour.

Websites linked with computerized reservations and ticketing systems are now used to drive information databases that can give marketers a rich source of knowledge about their customers. An on-line booking form, whether completed by the customer, the travel agent or a telephone sales person, can be used to provide essential management information on

- Type and class of products purchased.
- Frequency of purchase.
- Special needs requested-diets, disabilities, babysitting, business facilities, etc.
- Dates of booking – are they booking early or at the last minute?
- Source of booking – agency, telephone or on-line.
- Response to a promotional campaign or special offer.
- Full address and postcode as well as email address (on-line).
- Family or group size.
- Age – especially if there are special rates for children and senior citizens.
- Birthdays and other special occasions.
- Method of payment.

The addresses are very useful not only for mailing special offers to existing customers but also in suggesting where other potential customers might be found. A simple analysis can be used to identify the towns and types of postcodes within which existing customers live. By using the services of a geodemographic analysis system such as ACORN or Mosaic in the UK, or equivalent systems in other countries, addresses can be analysed into postal code districts and the types of housing and neighbourhoods where customers are most likely to be found be identified. From the wealth of census and survey detail at their disposal, these systems can produce a comprehensive picture of the residents of each type of housing area including age and family stage, occupation and education and consumption patterns of a range of products including holidays and travel.

USING CONSUMER BEHAVIOUR DATA FOR MARKETING

Database marketing

As a result of the development of database technology, marketers are now able to base much more cost effective marketing decisions on a detailed knowledge of the behaviour and preferences of their existing customers (and others that match the segment profiles). Through a process known as 'data mining', tourism firms can now target and contact their customers directly through the post or email with specific offers based on their previous buying behaviour. Websites can now greet repeat customers by name and a list of recommended products.

Relationship Marketing

Knowing that repeat customers are important is hardly a new marketing insight. It has been understood for centuries. What is new is the ability to recognize repeat buyers instantly and address them individually by name when organizations are dealing with tens of thousands or millions of customers a year. This ability provides the drive behind *Relationship Marketing*. Relationship Marketing switches the emphasis from the recruitment of new customers to the retention and recovery of existing ones. Although the cost of gaining a new customer is falling through use of the Internet, global players with large market shares cannot sustain profit unless their repeat levels of business are running at levels of 50% or more for key segments. For smaller companies such as niche tour operators Vacances Franco-Britannique, 80% of their business can come from repeat bookings and referrals from satisfied customers. Relationship Marketing has been one of the buzzwords of the last decade and it is primarily driven by knowledge gained and communicated by connected customer databases, often referred to as *Customer Relationship Management* (*CRM*) systems. Apart from the ability to target individuals, databases have a powerful market research value in generating detailed knowledge of repeat buyers and cutting out the cost of undertaking traditional usage and attitude studies among buyers.

These databases do need to be used with care or the effects will be counter-productive. The aim of CRM should be to create a long-term relationship with the customer, based on a high quality of service, 'the keeping of promises' as Grönroos put it. Gater captured the essence of what he termed the *database marketing approach*, as 'the building of a continuous relationship between principal and customer. That means not always selling when a communication is made and not always demanding a response... It means...obtaining loyalty through customer service and care, by building a relationship centred around the customer rather than the product' (Gater, 1986: 41).

Good relationships, whether in love or business, are based on trust and mutual need. If one party is continually pestering the other with unsolicited and unwanted messages, that is closer to stalking than a true relationship. Junk mail and SPAM emails give the whole direct marketing industry a bad name. To avoid this, a range of techniques known as *permission marketing* have been developed to make sure that the customer only receives the marketing messages that they have requested. Examples include loyalty cards and privilege clubs which give customers an incentive to sign up to receive advance notice of new products, special offers or prior booking for special events.

A further development of the use of software technology to retain and develop relationships with existing customers is known as *Customer Experience Management* (CEM). This too is based on long-standing marketing principles. As Jan Carlson of SAS said 'Any time a customer comes into contact with any aspect of your business, however remote, that customer has an opportunity to form an impression.' It makes sense therefore to ensure that each time the customer gets the same high standard of service. This is something hotel, restaurant and shop managers have always known instinctively, but is harder to achieve when the contact with the customers is through a website database or call-centre. CEM software can record every contact the customer has with the company so that when he calls, the employee has all the details on screen and can greet him as an individual, saving time and increasing the opportunity for further sales. It also enables managers to monitor the performance of their employees and the quality of the customer experience.

CHAPTER SUMMARY

This chapter:

- Deconstructs the way that consumers process information from marketing communications and informal sources in order to make decisions on travel and tourism purchases.
- Explains the psychological processes and the social influences that can aid marketers in designing effective plans for their target markets.
- Stresses that for higher value products, a purchase should not just be seen as an isolated occurrence but part of a developing long-term relationship between the customer and the company. A positive experience, of the booking process as well as the product benefits will influence the way in which future communications from a company will be received and processed.
- Explains how companies can use customer databases to build up a detailed knowledge of individual customers and make them specific and relevant offers.

QUESTIONS TO CONSIDER

1. What are the limitations of the stimulus–response model of consumer behaviour? To what extent can the human mind be compared to a computer?
2. Discuss the likely motivations and personality traits of the target customers for a special interest holiday of your choice.
3. Evaluate the influence of a visitor's experience on their subsequent holiday decision-making processes. What are the implications for marketers?
4. To what extent is choosing a holiday becoming a lower-involvement decision?
5. How has computer database technology changed the relationship between tourism organizations and their customers?

REFERENCES AND SUGGESTED READING

Beard, J. and Ragheb, M.G. (1983). Measuring leisure motivation, *Journal of Leisure Research*, **15**(3), pp. 219–228.

Bigne, J.E., Sanchez, M.I, and Sanchez, J. (December 2001). Tourism image, evaluation variables and after purchase behaviour: inter-relationship, *Tourism Management*, **22**(6), pp. 607–616.

Carlzon, J. (1987). *Moments of truth.* Harper Collins.

Crotts, J (1999) Consumer decision making and prepurchase information search. In: Consumer *Behavior in Travel and Tourism.* Mansfield Y, Pizam A, (eds.). Binghamton, N.Y.; Haworth Press: pp.149–168.

De Bono, E. (1977). *Lateral thinking.* Harmondsworth, Penguin.

Engel, J.F., Blackwell, R.D. and Kollat, D.T. (1978). *Consumer behaviour*, Hinsdale, Illinois. Dryden Press.

Fishbein, M. (1963). An investigation of the relationships between beliefs about an object and attitudes towards that object, *Human Relations*, **16**, 233–240.

Gabott, M., and Hogg, G. (1997). *Contemporary services marketing: a reader*. Dryden Press.

Gater, C. (October 1986). Database key to a direct hit, *Marketing*, **2**, 41–42.

Grönroos, C. (1989). Defining marketing: a market-orientated approach, *European Journal of Marketing*, **23**(1), pp. 52–59.

Gunn, C. (1972). *Vacationscape*. Austin: Bureau of Business Research, University of Texas.

Herzberg, F. (1959). *The motivation to work,* New York, John Wiley and Sons.

Hofstede, G. (1980). *Culture's consequences: international differences in work-related values*. London: Sage.

Holbrook, M.B. and Hirschmann, E.C. (1982). The experiential aspects of consumption: consumer fantasies, feelings and fun, *Journal of Consumer Research*, **9**(2), pp. 132–139.

Howard, J.A. (1989). *Consumer behaviour in marketing strategy*. Englewood Cliffs, N.J.: Prentice Hall, p. 34.

Iso-Ahola, S. (1982). Towards a social psychology of tourist motivation: a rejoinder, *Annals of Tourism Research*, **9**, 256–261.

Kim, H., Cheng, C.K. and O'Leary, J.T. (October 2007). Understanding participation patterns and trends in tourism cultural attractions, *Tourism Management*, **28**(5), pp. 1366–1371.

Maslow, A. (1970). *Motivation and personality*. NY: Harper and Row.

Morgan, M. (1996). *Marketing for leisure and tourism*. Hemel Hempstead: Prentice Hall.

Pizam, A. and Sussman, S. (1995). Does nationality effect tourist behavior? *Annals of Tourism Research*, **22**(2), pp. 901–917.

Plog, S. (1974). Why destinations rise and fall in popularity, *Cornell Hotel and Restaurant Administration Quarterly*, **14**(4), pp. 55–58.

Plog (2001). Why destination areas rise and fall in popularity, *Cornell Hotel and Restaurant Administration Quarterly*, **42**(3), pp. 13–24. Reprinted and revised as.

Rewtrakunphaiboon, W., and Opperwal, H. (2003). Holiday packaging and tourist decision making, *Tourism Analysis*, **8**(2), pp. 1893–1896.

Rogers, E. (1962). *The diffusion of innovations*. New York: Free Press.

Sirakaya, E., and Woodside, A. (December 2005). Building and testing theories of decision making by travellers, *Tourism Management*, **26**(6), pp. 815–832.

Xu, F. and Morgan, M. (2008). Students' travel behavior – a cross culture comparison of the UK and China, *International Journal of Tourism Research*.

'When Self-Challengers talk travel, they're not talking holidays on the beach'

CHAPTER 6

Market segmentation for travel and tourism markets

Market segmentation recognizes that people differ in their tastes, needs, attitudes, lifestyles, family size and composition, etc.... It is a deliberate policy of maximizing market demand by directing marketing efforts at significant sub-groups of customers or consumers.

(Chisnall, 1985: 264)

Chapter 3 stresses that a key role of marketing managers is to influence and, wherever possible, to manage demand: 'The more an organization knows about its customers and prospective customers – their needs and desires, their attitudes and behaviour – the better it will be able to design and implement the marketing efforts required to stimulate their purchasing decisions.' Building on Chapter 5, this chapter explains that market segmentation is the process whereby businesses organize their knowledge current and potential customer groups and select for particular attention of those whose needs and wants they are best able to supply with their products, both now and in the future.

In other words, because it is increasingly impossible to deal with all customers on a mass consumption or 'one size fits all basis,' market segmentation is the practical expression in business of the theory of consumer orientation. It is arguably the most important of all the practical marketing techniques available to marketing managers in travel and tourism. It is normally the logical first step in the marketing process involved in developing products to meet customers' needs. Segmentation is also the necessary first stage in the process of setting precise marketing objectives and targets and the basis for effective planning, budgeting and control of marketing activities. It is the basis for positioning, branding and communicating relevant images to targeted users.

In practice, apart from national tourism organizations, no individual business is ever likely to be much concerned with the whole or even many of a country's tourist markets. They will usually be closely concerned with particular subgroups of visitors within the total market or *segments*, which they identify as the most productive targets for their marketing activities. National tourism organizations also find it necessary to segment the total market of potential visitors in order to carry out the specific marketing campaigns they organize, although they may have to provide facilities, such as information services, for all visitors.

After studying this chapter you should be able to understand:

- The wide range of segments that typically exist for most producers of travel and tourism products.
- The process of market segmentation and the key criteria to be applied to any grouping of customers.
- The principal ways used in travel and tourism to divide up markets for marketing purposes.

MULTIPLE SEGMENTS FOR PRODUCERS IN TRAVEL AND TOURISM

Before considering the techniques used to segment markets we list below an indication of the wide range of subgroups with which businesses in the different sectors of travel and tourism are concerned. The list notes five broad consumer segments for each of the main sectors identified in Chapter 1 (excluding destination organizations that must have regard to all segments).

Hotels

1. Corporate/business clients.
2. Visitors on group package tours.
3. Independent vacationers.
4. Visitors taking weekend/midweek package breaks.
5. Conference delegates.

Tour operators

1. Young people, singles and couples, 18–30-year-olds.
2. Families with children.
3. Retired/senior citizens/empty nesters.
4. Activity/sports participants.
5. Culture seekers.

Transport operators

1. First-class passengers.
2. Club-class passengers.

3. Standard-class passengers.
4. Charter groups.
5. APEX purchasers.

Destination attractions

1. Local residents in the area.
2. Day visitors from outside local area.
3. Domestic tourists.
4. Foreign tourists.
5. School parties.

The segments listed above are not comprehensive, of course, but simply an illustration of the range of possibilities that exist for each sector. Readers may find it a useful exercise to extend these lists from 5 to around 15 segments for each sector, using the analysis discussed later in this chapter.

Even the minimum list above should make clear a very important point: *most businesses deal not with one, but with several segments.* Some segments are largely dictated by the location in which a business operates; other segments may be attracted by products designed and marketed specifically to them. It is also important to bear in mind that segments are often changing as demographics change, technology changes and world travel and immigration increases. For instance a few years ago there would have been only a very small market for organizing holidays to Poland. However, with so many Polish workers in the UK by 2008 a whole new market has opened up. Similarly with Chinese and Indian communities that have been resident in the UK for decades, whole new segments for holiday and visitor experiences have opened up. Segments change, grow and decline and they have to be monitored continuously.

Link article available at www.routledge.com/9780750686938

(1) Tkaczynski, A., Rundle-Thiele, S.A., Beaumont, N., in press. Segmentation: a tourism stakeholder view. Tourism Management.

A MARKETING AND OPERATIONS VIEW OF SEGMENTATION

At first sight it may appear obvious that all the managers in a business work closely together to create a range of products and market them to identified customer groups or segments. In practice there is often a real conflict between the needs of operations management and the view of marketing managers. Disputes are not unusual.

From an operational standpoint it is usually most cost-effective and easy to manage if a single, purpose-designed product, such as a standard airline seat or a standard bedroom, can be marketed to all buyers. In that way unit costs can be cut to the minimum, operational controls and training procedures can be standardized and more easily implemented. In such conditions segmentation is still relevant as the basis for separate promotional campaigns but it does not interfere with the smooth operation of production processes. Some large marketing-led organizations, most notably McDonald's family restaurants, budget hotels, budget airlines, major theme parks and other attractions, do provide essentially standard products for their customers. These are important exceptions but increasingly around the world, businesses are facing more competitive market conditions in which they are competing for shares of the same total markets and aiming their products at the same groups of prospective customers. The need to create and deliver *purpose-adapted* products for each defined user group is becoming more urgent in post-industrial societies with their greater affluence, wider choice and more demanding consumers.

In an ideal world each separate customer would receive special personal service or a custom-built product. They may still do so in travel and tourism if they are able to pay the necessary price, as in penthouse suites in luxury hotels. It is also possible in very small businesses, such as farmhouses taking in a few visitors to stay, in which the level of personal contact between visitor and host is very high and each service delivery unique. In the large-scale marketing of quality-controlled standardized products, however, such individual attention is not possible at the prices most customers are able and willing to pay. There is, therefore, often a considerable level of tension between the interests of marketing managers and the interests of operations managers. The former are committed to offering products designed to meet the needs of subgroups in the market as the best way to secure their custom; the latter are responsible for holding down or reducing unit costs while maintaining the highest possible quality standards of product delivery.

If significant product differentiation is required to meet the needs of different market segments, there are also likely to be management problems in servicing different needs at the same time on the same premises. Segments are often not complementary. To provide an example, a hotel may find it difficult or impossible to satisfy the needs of business people and coach parties of packaged tourists in the same restaurant at the same time; museums have similar problems with noisy school parties and older visitors requiring peace and quiet to achieve the experience they seek from a visit. The problems are very clear in the case of conference halls, which may be separately marketed as the venue for a pop concert one day, a political meeting next day, and a sales conference on the day after. In each case a different segment with different needs is dealt with, but they are not compatible on the same premises at the same time. Considerable strain and careful sequencing and separation requirements are imposed on those who manage such operations. (See also Chapter 7.)

To summarize, the task of marketing management, in close liaison with operations management, is to create and develop compatible products that meet the needs of compatible target segments. This usually has to be achieved on the same premises in a way that permits economies to be achieved in both operational and marketing processes and in ways that generate optimum income from the selected customer and product mix. Such optimization is never easy to achieve in service businesses. It requires compromises and readers should be aware of the conflicting management interests often existing in practice.

SEGMENTATION DEFINED

Segmentation may now be defined as the process of dividing a total market such as all visitors, or market sectors such as holiday travel or business travel, into subgroups or segments for marketing management purposes. Its purpose is to facilitate more cost-effective marketing through the formulation, promotion and delivery of purpose-designed products that satisfy the identified needs of target groups. In other words, segmentation is justified on the grounds of achieving greater efficiency in the supply of products to meet identified demand, and increased cost-effectiveness in the marketing process. It is also a shift in the direction of meeting the needs of individuals for product experiences that satisfy them and bring them back for more. In most cases travel and tourism businesses will deal with multiple segments and multiple products over a 12-month period but not necessarily simultaneously.

In the tourism industry most established businesses will often have no practical choice but to target certain segments because of the location and nature of their business. But usually there will be other segments that could be selected as targets if they contribute to needs of a business. For example, as a normal response to monitoring market trends and observing competitors' actions, a tour operator may decide to develop a range of specific products for segments of active people aged 55–75. If the operator is successful, the over-55s product may grow from, say 2% to, say, 20% of total turnover over a period of 5 years. The operator will have changed its segment/product mix as a result of a strategic marketing decision.

Most tourism businesses will have continuous scope and strategic opportunities for altering the mix of revenue generated by the current structure of segments, through targeting new segments and manipulating the marketing mix. They will have a strong incentive to do so in order to improve the profitability of their total portfolio of markets and products over time. The criteria for choosing new segments for marketing development will stem either from the producer's needs to utilize assets, e.g. to develop off-season business or find users for short-run capacity surpluses revealed by yield management programmes, or from recognizing attractive characteristics of the segments themselves, e.g. high relative expenditure per capita of some groups compared with others.

Actionable market segments

Drawing on the contributions of Kotler and Armstrong (1999), Chisnall (1985) and Middleton and Hawkins (1998) it is possible to focus on five main criteria that must be applied to any segment if it is to be usable or actionable in marketing. Each segment has to be

- Discrete.
- Measurable.
- Viable.
- Appropriate.
- Sustainable.

Discrete means that the selected subgroups must be separately identifiable by criteria such as purpose of visit, income, location of residence or motivation, as discussed later in this chapter.

Measurable means that the criteria distinguishing the subgroups must be measurable by available marketing research data, or via such new data as can be obtained at acceptable cost. Research is normally expensive and segmentation must be affordable within available budgets. Segments that cannot be adequately measured on a regular basis cannot be properly targeted. As noted in Chapter 11, if targeting is not measurably precise, it will be difficult or impossible to evaluate the effectiveness of marketing activities over time. From a marketing standpoint, if a segment cannot be measured, it does not exist, except as wishful thinking. Computerized booking systems and customer databases have greatly facilitated the segmentation process in recent years.

Viable means that the long-run projected revenue generated by a targeted segment exceeds the full cost of designing a marketing mix to achieve it – by a margin that meets the organization's financial objectives. In the short run it may be necessary to ignore segment viability in order to achieve other strategic organizational objectives such as growth. Viability, therefore, is a function of the costs of designing or adapting products for segments, promoting to target groups, and ensuring that prospective customers can find convenient access to such products, once they have been persuaded to buy.

Appropriate, reflects the inseparability of service product delivery (see Chapters 3 and 8) and means it is essential that segments to be serviced on the same premises are mutually compatible and contribute to the image or position in the market adopted by the business. An economy car with a Rolls-Royce label would be absurd, even if the company wished to make it. Similarly, downmarket coach tour business to the Savoy Hotel in London or to Crowne Plaza hotels could only damage those companies' reputations for exclusiveness and luxury at a price that maintains the expected standards. Meeting one segment's needs may sometimes not be achieved without alienating another.

Sustainable, in this context means assessing the extent to which segments contribute positively or negatively to the environmental mission and objectives of a business. If a resort business depends for its future on the quality of the coral reefs adjacent to which it is located, for example, it may have to limit the volume of segments shown to cause the greatest damage by their chosen activities. The choice of more sustainable segments and the avoidance of those associated with high impact and damage (and associated segment specific visitor management programmes designed to modify behaviour) are relatively new considerations for marketing. They are expected to become far more significant in the next decade.

To summarize thus far, market segments are identified target groups within a total market that are chosen because they are relevant to an organization's strategic mission statement, interests, skills and particular capabilities. In other words, selected segments have particular needs and profiles a producer feels especially competent to satisfy with relevant products that are both economically and environmentally sustainable into the future.

To be actionable in modern marketing, segments must meet all the five criteria noted in this section, which are as relevant to service organizations as to producers of manufactured goods. The next section discusses the ways or methods through which target groups may be identified and measured.

METHODS USED TO SEGMENT MARKETS

There are seven main ways of dividing up markets for segmentation purposes, all of which are used in practice in travel and tourism. They are usually based on some form of database analysis or marketing research and a commitment to segmentation implies a commitment to marketing information systems.

The methods are listed below and subsequently discussed. The sequence in which they appear is not that commonly found in marketing texts but it reflects an order of priority that the authors believe to be most relevant to international travel and tourism markets. The main methods of segmentation are by

1. Purpose of travel.
2. Buyer needs, motivations and benefits sought.
3. Buyer behaviour/characteristics of product usage.
4. Demographic, economic and geographic profiles.
5. Psychographic profile.
6. Geodemographic profile.
7. Price.

These seven methods are not to be seen as alternative choices for segmentation. They are overlapping and complementary ways in which it is possible to analyse a consumer market in order to appreciate and select from it the range of segments it comprises. Many businesses in travel and tourism will use at least three of the methods for any particular segment; all of them could be used if the segment being analysed is important enough to a business. Even if some of the variables are not used to select segments, they may well have a role in building up detailed consumer profiles for the segments that have been selected on other criteria.

Segmentation by purpose of travel

For any tourism business, practical marketing segmentation should always begin with a careful analysis of the purposes for which customers undertake travel and use its and competitors' products. Take, for example, business. Within the broad category of business travel there are many specific aspects of purpose that determine the nature of the products offered and the promotional approach to be used. Conference markets require different products to those supplied to other business travellers and meetings for groups of different sizes require special provision; some travellers may require secretarial services and business travel ranges from first-class to budget-priced products.

The range of segments noted under the main sectors of travel and tourism earlier in this chapter reflect some of the more obvious purposes. A little thought will indicate a wide range of possibilities. Provided the customer groups associated with any purpose meet the five essential criteria for effective segmentation, a detailed understanding of each purpose of visit will always be useful in practice. For smaller businesses in travel and tourism, segmentation by simple analysis of purpose may be all that is needed for practical or actionable purposes.

For a tour operator, customers' purposes and product needs will differ according to whether they are looking for

- Main summer holidays.
- Additional holidays and short breaks.
- Winter sun.
- Winter sports.
- Cruises.

Within the broad categories of main and additional holidays, typical subsidiary purposes would include sea and beach holidays (with and without children), cultural interests, walking and other activity or adventure interests, and an interest in exotic destinations. For larger tour operators, the products designed to appeal to such markets usually have their own websites and a separate brochure or separate sections within a brochure. The provision of different pages on a website and in brochures are therefore obvious signs of segmentation in practice. The flexibility and growing use of websites greatly facilitates and extends this type of segmentation.

For established tour operators and any other successful tourism businesses, the grouping of products currently provided is an accurate reflection of customer purposes served. In other words, and this is an important point, *market segmentation and product formulation are opposite sides of the same coin if they are correctly matched.* The widely used marketing terms *product/market mix* and *product/market portfolio* express this point succinctly.

The other segmentation methods discussed below are ways to refine and develop a clearer, more precise understanding of segments, which already exists in outline through the identification of travel purpose.

Segmentation by buyer needs and benefits sought

Within the purpose of travel, and obviously an underlying aspect of it, the next logical consideration for segmentation is to understand the needs, wants and motivations of particular customer groups, as discussed in Chapter 5. For reasons developed in the next chapter on tourism products, it is generally accepted in marketing that customers tend to seek particular benefits when they make their product choices. In the case of the tour operator example, the primary purpose is reflected in the type of holiday chosen; motivations may variously relate to opportunities to meet and mix with particular types of people, indulge in gastronomic pleasures, be highly active or take pleasures sedately, and so on. For organizations dealing with business markets, some business travellers may identify luxury and high levels of personal service as the principal benefits they seek when travelling away from home. Others may identify speed of service and budget prices as their principal benefits. Some business travellers, if they are paid a fixed sum of money for their travel expenses, may seek economy products, especially if they are able to retain the difference between their travel allowance and the actual cost they pay. Some travellers prefer to stay in large, modern, international hotels, while others choose older, more traditional establishments offering a more interesting environment or a more personalized service.

In the case of visitor attractions the benefits sought by family groups may relate to children's interests rather than those of the adults who purchase the admission tickets. In the case of museums, the benefits sought by most visitors are likely to be an hour or two's general interest and 'edutainment', since they have only a limited knowledge of the subject matter's intrinsic merits and depth. Many a museum management team has been misled by its own enthusiasm for its special collection into believing that most visitors are also very interested in the subjects displayed. Usually they are not and their threshold of patience is very easily crossed if the collections are not displayed in ways designed to stimulate general interest.

In many sectors of travel and tourism, the range and perceived importance of the benefits sought by customer segments may not be immediately apparent to marketing managers. Often they can only be discovered through market research among identified target groups, and consumer perceptions change over time. Segmentation by benefits makes it possible for marketing managers to fine tune the quality of the experiences that their products can deliver within the broad requirements of purpose noted earlier. Focusing on promoting the benefits sought is a logical objective for websites, brochures and other marketing communications.

An interesting example of both benefit and behavioural segmentation is offered by Inkbaran and Jackson (2005), who undertook research on people who travelled to resorts in Turkey. Through market research, they segmented the tourists into various clusters. These were

Resort incidental, recreation-focused (Romantics)

This was the smallest cluster, containing the second youngest membership and had the second highest percentage of tertiary-educated individuals. Cluster 1 has the highest percentage of singles and the highest percentage of couples without children. Their major reason for choosing a resort destination was the opportunity to pursue recreational activities without difficulty. This cluster is made up mainly of young people without families who are not interested in the resort or its general tourist activities, but in pursuing simple recreation activities.

Resort-centred, facilities focused (Immersers)

This was the second largest cluster with average age in the mid-30s, and included a large proportion of single members and couples with dependent children of all ages. They were regular visitors and chose the resort for recreation, tranquillity, convenience, combining adventure tourism with normal visitor activity, accommodation, family relaxation and safety and security. This group appeared to be focused on what the resort has to offer in terms of its location and facilities.

Resort-centred, family-focused (Tasters)

This was the largest cluster group, with more younger members, though spanning the whole age group. They had the highest education level and the highest percentage of first-time visitors to the resort. For reason of choice, this cluster group gave the highest rank to the resort as providing a good place for the family to relax and rejuvenate.

Resort-incidental, safety-focus (Veterans)

This group had the highest percentage of males, was the oldest group and the least educated. The membership did not include singles or young couples, but was made up of mature families, mature couples and mature singles. They had the highest percentage of re-visitations over the longest period of time. While they failed to rank any resort facility highly, they were above average in their ranking for safety and security reasons.

It is easy to see how this information can be translated into how the buyers could behave over a longer period of time. What such research does not necessarily uncover is the changing fashions in going to resorts and how some resorts can be very much in favour at certain periods and decline at other times. For instance Bournemouth was a very desirable seaside resort for many decades until the 1970s and 1980s when the UK's traditional main holiday markets were attracted to new Mediterranean resorts. However with the growth of the university, the attractions of living and having second homes by the coast and rapid expansion of the short holiday market, Bournemouth and some other coastal resorts are being revitalized and regaining popularity with new markets. Coupled with concerns about global warming and the negative impact of air travel, this type of UK resort has opportunities to develop in the coming decades.

Segmentation by buyer behaviour

Within purpose and benefits sought there is ample scope for refining the segmentation process according to the types of behaviour or characteristics of use of products that customers exhibit. One obvious example is the frequency of usage of products. Business users may be very frequent users of hotels with perhaps 20 or more stays in a year and even more frequent users of airlines and car rental companies.

Frequent users of the same product supplier, a buyer characteristic known as *product or brand loyalty,* may represent only 10% of individual customers in a year but could generate up to 60% of revenue for some hotel groups and airlines. *Loyal* customers are highly attractive to producers for obvious reasons and a combination of high spending, high frequency and high loyalty would be the best possible set of reasons for designing products and promotional campaigns aimed at securing and retaining these most valuable of customers. As such, they are always a key target segment for marketing attention and understanding the benefits they seek is an obvious focus for marketing research.

Visitor expenditure per capita, not necessarily directly associated with levels of income or socioeconomic status, is another dimension of behaviour or user characteristics that is highly relevant to segmentation decisions. For example, many British holidaymakers in Spain outspend German and Swedish visitors, although their per capita income may be less. Other things being equal, high expenditure segments are obviously seen as attractive targets in all sectors of tourism.

A little thought will soon indicate that there is a wide range of characteristics of buyer behaviour use that could be relevant for identifying and targeting particular

TABLE 6.1 Segment/buyer behaviour/usage characteristics by sequence of purchase and product usage

Before booking	Booking process	In use/consumption patterns	After use
Previous usage/experience/ expectation loyal/infrequent user	Package/independent arrangements	Utilization of facilities available, positive/negative impact on environment[a]	Customer satisfaction level and perceived value for money
Awareness/use of brochures/use of Internet	Via central reservation office/via website	Party size and composition, length of stay	Communication to friends/ relatives/positive or negative 'word of mouth'
Sources of travel information used	Booking direct with producer	Transport mode, accommodation types	Wish to buy again
Length of booking time before use	Sale discounts/special offers	Expenditure per head	Wish to buy again

Notes: This table indicates some of the variables in each of the four stages in the buying/usage process; the variables are expressed vertically in the columns, not by reading across.

[a] An indication of the relative sustainability of the consumption pattern of different segments.

segments, and developing or adapting products for their specific needs. These characteristics may be divided according to

- The timing and sequence of buyers' decisions prior to making a booking.
- Decisions made in the booking process.
- Product usage decisions during consumption, including the impact on sustainability.
- Buyer behaviour and decisions after using any travel and tourism product, reflecting the experience achieved.

Table 6.1 illustrates the range of characteristics in a context relevant to accommodation businesses or tour operators.

The aspects of behaviour noted in Table 6.1 are not fully comprehensive but they cover main aspects that can be adapted to the specific context of most businesses in travel and tourism. Pre-booking characteristics, for example, would be less important to many visitor attractions (but still relevant for group visitors), whereas details of visitor circulation patterns, features visited and rides used, division of time within the attraction during the visit, use of catering, retailing and so on, would be highly significant in product development and product positioning terms. Analysis of behaviour during product usage would indicate the comparative sustainability of one group of users compared with others.

Measuring and monitoring the user characteristics noted in Table 6.1 is the basis of many market research surveys of customers and prospective users (see Chapter 9). In their various forms, user surveys coupled with profile data are the most widely practiced type of market research used in all parts of the travel and tourism industry.

By the 1990s the increasing availability and capacity of inexpensive but powerful, networked PCs made it possible for growing numbers of marketing managers in travel and tourism to collect, analyse and retain information about their customers and their user characteristics in databases. Databases utilizing a unique record number for every buyer (or enquirer) are capable of recording and linking most aspects of customer profile and purchase patterns as they are revealed from telephone, Teletext and Internet enquiries and booking forms and invoices. Such databases (see also geodemographic segmentation) can now partially replace traditional market research methods based on sample surveys of customers and provide very much faster and cheaper ways to segment markets than was possible previously. The contact with customers on service business premises gives direct access to customer information in travel and tourism and provides a powerful marketing tool that is not generally available to manufacturers of goods using retail distribution systems to reach their customers.

MINI CASE 6.1 SEGMENTATION FOR AUSTRALIA IN THE UK LONG HAUL MARKET – SELF-CHALLENGERS

'Travel is a consuming passion for me. It's pretty much fair to say that I live for travel and so I'm always thinking about where I want to go to next' Penny, 27. Meet our Self-Challengers. For Penny, Darry, Simon and Kath, travel is an absolutely central part of life. And, when Self-Challengers talk travel, they're not talking holidays on the beach.

Courtesy of Dimitrios Buhalis.

As the name of this segment suggests, Self-Challengers have a drive to challenge themselves, are extremely experienced, passionate travellers and embrace the idea of exploring and immersing themselves in the culture and lifestyle of the destination. They seek destinations that are as different from home as possible and they don't mind roughing it a bit – it's all part of the challenge! Self-Challengers also don't mind going it alone if they can't find a travel buddy. For Self-Challengers the best travel experiences are the ones when they can immerse themselves into other cultures and understand how local people live.

Segment profile and highlights

The segment size is estimated at around 12% of the long haul market in the UK.

The segment motivation reflects a personal drive to challenge themselves and the reward is intensely personal experiences.

Compared with the profile of the rest of the long haul travel market in the UK, Self-Challengers:

- Are more affluent and highly educated.
- Have a higher income.
- More likely to be single.
- Have the greatest range of interests including eating out, reading, music concerts, hiking, DIY, theatre, self-education, outdoor and water sports, photography and more.
- Range between 18 and 75 years.

Approach to long haul travel

When travelling abroad, this segment appreciates immersion in the local culture, lifestyle and environment. They definitely perceive themselves as travellers, not tourists, and are focused on experiencing destinations before they become part of a heavily commercialized tourist trail. Self-Challengers are focused on self-discovery through challenging experiences and want to get 'under the skin' of a destination.

Australia as a destination

Australia is undoubtedly a very appealing long haul destination for Self-Challengers. This segment has no major barriers to visiting Australia. Instead they are attracted by the natural environment, the people and indigenous culture and are highly knowledgeable of Australia as a holiday destination.

What inspires them?

When deciding where to go on their next holiday, the top sources of destination inspiration for Self-Challengers are websites, blogs, TV documentaries and Travel books.

Source: http://www.tourism.australia.com/content/Research/UK_Segment_Guide_Dec04.pdf.

The above case illustrates the way in which the Australian Tourist Board has evaluated segmentation for a particular group that travels from the UK to Australia.

Segmentation by demographic, economic, geographic and life-cycle characteristics

If tourism businesses begin their segmentation process with an analysis of customer needs and benefits sought, within purpose of travel, they will have a clear understanding of the type of products their chosen customer groups want. If that understanding is backed up by information obtained by user surveys of the type noted in the preceding section, and/or database analysis, their knowledge of target groups will already be considerable. For the purposes of efficient promotion and distribution of products, however, especially to prospective new customers rather than to existing ones, they will also need to know the demographic profile and other defining characteristics of their target segments, including potential users.

At the simplest level of analysis, familiar to most readers, customer segments may be defined in terms of basic descriptions of age, sex, occupation, income grouping and place of residence. Known collectively as *customer profiles*, such facts are often easily obtained for existing customers in travel and tourism as a by-product of booking records, registration procedures and regular customer surveys such as the in-flight studies undertaken by airlines and tour operators. Descriptive information about buyers of travel products, generally, is usually also available in many countries from national tourist offices and commercial surveys of travel and tourism markets. These are commonly available for purchase in countries with developed tourism industries and are now increasingly to be found on NTO websites.

Simple demographic profiles still have their uses in segmentation, for example in deciding which media to choose for advertising purposes. Many smaller businesses in travel and tourism go no further. But on their own, without the prior analysis of purpose, benefits and user characteristics, basic demographic profiles are no longer an adequate basis for organizing effective marketing campaigns. Growing competition is shifting the goal posts and businesses relying solely on such simple data run the risk of being outmanoeuvred in the continuous preoccupation with winning new customers and retaining market share.

At a slightly more complex level of analysing customer profiles it is possible to group together a number of physical characteristics of people to form what is usually termed *life-cycle* analysis. This is based on the stages through which most people progress in life, from infancy, through adolescence and child rearing to different stages of maturity and old age. The travel behaviour of many people aged 18–35 may not vary much according to whether they are single or married, but it is likely to vary enormously according to whether or not they have children. Those with young children under the age of 4 have different travel needs from those with older children between the ages of 10 and 15. At the other end of the age scale the travel activities of those aged between 50 and 70 will vary enormously according to whether or not they are retired or still at work, and their activity patterns. All developed countries have market research organizations that analyse markets by *life-cycle* categories.

Segmentation by psychographic characteristics and lifestyle

Psychographics is the term used to denote measurement of an individual's mental attitudes and psychological make-up. It is clearly distinguished from demographics, which measures the easily quantifiable dimensions of age, sex, income and life cycle, noted in the preceding section. Dependent on sophisticated marketing research techniques, psychographics aims to define consumers on attitudinal or psychological rather than physical dimensions. The reason for segmenting buyers on psychological dimensions is the belief that common values among groups of consumers tend to determine their purchasing patterns – as illustrated earlier in the mini case for *Self-Challengers* to Australia.

The measurement of consumer attitudes and values is not new. It has been a preoccupation of market researchers on both sides of the Atlantic for decades. The methods of measurement, usually asking consumers to make complex ratings of items included in multiple-choice questions, are now greatly enhanced by the availability of software programmes to assess the results and identify respondents by clusters of associated attitudes. Software is readily available to measure the extent and strength of any correlations that exist between people's attitudes and values, and their behaviour patterns as buyers of travel and other products. Such measurements may be further refined by including specific questions about attitudes to, and perceptions of, individual travel companies and the products they supply. This type of research underlies the modern concept of product positioning, branding and image projection discussed later in this book.

Related to demographic characteristics and stages in the life cycle, the links between attitudes, perceptions and actual buyer behaviour, combine to determine the *lifestyle* which individuals adopt. An understanding of the lifestyle of target customers has obvious advantages when formulating new products, developing branding or creating messages designed to motivate such people. Among international operators in travel and tourism, Sandals resorts and Royal Caribbean cruise line, for example, clearly understand and have single-mindedly adopted a lifestyle segmentation approach, as any consideration of their websites and product brochures will confirm. Sandals targets the 'thirty somethings' offering an indulgent romantic holiday experience and Royal Caribbean focus on luxury, status and style for affluent empty nesters and younger wealthy couples.

Lifestyle segmentation reflects an understanding of individuals' needs, benefits sought and motivations. It normally requires significant expenditure on marketing research and it is used within the basic segmentation by purpose of visit noted earlier. Lifestyle-related choices for all kinds of products, including tourism, have become more important in the twenty-first century reflecting growing consumer affluence and sophistication. An interesting example of lifestyle segmentation is provided by Sharpley and Sundaram (2005) who undertook research into Ashram tourism in India. It is clear that there is a growing number of individuals for whom religious or spiritual beliefs play a great part in their lives. Given that most religions have a long history and spectacular architectural buildings and sites that have been constructed over centuries, an interesting area for tourism opens up. Religious and spiritual tourism is difficult to define and can mean different things to different people, but the Sharpley and Sundaram research identified some workable clusters, noted below. The study was based on the Sri Aurobindo Ashram in southern India. The clusters that they found were

(a) Spiritual seekers

These were individuals who knew something about the Ashram and were there in search of a spiritual experience. Some were devotees and some had visited the Ashram many years ago. In a sense these could be classified as devotees.

(b) Tourist trail followers

Many of the tourists who went to the Ashram did not do so for spiritual reasons. For them the architecture was important and also the fact that it was part of the tourist trail. Many were not drawn there for a specific need but were there to enjoy a wide range of experiences or out of a broad cultural interest.

(c) Yoga/meditation practitioners

This group knew exactly what they had come to the Ashram for. They came to meditate and to practice yoga in the hallowed areas. They also benefited from the practices and developed their 'inner self'.

It is likely that this type of historical/spiritual tourism will grow in the future and some of it may also develop into voluntary fund raising coupled with tourism. It is very much an expression of the lifestyle particular types of people want to follow.

Courtesy of Dimitrios Buhalis.

Geodemographic segmentation

In Britain since the early 1980s, and there are equivalent procedures in most other European countries and North America, a very productive and powerful segmentation tool was developed through combining an analysis of census data with the postal area (zip) codes that identify every group of households in the country. The UK has some 1.6 million postcodes each containing an average of 14.5 households. Allied to the power of modern computers to store and analyse data, the major marketing development was the classification of household/housing types into a total of 17 groups and 54 types in the UK, each with clearly defined characteristics which in turn correlate closely with population characteristics of age, family structure, life cycle and income. The housing types include, for example:

- Wealthy suburbs, large detached houses (2.6% of UK population).
- Affluent working couples with mortgages, new homes (1.3%).
- Council housing areas, high unemployment, lone parents (1.8%).

The UK's ACORN (A Classification of Residential Neighbourhoods) analysis of census data can be readily supplemented by data from major commercial surveys of purchasing patterns, including travel behaviour, which are routinely analysed by ACORN types. Provided that a business records the names and addresses of its customers and enquirers (including Internet contacts), it is now inexpensive and easy for research companies to pinpoint and map the typical household types in all the areas in which buyers with similar characteristics could be found throughout the country. A detailed consumer profile, including purchasing and media habits, can be provided at the touch of a button to match any selected postcode profiles.

The geographic aspect of geodemographics has been further enhanced in recent years by computerized mapping techniques based on satellite technology. The best-known software system, Geographical Information System (GIS), was developed in the USA. The GIS is expected to develop considerably in all countries and will provide improved linkages between mapping techniques and customer databases generally. This ability to combine mapping software with customer databases provided by census and market research survey data explains the generic title 'geodemographic'. Geodemographic segmentation tools, linked with data from websites are now capable of targeting individual buyers and households with great precision. To illustrate the usefulness in practice of the demographic, economic, geographic and life-cycle analysis of segments, it is interesting to consider the buyers of weekend and mid-week short-break leisure package holidays in hotels in Britain. Such products are now a core part of the business mix for nearly all hotel groups. The main target group of buyers are typically couples in the age range 30–60, professional people, college educated, affluent and living in cities or suburbs. They either do not have children living at home or are able to leave them with friends or relatives. It is also possible to define the typical distance in miles such couples are prepared to drive to reach their destinations, so that the catchment areas of target customers can be mapped for the location of any hotel with considerable precision drawing on most of the descriptive characteristics referred to in this section. With such information, linked to that in databases generated by website enquires and bookings it is easy to develop a targeted campaign best calculated to reach and motivate the target audience. To refine the segmentation further, market research would be needed to assess customers' reasons for taking breaks and their personal motivations and benefits sought for any particular hotel and its location.

Segmentation by price

In general, buyer behaviour in leisure travel and tourism markets in all countries appears to be highly price-sensitive and many tour operators still act on the assumption that price is the key segmentation variable. In other words, there are segments of customers to be identified and located who respond to different price bands. Strategically this is evidently true when major new tourism developments are planned, such as a new luxury hotel or resort complex. In such cases feasibility studies are required to identify the ability and willingness of sufficient customers to pay the prices that will generate the level of revenue required to pay back investment, cover fixed costs and create targeted profits. One may conclude that this is a form of segmentation by price but it will still rank below purpose, benefits sought and user characteristics in the hierarchy of segmentation modes.

For established businesses in tourism there will nearly always be room for price manoeuvre within broad price ranges in the short run and reducing price is often the major tool for promotional tactics. Yield management programmes for airlines and hotels have proved a fertile and flexible tool for segment targeted tactical pricing in the last decade, although limits are set by the strategic marketing mix decisions and the costs of operating the business and satisfying existing customers. Thus, although there is no doubt that, *other things being equal,* price continues to motivate very large numbers of customers, it is not a segmentation variable of the same kind as the others outlined in this chapter. The 'other things' include maintaining the competitive quality of product delivery needed to satisfy the demands of modern customers. Whatever the depth of the global economic recession being revealed as this book is written in 2008, price segmentation seems certain to assume a more important role in the next 5 years than in the previous decade.

CHAPTER SUMMARY

This chapter:

- Focuses on the role of market segmentation in tourism and the methods or techniques used to implement it in practice. Segmentation enables marketing managers to divide total markets into component parts in order to target and deal with them more effectively and more profitably.
- It notes that as consumer markets become more fragmented and the level of competition increases between producers seeking to maintain or increase their shares of the same market, the more that segmentation underpins business success.
- Outlines seven variables in the order of importance considered relevant to most businesses in travel and tourism. In particular it emphasizes the importance of segmentation by purpose of travel and of understanding the benefits that different

groups of customers seek. The implications for segmentation of researching user characteristics before, during and after purchasing travel products, are also stressed. The growing role of the Internet in communicating with customers and retaining their profile details on databases is now making an important contribution to management information.

- Explains why segmentation is a dynamic process. New segments emerge as older ones disappear or are no longer viable as a result of market change. At any point in time most organizations in travel and tourism will be dealing with a 'portfolio' of several different segments. All of these are likely to be in a state of continuous change, partly in response to shifts in the external market determinants and partly to changes in customers' needs, attitudes and motivations. In almost every case there will be opportunities for marginal improvements in what a business knows of its customers and, therefore, how best to promote to them and satisfy their product needs marginally better than the competition.

QUESTIONS TO CONSIDER

1. Outline the ways in which buyer behaviour patterns can be used to segment the market for a hotel group.
2. What are the key variables that should be taken into account when segmenting a visitor attraction?
3. Discuss the role that pricing plays in segmenting markets for a tour operator.
4. Discuss the ways in which web-sites can assist the segmentation process.

REFERENCES AND FURTHER READING

Arimond, G., Achenreiner, G. and Elfessi, A. (2003). An innovative approach to tourism market segmentation research: an applied study, *Journal of Hospitality and Leisure Marketing*, **10**(3/4), pp. 25–55.

Baker, M.J. (2000). *Marketing strategy and management*. Chapter 12 (3rd edn). Macmillan.

Brassington, F. and Petti, S. (2003). *Principles of marketing* (3rd edn). Prentice-Hall.

Davidson, H. (1997). *Even more offensive marketing*. Chapter 9. Penguin.

Dolnicar, S. (2002). A review of data-driven market segmentation in tourism, *Journal of Travel and Tourism Marketing*, **12**(1).

Dolincar, S. (2004). Beyond "Commonsense Segmentation": a systematics of segmentation approaches in tourism, *Journal of Travel Research*, **42**(3), pp. 224–250.

Dolnicar, S, Empirical market segmentation: what you see is what you get, in Theobald, W. (ed.) *Global Tourism: The Next Decade*, 3rd edn, Butterworth-Heinemann, Oxford, 2005, pp. 309–325. Copyright 2005 Elsevier.

Dolnicar, S. (in press). Market segmentation in tourism. In Woodside, A., Martin, D. (eds). Tourism Management, Analysis, Behaviour and Strategy. CABI, Cambridge, 2008.

Frochot, I. and Morrison, A.M. (2000). Benefit segmentation: a review of its applications to travel and tourism research, *Journal of Travel and Tourism Marketing*, **9**(4), pp. 21–45.

Inkbaran, R. and Jackson, M. (2005). Understanding resort visitors through segmentation, *Tourism and Hospitality Research*, **6**(1), pp. 53–72.

Kotler, P. and Armstrong, G. (1999). *Principles of marketing*. Chapter 7 (8th edn). Prentice-Hall.

Sharpley, S. and Sundaram, P. (2005). Tourism: a sacred journey? The case of ashram tourism, India, *The International Journal of Tourism Research*, **7**(3), pp. 161–171.

Smith, S.L.J. (1995). *Tourism analysis: a handbook*. Chapter 5 (2nd edn). Longman.

Tkaczynski, A., Rundle-Thiele, S.A., and Beaumont, N. (in press) Segmentation: a tourism stakeholder view. *Tourism Management*.

Destination images need not be grounded in experience or facts but they are always powerful motivators in leisure travel and tourism.

CHAPTER 7

Product formulation in travel and tourism

As far as the tourist is concerned, the product covers the complete experience from the time he leaves home to the time he returns to it.

(Medlik and Middleton, 1973)

Product formulation and design are crucial to marketing managers in tourism as they have to continually respond to market research about customer needs and interests as well as incorporate knowledge that they already have on their databases. Product decisions, with all their implications for the management of service operations and profitability, influence not only the marketing mix but also a firm's long-term growth strategy and policies for investment and human resources. Product specifications largely determine and reflect the corporate image and branding that an organization is able to create in the minds of its existing and prospective customers. They also determine the quality of the experiences that users can achieve for themselves.

To a great extent, decisions on the design of products also determine what prices can be charged, what forms of communication with the customer are needed and often what distribution channels are available. For all these reasons, customer-related product decisions are 'the basis of marketing strategy and tactics' (Middleton, 1983: 2). As the most important of the four basic Ps/Cs in the marketing mix, product formulation requires careful consideration in any branch of marketing. Because of the particular nature and characteristics of travel and tourism services, the subject is especially complex in the tourism industry and the concept of products extends to incorporate people, process and physical evidence as explained in Chapter 8.

This chapter is in three parts. The first part introduces the existence of two different dimensions for understanding tourism products, one of which is the overall product as perceived by customers and by destination managers, and the other is the narrower view of products taken by marketing managers of individual tourism businesses and other organizations. The second part explains product formulation on each of the two dimensions in terms of their component parts and the benefits they offer to customers. The third part explains two important concepts of co-creating value and co-branding or co-marketing that the authors believe will gain significance over the next 5 years as the ease of Internet access develops and extends.

After studying this chapter you should be able to understand:

- The differences between the two levels of travel and tourism products.
- How to de-construct tourism products and the complexities involved in product formulation.
- The important distinctions between core, formal and augmented products.
- The main marketing implications of product development.
- The role that co-production and co-branding can play in product formulation and collaborative marketing in the Internet era.

A COMPONENTS VIEW OF TRAVEL AND TOURISM PRODUCTS – FROM TWO STANDPOINTS

It follows from the definitions discussed in Chapter 1 that any visit to a tourism destination comprises a mix of several different *components*. These include transport, accommodation, attractions and other facilities, such as catering and entertainments. Sometimes all the components are purchased from one supplier, e.g. when a customer buys an inclusive holiday from a tour operator or asks a travel agent to put the components together for a business trip. Sometimes customers put the separate components together themselves, e.g. when a visitor drives his own car to stay with friends at a destination or uses the Internet to create his own choices for the bundle of components.

Conveniently known as a 'components view', the conceptualization of travel and tourism products as a group of components or elements brought together in a 'bundle' selected to satisfy needs is a vital requirement for marketing managers. It is central to this view that the components of the bundle may be designed, altered and fitted together in many different ways calculated to match identified customer needs.

The overall tourism product

Developing the components view from the standpoint of the visitor, Medlik and Middleton noted a quarter of a century ago that, 'As far as the tourist is concerned, the product covers the complete experience from the time he leaves home to the time he returns to it'. Thus 'the tourist product is to be considered as an amalgam of three main components of attractions, … facilities at the destination and accessibility of the destination'. In other words, the tourist product is 'not an airline seat or a hotel bed, or relaxing on a sunny beach … but rather an amalgam of many components, or a package'. The same article continued, 'Airline seats and hotel beds … are merely elements or components of a total tourist product which is a composite product' (Medlik and Middleton, 1973). With minor nuances to suit the views of different authors this original basic conceptualization of the product remains valid and has been adopted and used internationally.

The product of individual tourism businesses

Without detracting in any way from the general validity and relevance of the overall view of tourism products noted above, it has to be recognized that airlines, hotels, attractions, car rental and other producer organizations in the industry, focus on a much narrower view of the products they sell. They concentrate logically on their own services. Many large hotel groups and transport operators employ product managers in their marketing teams and handle product formulation and development entirely in terms of the operations they control. Hotels refer to 'conference products', for example, or 'leisure products', airlines to 'business-class products', and so on. For this reason, the overall product concept sets the context in which tourism marketing is conducted but it has only limited value in guiding the practical product design decisions that managers of individual producer organizations have to make. A components view of products still holds good, however, because it is in the nature of all service products that they can be divided or de-constructed into a series of specific service operations or processes, which combine to make up the particular products that customers buy. Thus for a visitor to a hotel (business or leisure), the hotel product is (or should be) a seamless entity but it is in fact a sophisticated bundle of service delivery experiences, which may be itemized as follows:

- Initial experience and reactions in selecting from a guidebook, brochure or website.
- Experience of the booking process – on-line or phone.
- First impression on entering the hotel – design of physical evidence.
- Reception process on arrival – front of house staff contact.
- Standard of room and its range of *en suite* facilities.
- Experience of customer – staff interactions during the stay.
- Provision of meals and any ancillary services.
- Checking out process on leaving.
- Any follow up, such as e-mails or direct mailing, received subsequently.

This is not a comprehensive list but it leads into the analysis of the services marketing mix set out in Chapter 8 and serves to stress the point that any individual product is composed of a series of elements or processes that combine to satisfy the purchasers' needs. Understanding, unravelling and fine-tuning the elements provide more than ample scope for marketing managers to increase their knowledge of customers' needs and thus improve their product presentation and delivery of satisfying services to prospective customers.

It is always highly instructive to analyse or de-construct any service businesses' operations in terms of the full sequence of contacts and processes between customer and business, from the time that they make initial enquiries (if any), until they have used the product and left the premises. Even for a product such as that provided by a museum, there is ample scope to analyse all the stages of a visit and potential points of contact that occur from the moment the customer is in sight of the entrance until he leaves the building, say 2 or 3 hours later. Putting the components view in slightly different terms, individual service producers designing products '*must define the service concept in terms of the bundles of goods and services sold to the consumer and the relative importance of each component to the customer*' (Sasser et al., 1978: 14). Shostack (1977) used the notion of a molecular product to convey the same idea, while blueprinting and scripting as described in Chapter 8 are further refinements of the service product concept.

To bring the two distinctive aspects of tourist products together – the *overall view* and that of *individual service businesses* – it is possible to consider them as two different dimensions. The overall view is a horizontal dimension in the sense that a series of individual product components are included in it. Customers as individuals, or tour operators acting as manufacturers (see Chapter 22), can make their selection to produce the total experience. By contrast, the service businesses' view is a vertical dimension of specific service delivery operations and processes organized around the identified needs and wants of target segments of customers. Businesses typically have regard for their interactions with other organizations on the horizontal dimension (networking and product collaboration) but their principal concern is with the vertical dimension of their own operations (this point is developed later in the chapter).

A BENEFITS VIEW OF PRODUCTS

Before discussing the two dimensions of travel and tourism products in more detail it is important to keep in mind the customers' views of what businesses of all types offer for sale. Levitt's classic statement is succinct: 'People do not buy products, they buy the expectation of benefits. It is the benefits that are the product' (Levitt, 1969). Developing this point, Kotler noted 'the customer is looking for particular utilities. Existing products are only a current way of packaging those utilities. The company must be aware of all the ways in which customers can gain the sought satisfaction. These define the competition' (Kotler, 1976: 25).

The processes of researching targeted customers' perceptions of product benefits and utilities, and designing or adapting products to match their expectations, lie of course at the heart of marketing theory and practice. There is no difference in principle between a benefits view of products applied to travel and tourism or to any other industry producing consumer goods. Pine and Gilmore (1999) developed the benefits concept further with their view that personal involvement and experiences are increasingly the benefits sought in service industries. They argued that in some ways Las Vegas could be considered one of the experience capitals of the world as virtually everything there is designed to create an experience, from slot machines at the airport to the gambling casinos that line the Strip. There are also themed hotels giving the experience of being in London or Paris and shows featuring magic, song and dance. This coupled with theme rides and ancient Roman experiences create something for all ages and interests. Even 'authentic' capital cities such as London draw on the experience concepts for visitors, for example, recreating the experience of what it was like to be in the Tower of London in the fifteenth century. Pine and Gilmore go on to conclude that as a key part of their marketing programmes, companies should create 'experience places' – absorbing, entertaining real or virtual Internet locations – where customers can try out offerings as they immerse themselves in aspects of the experiences on offer.

COMPONENTS OF THE OVERALL TOURISM PRODUCT

From the standpoint of a potential customer considering any form of tourist visit, the product may be defined as a bundle or package of tangible and intangible components, based on activity at a destination. The package is perceived by the tourist as an experience, available at a price. There are five main components in the overall product, which are discussed separately below:

- Destination attractions and environment.
- Destination facilities and services.
- Accessibility of the destination.
- Images of the destination.
- Price to the consumer.

Destination attractions and environment – and the visitor activities they generate

These are the component elements within the destination that largely determine consumers' choice and influence prospective buyers' motivations. They include

- *Natural attractions*: landscape, seascape, beaches, climate, flora and fauna and other geographical features of the destination and its natural resources.
- *Built attractions*: buildings and tourism infrastructure including historic and modern architecture, monuments, promenades, parks and gardens, convention centres, marinas, ski slopes, industrial archaeology, managed visitor attractions generally, golf courses, speciality shops and themed retail areas.
- *Cultural attractions*: history and folklore, religion and art, theatre, music, dance and other entertainment, and museums; some of these may be developed into special events, festivals and pageants.
- *Social attractions*: way of life and customs of resident or host population, language and opportunities for social encounters.

Combined, these aspects of a destination comprise what is broadly, if loosely, known as its *environment.* This is a wider concept that the physical environment although all are aspects now considered under sustainability of the destination. The number of visitors the environment can accommodate in a typical range of activities on a typical busy day without damage to its elements and without undermining its attractiveness to visitors is known as its *capacity.*

In the growth stages of a visitor economy in any country, tourism businesses are mostly able to plan their product strategies without much if any regard to either quality of the destination environment or capacity issues. They typically take it for granted. This is changing, however, and the development and practice of more environmentally responsible marketing conducted in context of the sustainability of destination environments appear certain to become increasingly important in the twenty-first century. Defining capacity with any accuracy remains a mystery but recognizing tourism damage to the environment is increasingly clear for all to see and marketing decisions are part of both the problem and solution (Middleton and Hawkins, 1998: Chapter 9). Damage is becoming a critical issue at many destinations and in today's world even getting there becomes an issue as many people are more aware of the global impact of climate change and some are willing to make sacrifices in terms of the mode of transport they choose to travel.

Destination facilities and services

These are the component elements located in the destination or linked to it, which make it possible for visitors to stay and in other ways enjoy and participate in the attractions. They include

- *Accommodation units*: hotels, holiday villages, apartments, villas, campsites, caravan parks, hostels, condominiums, farms, guesthouses.
- *Restaurants, bars and cafés*: ranging from fast-food through to luxury restaurants.
- *Transport at the destination*: taxis, coaches, car rental, cycle hire (and ski lifts in snow destinations).
- *Sports/interest/adventure/activity*: ski schools, sailing schools, golf clubs, trekking facilities, spectator stadiums; centres for pursuit of arts and crafts and nature studies.
- *Other facilities*: language schools, health clubs.
- *Retail outlets*: shops, travel agents, souvenirs, camping supplies.
- *Other services*: information services, equipment rental, tourism police.

For some of these elements the distinction between attractions and facilities may be blurred. For example, a hotel, skiing piste or a famous golf course may well be perceived as primary attractions in their own right and the reason for selecting a destination. Nevertheless, their primary function of providing facilities and services in the context of the specific attractions and environment of *place* remains clear.

Accessibility of the destination

These are the private and public transport aspects of the product that determine the cost, speed and convenience with which a traveller may leave his place of residence and reach a chosen destination (see Chapter 20). They include

- *Infrastructure*: of roads, car parking, airports, railways, seaports, inland waterways and marinas.
- *Equipment*: size, speed and range of public transport vehicles.
- *Operational factors*: routes operated, frequency of services, prices charged and road tolls levied.
- *Government regulations*: the range of regulatory controls over transport operations influencing routes and prices charged.

Images and perceptions of the destination

For reasons outlined in Chapters 5 and 10, the attitudes and images customers have towards products strongly influence their buying decisions. Destination images are not necessarily grounded in visitors' direct experience or facts but they are always powerful motivators in leisure travel and tourism. Images and the expectations of travel experiences are closely linked in prospective customers' minds.

For example, of the millions of people in North America and Europe who have not so far visited Las Vegas, there will be few who do not carry in their minds some mental picture or image of the experiences that destination provides. Through the media and through hearsay, most people have already decided whether they are attracted or repelled by the Las Vegas image. All destinations have images, often based more on historic rather than current events, and it is an essential objective of destination marketing to sustain, alter or develop images in order to influence prospective buyers' expectations. The images of tourism businesses within destinations, e.g. the hotels in Las Vegas, are often closely related to the destination image. The nature of the design or physical evidence (see Chapter 8) promoted by those who market Las Vegas is calculated to create and communicate the chosen image. Pine and Gilmore (1999) identify four different kinds of experience that visitors can undergo. These are entertainment, aesthetics, escapism and education in which visitors may participate either passively or actively. Education may not be high on the Las Vegas list but it certainly ticks the boxes in the other dimensions.

Price to the consumer

Any visit to a destination carries a price, which is the sum of what it costs for travel, accommodation and participation in a selected range of facilities and services. Because most destinations offer a range of products and appeal to a range of segments, price in the travel and tourism industry covers a very wide range. Visitors travelling thousands of miles and using luxury hotels, for example, pay a very different price in New York than students sharing campus-style accommodation with friends. Yet, the two groups may buy adjacent seats in a Broadway theatre. Price varies by season, by choice of activities and internationally by exchange rates as well as by distance travelled, transport mode and choice of facilities and services. The importance of pricing is demonstrated by Table 7.1 as presented by an article in http://money.uk.msn.com/guides/Holiday-Money/article.aspx?cp-documentid=5104199. The article assesses prices for various holiday expenditures once a person gets to his destination. In July 2007, the UK pound enjoyed a good exchange rate so many UK visitors chose travel to the USA, although America was still quite expensive in terms of holiday expenditure. According to the article, the Post Office

TABLE 7.1 UK Post Office Holiday Costs Barometer, 2007

Destination	Cost of ten basic items
1. USA	£69.41
2. Spain	£65.90
3. Canada	£65.15
4. France	£62
5. Australia	£52.76
6. Italy	£48.45
7. Croatia	£46.24
8. Turkey	£44.91
9. Cyprus	£41.30
10. Greece	£41.06

Holiday Costs Barometer found that although the exchange rate is good for picking up electronics and jewellery at a discount, everyday necessities are often expensive. There may be savings on iPods, laptops and designer clothes but the added cost on essentials like water, beer and sun cream make the USA quite expensive. The Post Office checked prices of ten basic items in favourite holiday destinations and found that America was the most expensive, with costs totalling £69.41. The cheapest destination was Bulgaria, whose total cost for all ten items was only £16.86 – a £52.55 difference. A 1.5-litre bottle of Evian water is almost three times more in the USA than in any other country surveyed, and is 15 times more expensive than in Egypt. Table 7.1 indicates how countries compare in terms of prices for essential items.

Price comparisons are notoriously difficult to make because price will also vary depending on where and at what time in a country the items were bought. It is certain, however, that price strongly influences visitors' perceptions of the experience they wish to achieve and their views on value for money. Price is also an aspect of image.

SOME MARKETING IMPLICATIONS OF THE OVERALL PRODUCT CONCEPT

With a little thought it will be clear that each of the five product components, although they are combined and integrated in the visitor's overall experience, are in fact capable of extensive and more or less independent variation over time. Some of these variations are planned, as in the case of the Disney World developments in previously unused areas around Orlando, Florida, or the purpose-built resorts at Cancun in Mexico. In both these cases massive engineering works have transformed the natural environment and created major tourist destinations. Center Parcs holiday village developments in the UK illustrate recent forms of destination engineering, providing covered, climate-controlled attractions within a central facility, as well as outdoor attractions and capacity-controlled accommodation in carefully landscaped surrounding areas. Center Parcs are planned to protect and in places enhance the environment. *In such cases all five product components are integrated under one management.*

By contrast, in New York, London or Venice, the city environments have not been much altered for travel and tourism purposes, although there have been massive planned changes in the services and facilities available to visitors and all have icon-status buildings designed or adapted for tourism purposes. Many changes in destination environments are not planned, however, they just happen. In Northern Europe the decline in popularity of traditional seaside resorts since the 1960s has been largely the result of changes in the accessibility and lower prices of competing destinations in the sunnier south of the Continent. Changes in the product components often occur in spite of, and not because of, the wishes of governments and destination planners. They occur because travel and tourism, especially at the international level, is a relatively free market with customers who are able to pursue new attractions as they become available and affordable. Changes in exchange rates, which alter the prices of destinations, are obviously not planned in any way by the tourism industry but have a massive effect on visitor numbers.

It is in the promotional field of images and perceptions that some of the most interesting planned changes occur and these are marketing decisions. The classic example of planned tourism image engineering may be found in the *I Love New York* campaign which, based on extensive preliminary market research, created a significant improvement in the 'Big Apple's appeal in the early 1980s. At a very different level of expenditure, industrial cities in Britain, such as Glasgow, Birmingham and Manchester, are working hard on their image projection to achieve the same type of change in visitors' perceptions and motivations.

The view of the product taken by leisure tourism customers, whether or not they buy an inclusive package from a tour operator or travel wholesaler, is essentially the same view or standpoint as that adopted by tour operators. Tour operators act on behalf of the identified interests of millions of customers grouped as segments and the design of their websites and brochures is a practical illustration of how to blend and communicate the five product components discussed in this section (see also Chapter 22).

The overall view of the product is also the standpoint of national, regional and local destination management organizations, whose responsibilities usually include the co-ordination and presentation of the product components in their areas. This responsibility is an important one even if the destination tourist organizations are engaged only in liaison and collaborative marketing and not in the sale of specific product offers to visitors.

In considering the overall product it should be noted that there is no natural or automatic harmony between components, such as attractions and accommodation, and they are seldom under any one organization's ownership and control. Even within component sectors such as accommodation there will usually be many different organizations, each with different and often conflicting objectives and interests. Indeed it is the diversity or fragmentation of overall control and the relative freedom of producer businesses to act according to their perceived self-interests, at least in the short term, which makes it difficult for national, regional and even local tourist organizations to exert much co-ordinating influence, either in marketing or in planning. Part of this fragmentation occurs simply because most developed destinations offer a wide range of tourism products and deal with a wide range of segments. It also reflects the fact that, for every large business in tourism at national or international level, there are up to a thousand small or micro-businesses, mostly pursuing individual goals. In the long term, however, the future success of a destination must involve co-ordination and recognition of mutual interests between all the components of the overall tourism product. Achieving such co-ordination is the principal rationale for much of the marketing work undertaken by National Tourism Organizations (see Chapter 18).

COMPONENTS OF SPECIFIC PRODUCTS – THE TOURISM BUSINESSES' VIEW

At this point in the chapter the focus shifts from the overall tourism product to that of individual businesses or other organizations delivering product offerings to visitors. As explained, the overall view of tourism products is still highly relevant to the marketing decisions taken by individual businesses in tourism. It determines the interrelationships and scope for co-operation and partnership between suppliers in different sectors of the industry, for example, between transport and accommodation. But in designing their product-specific offers around their service operations, there are internal dimensions of products for marketers to consider and plan. These are common to all forms of consumer marketing and part of widely accepted marketing theory. Marketing managers 'need to think about the product on three levels' (Kotler, 1984: 463).

Using Kotler's terminology, which is based on earlier contributions by Levitt, these three levels are

- The *core product*, which is the essential service or benefit designed to satisfy the identified needs of target customer segments.
- The formal or *tangible product*, which is the specific offer for sale stating what a customer will receive for his money. It is a marketing interpretation that turns the core into a specific offer.
- The *augmented product*, which comprises all the forms of added value producers may choose to build into their formal product offers to make the experiences they provide more attractive than competitors' offers to their intended customers.

Although many regard the labels applied to these three levels of any product as fairly unattractive marketing jargon, the value of the thought process underlying them is potentially very great indeed. The thought process can be applied by businesses in any of the tourism industry sectors and it is equally applicable to large and small businesses. It will repay careful thought and application in particular operations.

The following example of an inclusive weekend break in a hotel will help to explain what the three levels mean in practice. The product offer is a package comprising two nights' accommodation and two breakfasts, which may be taken at any one of a chain of hotels located in several different destinations. Because of the bedroom design and leisure facilities available at the hotels, the package is designed specifically to appeal to professional couples with young children. The product is offered for sale at an inclusive price through a brochure distributed at each of the hotels in the chain, through direct mail and on-line via the Internet. It is in competition with the products of other very similar hotels that are promoting similar products to the same market at much the same price levels. Products of this type are now widely available in many parts of North America and Europe and the total market for them grew substantially in the last 20 years. The example makes it possible to explore the three product levels inherent in what tourism businesses offer to their customers.

Core product is intangible not factual. It is an *idea* but it always comprises the essential need or benefit as perceived and sought by the customer – expressed in words and pictures designed to motivate purchase and communicate the essence of the experiences it can offer. For the weekend break under discussion the core benefit may be defined as relaxation, rest, fun and self-fulfilment in experiences that support an enjoyable family weekend away.

It should be noted that the core product reflects the characteristics and needs of the target customer segments, not the hotel. The core product establishes the key message that the hotel aims to communicate. The hotel aims to design and communicate its core product better than its competitors, and to achieve better delivery of the sought benefits. But all of its competitors are aiming at more or less the same basic customer needs and offering virtually identical benefits. Customers' core needs usually tend not to change very quickly, although a hotel's ability to identify, communicate and better satisfy such needs can change considerably. Since customer perceptions are never precisely understood, there is ample scope for improvement in this area.

Formal product comprises the formal offer of the product as set out in a brochure or website, stating exactly what is to be provided at a specified time at a specified price. In the example under discussion, the tangible product is two nights and two breakfasts at a particular location, using rooms of a defined standard with bathroom, television, telephone, etc. The provision (if any) of elevators, coffee shops, air-conditioning and swimming pool are all within the formal product and the name and brand of the hotel is also included.

In the case of hotel products generally, and certainly in the example cited, there is often very little to choose between competitors' formal product offers. In such conditions, products may be perceived as commodities and price may become the principal reason for choice. Blindfolded and led to the lobby or bedrooms of any one of, say, 20 competitors' premises, most hotel customers would not immediately or easily recognize the identity of their surroundings. The brochure description of the formal product forms the basis for the contract of sale, which would be legally enforceable in most countries. In Chapter 8 the use of design and 'physical evidence' is identified as one of the principal ways to differentiate, make more tangible and communicate the formal product in the minds of prospective buyers.

Augmented product. Both tangible and intangible, augmentation is harder to define with precision. It is driven by the search for competitive advantage and comprises the difference between the contractual essentials of the formal product and the totality of all the benefits and services experienced in relation to the delivery of the product to the customer. It can cover any or all of the stages – from the moment of first contact in considering a booking, to any follow up contact after delivery and consumption of the product. The augmented product also expresses the idea of *value added* over and above the formal offer. It represents a vital area of opportunity for producers to differentiate their products from those of competitors.

In the example under discussion there may be up to 20 'add ons' to the formal product – some fairly trivial such as a complimentary box of chocolates or glass of wine on arrival, and some significant, such as child minding services or entrance tickets to local attractions or entertainments. Some of the added benefits are tangible as indicated, but some are intangible, such as the quality of the service welcome provided, the friendliness of staff and the ambience created (see *People* and *Process* and *Physical evidence* in Chapter 8). In the example under discussion all the augmented elements would be purpose-designed and developed around the core product benefits in ways calculated to increase the appeal to the target segment's needs and help them achieve the experiences that research indicates they seek.

Other key dimensions of the augmentation process reflect the longer run strategic branding and images that hotels create to distinguish themselves from competitors and influence buyer behaviour. In the last decade, as global warming and related issues of sustainability have become more widely recognized, ways of providing and communicating more sustainable products and more sustainable business operations at destinations have also become important parts of the decision process for many customers. Examples are the emphasis given to the use of local produce and local suppliers for catering and contributions to benefit the local community and its environment. Linkages with destination management organizations to deliver a more sustainable product experience overall are also relevant. These are strategic issues explained in Chapter 10.

COMPETITIVE PRODUCT FORMULATION

To stay ahead of the competition, proactive marketing managers are constantly looking for product innovation and there are strong advantages in being first with product developments. In order to define the core product, the formal product and to identify the scope for product augmentation with some precision, frequent research into the perceptions and purchasing characteristics of segments is a necessary aspect of consumer orientation in the travel and tourism industry. There is normally considerable scope for creative innovation and for experimentation, especially in the area defined as product augmentation. Much of augmentation, including image, is under a marketing manager's control and it becomes the focus and primary rationale for persuading customers to choose between alternative products.

In the hotel example used to illustrate the three levels of the product it is interesting to note the potential for collaboration between the particular accommodation product discussed (the vertical dimension as it was defined earlier in the chapter) and other components of the overall tourism product (the horizontal dimension). The hotel, for example, may include access to local attractions at the destination as part of the augmented product. Similarly, hotel users may be offered public transport links to the destination with fares included as part of the formal product. Linkages between different product suppliers at the destination and their links with Destination Management Organizations are identified as forms of co-branding later in this chapter.

CO-CREATION OF PRODUCTS INVOLVING THE CUSTOMER AS A PARTICIPANT IN THE PRODUCTION PROCESS

Traditionally in travel and tourism as in other services provided for large-scale markets, even when consumer research was undertaken, managers decided what the product should be and customers were expected to buy what was provided. That is very much a *firm centric* approach determined by a top-down management decision process. It follows from Chapter 5 that many experienced travellers increasingly seek to exercise their choices and play a participating role in the purchasing of products. From the decision process involved in working out the various options of any visit, through the booking process and the delivery of services at a destination, individuals are becoming more involved in what is known as the value co-creation process. That is dubbed a *consumer centric* approach, which is participative and as much bottom-up as top-down.

To quote Prahalad and Ramaswamy (2004) 'No longer does value lie (solely) in products and services created by firms and delivered to customers. Increasingly value is being jointly created by the consumer and the company.' With the recent developments of the Internet and broadband access for communication, there is now much more emphasis on individuals creating their own products in conjunction with the supplier of the product. In this process there is co-creation of value that benefits the consumer and the company. Although not a tourism example, Dell, leading suppliers of computers, offer on their website a range of peripherals/components and the opportunity for customers to 'tailor' the product to their requirements. In this instance the customer is essentially in charge of determining the product specification.

In travel and tourism, luxury products such as those provided by five star hotels and first-class airlines have always responded personally to affluent customer expectations and requests. For customers in general there is now a range of ways in which the co-creation of value process can work. It is easiest to think of the process as a spectrum starting at one end with total product emphasis where individuals buy fully itemized package holidays from business centric operators. At the other end of the spectrum individual emphasis is encouraged and provided for in a consumer centric process and there is a very wide range of choice and flexibility in choosing rooms, meals, flights, etc. It is the ability of businesses and consumers to communicate and interact via the Internet that creates the new opportunities. Over time, as technology becomes ever more sophisticated with speedy Internet connections over mobile phones and other easily portable devices, it is clear that individuals will have more choices and will be able to participate in co-creating the values that meet their specifications – at any time and any location of their choice.

The following simple diagram (Fig. 7.1) makes the point.

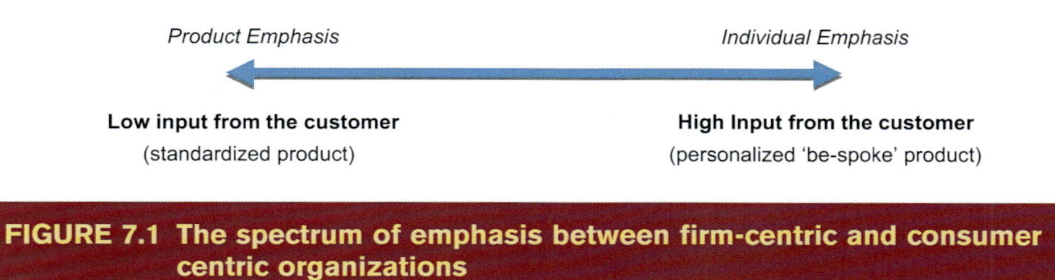

FIGURE 7.1 The spectrum of emphasis between firm-centric and consumer centric organizations

A recent example from the website of *Holiday Hypermarket* shows the co-creation of value process in operation.

MINI CASE 7.1 PRODUCT OPTIONS FROM HOLIDAY HYPERMARKET

PICK AND MIX FLIGHTS AND ACCOMMODATION TO CREATE YOUR PERFECT HOLIDAY

Build a holiday around your exact needs with the DIY holiday section of Holiday Hypermarket. With the introduction of our tailor made holidays page you can pick and mix from a range of airlines and hotels to create your own perfect holiday.

With a vast selection of flights from major European airlines and budget operators you can travel however you please. Spread your holiday budget exactly as you choose by booking your flights and accommodation separately. For example, you might prefer to book a cheap flight from one of the low cost airlines in order to spend more on your hotel.

CAN I STILL BOOK A TRADITIONAL PACKAGE HOLIDAY?

If you prefer the traditional package holiday then Holiday Hypermarket can still offer the same great service that we always have. Choose 'Package Holiday' in the search box to browse through a huge selection of fantastic deals from leading UK tour operators including First Choice Holidays, Thomson and Thomas Cook.

When you book 'bespoke' or tailor made holidays you should be aware that your bookings for flights and accommodation are made on a separate and independent basis with the airline and the accommodation provider (http://www.holidayhypermarket.co.uk/diy).

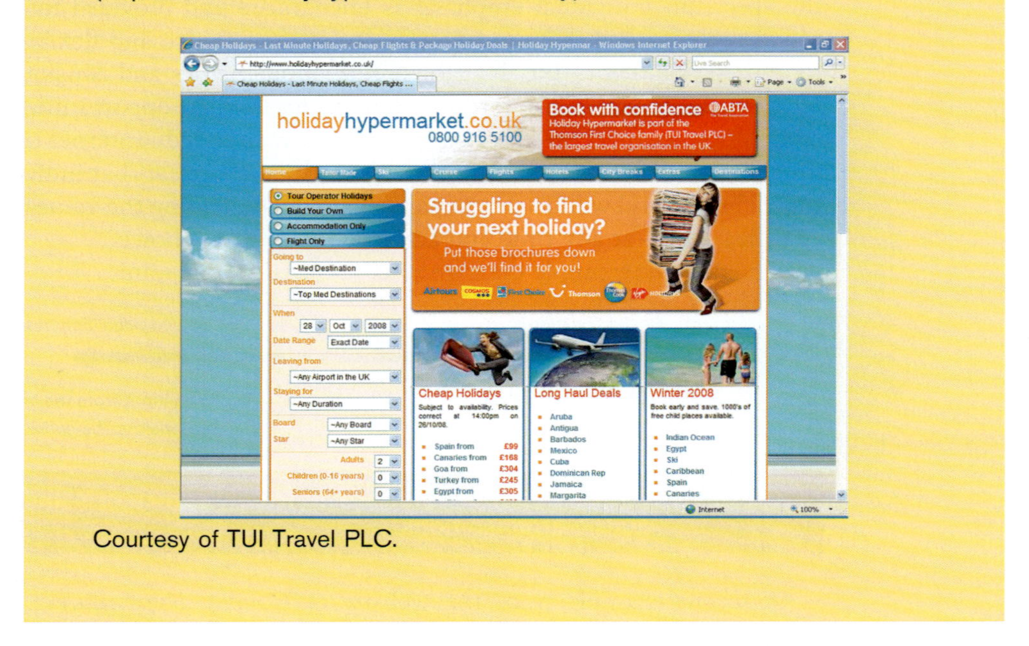

Courtesy of TUI Travel PLC.

The Holiday Hypermarket example above outlines a current approach to co-creation of value in the 'pick and mix' section, providing as much flexibility of choice as possible. In the traditional package section, buyers can still opt for a standardized package put together by tour operators.

Link article available at www.routledge.com/9780750686938

(1) Lee, S., Kim, W.G., Kim, H.J., 2006. The impact of co-branding on post-purchase behaviors in family restaurants. International Journal of Hospitality Management 25 (2), 245–261.

CO-BRANDING AND CO-MARKETING

In travel and tourism many brands are now household names either nationally or globally. Well-known examples are Accor, Disney, Marriott, Cathay Pacific, TUI, Sandals, Thomas Cook and Center Parcs. These brands and the products they deliver are under full management control. By contrast, leading destination brands such as London, New York and Singapore, even though they have become brands with their own developed and heavily promoted images, have to rely on persuasion and co-operation rather than the full management control available to individual organizations. It is, therefore, very much harder to make the destination branding work effectively. Powerful corporate brands, for example, Club Mediterranée or Sandals, are obviously big enough to override the values of weaker destination brands of the islands on which they are located. The more local the destination brand, the weaker it is likely to be, not least because of the level of budget available to research and communicate the brand as well as gain local support for it will be insignificant in international terms.

On the other hand, destination interests and corporate interests in the same location are increasingly likely at least to recognize interests in common. If customers expect to relate to the destinations they choose rather than be cocooned in a resort environment, the rationale for joint branding and marketing – also known as co-branding and co-marketing is obvious. Collaboration is also encouraged by the development of sustainable tourism awareness noted earlier. In most cases sustainable futures in travel and tourism mean better collaboration between the commercial and public sector players at any destination. This convergence of interests at the destination, supported by the growing modern emphasis on co-creation of value in which the lead is taken by customers not businesses, points to closer collaboration between businesses and destinations. In practice this means co-branding and co-marketing of tourism products. The processes for this are discussed in Part Five of this book.

CHAPTER SUMMARY

This chapter:

- Stresses the vital dimension of product formulation and design in the context of market segmentation and customer motivations. Marketing is nothing if not an integrated approach to business and students in particular should note the overlapping structure of the chapters thus far.
- Emphasizes a components view of travel and tourism products at two separate but related levels. At both levels the components view implies an ability, given adequate marketing research and product knowledge, to 'engineer' or formulate products to match the identified needs of target segments. Because needs are continuously shifting, and competitors' abilities to supply needs are constantly changing, product formulation is a continuous process. This holds good for new, purpose-built products that may be designed years before they are in operation, and for existing products, which may have to be adapted over time through rearranging and modifying product components.
- Explains the fact that product formulation has two sides, reflecting concerns with demand and supply. In terms of demand, the approach requires market research focused on customer needs, behaviour and perceptions in order to define target segments and to identify strengths and weaknesses of product design and images. In terms of supply, product formulation requires an analysis of product components and elements, and identification of the range of existing and potential products that could be improved or developed profitably to meet customer needs. These demand and supply implications apply equally to products developed by tourist destinations and to those of individual businesses. Matching supply to demand is, of course, the cornerstone of the modern marketing approach and integration between the two levels of the product is often

an essential part of the matching process in travel and tourism – communicated using images and brands.

- Explores the way in which sophisticated customers can co-create and 'tailor' the products they seek through the medium of the Internet. New technology facilitates this emerging new practice and provides individuals with a means of creating their own product options. This process is part of building relationships with customers and understanding their wishes.
- Discusses and explains the growing role of co-branding between businesses with compatible products and with destination management organizations. Given the inseparable nature of tourism production and delivery, and the intangibility of the product at the point of purchase, developing and communicating mutually supportive brand identities is a vital consideration in strategic and operational terms.

QUESTIONS TO CONSIDER

(1) Choose a typical tourism product and de-construct it in product formulation terms.

(2) Consider the way in which different product offerings may help to segment a market.

(3) Discuss how customers can play a role in co-creating value for a particular product or service.

(4) Why is pricing such an important component of product formulation?

(5) In what ways can co-branding augment the product offer?

REFERENCES AND FURTHER READING

Baker, M.J. (1996). *Marketing: an introductory text*. Chapter 11 (6th edn). Macmillan.

Brassington, F. and Pettit, S. (2000). *Principles of marketing* (3rd edn). FT Prentice-Hall.

Chernatony, L.de and McDonald, M.H.B. (1992). *Creating powerful brands*. Butterworth-Heinemann.

Chernatony, L.de and McWilliam, G. (1990). Appreciating brands as assets through using a two-dimensional model, *International Journal of Advertising*, **9**, pp. 111–119.

Clark, S. (2000). *The co-marketing solution*. McGraw-Hill Professional.

Davidson, H. (1997). *Even more offensive marketing*. Chapters 10 and 11. Penguin.

Dickinson, S. and Ramaseshan, B. (2004). An investigation of the antecedents to cooperative marketing strategy implementation, *Journal of Strategic Marketing*, **12**(2), pp. 71–95.

Doyle, P. (1989). Building successful brands: the strategic options, *Journal of Marketing Management*, **5**(1), pp. 77–95.

Gilmore, J.H. and Pine II, (2002). Customer experience places: the new offering frontier, *Strategy and Leadership*, **30**(4), pp. 4–11.

Jobber, D. (2007). *Principles and practice of marketing* (5th edn). McGraw-Hill.

Kim, W.G., Lee, S. and Lee, H.Y. (2007). Co-branding and brand loyalty, *Journal of Quality Assurance in Hospitality and Tourism: Improvements in Marketing, Management and Development*, **8**(2).

Kotler, P. and Armstrong, G. (1999). *Principles of marketing*. Chapter 1 (8th edn). Prentice-Hall.

Kotler, P., Wong, V., Saunders, J. and Armstrong, G. (2005). *Principles of marketing* (4th European edn). Pearson Prentice Hall.

Lee, S., Kim, W.G. and Kim, H.J. (2006). The impact of co-branding on post-purchase behaviors in family restaurants, *International Journal of Hospitality Management*, **25**(2), pp. 245–261.

Middleton, V.T.C. and Hawkins, R. (1998). *Sustainable tourism: a marketing perspective*. Chapter 9. Butterworth-Heinemann. For the sustainable issues surrounding tourism product formulation see also:

Weiermair, K. (2003). Product improvement or innovation: what is the key to success in tourism? In: OECD Conference on Innovation and Growth in Tourism.

Colourful morning market, Kota Bharu, Malaysia 'Visitors have to adapt, think and learn new 'scripts', in a tight time frame, which can be a stressful experience. A confused visitor in a foreign country unable to act out the national script for a simple service appears to be stupid'.

CHAPTER 8

The evolving marketing mix for tourism services

The marketing mix represents 'the four key decision areas that managers must manage so that they satisfy or exceed customer needs better than the competition'.

(Jobber, 2007: 18)

This chapter introduces the four basic variables – widely known as the *four Ps* – about which marketing managers have to make continuous decisions in their efforts to manage consumer demand. Known collectively as the *marketing mix*, these four core variables reflect and express in practical terms the decisions producers make concerning their production of goods and services for sale. These decisions have to be made, in the context of their business environment and long-term strategic objectives. In particular, this chapter sets the theoretical underpinning for many of the emerging electronic and Information and Communications Technology (ICT) developments in tourism marketing outlined in Chapter 14 and Part Four of this book.

After studying this chapter you should be able to understand:

- The meaning of each of the four core variables in the marketing mix as they were originally conceptualized in the 1960s for the marketing of physical goods.
- How the mix decisions fit within the marketing system for travel and tourism organizations.
- How the original four variables have been expanded to encompass *people*, *process* and *physical evidence* or design. In services marketing generally there has been extensive consideration of the meaning of 'product' and how the concept should be developed to reflect the modern, post-industrial context of service/experience industries.
- That a fundamental shift is taking place towards consumer centric marketing (CCM) and its impact on the future marketing of travel and tourism.

In every way, consideration of the marketing mix is central to understanding modern tourism marketing and the key variables discussed in this chapter are subsequently developed and referred to throughout this book.

MARKETING MIX DEFINED: THE ORIGINAL FOUR 'P'S

Defined as 'the four key decision areas that managers must manage so that they satisfy or exceed customer needs better than the competition' (Jobber, 2007: 18), the traditional concept of the marketing mix implies a set of variables akin to levers or controls that can be operated by a marketing manager to achieve a defined objective. By way of simple illustration the controls may be likened to those of an automobile, which has four main controls. A throttle or accelerator to control engine speed, a brake to reduce speed or stop, a gear shift to match the engine speed to the road speed required, or to reverse direction and a steering wheel with which to change the direction of travel. As every driver knows, movement of the controls must be synchronized in response to constantly changing road conditions and the actions of others. Effective progress requires continuous manipulation of the four basic controls.

Marketing managers are also 'driving' their products towards chosen destinations. The four controls are *product formulation*, which is a means of adapting the product to the changing needs of the target customer; *pricing*, which in practice tends to be used as a throttle to increase or slow down the volume of sales according to market conditions; *promotion*, which is used to increase the numbers of those in the market who are aware of the product and are favourably disposed towards buying it and *place*, which determines the number of prospective customers who are able to find convenient places and ways to gain information and convert their buying intentions into purchases. These four controls are manipulated continuously according to the market conditions prevailing, especially with regard to the actions of competitors. The destinations or goals, towards which products are being 'driven' by the four controls, are set by strategic decisions taken by organizations about their desired futures (see Chapter 10).

The central dynamic concept of continuously adjusting and synchronizing the four main controls according to constantly changing market conditions is the important point to grasp about marketing mix decisions. Continuous in this context could mean hourly decisions, especially of pricing, but in practice is more likely to mean weekly adjustments in the light of market intelligence about progress being achieved.

FOUR PS AND FOUR CS

As the focus of most marketing management decisions in practice, *product*, *promotion* and *place* warrant separate chapters in this book. Here the object is to introduce and explain them in an integrated way, which also serves as an introduction to market research and planning for marketing strategy and tactics. It will be noted that the four variables all begin with the letter 'P', hence the name *the four Ps* originally used to describe the marketing mix in 1960 by McCarthy (1981: 42). Perceiving that the original McCarthy principles are stated in producer orientated terms, Kotler restated the 'Ps' as 'Cs' to reflect the consumer orientation that is central to modern services marketing thinking in an era of growing competition (Kotler and Armstrong, 1999: 111).

- Product means *customer value* (the perceived benefits and quality of experience provided to meet needs and wants, quality of service received and the value for money delivered assessed against the competition).
- Price means *cost* (price is a supply-side decision, cost is the consumer-focused equivalent also assessed against the competition).
- Promotion means *communication* (embracing all forms of producer/customer dialogue including information and two-way interactive relationship marketing, not just sales persuasion).
- Place means *convenience* (in terms of consumer access to the products they buy).

The above classification underlies 'consumer-oriented marketing' in that the organization 'views and organizes its marketing activities from the consumer's point of view' (Kotler et al., 2005: 191). More recently this has developed further into the concept of consumer-centric marketing, an area, which is explored more fully towards the end of the chapter. Each of the four (or eight) mix variables are now outlined in more detail below.

Product – customer value

As explained in Chapter 6, product covers the shape or form of what is offered to prospective customers; in other words, the characteristics of the product as designed by strategic management decisions in response to marketing managers' knowledge of consumer wants, needs and benefits sought. For tourism, product components include

- Basic design of all the components that are put together as an offer to customers, for example, a short-break package marketed by a hotel group.
- Style and ambience of the offer. For service products dealing with customers on the premises where products are delivered, this is mainly a function of design decisions creating the physical environment, and ambience (also known as 'physical evidence') judged appropriate to the product's image and price.
- The service element, including numbers, training, attitudes and appearance of all staff engaged in the processes that 'deliver' the product to the consumer – especially front of house staff.
- Branding, the focus for communications, which identifies particular products with a particular set of values, a unique name, image and expectation of the experience to be delivered.

In current marketing practice, products in travel and tourism are designed for and continuously adapted to match the needs and expectations of target consumers and their ability to pay. Most organizations produce and market several products to match the identified requirements of several segments. For example, tour operators provide a range of products within their brochures and large hotels may have up to a dozen separate products ranging from conferences and business meetings to activity holidays and short-break packages.

Price – cost to the consumer

Price denotes the published or negotiated terms of the exchange transaction for a product between a producer aiming to achieve predetermined sales volume and revenue objectives, and prospective customers seeking to maximize their perceptions of value for money in the choices they make between alternative products. Almost invariably in tourism there is a published/regular price for a product and one or more discounted or promotional prices. Promotional prices respond to the requirements of particular market segments or the need to manipulate demand to counter the effects of seasonality or competition resulting from overcapacity. Topical in 2008, price also responds to economic crisis conditions leading to sudden, unplanned excess capacity.

Promotion – communication

The most visible of the four Ps, promotion includes advertising, direct mailing, sales promotion, merchandizing, sales-force activities, brochure production, Internet communications and PR activity. Promotional techniques are used to make prospective customers aware of products, to whet their appetites, stimulate demand and generally provide incentives to purchase, either direct from a producer or through a channel of distribution. A broader view of communication by producers also includes supportive 'relationship' information provided to reinforce awareness and build a positive attitude to products that helps customers, especially repeat purchasers, make their purchasing decisions. Received by customers through perceptual filters, as explained in Chapter 5, the available range of communication techniques is growing wider with the terms 'integrated communication mix', and 'promotional mix' frequently used in practice. Both these terms are developed in Chapter 16.

It is important for readers to appreciate the relationship between Promotion and the other three Ps to which it is integrally linked in the marketing process. However important and visible it is, promotion or communication is still only one of the levers used to manage demand. It cannot be fully effective unless it is co-ordinated with the other three.

Place, distribution, access – or convenience

Traditionally for marketing purposes, *place* is the term used to describe the location of all the points of sale that provide prospective customers with access to tourist products. For example, 'place' for Disney World in the USA is not only Orlando, Florida, but also the numerous travel agents and tour operators located in the northeast of the USA and worldwide who sell products that include admission to Disney World. Travel agents are of course only one of the ways in which 'place' or convenient access is created for Disney World customers, or indeed for most other products in travel and tourism. Convenience of place for a self-catering operator, for example, includes direct mail to the homes of prospective buyers, using free-phone numbers and easy access to products via computerized reservation/booking systems.

Over the past decade, for most travel and tourism businesses, the Internet and broadband access have revolutionized and globalized the concept of convenient access by bringing it directly into the homes of millions of prospective buyers. Chapters 13–15 examine in depth how trends in ICT are transforming the marketing of travel and tourism and drawing the traditional 4Ps together on line.

The four Ps/Cs, with illustrations drawn from hotels, a scheduled airline and a museum, are illustrated in Fig. 8.1. Readers may find it a worthwhile exercise to complete their own illustrations for visitor attractions, tour operators, a cruise ship or a car rental operation.

	Hotel	Scheduled airline	Museum
Product			
Designed characteristics/ packaging	Location/building size/ grounds/ design/room size/ facilities in hotel furnishings/decor/ ambience/ lighting/ catering styles	Routes/service frequency Aircraft type/size Seat size/space Decor, meals, style	Building size/ design/facilities Types of collection Size of collection Interior display/ interpretation
Service component	Staff numbers/ uniforms/ attitudes/ customer responsiveness	Staff numbers, uniforms/attitudes/ customer responsiveness	Staff numbers, uniforms/attitudes/ customer responsiveness
Branding	e.g. Holiday Inn, Marriott, Meridien	e.g. American Airlines, British Airways, Virgin Atlantic	e.g. Tate Gallery (London) Metropolitan Museum (New York)
Image/reputation/ position	e.g. upmarket, downmarket	e.g. reliable, exotic food, badly managed	e.g. dull, exciting, modern
Price Normal or regular price Promotional price (for each product offered)	Rack rates Corporate rates Privileged user rates Tour operator discount rate	First class/ business/tourist fares APEX/bulk purchase fares Standby Charter Consolidated fares	(assuming charge made) Adult rate, senior citizen rate Group/party rates Children rate Friends of the museum rate
Promotion (solo and collaborative) Advertising (television/radio/ press/journals/ web sites) Sales promotion/ merchandising Public relations Brochure production and distribution Sales force	Examples not provided since these are generally self-evident and specific to individual organizations (See Parts Four and Five)		
Place Channels of distribution including reservation systems, third party retailers and web sites	Computerized reservation systems (CRS) Other hotels in group Internet Travel agents Tour operators Airlines free telephone lines	Computerized reservation systems (CRS) Internet City offices Airport desks Travel agents Other airlines 800 telephone lines	Other museums Internet Tourist information offices Hotel desks Schools/colleges

FIGURE 8.1 Examples of the marketing mix in travel and tourism

MARKETING MIX: COST AND REVENUE CONSIDERATIONS

It is important to understand that all the marketing mix decisions represent costs to an organization and have direct implications for pricing and for sales revenue. Moreover, as consideration of Fig. 8.1 indicates, three of the Ps require significant expenditure to be committed in advance of the revenue it is expected to generate. Changes to the product, advertising, sales promotions, brochure production and the organization and servicing of distribution channels (both physical and online), all represent financial commitments made in the expectation of targeted sales. Investment in people, processes and physical evidence also require extensive 'up-front' investment ahead of sales. While pricing decisions do not cost anything in advance of sales, they obviously determine the level of revenue achievable. Any price discounting required to move unsold capacity represents a loss of anticipated revenue.

To illustrate this important point, if a tour operator decides to develop its existing product range by adding new destinations, there will be setup costs in investigating the options available and contractual obligations to be made months before the first customers make full payment. Advertising and brochure costs will also be committed months ahead of the first sales. To give a different example, the decision by a hotel group to provide improved access for customers through investing in a new, enhanced, interactive website may have to be made up to 3 years before the advantages of the new system secure enough additional bookings to pay back the cost and generate extra profit.

MARKETING MIX IN CONTEXT OF THE MARKETING SYSTEM

Figure 8.2 expresses the marketing system for any organization in three concentric rings. It is an alternative way to represent the marketing process and readers may wish to compare this diagram with Fig. 2.1 in Chapter 2. The two diagrams are compatible but illustrate the same process from a different standpoint. Figure 8.2 is designed to demonstrate how marketing mix decisions, strategic and tactical, operate around the core focus of targeted consumer segments.

As discussed earlier in the chapter, the four Ps in the *inner ring* are under the direct control of marketing managers but they are subject to the other resources and strategic management functions of an organization, shown in the middle ring.

The *middle ring* functions are influenced by and influence marketing decisions but are not usually under the direct control of marketing management. For example, initial choice of location and capacity for a hotel and its general corporate image will be heavily influenced by marketing inputs to the project appraisal process. But thereafter these aspects will be difficult or impossible to change in the short run. The management of personnel and operational systems, e.g. in an airline, will place constraints or limits for manoeuvre on marketing management. Financial resources will govern the size and scope of marketing budgets in all organizations. Corporate websites and e-marketing are part of operations management but are shown as a separate item because of their significance in tourism marketing.

In the *outer ring*, summarized under six headings, are the factors external to a business which are not controlled by or even much influenced by marketing managers of any one organization. The powerful effect of these external factors on

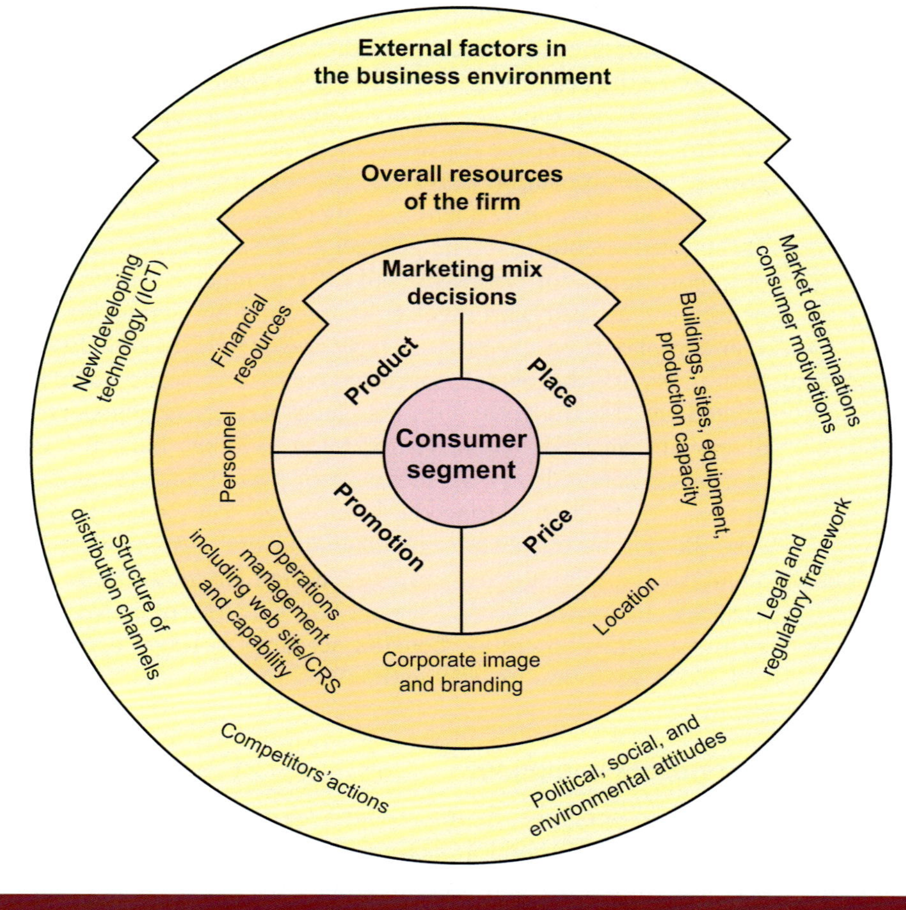

FIGURE 8.2 The core marketing mix in context of the overall marketing system. Adapted from Stanton: 1981

business decisions has already been made clear in Chapter 4 dealing with market determinants, and in Chapter 5 on buyer behaviour, so they are not repeated here. It is the combined influence of the six external factors in Fig. 8.2 that provides the context of opportunities and threats within which strategic and tactical marketing mix decisions have to be made. These are further developed in Chapters 10 and 11.

PEOPLE, PROCESS AND PHYSICAL EVIDENCE: EXPANDING THE MARKETING MIX

The second part of this chapter is structured around the expanded marketing mix that was originally devised by Booms and Bitner in the early 1980s. They added *people* or participants in the service delivery, *process* of delivery and *physical evidence.* The reader will discern overlap between these three additional 'Ps' and some justifiably consider them as part-product and part-communications mix. But the extra three-P framework is particularly useful for tourism, which is typically a high contact service (the people component), an extended and complex service (the process component) and a service that can only be evaluated by the consumer as they experience the delivery (incorporates the physical evidence component).

An inclusive tour, for example, involves extensive interaction with the tour operator's employees, with the staff of other organizations such as travel agency, airline, accommodation providers, restaurants, bars and clubs, with other tourists and with destination residents, many of whom do not perceive themselves as part of the tourism industry. The product is rich in human contact and there are plenty of opportunities for error especially if a product is consumed over a lengthy time period, say a week, and involves many different service providers. The product is also complex from a process perspective as it is the totality of the many services that make up the overall tourism experience. Some such services may be contracted out by the tour operator, such as airport transfers or excursions, while others are selected by the visitor, such as taxis, bars and cafés or tourist information centres. Clearly, an inclusive tour is difficult to assess at the point of sale but easy to evaluate during the holiday itself. To assist the prospective buyer and ease the purchase decision, inclusive tour operators need to provide tangible clues about their product offers and use design or 'physical evidence' to support the service delivery and provide satisfaction with the holiday during consumption. On all three counts, there are benefits accruing to travel and tourism marketers who pay close attention to the extra 'Ps' of the expanded marketing mix outlined below.

The people component

It is easy to recognize that most of the variability of the tourism product stems from the substantial human interactions inherent in the experience. It is a useful exercise to categorize the participants for marketing purposes. They are

- *Visitors*: the individual consumers of the product and the other visitors present at the same time and place. The interaction with other consumers of an inseparable experience will influence the experience and satisfaction or otherwise of each individual.
- *Employees*: the staff of an organization can be divided into front-line members with visitor contact and non-contact employees who provide support. Any third party organizations that supply different services to the principal provider will also be represented by front-line and support staff.
- *Host community*: the residents of a destination community who may not regard themselves as part of the tourism business but who, nonetheless, interact with visitors informally and whose friendly or hostile behaviour can make or mar a visitor's experience.

The elements of the marketing mix are traditionally viewed as controllable by the marketer. Clearly, the travel and tourism marketer has greatest control over product design and company employees, less over purchasers and very little if any direct control over the host community. Yet marketing activity can still influence behaviour in each of these categories. For example, two-way communication through strong public relations can foster positive attitudes and behaviour amongst destination residents.

Visitors

Holiday visitors are consumers with particular expectations. To deliver satisfactory experiences, travel and tourism marketers need to segment the market to ensure compatibility between consumers sharing the same premises at the same time (see Chapter 7). The consequences of mis-targeting a communications campaign can be dire in marketing terms because tourists are more than simply purchasers and users. They are also resources, assets and participants in parts of the service delivery whose activities need to be designed into the product offer and the delivery system. Compare the actions of a visitor in an intimate full-service restaurant with those of the same visitor in a self-service restaurant. Some of the activities carried out by consumers in self-service might logically be expected to form part of an employee's job. A low-cost budget airline will include more consumer participation in the product delivery process, reducing staffing and labour costs. For their part, certain tourist segments prefer the greater sense of control that more active participation in the service delivery process creates.

If the product design requires the customer to act in effect as a 'co-producer' in the service delivery, marketing managers must limit the risk and uncertainty for the service provider in three main ways: first, ensuring correct 'recruitment' (i.e. careful segmentation of the tourist market); second, providing unobtrusive clues for customers and 'training' (establishing awareness and expectations of the role in the consumer); and, third, encouraging 'motivation' (explaining the benefits of the design to the tourist and harnessing co-operation, just as the organization would be expected to do for a paid employee). The parallels with human resource management are not inappropriate.

Employees and interaction with visitors

For travel and tourism, it is hard to disagree with Zeithaml and Bitner's belief that employees *'physically embody the product and are walking billboards from a promotional standpoint'* (Zeithaml and Bitner, 1996: 304). In other words, staff *are* the organization in the eyes of the consumer. Hoffman and Bateson (1997) refer to front-line personnel as the 'public face' of the service firm. Their physical appearance, behaviour, knowledge and attitudes have a powerful impact on the customer's perception of the organization they represent. Logically, one can conclude that employee satisfaction is a prerequisite for obtaining long-term and consistent customer satisfaction. Happy employees give better and more responsive service that, in turn, triggers happy consumers. Placing staff satisfaction before customer satisfaction is the oft-quoted mantra of many CEOs. Indeed, an inverted view of the traditional organizational pyramid puts front-line contact staff at the top of an organization, with the various layers of management in a facilitating role beneath them.

In practice, many front-line contact staff in travel and tourism would struggle to recognize this portrait of an organization's appreciation of its most valuable resource. Many find themselves performing jobs below the status of the customer in a position that Shamir (1995) refers to as a 'subordinate service role'. This includes most waiters, bar staff, room service staff, cabin crew, bus and taxi drivers, tourist information staff, and so on. The list would be easy to extend. Only a minority of tourist-facing employees, such as airline pilots or instructors in a special interest activity, enjoy professional roles with the measure of control over the service encounter that a higher status affords. For many who serve tourists from a subordinate perspective on low pay, long hours, having little career structure and potentially minimal respect from the visitor, the idea of an inverted pyramid of management support below them would seem absurd. Resentful employees may develop their own methods to 'get even' and overcome perceived inequality between customers and themselves. For instance, the visitor information centre employee who speaks English when dealing with German visitors, despite being able to speak excellent German, is shifting the balance of power to give himself greater control over the situation.

Contact employees who have to reconcile the internal operational requirements of an organization with the expectations and demands of customers are required to show empathy with visitors while obeying the rules and regulations of the organization that employs them. There is often stress associated with these demands that can manifest itself in three types of conflict (Zeithaml and Bitner, 1996).

The first type of conflict may not be apparent to the visitor. It is the struggle between the personal feelings of the contact employee and the role required of them in doing their job. Role demands may grate against self-image. The female air stewardess who experiences lewd comments or physical harassment from male passengers is still expected to behave in role, although had such incidents occurred outside work her reactions would follow her personal feelings. Such conflict is particularly evident in subordinate staff where employees may be subjected to behaviour that lags behind accepted behaviour in society in general. Air stewardesses, for example, have been known to protest against airline advertising campaigns that present them in a sexual light. One might question what, if any, thought was applied to internal marketing in such cases.

The second type of conflict occurs when an employee is pulled between the wishes of the customer and the rules of the organization. The customer who requests a coach driver to make an unofficial stop or who brings over-sized baggage on to a full flight, or asks for more and more alcohol may initiate this type of conflict. Although the employee may attempt to apply the agreed regulations, given the person-to-person contact stress of the moment they are likely either to side with the tourist against the organization or to show signs of irritability. Frustration will increase if there is no logical explanation for the rule that can be relayed to the consumer. Consumers may interpret employee behaviour as 'bad attitude' even if they do agree to a request; this in turn will have a negative impact on product satisfaction.

The third type of conflict is linked to segment incompatibility. Differing expectations of the experience to be provided and personality differences can create problems between visitors who are sharing the same time and space, a phenomenon well recognized in museums, for example, where adults' interests and those of noisy parties of children are unlikely to be compatible. For destination representatives employed by tour operators, one of the key tasks they are allocated is to facilitate positive interactions between group members in order to enhance satisfaction with a holiday experience. Dealing with conflicts between customers is often stressful for employees, requiring good training and the development of strong interpersonal skills.

Internal marketing

In managing employees and harnessing their potential as an element of the marketing mix, there is an obvious requirement for co-operation between the human resources department and marketing management of a firm. Ideally, marketing should have input to the recruitment process, training, motivation and reward systems, which are the classic responsibilities of human resource management. For example, the communications mix should be directed in part at potential job applicants as part of the process of building an organization's reputation as a preferred employer. Reward systems should also recognize and reward qualitative aspects of the work as opposed to being geared only to productivity measures.

Known as *internal marketing* it is a logical extension of the marketing mix considerations to recognize that the employees of an organization are stakeholders too. Marketing is as applicable to internal audiences within a company as to prospective customers and others outside it, including the host community at a destination. In large organizations market research amongst staff can assess levels of satisfaction, identify problem areas and discover ideas for product improvement. In small- and medium-sized travel and tourism companies the encouragement of upward communication coupled with an open-door policy may suffice. Use of employees within prestigious advertising campaigns aimed at consumers also targets messages at staff and can be used to reward achieving employees and motivate others as well as creating a sense of ownership. Communication techniques such as newsletters, in-house magazines, electronic mail, notice boards and open meetings can also be used to transmit internal marketing messages, whilst a clear and credible mission statement can help develop a united sense of purpose amongst staff.

As well as establishing vision and strategy, good corporate leadership nourishes the right cultural environment for the organization and fosters the development of teamwork between employees. The quality of service delivered by contact staff is dependent upon the quality of the process supporting them and each employee in the chain needs to recognize their role in providing the final product and internal as well as customer satisfaction.

Participants, whether they are the visitors themselves, employees or other players in the process, are all operating within a service delivery system, or process. This component of the expanded marketing mix is discussed briefly below.

The service delivery process

The travel and tourism experience consists of both process and outcome. For leisure visitors the outcome is often intangible benefits, such as a sense of well-being, mental and physical recuperation, development of personal interests such as culture, or revived relationships. For individual service providers the outcome is rather more prosaic, for example, arrival at the airport/destination at the specified time. For travel and tourism, perhaps more than for any other service products, the outcome is highly dependent on the quality of service delivery as perceived by the user. A financial investment can be judged by the outcome of monetary return, a degree course by the grade of the award achieved, the advice of a law firm by legal success or failure. Yet travel and tourism only exists through the experience of its extended process of production and consumption. It is much harder to separate the outcome from the experience that delivered it.

Given the high contact nature of travel and tourism, staff and consumers form a vital part of the system of service delivery as discussed in the previous section. Consumers move through a series of encounters during the tourism experience. The obvious service encounters are those that involve the consumer interacting with an employee face-to-face on a firm's premises. But encounters may also be remote, by website, automated telephone service or, indeed, with physical evidence or equipment, such as a roadside sign or an automated check-in machine. Some encounters are of greater importance than others and these may be considered as *'critical incidents'*, or *'moments of truth'*. Critical incidents are also less memorably defined as *'specific interactions between a consumer and service firm employees (or equipment) that are especially satisfying or dissatisfying'* (Bitner et al., 1995: 135).

It is the *'moments of truth'* that stay in the consumer's mind and signify quality and satisfaction. Zeithaml and Bitner (1996), cite that Disney Corporation estimates that each visitor to its theme parks experiences around 74 'critical incidents', any one of which, if unsatisfactory, could result in a negative evaluation of the whole visit. A negative, or dissatisfying, critical incident necessitates an attempt at service recovery by the service provider, and this is better conducted at the time of the incident, rather than afterwards. Turning round a negative incident supports both consumer retention and positive recommendation; failure to do so may generate substantial adverse word of mouth and probable customer defection to competitors.

Planned service recovery systems, recognizing marketing as well as operational needs, provide opportunities to convert dissatisfied consumers into satisfied ones. Drawing on work by Bateson (1995), Zeithaml and Bitner (1996) and Jobber (2007), the following points for service recovery are judged to be particularly relevant to travel and tourism organizations.

- *Measure and track the costs of customer retention in* comparison with the costs of attracting new customers. Communication costs, the potential lifetime value of a customer, word of mouth recommendations and the value of familiarity with the service delivery process of customers as co-producers should enter into the cost calculation. It is commonly recognized that the costs of gaining new customers are at least three to five times greater than persuading current consumers to be repeat buyers. A keen commercial appreciation of the long-term value of existing customers is the rationale for implementing successful service recovery following a negative incident.
- *Encourage complaints* and use them as part of a comprehensive service management system that not only addresses consumers' concerns but also analyses and rectifies problems. Research suggests that for every complaint made to a company, there may be 20 other dissatisfied customers who refrained from voicing their unhappiness to the company itself. Yet, a customer with a complaint typically tells ten other people about it. Thus, one unfortunate incident drawing a complaint to the company from one consumer could, in practice, reverberate some 200 times through the word-of-mouth network. And this is before consideration of customer defection to a competitor and loss of lifetime value. Research also suggests that most service companies have ineffective complaint management systems with most companies spending 95% of their service time resolving individual complaints and only 5% of their time analysing and correcting the delivery fault that triggered the negative incident in the first place. Consumer and employee surveys, focus groups, 'mystery shoppers' and suggestion schemes can all play a part in gathering and analysing information useful for service recovery and complaint management.
- *Train employees in service recovery* using, for example, forms of 'empowerment' that simultaneously help employees show empathy for customer problems and understand managements' perceptions of what are

acceptable and unacceptable responses. Time is of the essence in complaints and swift decision and response is more likely to result in incident turnaround.

Link article available at www.routledge.com/9780750686938

(1) Briggs, S., Sutherland, J., Drummond, S., 2007. Are hotels serving quality? An exploratory study of service quality in the Scottish hotel sector. Tourism Management 28 (4), 1006–1019.

MINI CASE 8.1 MANAGING CUSTOMER RELATIONSHIPS

The travel and tourism industry, more than any other, has contributed exponentially to the growth in usage and influence of the Internet in recent years. This in turn hastened the need for airlines, hotels and tour operators alike to continue to develop their online strategies and improve the ease and security with which their e-commerce initiatives can be used by online customers. One outcome of this is the ever-increasing growth in self-serving technology with the consequent reduction in interaction between customers and the industry. This is particularly the case with online intermediaries who for much of the market are seen to provide facilitation rather than selling services. Despite the many benefits of online activity, one of the challenges for businesses is the means by which they are able to develop customer loyalty to particular sites. With the increasing trend towards 'bargain hunting' in many parts of the industry the search for loyalty is even more challenging than in off-line contexts as the Internet facilitates the ease with which 'switching' behaviour can and does take place. Up to 40% of people in the UK are estimated to have purchased travel products online while far more have used the Internet to search for information about their trip. This trend is also driven by shorter but more frequent trips and the ease with which product elements can be selected and combined by purchasers using the Internet. Interestingly, while on the one hand businesses wish to build relationships with customers on the other hand, consumer autonomy is growing via the use of self-servicing technologies.

Sometimes referred to as the 'post-service' economy, the above scenario poses a number of challenges to operators and businesses alike. Evidence of customers servicing their own information requirements, purchasing online at their convenience in a flexible and efficient manner is most noticeable perhaps in the context of airlines where online check-in is increasingly becoming commonplace and which in fact is now leading to the redesign of check-in facilities at airports; evidenced recently with the opening of Terminal 5 in 2008 at London Heathrow.

As with all systems the ease with which they can be used and are safe, will facilitate the ways in which they can then be used to manage customer relationships.

The principal challenge for the future is to integrate customer service strategies with customer service delivery and hopefully thereby increase customer satisfaction across the industry. In this regard a number of criteria have been identified as contributing to the successful management of customer relationships in self-service environments. The first aspect is to clearly *identify the online customer*. This will require a break down of the market into segments, which may relate to frequency of purchase, revenue per customer or socio-demographic factors. In essence, it is necessary to identify who the prime markets are, the IT capabilities of customers – as this will result in varying needs and levels of service – and the extent to which businesses themselves collect and manage customer data in a rigorous manner. Transactional data are easy to obtain but more insightful customer relationship data are far more difficult to get hold of. The design of websites is also crucial and must take into account the varying attention spans of different customer groupings. It is then necessary to *communicate effectively with customers*. Ideally, the next stage is the *development of loyalty and trust* and the need to overcome traditional face-to-face meetings. This can be achieved via brand development, the development of customer loyalty schemes and/or the development of online communities. This social dimension is particularly popular with younger segments where social networking sites are now commonplace. The challenge for the future is to find ways in which businesses from across the wider travel and tourism sectors are able to integrate these developments more fully into their customer relationship strategies.

Source: Based on Stockdale (2007).

Service delivery perceived as scripts

An alternative way to improve the performance of service delivery, at least for larger companies, is to draw analogies with the performance of a play or film. To see a play, for example, is to experience the writer's script in action. The words, movements and props are taken from a script and rehearsed to polished fluency. The notion is relevant in tourism because many services can, in effect, be scripted with the staff playing their roles as actors on a stage. A script is a sequence of actions, equipment and words that enables the service delivery process to run smoothly and seamlessly. So far only a very few tourism products are formally scripted. For example, the service delivery at Disney Corporation theme parks use written scripts but most scripting in travel and tourism is very informal, although it is often implicit in training schemes for employees.

To be used successfully, of course, it is necessary for all the participants, whether consumers or employees, to be reading from the same script. Visitors have to adapt, think and learn new 'scripts', in a tight time frame, which can be a stressful experience. The 'script' for an English pub will not apply to a French bar. Do you wait to be seated? When do you pay? Do you tip? And if so, how much? What behaviour on your part will obtain best service? The journey by bus can be equally daunting. Where do you buy the ticket? On the bus or at a kiosk? What type of kiosk? Does it require punching for validation? And so on. A confused visitor in a foreign country unable to act out the national script for a simple service appears to be stupid. One does not have to think long to remember personal anecdotes where a visitor hovering in uncertainty has irritated employees and other consumers alike. Unfortunately, this lack of understanding by the majority serves to reinforce the classic stereotypes of the ignorant tourist, so often parodied on postcards.

Marketers dealing with the interface between international visitors and developing informal 'scripts' should investigate ways of informing them before and on arrival of expected behaviour. Tools from the communications mix, such as travel guides, brochures, videos, in-flight magazines, post-purchase leaflets, websites and talks by tour representatives, can all serve to facilitate the process. In terms of services delivery processes, marketers should look at system flexibility and train employees to understand and manage customer expectations.

Courtesy of Dimitrious Buhalis.

Service blueprinting

Taking Levitt's original conceptualization of the service delivery processes to a logical conclusion some authors have concluded that improvements can be derived from constructing a formal service 'blueprint' or flowchart of the service delivery process (Hoffman and Bateson, 1997). It has also been described as *'a picture or map that accurately portrays the service system so that the different people involved in providing it can understand and deal with it objectively regardless of their roles or their individual points of view'* (Zeithaml and Bitner, 1996: 277).

Much of the work on services blueprinting from a marketing perspective was carried out by Shostack during the 1980s (Shostack, 1994), and the reader is referred to his work for further details. As a graphical representation of a particular service, any blueprint is likely to incorporate

- All relevant points of contact (or encounters) between the consumer and the service provider expressed in a flow chart.
- A dividing line between activity that is visible to customers and the support activity that is not.
- Activities of participants, both customers and employees, directionally linked in the flow chart.
- Support processes involved in the service delivery.
- Standard length of time for individual activities and any time targets based on consumer expectations. From these, labour costs and hourly or daily throughput can be calculated.
- Bottlenecks, or points in the process where consumers are obliged to wait the longest period of time.
- Points in the process where service failure might occur that is both rated as significant and observed by the consumer.
- Evidence of service that aids positioning and consumer evaluation of quality.

The blueprint idea is too complex to be of much use to smaller enterprises but the thinking process and analysis can produce better service and increased satisfaction for customers. It is more relevant for multi-site operators processing thousands of customers daily using standardized processes. The service blueprint concept is aligned to operations management, but, as sound marketing practice is an integrated function within management, it is a way to inject customer expectations and feedback into large-scale service processes.

Link article available at www.routledge.com/9780750686938

(1) Lopez Fernandez, M.C., Serrano Bedia, A.M., 2004 Is the hotel classification system a good indicator of hotel quality? An application in Spain. Tourism Management 25 (6), 771–775.

Managing physical evidence and design

Relevant to all sizes of operation, the third additional component of the services marketing mix is that of 'physical evidence' rooted in the five senses of sight (especially colour and aesthetics), sound, scent, touch and taste. Because tourism products are characterized by inseparability, visitors are present in the production premises and the design of the physical setting for the delivery process is a vital part of the product experience. Of course, the physical setting is sometimes the *raison d'être* for tourism in the first place but here it refers to the design of the built environment owned and controlled by a tourism organization, for example, a theme park or hotel, or to the efforts of an organization to design a natural or built area to meet particular visitor management objectives. Because tourism products are also characterized by intangibility, physical evidence is used additionally to 'tangibilize' the offer away from the place of consumption, especially at the point of sale, to influence purchasing. It is also used to reduce post-purchase anxiety, although with the notable exception of the brochure and more recently access to websites, the planning of remote physical evidence has often been overlooked.

The uses for physical evidence suggested by Hoffman and Bateson (1997) are relevant to travel and tourism. Physical evidence acts in lieu of the use of 'packaging' for products based on physical goods. It communicates messages about quality, positioning and differentiation, and it helps both to set and meet visitor expectations. Physical evidence can be used to facilitate the service delivery process through, for example, layout and signage that influence customer responses. By creating particular ambiences, physical evidence can help to promote social contact between customers and employees and facilitate desired emotional states or behaviours. As with any of the marketing mix components, the designing of physical evidence should be organized around stated goals. Skilful use of physical evidence can attract desired segments whilst deterring others, thus aiding demand management. Classical music played in public areas such as car parks or train platforms has been used, for example, to deter some groups of people judged undesirable from the premises. It is a means of enhancing the sense of security and satisfaction with the product enjoyed by targeted groups. For fragile resources such as cave paintings and other historic artefacts, physical evidence may be used as a form of virtual reality to create access while protecting the resource.

The power that the external and internal design of buildings influences over customers and employees is increasingly recognized in all sectors of travel and tourism. It is highly relevant to product augmentation (see Chapter 7) and its use in communicating corporate, brand and product values is becoming more important. Design features can influence the beliefs that a customer or an employee holds about an organization (the cognitive element), the emotions aroused in customers or employees (the affective element), the behaviour and actions of customers or employees (the behavioural element) and the physical comfort or otherwise of both parties (the physiological element). Yet, the use of physical evidence can be quite subtle, creating the designed effect without alerting the individual to the objective of the service provider. Ensuring consistency and co-ordination between the different tools of design is an inherent part of planning the physical evidence 'mix'.

CONSUMER CENTRIC MARKETING (CCM)

Developments in ICT generally and the Internet in particular are having a profound impact on the way in which organizations are able to communicate and develop relationships with their customers. Marketing is therefore 'called to capitalize on the emerging new tools and to enhance the relationship between companies and consumers towards adding value, improving service and ultimately contributing to the profitability of enterprises (Niininen et al., 2007: 265).

Defined as the 'discipline of capturing and deploying consumer insights to enhance marketing effectiveness and better serve those consumers that are brand's best prospects' (Manley et al., 2002: 3), CCM is a three-step process, namely

- The collection and arrangement of information and data on individual customers.
- The utilization of that information to target existing customers more effectively.
- Allowing buyers to customize and personalize the service to match their own needs and preferences.

On the one hand CCM allows organizations to obtain insight into the general characteristics of their clients and better understand their marketing-related behaviour (i.e. attitudes, beliefs and values) while on the other hand it opens up opportunities for consumers to customize products and so match their needs and wants more accurately. This, in turn, allows for far greater degrees of differentiation to be achieved, which also enhances value creation on the part of the consumer.

As discussed in Part Four, the Internet has enhanced the extent to which consumers have been empowered to make more informed purchases, join with others through networking to gauge opinion and/or actual experience of the product or destination, and enjoy new levels of interaction and development of personalized products and experiences. Often referred to as a 'positive cycle of learning', CCM is ideal for many tourism-related products and experiences in that it facilitates the flexible packaging of the destination product and the flexibility and choice of various media channels. Building on the origins of customer relationship management, for CCM to be achieved a number of prerequisites need to be met. First, organizations need to have a significant amount of relevant information about customers on their databases. Second, organizations need to offer their clients suitable communication platforms or selling points where the client can select the elements of their product. Finally, the accumulated knowledge allows the design of personalized and meaningful messages to the customer regarding the features of the brand.

A variety of trends have contributed to the origin of CCM, namely: brand and product proliferation; the fragmentation of traditional media and the emergence of new communication methods; the changing consumers; the increased channel power and developments in ICT more broadly (Niininen et al., 2007: 269).

In essence, what is now occurring in the marketplace is one-to-one ICT-enabled marketing whereby the combination of technology and dynamic interaction for the first time are creating cost-effective customization on a large scale. Data gathering, evaluation and decision-making have been transformed by the empowerment offered by the Internet. It is now commonplace for many companies to actively encourage customers to register online, to declare personal information and travel preferences with all this information then serving as a driver for target-driven marketing. Despite the focus on the importance of ICT, integral to the success of CCM is a broad understanding of many of the lessons identified in this chapter in terms of getting the 'product' and other elements of the marketing mix correct. The current focus is on the pre-visit experience. But the growing availability of wireless technologies and provision of 'two-way-always-on connectivity' in more and more destinations around the world means that the impact of CCM will begin to be felt more fully when on location. More significantly from a marketing standpoint it will also be felt in the post-visit experience. Still at a relatively early stage in development, CCM embraces and reflects all aspects of the marketing mix outlined in this chapter using the latest website technology.

CHAPTER SUMMARY

This chapter:

- Introduces the essential components of the marketing mix and discusses how the four Ps or Cs have dominated marketing thinking for over 40 years. They are discussed as the main levers or controls available to marketing managers in their continuous endeavours to achieve objectives and targets, expressed as sales volume and revenue from identified customer groups. The mix decisions are based on a combination of marketing research, marketing planning procedures and the judgement of individual managers engaged in a strategic battle of wits with their competitors.
- Sets the four Ps/Cs in the wider context of non-marketing resources within organizations, and the continuously changing external influences to which marketing managers have to respond. This very important concept of marketing response was succinctly summarized in Stanton's view that: *A company's success depends on the ability of its executives to manage its marketing system in relation to its external environment. This means (1) responding to changes in the environment, (2) forecasting the direction and intensity of these changes, and (3) using the internal controllable resources in adapting to the changes in the external environment* (Stanton, 1981: 32).
- Drawing on the broader services marketing literature, explains the three additional Ps that are especially appropriate to managing service delivery in travel and tourism. These are People, Process and Physical evidence. Much of the thrust for this elaboration of the original four Ps has come from larger international and global multi-site businesses in the ceaseless pursuit of a competitive edge in the markets they serve. To achieve and sustain such an edge has to be based on product consistency, quality controls and customer satisfaction, and it has to be managed over multiple sites in different countries and cultures. To achieve that, organized operational systems for service delivery have to be applied.
- Stresses that marketing-mix decisions, including design, mostly imply significant costs that have to be met or committed in advance of the revenue such decisions are expected to achieve.
- Introduces the emerging concept of CCM and the many benefits it offers marketers including the potential that exists with wireless technologies in destinations all around the world.

QUESTIONS TO CONSIDER

1. How have developments in the Internet and web-based technologies impacted on the use of the four Ps as advocated by McCarthy nearly 50 years ago?
2. Provide some examples that demonstrate how 'Price' can be used successfully, both strategically and tactically, in a sector of your choice (i.e. airlines, tour operations, accommodation).
3. How important are 'People' in the increasing electronic and self-service environment of the new century?

4. Discuss alternative internal marketing strategies that may be adopted in destinations and the circumstances that could necessitate their implementation.
5. How may complaints from customers be used positively by marketers?
6. Think of examples whereby 'service blueprinting' may be used in the operation of a theme park targeted to family groups.

REFERENCES AND FURTHER READING

Augustyn, M. and Ho, S.K. (1998). Service quality and tourism, *Journal of Travel Research*, **37**, pp. 71–75.

Managing Services Marketing: Text and Readings (Ed. by J.E.G. Bateson) (3rd edn). Dryden Press.

Bitner, M.J., Booms, B.H. and Tetrealt, M.S. (1995). The service encounter. In: *Managing Services Marketing: Text and Readings* (Ed. by J.E.G. Bateson) (3rd edn). Dryden Press.

Briggs, S., Sutherland, J. and Drummond, S. (2007). Are hotels serving quality? An exploratory study of service quality in the Scottish hotel sector, *Tourism Management*, **28**(4), pp. 1006–1019.

Gilbert, D., Child, D. and Bennett, M. (2001). A qualitative study of the current practices of 'no-frills' airlines operating in the UK, *Journal of Vacation Marketing*, **7**, pp. 302–315.

Hoffman, K.D. and Bateson, J.E.G. (1997). *Essentials of services marketing*. Dryden Press.

Jobber, D. (2007). *Principles and practices of marketing* (5th edn). McGraw Hill.

Kotler, P. and Armstrong, G. (1999). *Principles of marketing* (8th edn). Prentice Hall.

Kotler, P., Wong, V., Saunders, J. and Armstrong, G. (2005). *Principles of marketing* (4th European edn). Pearson Prentice Hall.

Law, R. and Leung, R. (2000). A study of airlines' online reservation services on the Internet, *Journal of Travel Research*, **39**, pp. 202–211.

Lopez Fernandez, M.C. and Serrano Bedia, A.M. (2004). Is the hotel classification system a good indicator of hotel quality? An application in Spain, *Tourism Management*, **25**(6), pp. 771–775.

Manley, R., Flink, C. and Lietz, C. (2002) White paper on consumer centric marketing: how leading consumer packaged good companies are transforming the way they market. Available at: crm:ittoolbox.com/documents/documents.aspi

McCarthy, E.J. (1981). *Basic marketing: a managerial approach* (7th edn). Irwin.

Niininen, O., Buhalis, D. and March, R. (2007). Customer empowerment in tourism through consumer centric marketing (CCM), *Qualitative Market Research: An International Journal*, **10**(3), pp. 265–281.

Shostack, G.L. (January–February 1984). Designing services that deliver, *Harvard Business Review*.

Stanton, W.J. (1981). *Fundamentals of marketing* (6th edn). McGraw Hill.

Stockdale, R. (2007). Managing customer relationships in the self-service environment of e-tourism, *Journal of Vacation Marketing*, **13**(3), pp. 205–219.

Weber, K. (2005). Travelers' perceptions of airline alliance benefits and performance, *Journal of Travel Research*, **43**, pp. 257–265.

Whyte, R. (2003). Loyalty marketing and frequent flyer programmes: attitudes and attributes of corporate travellers, *Journal of Vacation Marketing*, **9**, pp. 17–34.

Zeithaml, V.A. and Bitner, M.J. (1996). *Services marketing*. McGraw-Hill.

Planning for Marketing Strategy and Short-term Operational Objectives and Campaigns

Part Three focuses on the tools of marketing research and marketing information needed for the planning of effective marketing strategies that provide directional stability to commercial and not-for-profit organizations in an ever-changing business environment. Chapter 11 identifies the marketing planning process with a focus on short-term objectives and action plans. Chapter 12 focuses on marketing campaigns; the way they are costed and results evaluated in travel and tourism.

In the Balearics... nearly... 80% of.. companies.. are engaged in activities that are either directly or indirectly related to the tourism industry

CHAPTER 9

Marketing research in travel and tourism

Imagination, judgement and courage remain important qualities for the successful decision maker. Research is the handmaiden of competent management but never its substitute.

(Luck et al., 1970: 8)

What marketing managers know of market trends, consumer segments, buyer behaviour, product performance and consumers' response to all aspects of marketing campaigns, is mostly derived from one or more aspects of marketing research activity. Other than for very small or micro-businesses the planning processes at both strategic and operational levels are research based, as discussed in Chapters 10 and 11. This chapter, therefore, focuses on techniques that are essential in successful marketing practice. The term *marketing research* is used in its broad sense of embracing all forms of research-based information used in making marketing decisions, including consumer research, database analysis and marketing information systems (MIS).

In using computers most readers will be aware of the maxim, 'garbage in, garbage out'. In other words, if the information or data fed into a computer are inaccurate or inadequate, one cannot hope for useful results. There is a marketing research parallel because the whole of marketing strategy and operations are also calculated responses using information input. The lower the quality (or absence) of information used for marketing decisions, the higher the risks of marketing failures, especially in strongly competitive markets.

Commencing with an initial definition, this chapter identifies the six main types of marketing research. It next describes ten kinds of marketing research activity, widely used in travel and tourism, which readers can expect to find in practice. The next section explains a typical 'menu' of marketing research choices available to operators, and illustrates it in a tourism context. The final part of the chapter indicates how to use a market research agency and comments on test marketing and monitoring for travel and tourism products.

After studying this chapter you should be able to understand:

- What marketing research means in its travel and tourism context.
- The types of market research that can be undertaken within the sector.

- How to develop a brief to commission market research.
- The special advantages for research and test marketing innovation of multi-site operations having customers on their premises.
- The research role of the Internet.

MARKETING RESEARCH DEFINED

Marketing research is an organized information process, which deals with the gathering, processing, analysing, storage and communication of information to facilitate marketing decision-making. This description of the core rationale for undertaking marketing research has hardly changed in a century of practice. Recently, however, information gathering has been massively facilitated through the advent of computer technology, faster data processing and sophisticated database software. Vital information gathering takes place via sources such as the Internet, mobile phones and telephones as well as the traditional use of questionnaires and interviews.

Most marketing decisions require answers as to 'who, what, when, where, how and why'. Marketing research typically starts with the information held on customer databases and flows of 'intelligence' data gathered through B2B and other websites, trade publications – and for tourism – destination management organizations. It includes regular analysis of traffic through corporate websites and call centre data. It proceeds with primary research ranging from focus groups to full-scale sample surveys on a local, national or international scale. Increasingly now, data from mobile sources are also utilized in order to understand details of how individuals undertake purchasing decisions.

Most authors stress that marketing research cannot, as is sometimes supposed, provide solutions to management problems. Research can seldom ensure correct decisions. What it can do, as the quote at the head of the chapter notes, is reduce the amount of uncertainty and risk associated with the results of marketing decisions and focus attention on the probable implications of alternative courses of action. In general marketing research provides businesses engaged in tourism with an ability to make *informed* decisions.

From observation of the way that travel and tourism businesses are conducted in many countries around the world, it appears to be a distinctive feature of the industry that the use of marketing research is still generally less effective than in other major industries dealing with consumer products. Of course there are exceptions, although they are mainly the very large international corporations in air transport, tour operations, car rental and some hotel groups. The reason for this weakness appears to be rooted in the increasingly irrelevant assumption that research is not needed when producers and customers meet face to face on the producer's premises. In other words, through such contact, managers 'know' their customers without the need for expensive research. This may still be true for guesthouses, small attractions and neighbourhood travel agencies but it was never true for larger businesses, especially those with multi-site operations and management teams not directly involved in daily service delivery. The presence of customers on the premises is, however, a most important marketing strength or asset to be exploited systematically by producers and this point is developed at the end of the chapter.

Using judgement or research?

In practice it is nearly always the case that managers have to take most decisions with less than adequate information, especially in times of crisis. The cost of obtaining additional information has to be measured in time as well as money and is always related to the prospective gain or loss at risk in the decisions that are made. For example, faced with a decision between two alternative designs for a brochure cover, a marketing manager for a tour operating company has either to exercise judgement or commission research to evaluate target customers' responses to the two designs.

Where millions of brochures are to be printed, a 10 per cent better customer reaction to one of the designs could pay off in thousands of additional bookings. Research in this case would be justified if waiting for results did not delay production and distribution. For smaller operators the expense would rarely be justified by the potential extra business, and close attention to the print design brief (itself research based) would have to suffice, together with experience and judgement gained with other brochures.

By contrast, a strategic decision by a business such as a theme park to restructure its product by making major investment in new facilities would always justify marketing research studies at a cost related to the size of the investment. Such research would be needed to inform decisions about the scope and range of the new facilities, and the design of the new product in terms of identified market needs, behaviour patterns and visitors' capacity to pay. For example, if research indicated that visitors would be likely to spend only 2 hours at a new attraction and not 4 hours, the implications for car parking, prices, display and content, would be critical. In practice there is always a requirement to balance the need to know against the cost in time and money. But the reasons for using marketing research as well as the techniques available are the same in principle for travel and tourism as for any other form of consumer marketing.

SIX MAIN CATEGORIES OF MARKETING RESEARCH AND THEIR USES

Table 9.1 is capable of almost endless extension and technical detail but an understanding of the six main categories of marketing research noted will be adequate for most marketing decision purposes. The six categories correspond exactly with the information needs required to make efficient decisions for marketing-mix programmes, and the strategic and operational plans within which they are implemented. The categories in Table 9.1 are common to any marketing organization dealing with consumers, although the uses noted are specific to travel and tourism.

NINE TYPES OF MARKETING RESEARCH COMMONLY USED IN TRAVEL AND TOURISM

Marketing research has become a large and complex sector of economic activity in its own right and it has inevitably produced its own technical vocabulary. To achieve the information most commonly needed in travel and tourism, the types of research methods most commonly used are noted below and discussed in this chapter. They are

- Continuous and ad hoc.
- Quantitative and qualitative.

- Primary and secondary.
- Omnibus and syndicated.
- Occupancy studies.

TABLE 9.1 Six main categories of marketing research and their uses

Research category	Used in/for	Typical research content and methods
1. Market analysis and forecasting	Marketing planning	Measurement and projections of market volumes, shares and revenue by relevant categories of market segments and product type
2. Consumer research	Segmentation, branding and positioning	(a) Quantitative measurement of consumer profiles, awareness, attitudes and purchasing behaviours including consumer audits (b) Qualitative assessments of consumer needs, perceptions and aspirations
3. Products and price studies	Product formulation, presentation, pricing and market assessment	Measurement and consumer testing of amended and new product formulation, and price sensitivity studies
4. Promotions and sales research	Efficiency of communications	Measurement of consumer reaction to alternative advertising concepts and media usage; response to forms of sales promotion, and sales-force effectiveness. Measurement of website responses
5. Distribution research	Efficiency of distribution network/ channels	Distributor awareness of products, stocking and display of brochures, and effectiveness of merchandizing, including retail audits and occupancy studies, analysis of website usage and of call centres
6. Evaluation and performance monitoring studies	Overall control of marketing results and product quality control	Measurement of customer satisfaction overall and by product elements, including measurement through marketing tests and experiments and use of mystery shoppers

Continuous and ad hoc

Commercial organizations have to measure key trend data on a regular or 'continuous' basis. 'Continuous' in this context typically means daily, weekly or monthly, although the growing use of the Internet permits literally continuous data review. Data covering enquiries, sales, booking types and patterns, market shares, customer satisfaction and seat or hotel bed occupancy, are typical examples of 'continuous' marketing-research measures in travel and tourism. Continuous information is increasingly incorporated into databases that provide a fertile source of information for user satisfaction with products and for marketing-mix decisions generally.

There are also many specific problems in marketing that require research relevant to a particular circumstance. For example, could a redesigned guidebook for a visitor attraction, with a print life of say 3 years, produce extra sales revenue? Would the introduction of a buffet-style instead of full-service breakfast reduce customer satisfaction or increase it? Does the market potential warrant investment in a new hotel and, if it does, what size of hotel and what level of service would be justified? To inform such management decisions a specific or ad hoc investigation would be needed.

Most marketing research programmes are a mixture of continuous research involving ongoing investment in the monitoring of trends, and ad hoc surveys when the cost of research is justified to illuminate specific problems or opportunities as they occur. A modern way in which continuous research takes place is through websites and advertisement links on the Internet. Sites are monitored continuously for traffic and the number of clicks and page uses generated. This enables websites to be adjusted and fine tuned or configured slightly differently based on the information obtained. For example, the search terms most used by Google indicate the language most used by prospective buyers. The volume of responses that searches on keywords generate also indicates the level of competition.

Quantitative and qualitative

Traditionally, most consumer research studies are based on questions identified in marketing decision-making to be asked of random samples of existing or potential customers. For example, a coach tour operator will be aware from national surveys that some 60% of adults take a long holiday in a given year, of whom a third travelled abroad, stayed an average of ten nights away from home and spent £600 per person. The operator would need to know what proportion used coaches and cars, how that proportion varied year by year and by month, the profile of coach clients compared with users of other transport, their preferred destinations, and so on. With due allowance for statistical variation all these are quantifiable dimensions that can be projected into percentages and volume estimates for the coach tour market. Hence quantitative research, meaning studies from which numerical estimates can be estimated. Quantitative research is always based on 'structured' questionnaires in which every respondent is asked the same questions. Mostly, because the range of possible answers is also printed on questionnaires drawing on previous experience, variations to suit individual respondents are not possible.

Quantitative methods are often also used to give some basic indications of motivations. But generally, research companies cannot predict the ways in which people think about different products and such methods are unsuitable for exploring consumer attitudes, feelings, desires or perceptions. It is always possible to construct hypothetical answers and ask people to agree or disagree, but these may not get at what really matters to prospective buyers.

Qualitative studies commence from the standpoint that there are consumer (or staff) attitudes and motivations to be explored for which the answers cannot be predicted. How customers feel about Brand A compared with Brand B; what attributes and values are perceived as adhering to Brand A and not Brand B; what sort of people are thought most likely to buy Brand A rather than B; and so on. To understand and communicate positioning and branding values, qualitative research is usually essential for larger companies.

Most qualitative studies commence with exploratory or open-ended research in which small samples of carefully targeted individuals are asked to express their views. This may be done on a one-to-one basis or in a focus group where interaction between a small group of individuals is part of the research process. The interviewer or focus group leader is typically an experienced researcher, often with some training in social psychology. He is responsible for introducing the subjects for discussion and encouraging views but not imposing any preconceived ideas. What emerges, recorded for analysis on tape, is a discussion in consumers' own words concerning what matters to them. Summarizing an hour-long tape and producing two or three pages on the main attitudes emerging is much harder than it sounds and it involves considerable skills and experience.

By definition, individual and focus group sessions cannot be quantitative because the ideas are not tied down to structured questionnaires or based on adequate samples of the target group. They are often used, however, to structure subsequent quantitative surveys, or they can be used in their own right to help marketing managers understand the ways in which existing and potential customers think, and what matters to them.

In recent years, given adequate continuous quantification of the main patterns of visitor profiles and behaviour using databases as explained above, qualitative research has been more widely used. It is expensive but relatively quick to implement and especially useful in image and branding development, designing advertising messages, websites and brochure contents in ways best calculated to communicate with prospective customers in their own terms.

Primary and secondary

Primary data, covering both quantitative and qualitative data, is the label applied to marketing research that is specifically commissioned by a business to contribute to its decisions. It requires the gathering of data not available from any other (secondary) source. For example, a survey commissioned by one airline to study the current attitudes of business travellers towards its own and other airlines competing on the same route, would be primary data.

Secondary data are information gathered originally for a purpose not related to the needs of a particular business, but which may be used by it as part of its market information system. All published sources, including Internet usage data, government statistics, trade association surveys and commercial publishers' market surveys, represent secondary data.

Common sense dictates that it will always be quicker and cheaper to obtain and use secondary rather than primary data. For any decision requiring research information, initial investigation should always begin at the secondary level before proceeding, if necessary, with primary research. The more efficient a marketing information system based on secondary data is, the less need there may be to commission (and wait for) expensive new data.

Omnibus and syndicated

Not only in travel and tourism, but also in consumer markets generally, large market research companies operate their own regular (continuous) sample surveys and sell space in them to a range of customers. Such surveys are known technically as 'omnibus' surveys because they are potentially open to all users. Where an organization seeks answers, say, to just four or five key questions, it may be possible to get access to a nationally representative sample of 2000 adults for a tenth of the cost of commissioning its own survey. For the price, a client would not only get answers to his specific questions but also fully cross-tabulated data, using profile characteristics, such as age, postcodes and readership of media, which are a standard part of any 'omnibus' survey. The United Kingdom Tourism Survey (UKTS) is probably the best-known survey of UK tourism. Until recently it was in fact a series of questions asked regularly throughout the year on a national weekly omnibus survey. Jointly sponsored by VisitBritain, VisitScotland, Visit Wales and the Northern Ireland Tourist Board, the UKTS is a national consumer survey designed to measure the volume (visits and nights spent), expenditure on visits and the main characteristics of tourism visits taken by UK residents. The characteristics covered include choice of accommodation, transport mode and areas and type of destinations visited. The survey measures visits away from home lasting one night or more for the purpose of holidays, visits to friends and relatives, business and conferences, and other purposes. The data is cross-tabulated by the usual range of socio-demographic profile data. Reflecting concerns about the reliability of its data, UKTS has undergone a series of methodology changes this century and is expected to change again as this book goes to press. There are other omnibus surveys available, covering not only adults in general but many specific segments, such as motorists, business travellers, frequent users of hotels, and so on.

Syndicated surveys serve much the same purpose as omnibus surveys but are usually commissioned by a group of clients on a cost-sharing basis. The regular survey of customer value for money and satisfaction, co-ordinated for its members by the Association of Leading Visitor Attractions (ALVA) in the UK since the late 1990s, is an interesting example. Members not only share costs and receive details for their own attraction; they also gain access to relevant comparisons with competitor sectors in the context of overall trends in the attractions market.

Both omnibus and syndicated studies provide cost-effective forms of research, especially for smaller businesses, for whom the costs of an ad hoc survey would usually be prohibitive. By using such studies, firms can also obtain technical assistance from research agencies with the wording of questions and interpretation of results. The omnibus method is especially suitable for achieving quantified results much faster than would be possible with ad hoc surveys.

Occupancy studies

In any developed country, the travel and tourism sector nationally or regionally typically comprises hundreds or even thousands of different businesses, most of which have no direct contacts with each other. There is no easy way in which destination managers, tourist boards or even trade associations such as hotels can know what is happening in the sector in terms of monthly or quarterly business trends. Trends could be obtained from surveys of consumers but, as noted earlier, these are highly expensive and would take months to process. Key trend information for marketing planning and strategic decisions is typically, therefore, not available in the tourism sector. A common solution is to recruit a small but representative sample of businesses in a sector such as hotels and ask them to maintain daily records, for example, of arrivals and departures and rates paid by the main segments of the market they deal with. These data can be analysed to provide a rich source of data for marketing planning purposes that can be measured on a weekly, monthly or quarterly basis. They can be communicated to the sector as a whole to help their own decision-making. When the results are grossed up to represent the industry sector as a whole they provide valuable supply side indicators of trends to be interpreted alongside results of consumer surveys. The samples are not often easy to recruit and there is always fall-out over time but the methodology is valuable and well tested. Similar methodology based on small business samples can be used to assess customer satisfaction levels with the range of experiences they receive. Far from perfect, these occupancy studies with parallels for monitoring trends in attractions, can provide vital early warnings by detecting shifts from normal trading patterns that require a marketing response.

A MENU OF MARKETING RESEARCH METHODS

Drawing together the different categories of marketing research noted earlier and the research methodologies that are commonly used, it is possible to present the wide range of methods available to any business as a 'menu'. This 'menu' or tool kit is a listing of research techniques from which it is possible to make a selection according to need and circumstances. Each technique is available at a price. The menu, in a form relevant to businesses in travel and tourism services, is shown in Table 9.2. The menu concept is developed from papers originally presented on a UK Market Research Society training course. It is important to stress that the menu means prospective users can select items according to their needs and budget. Only large organizations with in-house research staff are likely to need or be able to use all the items over a period of 12 months.

TABLE 9.2 The marketing research menu or tool kit

A. Desk research (secondary sources)

1. Sales/bookings/reservations records; daily, weekly, etc. by type of customer, type of product, etc.
2. Visitor information record, e.g. guest registration cards, booking form data, call centre or website data
3. Government publications/trade association data/national tourist office data/abstracts and libraries
4. Commercial analyses available on subscription or purchase of reports
5. Previous research studies conducted; internal data bank
6. Press cuttings of competitor activities, market environment changes

B. Qualitative or exploratory research

1. Organized marketing intelligence, such as staff feedback, sales-force reports, attendance at exhibitions and trade shows
2. Focus group discussions and individual interviews with targeted customers/non-users, especially to identify the perceptions and attitudes of key users and non-user groups
3. Observational studies of visitor behaviour, using cameras, electronic beams or trained observers
4. Marketing experiments with monitored results

C. Quantitative research (syndicated)

1. Omnibus questions to targeted respondents
2. Syndicated surveys, including audits

D. Quantitative research (ad hoc and continuous)

1. Studies of travel and tourism behaviour and usage/activity patterns
2. Attitude, image, perception and awareness studies
3. Advertising and other media response studies
4. Customer satisfaction, value for money and product monitoring studies
5. Distribution studies amongst the range of distribution channels being used or investigated for future use

Using the 'menu': a holiday-park operator

To help explain the possible selective use of the menu in travel and tourism practice, consider a holiday-park business with eight parks comprising a mix of owned holiday home lodges and caravans with, using notional figures, 1000 caravans and other units for let on a weekly or part-weekly basis. The turnover from the holiday lets would justify a budget of around £50,000 at most, even for a proactive marketing owner. Such a budget could be deployed as follows:

A1. A computerized database would show forward bookings for each park on a weekly basis, with analyses of areas from which bookings flow, postcodes of bookers, type of caravan most or least in demand, size of party, repeat business, etc. Many of these data would be collected automatically through the process of keeping business accounts and setting up customer invoices. Profiles of customers using a website or using a call centre would be part of this process.

A2. On a continuous or a sample basis, customers checking in on arrival could be asked to provide simple key information establishing, for example, how they heard of the park, whether the park website or brochure was seen and used, and the number of repeat visits (if any).

A3. Published results of tourist board surveys would throw useful light on trends for the self-catering market nationally and by region. Occasional other inexpensive analyses of the self-catering market would be available from time to time (*A4*). B2B websites and trade journals for the holiday parks and caravan industry provide valuable insights into current events and trends in the market (*A6*).

A5. Previous years' records (as in *A1* and *A2*) would provide valuable benchmarks against which to view current patterns on a weekly or monthly basis.

B1. There are numerous trade shows and travel workshops available for the holiday-park operators, as well as national conferences. All provide opportunities to gain market intelligence and to learn what others in the industry are doing, especially in terms of park design, accommodation unit design, product presentation in brochures, and so on.

Assuming that management time is excluded from the cost, and that business records are a by-product of essential Internet operation and accounting procedures, the cost of information collected up to this point would be measured in hundreds rather than thousands of pounds. To proceed beyond this point calls for more significant expenditure, to be set off against the expected value of results:

B2. Not affordable on an annual basis in this example, the decision to renew the main brochure and website communications could repay discussion of alternative covers, contents and formats conducted with small focus groups of existing and prospective clients. Such group discussions would also generate ideas and concepts for advertising and image presentation. With 1000 units to let, this operator might distribute 150,000 brochures per annum so that up to £20,000 on group discussions could be productive spread over a 3-year brochure life span, assessed against sales revenue achievable. The same research would help to identify ways to develop and communicate on the park owner's websites.

B3. If, for example, the capacity and quality of showers and laundry facilities were judged to be an issue at one or more of the parks, cameras or simple observation of queues and their reactions would be a cheap but effective form of research before any investment is made.

B4. In terms of pricing, different advertising formats, and product developments, e.g. mini-breaks, this holiday-park operator is perfectly placed to engage in systematic test marketing and monitoring (see later in this chapter) at low cost.

C2. Park owners of this type may be able to purchase packs of printed, standardized, self-completion questionnaires, organized for them by their trade association and designed by a commercial market research agency. Owners would be responsible for distributing and ensuring completion by samples of visitors, and collecting questionnaires. The price per thousand of using these standard questionnaire forms (similar in concept to those used by tour operators to measure customer satisfaction at the end of a holiday) would usually be less than 10% of the cost of conducting surveys with trained interviewers on site. These forms may be designed for electronic scanning directly into computers to reduce the costs still further.

D4. Of all the research options, *D4* would be particularly important for this type of operator. Administered either as part of a syndicated (*C2*) survey or as a separate entity during, say, six selected weeks of the operating year, measuring satisfaction and value for money would probably account for the largest portion of annual marketing research expenditure in this example. E-mailed questionnaires to customers who booked on websites offer a much lower cost option and are now widely used. Analysed by type of product, customer segments, time of year and in association with any test marketing initiatives, the value of this research in marketing planning would be considerable. Tracking and analysing the trends in customer reaction over time are essential data for strategic planning.

MINI CASE 9.1 THE BALEARICS TOURISM SECTOR SURVEY (2004)

An illustration of an industry collaboration research methodology is provided in Fig. 9.1 in the mini case study below. It was undertaken in 2004 by the Centre of Tourism Research and Technologies of the Balearic Islands under the auspices of the Organization for Economic Co-ordination and Development (OECD).

In the Balearic Islands nearly 80% of businesses belong to the service sector and are engaged in activities that are either directly or indirectly related to the tourism industry. In undertaking tourism research, therefore, it was critical that a research sample had to be carefully defined. With OECD involvement, the criteria for selection were identified as

1. Enterprises clearly representative of tourism in the Balearic Islands. As a result of its importance and its representative role, or its innovation or its wide and deeply rooted tradition, each enterprise should have an obvious and significant weight within the tourism business framework of the Balearic Islands.
2. Enterprises complying with the above requisite, which should, by virtue of their size, also configure a valid and representative sample of the different sized companies existing in the Balearic Islands.
3. Enterprises whose specialization in their sphere made them representative of the different tourism products supplied by the Balearic Islands as a destination.

The sample comprised 25 enterprises and the response rate was 72%. Figure 9.1 illustrates the processes that were undertaken to develop the research. The key findings indicated that the enterprises regarded the following as being highly important:

- The brand name is the most important attribute, in spite of its intangible nature.
- The buildings and the surrounding environment.
- And lastly its information systems and know-how.

The most important attributes in each sector are indicated below.

In the accommodation sector, the key important attributes were

- Service by the personnel
- Location and facilities
- Quality and excellence in the service
- Brand and know-how
- Customer satisfaction and individual treatment

In the travel agencies sector the most important attributes were

- Personalized service
- After-sales service
- Quality

In the transport sector the key attributes were

- Security
- Quality

In the leisure and catering sector it was

- The human team

Each area works within the tourism value chain and in terms of relative lifecycles the enterprises aimed to position themselves as shown in Fig. 9.1.

Courtesy of Dimitrios Buhalis.

This research was used to help the organizations to understand how to develop their markets and marketing strategies.

Source: http://www.oecd.org/dataoecd/44/56/40122412.pdf.

The Centre of Tourism Research and Technologies of the Balearic Islands undertook the study, which took approximately 1 month. Members of the Board of Directors were interviewed in every case. The average length of each interview was two and a half hours. The above case is one illustration of the way in which collaborative market research can be carried out across different sectors and the impact it can have on particular locations.

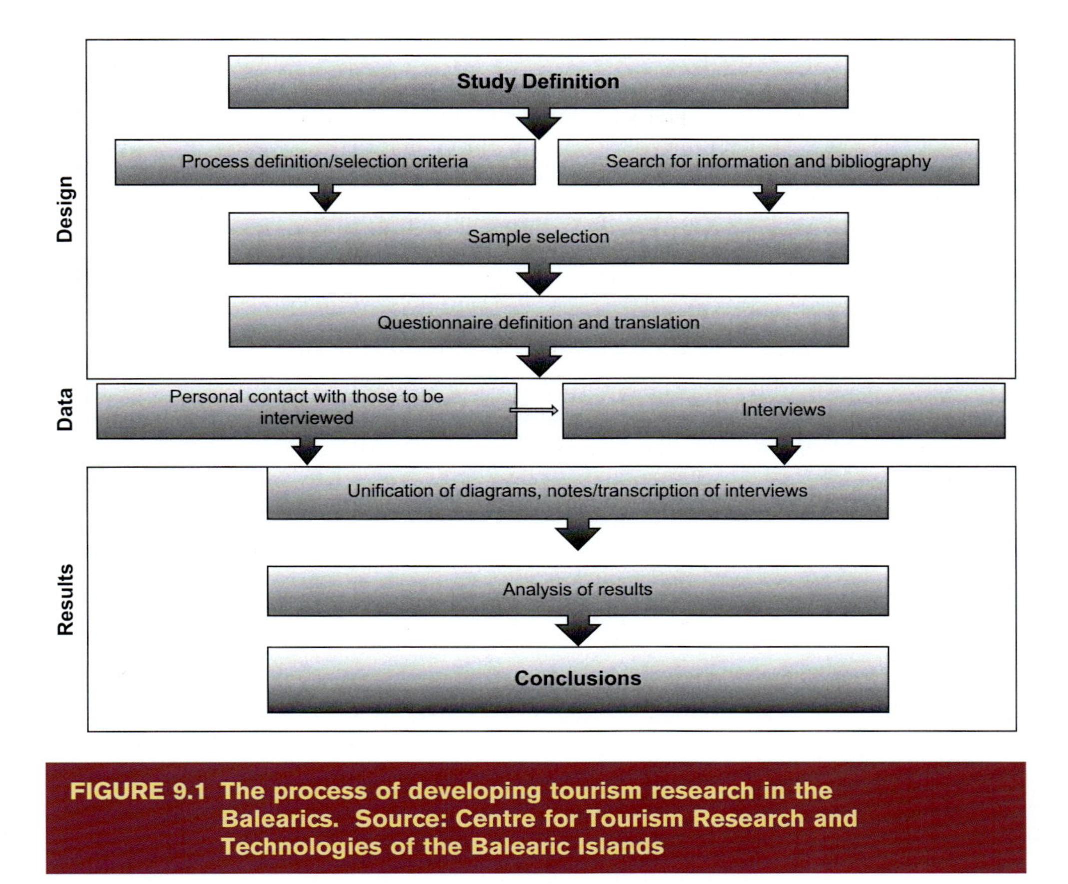

FIGURE 9.1 The process of developing tourism research in the Balearics. Source: Centre for Tourism Research and Technologies of the Balearic Islands

COMMISSIONING A MARKET RESEARCH AGENCY

While most marketing managers are expected to be competent in the analysis of marketing research data, relatively few will also be engaged in organizing and conducting surveys. Large organizations such as airlines, tourist boards and major hotel corporations have their own research departments. But most survey work will be commissioned from specialist market research agencies, of which there were some 2000 in the UK alone in 2008 to choose from. It is therefore important that marketing managers should be aware of what agencies do and how to get the best response from them.

In the UK the Market Research Society (MRS) is the professional body for all individuals using survey techniques for market, social and economic research. With some 7000 members, in some 70 countries the MRS is the largest professional body of its kind in the world (MRS website, 2008) and it has developed and published detailed codes of professional conduct over many years. These codes are designed to protect and enhance the integrity with which research is practiced, and to safeguard the interests of the general public and clients as well as the interests of agencies offering research services. Similar codes exist in several other European countries.

In research, as in most of marketing practice, the best way to achieve cost-effective work is to specify the problem with as much precision as possible, setting it in its wider marketing context. Unless a client and an agency have worked together on a regular basis, it is unlikely that agencies asked to quote for surveys will be experts on the client's business. Unless the budget is unusually large in travel and tourism terms, there will not be many hours available for the agency first to absorb the key details of the clients' current marketing information (expressed as 'diagnosis' and 'prognosis' in Chapter 11 on the use of research data in marketing planning) and the objectives of its marketing programmes. The agency will need a helpful initial brief. Time spent learning about the business will be time not available for developing the research approach.

'Problems' in marketing are seldom clear-cut. They are frequently matters of perception and judgement and two managers may well see the same problem in different ways. Time spent systematically analysing the problem, therefore, is seldom wasted. It focuses managers' minds and often changes the way the problem is perceived, or switches attention to a different problem area not at first sight apparent. An essential part of the process of thinking through the problem is a realistic consideration of how the survey results are to be used in the business. For example, if a survey of visitors to a visitor attraction is required to reveal ways to achieve higher spending in shops on site, the agency must be given details of current retail sales policies and detailed trading results before they design their research methodology and the questions to be asked. The expected use of results also determines the nature of the questions to be asked, but surprisingly few research buyers recognize this basic truth when defining the 'problem'.

Problem specification, together with other information noted in Table 9.3, should always be put in writing and filed for future reference. At this stage, with a clearly expressed 'research brief', clients can approach agencies and invite them to tender for the work. Where an agency's work is well known to a client, competitive tendering may be unnecessary. Where it is not, it is usual practice to invite a maximum of three or four agencies to submit tenders, informing them that others have been approached. The commercial market research world is highly competitive and tendering is the usual route to new business.

Preparing tenders is a costly process for agencies; it may take several days' work for larger projects. Unless otherwise agreed the cost of research tenders is not charged but absorbed as a business overhead. In preparing a tender the agency would normally expect at least one meeting to clarify and interpret the way the problem is expressed in the client's brief. Through experience with similar problems, agencies may well be able to restate the problem or illuminate it in ways not obvious to the client. They may also have access to secondary data not known to clients, which can considerably reduce the costs of primary research.

TABLE 9.3 Basic requirements of client and agency in commissioning marketing research

The client brief
Identifies the marketing context and perceived problem to be researched
Specifies the expected use of results
Indicates the timescale for completion
States the approximate budget limits
The agency tender
Defines or redefines the problem in research terms
Proposes a methodology relevant to the problem
Specifies a realistic programme for completion, including client liaison
Recommends a reporting format and procedure
Sets out the terms and conditions of business, including costs and timing of payments
Specifies personnel involved, their qualifications and experience, and their respective involvement in the proposed study
Indicates agency experience relevant to the problem, including reference to previous studies and other clients whose needs were broadly comparable

Tenders should cover all the points noted in Table 9.3, and clients will often find broad similarity in the methods and costs proposed by competing agencies. Accordingly, selecting which agency to use will normally be based on the extent to which each one demonstrates comprehension of the problem, and the effectiveness and creativity of the proposed methods of tackling it within stipulated budget limits. A proven track record in travel and tourism research may be helpful but much more important is the quality of the rapport between the client and agency. This will be evident from the first meeting and reflected in the tenders. It will always be wise for clients to meet the research executive directly responsible for their job as well as the agency director or senior researcher who is likely to produce and present the tender. If meetings are necessary, visiting the agency's premises will often reveal much more about the nature and quality of its operation than the usual glossy brochure with its predictable claims of all-round excellence and deep expertise.

Successful research depends on trust between the client and agency akin to that which develops between advertising agency and client (though on a smaller scale). Reputable agencies will normally reveal names of previous clients and it is quite usual for prospective clients to talk in confidence to previous clients about their experiences with particular agencies.

CUSTOMER ACCESS: A PRICELESS ASSET OF SERVICE BUSINESSES

A massive potential research advantage inherent in marketing most service products in travel and tourism is the presence of customers on producers' premises. In the authors' view it is a grossly underestimated advantage.

Anyone who has owned, worked or been brought up in a small business, such as a hotel, travel agency, restaurant, pub or caravan park, will recognize the powerful immediacy of customer contact. They will know the ease with which it is possible to detect (or impossible to avoid) evidence of customer needs, behaviour and satisfactions or complaints. Such businesses hardly need market research surveys because, in a very real way, their customer knowledge and 'feedback' are more immediate, better, more natural and more continuous than any researcher, self-completion questionnaire or database could ever provide.

Once a business grows large enough to have multiple units, however, or is run by managers generally remote from day to day customer contact, direct customer-management communication is lost. The Board of Directors of an airline or large hotel company may not speak at all to customers for months or years and, if they do, may so intimidate them as to negate any research value of the contact. In these management circumstances systematic research is necessary but it can still take advantage of the inherent benefits of customer/product inseparability and the relative ease of communication 'on site' or 'in-house'.

By contrast, manufacturers of most consumer goods usually have either no contact at all with their customers, who purchase anonymously in retail outlets, or at best have access to names and addresses provided for warranty or servicing purposes. Knowledge of who is surfing their websites and using call centres is now assisting manufacturers to know more about their final consumers but in travel and tourism all making enquiries and booking services in advance immediately and automatically supply useful marketing information about themselves as part of the process. Visitors using commercial accommodation sign registers and/or enter details on a registration card. Airline customers spend many hours waiting in terminals and in planes for their journeys to start or to end. Visitors to attractions stroll around reception areas and car parks, travel agencies have many opportunities to seek out and record customers' needs and interests, and so on. At the start of the new century it is quite extraordinary that with the exception of some large tour operators and a very small proportion of other large companies, these easy opportunities for research are for the most part still overlooked and certainly underutilized.

Similarly, all service producers with customers on the premises have a major opportunity to organize internal research both with customers and especially in gaining marketing intelligence feedback from staff with direct customer contact. Researching the knowledge as well as the attitudes of employees provides a valuable stream of marketing decision information that is also often overlooked.

RESEARCHING CUSTOMER SATISFACTION AND VALUE FOR MONEY

Using their on-site customers to good effect, large tour operators typically hand out self-completion customer satisfaction questionnaires to all travellers returning from holidays abroad, generally on the flight home. Such questionnaires request rating of all aspects of the holiday, using numeric scales such as 4 = excellent, 3 = good, 2 = fair and 1 = poor, which can also be communicated by words or cartoons. The responses can then be computer-processed to produce numerical ratings or scores. From this information, if plotted on a week-by-week basis, it is possible to detect comparative satisfaction with individual resorts and hotels, check the performance of specific flights or evaluate customer appreciation of particular aspects of products such as food, excursions or the service provided by resort representatives.

Because 'profile information' is included in the questionnaire, it is possible to analyse satisfaction and value for money by age of respondent, region of origin, postal codes, cost of package, and so on. These questionnaires, mostly scanned and processed by computers, provide a vast range of continuous management information. Such information is both a management control tool for service operations and a fertile database for marketing mix decisions, such as product formulation and pricing. Airlines use in-flight survey questionnaires in the same way for the same purposes. So do some hotel companies and major attractions. In the UK, Thomson Holidays (now TUI) first used customer satisfaction questionnaires in 1972, well ahead of their competitors. By the mid-1990s they had processed over 12 million forms, using the information systematically to retain their competitive edge as a market leader.

Questionnaires to visitors are not welcome in all businesses, however, and the use of so-called *mystery shoppers* is an alternative research technique whereby multi-site service providers can evaluate and compare the quality of their service delivery over the full range of their sites. The technique is widely used, especially in the accommodation and restaurant sectors of the tourism industry. Provided they are systematically organized, mystery buyers of meals, rooms, users of call centres and front-of-house telephone systems, can provide vital insights into the quality of service delivery systems, exploring both the weaknesses and the strengths of service provision (See also Chapter 8.)

Link article available at www.routledge.com/9780750686938

(1) Oh, H., Kim, B., Shin, J., December 2004. Hospitality and tourism marketing: recent developments in research and future directions. International Journal of Hospitality Management 23 (5), 425–447.

OPPORTUNITIES FOR RESEARCHING MARKETING INNOVATIONS

Especially with multi-site operations, the opportunities for managers to innovate and test market service products are virtually limitless. A hotel corporation might, for example, vary menus and prices, vary the formality of food service, offer new facilities for business or leisure customers, change room furniture and decor or promote a particular type of inclusive weekend-break product. Provided always that the results are measured in enquiries and sales, and that satisfaction is monitored, there are many opportunities to carry out 'live' market research through conducting controlled marketing tests. Through a process crudely but accurately dubbed 'suck it and see', most service producers can test, learn and modify product developments on a limited scale before wider implementation in other sites or premises.

Tour operators can offer new destinations or new product types in the pages of an existing brochure or trial them in pages on the Internet (see below). If the development is popular and sells well, it can often be extended quickly and modified as necessary by evidence gained from customer satisfaction questionnaires. This 'learning' opportunity to set up and read the results of marketing tests at low cost is usually not available to manufacturers of physical goods, especially where powerful retailers control distribution outlets and the shelf space allocated to producers. Test marketing of physical goods is generally a far more costly and time-consuming process than test marketing of services.

If they approach the issue systematically, most businesses in travel and tourism can create an almost infinite range of opportunities to experiment and monitor. Above all they can build up their marketing knowledge of buyer behaviour by obtaining relatively inexpensive feedback from the customers using their premises. These are powerful opportunities for cost-effective marketing research, which other industries must envy.

Since the start of this century consumer access to the Internet and corporate websites has provided a whole new medium for research and innovation. It makes the process of testing product and segment options relatively easy and cheap to organize. Even more importantly, it provides almost instant and continuous feedback from customers. The combination of Internet experimentation with systematic on site/in premises research is a very powerful marketing tool indeed.

CHAPTER SUMMARY

This chapter:

- Identifies the role of marketing research and its value as the essential information base for making effective marketing decisions. It explains the main categories of marketing research that practitioners in travel and tourism are most likely to encounter and describes the commonly used survey techniques. In particular, it draws a distinction between continuous and ad hoc research, 'continuous' implying the creation and use of databases organized as marketing information systems for marketing decision purposes, a very important development explained further in Chapter 11.

- Indicates how the different types of market research can be used in practice drawing on a 'menu' of options summarized in Table 9.2, which may serve with Table 9.3 as a useful checklist for those who have to commission research to fulfil particular purposes. In practice each method has strengths and weaknesses that vary according to the company undertaking the research, the size of its budget and the particular decisions they have to make. The combined use of several methods is normal, as noted in the holiday-park example.
- Highlights the remarkable scope in practice that all travel and tourism businesses have for experimentation in the marketing mix. Combined with detailed monitoring of results, market testing is a particular form of low cost research that is relevant in a strategic as well as a tactical context. Innovation through market testing exploits the advantages of having customers on business premises or sites and it is greatly facilitated by recent Information and Communications Technology (ICT) developments, especially the Internet. Innovation is now even easier 'off site' by making virtual offers possible in a primary promotion and distribution channel that incorporates immediate evaluation of customer response.
- Stresses that marketing research is used to throw light on marketing decisions and reduce the level of risk and uncertainty associated with them. But it does not and cannot replace the essential quality of judgement from managers.

QUESTIONS TO CONSIDER

1. For a medium to large-scale travel and tourism business of your choice, draw up a menu of research methods that could help its marketing decisions.
2. Why are qualitative market research techniques becoming more important?
3. As the Internet is becoming a widely used way to book holidays, how can it help in market research?
4. Elaborate the key processes that are required in submitting a tender for market research.
5. Explain how market research can help to segment customers.

REFERENCES AND SUGGESTED READING

Baker, M.J. (1996). *Marketing: an introductory text*. Chapter 10 (6th edn). Macmillan.

Brassington, F. and Pettit, S. (2000). *Principles of marketing* (3rd edn). FT Prentice-Hall.

Carson, D., Gilmore, A. and Gronhaug, K. (2001). *Qualitative marketing research*. SAGE.

Crouch, S. and Housden, M. (1996). *Marketing research for managers* (2nd edn). Butterworth-Heinemann.

Jobber, D. (2007). *Principles and practice of marketing* (5th edn). McGraw-Hill.

Kotler, P. and Armstrong, G. (1999). *Principles of marketing*. Chapter 1 (8th edn). Prentice-Hall.

Kotler, P., Wong, V., Saunders, J. and Armstrong, G. (2005). *Principles of marketing* (4th European edn). Pearson Prentice Hall.

Moutinho, L. (2000). Tourism marketing research. In: (Ed by Moutinho, L.), *Strategic Management in Tourism*. CABI Publishing.

Oh, H., Kim, B. and Shin, J. (December 2004). Hospitality and tourism marketing: recent developments in research and future directions, *International Journal of Hospitality Management*, **23**(5), pp. 425–447.

Ronald, A. Nykiel (2006). *Handbook of marketing research methodologies for hospitality and tourism*. New York: The Haworth Hospitality & Tourism Press. 368 p.

Wright, L.T. and Crimp, M. (2000). *The marketing research process* (5th edn). Financial Times/Prentice-Hall.

Branding reduces perceived risk for the consumer at the point of purchase by signalling the expected quality and performance of an intangible product.

Courtesy of www.baa.com/photolibrary

CHAPTER 10

Planning marketing strategy

The future is now. The short term and the long term don't abut one another with a clear line of demarcation five years from now. The short term and the long term are tightly intertwined.

(Hamel and Prahalad, 1996: 30)

A strategy is a plan for an organization that sets the overall direction to be taken. It is broad in scope and takes a long-term perspective. Within this strategy there has to be flexibility to adapt short-term plans to deal with unforeseen circumstances. In marketing, strategy involves directing all of a company's resources to meet customers' needs. This is achieved through market analysis, an understanding of competitor actions, governmental actions and the global business environment, together with the implications of technological and environmental changes. The management of these complex inter-relationships is vital within the travel and tourism sector.

Strategic marketing planning involves careful analysis of an organization's environment, its competitors and its internal strengths, in order to develop a sustainable plan of action which will develop the organization's competitive advantage and maximize its performance within given resource availability.

(Ranchhod and Gurau, 2008)

Today, strategic planning needs also to consider the ethical and ecological implications of the company's actions, and to be flexible enough to adapt to rapid changes in the business and social environment. As this book is being written the greatest global financial and economic crisis since the Great Depression of the 1930s is being played out. Companies that planned on maintaining the continuous economic growth of the early years of the twenty-first century now have to revise their plans rapidly to adapt to this unprecedented downturn.

In the face of such uncertainties, and there have been several in the last two decades, the focus of strategic management over the last 20 years has changed. Until the 1980s, relatively stable models of growth were in place and strategic marketing was very much concerned with planning. Over the last two decades the advent of the Internet has changed the planning model considerably with companies having to adapt to faster changing markets. This has rendered pointless many of the long-range econometric forecasting models that developed with computer modelling techniques in the 1980s. Old concepts of 'top-down' centralized head office planning departments for large organizations do not work in modern market conditions and new models of delegated planning for separate sectors of a business (known as strategic business units or areas – SBUs or SBAs) have emerged. These new approaches heighten the need for corporate vision, leadership, co-ordination and support, at the same time restricting the direct involvement of corporate headquarter staff in day-to-day operations.

Strategic marketing planning is just one of the core business functions contributing to an organization's corporate strategy. In a customer-orientated organization, however, marketing is a dominant element because of its focus on balancing the delivery of customer satisfaction and value with the generation of sales revenue. Marketing also has a vital contribution to make in the formation of the corporate vision for the future, through its role in interpreting customers needs' and market trends.

After studying this chapter you should be able to understand:

- The need for planning within the tourism sector.
- The key components of the strategic planning process.
- The place of marketing within the overall corporate strategy.
- What is involved in analysing the external environment and the competitive forces in the market.
- How marketing strategies are based on competitive positioning and how that positioning is communicated through effective branding.

This chapter deals with marketing planning at the strategic level, while Chapters 11 and 12 develop the actual planning process in more detail focusing on shorter-term action plans for effective marketing campaigns.

THE NEED FOR STRATEGIC PLANNING

In many companies the very notion of strategy has become devalued... what is being rejected is strategy as pedantic planning ritual... Strategy as foresight, architecture and intent, and industry redefinition to create new competitive space, is the greatest value added that senior management can contribute. (Hamel and Prahalad, 1994: 308)

To provide vision for the future, leadership and an agreed framework for the conduct of business in an ever more rapidly changing and globally competitive market environment, it is essential for any organization to plan its activities. The larger the business and the more products and markets with which it has to deal, the deeper its need to understand the nature of future change and competition, and the greater the importance of effective planning processes. The more volatile a market is in terms of monthly and annual fluctuations in customer demand, the more important it is to work within a framework of agreed objectives.

In travel and tourism, years of market growth have often tended to obscure the perceived need for planning, although discontinuities in market trends, unpredicted economic recessions and sudden market decline bring planning issues sharply into focus. The current issues surrounding globalization, mergers, strategic alliances and investment in new developments – or response to business failures – also heighten the focus on strategic decision processes. Strategic thinking is also an essential part of the process by which organizations convince their investors and other stakeholders about the directions they seek to pursue.

In essence, any strategy comprises a statement of goals and objectives, a framework of resources needed and a programme of activity intended to achieve the goals. In all but the smallest companies, setting the goals will require market research and analysis, and the programmes of activity will have to be costed and monitored to work out how well the objectives are actually achieved. All planning is conducted on the assumption that the effort in time and money is essential to produce profitable results and an increasing recognition that future growth must be planned and prepared for now and implemented over several years.

Managers will recognize how these simple truths tend to disappear in the complexities of planning analysis and techniques, but students should hold on to this simple definition in understanding this chapter.

A MODEL OF THE STRATEGIC PLANNING PROCESS

Stripped of its mystery and techniques, all forms of strategic corporate planning attempt to answer four outward looking questions:

- Where are we now, in the industry and market spaces we occupy?
- What opportunities are emerging in a changing world, which we could develop and aim to lead?
- Where do we want our organization to be in 5 or more years' time?
- What decisions do we have to make now to get to where we want to be?

The four questions lead naturally to the idea of a *position*, meaning the 'place' that an organization occupies in an industry sector compared with its competitors and in the minds or perceptions of customers and prospective customers (see later in this chapter). The questions also help to explain three concepts in corporate planning (adapted from Davidson, 1975: 109):

- Vision, goals and objectives (where do we want to be?).
- Strategies (chosen routes for achieving goals).
- Plans (action programmes for moving along the route and evaluating achievement against targets).

Although the formality of the process is obviously very different, these strategic planning questions are as relevant to small businesses as to large ones. For marketing purposes, strategic planning may be defined as the process whereby an organization

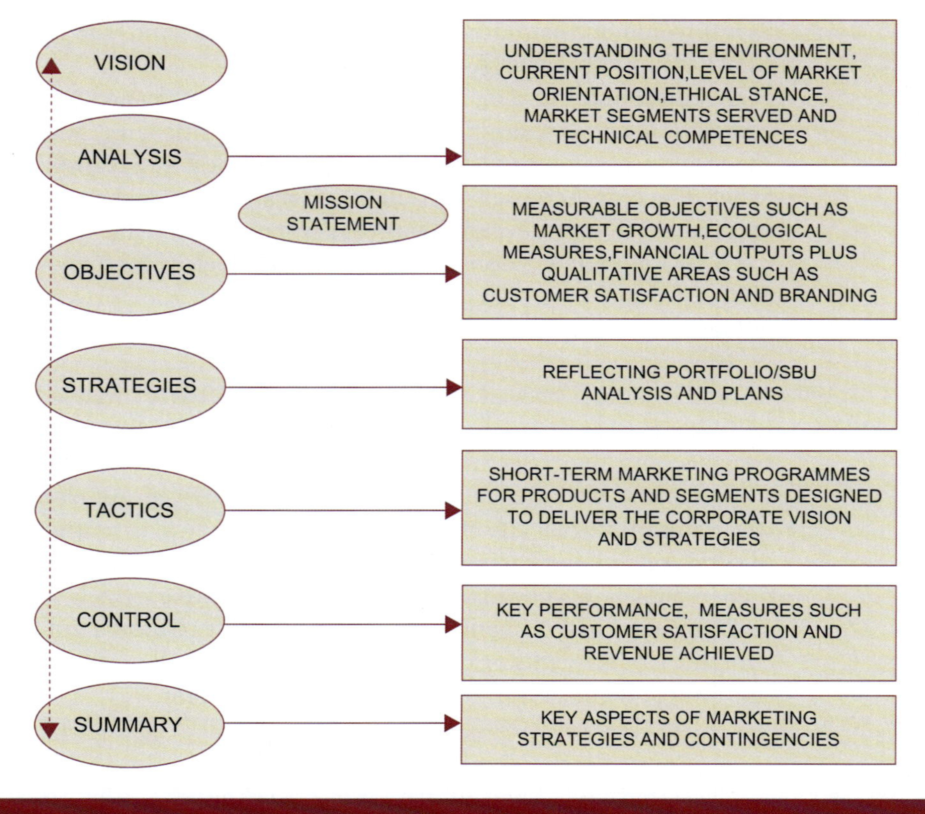

FIGURE 10.1 The key stages in developing marketing strategies. Adapted from Ranchhod and Gurau (2007)

analyses its strengths and weaknesses in its current and prospective markets, identifies its aims and the opportunities it seeks to develop, and specifies strategies and costed programmes of activity to achieve its aims. Figure 10.1 illustrates the key stages within the marketing strategy development process. The stages illustrated in the figure are discussed in this and in the next two chapters. The stages are

- Vision
- Analysis
- Objectives
- Strategies
- Implementation
- Tactics
- Control

Strategic decisions are always focused on the longer run, usually defined as 3 or more years ahead and looking wider than the existing range of products provided for a current group of segments. For larger, global corporations a timescale of up to 20 years may be needed to achieve strategic goals that involve major investment decisions and the development of new technology. Larger organizations with multiple products in multiple markets, such as hotel chains or international car rental companies, also require strategic planning to achieve effective relationships and allocation of resources between the component parts of their businesses. The co-ordination of these 'strategic business units' is discussed later in this chapter.

Strategy aims to be proactive in the sense that it defines and wills the future shape of the organization as well as responding to changing industry patterns, technology, market conditions and perceived consumer needs.

VISION AND MISSION

Strategic planning should be founded on the mission and the values of the organization.

Corporate values drive the purpose and strategy of a company with the objectives being actionable and measurable (such as customer satisfaction and service quality). The Ashridge model shown in Fig. 10.2 illustrates the key areas that shape the mission or values of an organization. These are

(a) *Why a company exists*. In tourism-related industries companies exist to provide a service to consumers in areas such as flights, cruises, hotels, historical sites, etc. These services enable the consumers to enjoy unique and memorable leisure experiences or to achieve their business objectives.

(b) *What the company believes in*. Each company will have its own set of beliefs about how it engages with the consumer. British Airways sees itself as embodying traditional British quality. Virgin sees itself as the fresh-thinking challenger to conventional competitors. Ryanair and other budget airlines believe in making travel affordable to a wider market.

(c) *The competitive position and distinctive competence*. Companies may have certain competences be they competences related to the service provision or to the speed at which they can satisfy the customer. Each company may specialize in particular competences and competitively position itself that way. To achieve

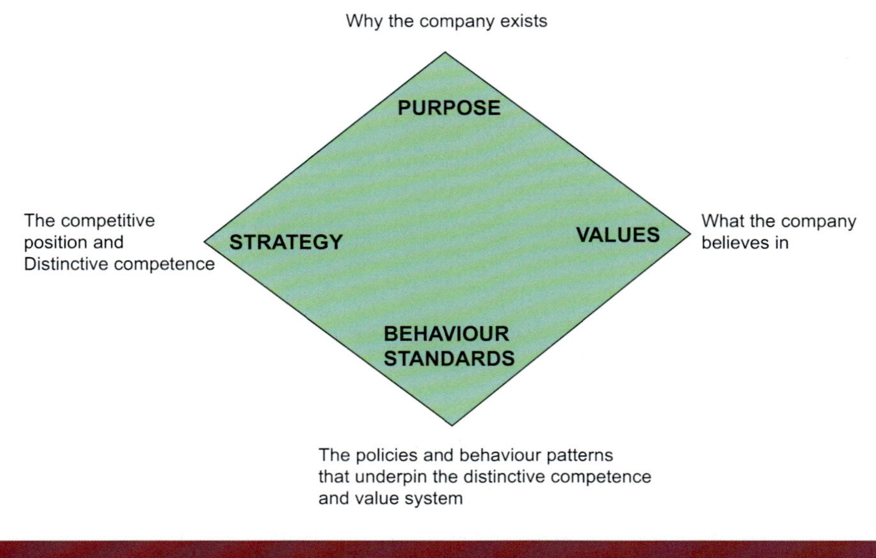

FIGURE 10.2 Corporate purpose, values, policies and positioning: the Ashridge Model

its low-cost leadership position, Ryanair has developed a business model based on high utilization of aircraft, use of cheaper secondary airports and direct distribution over the Internet.

(d) *The policies and behaviour patterns that underpin the distinctive competence and value system*. Companies tend to create a set of behaviour patterns and also set the culture within the organization that sets the tone of how individuals interact with the consumer. For instance for years Singapore Airlines has won awards for the way in which treats its customers.

The vision of a company is often expressed in a formal Mission Statement which communicates to all employees what the company stands for. In tourism, for instance, Thomas Cook's mission statement embodies in modern day terms, the values of its Founder Thomas Cook a former Baptist preacher and Temperance supporter. The company was launched in the dawn of the railway era in 1841.

Thomas Cook's mission is to:

Perfect the Personal Leisure Experience. As part of this mission the company is committed to working towards developing, operating and marketing our business in a sustainable manner i.e. in a way that makes a positive contribution to the natural and cultural environment, which generates benefits for the communities in which the company operates, and which does not put at risk the future livelihoods of the people in those communities.

As a business Thomas Cook believes that it can be an important contributor to the global society. The company will, therefore, strive to anticipate and prevent economic, environmental, social and cultural degradation. It works towards integrating these considerations into its operations and activities.

Source: http://www.neilson.co.uk/Responsible-Travel-Thomas-Cook.aspx.

A mission statement, therefore, sets the agenda for a particular type of strategy that a company will follow and encapsulates the raison d'etre for the company. See also the Thomas Cook mini case later in the chapter.

ANALYSIS

The first stage of the strategic planning process is to carry out a thorough analysis of the factors in the external environment which will affect a business. The analysis should evaluate the macro-environment; the global influences that affect all businesses and the micro-environment; the factors specifically affecting the company, its customers and its competitors.

The external business environment

The trends in the macro-environment have already been discussed in Chapter 4. The information revolution, the terrorism agenda and global warming pose serious and ongoing problems within the price-sensitive international travel and tourism markets. Without strategies to guide their responses to inevitable changes in the external business environment, organizations can lose sight of their future development goals in the time-consuming and urgent tactical decisions called for in the day-to-day management of demand that all service industries require. Marketing strategy has to be flexible to cope with change.

The analysis of the macro-environmental factors is often structured under headings such as PESTLE – Political, Economic, Social, Technological, Legal and Environmental. While such headings are useful in stimulating discussion, it should be remembered that the divisions are artificial. As discussed in Chapters 4 and 13, technological changes in Information Communications and Technology (ICT) have economic and social effects in changing people's behaviour. This in turn may have environmental or social impacts that require politicians to amend legislation to regulate business activities.

What such analyses focus on is how these changing factors will affect the company and its markets. These effects are often expressed as Opportunities and Threats. The same trend may offer both. The increasing acceptance of the reality of man-made climate change, coupled with diminishing reserves of fossil fuels, presents obvious threats to the travel and tourism industries because they are heavy consumers of energy and produce large amounts of CO_2 and pollutants. The strategic plan of most companies will have to take into account likely rises in fuel prices, legislation and taxation policies aimed at reducing their carbon footprint. This is an obvious threat to their existing ways of doing business but it may also create opportunities. These include the development of new 'greener' technologies by construction and engineering companies but there may also be opportunities to develop new products within the visitor economy. For example, 'slow travel' packages by train or even cycling may offer tourists not only a way of doing less damage to the environment but also a different, richer experience of the places they visit.

One way of dealing with the uncertainties of the future when preparing a strategic plan is to use scenarios. Ringland (2002) defines them as follows:

Scenarios are possible views of the world, providing a context in which managers can make decisions. By seeing a range of possible worlds, decision makers will be 1/10 better informed, and a strategy based on this knowledge and insight will be more likely to succeed. Scenarios may not predict the future, but they do illuminate the drivers of change: understanding them can only help managers to take greater control of their situation.

Scenario planning has become important in recent years as a way of coping with unexpected events such as the SARS and disruption caused by terrorism. In each case normal planning processes are disrupted and it needs a more visionary approach to understand how the future could be planned to deal with such drastic changes.

At the micro-environmental level, the analysis often takes the form of a market analysis, which looks at the trends in demand for the organization's products and the activities of direct and indirect competitors. A commonly used model is

AN EXAMPLE OF QUALITATIVE SCENARIO PLANNING FROM COPENHAGEN (DENMARK)

Since 2003, Wonderful Copenhagen, the tourism organization of Greater Copenhagen, has used scenario planning as a framework to communicate with policymakers. Two or three scenarios, typically one with no political initiative or investment compared with one with great political initiative, are developed each year. These scenarios are then quantified by the tourism organization's analysts using a basic model to estimate the impact of tourism on economic growth. For example, in developing the organization's tourism strategy for 2007–9, Wonderful Copenhagen developed two scenarios. In one scenario, the sub-national government does nothing to promote tourism, and the short-term growth rates continue at the level of the past decade. However, in the medium-term, the city experiences declining growth due to capacity problems and international competition. In the alternative scenario, the sub-national government invests in facilities, infrastructure, and city marketing, which results in a projected doubling of the city's projected long-term growth.

Source: *http://www.citiesalliance.org/doc/resources/led/9.pdf.*

Porter's (1980) five forces of competition. This requires an assessment of the power of competition, not only from the current direct rivals but also the threat of new entrants and the development of substitute product categories. For example, a tour operator such as Thomas Cook needs to take into account not only the actions of its direct rival in Europe, TUI, but the possibility of new entrants from other continents or industries taking advantages of gaps in the market. More pressing in this example would be the threat of substitutes to the conventional package holiday from low-cost airlines and their affiliate networks and new types of on-line intermediaries. (See Chapters 13 and 15 for a fuller discussion of these trends.) They would also need to take into account the trend towards independent travel.

Porter's model also takes into account the power of suppliers and buyers to influence the market. The large tour operators depend on a supply of low-cost accommodation and flights and until recently have needed retail travel agents to reach their customers. Their strategies have therefore sought to gain power over their suppliers and outlets through consolidation into large groups with high bargaining power, and through vertical integration – protecting their supply and distribution chains by acquiring their own airlines, hotels and travel agents.

Porter's model fitted a mature consolidated sector such as tour operating in the 1990s but can seem rather over-simplified in the light of recent developments in the travel and tourism industries. The emergence of new forms of tourism, alternative on-line distribution channels and a fragmentation of the former mass market into individualistic niches require more flexible forms of analysis that see the visitor economy as a complex network of interdependent organizations. One of the ways in which organizations cope with this complexity is to divide their business into a number of SBUs. Known as a 'portfolio' each SBU develops its strategy for a specific set of products and market segments.

SBUS AND BUSINESS PORTFOLIO ANALYSIS

The strategic planning process for a large international company requires continuous analysis of its current portfolio of SBUs and a much more difficult set of higher risk decisions on what changes are needed to secure future growth and profit in the light of projected international market conditions.

Within any portfolio of SBUs, some will be in growing and some in declining markets. Some are more profitable than others. Portfolios are therefore continuously evaluated according to key variables of

- Shares of current markets held by own and competing companies and trend patterns.
- Perceived market size, growth prospects and product life cycles – including assessment of emerging and predicted markets.
- Cash-flow generation.
- Return on investment compared with other major competitors.
- Strength of competition and probability of others entering markets under consideration.
- Knowledge and core competencies developed within a corporate entity that might be utilized in additional directions.

In any established successful large business it will usually be obvious from analysis that some SBUs in the corporate portfolio have a relatively large share of expanding markets with good profitability. Such products, typically developed as a result of foresight some years earlier, are obvious candidates for strategic support if the general projections remain favourable. Other products, perhaps because the market sector is declining, and not because the product is inadequate, will be in decline and generating little profit, especially if prices are being reduced to maintain volume and market share in the face of aggressive new competition.

Corporate portfolios will typically also comprise some relatively new product-market groupings or SBUs with good shares of growth markets ('stars') and some profitable products with well-established shares of mature markets ('cash cows'). In practice portfolios will frequently also contain products with low shares of declining markets and poor profitability ('dogs'), which are candidates for disposal or liquidation. The labels (in brackets) are those created by the Boston Consulting Group in the USA, which developed one of the best-known techniques for portfolio analysis.

MINI CASE 10.1 THE THOMAS COOK GROUP

Thomas Cook is one of the world's largest travel related group and is based in most of the key regions around the globe. Thomas Cook began his travel business with the advent of the first railway system in the United Kingdom in 1841. In 1865 he opened his first High Street shop in Fleet Street in London and in 1872 he led the first 'Round the

World' tour using ships and trains. As air travel improved and became established that was the next logical development. Since the Second World War the company was nationalized then privatized, being bought by a consortium consisting of the Midland Bank, Trust House Forte and the Automobile Association. In 2001 Thomas Cook was acquired by C&N Touristic AG and changed its name to Thomas Cook AG. In 2007 Thomas Cook merged with MyTravel and became the Thomas Cook Group plc. These events illustrate how a group such as Thomas Cook evolves and becomes a group with a diversified portfolio within the travel and tourism industry.

'Now, the newly-formed Thomas Cook Group has created an international company with 30,000 employees. In less than a year since the merger with MyTravel to form the Thomas Cook Group it announced higher than anticipated operating profits of €375.3 million, fully integrated the two businesses, identified at least €200 million in synergies, laid the groundwork for a major share buy-back programme and been elevated to the upper ranks of the FTSE 100' (from the 2007 Company Report).

The company organizes travel to 2000 destinations, employs 30,000 staff, possesses 97 aircraft and owns 3,000 shops around the world. Its portfolio includes, flights, travel agencies and financial services related to the travel sector (insurance, currency exchange and credit cards). In each market/product segment (SBU) that the company operates in it has a brand portfolio to be managed. The segments are divided into the key regions such as, UK and Ireland, Continental Europe, Northern Europe, North America, Airlines Germany and Corporates. The main brands in the UK are Airtours, Club 18-30, Cresta, Direct Holidays, Going Places, Neilson, Panorama, Sunset, Thomas Cook and Thomas Cook Signature. In Northern Europe the key brands are Spies, Tjaereborg and Ving. The company manages a complex portfolio that crosses its main segment boundaries and is generally a brand portfolio. According to the company:

'Our new UK and Ireland brand strategy has been implemented, with Thomas Cook as our leading brand, supported by a strong portfolio of brands including Airtours in the mass market segment; Direct Holidays, the UK's number one brand for holidays sold direct to the consumer, and specialist brands such as Thomas Cook Signature, Cruise Thomas Cook, Cresta, Tradewinds, Neilson and Club 18-30.'

Thomas Cook thus slices its business in two different ways. Its portfolio of Strategic Business Units comprises market segments and brands/products. For each geographical region the portfolio of brands maybe slightly different reflecting the heritage and history of each brand within that location. For instance the Northern European brands are not likely to be well known in the UK for instance, whereas brands such as Thomas Cook Signature may be more universally accepted. This indicates the dilemma that large companies face when developing a strategic marketing plan that straddles many parts of the world.

In terms of the industry sector/market spaces they occupy and the specific products and market segments they serve, these are essentially quite separate businesses, each marketed under its own distinctive brand. But they share in common the strength of the corporate entity and its value in delivering strategic alliances, the economies and advantages of bulk purchasing and access to investment finance.

Table 10.1 illustrates the key regions that Thomas Cook operates in and within each of these regions the company manages a portfolio of brands for targeted segments.

TABLE 10.1 Revenue by market regions/segments for Thomas Cook Group

	Year ended 31 October 2007 (millions of Euros)	Year ended 31 October 2006 (millions of Euros)	Revenue change (%)	Profit change (%)
Revenue				
UK	4714.3	4736.6	−0.5	+36.2
Northern Europe	1119.8	1151.9	+3.7	+18.5
Continental Europe	4477.4	4567.8	−2.0	+0.3
North America	559.8	684.6	−18.2	−49.7
Airline Germany	767.8	694.4	+10.6	+78.7
Corporate	0.4	35.3	−98.9	+15.4
Group	11,714.5	11,870.6	−1.3	+26.1

Table 10.1 illustrates the fact that although revenues were either static or have decreased slightly in all the major areas, the profitability has been largely up in most cases except North America. The major cause for concern has been the corporate area which represents unallocated head office costs and the results of businesses held for sale. The significant reduction in revenue in the year reflects the completion of planned divestment of non-core businesses within Thomas Cook AG. Overall the figures indicate that Thomas Cook has probably benefited from bulk buying and that may have contributed to increased profitability across its SBUs. Table 10.2 shows the segments and portfolios at a glance.

CORPORATE STRATEGY AND OBJECTIVES

The discussion of the analysis above makes it clear that objective setting must be undertaken at more than one level within an organization. Corporate strategy defines a vision for an organization as a whole and its place in an industry and markets. It sets objectives for all the strategic business units and also the functions that are needed to get the organization as a whole from where it is now to where it wants to be at some future date. Figure 10.3 shows the two main levels of business objectives and

TABLE 10.2 Thomas Cook – International product portfolio

	UK and Ireland	Continental Europe	Northern Europe	North America
Mainstream	**Thomas Cook, Airtours, Direct Holidays, Panorama Manos Holidays, Sunset, Thomas Cook Tours, Sunworld Holidays Club Style-Art of Villa holidays, Cruise Thomas Cook, Neilson**	**Pegase, Thomas Cook, Neckermann Travel, Aquatour, Bucher**	**Spies, Ving, Tjoereborg**	**Sunquest, Alba Tours**
Distribution	**Thomas Cook, Thomas Cook Sport, My Travel, Going Places, flythomascook.com,**	**Thomas Cook, Neckermann, Travel**	**Spies, Ving, Tjoereborg**	**ABC Corporate Services, BelAirTravel.com, The cruise Store**
Independent	**Flexible trips, Cresta, Flight Savers, Tradewinds-worldwide holidays, Thomas Cook signature**	**Thomas Cook, Neckermann, Vrij Uit, Condor**	**Ving, My Travel (Tango), Globetrotter, Tjoereborg**	**Holiday House, Network, Encore Cruise Escapes, Lifestyle Vacation Incentives**

serves also to put marketing strategy into the wider context of future planning for an organization.

Figure 10.3 notes seven common elements that are systematically assessed and integrated in most corporate strategies. As noted earlier, marketing is always a key consideration but only one of the seven. It is shown in the centre of the figure with a separate input below it to demonstrate the linkages with tactical or operational marketing planning shown as level 2.

A brief description of the non-marketing elements is provided below with airline illustrations simply to set a context for the marketing strategy issues, which follow. Other than as context, however, the other elements are not the subject of this chapter and are not referred to further.

While hierarchies of objectives may not appear relevant to small proprietor-run businesses, the thought process and principles discussed in this chapter are fully appropriate to any size of operation. It is often the failure to think strategically, and evaluate and respond proactively to long-term trends and opportunities, which causes so many smaller businesses to founder.

Corporate strategy in an airline context

In the context of a scheduled airline with an international network of routes, the decisions to be brought together in a strategy can be explained briefly as a series of questions:

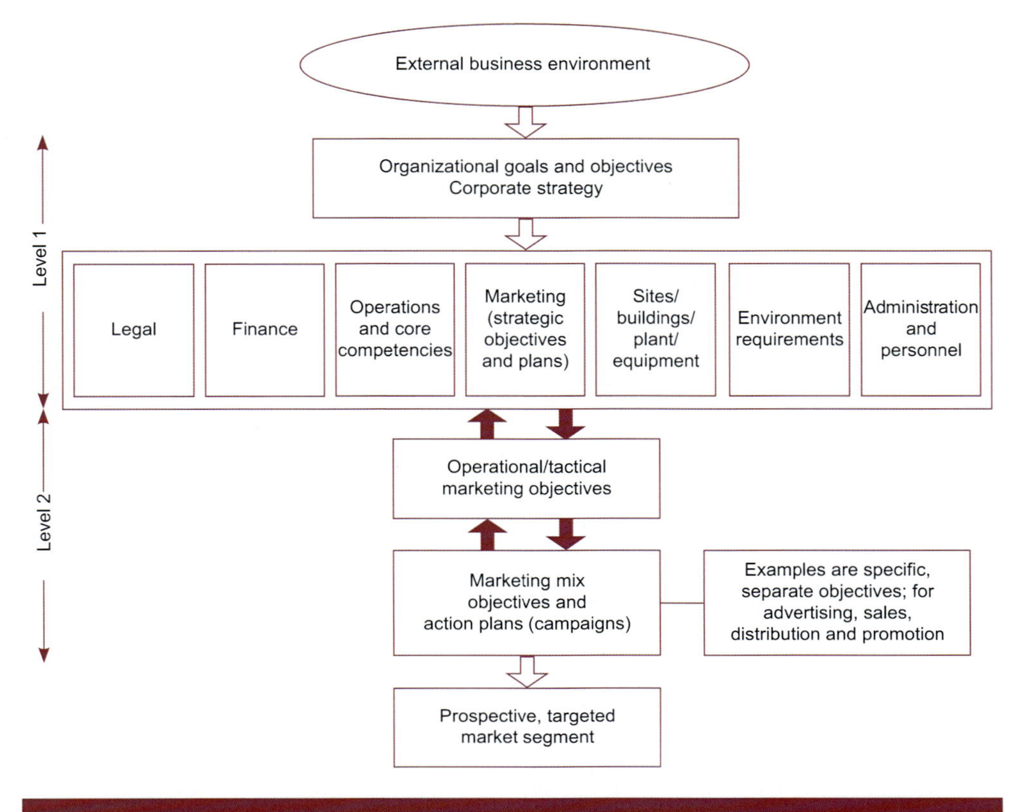

FIGURE 10.3 Elements and stages involved in a corporate business strategy: the hierarchy of objectives

- *Legal*. What agreements between countries are required to maintain and develop services on agreed route networks? How far and how fast might deregulation proceed? What are the legal implications of possible alliances, mergers and acquisitions? What action is needed to comply with existing and perceived new legal requirements?
- *Finance*. What asset and loan structure is needed by the airline? What returns on capital are required to service the investment, meet the stakeholders' interests and fund new investment in aircraft, ICT and facilities?
- *Operations*. What number, type and size of aircraft are required to perform agreed services, on which routes at what times? How to optimize the scheduling of the fleet? What are the future requirements for the services network looking 10 years ahead?
- *Sites, buildings, plant and equipment*. What ground facilities are required at airports and operational bases? What servicing (engineering) facilities are needed for aircraft, etc? What computer facilities are needed to service business operations?
- *Environment*. What changes to aircraft and other operational developments are needed to meet regulations concerning noise, emissions, waste control, night flights and energy consumption? What are the implications for

conducting environmental audits and carrying out impact assessments for major new projects? How will future operations be affected by new environmental policies?

- *Administration and human resources (HR).* What core competencies and facilities for management, buildings, equipment and general organization are needed to service the airlines' current operations and assist it to develop in targeted new areas to achieve planned goals and objectives? What competencies, numbers, remuneration levels, qualifications, organization, training and career structure are required for employees, to provide and sustain effective quality assured service delivery across the network?
- *Competitive pressures.* What are the competitors doing? How much have they invested in resources? Competitive pressures generally drive the need to take a strategic approach to planning.

Marketing strategy in an airline context

Marketing strategy identifies and is primarily responsible for future sales revenue generation by specifying the segments, products and associated action programmes required to achieve sales and market share against competitors – and deliver customer satisfaction.

Each of the other elements in the corporate strategy requires expenditure out of projected revenue. However vital these elements are to the conduct of the business, they are ultimately conditioned by the organization's ability to persuade sufficient existing and new customers to buy enough of its products to secure a surplus of revenue over costs in the long run. While it is obviously incorrect to conclude that business strategy is only about marketing, it is undeniable that all strategy for commercial organizations has its bottom line in the sales revenue which results from customer satisfaction. Marketing managers are employed to achieve revenue targets through their specialist knowledge of market needs and circumstances.

To illustrate the point, the decision by an airline to buy or lease new aircraft, such as the new double-deck 550-seater airbus A380, rather than additional 'stretched Boeing 747 400s', has strategic implications for each of the seven elements, noted in Fig. 10.3. But unless marketing managers can commit to achieving daily seat-occupancy levels (load factors), at average prices (yield) that will exceed average costs, the decision to buy cannot be taken. In practice there is always an element of risk in the decision to buy equipment because the speed and location factors of global market growth cannot be predicted with precision. Currently (2008) rising fuel prices and financial credit crises have meant that many airlines have already gone to the receiver and others are expected to follow or merge. But the principal challenge lies in projecting future customer demand and having the marketing competence to secure the demand against aggressive competition – and cope with unexpected shifts in market conditions.

THE MARKETING STRATEGY PLANNING PROCESS

The key components of marketing strategy are:

- *Goals and objectives.* As outlined above marketing strategy reflects and at the same time informs corporate vision and leadership. It is related to the external business environment, its view of customer needs and competitors' actions. It is also concerned with the overall corporate values that a business seeks to develop and communicate to customers and stakeholders. These goals have to be translated into objectives for the position in its chosen markets that an organization seeks to occupy, usually defined broadly in terms of sectors of business, target segments, volume of sales, product range, market shares and profitability.

- *Positioning and branding.* Where the organization seeks to be in terms of customers' and retailers' perceptions of its products and the values in its mission statement. Includes choice of corporate image and branding in relation to competitors. (See later in the chapter.).
- *Strategies and programmes.* Broadly what actions, including product development and investment, are required to achieve the goals and objectives?
- *Budget.* What resources, staff and money, are needed to achieve the goals?
- *Review and evaluation.* Systematic appraisal of achievement of goals in the context of competitors' actions and the external environment.

The last three points are discussed in more detail in Chapters 11 and 12.

Within the limits of this book it is only possible to draw attention to main issues but three strategic factors in particular, drawn from the extensive literature on business management, will assist in making the important distinctions. These are:

- Product-market growth and development.
- Corporate and product positioning.
- Branding.

Strategies for product-market growth and development

As noted earlier, the start of the twenty-first century has been a time of unprecedented turmoil and change in all industries – not least in travel and tourism. No organization can rest on past progress and expect to maintain the structure of existing product-market portfolios and profitability levels, even over a period as short as 2 years. Profitable product-market portfolios are certain to be targeted by aggressive competitors and businesses also have to respond to other pressures, such as unfavourable exchange-rate movements, changes in regulatory requirements and new technology options.

For competitive businesses the process of reviewing their portfolios is continuous. The options for growth for each product can be neatly summarized in an elegant, four-box model, originally devised by Ansoff and much copied and developed since (see Fig. 10.4). Each of the strategies summarized in the four boxes has radically different implications for marketing.

The four-numbered boxes in the model may be illustrated with typical travel and tourism examples as follows:

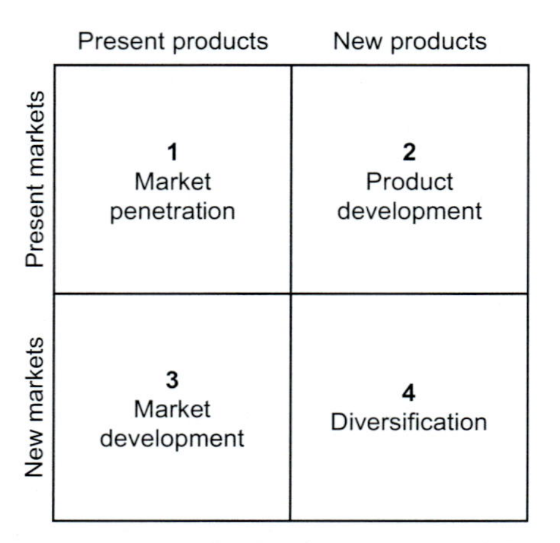

FIGURE 10.4 Product–market growth strategies (four basic options). Source: Ansoff (1987)

1. The case where a hotel group, already servicing the corporate (business) market as its principal market segments, decides that it is well positioned to expand in this market through aggressive marketing campaigns. With its existing portfolio of products, any expansion above natural market growth would represent an increase in market share, which is also known as increased 'penetration'. This is a relatively low-risk strategy.
2. The case where a European tour operator, already operating a portfolio of inclusive tours to European destinations, decides to expand its operations by developing long-haul tours to destinations in Asia, targeting its existing market segments. This decision represents an addition to the product portfolio and is known as product development (new products for present markets). Its knowledge of and competencies with existing segments will be a valuable platform for expansion.
3. The case where what was originally a Dutch company based in the Netherlands with a largely continental European clientele, first marketed its existing continental villages to the UK market (market development). In the late 1980s Center Parcs was purchased by British owners and developed its holiday village concept in four locations in England. This was an existing (albeit modified) product concept targeted at new markets and it therefore represented market development.
4. Finally, when an airline company (Virgin Atlantic) decided to buy and brand a UK railway operating company (Virgin Rail) through acquisition, it stepped outside its existing product-market portfolio and effectively diversified its business activities with a completely new set of SBUs in a new market sector. In this case, Virgin brought its core passenger-handling competencies to bear on a different form of transport. This represents a relatively high-risk form of diversification.

Each of these choices is a strategic decision usually undertaken on the basis of a detailed analysis of potential revenues and advantages as well as potential costs and disadvantages. The choices also reflect the strategic vision a company has of the direction in which it wishes to proceed for future profitability.

Competitive strategy and product positioning

For each product or business unit and for organizations communicating to stakeholders, decisions have to be made about the position to hold in chosen marketplaces. Always a strategic decision, the position that a product or brand or an organization adopts as an entity is ultimately determined by how its target customers perceive it in relation to the alternatives offered by its competitors. As two of the early exponents of positioning as the basis of marketing strategy said, 'It's not what you do to the product that matters, it is what you do in the mind of the prospective customer'.

The first stage of positioning is to decide on how a product will compete with the alternatives offered by competitors. According to Porter (1980) this comes down to a combination of three elements. The product can either be aimed at a broad market or a focused niche segment, and within that market it can either compete on price or differentiation.

Price-led strategies are termed 'low-cost leadership' emphasizing that low prices are only sustainable if underpinned by low operating costs. Examples in tourism are the broad cost leadership strategies of the major tour operators who under-cut their smaller rivals through negotiating high volume/low rate deals with suppliers; or the focused cost leadership of budget airlines who achieve efficiencies through their 'no-frills' operations on a limited number of routes.

Differentiation strategies can be based either on tangible product features, superior service or on a better image, more fashionable, more reliable or associated with a particular lifestyle or country of origin. Such differentiation can be the result of a strategic analysis of customer needs, values and aspirations matched against the characteristics of competitors' products. For example, the accommodation sector in the UK was until the 1990s dominated by standardized global hotel chains offering three or more star accommodation, with the only alternative being the independent sector private hotels and guest houses. This created a gap in the market for branded budget hotels which combined the reassurance of a well-known name and the convenience of centralized reservations with a lower, no-frills price. The consolidation of the sector at both budget and higher-class levels created another gap in the market for hotels which were differentiated from the chains by local distinctiveness or original design features. The result has been the growth of what are known as 'boutique hotels.'

Once the customer need and a potential gap in the market have been identified, the next stage is to design a product that is positioned to fill that gap and then to make the positioning the core of the marketing communications strategy. This is done most effectively if the distinctive positioning of the company or product is the basis of the brand image.

Branding and image

The brand image or 'position' that products occupy in customers' minds is always part of the product augmentation process (see Chapter 7) and in the case of a group hotel this will be closely related to the corporate image and branding of the group.

Branding obviously plays an important role in developing a marketing strategy because a brand image actually 'positions' a company or a destination vis-à-vis its competitors. In common with most services, the benefits provided by travel and tourism products are essentially intangible and need to be communicated in ways that influence consumers' perceptions. The origins of branding can be traced all the way back to Greek and Roman times, through craftsmen in the Middle Ages, to the branding of cattle on nineteenth-century American ranches. All these early notions of branding demonstrated the core attributes of

- Statement of ownership.
- Means of identifying a product or service for purchasers and distinguishing it from that of competitors.
- Symbol or shorthand device to which expectations of quality could be attached.

Doyle described a brand as '*a name, symbol, design or some combination, which identifies the "product" of a particular organization as having a sustainable differential advantage*' (Doyle, 1989: 78; emphasis added).

Doyle's definition is useful but it does not capture the modern concept in its entirety. It reads as if the brand is added to the product. In fact, a strong brand reflects and guides the development of core values throughout the product, staff and organization. The definition also reads from a producer, rather than a consumer perspective. In practice a strong brand has to exist in the minds of consumers as a fusion of readily understood values and benefits and is used by them to achieve their perceived needs and in some cases to make statements about themselves and their personal values.

Figure 10.5, drawn from work by de Chernatony and McDonald (1992), explores the branding concept further. A *commodity* has many substitutes and is compelled, especially through websites, to match the prices set by competitors. Many bed and breakfast businesses are perceived as commodities and have difficulty breaking away from a competitive-parity pricing that mirrors the rates set by other accommodation providers in the same location. One step up from the commodity is the *product with a brand identity system* bolted on. The use of a design incorporating a name, logo and slogan that is attached to a product is commonly mistaken for branding. It is arguable that many would-be tourism brands fall into this trap. Davidson (1997) refers to the

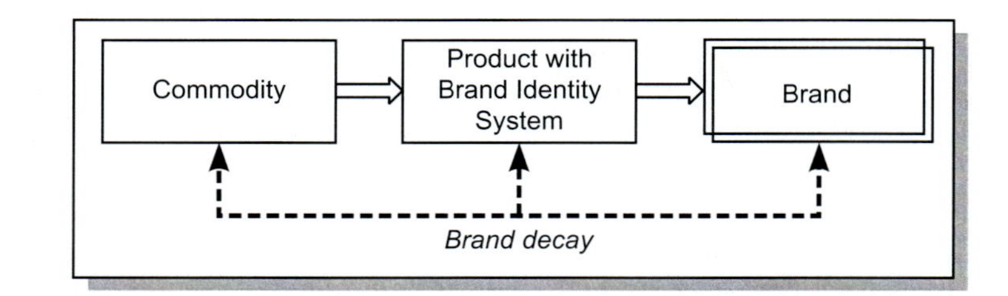

FIGURE 10.5 A simplified concept of branding. Based on de Chernatony and McDonald (1992)

frequent use of 'labels' attached to 'me too' products, whilst de Chernatony and McDonald (1992) claim that a primary management error in branding is the reliance on the brand name as the differentiating device, rather than the development of genuine competitive advantage. A brand in the modern marketing sense offers the consumer relevant *added values*, a superior proposition that is distinctive from competitors and imparts meaning above and beyond the functional aspects. It is also a total entity developed by the integration of the resources, processes and marketing decisions of an organization and much of the effort and input to developing a brand remain invisible to the consumer. As tourism is a chain of service encounters spread over hours for visitor attractions, days for hotels or even weeks for a tour operator, the added values should be integrated into every point of contact with the consumer from pre-purchase through to post-use.

A competitive brand is a live asset, however, not a fixture and its value will depreciate over time if starved of investment and marketing management skill. Brand decay may begin if a brand is over-stretched into new products that damage its essence, or following a merger or takeover. Some writers query, for example, whether the international Virgin brand has been over-stretched by the diversification into dozens of products ranging from air transport, rail transport and financial services, to compact discs (CDs), cola and entertainment.

Advantages of branding for travel and tourism

In addition to the initial advantages of branding already mentioned, the characteristics of travel and tourism suggest that other specific benefits may be gained from successful branding.

- Branding helps reduce medium and long-term vulnerability to the unforeseen external events that so beset the tourism industry. Recovery time after a crisis may be shorter, whilst resilience to price wars or occasional hiccups may be improved.
- Branding reduces the risk for the consumer at the point of purchase by signalling the expected quality and performance of an intangible product. It offers either an implicit or explicit guarantee to the consumer.
- Branding facilitates accurate marketing segmentation by attracting some and sending negative signals to other consumer segments. For an inseparable product, on-site segment compatibility is an important marketing issue. The British tour operator *Club 18–30* attracts certain segments of the youth holiday market while it dissuades others; the resulting mix of clients ensures that the clubbing atmosphere of the product that target users want is experienced at the destination.
- Branding provides the focus for the integration of stakeholder effort, especially for the employees of an organization or the individual tourism providers working within a destination brand. In popular destinations, reflecting the complexity of the overall tourism product, local residents are also stakeholders in the meaning and values of 'place' even if they consider themselves to be uninvolved in tourism. A strong brand can help provide a common understanding and some unity of purpose for staff, residents and businesses alike.

- Branding is a strategic weapon for long-range planning in tourism, a means of changing the way that the country is perceived as a destination (See the New Zealand case study in Part Six.) Singapore Airlines has repositioned itself as both a global airline and the key airline for South East Asian destinations.
- Clearly recognized international branding is an essential attribute for effective use by businesses of the Internet. With millions of websites available, consumer are likely to choose and trust those of recognized and reputable brands over those of unknown names, as the collapse of many new dot.com companies in the late 1990s illustrated. The linking of brands and banner advertising to relevant portals and sites depends on consumer's awareness of brands for its effectiveness.
- Branding is also an essential element of distribution strategy. In many sectors including holiday tourism, customers may be more familiar with the brands of the retailers than those of the producers. They may accept whatever airline, hotel or car-hire firm is offered by a travel agent or on-line intermediary because they trust that retailer brand, be it Thomas Cook or Expedia. If a supplier wishes to by-pass the retail channel and sell direct, they will need to invest in advertising and direct marketing to establish their own brand as a symbol of quality and reliability.

THE INTERPLAY OR DIALOGUE BETWEEN STRATEGY AND TACTICS

Traditionally in all large hierarchical organizations, goals reflecting corporate values would be drafted by planning departments, debated and set by a board of directors and handed down to managers who were expected to achieve them. But it is increasingly recognized that achievable corporate goals cannot be set without participation by those who have to implement them, especially in service businesses which are so dependent on the knowledge of line management and customer facing staff and the quality of services they are motivated to deliver.

It is increasingly the business of managers, therefore, to work out practical trade-offs through a dialogue between board level aspiration and the operational knowledge and industry expertise of those directly responsible for service delivery. Also known as a 'goals down/plans up process' these trade-offs have both strategic and tactical implications. Resolving the differences between desired, especially long-term goals and achievable, especially short-term, objectives and targets, is a now a key role for management and staff in any large organization. This process brings together and modifies both strategic and operational decision processes and harnesses all the competencies in the organizations around achievable goals. Since strategic goals are also intended to motivate managers and always relate to desired future states, it is normal for there to be some tension and dispute between short-term and long-term planning requirements.

CHAPTER SUMMARY

This chapter:

- Introduces the basic concepts and processes of strategic thinking that are central to the efficient conduct of marketing-led organizations in travel and tourism. It stresses the need for future orientation of strategy in an era of globalization, constant change and the redrawing of traditional industry sector boundaries facilitated by information technology.
- Explains how the process of strategic planning should be based on a clear vision of what the organization exists to do and a thorough analysis of trends in the macro-environment affecting the business and its immediate market.
- Shows that marketing strategy is one element in the overall corporate strategy of the organization which is implemented through its various business units and through co-ordinating the various functions of the organization of which marketing is just one.
- Explores the development of a marketing strategy based on a clear competitive strategy which creates a distinctive and sustainable position for the company and the values it stands for in the minds of its existing and potential customers.
- Outlines the role of branding in communicating the marketing and positioning strategy to the target market and discusses the importance of branding for organizations in travel and tourism.

QUESTIONS TO CONSIDER

1. What are the main issues that need to be considered in developing a strategic plan?
2. What are the key components of the marketing strategy process?
3. Choose a sector with a number of leading brands and identify the different positioning and branding strategies of each of the competing companies.
4. What values are these brands seeking to communicate to customers?
5. Why is branding especially important in travel and tourism?

REFERENCES AND FURTHER READING

Baker, M.J. (1996). *Marketing: an introductory text.* Chapters 2 and 3 (6th edn). Macmillan.

Brassington, F. and Pettit, S. (2003). *Principles of marketing* (3rd edn). FT Prentice-Hall.

Chernatory, L. de and Mc Donald, M.H.B. (1992). *Creating Powerful Brands.* Butterworth-Heinemann.

Doyle, P. (1989). Building successful brands. The strategic options. *Journal of Marketing Management*, **5**(1): pp. 77–95.

El-Ansary, A. (2006). Marketing strategy: taxonomy and frameworks, *European Business Review*, **18**(4), pp. 266–293.

Hamel, G. and Prahalad, C.K. (1994). *Competing for the future*. Harvard Business School Press.

Jobber, D. (2007). *Principles and practice of marketing* (5th edn). McGraw-Hill.

Keegan, W.K. and Davidson, H. (2005). *Offensive marketing: gaining competitive advantage*. Butterworth-Heinemann.

Kotler, P. and Armstrong, G. (1999). *Principles of marketing*. Chapter 1 (8th edn). Prentice-Hall.

Kotler, P., Wong, V., Saunders, J. and Armstrong, G. (2005). *Principles of marketing* (4th European edn). Pearson Prentice Hall.

Li, S. (2005). A web-enabled hybrid approach to strategic marketing planning: group Delphi + a web-based expert system, *Expert Systems with Applications*, **29**, pp. 393–400.

Porter, M. (1980). *Competitive Strategy: Techniques for analyzing industries and competitors*. Collier Macmillan.

Ranchhod, A. and Gurau, C. (2007). *Marketing strategies: a contemporary approach*. Pearson Education.

Although systematic planning processes and entrepreneurial market flair are usually seen as opposites, they can, and should be mutually supportive.

CHAPTER 11

Marketing planning: the process

The problem...is not that the philosophy of marketing is not believed; rather it is that most companies...have difficulty in making it work. This is largely because of ignorance about the process of planning their marketing activities.

(McDonald, 1995: viii)

The previous chapter identifies the differences and links between long-term marketing strategy and short-term marketing tactics and programmes, explaining the relationship between them in the overall hierarchy of corporate objectives. This chapter continues the marketing planning theme with a focus on marketing objectives to be implemented in the short run through specified action programmes. Corporate objectives have been described earlier as 'destinations', strategies as 'routes' and plans as 'action programmes' for moving along agreed routes. In other words, strategy sets the framework within which tactics are planned and, in practice, much of the work in marketing departments is concerned with drawing up, implementing and measuring the effects of action plans.

This chapter identifies eight stages of the process common to marketing planning in any industry. It emphasizes that the planning process for strategy and tactics covers the same essential stages, usually drawing on the same research sources and often undertaken by the same people. For strategic purposes, the analysis and forecasting of trends in the external business environment and the implications of demand for the development of future competitive product/market portfolios are the most important parts of planning. For operational tactical purposes, the setting of precise objectives and targets for the existing product/market portfolio and devising action programmes for 6–12 months ahead are the main focus.

After studying this chapter you should be able to understand:

- Each of the stages in the planning process, which are summarized in Fig. 11.1.
- The objectives, resources and tactical budget dialogue that are part of the process of marketing communications within all marketing-led businesses and the means of bringing marketing together with other parts of an organization.
- That the process, although obviously most relevant to larger organizations, is in fact ultimately a logical thought process that is just as applicable in principle to small businesses.

THE PARTICULAR SIGNIFICANCE OF MARKETING PLANS

In its principles, marketing planning is no more than a logical thought process in which all businesses engage to some extent. It is an application of common sense, as relevant to a small guesthouse or caravan park as it is to an international airline. The scale of planning and its sophistication obviously vary according to the size of the organization concerned but the essential approach is always the same.

Building on the purposes of strategic planning outlined in Chapter 10, it is helpful to emphasize seven main reasons why staff time and resources are allocated to marketing planning at the tactical or operational level:

- To identify and focus management attention on the current and targeted costs, revenues and profitability of an organization, in the context of its own and its competitors' products and segments.
- To understand the role of stakeholders in the development of strategic marketing planning for the organization.
- To focus decisions on implementing the strategic objectives of an organization in their market context and specifying competitive short-term action plans relevant to the long-term future.
- To set and communicate specific business targets for managers/strategic business units (SBUs) to achieve in agreed time periods.
- To schedule and co-ordinate websites, booking systems, promotional and other marketing action required to achieve targets and to allocate the resources required as effectively as possible.
- To achieve co-ordination and a sense of joint direction between the different departments of an organization, and to communicate and motivate all levels of staff.
- To monitor and evaluate the results of marketing expenditure and adjust the planned activity as required to meet unforeseen circumstances.

Are there alternatives to marketing planning?

The only alternatives to the systematic commonsense planning processes outlined in this chapter are guesswork, hunch, 'gut feel' for the market, simple intuition or vision. Sometimes hunches and intuition are implemented with brilliant success by highly energetic and determined business entrepreneurs. Many of these dismiss systematic planning as bureaucratic, rigid, time-consuming, expensive and often wrong. But hunch and guesswork also have their disadvantages, and the history of travel and tourism reveals many illustrations of brilliant entrepreneurs whose businesses grew rapidly and successfully for some years, only to crash spectacularly in the wake of unpredicted events. The recent collapse of Zoom in Canada and XL in the UK as a result of the sustained increase in the cost of fuel are two prime examples of sudden environmental shocks to the system. In 2008/2009 there are doubtless thousands more small businesses that will fall at the same hurdles but whose names are unlikely to attract media attention.

In principle, although systematic planning processes and entrepreneurial market flair are usually seen as opposites, they can, and should be mutually supportive. Provided they are not inflexible and the cause of delays, planning procedures may be used to provide a framework of objectives and an information base that support and give a sense of direction or roots in which marketing judgement and flair can grow. 'Entrepreneurial planning' may sound like a contradiction in terms but it is nevertheless a desirable goal to which most modern large businesses aspire (they call it intellectual foresight and vision) and which they seek to build into their internal management procedures. There is very clearly a balance to be struck in marketing management between analytical procedures and creative flair. Both are essential qualities for long-run survival and profitability. Creative flair and vision will always be a vital quality in successful marketing strategies and tactics. Unbridled by agreed strategies and a common sense of direction that commands internal support, such flair can also be self-destructive.

LOGICAL STEPS IN THE MARKETING PLANNING PROCESS

There are eight logical steps in a systematic marketing planning process. Each step feeds into the next one with feedback loops built into the process, as noted with arrows in Fig. 11.1 and explained in the text that follows.

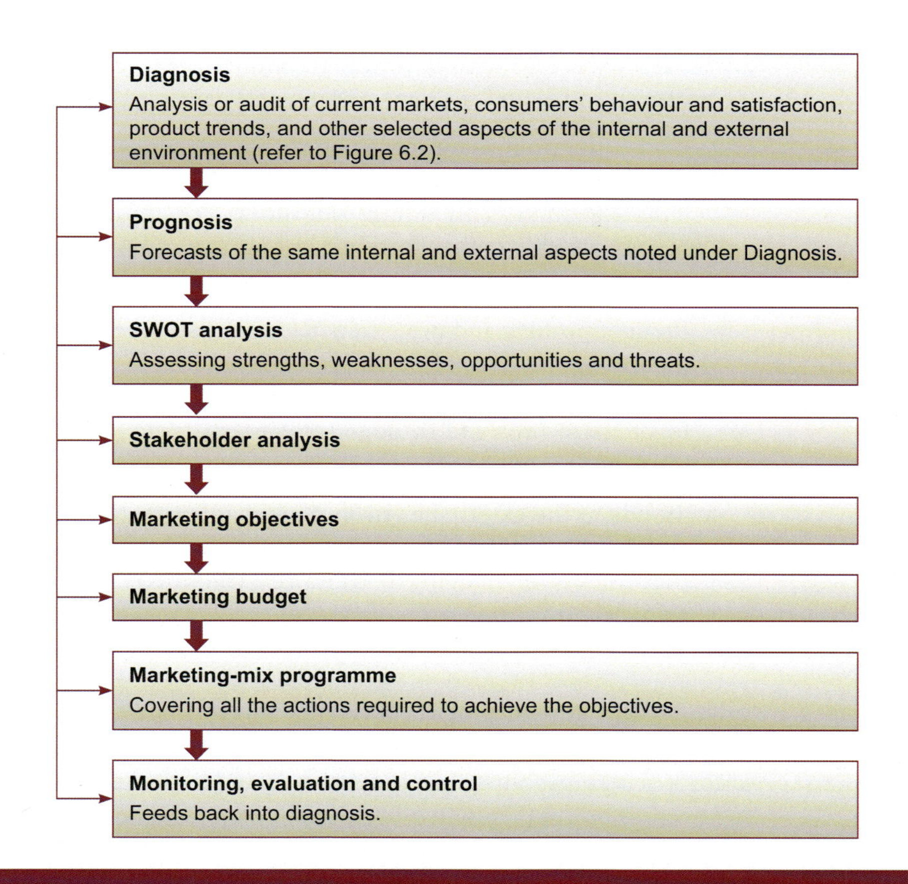

FIGURE 11.1 Stages in the marketing planning process

Explaining marketing planning as a series of logical steps runs the risk of missing the holistic contribution to the decision processes of a business. As Leppard and McDonald put it: 'While the marketing planning process appears on the surface to be just a series of procedural steps, it does in fact embrace a series of underlying values and assumptions' (Leppard and McDonald, 1991: 213). They stress that a marketing-led corporate culture in an organization is a precondition for successful marketing planning in which the process should be an integral part of corporate decisions and communication. The underlying values and assumptions are explicit in the long-term strategy of the business. At worst, if marketing planning is no more than a 'bolt-on' procedure, it will scarcely be recognized outside the marketing team and have no real impact on the conduct of a firm in the long or short run.

Diagnosis

Described in some texts as part of a 'marketing audit', the first stage in the planning process is based on the analysis of company databases, supplemented by marketing research as necessary and drawing on available published and unpublished data for analysis of trends under four main headings.

1. Sales volume and revenue trends over at least a 5-year period to identify total market movements and market shares for particular segments and for own and competitors' products. A UK tour operator would, for example, compare its own sales data with Civil Aviation Authority data for charter airline passengers and with government and national tourist office survey data for overall travel and tourism volume and value.
2. Consumer profiles for own customers and competitors' customers, including detail of demographics, attitudes and behaviour, as outlined in Chapter 6. This information, including indicators of customer satisfaction and value for money, usually comes from a combination of business records and through market surveys.
3. Product profiles and price trends for own and competitors' products, identifying product life-cycle movements and in particular noting growing and declining product types. Such information comes from analysing internal business records and through trade press, trade research and other forms of marketing intelligence.
4. Trends in the external environment as identified in Chapters 4 and 10, such as changing technology, changing regulatory requirements, exchange rate movements or changing distribution structure. This information also derives primarily from government sources, trade press and trade research, although some aspects may justify undertaking marketing research studies.

Under the four headings above, the process of *diagnosis* represents a factual platform, which is the basis for all marketing plans at tactical level. The same platform serves also for strategic appraisals and for long-range scenario planning but may need to be supplemented by specially commissioned analyses of future trends and opportunities. Since the travel and tourism industry has access to data from many sources, the way in which data are selected, organized and presented for decision purposes is an important marketing management skill.

The level of detail in the diagnosis is a matter for each individual business, reflecting its size and the range of its operations. Diagnosis is likely to extend beyond the products and markets of immediate concern to a business, into adjacent markets. For example, a budget hotel chain would expect to diagnose budget-sector accommodation markets and products in full detail. It might also need to monitor trends in the sectors above and below its chosen market sector in order to assess relative changes in the sectors which could have future strategic implications. Similarly an airline without its own low-cost operator, or links to a low-cost partner operator, would monitor international budget transport market trends to decide whether, when, how and to what extent it might enter that sector in the future.

Prognosis

Summarized in many texts as 'forecasting', the second stage in the planning process is also market-research based but future orientated. It relies on expectations, vision, judgement and forecasting for each of the four headings already covered under 'Diagnosis'. Because the future for travel and tourism products is subject to volatile, unpredictable factors and competitors' decisions, the purpose of prognosis is not accuracy but careful and continuous assessment of probabilities and options with a focus on future choices. It recognizes that most marketing mix expenditure is invested weeks and months ahead of targeted revenue flows. Diversification into other products and markets may require investment years ahead of estimated revenue flows. Since marketing planning is focused on future revenue achievement, it is necessarily dependent upon skill, judgement, foresight and realism in the prognosis process.

Both for diagnosis and prognosis the quality of the management information systems created through the marketing research process (Chapter 9) will make a critical contribution to the effectiveness of the processes of evaluation. A key part of marketing management skills lies also in the way that the essential information is presented so that other managers are able to use data and future scenarios and respond to them in their own strategic and operational decisions.

SWOT analysis

Equipped with relevant information through the process of diagnosis, and the best indications of developing trends through prognosis, the next task is to assess what the information means for marketing strategy and tactics. A framework for this assessment is contained in the traditional but still useful acronym SWOT, which stands for strengths, weaknesses, opportunities and threats.

Strengths are normally expressed as inherent current advantages, whether by earlier strategic decisions or historic good fortune. Strengths may exist in an organization's market/product portfolio and its operations in relation to competitors. Products with increasing shares of markets predicted to grow are obviously strengths. Dominance of market share among key market segments is another strength while strategic alliances with other companies may have achieved a particular set of competencies and value-added for which customers are willing to pay premium prices. For hotels and visitor attractions, location may be a major strength. Strength may lie in historic artefacts or architectural style and it may reflect a particularly favourable consumer image. Strength may lie in the professional skills of a marketing team or a distribution system, or in the future orientated competencies of key staff, or in customer service staff with a recognized reputation for being especially helpful and friendly.

It is impossible to indicate all the possible dimensions of an organization's strengths, but such dimensions are always identifiable and recognizable characteristics, which an organization is uniquely positioned to deliver, or has more of or does better than its competitors. Strengths will usually be reflected in the chosen values of an organization and be part of its positioning in the market place and branding. Once identified, strengths are the basis of corporate positions (see Chapter 10) and can be developed within a strategic framework, enhanced through product augmentation and promoted to potential customers.

Courtesy of Dimitrios Buhalis.

Weaknesses, ranging from ageing products in declining markets to surly customer contact staff, must also be clearly identified. Once identified, they may be subject to management action designed to minimize their impact or to remove them where possible. Weaknesses and strengths are often matters of perception rather than 'fact', and may often be identified only through consumer research.

If, for example, an historic hotel in a market town is perceived by many of its customers as an attractive building but old-fashioned, noisy and uncomfortable for its users, it may be possible to highlight its strengths by repositioning the hotel to stress old-world charm, convenience of location and atmosphere. Such a repositioning may necessitate extensive refurbishment, including double glazing and refurnishing, but it could provide a strategic route to turn a weakness into strength. If a modern competitor hotel were to be built on the outskirts of the market town, the historic hotel would probably lose some of its non-leisure clients and might be forced to reposition its products and develop new leisure market segments in order to survive.

To enhance their own foresight and bring to bear an independent, fresh vision, it is common practice in large marketing-orientated businesses for managers to commission consultants to carry out regular audits of all aspects of their business, including SWOT analyses.

Opportunities in a marketing context may arise from elements of the business under direct control, such as a particular product or process, or a particular set of staff competencies. They may also arise from shifts in the external environment, which a firm may exploit. For instance companies such as eBookers understood the value of the Internet and created a first mover advantage for flight bookings on the Internet. EasyJet over the last 10 years has carved itself a strong position as a low-cost airline taking people to popular holiday destinations. This opportunity opened up with the deregulation of the airline industry, which paved the way for smaller more agile operators to enter the market. As this book is being written, spiralling fuel costs are creating problems for domestic airlines in Europe but may open up new opportunities for rail operators. SwimTrek is a company specializing in swimming holidays for individuals who are good but not outstanding swimmers. The opportunity arose because the founder realized that there was an opportunity to offer the large number of regular swimmers an interesting holiday experience of swimming from island to island in the open sea. After starting the first swimming holidays in Greece it has now expanded its operations to the Virgin Islands, Malta, Sardinia, Croatia, the Lake District, the Shetland Islands, Malta and New Zealand, indicating how well it has capitalized on a hitherto 'hidden' opportunity.

Currently in the United Kingdom the advent of the 2012 Olympics is creating a major opportunity to market the UK brand as a destination and at the same time to develop the visitor economy to help revive East London. A combination of world class sporting facilities, infrastructure and media exposure is expected to provide opportunities for new businesses in travel and tourism.

Courtesy of Richard Shipway.

Threats may also be presented by internal elements within the business's control or by external events such as exchange rate changes, rising oil prices or acts of international terrorism. In Britain, traditional seaside resorts offering beach-based summer holidays have been under heavy threat for three decades from seaside resorts along the Mediterranean coastline. They have also suffered from a form of management inertia implicit in the traditional public sector structures that are responsible for their futures. The competition has severely eroded their customary markets and, some would say 20 years too late for many, is finally forcing a strategic reappraisal of their futures in the twenty-first century.

Although it is not easy to justify the point theoretically, practical experience of marketing proves that the time and effort spent in a systematic, wide-ranging and creative SWOT analysis are invariably productive. It is much more than routine analysis of market statistics. There is ample scope for creative interpretation, judgement and lateral thinking, both at the strategic and tactical levels of planning. There is also good reason and ample scope for marketing managers to bring other managers into this process and also to involve the staff of an organization in the process, to draw out their expertise and perceptions of a business and its customers.

Because information is never perfect and the future is always unknown, there is never one right conclusion to be drawn from the evidence gathered in the SWOT process. Best guesses are required. Managers change and their memories are often faulty so, whenever strategy and tactics are reviewed, it is essential for larger businesses to record the assumptions made and conclusions drawn. Establishing a formal record, however succinct, is equally valuable for small businesses.

Stakeholder analysis

Stakeholders are an important part of an organization, ensuring its well-being and future prospects. Most organizations in travel and tourism have several different groups of stakeholders that have to be considered when developing plans. One of the key stakeholders are shareholders who provide resources for company growth through shareholding or loans. These enable an organization to develop and execute marketing planning effectively. Customers are another important stakeholder group that enable an enterprise to grow and flourish. Companies that are therefore customer oriented and manage these stakeholders well tend to perform better in the marketplace. Another important stakeholder in tourism is the local community at visited destinations that either benefits from a particular tourism planning strategy or suffers from it through congestion, pollution or degradation of the land and other resources. In this connection, issues of sustainability are becoming more significant and other stakeholders such as Non-Governmental Organizations (NGOs) may take an active interest in the effect that an organization's marketing planning may have on a particular environment. The marketing of developments that extract local water resources for golf courses, or disturb local wildlife habitats are examples. Organizations such as Greenpeace and the World Wildlife Fund are often active in this area. Other stakeholders are suppliers, such as hotels for tour operators or local government on behalf of local residents. A thorough analysis of the stakeholders' involvement enables an organization to develop a sensible marketing plan that is most likely to gain approval and support.

Marketing objectives and targets

Marketing objectives and targets at operational or tactical level derive logically from the previous stages of the planning process. Targets express what managers believe can be achieved from a business over a specified time period.

To be effective and actionable in practice, tactical marketing objectives must be

- Integrated with long-run corporate goals and strategy.
- Precise and quantified in terms of sales volume, sales revenue and, if possible, market share.
- Specific in terms of what products, which segments, what prices.
- Specific in terms of the time period in which they are to be achieved.
- Realistic and aggressive in terms of market trends (revealed by prognosis and SWOT) and in relation to budgets available.
- Agreed and endorsed by the managers responsible for the programmes of activity designed to achieve results and clearly communicated to staff.
- Measurable directly or indirectly.

If these seven criteria are not fully reflected, the objectives will be less than adequate for achieving the success of the business and the marketing programmes will be harder to specify and evaluate. The more thorough the diagnosis, prognosis and SWOT, the easier the task of specifying precise objectives.

To give an example, consider the case of a medium-sized European tour operator with a capacity of say 500 000 packages sold to European destinations in the previous year and a 5-year strategy to grow through a combination of market penetration and product development. Assuming that favourable market circumstances are revealed by diagnosis and prognosis, and starting from a good competitive position, the operator might look for a 15% increase in volume in the following year, e.g. to achieve sales of 575 000 tours over the next 12 months.

Even if revenue targets and market share were added to this statement, it could not be considered fully actionable in marketing terms. To meet the seven criteria previously noted, and drawing on a notional analysis of the operator's business for the sake of the example, the same objective would have to be developed as follows.

To achieve sales of 575 000 tours in targeted European destinations between April and September, at average 95% occupancy, to achieve total revenue before costs of, say, £12 million, with an overall market share of 3%:

(a) *by sales of 355 000 summer sun tours (+2% on previous year)*

(b) *by sales of 115 000 lakes and mountains tours (+15% on previous year)*

(c) *by sales of 30 000 coach tours (+5% on previous year)*

(d) *by sales of 75 000 city breaks (+25% on previous year)*

The figures in brackets represent target increases on previous years' sales, reflecting the diagnosis and prognosis stage of planning as well as a particular growth strategy, in this case to extend penetration in the city breaks market and develop new products in that sector of the market.

This level of precision would be the basis for planning weekly capacity for airports of origin, resort destinations, flight and bed capacity and contracting for the necessary seats and rooms. In tour-operating practice the process of targeting numbers is built up on the basis of aircraft flight capacity and schedules, so that the operational implications of targeted increases for contracting purposes are immediately apparent to managers.

From these quantified capacity targets, the promotional and other marketing tasks in achieving the targeted volumes can be drawn up and costed for budget purposes. Subsequently, the marketing effort can be evaluated in terms of bookings against target sales on a weekly basis.

It should be apparent, even from this brief consideration of setting objectives, that precision of this kind cannot be achieved without prior analysis in some depth (diagnosis and prognosis) and evaluation of SWOT. In every case, except for very small operators with one product and one segment, it will be found necessary to disaggregate the objectives into specific products and segments. Once this is achieved, the specification and costing of marketing-mix tasks immediately become easier.

Marketing budget: a dialogue

The marketing budget (discussed in more detail in Chapter 12) determines the amount of money that has to be spent in advance of bookings, reservations and purchases in order to secure targeted sales volume and revenue. In the tour operator example noted above, costs of website operations and bookings, brochure production, servicing retail distributors and advertising would be committed months before the full payments were made for bookings or even most of the deposits were received from customers. Only the retail commission would be a variable element in the marketing budget.

The budget thus represents the sum of the costs of individual marketing-mix elements judged necessary by marketing managers to achieve specified objectives and targets. There can never be total precision between costs spent up-front and results achieved but this does not alter the principle of allocating money to specific tasks in order to achieve targeted results.

Because the budget is required to achieve volume and revenue objectives through expenditure on a marketing-mix programme, there is a vital feedback or 'dialogue' loop between target setting and marketing management agreement on what can realistically be achieved with affordable budgets (see Fig. 11.2).

Fig. 11.2 demonstrates the essential systematic interaction that takes place in marketing planning between goals, objectives, budgets and programmes. The proposed objectives reflect business goals and strategy, as previously described. The marketing resources include the numbers, competencies and skills of staff to undertake programmes. Also in resources are the size, structure and costs involved in providing websites, booking systems, servicing distribution channels and undertaking a realistic integrated communications and promotion mix (see also Chapter 16).

For each marketing objective there will normally be a range of options as to how it will be achieved – more or less advertising, more or less price discounting, and so on. Marketing managers are required to consider these options and the associated costs,

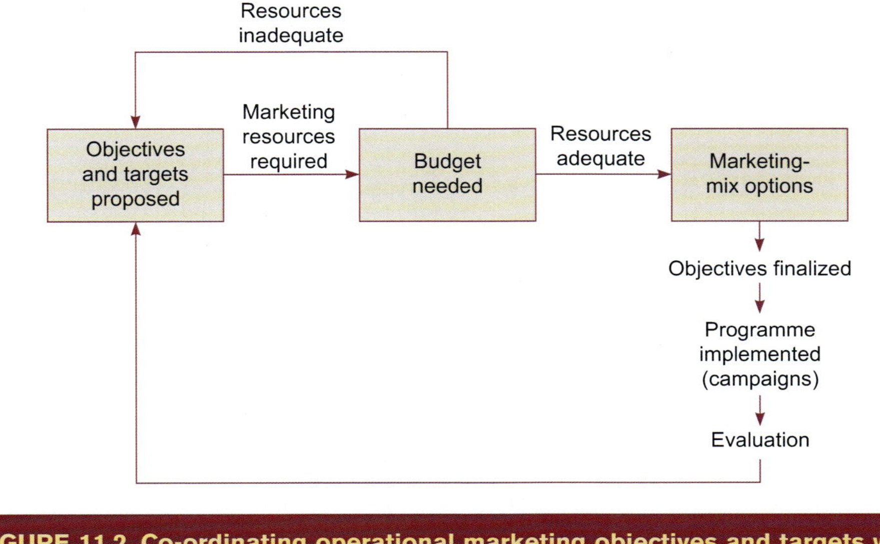

FIGURE 11.2 Co-ordinating operational marketing objectives and targets with budgets and marketing mix programmes

using judgement, experience and analysis of previous results. If an evaluation of objectives and the cost of marketing tasks demonstrates that planned resources are inadequate, then additional budgets will be needed or the objectives must be amended.

Over the space of several days or weeks, each of the interlocking elements in Fig. 11.2 will be modified until an agreed marketing mix programme is finalized for implementation. The essential features of targets are that they should be meaningful and that they should be acceptable to those taking on responsibility for striving to achieve them.

Marketing-mix programmes

Action programmes comprise the costed mix of marketing activities that are undertaken to influence and motivate buyers to choose targeted volumes of particular products. These include

- Internet marketing and booking system costs.
- Promotional literature and electronic information provision.
- Advertising.
- Direct marketing.
- Sales promotion and merchandizing.
- Public relations.
- Retail distribution (if relevant) and use of sales-force to service selected channels.
- Commissions to retailers.

- Planned price discounts.
- Payment to search engines such as Google and selected portals making charges.

Link article available at www.routledge.com/9780750686938

(1) Lichtenthal, J.D., Eliaz, S., 2003. Internet integration in business marketing tactics. Industrial Marketing Management 32, 3–13.

A marketing-mix programme or marketing campaign (see next chapter) expresses exactly what activities will take place in support of each identified product/market subgroup on a week-by-week basis. Because website operations, brochure production and distribution, retail distribution channels, advertising and sales promotion all have different timescales, there is a considerable management art necessary in scheduling programmes of work to make the best use of the marketing department staff's time.

Link article available at www.routledge.com/9780750686938

(1) Westwood, S., Morgan, N.J., Pritchard, A., 1999. Branding the package holiday – the role and significance of brands for UK air tour operators. Journal of Vacation Marketing 5 (3), 238–52.

Monitoring, evaluation and control

Chapter 10 posed three key strategic questions of: where are we now? Where do we want to be? How do we get there? Implicit in that is another question, how do we know if we arrived? Perhaps the most important reason for insisting on precision in setting objectives is to make it possible to measure results. In the case of the tour operator business discussed above under 'marketing objectives and targets', it would be possible to monitor results for each market/product sector under at least seven headings, most of them daily or at least weekly:

- Consumer use of websites and flow of bookings achieved.
- Other flows of bookings against planned capacity.
- Enquiries and sales response related to any advertising.
- Customer awareness of advertising messages measured by research surveys.
- Sales response to any price discounts and sales promotions.
- Sales response to any merchandizing efforts by travel agents.
- Customer satisfaction with product quality measured by customer satisfaction questionnaires.

Chapter 12 deals with evaluation and control in more detail. Suffice it here to note that marketing staff in the tour operator illustration would be expected to have records of weekly booking flows for several previous years as a guide to expected flows of bookings in a current year.

THE CORPORATE COMMUNICATION ROLE OF MARKETING PLANS

As noted earlier, involving as many staff contributions as possible in the process of setting objectives and drawing up plans that communicate well is an important aspect of motivating staff at all levels and securing enthusiastic participation in the implementation process. It is a subject of increasing attention in many travel and tourism organizations; it is especially important for service businesses in which so many staff have direct contact with customers on the premises (see Chapter 8). It is usually possible to time the stages in marketing planning so that managers and as many staff as possible in all departments can take some part in initiating and/or commenting on draft objectives and plans. It is common sense that those who have to carry out plans should identify themselves with their success and not see them as impositions laid down by senior managers who may not have recent practical experience of what can be achieved within known constraints. Where target setting and evaluation are linked with some form of performance incentives, the motivation of staff is likely to be easier to secure.

Many managers will be aware of the damaging effect on staff morale of working within an organization where the objectives appear to change according to management whim, or where directives are issued by planning departments and there is no opportunity to debate their practicality in operation. While marketing planning is conducted primarily to achieve more efficient business decisions, its secondary benefit is to provide a means of internal participation and communication, vital in creating and sustaining a high level of organizational morale.

Marketing plans are also important in communicating to stakeholders outside the company. An approach to banks or other investors, for example in tourism projects funded by EU sources, invariably requires a business plan in which marketing objectives and outputs are a primary component. Where money is granted, evidence of results will always be required through a formal evaluation process.

DISTINGUISHING BETWEEN MARKETING PLANNING FOR STRATEGY AND TACTICS

Earlier in the chapter it was noted that the eight-stage process for drawing up marketing plans is the same in principle for both strategy and tactics. Strategic planning usually focuses mainly on diagnosis, prognosis and the SWOT analysis, and is likely to look backwards over the trends of several years as well as forward to the extent that projections are sensible. As explained in Chapter 10, strategic planning is much broader in its approach than tactical planning, and strategic goals are normally not expressed in quantifiable terms. Strategic goals state where an organization wishes to be with regard to its markets, expressed in broad terms of corporate missions and objectives and evaluation of opportunities that can be turned subsequently into short-term operational plans. Strategic goals may be expressed in terms of projected growth and profit, organizational structure or in relation to competitors. Strategies may be expressed in terms of the four main Ps of the marketing mix or any other aspect influenced by marketing managers and ultimately measurable in customer attitudes and purchase behaviour. For any large organization they will be concerned with the way a company does business looking at least 5 years ahead.

Effective marketing strategies always require considerable organizational commitment and effort. 'Strong, offensive strategies do not come easily. They are usually the result of prolonged and painstaking analysis of the market, competitors and the trend of change' (Davidson, 1975: 115).

By contrast operational or tactical marketing planning is a 'practical exercise in deciding what a business is to achieve through marketing activity in the year ahead. It is a logical thought process and an application of common sense. It provides a basis of objectives around which marketing tasks are set, budgets drawn up and results measured' (Middleton, 1980: 26). Operational plans express in precise, quantifiable, short-run terms what an organization is seeking to achieve for its portfolio of products and segments within the context of an established long-run strategy.

CHAPTER SUMMARY

This chapter:

- Considers the need for and the process of marketing planning for travel and tourism organizations, now undertaken in some form by all medium to large organizations. Unless they need to approach banks or other investors, most smaller businesses still rely on 'feel for the market' to guide their decisions on objectives and the ways in which they intend to achieve them. In the authors' experience, only very large organizations have established systematic planning processes comparable to those in manufacturing and leading service industries such as the retail and financial sectors. For most organizations, therefore, there is great scope for significant improvement in the time, effort and expertise that is employed to undertake what is perhaps the most important single aspect of conducting any business.
- Compared with the constant preoccupation in most companies with cutting current costs, more time allocated to the processes best calculated to generate future revenue would be well spent. The marketing process offers the best available route to increasing performance at the margin.
- Explains how systematic marketing planning establishes operational objectives and action programmes that are adapted to changing circumstances. Planning does not replace flair and judgement. It certainly does not provide certain ways to cope with crisis. But it does provide a fertile base of the best available information and a broad strategic direction within which imagination, flair and vision can be harnessed to produce their best results.
- Considers the role that stakeholders play in the marketing planning process. All tourism-based organizations have to work with stakeholders, especially now when there are growing concerns about climate change, degradation at destinations and the proportions of visitor expenditure retained in local economies. Stakeholder participation is crucial to longer run success of businesses and a key part of the public and private sector collaboration covered in Chapters 10 and 18.

QUESTIONS FOR DISCUSSION

1. Summarize the differences between strategic and tactical market planning.
2. Drawing on a tourism business example of your choice, indicate the main components to be identified in marketing objectives for the year ahead.
3. Explain why environmental impact assessment will become more important in future years.
4. Why are stakeholders so important in marketing planning?

REFERENCES AND FURTHER READING

Brassington, F. and Pettit, S. (2003). *Principles of marketing* (3rd edn). FT Prentice-Hall.

Davidson, H. (1997). *Even more offensive marketing*. Chapter 8. Penguin.

Fyall, A., Callod, C. and Edwards, B. (July 2003). Relationship marketing: the challenge for destinations, *Annals of Tourism Research*, **30**(3), pp. 644–659.

Jobber, D. (2007). *Principles and practice of marketing* (5th edn). McGraw-Hill.

Kaynak, E., Bloom, J. and Leibold, M. (1994). Using the Delphi technique to predict future tourism potential, *Marketing Intelligence and Planning*, **12**(7), pp. 18–29.

Kotler, P. and Armstrong, G. (1999). *Principles of marketing*. Chapter 1 (8th edn). Prentice-Hall.

Kotler, P., Wong, V., Saunders, J. and Armstrong, G. (2005). *Principles of marketing* (4th European edn). Pearson Prentice Hall.

Lichtenthal, J.D. and Eliaz, S. (2003). Internet integration in business marketing tactics, *Industrial Marketing Management*, **32**, pp. 3–13.

McDonald, M.H.B. (2007). *Marketing plans*. Chapters 2–6 (6th edn). Butterworth-Heinemann.

Ringland, G. (2002). *Scenarios in business*. New York: John Wiley.

Westwood, S., Morgan, N.J. and Pritchard, A. (1999). Branding the package holiday – the role and significance of brands for UK air tour operators, *Journal of Vacation Marketing*, **5**(3), pp. 238–252.

Yeoman, I. and McMahon-Beattie, U. (2005). Developing a scenario planning process using a blank piece of paper, *Tourism and Hospitality Research*, **5**(3), pp. 273–285.

ARRIVED IN SEARCH OF THE ULTIMATE BREAK.

DEPARTED HAVING FOUND PARADISE.

It's true what they say: to find yourself sometimes you need to lose yourself. In Australia they call this going 'walkabout'. And with the most incredible beaches, the ultimate lifestyle and one of the best climates in the world, it's no wonder people are finding themselves here every single day. Visit Australia.com to find out how you can go walkabout.

Destination marketing campaigns typically aim to influence the numbers, type and spending of visitors.

Courtesy Tourism Australia

CHAPTER 12

Planning marketing campaigns: budgeting and evaluating marketing performance

Marketing is a learning game. You make a decision. You watch the results. You learn from those results. Then you make better decisions.

(Kotler, 1999: 185)

This chapter draws the other chapters of Part Three together in a practical focus on the meaning and nature of marketing campaigns. The broad, unifying concept of campaigns is explained here and developed subsequently throughout Parts Four and Five of the book. 'Campaign' is not a term widely used in marketing texts except in the specific contexts of advertising or public relations. For all forms of travel and tourism, however, production operations, service delivery and marketing are very closely interlinked. We believe the marketing campaign concept is especially valuable for the practical insights it provides into organizing and controlling marketing tactics and programmes, and the term is strongly recommended to readers.

The word *campaign*, with its connotations of military action, is well suited to the activities of marketing managers aggressively promoting their organizations' interests and aiming to defeat their competitors. Marketing managers, or product managers responsible for undertaking campaigns, have been aptly described as the 'storm troopers of marketing' (Davidson, 1975: 95). For modern readers, the concept of storm troopers is rather too business centric to chime with consumer-centric thinking, but the idea of focused teams aggressively pursuing campaign objectives is still valid. Campaigns create a sense of purpose and urgency for the brand that is being promoted, but the competitive thrust can, and should be, adapted to embrace information for customers about the quality of experiences that can be expected and it must also accommodate ideas of dynamic packaging and customer participation. Usually, before campaigns are developed, extensive market research about a product and its expectations among the consumers needs to be carried out. The target markets need to be understood and campaigns have to be developed to enable the potential targets to appreciate the experiences that they may expect at particular destinations.

After studying this chapter, you should be able to understand:

- The definitions of marketing action programmes relevant to the whole of Part Four.
- How to identify and specify the techniques that marketing managers deploy in their campaigns to influence consumer demand and generate sales revenue.
- The basic methods used for budgeting in marketing by working through typical campaign budgets.
- The approaches used to measure performance including practical ways to monitor results.

MARKETING CAMPAIGNS ARE ACTION PROGRAMMES

Marketing campaign describes any coordinated programme of marketing activities in the general field of product design, pricing, promotion, communication and distribution that is designed to influence, mould and respond to customers' behaviour.

In marketing practice and in texts, the term is often used only in a restricted sense of advertising, sales promotion or public relations. In fact, the term is not used by Kotler, but Stanton defined a campaign as 'a co-ordinated series of promotional efforts built around a single theme or idea and designed to reach a predetermined goal ... we should apply the campaign concept to the entire promotional programme' (Stanton, 1981: 391).

Without challenging the principle underlying Stanton's definition, the authors believe it makes sense to broaden it further and to tie it specifically into the implementation phase of the marketing planning process. Thus:

A marketing campaign is a planned, integrated action programme designed to achieve specific marketing objectives and targets, through the deployment of a budget on the promotion and distribution of products over a specified time period.

Campaigns may be aimed directly at consumers, or indirectly through a distribution network, or both. The focus of a marketing campaign is a short-run action programme and several campaigns would normally be necessary to achieve particular strategic objectives.

THE MENU FOR MARKETING CAMPAIGNS IN TRAVEL AND TOURISM

The full range of marketing techniques to be woven into campaigns is set out in Table 12.1 as a *menu*. Each technique has its own methods, skills and implications for action, which are explained in subsequent chapters in Part Four of the book. The implications for campaigns are generally perceived to lie in the promotional aspects of the marketing mix but price is included in its discounted sense, product augmentation is included where it overlaps with sales promotion, and distribution is both a target for campaigns and increasingly a part of the promotional process. The menu represents choices from which marketing managers will select according to their particular targets and market circumstances.

Marketing campaigns in travel and tourism have two main dimensions:

1. Promotional techniques designed to motivate and move or 'push' prospective customers towards a point of sale and also to provide incentives to purchase (includes promotion to distributors). Such techniques include websites as part of the promotion.

2. Facilitation of access techniques designed to 'pull' and make it as easy as possible for motivated people to achieve their intended purchase, especially at the point of sale (access is defined in Chapter 15). Here too, access via websites is now a central part of any modern access decision.

Where products are normally purchased ahead of consumption, as is the case, for example, in accommodation, transportation, tour operation or car rental, it

TABLE 12.1 The principal marketing campaign techniques used in travel and tourism

Activity	Notes
Paid for media advertising	Includes television, press, radio and outdoor. Also includes tourist board and other travel guides, books and brochures.
Internet	Web sits/banner advertising and links to other sites.
Direct mail/door to door	Includes sales literature and print items specially designed for distribution for this purpose.
Public relations	All media exposure achieved as editorial matter. Also other forms of influence achieved over target groups—customers and stakeholders.
Sponsorship	An alternative form of media to reach specified target groups.
Exhibitions/shows/workshops	Important alternative forms of distribution and display for reaching retail, wholesale and consumer target groups.
Personal selling	Via meetings, telephones, e-mail and workshops. Primarily aimed at distributors and intermediaries purchasing on behalf of groups of consumers.
Sales literature (print)	Expecially promotional brochures and other print used in a servicing/ facilitation role.
Sales promotion	Short-term incentives offered as inducements to purchase, Including temporary product augmentation. Covers sales force and distribution network as well as consumers.
Price discounting	A common form of sales promotion. Includes Internet offers and extra commission and bonuses for retailers.
Point of sale displays and merchandising	Posters, window dressing, displays of brochures and other materials both of a regular and temporary incentive kind.
Familiarization trips and educationals	Ways to motivate and facilitate distributor networks through product sampling. Also used to reach and influence journalists.
Distribution networks and commission	Organized systems or channels through which prospective customers achieve access to products. Includes CRSs and the Internet.

always makes sense to programme and include the full cost of access facilitation in the total campaign budget. Where multiple distribution channels exist and are diversifying rapidly, as again is the case for much of travel and tourism, creation of consumer access for products is getting much closer to what is conventionally discussed as promotion than it is to what was conventionally described as distribution.

Access to the Internet as a marketing tool since the mid-1990s has provided a wholly new means of bringing the two dimensions together by integrating promotion and access within the same medium. The power of websites is that they can simultaneously advertise, inform, display, promote special offers, make a sale and provide instant booking and confirmation – in customers' homes or while they are on the move (see Part Four of the book).

In summary, marketing campaigns include all four variables of the marketing mix (four Ps or four Cs), where their use is designed in the short term to influence and facilitate buyer behaviour to achieve targeted campaign objectives. To focus only on promotion, however, is seriously to underestimate the cost of marketing. The campaign menu in Table 12.1 is provided as an indication of what lies within the spectrum of choice for marketing managers. The main techniques are all discussed separately in Part Four of the book.

Courtesy of Dimitrios Buhalis.

MARKETING CAMPAIGN BUDGETS

The marketing budget may be defined as *the sum of the costs of the campaign action programme judged necessary to achieve the specified objectives and targets set out in the marketing plan.*

In practice, the most difficult decisions in a marketing manager's year lie in estimating and agreeing the budget. The budget, usually drawn up on an annual campaign basis for each major product/market in an organization's portfolio, represents money that has to be spent 'up front' or ahead of the targeted volume and sales revenue it is expected to generate. Every $1000 spent on campaign action programmes has to be paid for out of reserves, current cash flows or by borrowing. It is money that can only be recovered at some future point from the projected surplus of income over operating expenditure, that is, gross operating profit. On the other hand, as marketing managers are expected to demonstrate, if the money is *not* spent, revenue targets will not be achieved. Perhaps, the hardest decision to justify is that of borrowing thousands or millions of pounds to spend on marketing campaigns, not to secure a projected operating surplus, but to reduce the probable size of an expected loss. Such decisions had to be taken by most airlines and many hotels in the international economic crises of the early 1990s, and again in the Asia Pacific region in the wake of the massive downturn in 1997 of the Asian 'Tiger' economies. As this book goes to press, these hard decisions are being taken again in the light of the 2008 global financial crisis and expected recession in 2009.

In practice, setting campaign budgets depends on finding answers to three fundamental questions.

- How much money must be spent *in total* on a marketing campaign, in order to achieve objectives? This amount will usually be expressed as a percentage of total sales revenue or as a ratio. Thus, a £50 000 marketing budget on a sales turnover of £1 million will be 5 per cent or a ratio of 1:20.
- How will the total be *split between the products and segments* included in the campaign? In practice, it is essential to divide a total budget between the specific sets of targets it is expected to achieve. The process for analysing product/market groupings, discussed in Chapters 10 and 11, provides a logical basis for such division. Naturally, if an international organization, such as an airline, is marketing itself in several countries, then the budget also has to be divided between the targeted countries. In larger organizations, each strategic business unit (SBU) as well as each product/market grouping will have a separate campaign budget.
- How will the total be *divided between the component parts* of the action programme? The component parts of the action programme are the marketing tools or techniques shown in Table 12.1. The choices and the costs will be different for each of the targets within a campaign and for each of the countries included in a campaign.

With a few moments' thought, it should be clear that the apparently simple tasks implied in the three fundamental budget questions become very complicated in practice for large businesses marketing their portfolio of products to a range of segments in different countries.

BUDGETING METHODS

Kotler (1984: 621) noted basic methods of setting both the total budget and any of its sub-divisions. Each of these is still commonly used:

- Affordable method.
- Percentage of sales revenue method.
- Competitive parity method (matching competitors' spending).
- Objective and task method.

The first three of these methods are, in fact, quite closely related and rely primarily on historic information (previous budgeting levels), marketing intelligence about competitors' actions and received wisdom about 'industry norms' based on experience. In essence, they are all 'rule of thumb' or 'gut feel' methods, which commence with a fairly broad notion of an appropriate marketing expenditure considered affordable, expressed as a proportion of targeted sales revenue or turnover, such as 5 per cent. Over time, such aggregate percentages often become a 'norm', which sets an expenditure ceiling not to be exceeded unless a company is forced to do so to match the competition, or to respond to other unforeseen events. Although they are still widely used in practice, especially by small businesses, these are aggregate or top-downwards methods that shed no light on how total expenditure *should be* allocated between product–market groupings or divided between campaign elements, two of the three basic questions posed earlier.

The objective and task method is quite different. It begins with a specification of what is to be achieved (objective) and proceeds by stating and costing the techniques (tasks) required to achieve it. This method, which is closely related to so-called zero-budgeting methods, is obviously the one most closely associated with the systematic marketing planning approaches discussed in this book. If there are precise objectives for each product/market grouping, the objective and task method can be used to construct a budget from the bottom upwards through specification of tasks, so that each of the three budget questions posed earlier are answered. Objective and task methods are, however, time-consuming, and the procedures for costing are often dependent on marketing judgement. The tidy logic of the textbook may not be easily implemented in practice, especially for organizations with multiple objectives and several product/market groupings.

The next section explains and illustrates how these methods work in practice.

A marketing budget for a tour operator

An illustration of a hypothetical British tour operator's budget is shown in Fig. 12.1 to indicate how budgeting methods often operate in practice. The example assumes that sales are achieved at targeted load factors (typically around 90 per cent of the capacity put on sale) and the items, representing the essentials of a typical trading, profit and loss account, have simplified headings for the sake of presentation. The budget is based on hypothetical figures but it broadly represents British tour operator cost structures of the mid to late 2000s. No operator will release data of this sort, which has to be commercially confidential. The authors have been assisted in producing broadly realistic budget estimates by two organizations shown in the Acknowledgements in the Preface to this book.

It needs to be stressed that before this process of budgeting begins, decisions have already been made on corporate vision and the values to be communicated – positioning in the market place and the brand propositions to be fully reflected and built into all aspects of promotion and distribution. See Chapters 8, 10 and 11. These are taken for granted in this example and not separately dealt with in the chapter.

In this illustration, it is estimated that approximately two-thirds of all the sales are derived from retail travel agents and a third from the Internet. The website proportion has been rising every year this century. The thinking implicit in Fig. 12.1 can be adapted to suit the budget circumstances of most travel and tourism businesses and is offered as a useful model for examining budgeting issues. For example, one could apply the model to a large tour operator with over 1 million packages in a market/product portfolio and an average package price of around £600. Equally, it would work for a domestic tour operator with 100,000 weekend packages with a brochure price of around £200. See also the explanatory notes accompanying Fig. 12.1.

While the percentages or proportions of the budget allocated to the items shown in Fig. 12.1 will certainly fluctuate from year to year and from one firm to another, the broad orders of magnitude hold good over time and the following points can be made:

- Of the total sales revenue, some 80 per cent is absorbed in contracted product component costs and a further 4 per cent is committed in fixed costs of operation and investment in systems. For some tour operators, the contracted costs would exceed 80 per cent, which – considered with the cost of achieving sales – gives some idea of the knife-edge of profit or loss affecting most operators. Of the remainder, the brochure commitment is inescapable, and so also is the retail agency support system to achieve the targeted volume of sales (assuming 66 per cent of sales through this form of distribution channel in the example). In other words, some 90 per cent of sales revenue is, to all intents and purposes, committed in advance of any revenue received.
- In Fig. 12.1, advertising, sales promotion and other discretionary campaign costs to be decided by the marketing manager, represent well under 1 per cent of total turnover. As it is most unlikely that, in practice, such costs would be either halved or doubled in any one year, the real level of budget discretion is remarkably small, probably under 0.5 per cent of projected sales turnover.
- In this example, the contingency reserve for tactical discounts at £1 million is not much bigger than the itemized discretionary expenditure (on advertising, sales promotion and PR), although it represents only £2 per tour package. In practice, if bookings fell seriously below targeted levels, the contingency reserve would be increased by a factor of two or more but the money could only come from the £6.75 million targeted gross operating profit – or from reserves. In the mid-2000s large UK tour operator struggled to achieve 5 per cent gross profit on trading operations, because of fierce competition and the need to spend contingency money on marketing, especially tactical price discounting. Figure 12.1 is based on a target gross profit of 4.5 per cent.
- There is no consensus as to exactly what items should be included or excluded from a marketing budget. The websites, CRS systems and associated call centres are clearly essential for the achievement of sales, and

The company

This is a notional company with national sales of packages via travel agents and Internet targeted at the British market with package offers mostly for short breaks to European destinations. This illustration covers the campaign for one product/market portfolio.

Budget summary	**Year** (£000s)	%
Total turnover @ £300 (arsp) [1] on 500,000 packages sold assuming sales of 90% capacity	150,000	
Less cost of contracting components [2], say	- 120,000	= 80%
= Gross trading surplus	30,000	
Less targeted operating profit before tax @ say 4.5% turnover	- 6,750	= 4.5%
= maximum sum to cover all admin and marketing costs	**23,250**	= 15.5%

Specific costs of administration, operations and marketing

(Essentially fixed costs for a year ahead)		
Committed costs of operation	1,800	
Reservation system and overheads [3]	1,500	
Non-marketing administration costs [4]	1,200	
Marketing staff and overheads	1,320	
Support staff at destinations	180	
	6,000	**=4%**

Marketing campaign costs

(Fixed and *variable costs for year ahead but dominated by variable costs)*		
Advertising, sales promotion and PR [5]	750	
Brochures and marketing print	1,650	
Cost of sales		
Retail sales commission (@ average of 13 % [6]	11,000	
Web site costs and fees payable [7]	2,800	
	16,200	**=10.8%**
Planned contingency reserve [8]	**1,000**	**= 0.7%**
	23,250	

Notes

1. The average retail sales price achieved. In practice this would vary between planned brochure price and discounted prices either at retail agents or on the Internet
2. Accommodation and any transport , transfers and options included in the package
3. Includes Internet , CRS and Web site investment, computer systems and all staff engaged
4. Office expenses, heating/lighting/rates etc, staff and equipment including general administration
5. Covers all elements of the integrated promotions mix noted in Chapter 16
6. Payments based on 66 per cent sales via retail agents and 33 per cent via Internet. This is an *average* discount figure, which allows retailers to undertake some of their own discounts to customers
7. Covers 'pay per click' and search engine optimization costs,
8. Held in reserve, especially for tactical discounts if sales fall below targets

The estimates in this illustration make realistic allowance for factors such as the cost and number of brochures needed, discounts that in practice vary the commission paid to retail agents and the price discounts implicit in achieving a third of sales via the Internet.

FIGURE 12.1 A marketing budget campaign model for a tour operator. (Adapted from the 3rd edition of this book with current advice from two tour-operating companies.)

are shown as reservation systems and overheads and committed costs of operations. The concept of integrated communications that would be involved in practice in this budget is discussed in detail in Chapter 16.

- In this example, brochure production and distribution costs plus agency commission costs are well over 15 per cent of turnover, which is over three times the size of the targeted operating profit.
- Much attention is currently being focused on the alternative costs associated with investing in systems that use the Internet. In 2008, the use of the Internet for booking, as a percentage of total sales had grown massively since 2000, and in this example is estimated to be around one-third of sales. Internet sales, however, are not calculated simply as the cost of setting up and operating systems. There are payments to search engines, costs of banner advertising and costs per click to be paid. More significantly, many customers use the Internet to find lower-cost options (after all they are doing the work themselves), and there is an element of general and last-minute price discounting on website sales, which is likely to amount to 5 per cent or more of the brochure price. These considerations are reflected in the estimates shown in Fig. 12.1.

THE OBJECTIVE AND TASK METHOD

From Fig. 12.1, it should be clear that the so-called affordable and percentage of turnover methods of budgeting are at least relevant and practical. Apart from establishing upper limits to expenditure, however, such methods do not provide guidance as to how best to apportion the affordable sums. For that, it is necessary to use the objective and task method discussed next.

To illustrate this method, consider the case of a hotel consortium acting for marketing purposes as a group but comprising 100 individually owned hotels with a combined capacity of 6000 rooms. Assume that, through careful diagnosis and prognosis, the consortium has set itself a marketing objective to sell 45 per cent of its aggregate capacity (equivalent to 2700 rooms) as weekend packages over 20 selected weekends between October and April. The group plans to do this via its own promotional and distribution efforts centred around its group of hotels as points of promotion, access and sales, plus website sales and its own CRS system. For ease of calculation, assume that each package lasts for two nights and covers two people. Also for ease of calculation, assume the average price, published in the consortium's brochure, is £100 per person/package, which includes breakfast and dinner for the two nights – but not additional expenditure in the hotels.

The sales revenue target is, therefore:[a]

2700(rooms) × 20(weekends) × 2 persons × £100 per person
= total weekend package sales revenue = £ 10,800,000

2700(rooms)×20(weekends)×2 persons × 2(days) × £ 20 per day
= additional revenue spent in bars, etc. = £ 2,160,000

***Total sales revenue* = £ 12,960,000**

[a]All quoted billions come from European Sources and so are 10^{12}

Because the fixed costs of hotel operation are already committed, the hotel consortium stands to achieve a gross contribution (additional revenue over variable costs) of around 45 per cent on this business, say £6 million.

The question to resolve is how much should the consortium spend on marketing in order to achieve the £6 million additional revenue? By applying conventional ratio methods, it is easy to calculate (using rounded figures) that:

5 per cent of total sales revenue (including additional spending)	£648,000
10 per cent of total sales revenue (including additional spending)	£1, 296,000
20 per cent of total sales revenue (including additional spending)	£2,592,000

Even beyond the 20 per cent level of expenditure on marketing, the consortium would still find it advantageous to invest assuming that, without the calculated marketing effort, at least a half of the potential £6 million gross contribution would not be achieved. In practice, if the hotel consortium were to negotiate with a tour operator to sell its packages, the contract discount required could easily be 25 per cent or more.

With clear objectives set, which in practice would be split by area of the country and the projected profile of target buyers, the next step is to itemize and cost the tasks in an effective marketing campaign.

Task-based campaign budget

The following costs are indicative of what would be spent in practice (2005 prices) by the consortium to meet the objectives noted in the preceding section:

Cost of producing, say 250, 000 brochures (allows for costs of distribution via hotels own lists, direct mail, and via e-mail requests)	£350,000
Advertising in consumer media	250,000
Advertising in tourist board guides etc.	7,500
Point of sale material (hotels in the group)	5,000
PR campaign costs	15,000
Others, including costs of website promotion and allowance for promotional price offers averaging 7%	600,000
Total	**£1,227,500**

The following points can be made:

1. Selecting the itemized tasks and estimating the expenditure required are based on a mixture of *fact* (brochure production and distribution costs, website costs and discounts needed,), *experience* (knowledge of which activities are most relevant for selling weekend packages and the costs and quantities of any previous campaigns) and *judgement* (especially in relation to media expenditure and level of discounting needed but drawing on advertising agency knowledge and expertise and close monitoring of website sales)

2. There can be no absolute certainty that £1,227,500 will produce the targeted bookings for the consortium. There is, however, a systematic method and framework for making decisions within which it is possible to focus facts, experience and judgement. Given adequate evaluation of the campaign's

results (see later in this chapter), the systematic framework would also serve as a learning mechanism to refine the decision process for any subsequent campaigns.

3. If the sales target is achieved, £1,227,500 will be 11.8 per cent of £10,800,000 (the sales revenue from selling the product packages) and 20.5 per cent of the gross contribution of £6 million. The advertising (paid space in the media) is 2.3 per cent of the package sales revenue. In the end, these ratios have little meaning except to establish that the bottom line return is worth the investment. The cost of the campaign can be seen as the price for achieving the targeted business, and at that point, the ratios are only of interest for control and evaluation purposes – they were not used to determine the size of the marketing budget.
4. In practice, in monitoring and evaluating a campaign of this sort, the hotel group would wish to analyse the proportion of its bookings that came from previous customers. It may be possible to adapt the components of the campaign to achieve a higher proportion of sales from repeat bookers, thereby lowering marketing costs. The group would also wish to evaluate the relative cost and revenue generation of sales via retail outlets versus sales over the Internet.
5. If the hotel consortium chose the alternative route of retail sales for around two-thirds of its product offer, the total campaign budget including commission and servicing would be of the order of 12–15 per cent of sales revenue and substantially higher than shown in this example. By the methods shown, the group would also refine its database knowledge for future marketing activity.
6. The functional relationship between marketing expenditure and targeted revenue should be clear.

Link article available at www.routledge.com/9780750686938

(1) Trembath, R., 1999. Best kept secrets: an evaluation of South Australia's direct marketing campaign. Journal of Vacation Marketing 6, 76–85

PERFORMANCE MEASUREMENT: EVALUATION, MONITORING AND CONTROL

Kotler states that 'marketing control is the natural sequel to marketing planning, organization and implementation' (Kotler, 1984: 773). All marketing texts stress the importance of measuring the results achieved by action programmes against the planned targets. But, given the importance of the subject, it is surprising how little space most books offer on measurement and there are no recognized guidelines for travel and tourism. The subject is too often seen, as in most hotel groups, as the responsibility of accountants and financial controllers. It is far too important for that.

Good performance measurement provides the vital information for marketing managers to:

- Respond quickly and effectively if actual sales and other indicators vary significantly from targets.
- Learn from current experience in ways that will make the subsequent year's campaign targets and budgets more cost-efficient.
- Adjust strategic objectives in the light of current results.
- Integrate marketing decisions with those of other key business functions, especially accounting and finance and operations management.
- Make the vital marginal adjustments to campaigns, which in high fixed-cost businesses will always have a major impact on profit or loss.

It is not too much to claim that the effectiveness and efficiency of marketing is actually determined by the quality of the performance measurement techniques used. It is also worth repeating that it is impossible for marketing managers to respond effectively to aggregate measures of the total volume or revenue. In other words, the number of airline passengers carried over a year is a useless measure in practice, except perhaps for annual reports and PR purposes; the total number of room nights sold by a hotel, or total bed occupancy, is just an academic statistic of no marketing management value. What matters is how many first-class passenger bookings were received against monthly targets; which of the routes flown were up or down; how conference bookings for events for over 100 persons responded to the action programmes targeted at conference organizers and so on.

The all-important linkage between targeting, budgeting and measuring performance *disaggregated by product/market groupings* is a constant theme throughout this book. It is reflected in the hotel example used in this chapter and further illustrated in Part Five. As Kotler put it 'market-share analysis, like sales analysis, increases in value when the data is disaggregated along various dimensions. The company might watch the progress of its market share by product line, customer type, region, or other breakdowns' (Kotler, 1984: 748).

In travel and tourism, it will be found helpful to distinguish between three aspects of performance measurement that are the responsibility of marketing managers. There is a fourth related form of measurement outlined as follows under innovation, experimentation and test marketing:

1. *Evaluation* – defined as the systematic periodic evaluation of achievement of stated objectives. Evaluation is usually an annual process and often a focal part of regular marketing audits carried out as part of the strategic planning process described in Chapters 10 and 11. Evaluation is crucial in measuring the competitive or relative performance of one company against another in the same market.
2. *Monitoring* – the systematic measurement of performance on a daily, weekly or monthly basis, which assesses actual results against targeted sales. The results of monitoring are typically collated through a marketing information system, used immediately for marketing control and also fed into the annual evaluation process.

   As with so many elements in the marketing mix, the advent of the Internet provides readily available measures of the total number of hits that websites receive, the number of individuals making the hits and the flow of those hits, yielding a continuous stream of low cost data with which to monitor campaigns.

The monitoring process may also rely to some extent on market research where the effectiveness of campaigns can be assessed, for example, in awareness studies of a campaign and satisfaction with the product studies. In some instances, campaigns can play a longer-term role, where a particular campaign can capture a person's imagination but his or her intention to go to a particular destination may be delayed because of personal circumstances. Hence, the full effect of the campaign would be delayed and the routine monitoring process would not be able to pick this aspect up readily – even annually.

Although not directly related to the key issues of monitoring sales performance and revenue against targets, monitoring for all organizations is increasingly expected to have regard to sustainable performance measures, such as energy usage, water usage, waste creation and proportion of food sourced locally. Where an organization positions itself and its brands as delivering sustainable values and practice, such monitoring will be essential to support its claims.

For effective evaluation and monitoring, it is essential that the practicalities of measurement are included in the process through which marketing targets are drawn up. It is a central criterion of the planning process described in Chapter 11 that no target is accepted unless the method of measuring it is defined in advance. In this sense, performance monitoring is more than a 'sequel of marketing planning, organization and implementation'; it is an integral part of the targeting and objective setting process. If objectives cannot be monitored and assessed by affordable methods, they should not be selected.

3. *Marketing control* – means tactical marketing management actions taken continuously in response to the information provided by monitoring. Generally this action will be funded out of contingency sums in marketing budgets, although in crisis conditions additional funding will be required. Such actions normally focus on tactical pricing, sales promotion and advertising, and sales achieved on the Internet. The control aspects will build on the monitoring process and give an opportunity to marketers to curtail particular campaigns or to enhance and improve others.

Innovation, experimentation and test marketing

Not normally seen as part of performance measurement, the opportunities for systematic innovation and testing represent a massive and underutilized asset to most marketing managers in travel and tourism. It can and certainly should be used regularly as a highly cost-effective form of both testing and measuring the effectiveness of marketing programmes for travel and tourism products, as well as in the more traditional role of product testing and evaluation.

The opportunities arise in two ways. The first is because customer contact on premises or sites is a normal part of service-delivery operations, and the feedback can be virtually instantaneous. Where an organization, such as an airline or hotel group, operates multiple sites, it is possible to test market innovations and compare responses between outlets, often very quickly. The change may be to the room design, new staff procedures, uniforms or any of the many components that make up the formal and augmented product outlined in Chapter 7. The second way reflects the fact that much of travel and tourism is booked in advance on the basis of information provided. A tour operator can offer a small number of new products or a new destination and monitor the response; any firm can experiment with pages and the layout on their websites as promotional tools and, again, monitor the response; a hotel can collaborate with local heritage attractions and build them into a product offer, and so on. There are countless ways in which forms of test marketing are easier in travel and tourism than in most other industries. It should be built into the performance-measurement programme.

CAMPAIGN PLAN MONITORING

Sales variance

In several parts of this book, reference is made to 'marketing the margin'. Because of the effects of operating on high fixed costs, it means concentrating marketing effort on the incremental percentage occupancy, load factor or visitor numbers, which in travel and tourism usually generate additional revenue at very little or no additional variable cost. If a business loses sales at the margin – sales falling below targets – the margin typically represents a significant loss. In the case of a rail operating company, for example, an additional 1 per cent extra seats sold on a train with available capacity represents 'pure' profit at zero additional cost. One per cent fewer sales reflect a complete loss. Performance measurement must be designed to highlight those margins and the effectiveness of marketing programmes in influencing them.

The more that operational marketing objectives are made precise in terms of volume and revenue targets, time periods, and specific products and segments (discussed in Chapter 11), the easier it is to measure results. Airlines, for example, forecast their passenger volume over a long-run period, by product type, for example, first class, business class and by types of economy fare offered, and by route, making projections on a daily basis. With modern yield-management programmes, they are able to read advance bookings and current sales on an online basis for every flight on every route. The information is used to drive the tactical pricing responses involved in marketing control processes.

In Fig. 12.2 the projected sales represent weekly planning targets, based partly on previous years' operations and partly on diagnosis, prognosis and SWOTanalyses. Airline capacity and operations are scheduled on such projections, timetables are published, seats are made available through CRSs and on websites, and marketing campaigns are carried out ahead of sales. In weeks 4–6, the graph showing 'actual sales' achieved drops significantly below projected sales. As soon as the fall is detected, marketing managers must establish the cause of the drop and consider action to generate more sales, employing contingency reserves if necessary. This type of monitoring is known as variance analysis and, in forms suitable to the products in question, it is the cornerstone of most marketing control. A visitor attraction would target its weekly sales by key segments, such as school groups, holiday visitors, day visitors and coach parties, and monitor actual sales against those targets. The management would separately analyse actual shop and catering sales against their targets to measure variance, and so on.

Sometimes, sales may move far enough ahead of target to make it possible to reduce marketing budgets. When Center Parcs opened their first enclosed resorts in

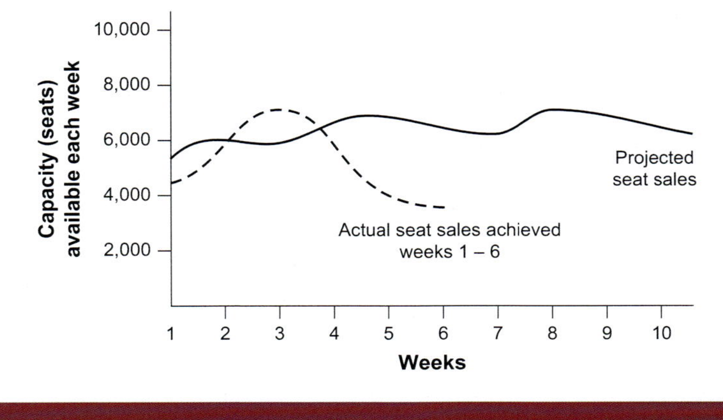

FIGURE 12.2 Variance of sales against targets for an airline

the United Kingdom, they were able to cut back on national advertising because of the initial volume of response. This does not often happen in travel and tourism.

Market share variance

In consumer goods marketing, market share analysis and variance over time are a second basic aspect of marketing monitoring. Own sales analysis, without knowledge other than general marketing intelligence of competitors' sales, can of course provide misleading information. There is no satisfaction in knowing that a business has created a 5 per cent increase in its sales revenue, for example, if its two main rivals have increased by 10 and 15 per cent, respectively, in the same period. In much of travel and tourism, however, apart from transport and tour operations that are legally required to register capacity and carryings, share data is often not known at all, or has to be estimated months afterwards, too late to trigger a variance response. Large hotel groups commission surveys to monitor brand share performance, but such information is not available to smaller businesses.

Customer satisfaction variance

The third principal element in variance analysis can be achieved by regularly monitoring customer satisfaction, both overall and by product components. As described in Chapter 11, providers of travel and tourism service products with customers on their premises are particularly well placed to exploit opportunities to measure customer satisfaction on a regular basis and to read any shifts from average scores. Figure 12.3 illustrates the point in the context of a tour operator monitoring the performance of one of the resort hotels included in its programme.

In Fig. 12.3, based on data collected and analysed over many months, normal customer satisfaction ratings for hotels overall typically vary between 4.8 and 5.5. In that band hotels are generating good satisfaction in the judgement of customers using them. In weeks 1–4, satisfaction is normal. In week 5, it plunges and stays down. Why? Analysis of other scores may reveal a particular problem with food or service, and management action can be taken to rectify the problem and return scores to the average band. To be useful, such variance must be known within hours of its occurrence. Modern computer technology is of increasing value in making such rapid response possible. In this case, marketing research methods to monitor satisfaction also operate as management control mechanisms.

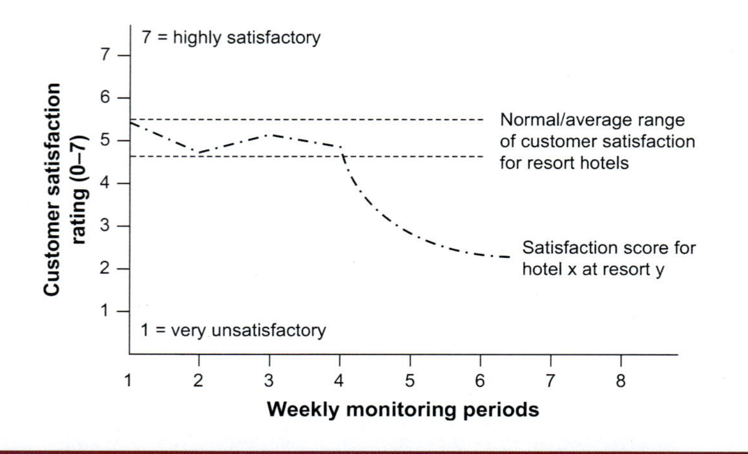

FIGURE 12.3 Variance of satisfaction over time for a tour operator

The growing importance of retaining repeat or loyal customers means that particular attention is likely to be paid to their satisfaction. Any downward variation in this group is a matter of immediate concern and its responses should be separately analysed in all types of tourism business. The YOTEL case in Part Six utilizes satisfaction ratings as a management tool in this way.

Ratio variance

Once the marketing campaign budget is agreed, it is possible to calculate a series of financial comparisons between marketing expenditure and revenue targets, and they can, subsequently, be reviewed against actual revenue achieved. Provided that an organization divides its total portfolio of product markets into logical groupings or profit centres for management purposes, it is possible to establish the costs and revenues attributable to each grouping and then calculate for each:

- Ratio of total marketing expenditure: total sales revenue.
- Ratio of total marketing expenditure: gross contribution.
- Ratio of total marketing expenditure: net profit.
- Ratio of total marketing expenditure: unit cost of production.

The comparisons of current and historic ratios and of ratios between product/market groupings in the total portfolio, yield very useful evaluation data. It helps to establish growth and decline trends in product life cycles and revenue generation. Total marketing expenditure can also be divided into the main component parts noted in Table 12.1 to establish separate ratios for each of the main techniques used.

As with other variance measures, the purpose is to alert managers to any deviations from normal that may require marketing action, both within the campaign period and strategically in the longer run.

CHAPTER SUMMARY

This chapter:

- Defines marketing campaigns as 'integrated action programmes designed to achieve specific marketing objectives through the deployment of a budget ... over a specified time period'. Within the deliberately broad definition adopted in this chapter, campaigns can be seen as the final stage in an interlinked framework of business goals, strategies and plans, introduced in Chapters 10 and 11.
- Explains why effective action programmes must be carefully researched and costed before implementation, and this requires marketing managers to find answers to three vital questions concerning the budget: how much to spend in total, how the total should be split between the products and segments in an organization's total product portfolio, and how it should be allocated among the wide range of promotional and other marketing-mix techniques presented as a menu in Table 12.1.
- Works through two different tourism-related marketing budget models to explain the process and methods of budget setting, and especially to explain the important *objective and task* method. This is the budgeting process that most closely meets the needs of modern marketing-led organizations. It is relevant in its principles to all sectors of the travel and tourism industry, both commercial and non-commercial. In particular, this method is the only one that directly facilitates the systematic processes for performance measurement and control defined later in the chapter. The form and main aspects of performance measurement are noted and their role in *marketing the margin* is highlighted. Stress is laid on the size of the opportunity and the potential value of continuous innovation and test marketing for travel and tourism businesses.
- Develops the arguments related to the adoption of measures and their acceptability, suitability and feasibility in an age where social and environmental issues are becoming increasingly important.
- Serves as a bridge between Part Three, which explains the meaning and processes of strategy and tactics and the role of marketing managers, and Part Four, which reviews each of the main promotional techniques, and the way they are implemented effectively in practice. The marketing campaign is the coordinating framework for all the marketing mix techniques included in action programmes and the platform for evaluation levels of success or failure.

QUESTIONS TO CONSIDER

1. Take a brochure or website package offer from any leading international or domestic tour operator, and using their prices and your own broad estimates of the volume of sales they are likely to be targeting, devise a budget using Fig. 12.1 as a template for the likely cost of items.
2. With an example, such as a local visitor attraction, develop an objective and task approach in devising a campaign for one of its targeted segments.

3. In relation to Fig. 12.1, consider the thought process and considerations that managers would apply in deciding between the choice of Internet or retail travel agents to market their products over a campaign period.
4. Summarize the reasons why performance measurement is essential to effective marketing campaigns.

REFERENCES AND FURTHER READING

Brassington, F. and Pettit, S. (2000). *Principles of Marketing* (3rd edn). FT Prentice-Hall.

Davidson, H. (1997). *Even More Offensive Marketing. Chapters 1 and 2.* Penguin.

Jobber, D. (2007). *Principles and Practice of Marketing* (5th edn). McGraw-Hill.

Kotler, P. and Armstrong, G. (1999). *Principles of Marketing.* Chapter 1 (8th edn). Prentice Hall.

Kotler, P., Wong, V., Saunders, J. and Armstrong, G. (2005). *Principles of Marketing* (Fourth European edn). Pearson Prentice Hall.

Kotler, P. (1999). *Kotler on Marketing.* Simon and Schuster. London.

Medlik, S. (1994). *The Business of Hotels* (3rd edn). Butterworth Heinemann.

McDonald, M. (2002). *Marketing Plans* (5th edn). Butterworth Heinemann.

Ranchhod, A. and Gurau, C. (2007). *Marketing Strategies: A Contemporary Approach* (2nd edn). Pearson Education.

Trembath, R. (1999). Best kept secrets: an evaluation of South Australia's direct marketing campaign, *Journal of Vacation Marketing*, **6**, pp. 76–85.

Communicating with and Influencing Consumers

The unifying theme of this section is integrated marketing communications – the philosophy of integrating and coordinating all the promotional tools and communication channels to deliver a clear consistent and compelling message about the organization and its products. While media advertising used to be the dominant form of promotion, now marketers can select from a range of above- and below-the-line tools, new digital media and traditional publications, and one-to-many or one-to-one communications, to reach their chosen target audience.

One important factor in this change, but not the only one, is the growth of ICT, and in particular, the Internet since the mid-1990s. This has widened the choice of products available to the customers and made the booking process quicker and easier. It could be argued that this has only served to accelerate underlying trends in our consumer society that were already beginning to create significant changes in travel and tourism behaviour. However, as the Internet becomes the main source of travel and tourism information for an increasing percentage of the population, an organization's website is now the centre of the marketing communications strategy around which all the other promotional activities are integrated.

Chapter 13 outlines the factors, both supply and demand, which have created this paradigm change in the way travel and tourism organizations communicate with their potential customers. Chapter 14 goes on to explain how these organizations can make effective use of e-marketing media and techniques. Chapter 15 examines how the digital revolution has created new distribution channels for tourism products and outlines the principles of marketing channel management. Chapter 16 covers the range of promotional tools that are used to communicate with customers as part of an integrated marketing communications strategy. Chapter 17 examines the continuing role of brochures and other printed materials as part of the strategy.

To students brought up in the computer age it must seem strange that well into the 1970s, most travel reservation systems were still manual.

CHAPTER 13

The growth and role of information and communications technology and the rise of the dominant consumer

The Internet is turning business upside down and inside out. It is fundamentally changing the way that companies operate. This goes far beyond e-commerce and deep into the process and culture of an enterprise.

(Business and the Internet, *Economist*, 26 June 1999:54.)

Any book that attempts to deal with developments in information and communications technology risks becoming out of date before it is published. The previous edition of this book had the foresight to predict that information and communications technology (ICT) would have a major influence on nearly every aspect of services marketing. The convergence and 'connectivity' now available through ICT appeared, as we said, to signal one of the historic 'discontinuities' in the way business is conducted. We noted that this would provide massive growth opportunities for the proactive and overwhelm those too slow to adapt. The only doubt expressed was regarding how quickly people, businesses and customers would change the ways in which they behaved.

In reality, the speed at which the Internet, in particular, has become a central part of everyday life would have surprised the authors writing in 2000. For the latest statistics, readers are advised to consult government and commercial research reports in their library systems, but the trends are clear. From being the domain of young, well-educated and affluent early adopters, the Internet is now used regularly by all age groups and socioeconomic classes in developed countries, often helped by government schemes to ensure that all families have access. In Britain in 2007, Mintel research indicated that almost all teenagers have a home computer, Internet access, DVD player/recorder, video games console, mobile phone and MP3/MP4 player. All school children are expected to be computer familiar by the age of 5 or 6 years. The European Travel Commission (ETC) predicts that around 20% of the world's population will be online by the end of the first decade of the century, making a global market of around 1.4 billion people accessible to marketers. The figures for North America, Western Europe and Australasia appear to be reaching saturation at around 70% of all homes, but the ETC predicts rapid growth in countries, such as China, Russia, India, Brazil and Mexico, where the figures are currently below 20%. These people will all have instant access to information and purchasing systems that will give them a very wide choice of products in travel and tourism as in other markets. There are still, however, concerns for the splits in society between those who are computer literate, employable and well paid, and those who are not – the so-called 'Digital Divide'. Similarly, there are millions whose livelihoods in long-established industries in the 'old' economies of the developed world will be lost as the traditional geographical logic for industrial location are overturned and production shifts to low-cost countries.

This chapter sets out the scope of the ICT revolution, stressing that commercial use of the Internet is only possible because of the parallel developments in database technology, which are equally profound in marketing terms. It proceeds to indicate at least some of the influences in ICT on both the supply and the demand for travel and tourism. None of the authors claims to be an ICT expert, nor are the great majority involved in tourism marketing. It is, however, possible to see at least the direction of opportunities and threats, through observation and analysis of events as they occur. By applying the ideas that emerge to the basic principles of tourism marketing, *which have not changed*, it is possible to identify some of the issues that will shape the future of visitor economies.

After studying this chapter, you should be able to understand:

- How the evolution of ICT has profoundly changed the ways in which travel and tourism are managed and marketed.
- The range of technologies and applications that make up an integrated ICT system.
- The main current trends in ICT and their implications for marketing.
- The wider impact of ICT and related social and market trends on the visitor economy.

ICT DEFINED

ICT is a deliberately broad term to encompass any technology that helps to gather, store, analyse, communicate and disseminate information. Having accurate and up-to-date information has always been the basis of good decision-making in any business, and computer technology has developed to supply this need. As described later, ICT was first used to speed up the processing and communication of information within companies, then between the company and its trade partners, and more recently, through the Internet, between the company and its end-user customers. This has had a powerful effect in service industries, such as tourism, because information is fundamental to the creation and selling of intangible holiday and travel experiences. Information is the life-blood of tourism.

While computer processing of information is at the heart of the ICT revolution, of equal importance is the development of telecommunications technologies, such as satellite transmission, cell phone networks and Broadband data cables, which have dramatically increased the speed and volume of data that can be transferred. This enables not just words and figures but video film and music to be communicated from companies to individual customers on the move and in their homes.

Figure 13.1 shows the three main elements of the multimedia convergence that is transforming business and leisure activities in the twenty-first century. Companies like AOL Time Warner, Sony, Microsoft and Google have created global businesses that span the three realms, producing the entertainment content, the technology needed to enjoy it and the networks to distribute it. Travel and tourism products provide an attractive element of the content that draws consumers to particular portals and networks, and hence, multimedia organizations are increasingly becoming significant players in tourism marketing.

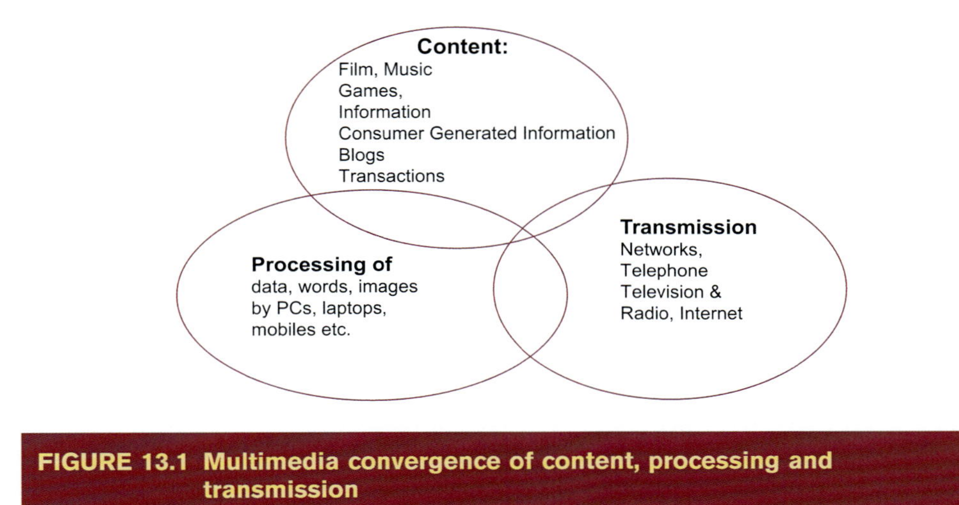

FIGURE 13.1 Multimedia convergence of content, processing and transmission

THE EVOLUTION OF ICT

In the next section, we trace the evolution of ICT from its initial use within organizations through the development of external business-to-business (B2B) networks to the widespread use of the Internet for business-to-consumer (B2C) and consumer-to-business (C2B) communication. As this edition is being written, a second generation of web-based applications, known as Web 2.0, is enabling consumers to communicate with each other (C2C) more easily. This has led to commercial websites based on 'user-generated-content', that is, material provided by consumers rather than the organization running the site. At each stage of this evolution, tourism businesses have been major users of the technology, which in turn has transformed the way they do business.

How it used to be before ICT

To students brought up in the computer age, it must seem strange that well into the 1970s, and within the working life of at least one of the authors, most travel reservation systems were still manual. Even in the USA, in large and small businesses, teams of clerks using telephones toiled like ants around massive pegboards, blackboards, ledgers or charts that filled the whole wall space of large offices. Such charts physically represented production capacity for hotel rooms, campsites and so on, for several months ahead. Although such systems could handle several destinations, the geographical coverage was inevitably limited by administrative difficulties and communication delays.

Such manual systems were slow, inflexible, liable to failure through human error and very costly in labour employed. They could not cope easily with changes as they occurred, nor identify and suggest alternatives if a particular slot was already booked. They required elaborate paperwork support systems, and the physical capacity of such manual systems set limits to the volume of transactions that a business could handle. The first use of mainframe computers for reservation systems in the tourism industry started with the airlines in the 1960s and developed quickly into global distribution systems (GDS). By the mid-1970s, the manual systems had disappeared from large- and medium-sized producers, to be replaced by online electronic information systems, operating through each principal's main computer via as many peripheral terminals as the flow of business could justify. Manual systems did not disappear from most small businesses; however, they would have to wait for nearly another 20 years before the advent of low-cost, highly efficient, Internet-enabled PCs would make it possible for them to join the information revolution and begin to exploit its opportunities.

The new ICTsystems made business growth possible, and the growth in revenues justified the technology and personnel investment required. This 'win–win' cycle has been repeated many times since, but it traces its origins to the 1960s and 1970s. It underlies the globalized economy of today.

Data processing

The initial use of ICT in tourism marketing was for data processing. As outlined in Chapter 5, using computer databases enables data on customers to be analysed and used as the basis for segmentation and direct marketing. This led to a gradual shift from mass marketing based on broad demographic segmentation and newspaper readership to precision marketing, where individuals are sent messages and promotional offers based on their previous buyer behaviour with an organization. In travel and tourism, a major breakthrough can be seen in the airline, car rental and hotel loyalty membership schemes designed to reward repeat buyers that stemmed from the computer technology of the 1980s.

Management information

The speed of computer data processing has also meant that management information is available almost instantaneously, enabling the fine-tuning of marketing and operational decisions as bookings come in. Close monitoring of booking patterns forms the basis of yield management systems in which prices are raised or lowered daily or hourly to encourage bookings on less popular dates or increase the revenue yield from popular ones. In travel and tourism, it is the collection and analysis of data streams that now flow continuously through distribution channels and booking systems, which provide the information base for the strategic and operational decisions of large organizations.

Internal networks

The ability to link or network computers is, therefore, a vital part of the exploitation of data for tourism marketing. The technology was first used for internal 'intranets' linking different parts of the same organization. These have made it possible for large multi-site companies to consolidate their management into fewer offices and to relocate or outsource reservations, enquiries and other functions. The internal computer network has increased the effectiveness of telephone sales staff and made possible the creation of the modern call centre.

Call centres

Use of telephones to service customer enquiries and make reservations and bookings has been a traditional distribution channel for over 75 years. But around the end of the 1980s, a number of trends justified the investment by larger multi-site businesses, such as airlines and budget hotels, to create separate call centres for the more efficient processing of telephone calls. These trends were the increasing volume of telephone use, the demand for services around the clock, growing corporate use of direct response marketing, the growing trend to last minute bookings, the rapid expansion of mobile phone use and, of course, the developments of ICT, including satellite relay stations for global communications. It is now possible to establish call centres almost anywhere in the world, certainly in areas far removed from a businesses headquarters, to take advantage of lower wages and lower communication costs.

Modern call centres work on shift systems, with fully computerized customer databases and training programmes to maximize efficiency. Shared call centres are common for smaller businesses that cannot justify the full investment, another example of ICT enabled outsourcing for business purposes.

Call centres are now part of the standard reservation processes for all larger businesses in travel and tourism, appealing particularly to customers who lack confidence to book online or prefer to deal with a human voice. They have become a major international development, with India and China especially attractive as locations. Salaries in India, for example, are currently lower than in the advanced economies; hence, unit costs per call are lower and there is a ready supply of well-educated workers who speak good English. The time zone occupied by India often means that communications can take place at cheap phone rates in the countries from which the business flows. Call centre operations and the associated technology lend themselves naturally to undertaking other back office functions, such as accounting, data processing and invoicing. British Airways (BA), for example, was employing some 2000 employees in Bombay and Poona by the end of 2000. The operation, producing cost savings of at least a third compared with locations in the United Kingdom, initially focused on servicing BA and other contracted airlines but expanding to provide services for other industries.

External networks

Including trade partners in computer network was an obvious next step. The airline industry investment in Central Reservation Systems (CRS) to link or connect businesses' inventory directly to intermediaries in the distribution chain was a vital first step in the tourism ICT 'connectivity' process. It paved way for subsequent change. The level of investment required to set up the new systems was one of the first underlying reasons behind the emergence of the international/global links, alliances and acquisitions that dominated so much of the tourism industry in the last quarter of the twentieth century and continues today.

The airline CRS or Global Distribution Systems (GDS) became the major channel linking not only airlines but also hotels, car hire firms and other services with retail travel agents in high streets around the world. The three GDS – Amadeus, Sabre and Galileo/Worldspan – have been referred to as the backbone of the modern travel distribution. According to Mintel (2006), they have processed more than 1 billion air bookings each, and another 250 million for hotels, cruises and other non-air content, generating over US$6 billion in revenues. The volume of global transactions through the GDS had risen 4% year on year to 343 million in 2005. Worldwide, the GDS reaches some 230,000 points of sale. Until recently, the high entry costs required to create the IT booking systems linking airlines, hotels and car rental operators with travel agents and consumers had given the big three GDS an oligopolistic control over travel distribution. However, as some 70% of their business depends on retail travel agents, the widespread consumer adoption of the Internet has led some to forecast that they may soon become unwieldy dinosaurs threatened with extinction unless they adapt to the new environment.

The World Wide Web

The significance of the Internet and the World Wide Web for tourism is that information once accessible only to travel agents with links to GDS is now available to the general public 24 hours a day, 7 days a week (part of what is known as the '24/7' economy). It has created a global marketplace based entirely on information provision and exchange transactions in which detailed information, for example, on prices and availability, is changing every few seconds. It comprises multimedia information to support consumer decision-making; it supports global transactions and bookings, distributes ticketing and invoices, and collects information about customers that is transferred immediately on to databases available for marketing research. Related information flows occur at check-in for transport and registration for accommodation. Other than printed information, some of it via 'downloads', there are no tangible elements in the service delivery process until a customer departs from home and arrives at the destination. Because travel and tourism is an information industry and customer decisions are highly price-sensitive, it has become one of the natural lead industries on the Internet.

E-businesses

As well as changing the way that existing businesses, such as hotels, airlines and tour operators communicate with each other and the final customer, the Internet has also led to the creation of virtual companies that are branded and exist in cyber space but outsource most of their inputs using B2B methods. The wave of *dot.com* Internet companies that launched themselves in travel in the late 1990s were in many ways virtual marketing companies, providing a platform for the exchange of information and for e-commerce transactions for a wide range of products but producing no products themselves. They simply provided distribution and marketing services, acting as infomediaries (also known as travel e-mediaries) for other service provider businesses. While many of these new companies have proved short-lived, partly due to the marketing investment needed to establish themselves as trusted brands, some, such as Lastminute.com, have survived and challenge the supremacy of the traditional intermediaries.

The Internet has also been a major factor in the rise of another challenge to traditional travel and tourism marketing systems from low-cost airlines. Reducing the cost of reservations by eliminating both travel agency commission and conventional telephone bookings and call centres is an important part of the low-cost model. So too are the yield management systems that maximize the occupancy and revenue from each flight (see Chapter 20). Low-cost airline websites not only offer customers the choice of an alternative flight (often but not always cheaper than the traditional airlines), but also the options or linkages to a hotel-finder website, car rentals, airport parking and so on. Thus, travellers are given the option of booking their entire holiday online without using a conventional inclusive tour operator or a travel agent with links to one of the major GDS.

User-generated content

The latest development in ICT as this edition was being written is the growth of 'user-generated content', sometimes known as Web 2.0. These terms are used to reflect the way that the web has developed from its original role as a place where commercial organizations (e.g. tour operators and hotels) and public-sector bodies (e.g. tourist boards and destination management organizations) provided information for prospective customers on their websites. Initially these were often little more than animated brochures. Today, many prospective travellers will compare the information on these official sites with the views and experiences of other visitors on unofficial sites using blogs and message boards, such as Tripadvisor. As we shall discuss in Chapter 14, these present both opportunities and threats for tourism marketing. Web 2.0 is part of the shift away from company-centric towards consumer-centric approaches to modern marketing (see also Chapter 8).

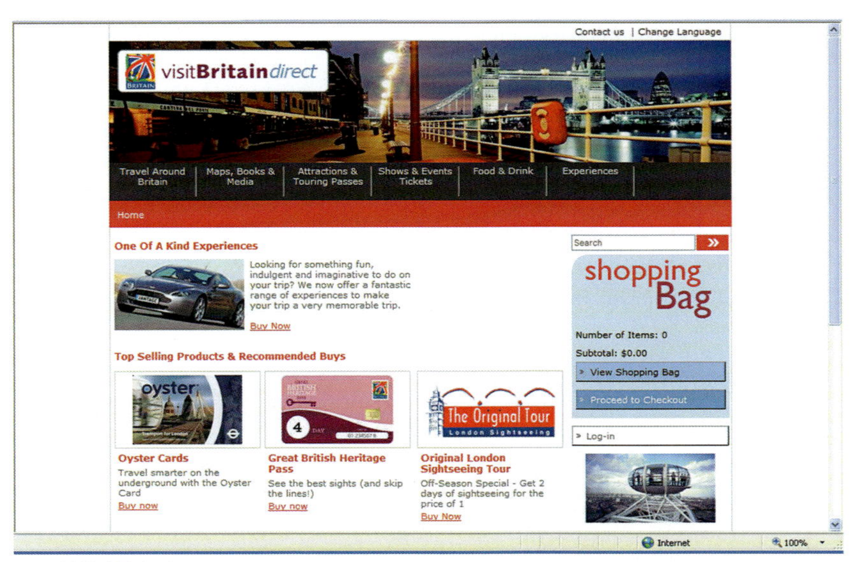

Courtesy of VisitBritain.org

PREDICTING THE FUTURE OF ICT

Link article available at www.routledge.com/9780750686938

(1) Buhalis, D., Law, R., 2008. Progress in information technology and tourism management: 20 years on and 10 years after the Internet – the state of eTourism research. Tourism Management 29 (4), 609–623.

The continued development of ICTwill depend on the technological advances in the four interrelated areas of hardware, software, networks and netware (Buhalis, 2003).

Hardware trends

By hardware, we mean the physical equipment, the computers, mobile phones, television receivers and monitors etc. Here, the current trends are towards smaller portable devices with the capabilities once only found on larger desktop computers. Laptops are now a standard part of business travellers' luggage. Hand-held devices, such the Blackberry or I phone, can be used to make phone calls, access email and the Internet, or download data from corporate computer systems, as well as for playing games and listening to music. Cameras, music players and Internet access are now standard features on all but the most basic mobile phones. Such developments change the ways in which business travellers work and leisure travellers interact with their surroundings. This creates new opportunities for tourism organizations to communicate with visitors and enhance their experience of a hotel, attraction or destination. It also creates new opportunities for customers to interact with businesses (C2B) to achieve the experiences they seek from product purchases.

Software trends

The development of software over the last two decades has enabled any computer user to create documents, spreadsheets and databases that would have in the past been the preserve of specialists. Now anyone can create a presentation, a poster, brochure or website using images from their digital camera manipulated by an affordably priced software package. The more advanced can also do the same with sound and video. This has reduced the marketing costs and the barriers to entry for small businesses and voluntary organizations, but there is a danger that it will lead them to undervalue the importance of design skills and marketing planning. In reality, as marketing communications, online and in print, increase in volume and in visual quality, it becomes harder for a company to be noticed above the 'clutter' without the expertise of professional designers and marketers.

Network trends

As noted earlier, it is the ability of networks to connect individuals and organizations that has transformed the way that tourism marketing is practised. Technologically, the only constraint on the development of networks is the availability of the cables or radio frequencies to carry high-speed, high-volume data flows. As Broadband access to the Internet becomes the norm in Europe and North America, the downloading of high-quality video films will become a standard part of home entertainment and an important tool of marketing.

Future trends are likely to be towards ever-greater connectivity and sharing of data between organizations. In addition to their marketing uses, linked databases can be used to verify individuals' identity and credit ratings. The use of identity cards or passports with biometric data, such as fingerprints, eye or facial scans stored on national databases, is being introduced by many countries to help police and immigration officials combat the threat of terrorism. Critics say identity cards interfere with civil liberties, and might cause friction among ethnic minority communities particularly affected by police stop and searches.

Netware trends

Perhaps the most significant developments of the last 5 years have been in the area of netware, the software systems that support and enhance the use of computer networks. The millions of websites that are now on the Internet would be of very limited use without the search engines that can select the ones that are relevant to the user's current interests. Google has become the dominant 'portal' through which people search for information on travel and holidays as in every other aspect of life. Search engine technology is also vital in the development of social networking sites, such as My Space and Facebook. These provide users with their own readymade websites into which to put details of themselves and their leisure interests. They can then link up with a network of friends and search for others who share a particular interest, for example, in a particular type of music or sport. All these sites are funded by advertising, because they offer the opportunity to target very precise segments of special-interest groups. The marketing use of these sites is explored in Chapter 14.

THE FUTURE OF TV

The Internet is not the only factor behind the fragmentation of consumer markets into smaller special-interest segments. TV has also changed as the traditional terrestrial channels now compete for viewers with satellite and cable networks offering a choice of up to 200 channels, and the alternative use of the TV monitor to watch films on DVD or play computer games. While advertising on the main channels may now reach fewer viewers, the new digital channels offer opportunities for tourism companies to reach niche markets by placing adverts in travel programmes or related subjects, such as history, the arts, food, music, wildlife and sport. Some companies, such as Thomas Cook, have their own digital television channels from which customers can watch films of destinations and then make their bookings via interactive connections.

The latest technological trends suggest that the way households use TV is taking two divergent directions. On one hand, larger, wider screens and sound systems can create a cinema-quality experience in the living room, offering serious competition for out-of-home leisure attractions. On the other hand, a single monitor with a PC and Broadband Internet connection can be used to watch television programmes 'on-demand', interact with shopping channels to place orders, buy or sell items on Ebay, play computer games with someone in another location, or enjoy an almost infinite choice of music and video clips through websites like MySpace and YouTube. The effect on family life has been described as creating a cellular household, where individuals follow their own tastes and interests in separate rooms, except for special occasions when they come together to watch a DVD in the home cinema. This further weakens the effectiveness of traditional TV advertising.

HOW ICT IS INFLUENCING TOURISM MARKETING

Having outlined what at the time of writing appear to be the significant technological developments, we will next examine the impact of this ICT revolution on consumer attitudes and behaviour and on the visitor economy.

The dominant consumer

As explained, the initial benefits of ICT were to companies, increasing the efficiency with which they communicated with customers and processed their bookings. This had the effect of accelerating the consolidation of the tourism sectors into large multinational companies or alliances, linked by GDS. However, the longer-term marketing effects of ICT appear likely to increase the power of the consumer. The widespread adoption of the Internet and the use of search engines have given people the ability to 'shop around' for bargains and choose from a much wider selection of travel opportunities than those offered by the main travel-agency and tour-operator chains. The consumer, it is argued, is now becoming the dominant partner in the marketing exchange and companies have to tailor their products, prices and communications to meet individual needs.

The freedom of choice provided by the Internet is just the latest factor in the underlying changes in the tourism market outlined in Chapter 4. Many of today's travellers are likely to be the third generation of their families to enjoy foreign holidays. Better educated and more experienced than their parents, they are no longer deterred by the three Fs of flying, foreign food and foreign languages. Instead, they are sophisticated consumers used to expressing themselves through their lifestyle and by what they buy and consume. This trend is evident, for example, in food, fashion and home improvements as well as in holiday destinations and choice of travel products. Many modern customers are in demanding jobs, are 'money rich but time poor', and are looking for new experiences to get the most out of their precious limited free time. The Internet simply provides them with a more convenient means of satisfying these aspirations.

The choice available to consumers has increased owing to a number of other supply-side factors alongside the Internet. Deregulation of air travel and the rise of the low-cost carriers have encouraged the growth of the impulse-buy short-break market, offering new destinations near regional airports. Political changes, such as the opening up of Eastern Europe, the abolition of visa requirements and the adoption of a common European currency, all reduce the need to plan ahead. The fact that there is often little to choose between competing hotel or airline brands, and that an acceptable quality of service can often be taken for granted, means that short breaks booked over the Internet are seen as relatively low-risk purchases.

The result is that the market is increasingly dominated by a new type of visitor, one that Poon first noted as early as in 1993: affluent, independent, confident and curious to discover other places and cultures, and for part of the holiday at least, looking for something more active than the four Ss of the traditional beach holiday – sun, sand, sea and sangria (or sex).

Evidence of this can been seen in the tourism statistics showing a faster growth of independent compared with package holidays and in the growth in special interest and activity holidays of all types. Even traditional resorts like Bournemouth are seeing a new type of visitor, who books a short-break online at very short notice, specifically, to enjoy a particular type of experience, for example, watersports, nightlife and entertainment, or eating out.

Consumer adoption of the Internet for travel

With Broadband access now available to most households across age, class and income groups, home shopping has become a routine activity. Concerns for the security of credit card and bank details when buying online appear to have diminished as people are used to ordering in sites like Amazon without problems. The Paypal system developed for transactions on the auction site Ebay allows people to transfer money safely to companies or private individuals. It is not surprising, therefore, that booking flights, hotels and event tickets on the Internet has become commonplace. Travel sites are among the most popular on the web in terms of 'hits'.

In the early 2000s, these sites were used more for obtaining information than for online purchase, with travel agencies still often being used for the final booking of holidays. Latest data indicate that the number of buyers taking the final step of booking is growing rapidly, and in some sectors of travel and tourism, has already become the normal pattern.

IMPACT OF THE ICT REVOLUTION ON THE VISITOR ECONOMY

The recommoditization of services

The increase in consumer choice is resulting in strategic changes in the structure of tourism. One aspect of the 'knowledge society' is that the majority of potential customers can compare online prices to find bargains in flights, accommodation, car hire and other components of their travel choices. Other factors have also contributed to the evolution of this price-transparent, price-sensitive market in services – the harmonization of regulations and standards, the removal of barriers to the trade in services and the adoption of the single currency in most of Europe. Measures to protect the consumer and the almost universal application of service quality management have meant that consumers take quality and reliability for granted, and hence, make their choice solely on price and availability. This threatens to reduce tourism products in some sectors of travel and tourism to the status of commodities like oil or potatoes.

In this kind of commodity market, differentiation, quality of service and brand image may no longer be perceived to add value or competitive advantage. Instead, companies trapped in a price war may be forced to make cost savings through less labour-intensive modes of operation, through employing low-wage migrant labour or through transferring or outsourcing part or all of their operations (e.g. call centres) to lower-wage economies outside Europe.

Another result of the ICT revolution has been to make a much greater choice of destinations affordable and accessible to visitors, often to the detriment of established destinations. Traditional coastal resorts and rural recreation areas, especially those providing services aimed at people on main holidays of seven or more days have been particularly affected and, unlike other industries, are unable to relocate to reduce costs or access new markets. Some have the option to regenerate their offer with new products for new segments, but these trends can have profound implications for employment, quality of life and social cohesion in some parts of both Northern and Southern Europe.

The emergence of an experience economy

The trends we noted in the previous section towards affluent-lifestyle consumers using the Internet to search for new experiences do suggest an alternative strategy for tourism businesses and destinations. This strategy is based on the argument that European and other developed countries are moving from a service to an experience economy (Pine and Gilmore, 1999) in which experience-based products, for example, admissions to recreational events, have outperformed other services and goods in terms of price inflation, employment and gross domestic product (GDP). In this new economy, they argue, sustainable competitive advantage can only be gained by offering the customer unique and memorable experiences.

Examples of experience-based products can include the hedonic thrills of the theme park, the physical challenge of adventure and activity, the sensual delights of gastronomy or wine tasting, the intellectual discovery of arts and cultural events or even the excitement of shopping. Destinations need to emphasize what makes them distinctive rather than market themselves as a generic beach resort (King, 2002; Williams, 2006).

New opportunities for smaller businesses

In the experience economy, the Internet offers significant new opportunities for small businesses offering niche products. Chapter 3 explains that one of the defining characteristics of the travel and tourism industry is the marketing paradox of, on one hand, the consolidation of power and influence in a small number of global players in the industry and, on the other hand, the growth in the tens of thousands of small businesses that provide so much of the character and 'specialness' of place to be found at destinations. Until the mid-1990s, most small businesses were unable to take advantage of the developments in ICT, which were increasingly available to the dominant large international players. The investment was too great and they lacked the specialist skills.

However, the position is rapidly changing. The remarkably low cost of designing small business websites and the growing willingness of customers to surf the Internet for options is helping even the smallest of businesses to go global. The Internet empowers micro-businesses to make the most of their individuality and enterprise. It offers them access to markets and to a supply of lower-cost business necessities that was previously unthinkable. Forward-looking micro-businesses are especially well placed to participate in the co-creation of value process of their products because of the ease of direct personal communication they can provide.

ICT will also help small and medium sized enterprises (SMEs) to achieve a collective voice and help them move themselves up the political agenda. To maximize the potential of the Internet, SMEs need to collaborate with destination management organizations to create portals and links that place their websites where potential visitors will find them. For an example of collaborative online marketing, see the mini-case study on the Association of Independent Tour Operators (AITO) website.

Destination management systems

Destination management organizations, such as local-authority tourism departments, have an important role in facilitating the growth of micro-businesses. The previous edition of this book stated that governments and national tourist boards had paid lip service to micro-businesses but, in many ways, simply ignored them other than by imposition of regulatory burdens. The developments of ICT and the key role that small businesses can play in creating local distinctiveness are gradually changing this attitude. As Buhalis (2003) notes, SMEs need the support of public tourism organizations and associations of local tourism enterprises to make strategic use of the Internet. Between them, they can create a destination management system that not only communicates the 'brand personality' of the destination but also allows potential visitors to search for information and make reservations from the same 'one-stop' website, whether for a four-star hotel, a bed-and-breakfast or a backpacker hostel.

BARRIERS TO THE GROWTH OF E-TOURISM

A number of factors still inhibit the adoption of the Internet as the main channel for tourism marketing and sales. We have already mentioned the issue of the security of transactions, which involves the customers giving out their credit card and other personal information over the Internet. The battle between those developing secure encrypted systems and those determined to break into them is an ongoing one, and the scale of tourism e-commerce will depend on which side customers perceive to be winning.

This is linked to the wider issue of how far consumers will trust a company they know only from its website. Establishing a well-known brand name is as important in Internet business as in more traditional channels of distribution. Amazon, for example, ran at a loss for many years, which its owners and backers accepted as the price of establishing it as a trusted brand. The websites of long-established brands, such as Thomas Cook, continue to be among the most frequently used in the travel sector.

Another thing that works to the advantage of established brands is that too much choice can be bewildering and stressful. As noted in Chapter 5, most consumers make their final choice from a very limited set of alternatives. An Internet search may result in 'information-overload' and drive the customer to seek help in simplifying the decision. This help may come from friends, from the local travel agent, or by restricting the choice set to well-known brands. In the era of Web 2.0, it may alternatively come from other Internet users via advice sites like tripadvisor.com or a special interest discussion board. We will return to these issues in more detail in subsequent chapters.

MINI CASE 13.1: COLLABORATIVE E-MARKETING FOR SMALL TOUR OPERATORS

AITO is an organization representing over 150 of Britain's specialist tour operators. **AITO members are independent companies**, most of them owner-managed, specializing in particular destinations or types of holidays. This means that they are able to provide personalized advice based on first-hand experience. As their website says, every AITO member is passionate about its chosen destinations or activities and keen to share that enthusiasm with discerning holidaymakers.

The common aim of all AITO members is to provide the highest level of customer satisfaction by concentrating on three main pillars: Choice, quality and service, enshrined in the association's **Quality Charter**. It is a source of pride to the association that AITO companies dominate the consumer-voted travel awards every year in various categories.

The association promotes the unique range of its members' holidays and encourages the highest standards in all aspects of tour operating. It insists on its members being part of a scheme to provide financial protection for all their customers' holidays if a member company goes out of business. It provides marketing services and advice for its members and also represents their interest to government, industry and media.

The AITO website provides a portal through which customers can search for holiday ideas to a wide choice of destinations, activities and types of accommodation. In 2006, the site was relaunched as outlined in the following user-friendly style press release:

Courtesy of The Association of Independent Tour Operators Limited.

Navigating your way around unfamiliar websites can be confusing and time-consuming. Now AITO (The Association of Independent Tour Operators+) has made life easier for holiday-seekers. New mini-sites take you straight to the

heart of the holiday topic in which you are interested. With 150 of the best specialist holiday companies' wares on offer and well over 350 brochures to choose from, you can be assured of finding your perfect holiday, be it tailor-made or a carefully crafted off-the-shelf trip.

There are eight of these new mini-sites: ones for France, Italy, the Caribbean and Bermuda, Spain and Portugal, Greece, Central and South America, North Africa and Skiing & Wintersports Holidays.

Each mini-site comes with the same helpful features available on the main AITO website. There is a search engine, where you can find holidays in a particular town or resort in the mini-site's region, or on a particular theme, such as a cultural tour or a wildlife-watching break. Just like on the main AITO website, there is also a list of special offers from AITO members, focusing just on the particular area covered by each mini-site.

These new AITO websites make searching for holidays in these most popular of areas an easier, and hopefully even quicker, process. Coupled with the high level of customer service offered by AITO members, the new mini-sites ensure you can be jetting off on your dream holiday in record time.

- What are the advantages to the AITO members, and to potential tourists, of linking their sites with the AITO website?
- What are the limitations of this form of collaborative marketing?

Source: AITO websites, 2008

CHAPTER SUMMARY

- The ICT revolution has been created by the development and convergence of technologies for the processing, transmission and display of data, images and sounds.
- In travel and tourism, its initial uses were for data processing and management information, leading to greater efficiency in the handling of reservations and better utilization of capacity through yield management systems. The ability to connect computers over long distances led to the development of GDS linking principals,

intermediaries and retailers, and encouraging the growth of multinational companies and strategic alliances.

- The rapid adoption of the Internet since the mid-1990s has enabled individual travellers to access these distribution networks and search for bargains and niche products around the world. Linked to underlying social and political changes encouraging the growth of independent travel, the Internet has resulted in changes in the way consumers search for and book holidays that have profound implications.
- On one hand, the increased choice and price transparency may change some sectors, such as budget flights and hotels, into commodity markets where decisions are made primarily on price and availability. This places greater emphasis on images, branding and positioning to communicate specific company values and strengths.
- On the other hand, the Internet can connect small businesses with niche, special-interest market segments and encourage the development of new products offering unique and memorable experiences.

Whatever competitive strategy companies adopt in these changing markets, the key to success will be to be based on effective websites that are accessible to the target market through well-chosen links and promotional strategies. From being an additional channel of distribution, the website has now become the centre of the marketing communications' mix. In the following chapters, we will first examine how the website itself can be used for effective marketing, and then its place in the distribution and promotional strategy of the organization.

QUESTIONS TO CONSIDER

1. 'Though the technologies have changed, the principles of tourism marketing have not'. Show how the principles of marketing can be applied to tourism in the age of the Internet.
2. Choose one of the elements of ICT – hardware, software, networks and netware – and discuss how the latest technological developments could be used for tourism marketing. Use your own current knowledge to update the suggestions in this chapter.
3. How has the continuing evolution of ICT affected the balance of the relationship between large tourism organizations and their customers?
4. What are the opportunities and threats to small and medium-sized tourism enterprises from the current developments in ICT?

REFERENCES AND FURTHER READING

Buhulis, D. (2003). *eTourism: information technology for strategic tourism management.* London: FT Prentice Hall.

Buhalis, D. and Law, R. (2008). Progress in information technology and tourism management: 20 years on and 10 years after the Internet – the state of eTourism research', *Tourism Management*, **29**(4), pp. 609–623.

Hastings, G. and Saren, M. (2003). The critical contribution of social marketing, *Marketing Theory*, **3**(3), pp. 305–322.

Hughes, T.J. (2002). Marketing principles in the application of e-commerce, qualitative market research, *An International Journal*, **5**(4), pp. 252–260.

King, J. (2002). Destination marketing organizations – connecting the experience rather than promoting the place, *Journal of Vacation Marketing*, **8**(2), pp. 105–108.

Pine, B.J. and Gilmore, J.H. (1999). *The experience economy: work is theatre and every business is a stage*. Boston, Mass: HBS Press.

Poon, A. (1993). *Tourism, technology and competitive strategies*. Wallingford: CAB.

Williams, A. (2006). Tourism and hospitality marketing: fantasy, feeling and fun, *International Journal of Contemporary Hospitality Management*, **18**(6), pp. 482–495.

Why not head Eastbound?

4★ Hong Kong,
5 nights from £572

4★ Singapore,
4 nights from £635

4★ Kuala Lumpur
4 nights from £530

lastminute.com

Prices correct at time of going to print, subject to availability & conditions. Offers are limited, once it's gone, it's gone. Prices include flights based on 2 sharing accommodation, departing in April 2008 (Singapore, indirect flight). Booking fees may apply. lastminute.com acts as an agent for ATOL protected operators.

Lastminute.com's Culture Spell advert from the Culture Vulture campaign. For leading marketing organizations the website is now the centre of the marketing communications mix. The rest of the marketing communications activities should all be aimed at drawing the customer to the website.

Courtesy of lastminute.com, produced by Farm Communications, April 2007.

CHAPTER 14

E-marketing: the effective use of ICT

As the number of users intent on booking their flights online is set to increase in 2008, the opportunity for travel agents and carriers can only be realised by delivering a first class user experience. If users can't find the flights they want and successfully get through your booking process they'll go somewhere else.

Webcredible report, 2008

In the previous chapter, we traced the way that ICT is causing profound changes to the whole business environment for travel and tourism organizations and restructuring the approach to marketing. This chapter goes on to explain how businesses can make effective use of e-marketing media and techniques.

After studying this chapter you should be able to understand:

- The impact of the Internet on the marketing process and the marketing mix.
- How to select a range of e-marketing tools to make effective use of a company website.
- The marketing potential of the growth of user-generated-content websites and online communities.

THE IMPACT OF ICT ON THE MARKETING MIX

According to Jobber (2007), the digital technology we outlined in the previous chapter is reshaping the entire marketing mix. Drawing together the four Ps (see Chapter 6), Fig. 14.1 summarizes the changes discussed in this chapter. These changes are illustrated in the following section with examples drawn from travel and tourism.

Product

Many travel and tourism products may be customized for each individual and delivered digitally. For example, customers can create or assemble their holiday or travel itinerary to suit their individual requirements either by using the website of

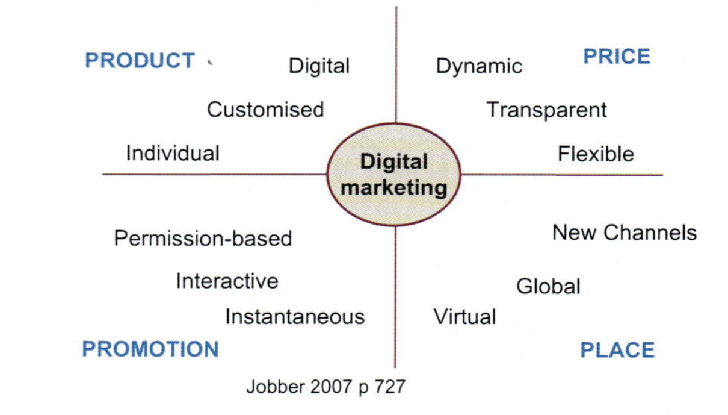

FIGURE 14.1 The impact of ICT on the marketing mix. Based on Jobber 2007 page 727

a travel agent or tour operator or by using linked airline and hotel websites. This has been referred to as mass customization or dynamic packaging as outlined below.

Dynamic packaging

Dynamic packaging is a travel industry term for a more flexible way of booking a holiday. Instead of offering customers a set package off the page of a tour operator's brochure, travel agents assemble the elements of the holiday to meet the customer's requirements. By using 'bed-banks' – companies that offer a database of hotel rooms at a discounted rate – the agents can match the prices of traditional tour operators while achieving better profit margins for themselves.

For an example of a bed-bank company see www.travelberry.co.uk

Traditionally, the physical evidence of intangible tourism products used to be available only in the form of pictures in a brochure. Now, for the first time, potential customers can browse a gallery of pictures on the website, or in some cases, take a virtual tour through video clips or watch what is happening there live on a webcam. The Wales Tourist Board website recently included a computer game in which people piloted a hang-glider over the mountains and watched the changing views below. As broadband capacity for moving images increases, this kind of 'virtual experiential marketing' is likely to become more common.

Pricing

Prices become more transparent, as customers can use the Internet to compare prices and search for bargains. In response, companies can adjust prices dynamically in response to fluctuations in demand. Ferry companies, for example, have moved from brochures setting out a complex tariff of prices for different dates, times and lengths of stay to a web-based booking system similar to those of low-cost airlines. Here the customer chooses the times of travel and is quoted a price which is set by the company's yield management system. Currently, a website called Farecast monitors the online yield management of major airlines and will advise users whether to buy at the current price or wait for later reductions.

Company pricing and refund policies now also have to take account of the way in which holiday packages, travel or event tickets are now resold on auction sites like eBay. This can be a convenient way for people to avoid cancellation charges if they are unable to use the tickets themselves, but it can also lead to 'online ticket touts' buying scarce tickets and reselling them for profit, especially for popular events.

Place or distribution

Once a booking has been made, travel tickets and accommodation vouchers or access codes can be downloaded and printed out by the customer, speeding up the process by eliminating the need to send documents by post.

Visitors can book timed tickets for attractions such as the London Eye or major art exhibitions, which guarantee admission at a particular time, eliminating the long and frustrating queues that can mar the experience.

The way that the Internet now provides alternative distribution channels for travel, accommodation and other tourism products, and the effect on the traditional tour operator/travel agency channel, has already been mentioned and will be developed further in Chapter 15.

Promotion

Online promotion, as outlined by Jobber (2007), has the advantages of being instantaneous, interactive and permission-based. Traditional advertising has to attract attention and create a memorable impression on someone who is watching TV or reading a newspaper, in the hope they will later remember the brand when visiting a travel agency. Instead, a website is there to be consulted when the customer is actively looking for information, with the opportunity to consult *Frequently Asked Questions* pages, e-mail for more information or make an electronic booking. They can also sign up for regular e-mail messages or Really Simple Syndication (RSS) feeds to alert them on special events and offers. The role of websites as the basis for direct marketing is discussed in detail later in the chapter.

RSS feed (Really Simple Syndication) – a system that alerts subscribers to new content or changes in a web site by placing a short headline on their homepage or other nominated site. Originally developed for news media websites, it can also be used for news of events or marketing offers.

THE WEBSITE AS THE CENTRE OF THE MARKETING COMMUNICATIONS MIX

Jobber's model in Fig. 14.1 demonstrates that the website is now the centre of the marketing communications mix. It is the place where the product is offered or customized, where the price is set and, increasingly, where the transaction is made and the documents delivered. The rest of the marketing communications activities of the organization should all be aimed at drawing the customer to the website.

Clearly, alternative channels need to be provided for those who cannot or do not wish to use the Internet, but these are increasing likely to be in the minority.

It is, therefore, important to decide the role and functions of the website, how to link it to the Internet and how to maximize its effectiveness.

The uses of a website for marketing

Angehrn's model (1997) summarizes four uses of cyberspace for marketing.

- Information
- Transaction
- Distribution
- Communication

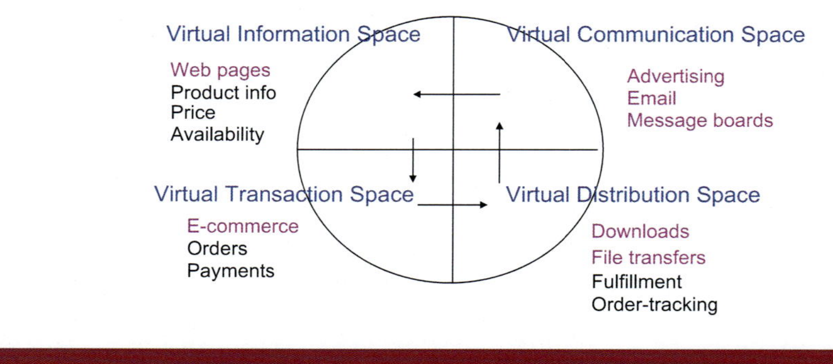

FIGURE 14.2 Four uses of cyberspace for marketing. Based on Angehrn 1997.

Companies need first to decide how they design their web presence to achieve their strategic goals. The basic use of a website is as a source of information, a kind of online advertisement or brochure. This is still the main purpose of many small business websites. The marketing effectiveness of the site is greatly increased if the customer is able to make a transaction from the web page, placing an order and making payment. Not all products can be electronically delivered as is possible with music or video files, but a website can, nevertheless, fulfil the distribution process by providing downloadable confirmations, tickets or vouchers or by enabling people to check and monitor the progress of their order. The communications element has two parts: using traditional or online media to communicate the existence of the site to potential customers and then encouraging continuing communication between the company and its users as a way of establishing a lasting relationship.

Attracting people to the website

The Internet is what is termed a pull rather than push medium – the customer has to find one's website among the thousands of travel-related sites available. The communication features of the site are, therefore, vital to its success. Traditional media advertising can be used to create awareness and interest, and give the website address for further information. Online travel agencies, Expedia and Travelsupermarket, have invested heavily in TV and press advertising to create brand awareness and attract people to their sites.

Display advertising on other websites, in the form of banners or pop-ups, can be used to tempt people to 'click-through' to your site. Such adverts have the advantages of being colourful and animated but can be dismissed as a distraction and ignored in the same way as other media advertising.

To overcome this, a more targeted and subtle form of online marketing is known as affiliate marketing. This is where a link is placed on a website for a product or topic where there is something in common between a company's products and the interests of the users of the other site. Amazon has nearly a million Associates who place specially designed links on their sites to specific books for sale by Amazon in return for up to 10% commission per sale.

Affiliate marketing is a web-based marketing practice in which a business rewards one or more affiliates for each visitor or customer brought about by the affiliate's marketing efforts. Jeff Bezos, the founder of Amazon, is said to have come up with the concept of affiliate marketing after chatting with a woman at a party about how she wanted to sell books about divorce on her website. According to this version of history, affiliate marketing was then born after he thought about how the woman could link her site to Amazon.com and receive a commission on book sales.

Along with financial services, retail and mobile phones, the travel sector is one of the major spenders on affiliate marketing. A good example of an affiliate network is the links between the website of a low-cost airline like Easyjet and companies offering hotels, car hire, taxi and other services.

EASYJET'S AFFILIATE NETWORK (2008)

Airline: Easyjet
Hotels: Hotelopia (part of the TUI Group)
Car rental: Europcar (part of Volkswagen Group)
Ski Breaks: Erna Low (independent specialist tour operator)
Chalet rental: Chaletgroup (consortium of Chalet owners)
Skiwear: BornForSports (community marketplace for sportswear)
Travel Insurance: Mondial Assistance (part of Allianz Group)
To/from the airport: Holidaytaxis
Airport parking: NCP
Travel guides: Arrivalguide.com in association with Fastcheck AB

Search engine marketing

The most common ways that people use to find information online are search engines, such as Google and Yahoo. The largest of these, Google, claims 82 million unique users a month providing results in 35 languages. These search engines use a bank of computers to 'crawl' the Internet looking for sites with words that match those of the enquiry. (See also the Epilogue for this book.)

Google's Guidelines for Webmasters explains the process:

When a user enters a query, our machines search the index for matching pages and return the results that we believe are the most relevant to the user. Relevance is determined by over 200 factors, one of which is the PageRank for a given page. PageRank is the measure of the importance of a page based on the incoming links from other pages. In simple terms, each link to a page on your site from another site adds to your site's PageRank. Not all links are equal: Google works hard to improve the user experience by identifying spam links and other practices that have a negative effect on search results. The best types of links are those that are given based on the quality of your content.

Search engine marketing is the term given to actions taken by a company to improve the ranking of their website on a search engine. Sixty per cent of all online marketing expenditure is on search engines. One action can be to make sure that the site has the right keywords, those that potential customers of their products most commonly use in their searches. Another is to develop links from relevant sites in order to improve the page ranking. These activities are called search engine optimization.

It is also possible to pay the search engine company to ensure that your website is listed on the first page of the search results for your chosen keywords. This is usually on a pay-per-click basis – in other words, you only pay when someone clicks on the advert, not when it is displayed but ignored. Reflecting the exponential growth of Internet usage in the last decade, the revenue from these 'AdWords' has made Google one of the biggest media companies in the world, outstripping the advertising revenue of most television and newspaper companies.

Another way of improving the accessibility of the website is to have an easily remembered website address (known as a domain name, hostname or URL – unique resource locator). Larger companies may have a separate address for each product or each promotional campaign. These names are allocated on a first-come basis and speculative 'squatters' may have already registered promising names in the hope of selling them on to companies who need them.

There are now numerous specialist agencies offering to improve the ranking of companies' websites. However, in essence, successful search engine marketing is based on one of the fundamental principles of marketing – understanding precisely what your customers want and where they will look for it.

What makes an effective website?

There are also many agencies specializing in website design, each with their own trademarked model of the formula for a commercially effective website. The main considerations for website design can be summarized in the following questions:

- Does it have the content that our customers are looking for?
  - Is the information relevant and up to date?

- Can users navigate around the site easily to reach what they need?
  - A guideline often used is that it should never take more than three clicks from the homepage to reach the relevant information.
- Is the page designed to make information and links easy to understand?
  - Or do design features and animations distract from the content?
- Will visitors enjoy the site and want to return?
  - Does it 'speak the same language' as the users and share their sense of humour?
  - Does it need to entertain and inform them?
- What level of interaction is needed?
  - Should visitors be able to e-mail questions, place orders or make comments on a message board?

Adapted from the Insites model in de Pelsmacker et al., 2001

How these questions are answered will depend on the objectives of the website as part of the communications strategy. Websites are very effective at giving information and enabling transactions for customers who already know what they are looking for. They are perhaps less good at giving people ideas and inspiration on what to do and where to do it. Expedia's Inspiroscope is an attempt to do this by inviting users to click on keywords that float across the screen to the sound of waves on shingle. It then delivers five holiday package ideas to match the chosen keyword.

Managing the customer experience online

A mistake sometimes made by small (and not so small) businesses is to see the creation of a website as a one-off activity, forgetting that it needs to be kept up to date, and that efficient systems for dealing with orders and responding to questions need to be in place. The concept of customer experience management mentioned in Chapter 5 – 'the process of strategically managing a customer's entire experience with a product or company' (Schmitt, 2003) – has been taken up by specialist agencies that examine every point of contact customers have with a company. Their aim is to improve the quality and efficiency of the interaction throughout what has been termed the service journey, from the initial browsing to the choice, purchase and post-sale experience.

Analysing the customers' online experiences should include consideration of when they need to be in contact with a real person. According to Friedman and Goodrich (1998), when given the choice, customers often prefer to avoid face-to-face or voice-to-voice encounters with sales staff, because they can take greater control of the buying process using impersonal channels, such as online shopping. However, particularly in the period between booking and taking a holiday, the ability to contact the company to ask questions can help to reduce 'post-purchase dissonance'.

Link article available at www.routledge.com/9780750686938

(1) Bill Doolin, Lois Burgeus, Joan Cooper, 2002 Evaluating the use of the web for tourism marketing: a case study from New Zealand. Tourism Management 23(5), 557–561.

THE NEXT PHASE OF INTERNET MARKETING: WEB 2.0

An alternative source of reassurance can be found in reading the comments or asking the advice of previous customers. Companies have always included testimonials from satisfied customers in their promotional literature. The interactive nature of the Internet has made it possible to receive and publish customer feedback on a much larger scale and in a way that is more credible than the brief comments selectively quoted in a brochure.

Some tour operators now invite customers to write reviews of the hotels and resorts they stayed in to help others make the right choice. Visitors to the website are invited to 'check out these honest holiday reviews from past travellers and get the low-down on the food, the location and pretty much the whole shebang' (Thomson website: http://www.thomson.co.uk/holiday-reviews/holiday-reviews.html).

If the suspicion remains that reviews on the tour-operator sites may be edited and censored by the company, there are also more apparently independent sites offering travel advice. One of the biggest of these is Tripadvisor (see box).

TripAdvisor attracts nearly 30 million monthly visitors (July 2007) across eight popular travel brands, namely TripAdvisor® sites, bookingbuddy.com™, cruisecritic.com™, independenttraveler.com™, seatguru.com®, smartertravel.com™, travel-library.com™ and travelpod.com™. TripAdvisor-branded sites make up the largest travel community in the world, with more than 25 million monthly visitors, 5 million registered members and 10 million reviews and opinions. Featuring real advice from real travellers, TripAdvisor-branded sites cover 280,000+ hotels and attractions and operate in the United States (http://www.tripadvisor.com/), the United Kingdom. (http://www.tripadvisor.co.uk/), Ireland (http://www.tripadvisor.ie/), France (http://www.tripadvisor.fr/), Germany (http://www.tripadvisor.de/), Italy (http://www.tripadvisor.it/) and Spain (http://www.tripadvisor.es/).

While it is free for travellers to use and for companies to be listed, TripAdvisor® Media Network offers travel suppliers advertising opportunities on a cost-per-click basis. After reading the reviews, travellers can click through to make bookings through an affiliate network of leading online travel agencies, tour operators, airlines and hotel groups. TripAdvisor and the sites comprising the TripAdvisor Media Network are operating companies of the online travel agency Expedia.

Source: http://www.tripadvisor.co.uk/PressCenter-c4-Fact_Sheet.html

User-generated content

Tripadvisor is an example of the type of Internet application which O'Reilly (2005) christened *Web 2.0*. In this second stage of the development of Internet, the software is only important because of the services it can deliver. These services are based on 'user-generated content' – reviews, photographs, music, information or software applications provided by the public. O Reilly calls this 'harnessing collective intelligence'. The data sources created in this way get richer as more people use them. The most ambitious example of this 'collective intelligence' is the online encyclopedia Wikipedia, which allows anyone to submit or amend entries on any subject known to mankind. (As the site explains, 'A ***wiki*** is a software that allows users to collaboratively create, edit, link, and organize the content of a website, usually for reference material. Wikis are often used to create collaborative websites and to power community websites.')

Blogs

While Tripadvisor and Thomson's sites are owned and developed by the travel industry for commercial purposes, much of the user-generated information and advice to travellers online takes place on sites with no direct links to the industry. Any traveller can get free web space to start his or her own online travel diary, known as a weblog or *blog*. Most have little chance of being read outside a small group of friends and family – an extension of the traditional spread of consumer information by word of mouth. However, a number of specialist travel blog sites allow visitors to search for blogs on a particular destination or mode of travel. Blogs are no longer just the work of amateurs. The blog format – an article followed by a discussion forum – is now used by journalists in online media and by companies as a way of keeping customers up to date with the latest products. According to Schmallegger and Carson (2008), 'company blogs have to provide some added value to the visitor, either in the form of interesting stories, unique insider information, good networking opportunities or even time and cost saving opportunities, to make them visit and contribute to the blog. The content of a blog should be more casual and entertaining instead of factual information and highly scripted marketing messages.'

Online communities

Travel blogs are part of another phenomenon of the Internet, the development of what Cova called *'communities of consumption'*, groups of people who come together because of a special interest in a particular product or activity. These communities are sometimes termed neo-tribes, interlinked and held together by a shared passion but otherwise heterogeneous in their demographic, economic and geographic characteristics (Cova and Cova, 2001). What unites them is a shared experience, expressed through the values they place on certain objects, events and spaces. These groups meet in forums, message boards and chat rooms, with the main purpose of discussing their common interest. However, as in any community, regulars soon start sharing views, experiences, gossip, jokes and advice on topics far removed from the one that brought them together. Travel tips can be part of this general conversation. Sports fans can discuss how to follow their team abroad, while music fans may plan to meet in a foreign city for a concert. Such communities can provide opportunities for research and targeted marketing, particularly for specialist travel companies.

Social networking sites

Social networking sites, such as Facebook and MySpace, take user control a stage further, allowing people to construct their own online communities by linking their personal page to those of their friends. In addition to communities based on offline relationships – with classmates or work associates – users can join groups linked by an experience, an opinion or an allegiance to a sports team or a singer or band. For example, a Facebook group called 'I looove to travel' has 2700 members. On its group page are links to travel company sites, and among the messages of advice are some that have been posted by companies recommending their services.

Travel companies can also pay for adverts, sponsor their own Facebook page to create their own community of customers, run polls to find out what a particular segment thinks, or create applications which users can include on their own pages (see http://www.facebook.com/business/). An example of these applications is the 'Cities I have visited' map sponsored by Tripadvisor, which enables users to stick virtual pins in a map of the world, showing their friends where they have been. There is a link to Tripadvisor so they can share stories and pictures about the places they have visited. The student travel firm STA Travel has another prominent presence on Facebook.

All these pages, groups and applications spread through the Facebook communities by being recommended by one user to their friends, examples of what is called '*viral marketing*', as it spreads in the same way as an infectious disease – from person to person. Links from the 'Cities I have visited' map make it easy for users to recommend it to others or to compare their map with their friends'.

WAYN (where are you now) is a social networking site specializing in putting travellers in touch with each other. With an estimated 11 million members, it offers targeted advertising opportunities, and also 'white-labelling' of WAYN content on other sites. For example, city or hotel websites can show the WAYN members currently in the city their photos of the area and suggestions on things to do.

Other forms of 'user-generated content' sites that might be useful for travel companies' advertising include photo storage sites like Photobucket and Flickr and the hugely popular video site YouTube.

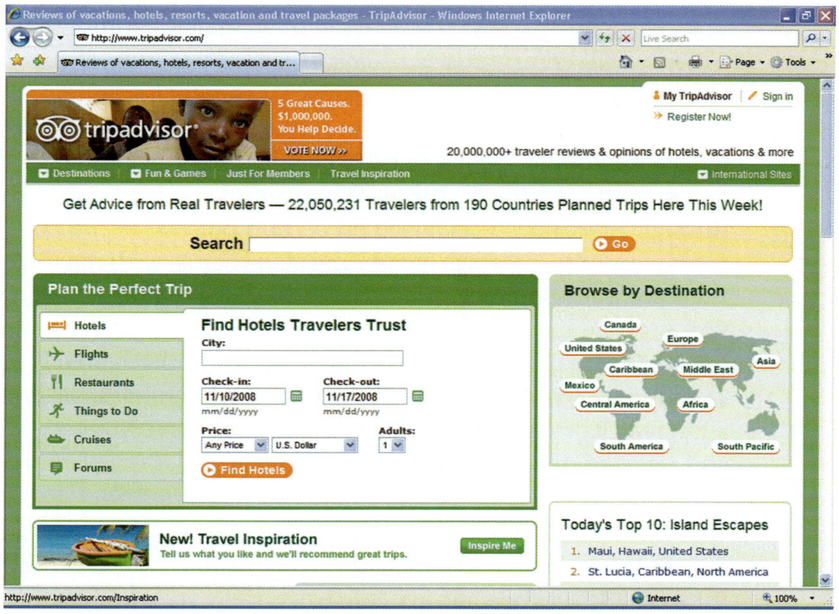

Courtesy of TripAdvisor LLC.

Marketing through Web 2.0

From the aforementioned examples, it can be seen that the latest developments on the Internet are creating networks or communities of people, often linked only by their shared interests in a particular form of consumption activity. This presents the marketer with the opportunity to observe, contact or interact with people who have revealed a strong interest in their product category.

This can be used for marketing research purposes to gain insight into consumer attitudes, preferences and trends, either by online polls or by using ethnographic methods to observe the community over a period of time. Internet ethnography or 'Netnography' can be a way of gaining insights into the experiences of a group of participants without the problems of inhibition and influence that come from the presence of a researcher, since the information is publicly available (Arnould and Epp, 2006). According to several authors (Kozinets, 2002; Arnould and Epp, 2006), the advantages of netnography are that it is not only less time consuming and less costly than traditional techniques, but is also less obtrusive and provides a window into naturally occurring behaviours in a context that is not fabricated by the researcher. There are limitations in that these communities represent only the most involved and committed enthusiasts rather than the total market for a product, and that members may hide their identities and play characters rather than reveal their everyday selves.

Website review pages can provide another source of marketing research, but again, these are unlikely to be representative, as only those with strong views, favourable or unfavourable, are likely to be motivated to post their views.

The websites where the communities meet can provide opportunities for carefully targeted advertising, sponsorship and affiliate marketing links. However, the best way to understand the role of these user-generated content sites in marketing is to regard them as a new medium for the spread of news and opinion alongside, and for many people replacing newspapers and magazines. Bloggers and other self-appointed reviewers are replacing journalists and critics as trusted sources for unbiased advice. Managing the way the image of the company was represented in the old media was the job of the Public Relations department, which established good relations and fed stories to a small number of influential contacts. The 'democratisation of criticism' in the new media makes this much more difficult. Online communities are likely to be quick to spot and expose company attempts to plant favourable stories. Even company-sponsored message boards can attract negative and positive comments, especially if posts are not continually monitored and moderated. The best source of positive public relations, in the Internet age as in the age of printed media, is still good-quality products and satisfied customers.

DIRECT/DATABASE MARKETING AND THE INTERNET

Once someone has visited a website or placed an order through it, his or her details can be stored on a database and used for direct marketing. Direct marketing is a highly cost-effective tool for marketing research, segmentation, market innovation and test marketing, as well as a means of reaching customers, making sales and monitoring sales revenue. The data can be part of a *customer relationship management* (CRM) system, the name given to the systematic use of database systems to manage and develop relationships through the relevant and personalized communications with customers.

Websites can help to build this continuous relationship by encouraging the customer to return. Details of the customer's address, credit card and purchases are recorded on the database and a *cookie* planted on the customer's computer. Cookies are pieces of data that are recognized by the company's web server so that on the next visit, the customer's details are retrieved from the database. This allows the web page to be personalized, greeting the users by name, offering them information and recommendations based on their previous purchases, and speeding up transactions by recalling the address and credit card details.

To capture consumer data even where there is no purchase, many websites encourage users to register in order to gain access to added-value facilities, such as priority booking or the ability to take part in user forums and discussion boards. As we said earlier, such forums can encourage a sense of community among regular users, giving them a reason to visit the site often and providing the company with insights into their attitudes and behaviour.

In using the Internet for direct marketing, care needs to be taken only to send customers communications that they find interesting and relevant. Unsolicited e-mail messages, known as spam (a term derived from a Monty Python sketch), are the curse of the Internet. Most are instantly deleted either automatically by 'spam filters' on servers or manually by the irate user. Over-frequent marketing messages can be seen as spam and meet the same fate. To ensure the message gets through, marketers should use '*precision marketing*', carefully targeting only those who are known to be interested in the particular type of product, and '*permission marketing*' – allowing people to opt in or out of receiving the messages.

Viral marketing

Viral marketing is another means of overcoming the problem of spam as the message is relayed not by the company but by a known and trusted friend. For that reason, many websites now have a 'send-to-a-friend' button prominently displayed.

Viral marketing is the term used for activities that encourage individuals to pass on marketing communications to their friends. Its name reflects the way the marketing message spreads from person to person rather like a virus. It is not entirely new in principle as creating word-of-mouth recommendation and using incentives for customers to recruit their friends have always been part of marketing. The Internet and the mobile phone, however, have made it much more prominent with potentially global coverage. While incentives and rewards are still used, the most effective way of stimulating viral marketing is to produce something that users want to pass on because their friends will find it amusing or interesting.

A series of amateur videos showing a young man called Matt dancing in front of the world's great tourist views attracted 100,000 visits on YouTube through viral recommendation. The chewing gum manufacturer Stride then paid him to do more trips and the new series of 'Where the Hell is Matt?' featuring the Stride logo in the credits, has now delivered them 8 million viewers.

PERMISSION MARKETING

Data-protection laws in many countries require organizations to seek the permission of people before storing data about them or using them for marketing purposes. There are also voluntary or statutory systems that allow individuals to opt out of all direct mail or telephone marketing calls. For this reason, there is often a box on order or enquiry forms, which the customers have to tick if they agree to receive further information and offers from the organization or third parties.

Permission marketing (Godin, 1999) refers to ways in which organizations try to encourage people to agree to, or to actively request, being sent marketing messages. This is done by offering them some added benefit, either in terms of useful information or a monetary benefit. A common form of permission marketing is the consumer survey, in which people give details of the products and brands they use regularly in return for the promise of receiving discount vouchers and special offers for those products.

According to Brey et al. (2007), the main reasons why people give their name and e-mail address to a tourism website are to personalize a site, to obtain a login or password, to subscribe to a newsletter, to receive notification of discounts, to enter a contest, to purchase online, or to request a travel brochure.

Link article available at www.routledge.com/9780750686938

(1) Eric, T. Brey, Siu-Ian (Amy) So., Dae-Young Kim, Alastair, M. Morrison. 2007. Web-based permission marketing: segmentation for the lodging industry. Tourism Management 28 (6), 1408–1416 .

CHAPTER SUMMARY

- This chapter examines ways in which an organization can use its website as the centre of its marketing communications, embracing all elements of the traditional marketing mix explained in Chapter 8.
- It outlines ways in which people may be attracted to the site, through affiliate networks and search engine marketing.
- The guidelines for effective website design are set out, and the importance of monitoring and managing the customer's online experience of the organization is stressed.
- The use of websites to collect data for permission-based direct marketing and to develop continuing customer relationships has been discussed.
- The chapter also explores some of the marketing implications of the latest developments of the Internet, the growth of sites dependent on user-generated content. The development of blogs, wikis, forums and social networking sites all encourage the formation of 'communities of consumption', drawn together by a shared interest. The communities present readymade behavioural segments to be targeted by marketers through sponsorship, advertising and affiliate links.

- It notes that the rapid spread of news, opinions and reviews through these networks creates not only marketing opportunities but also threats to organizations whose failings may be quickly exposed and dissected by a global audience.

QUESTIONS TO CONSIDER

1. To what extent is it possible for a tourism organization to rely entirely on online media for its marketing communications?
2. Using the criteria outlined in the chapter, evaluate the effectiveness of a travel or tourism website of your choice, and recommend ways in which it could be improved.
3. Evaluate the advantages and limitations of social networking sites as a medium for commercial organizations to interact with their target markets.
4. What strategies should organizations use to cope with the 'democratization of criticism' encouraged by user-generated-content sites?

REFERENCES AND FURTHER READING

Angehrn, A. (1997). Designing mature Internet business strategies: The ICDT model, *European Management Journal*, **15**(4), pp. 360–368.

Arnould, E.J. and Epp, A. (2006). Chapter 4: Deep engagement with consumer experience: listening and learning with qualitative data. In: *The Handbook of Marketing Research: Uses, Misuses, and Future Advances* (Ed. by Grover, R. and Vriens, M.), p. 41. London: Sage.

Brey, E.T., So, S.I., Kim, D.-Y. and Morrison, A.M. (2007). Web-based permission marketing: segmentation for the lodging industry, *Tourism Management*, **28**(6), pp. 1408–1416.

Chin-Sheng, W., Sheng-Hshiung, Ya-Li C. and Wen-Bin, C. (2007). Is the advertising effect of virtual experience always better or contingent on different travel destinations?, *Information Technology and Tourism*, **9**(1), pp. 45–54.

Cova, B. and Cova, V. (2001). Tribal aspects of post-modern consumption research: the case of French in-line roller skaters, *Journal of Consumer Behaviour*, **1**(1), pp. 67–76.

De Pelsmacker, P. Geuens, M. and van den Bergh, J. (2001) Marketing Communications, FT Prentice Hall. pp. 423-424.

Doolin, B., Burgess, L. and Cooper, J. (2002). Evaluating the use of the Web for tourism marketing: a case study from New Zealand, *Tourism Management*, **23**(5), pp. 557–561.

Friedman, L. and Goodrich, G. (1998). Sales strategy in a multi-channel environment, *The Journal of Sales and Major Account Management*, **1**(1), pp. 38–48.

Godin, S. (1999). *Permission Marketing: Turning Strangers Into Friends and Friends Into Customers*. New York: Simon Schuster.

Jobber, D (2007) Principles and Practice of Marketing. 5th edn. McGraw Hill 727

Kozinets, R.V. (2002). The field behind the screen: using netnography for marketing research in on-line communities, *Journal of Marketing Research*, **39**(1), pp. 61–73.

O'Reilly, T. (2005) What is Web 2.0: design patterns and business models for the next generation of software. O'Reilly Media website. Accessed March 2008. http://www.oreilly.com/pub/a/oreilly/tim/news/2005/09/30/what-is-web-20.html

Ranchhod, A. (2004). The changing nature of cyber-marketing strategies, *Business Process Management Journal*, **10**(3), pp. 262–276.

Schmallegger, D. and Carson, D. (2008). Blogs in tourism: changing approaches to information exchange, *Journal of Vacation Marketing*, **14**(2), pp. 99–110 [this edition also contains several other interesting articles on travel blogs].

Schmitt, B.H. (2003). *Customer Experience Management: A Revolutionary Approach to Connecting with Your Customers*. Hoboken NJ: John Wiley and Sons.

Wang, Y., Yu, Q. and Fesenmaier, D.R. (2002). Defining the virtual tourist community: implications for tourism marketing, *Tourism Management*, **23**(4), pp. 407–417.

Zhang, Z. (2005). Organizing customers: Japanese travel agencies marketing on the Internet, *European Journal of Marketing*, **38**(9/10), pp. 1294–1303.

An advert from the internet travel agency LateRooms.com, 'Dizzy with choice' advertising campaign 2008' 'the impact of ICT is that consumers now have easier, more convenient and faster access to a much wider choice of holiday and travel possibilities'.

Courtesy of LateRooms.com and BMB Advertising Agency.

CHAPTER 15

Distribution channels in travel and tourism: creating access

LateRooms.com
DIZZY WITH CHOICE

Once the Cinderella of the marketing mix – unglamorous but essential – distribution is now seen as central to many economic sectors

Cooper and Lewis in Buhalis and Laws, 2002

The new competition is not between individual companies but between networks of value-delivery systems and the winners will be the companies with the best networks

Kotler, 1998

This chapter considers the last of the basic four Ps in the traditional marketing mix, *place* or distribution as introduced in Chapter 8. Distribution aims to provide 'access', meaning points of sale convenient for customers. In revising this chapter for the fourth edition, the focus has changed from regarding the Internet and digital communications channels as an emerging challenge to the traditional distribution channels, to one where the Internet has become the *primary* channel for consumer access, distribution and direct marketing. However, this chapter will stress that the principles of distribution remain the same: there is a continuing need to provide access for consumers at multiple points of sale away from the places of service production.

After studying this chapter, you should be able to understand:

- The key strategic choice between direct and indirect marketing.
- The role of distribution channels in travel and tourism.
- How to evaluate and select appropriate marketing channels for a tourism business.
- The impact of the Internet on the evolution of tourism distribution systems.

DIRECT OR INDIRECT MARKETING – A STRATEGIC DECISION

Because of the large costs incurred in providing access, the fundamental strategic choice now facing all travel and tourism businesses is between direct and indirect marketing. Direct means that a business promotes to and deals directly with its customers. Indirect means that sales are achieved through third-party distribution. The choice is seldom clear-cut, and the balance of advantage is shifting continuously through the influence of new developments in ICT. A combination of both strategies for achieving sales response is common in the travel and tourism industry.

Because of the traditional importance of travel agents in the transport and tour-operating sectors of tourism, most texts on travel and tourism marketing have dealt with the distribution function from the standpoint of the retailer. In reality, they have never been the most important channels for most businesses in the visitor economy. Their share of the holiday and business travel markets differs from country to country, higher in Britain than, for example, in Germany or the United States because of the need to book air or sea transport as part of the package. Most businesses, hotels, attractions or holiday companies, use more than one form of distribution. Smaller businesses, which are numerically the largest part of the industry in all developed countries, are effectively excluded from retail distribution channels, because individually they are too small.

While travel agents are still important in specific sectors of the industry, their influence within the overall distribution pattern has declined in importance in recent years as all businesses are forced by competition and ICT to re-evaluate their distribution costs and options. As explained in Chapter 13, the impact of ICT is that the consumer now has much easier and more convenient access to a much wider choice of holiday and travel possibilities, while businesses are enabled to reach their target markets directly with reduced marketing and operations costs. In this climate, the traditional intermediaries and retailers need to offer clear advantages and added value if they are to survive in competition not only with direct marketing alternatives but also with new forms of online intermediaries or e-mediaries.

This chapter, therefore, explores the choices marketing managers in travel and tourism have to make in choosing the best combination of distribution channels for their products. It first outlines the function of distribution channels and the roles of the intermediaries within them as illustrated by the traditional distribution channels in travel and tourism, setting out the advantages and disadvantages of direct and indirect distribution both from the company and from the customer perspectives. It then discusses the extent to which these principles remain unchanged by the emergence of new online channels and intermediaries.

STRATEGIC CHOICES IN DISTRIBUTION

The marketing triangle for producers, distributors and customers

Distribution channels do not just convey products, but they also transfer marketing communications, bookings, payments and management information. Figure 15.1 is used to represent the main transactions and flows of information in marketing that take place between producers (or 'principals'), distributors and customers. The diagram is valid for the marketing of all types of travel and tourism companies, whether in accommodation, transport, attractions or tour operation. The shape of the triangle reveals the two basic options:

- Two-way direct response between producer and prospective customer.
- Indirect response, with distribution channels as third parties.

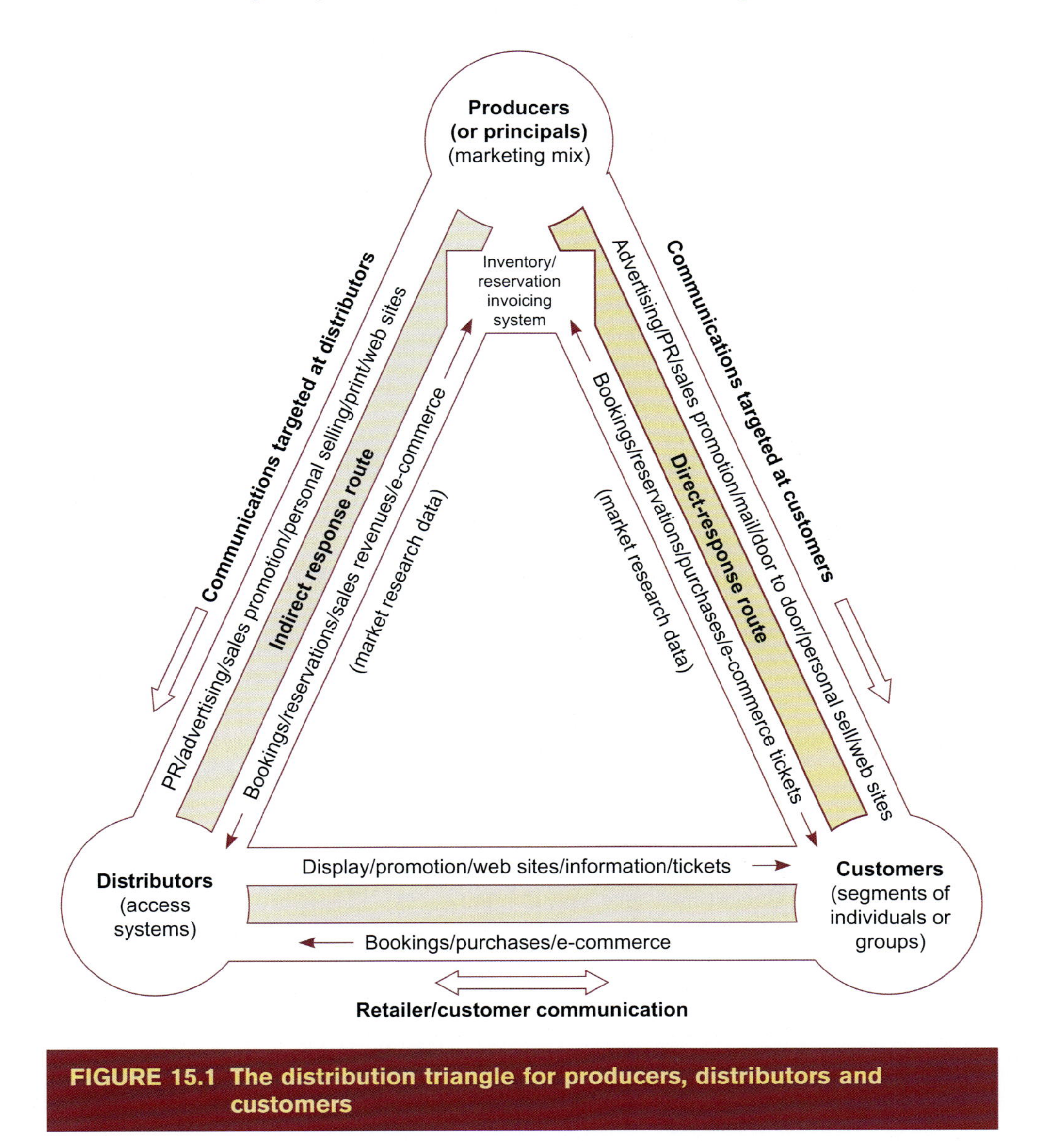

FIGURE 15.1 The distribution triangle for producers, distributors and customers

Within the triangle, there are three types of transaction:

1. **Business to customer direct:** On the right-hand outer leg of the triangle, outwards from producers, is the whole of the communications mix targeted at existing and prospective *customers*. It includes media advertising, PR, and sales promotions as well as any direct mail and telephone marketing. It also now includes B2C Internet communications via PCs, mobile phones and

interactive digital televisions. If businesses choose to market direct to customers, their bookings and money transactions flow back inwards also on the right hand of the triangle to be serviced via e-commerce, e-mail, call centres and direct mail, operating through an inventory management system. The tickets/confirmations flow back along the same route. This process is a rich information source for businesses and a very important feeder for customer databases, which are also a source of marketing research. Databases may be used to identify responses from different forms of promotional techniques, such as bookings from advertising in different media, and response to specific sales promotions. The information, including names and all the information that flows from addresses (see Chapter 9), is a by-product of modern reservation systems and it costs very little to collect once the inventory/database system has been set up to record and analyse the flows of routine data within a management information system.

2. **Business to business:** On the left-hand outer leg of the triangle, outwards from producers, is the communications mix targeted at business intermediaries in the distribution system. It includes online B2B communications and intranets accessible only to distributors. If customers purchase through distributors, bookings and money transactions flow inwards on the left hand of the triangle to an inventory management system, and tickets/confirmations flow outwards on the same route.

3. **Distributor to customer:** The base leg of the triangle represents the two-way flow of transactions between customers and distribution channels where the customer has no direct contact with the producer at the point of sale. Distributors include travel retailers and other channels that offer display space and access to products, and pass title on behalf of principals in return for a commission on sales. Distributors deal directly with customers in providing information, displays and promotional materials; they take money and supply tickets and other services. On the base leg, businesses have no access to their final customers or the flow of continuous market research information they represent.

Except for very small businesses, all inward flows of bookings and revenue, whether direct or indirect, are managed within an inventory or reservation system, often linked to call centres and or websites. Such systems are typically set up to handle the provision of options if the customer's first choice is not available, as well as confirmations, ticketing and invoicing.

The strategic choice and its implications

The triangular concept of flows makes it easier to understand the importance of the strategic question whether, and to what extent, producers should distribute and promote their products direct to the customer or organize sales through third-party channels of distribution. With few exceptions, there is rarely a simple answer to this question, and the answer varies over time and for different products within the same principal's portfolio. Thus, it may be advantageous for a hotel to market most of its domestic business travel direct to corporate clients than to market the bulk of its International business and weekend packages through retail travel agents.

At any point in time, a principal has to make a judgement on the marginal revenue and the marginal costs implied by the balance between direct and indirect sales, taking into account external and internal constraints, especially the rapid developments in ICT summarized in Chapters 13 and 14. The decision is mainly a financial one, reflecting the fact that any use of retailers has traditionally cost a minimum of 10% of the sales revenue generated, usually deducted at source. Commission has been as high as 15% and there are additional costs of servicing retailers with brochures and online connections, promoting to them and possibly employing a sales force to maintain product awareness and levels of display. On the other hand, commission is a variable cost that is not paid until sales are actually made and the principal's cash flow is not affected ahead of the sale, in contrast to the costs of advertising and direct marketing.

Link article available at www.routledge.com/9780750686938

(1) Pearce, D.G., 2008. A needs-functions model of tourism distribution. Annals of Tourism Research 35 (1), 148–168.

PRINCIPLES OF DISTRIBUTION

The principles of distribution were originally developed from the physical transportation and storage of tangible products. Paradoxically, the inability in travel and tourism to create physical stocks of products is exactly the reason why the distribution process has now become so significant in the information age. It creates innovative opportunities and a flexibility that manufacturers must envy. Creating and manipulating the distribution systems that provide access for consumers is one of the principal ways to manage demand for highly perishable products, and distribution has become the primary area for seeking competitive advantage in both cost reduction and service improvement.

The function of distribution is to make the product available for purchase by potential customers. Although with tangible goods this is achieved mainly by moving the product to make it available in retail shops, with services, it is often the customer who moves in order to enjoy and experience the product. In either case, the marketer's task is to give the customer easy and convenient access to the means of purchasing and enjoying the product. Thus, in travel and tourism, distribution decisions include the availability of information, the systems for reservations and payment, and the physical access to the place where the service or experience is performed.

An illustration of the distribution options open to businesses in travel and tourism is outlined in Figure 15.2.

THE IMPORTANCE OF LOCATION

For most small or micro-businesses with only one 'production unit', such as proprietor-owned guesthouses, small visitor attractions, recreation equipment hire operators or indeed independent travel agents, the choice of location is still likely to be the most important business decision. A well-located small business can expect a good flow of customers to its area and past its doors. Product formulation, promotion and, above all, pricing have always been vital marketing considerations

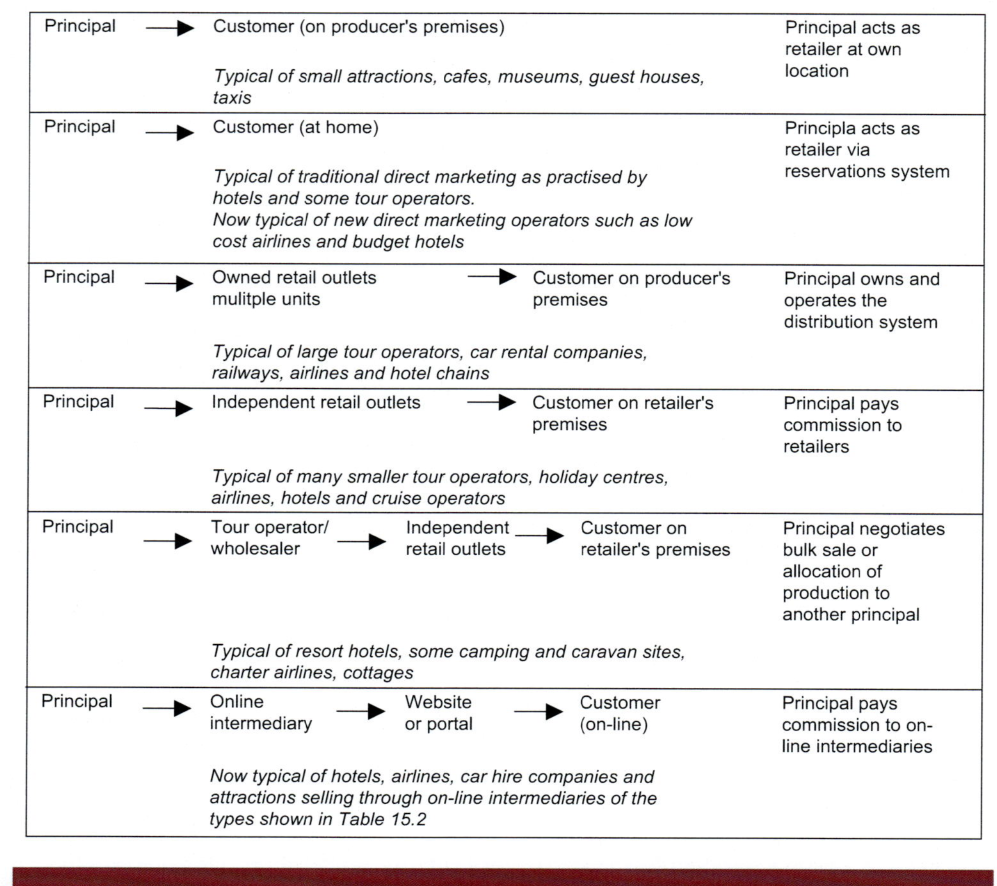

FIGURE 15.2 Distribution options in choosing channels for travel and tourism products (Adapted from Kotler: 1984)

for small businesses, but not distribution. Traditionally, location is both place of production and the primary point of sale. As noted later, however, even the established distribution certainties of the smallest business are increasingly challenged and undermined by a combination of excess capacity in mature markets and the new competitive opportunities provided by the Internet.

The fundamental requirement for well-located sites remains vital for large tourism businesses also. The continuing search by international hotel companies for suitable development sites in the major cities of Europe provides some illustration of its importance. However, location of production units is seldom, if ever, a *sufficient* source of sales volume for bigger businesses; one or more distribution channels are nearly always required to provide supplementary points of sale away from the locations of service production and consumption, especially where seasonal flows of business create spare capacity.

As this chapter indicates, there are other good marketing reasons for developing new distribution or access systems, especially cost reduction and control, protecting market share and matching competitors. But the over-riding reason is usually to generate sales revenue additional to that which may be sustained solely by a good location. While, to some extent, additional expenditure on advertising or other communications is an alternative to developing points of sale, in practice, there is a balance to be achieved between promotion and place. A massive demand generated by advertising would be lost, for example, if convenient points of access were not available to turn demand into sales. As modern distribution systems increasingly embrace both advertising and sales promotion functions, the balance has tilted strongly towards investment in distribution in the last decade.

DISTRIBUTION CHANNELS OR ACCESS SYSTEMS: THE NOTION OF PIPELINES

To achieve sales away from the location may require the involvement of other organizations, for example, tour or coach operators, travel agencies or tourist information centres. These are known as 'intermediaries', because they come between the 'principals' – the hotels, attractions or transport companies – and the customer. Together they provide a channel through which information, promotion, bookings and payments flow between the principal and the customer.

The main types of intermediaries and the alternative distribution channels through which an international visitor can purchase travel products are shown in Fig. 15.3. The customer can either book each element of a foreign trip direct with the principal suppliers or use the services of a tour operator, again either directly or through a retail or online travel agent. The tour operator in the originating country can either deal directly with the principals or employ a local company to do so. National Tourist Offices and destination management organizations do not normally act as a channel for sales but as a facilitator to help the channel members work together more effectively.

Although the figure uses the traditional terminology of tour operators and travel agents, the basic choice facing the customers remains the same whether the means of communication is face to face, by telephone, post or online. They can either contact the principal suppliers direct or use intermediaries. Those principal suppliers,

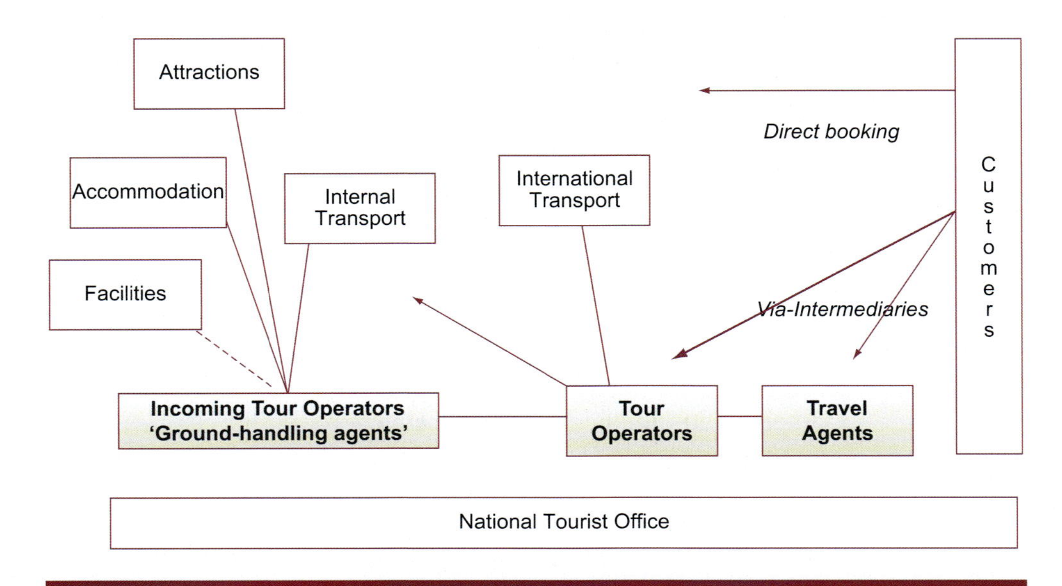

FIGURE 15.3 Distribution channels for international tourism

therefore, need to know which channels their particular target customers are more likely to use and how they may have shifted preferences over the last 5 years or so.

Other businesses in travel and tourism have their own channels and intermediaries. Thus, a car rental business may establish its own corporate desks at airports to service travellers arriving and departing by air; it will provide direct 'pipelines' for its frequent 'loyal' users; it will usually offer commissions on sales made by travel agents and provide allocations of cars to tour operators that include car rental in their holiday packages. The same company will create and maintain websites including details of products and prices and how to book, with or without an e-commerce option. By contrast, a guesthouse or a small tourist attraction traditionally dealt only directly with customers and tourism information centres as a channel for display and bookings. Now, however, even very small businesses have their own websites to promote what they offer, and provide low-cost information and booking services. Typically, such small businesses would take space on destination management organization websites open to them, thus, potentially extending their access globally.

Definitions

To encompass these many different types of channels, a broad definition is needed.

A distribution channel is any organized and serviced system, paid for out of marketing budgets and created or utilized to provide convenient points of sale and/or access to consumers, away from the location of production and consumption (Middleton, 1994a: 202).

The channels are carefully planned by marketing managers and serviced regularly through a combination of online access, call centres, sales visits, sales literature, multimedia options, educationals, familiarization trips and trade shows. Each channel, once established, organized and serviced at a cost to be paid for out of marketing budgets, becomes in effect a 'pipeline'. Through these pipelines flow, in one direction, information, promotional materials and marketing expenditure, and in the other, bookings and payments (see Fig. 15.1).

When the distribution channel involves an ongoing relationship with one or more intermediaries, it is sometimes referred to as a marketing channel. Marketing channels were defined by Stern and El Ansary (1996) as 'sets of interdependent organisations involved in making a product available to the end-user customer'.

The key word here is interdependent. While both sides gain benefits from cooperating, the distribution costs will be justified. If the benefits are greater for one party than the others, then alternative channels will be considered. For most travel and tourism businesses, the cost of distribution is, by far, the largest element in the marketing budget; hence, the effectiveness of the channels needs to be under continuous review.

Another way of understanding the distribution channel is to see it as an extended value chain (Porter, 1980) or value-delivery system. This approach involves in assessing what added value each intermediary or retailer adds to the end product, in order to judge whether this justifies the additional costs they create. This added value is created by the benefits the intermediaries offer to suppliers and consumers.

The benefits of using intermediaries: the supplier perspective

The main benefit to the suppliers, the tourism principals, is that each selected channel offers an efficient way of making contact with the end-user customers (Rosenbloom, 1995), thereby extending its points of access and sales away from the location. Through a single relationship with a tour operator, a hotel in Spain can get bookings from thousands of visitors through brochures displayed in travel agencies in every shopping centre in Britain. Using a distribution agent, a visitor attraction can get its leaflets to every hotel, holiday cottage and campsite in its region.

Another important function of marketing channels is to facilitate the purchase of products in advance of their production. 'Advance' could be anything from 2 to 3 hours (for transport bookings) and up to 2 or 3 years or even longer (for major conventions or exhibition venues). The greater the volatility of daily demand, the greater the imperative to sell in advance if possible. For a seasonal resort hotel, daily or weekly demand is open to very wide fluctuation, and some bookings are made months ahead of delivery. The logical marketing response is to focus maximum effort on advance sales and organize reservation systems to that end.

However, if there is unsold capacity left at a later stage, the channel can also be an effective way of bringing discounts and promotional offers to the notice of a greater number of potential customers. Travel agency windows always carry cards advertising last- minute bargains, and hence, become the place where many people look for holiday ideas. Nowadays, of course, the Internet offers the same facility.

Finally, selected channels provide a range of marketing and customer services for the principal as shown in Table 15.1

The benefits of using intermediaries: the customer perspective

For the customers, the value of the channel is that it makes the product available in the form, and at the time and place they require (Bucklin, 1966). For example, the

TABLE 15.1 Services provided by distribution channels

1. Points of sale and convenient customer access, either for immediate purchase or for booking in advance.
2. Display and distribution of product information, such as brochures and leaflets – or multimedia information that may be accessed and downloaded via the Internet (providing choice for customers).
3. Sales promotion and merchandising opportunities, especially special deals on prices responding to yield management programmes.
4. Advice and purchase assistance, e.g. itinerary planning, suggestion of options and helpful product knowledge.
5. Arranging transfer of title to a product through ticketing and travel documentation, or provision of a unique reference number that can be presented at the point of delivery.
6. Receiving and transmitting sales revenue to principals.
7. Possible provision of ancillary services, e.g. insurance, advice on inoculations, passport assistance.
8. Sources of marketing intelligence for producers, often including building up consumer databases.
9. May be used as part of a principal's advertising and PR campaigns.
10. A route for receiving and assisting with complaints from customers, or directing them to another source.

customer can pick up a brochure in his or her own language, with flights included from his or her nearest airport, with coach transfers, insurance and as optional extras car hire or excursions all included. The booking can be made in their own town centre as part of a regular shopping trip.

Using intemediaries also offers the customer convenience. The travel agent, whether on the high street or online, provides the opportunity to compare a number of alternative products and to get advice from experienced staff. Choosing a package simplifies a potentially time-consuming and stressful decision.

Booking an intangible service months in advance can lead to post-purchase anxiety. Dealing with a local retailer face to face offers the reassurance that if problems occur, there will be someone there to help. Choosing a well-known brand promises quality, consistency and reliability. As a campaign for Thomson Holidays (now TUI) stated in their advertising:

If Thomsons do it, do it. If Thomsons don't do it, don't do it

Even on the Internet, the consumer is more likely to choose the website of a well-known brand, whether TUI or Expedia, than one they have no previous knowledge of.

The costs of using intermediaries

The benefits of using a marketing channel are clear but they come at a price. To create the marketing offer that the customer demands may require members to subordinate their own needs to the success of the channel (Coughlan et al., 2008). For a hotel to be included in a tour operator's brochure displayed in a nation-wide chain of travel agents, it must accept the rate per room demanded by the tour operator. This will certainly be well below the 'rack rate' offered to individual members of the public. Tour operators, online intermediaries and other group travel organizers demand discounts for volume business, while travel agents and other sales outlets will require commission of 10% or more. Both channels will affect the revenue yield to the hotel.

As we have emphasized in earlier editions, the fixed and variable costs of distribution are typically, by far, the biggest element in the marketing budget of any large travel and tourism business. Seldom less than 15% and usually far higher than advertising expenditure, in some circumstances, channel costs can amount to between a quarter and a third of turnover.

For hotels, it was estimated in 1999 that for a standard $100 hotel booking, the cost of using the basic pipelines specified below could be around 27.5% (*Financial Times*, 1999). The sum comprised:

Credit card charge	$3.00
Hotel CRS charge	$10.00–12.00
Ultra switch	$0.50
GDS charge	$3.50–4.00
Travel agent's percentage	$10.00
Total	$27.50

Because the booking was a notional $100, the figures above are also percentages. Although this example is now dated, the orders of magnitude for using standard pipelines of this type remain broadly true. The incentive to find less expensive pipelines is powerful. Hotels and other principals need to weigh up carefully the comparative costs of each distribution channel, and seek to reduce them wherever possible. The biggest changes since 1999 has, of course, been in online distribution. In the right conditions, this can generate a booking for a cost of less than $1, but it does not reach all customers at the present time.

In using intermediaries, a hotel also relinquishes full control over the image that is presented in the brochures or websites of intermediaries, and may have to adapt its services to meet the demands of the tour operator's customers. It needs to decide whether it is preferable to accept a regular supply of low-yielding guests from the tour operator or withhold some or all of the capacity in the hope of filling it with high-yielding customers through its own direct marketing efforts. Prior to the Internet, the costs of advertising or direct marketing would probably have been judged too high. Now, using bed-banks or search-engine marketing as well as its own websites can provide an affordable alternative.

This example illustrates the issues of control and power that exist in any distribution channel. Power in this context means the ability to influence the way in which the product is presented to the end user. The power, for example, of travel agents, is stronger if other members of the channel are dependent on them for business. If this dependency is lessened by the development of alternative channels,

Courtesy of LateRooms.com and BMB Advertising Agency, from the 'Dizzy with choice' advertising campaign 2008'.

then the power will also be weakened. In recent years, we have seen the airlines renegotiate the payments they make to travel agents from a commission basis to a flat fee, and many analysts expect the major hotel chains to follow suit.

Criteria for channel choice

Which distribution channels a business chooses for its marketing campaigns will depend on:

- **Consumer preference and habit:** The first question to ask is where their target group of customers normally look for information on this type of product. Until recently, British people used travel agents for overseas holidays but booked domestic holidays direct with the suppliers. Now, according to research reports at the time of writing this chapter, the situation is more complex with increasing numbers booking overseas holidays online but many using several sources – travel agents, phone calls to tour operators and the Internet – during their decision-making process. The majority of Germans taking foreign holidays still book package holidays through travel agents

- **Coverage of target market**: Depending on the size of the business and the capacity they have to fill, the company has to decide between three types of strategies:
  - Extensive distribution – blanket coverage of all the outlets in a catchment area
  - Intensive distribution – supplying only those outlets proven to be cost-effective
  - Or an exclusive distribution deal with one chosen partner.

The costs of printing and distributing brochures means that tour companies carefully monitor the performance of their agents and allocate the brochures accordingly.

These first two considerations will suggest where the company should ideally be targeting its distribution. However, other factors may lead them to modify their strategy.

- **Comparative cost:** Distribution is the largest cost in the marketing budget. In deciding between distribution options, it is necessary to compare the expenditure needed in the following areas
  - Printing and physical distribution of brochures and other promotional literature
  - Reservations and enquiry office staffing to service each channel
  - Sales and trade support staffing to motivate each channel
  - Advertising and publicity costs targeted to each channel
  - Discounts for trade and group bookings to support each channel
  - Commission and incentives for retailers and any other intermediaries

In marketing terms, the choice is between a push strategy, which rewards the intermediaries and retailers for carrying out much of the promotional and sales work, and a pull strategy, which puts more resources into advertising and direct marketing to the end consumer. After staffing, the cost of printing and distributing brochures is generally the biggest element; hence, making the most cost-effective use of them is a key consideration in deciding the distribution strategy.

- **Control of the channel**: While travel agencies may be the place where the majority of consumers look for holiday ideas, the majority of retail agencies is now part of vertically integrated travel companies, and give priority to selling their own group's branded products (Hudson et al., 2001). To fill their remaining shelf space, they will choose the products that will give them the best return, a decision made centrally rather than left to the branch manager. Their nationwide coverage and brand-loyal customers give them 'retailer power' to dictate terms to independent tour operators. These smaller tour operators may not be able to provide the year-round capacity needed to service all the branches of the travel agency chain, nor will they have the marketing budgets to create high brand awareness or take part in joint promotional campaigns. The high rates of commission demanded by the multiple agencies may take an unacceptably large proportion of their profit margins. For these reasons, the smaller companies have to seek alternative ways of reaching their markets.

THE EVOLUTION OF DISTRIBUTION SYSTEMS

To illustrate the principles of distribution in travel and tourism as they developed over the second half of the twentieth century, this chapter so far has concentrated on the traditional multi-level channels. However, these systems were the result of a particular business environment and, as we discussed in Chapter 13, that environment has changed dramatically since the mid-1990s. For as long as the gateway to mass tourism holiday markets was through retail travel agencies owned by vertically integrated travel companies and linked to airline global distribution systems, suppliers and smaller independent intermediaries had either to accept the terms these companies demanded or find alternative direct marketing routes to niche markets.

Now, of course, consumers have a much wider choice of electronic gateways through which they can obtain information and make bookings, as Table 15.2 shows.

TABLE 15.2 New gateways for travel and tourism information and bookings

Airlines	Individual airline websites and their affiliate networks – e.g. easyjet.com.
	Sites owned by airline consortia – e.g. opodo, orbitz
Hotel sites	Websites of individual hotels, groups or consortia – e.g. Best Western
Bed banks	Hotel booking companies – e.g. Utell, Hotel Connect, Hotelopia
Destinations	Websites run by national, regional or local destination management organizations
Online travel agencies:	Expedia, Travelocity
Review sites	Tripadvisor
Late booking sites	lastminute.com
Travel search engines	Cheap Flights, Sidestep, Kayak
Portals*	Travel pages of internet service provider portals – e.g. Yahoo, Orange
Vortals*	Travel pages of specialist portals – e.g. tennis.com, igolf.com
News media	Online newspapers and other media – e.g. Telegraph, Guardian, CNN
Auction sites	eBay, Qxl
Social networks	Facebook, mySpace

Adapted from Buhalis, 2003.

* Portals – a website that draws together links from a range of other sites to provide users with a summary of current news or a directory of relevant pages and sites. It thus provides a portal or doorway into cyberspace for them. The first portals were provided by Internet service providers for their subscribers. The concept of a front page with current news, links and special offers is used by companies both for internal and external communication. Vortals, or vertical portals, are portals designed for a specific industry or leisure interest.

MINI-CASE 15.1: OPODO

Opodo is a Pan-European company owned by nine of Europe's leading airlines – Aer Lingus, Air France, Alitalia, Austrian Airlines, British Airways, Finnair, Iberia, KLM, Lufthansa – and by Amadeus, the GDS, and travel industry technology provider. It links to airline central reservations systems and global distribution systems to give the public the ability to choose and book flights and other services in a way previously only available through travel agents. It was created by the European airlines in response to the growing power of online travel agencies, such as Expedia, and to the launch of a similar venture by the American airlines with Orbitz.

Opodo launched its first site (www.opodo.de) in Germany in November 2001, its UK site (www.opodo.co.uk) in January 2002, its French site (www.opodo.fr) in April 2002 and its Italian site (www.opodo.it) in January 2006. Having established a presence in Spain and Scandinavia, Opodo now operates in nine markets. Its turnover is estimated at over €1 billion.

Opodo claims to address the real needs of today's traveller by offering a competitively priced online travel service for world travel, with access to flights from over 500 airlines, over 65 000 hotel properties and over 7000 car-hire locations worldwide, as well as travel insurance. Although owned by the airlines, it is managed independently, and stresses that it provides unbiased information on the best available routes and prices.

The name "Opodo" was chosen because it does not mean anything in any of the European languages, thus ensuring that all of the countries treat it as a 'foreign' website. The word Opodo stands for "OPportunity tO DO"

Source: www.opodo.co.uk.

Disintermediation or reintermediation?

Do the developments of the last decade mean that the traditional channels and intermediaries are obsolete? When the Internet first became widely used, there was a prediction that it would lead to a 'disintermediation' of distribution channels, with more and more customers booking direct with suppliers and cutting out the intermediaries. Although direct booking and independent travel has certainly grown massively, what has actually happened is more complex. As Table 15.2 shows, the Internet has created business opportunities for a range of different infomediaries or travel e-mediaries offering essentially the same services online as their traditional rivals did on the high street.

At the same time, the established companies have reinvented themselves online, offering the customer additional benefits, including the ability to tailor their own holiday through dynamic packaging and to compare their experiences with others on the review pages or blogs. The websites of Thomas Cook and Thomson rival those of Expedia, Opodo and Lastminute in the top 10 travel sites used by British people in a Mintel survey.

This 'reintermediation' suggests that the principles of distribution we outlined earlier still apply in the now dominant online era, in particular:

- Many customers with busy lives value the convenience of a 'one-stop-shop' for all their travel purchases – both online and off it.
- Faced with a bewildering choice, consumers value the reassurance provided by a well-known brand.
- Suppliers value the efficient access to wide consumer markets provided by intermediaries.
- The purchasing power and marketing spend of the large consolidated companies continues to give them a competitive advantage over their smaller rivals.

While retail travel agents are losing business to online and call-centre-based rivals, there will still be people who prefer the reassurance and personal service of the face-to-face contact.

The core activities of tour operators are to:

- Purchase in bulk the components of holidays.
- Package them into a standardized, repeatable, quality-controlled product.
- Brand them into a single entity.
- Offer them to the public at an inclusive price.

These services will still give operators advantage in a market where customers are able to search for the best bargains. They may well use these advantages to offer their products through new channels. In Chapter 14, we saw that TUI, the parent company of Thomson, also owns the hotel bed bank Hotelopia and markets it through the affiliate network of Easyjet and other airlines. These new marketing alliances and networks facilitated by the Internet will further increase the volume of business and, therefore, the buying power of the group.

Link article available at www.routledge.com/9780750686938

(1) Buhalis, D., Licata, M.C., 2002. The future of eTourism intermediaries. Tourism Management 23 (3), 207–220.

MANAGING THE MARKETING CHANNEL

We have described distribution channels as pipelines. Pipelines mostly carry their flows unseen and without human intervention; yet, if a blockage occurs and is undetected, the results can be disastrous. As we saw in Chapter 13, companies have used ICT to computerize their routine transactions with their suppliers and intermediaries to reduce the cost and the possibilities of human error. Nevertheless, tourism remains an industry based on human interaction. Satisfying and retaining a customer may depend on the service provided by someone employed by another company. Dealing with the crises that inevitably arise will be easier if there are close relationships between the members of the marketing channel.

For this reason, the principles of relationship marketing – establishing long-term relationships through the making and keeping of promises, as Grönroos (1989) puts it – apply in managing the distribution channel. The key accounts need to be identified and developed from the early stages where contact is between a single sales executive and purchasing officer to one where there is regular interaction, communication and trust through every level of the two organizations (Macdonald and Woodburn, 2007). The tourism industry has always used incentives and familiarization visits or 'educationals' as the means of developing business and cooperation between suppliers, intermediaries and retailers.

CHAPTER SUMMARY

- The aim of every distribution strategy is to provide targeted customers with easy access to the means of obtaining information and making a purchase.
- Although location is still an important factor in travel and tourism, creating and using distribution channels is normally essential to provide an efficient way to reach a wider market and generate advance sales.
- For customers, distribution channels can simplify the purchase decision by offering products in a convenient form from a trusted source at a time and place of their choosing.
- In deciding which channels to use, companies need to consider
  - Where their target markets look for information.
  - The relative coverage of each channel.
  - The comparative costs, revenue and net contribution of each channel, which change frequently.
  - The extent to which access is controlled by vertically integrated companies and the implications of that for businesses not directly connected.
- The Internet has both provided a direct channel between buyers and sellers and at the same time increased the choice of channels and gateways through which travel bookings can be made.
- Although direct booking with suppliers have increased rapidly, so too have the number of new online intermediaries offering services similar to those of the traditional intermediaries and retailers.

QUESTIONS TO CONSIDER

1. Using the criteria outlined in this chapter, evaluate the range of distribution options available to one of the following:
   i. A conference and exhibition centre.
   ii. A museum or heritage centre.
   iii. An adventure holiday company.
   iv. A medium-sized hotel group of around 75 hotels geographically spread across a country.
2. Will the widespread adoption of the Internet eventually lead to the demise of tour operators and travel agents?

REFERENCES AND FURTHER READING

Alamdari, F. and Mason, K. (2006). The future of airline distribution, *Journal of Air Transport Management*, **12**(3), pp. 122–134.

Bucklin, L.P. (1966). *A Theory of Distribution Channel Structure*. IBER Special Publications.

Buhalis, D. (2003). *eTourism: Information Technology for Strategic Tourism Management*. FT Prentice Hall.

Buhalis, D. and Laws, E. (2001). *Tourism Distribution Channel, Practices, Issues and Transformations*. Thomson Learning.

Buhalis, D. and Licata, M.C. (2002). The future of eTourism intermediaries, *Tourism Management*, **23**(3), pp. 207–220.

Coughlan, A., Anderson, E., Stern, L.W. and El-Ansary, A. (2008). *Marketing Channels* (7th edn). Pearson education.

Grönroos, C. (1989). Defining marketing: a market-orientated approach, *European Journal of Marketing*, **23**(1), pp. 52–59.

Hudson, S., Snaith, T., Miller, G. and Hudson, P. (2001). Travel retailing: switch selling in the UK. In: *Tourism Distribution Channel, Practices, Issues and Transformations* (Ed. by D. Buhalis, E. Laws). Thomson Learning.

Macdonald, M. and Woodburn, D. (2007). *Key Account Management: The Definitive Guide*. Butterworth–Heinemann.

O'Connor, P. and Frew, A.J. (2004). An evaluation methodology for hotel electronic channels of distribution, *International Journal of Hospitality Management*, **3**(2), pp. 179–199.

Pearce, D.G. (2008). A needs-functions model of tourism distribution, *Annals of Tourism Research*, **35**(1), pp. 148–168.

Porter, M. (1980). *Competitive Strategy*. Free Press.

Rosenbloom, B. (1999). *Marketing Channels: A Management View* (6th edn). Dryden Press.

English Harbour, Antigua was a filming location for Pirates of the Caribbean – 'Destination tourism officers encourage filming in their locations as successful television or film productions can boost visitor numbers at a fraction of the cost of an advertising campaign'.

CHAPTER 16

Integrating the promotional and communications mix

Advertising, public relations (PR) and sales promotion have always been the most visible outputs of travel and tourism marketing but, generally, not the most important or the largest elements in the marketing budget. Distribution and location have always been the keys to success. As discussed at length in Part Four of this book, in the twenty-first century, the Internet has become the distribution channel of choice for a growing number of people, and companies are, therefore, making websites the centre of their marketing communications activities.

Tourism organizations are constantly communicating, whether intentionally or unintentionally, through each personal and non-personal interaction with the public. The role of marketing is to coordinate all the elements under the control of the organization in order to deliver consistent messages that enhance the chosen positioning. Although it is not under the immediate control of marketing management, taking steps to influence positive 'word of mouth' by satisfied customers is an additional important aspect of communications activity for service businesses. Most travel and tourism marketing communications are product focused and targeted either at the public or the travel trade. But large organizations, such as airlines and hotel groups, also buy media space to communicate with shareholders, politicians or the financial sector. Here, the emphasis is on corporate name and image.

This chapter examines the continuing role of the traditional media as part of an integrated marketing communications (IMC) strategy. It will first outline the principles of IMC and the stages of developing a marketing communications campaign. It then examines the contributions that advertising, PR and sales promotion can make to the strategy alongside the Internet communications outlined in Chapter 14.

After studying this chapter, you should be able to understand:

- The principles of IMC.
- The process and stages of devising a communications plan for a tourism business.

- How to identify the uses and planning processes for each of the main marketing communications tools.
- The continuing role of traditional communications in conjunction with the Internet.

THE PRINCIPLES OF IMC

Getting the message across to the target market is not easy. For reasons introduced in Chapter 5, all of us have barriers and filters in our minds. These barriers and filters, themselves products of our personalities, experiences and attitudes to life, condition our perception of the world around us. Bombarded by a continuous background 'noise' of up to 2000 advertising messages a day in developed countries, we use these barriers and filters to select the messages of interest to us. In other words, we only see what we want to see.

The normal length of a television commercial is 30 seconds, which is longer than most people spend looking at a newspaper or website advertisement, poster or direct marketing 'flier'. It is vital that these brief opportunities to communicate with the target market are not wasted.

Therefore, the principle of IMC is that, every time the consumer comes into contact with the organization, he or she should receive the same clear consistent message about the brand. A useful analogy is with the work of a continuity assistant in a film who ensures that each scene contributes to the story and there are no jarring inconsistencies of lighting, costume, weather or behaviour, no wristwatches on the Roman charioteers. In the same way, each communication from the company should be a variation on the same theme building a consistent brand image and personality. These communications do not just include the paid-for adverts, literature and web pages but other contacts with the company through media reports or interaction with reservations, reception staff or resort representatives. Other parts of the marketing mix, the price positioning and the type of outlets where the product can be accessed, can also be used to convey a message about the brand.

IMC – a definition

The concept under which a company carefully integrates and co-ordinates its many communications channels to deliver a clear, consistent and compelling message about the organization and its products.
Kotler et al., 1991

IMC has become an important concept partly through the changing relationships between marketing agencies and their clients, and also in response to changes in the business and media environment.

As discussed in earlier chapters, people in developed countries are increasingly experienced and sophisticated in their consumer behaviour and are less likely to be persuaded by 'hard-sell' advertising techniques. The proliferation of choice in every market, including travel and tourism, means that it is harder for companies to establish unique selling points or differentiate themselves from their rivals.

The proliferation of media outlets has led to intense competition for audiences and advertising spend. Advertisers can choose from hundreds of digital TV channels, thousands of consumer, special interest or business magazines, and millions of websites. The audience too has fragmented so that advertising has to be spread over more outlets to reach the target market. The implications of this for marketing are not just that each advertisement must be clear, consistent and compelling, but also that media advertising may not be the most cost-effective way of reaching the target market.

One principle of the IMC approach is to avoid presumptions in favour of any one promotional tool or medium, but instead, to select the most appropriate one for the objectives of each specific campaign.

The adoption of IMC was, in part, the response to a trend in marketing away from full-service agencies, which offered clients the complete range of services from campaign planning, creative design, to media buying and evaluation research as well as PR, sales promotion, exhibition and brochure design. Instead, companies can buy services from competing specialist agencies offering just one of the functions. This had obvious advantages to the client companies in terms of driving down costs and regaining control, but it also created the danger of diluting the message through a number of unrelated and uncoordinated ideas and executions. IMC argues for the whole marketing communications strategy to be coordinated either by a single full-service agency or by strong control by the client company, resulting in a more economic and efficient selection of promotional methods and a more effective communication of the brand message. For this reason, the traditional distinction between 'above'- and 'below'-the-line expenditure is now largely historic. Advertising was traditionally referred to as 'above-the-line' expenditure, because agencies used to earn commission from the purchase of media space, whereas other activities were conducted on a fee-paying basis, hence the term 'below-the-line' expenditure. With the shift towards alternative approaches to agency remuneration, the advent of the Internet and the increased expenditure on so-called 'below-the-line' activities, such as direct marketing and sales promotions, these original distinctions are less helpful in today's environment.

In summary, IMC means integration on three levels. First, it requires the integration of marketing objectives and messages across the range of promotional tools and communication channels. Secondly to achieve this, it requires integration or coordination of the marketing work within the company and with its agencies supplying marketing services. Thirdly, more fundamentally, it requires the integration of the one-to-many communications of the company with its one-to-one contacts with the customers throughout their relationship with the company (Pickton and Broderick, 2001). This involves not only the marketers responsible for advertising and promotion and the often separate PR department, but also with the departments responsible for sales and operations who form the front line of the company's interaction with its customers.

Courtesy of Dimitrios Buhalis.

THE DIMENSIONS OF MARKETING COMMUNICATIONS

IMC involves making the most appropriate selection from a range of promotional tools, including advertising, PR, direct marketing, sponsorship and sales promotion. Each of these will be explained in more detail later in the chapter, but an overview is offered as follows to guide the reader through the content of this chapter.

Advertising includes any paid-for communication in media aimed at the public, traditionally TV, radio, print, film and poster sites, but now, also websites and other digital media. This definition distinguishes advertising, where the media space is purchased for carefully controlled messages by an organization, from PR that seeks to obtain publicity for a company and its products through news stories and features in which it does not have direct control over the way messages are used. It also distinguishes media advertising (one-to-many) from direct marketing, which involves one-to-one communications with potential customers through the mail, Internet or telephone.

The dimensions of the marketing communications sector can be seen from Table 16.1 drawn from the British Advertising Association figures showing UK advertising expenditure in 2006. The press accounted for, by far, the largest share of total advertising expenditure (43.7%), with television the second largest medium (24.1%), followed by direct mail (12.2%), Internet (10.6%), outdoor (5.7%), radio (2.8%) and cinema (1.0%). But, while the traditional media showed little or no growth, expenditure on the Internet (including search engine marketing) grew by 47% in 1 year. Sponsorship has also shown sustained growth in recent years. The figures also reveal that expenditure on sales promotion, an essential short-term tactical tool, is greater than that on display advertising, which often has a longer-term brand-building objective.

TABLE 16.1 Advertising options in the United Kingdom in 2006 – Advertising Association figures

	£M (2006)	Number of outlets
Television	4594	Over 200 digital channels
National newspapers	1489	21
Regional newspapers	883	632, excluding freesheets
Consumer magazines	665	3200
Business and professional journals	630	5100
Directories (including Yellow Pages)	1174	
Press production costs	647	
Outdoor and transport	1084	
Radio	534	371 commercial stations
Cinema	188	3500 screens
Direct mail	2322	
Internet	2016	
Sponsorship	871 (Mintel estimate)	
Sales promotion	19 000 (IPA [Institute of Practioners in Advertising] estimate)	
Public relations	6500 (estimated turnover of the industry CIPR)	

Newspaper and magazine figures are for display advertising only – excluding classified small advertisements.

STAGES IN THE MARKETING COMMUNICATION PROCESS

Whichever promotional tools and media are chosen to get messages across, the principles of planning a marketing communication campaign and the stages involved are essentially the same. The seven main stages in the marketing communication process are noted in the following and explained in the pages that follow. Complete explanations can be found in the recommended texts at the end of the chapter.

1. Communications objectives.
2. Target audience identification.
3. Choosing the marketing communication tools.
4. Creative planning.
5. Media planning.
6. Media costs.
7. Measuring the results.

1. Communication objectives

Any marketing communication campaign needs clearly stated objectives about what it is setting out to achieve, related to the processes expected to take place in target segments' minds, such as awareness, interest and positive feelings.

All forms of marketing communications are primary means of manipulating demand and influencing buyer behaviour. Simply stated, they enable businesses to *reach* people in their homes or other places away from the places of production and delivery, and to *communicate* to them *messages* intended to influence their *purchasing behaviour.*

The communication process is shown in Fig. 16.1 using the analogy of a radio or television broadcast. The advertiser, the sender, transmits a message converted into a form that can be received and understood by the target consumer. The primary problem for marketing managers is to devise *messages* in a form most likely to communicate with the desired audience. The messages may be received, but if they are not 'decoded', that is, understood or remembered, effective communication will fail to take place and the communications budget will be wasted. Once an advertiser has identified the audience he hopes to influence, the *reach* part of the process is relatively straightforward, though also the most expensive part, requiring money to buy space in advertising media.

Not surprisingly, given their importance and cost, decades of research have been conducted into the process of creation and interpretation of messages. Semiotic studies interpret the meaning attached to advertising signs and symbols, in other words, how the message is coded by the sender and decoded by the receiver.

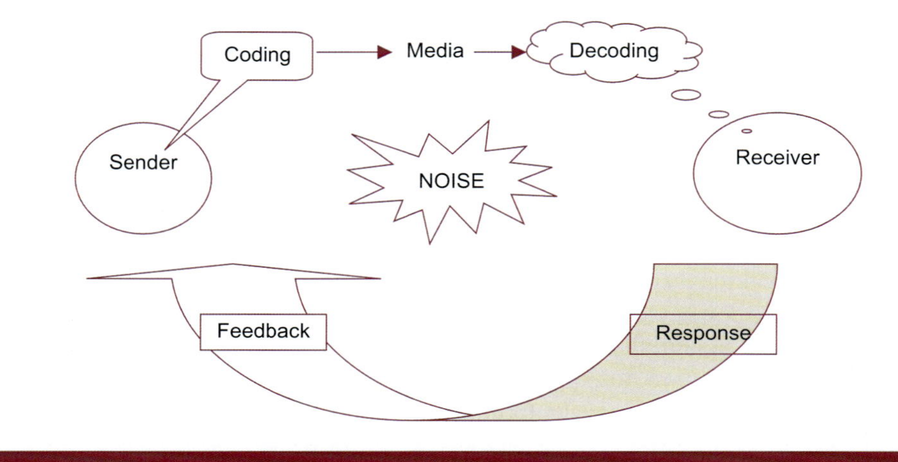

FIGURE 16.1 The Communications process (after Schramm 1955)

Another area of study is the response – the effects that advertising has on the consumer's decision process. Some much-quoted models assume that it should work by moving prospects through the consecutive stages of Attention, Interest, Desire to purchase and purchase Action (Strong's [1925] Awarness Interest Desire Action (AIDA) and similar models). Others deny that advertising can have such a powerful effect, arguing that it simply serves to tell or remind people that the brand exists in order to encourage them to find out more or to try it (Ehrenberg et al., 1998). In the Internet era, this 'weak' theory of advertising would argue that its role is simply to reassure the potential consumer that the travel website and the airline or hotels it offers are owned by well-known companies and can, therefore, be trusted.

Such research is important but the exact ways in which both advertising and PR work on buyers' minds and influence their behaviour are still not fully understood. The communication process is highly complex and remains something of a 'black box'.

An example of the complex communication process and the barriers to overcome

The process of setting communication objectives is represented in Fig. 16.2 in a linear model form. To understand it, consider the example of a national hotel group with a 10% share of the market for sales conferences. The hotel group has decided to use press advertising to supplement its website pages to reach and gain an increased share of this target audience. Using data that would be derived in practice from consumer research, Fig. 16.2 shows how the original message filters its way through several stages to the purchase decision, illustrating the filters and barriers that diminish the impact of advertising.

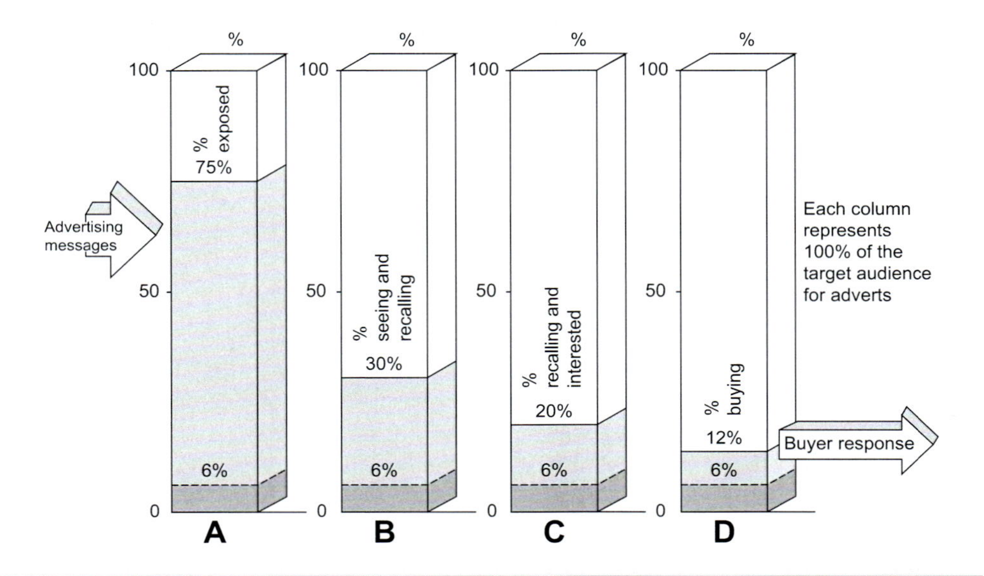

FIGURE 16.2 Filters in awareness and interact that blunt the communication process

Column A represents 100% of the potential target market of people who attend sales conferences; their profiles would be detailed in the marketing plan. With a realistic budget, the hotel group might hope to reach and expose its message to, say, 75% of this total. This entails buying media space in magazines and other press that three-quarters of the target are known to look at, at least once during the campaign period.

Column B indicates that, in this case, 30% of the target audience is able to recall seeing the hotel group's advertising. The remaining 45% may not have glanced at the right page or have simply ignored it as irrelevant or uninteresting to them.

Column C reflects the proportion of the target audience (20%) who remember the advertising and were additionally sufficiently interested to consider using the hotel at some time. This suggests a potentially positive attitude (recall alone may be for negative reasons!).

Column D represents the final stage of actual use and shows the 12% of the target audience that attended a sales conference at one of the group's hotels in the 12-month duration of the campaign. The dotted line in all four columns shows the 6% of existing buyers for whom the advertising may have served to reinforce their intentions, but who would have purchased anyway – they are satisfied, repeat buyers. The additional 6% represents first-time buyers or lapsed buyers. The total 12% market share is two percentage points higher than the original 10%.

Assuming that the objective was to raise market share to 12% over 12 months, the advertising can be judged as successful. Its costs, with data from the hotel group's website, can be evaluated against the additional revenue gained.

Figure 16.2 explains why businesses have to monitor conversion rates between the stages to help measure and develop the effectiveness of their communication campaigns. The expertise implicit in Fig. 16.2 includes:

- Media purchase decisions best calculated to reach the target cost-effectively (percentage of A).
- Design of appealing messages and symbols best calculated to arrest and capture attention (percentage of B).
- Communicating memorably the key points that matter to buyers (percentage of C).
- Motivating prospective buyers and turning interest into purchase (percentage of D).

2. Target audience identification

For all the reasons set out in Chapter 6, the target audience needs to be profiled in detail, including the media and purchasing habits that will facilitate *reach*. Although the target audience may be the intended purchaser and user, other members of the decision-making unit must not be ignored. Opinion leaders, stakeholders and the travel trade are also potential audiences.

3. Choosing the marketing communication tools

In order to achieve the desired effects of the campaign, marketers must select the most appropriate combination from a range of different techniques, often called promotional or marketing communication tools. These include advertising and PR, direct marketing, sponsorship and sales promotion. Each is outlined under 'IMC' later in this chapter.

Attempts to distinguish between the tools only serve to emphasize how in practice they overlap and are most effectively used in combination with each other in an integrated campaign. The launch of a new product, such as a visitor attraction, will involve PR activity to gain media coverage and create awareness, advertising to communicate what the attraction has to offer and give details of location and opening times, direct mail or distribution in the catchment area and sales promotion discounts to encourage people to visit and sample the attraction. The same logo, images and messages would also be included on the attraction's website, which is likely also to have pages carrying news releases and other useful information for journalists.

National tourist offices have to make best use of limited budgets to reach a potentially worldwide market. Even after prioritizing selected countries, they can only afford a limited amount of television, national press or outdoor billboard advertising to communicate the main theme of the campaign. They, therefore, rely on their relationships with the media to generate stories in newspaper travel sections, magazines and TV holiday programmes, and with the travel trade to fund collaborative marketing through print, online media, exhibitions and direct mail.

The objectives of any campaign have to be translated into specific objectives for each of the promotional tools outlined.

4. Creative planning

The aim of any campaign is to produce a creative execution using pictures, symbols and words that capture the message in a way judged best able to penetrate the barriers and filters of the target audience. Memorable examples of creative executions in travel and tourism include:

- 'I love New York' (New York State).
- 'We try harder' (Avis).
- 'What the bloody hell are you waiting for?' (Australia).
- 'Mind Body Spirit' (Champneys).

Because of the cost of creative execution, concepts are often tested as they are developed. For example, storyboards and key frames may be used as visual stimulation to gain the reaction of audiences using focus groups. Advertising agencies often require clients to 'sign off' at key stages in creative planning to avoid backtracking that can undermine the whole process.

Over the years, many businesses in the travel and tourism industry have been damaged by a reputation for over-promising in advertising, creating expectations among buyers that cannot be matched by the reality of the experience. The intangible nature of leisure tourism, in particular, makes such behaviour tempting and hotels, destinations, airlines and attractions have all succumbed. But such practice runs contrary to the fundamental principles of marketing centred on delivering customer satisfaction; it creates bad word of mouth and negative media interest, and may damage or destroy the prospect of creating repeat business.

As Morgan and Pritchard put it, 'tour operator advertising has frequently proved to be a fertile breeding ground for clichéd and even bad ads as operators have focused on sun, sand and sex clichés or value for money concepts. Originality has tended to play a very minor role' (Morgan and Pritchard, 2000: 34).

5. Media planning

Concurrent with creative planning is media planning, which is concerned with programming the ways in which advertisements will be seen and heard through media selection, scheduling and buying. The choice of *media type* is wide for travel and tourism, as indicated in Table 16.1 earlier.

Modern media planners use sophisticated software to aid decision-making in media selection, buying and scheduling. The fundamental principles, however, rest on two basic requirements:

1. That the target audience can be identified and profiled with some precision, using key demographic, socioeconomic and psychographic variables (see Chapter 6).
2. That media owners can provide reader/viewer numbers and characteristics with considerable precision. Because revenue from advertising generally far exceeds revenue from sales to readers/viewers, the media have a vested interest in providing such analysis.

According to Smith and Taylor (2004), media planners need to resolve a number of issues relevant to buying advertising space:

- Cost-effective coverage of the target audience.
- Creative scope of the different media in terms of colour, contrast, sound and movement.
- Compatibility of media type and vehicle with product positioning, hence the old adage 'the medium is the message'. The image of the media vehicle itself should 'rub off' on the product to positive effect.
- Anticipated activity of competitors to advertising; will they aim to copy or counter it?
- Audience's state of mind or receptivity at the time of receiving the message. It is no accident that holidays feature heavily in Sunday newspapers when the recipients are likely to be in a relaxed frame of mind.
- Regulations and restrictions in operation, including lead time and clearance procedures (varies with media type).

Some authors refer to the creation of a 'personal media network', where the aim is to wrap the messages around the target audience throughout the day. Target X wakes in the morning to the message on his local commercial radio station, sees the advertisement in a newspaper over breakfast, drives to and from work past the poster advertisements, and relaxes in the evening to the cinema or television advertisement. It may also flash up at intervals on e-mail and on his mobile phone.

6. Media costs

The critical issue for media planners is juggling *media costs.* As much as travel and tourism companies wish to screen television advertisements, a national television campaign that gives potential customers sufficient opportunities to see and remember the advertising message would probably cost several million pounds. National television coverage would only be justified where the potential net sales resulting from the campaign would substantially exceed the cost. Only airlines, major tour operators and hotel chains have this kind of turnover, although some national tourist offices may also invest in limited television advertising to build the image of their country as a tourist destination.

Television advertising rates are determined by a complex bidding process taking into account the audience figures and demand for particular times and programme slots. Most other commercial media publish rate cards showing their regular prices for advertising spaces. These prices reflect the size of an advertisement and the numbers of readers/viewers that the media vehicle reaches. The standard measure in the industry is the cost per thousand (CPT) people reached. If a double-page colour advertisement in the *Sunday Times* magazine is seen by 4 million adults and costs £60 000, the CPT for that media vehicle would be £15.00. In the more down-market *News of the World* magazine, the advertisement would be seen by nearly 8 million and would cost £75,000, a CPT of £9.37. In choosing between the two, however, it would also be important to know which paper offers the most cost-effective coverage of the company's actual target market, as it would be wasteful to advertise a niche product in a mass-market paper. It is also important to know where and when that target market looks for ideas and information about holidays. Some British media, such as *TV Times* and *Radio Times* have traditionally been known to be especially effective in travel and tourism around December and January time. Accordingly, their CPT rates are higher, but may still represent good value for money calculated in responses and subsequent bookings per £1000 spent.

As with any perishable product, the rate card prices are indicative only. They change as the time of production approaches and agencies are highly skilled at bargaining and negotiating discounts. Few agencies pay anything like the nominal rate card prices. As the number of media opportunities escalates, including the Internet, the expertise available to advertisers for cost-effective media purchasing is becoming an ever more important criterion in agency selection.

7. Measuring the results of the marketing communication campaign

It is seldom possible to isolate the effect on sales of such expenditure with any precision. Price cuts, competitor activity, sales promotions, political events and even the weather can all distort the relationship between advertising and outcomes. Yet, advertisers are increasingly demanding accountability for the results of their advertising and, without measurement, there is no way of knowing how effective communication expenditure has been and no evidence on which to justify a budget allocation in the following year.

Standard techniques available to large firms include:

- *Response measurement* – where advertising is designed to produce an enquiry, brochure request or booking, it is common practice to code advertisements with letters or numbers that identify the media used and the date of insertion. Replies can then be assessed against the original expenditure. The use of coupons to generate responses is common in travel and tourism, and monitoring telephone calls and website hits are also closely monitored. Ratios of enquiries/bookings and others to advertising expenditure can be calculated and used for comparative purposes across media, as can the average advertising cost per enquiry and so on.
- *Market research measures of the communication effect* – before and after sample surveys of the target audience can be used to quantify changes in awareness, interest, attitudes and preferences. Many advertising agencies conduct recall tests, either unprompted where no stimulus is given, or prompted where respondents are shown a card naming or illustrating recent advertising campaigns and asked to indicate which they remember seeing.
- *Pre-testing of communication effects* –prior to full implementation of a large campaign, focus groups of the target audience can be used to test the proposed creative ideas. Equipment in laboratory settings can be used to measure eye movement, pupil dilation and other physiological responses to images shown.

THE PROMOTIONAL MIX: THE MAIN TOOLS OF IMC

As we have said, an effective marketing communication campaign requires a blend of a number of different promotional methods or tools, as they are often known. The definitions and key characteristics of each of the main tools are outlined in the following section.

Advertising

Definition

The American Marketing Association defines advertising as 'any paid form of non-personal presentation and promotion of ideas, goods or services [to a targeted] audience by an identified sponsor'. The words in brackets are inserted by the authors to convey the fact that segmentation and targeting always precede advertising. Several points help to unwrap the definition. First, 'non-personal' implies the use of media to access a large audience, as distinct from individually targeted forms of communication using a name and address (direct marketing). Second, an 'identified sponsor' means that the communication is easily recognizable as an advertisement paid for by the organization whose name or logo it displays.

The advantage of paid-for advertising is that the advertiser has full control over the message content and, depending on the budget size, can choose advertisement size, position and insertion frequency. However, advertising space in print and advertising breaks in broadcasting are often ignored or given little attention, and the message may seem to be biased. Communication theory holds that the credibility of the source is an important factor in influencing whether a message is listened to and accepted.

The cost of media advertising and the difficulties of being noticed and remembered among so many other competing messages are also drawbacks, particularly for organizations with limited budgets.

Advertising objectives

Classically, advertising is best at creating awareness, informing, persuading and reminding. Thus, the objective might be to *inform* the audience of product benefits, a new product launch or a revised pricing structure; to *persuade* them by changing attitudes towards the brand, building product preference or altering product positioning; or to *remind* the consumer after purchase to reduce post-purchase anxiety, trigger word-of-mouth recommendation or keep a brand name front of mind for future purchases. Objectives must be fixed to a specified time period and be amenable to measurement. For example, 'to raise awareness of business-class upgrade in a target audience from 30% in January 2009 to 60% by April 2009' is specific enough to be evaluated.

Some advertising in travel and tourism is designed to stimulate 'immediate' action. Direct response advertisements with a website address or free-phone telephone number may seek to increase brochure request rates and generate specific enquiries or bookings. Similarly, classified advertisements are often linked to late deals and price cuts. But, generally speaking, advertising is chiefly about consumer, travel trade or stakeholder awareness of and interest in the brand and, like all marketing mix objectives, relates back to the marketing objectives and strategies that drive management decisions.

The role of advertising agencies

Only very small businesses, such as guesthouses or local visitor attractions, are likely to undertake their own advertising without professional help. At the very least, as noted earlier, advertising agencies can assist with the purchase of advertising space at discounted rates. Even small- to medium-sized clients with about £20 000 to spend on media may find it advantageous to approach regional or local advertising agencies. Large organizations prefer multinational agencies whose offices or networks reflect their patterns of business. Most advertising agencies enjoy working on travel and tourism accounts as intrinsically interesting products and may welcome the account as a stimulating break from their usual subject matter.

As well as full participation in the marketing planning process, advertising agencies typically provide:

- Creative planning and execution for online and other messages, including developing original concepts and ideas, design of all visual material and copy, and any pre-launch research.
- Media planning, scheduling and buying, and negotiating discounted rates.
- Advertising production services and implementation of agreed campaign elements and materials.
- Monitoring and evaluation of advertising performance.

Advertising agencies are usually selected through competitive tender and, once selected, seek to build up long-term relationships with their clients. The relationship between agency and client is handled by an account director or executive, who ensures that creative and media briefs are adhered to, and liaises between the agency team and the client. In addition to the creative and media team, 'traffic control' staff are needed to ensure that advertisements get to the right place at the right time and that deadlines are met.

As we discussed earlier, there are also many specialist agencies offering expertise in specific areas. Choosing more than one agency increases the workload for the marketing department, however, in coordinating the brand strategy and the campaigns. Many agencies can provide all the services required to plan and implement an integrated communication campaign.

Terms commonly used in advertising practice

Being technical subjects, advertising and PR are accompanied by their own terminology. Eighteen commonly used terms are presented in annotated form in a glossary at the end of this chapter. They are intended to serve as an aide-mémoire.

Public relations

Definition

PR, in contrast to advertising, does not involve the purchase of media space. The aim of marketing PR is to obtain favourable publicity for an organization and its products in the media through news reports, features and reviews. This means that the organization has less control on what exactly is said or shown, but the message may have greater credibility as it is perceived as coming from an unbiased third party.

Marketing PR is only one aspect of PR, which is also concerned with the corporate image of the company. Indeed, within a large organization, the two are treated quite separately, with corporate PR funded from corporate resources as opposed to a marketing budget allocation. The British Institute of Public Relations defines PR as 'the discipline which builds and maintains reputation, with the aim of earning understanding and support and influencing opinion and behaviour. It is the planned and sustained effort to establish and maintain goodwill and mutual understanding between an organisation and its publics.'

Two points from the definition need clarification. First, professional PR is about building 'mutual understanding' or trust between an organization and its publics; it is about two-way communication, and is strongly rooted in the idea of developing credibility ahead of raising visibility. Second, the range of 'publics' or target audiences is typically much wider than for advertising. In travel and tourism, it is important to develop mutual understanding with publics, such as local residents and businesses, other industry sectors, environmental pressure groups, politicians and suppliers of service components.

PR in travel and tourism

PR programmes are usually thought of as complementary to media advertising. They are, but it is to miss an important part of its role in marketing to perceive PR only in its narrow role of generating non-paid-for media coverage. Effective PR starts by developing *credibility* across an organization as a whole before seeking to raise its *visibility* through media relations and other techniques.

As much of tourism is inherently interesting, with professional handling, most travel and tourism organizations should be able to exploit a wide range of creative subjects. This is not to say that achieving media attention is uncompetitive, however. Of the 125 million press releases distributed in the United Kingdom every year, around 121 million are estimated to be thrown by editors into the waste bin (Smith and Taylor, 2004).

However, the high visibility of tourism can also mean it is vulnerable to negative publicity. For this reason, as environmental issues and the implementation of sustainable tourism continue to cause public concern, tourism organizations need to

TABLE 16.2 Types of public relations activity in travel and tourism

Writing and editing	Press releases and feature articles for busy editors, annual reports, shareholder reports, newsletters and in-house magazines, film and video scripts, press packs.
Building press relations	Mailing lists and databases of media contacts, liaising with media.
Public speaking	Meetings, presentations, platform participation, after dinner speaking, seminar papers, television and radio interviews, community events.
Training, briefing and counselling executives	In handling media interviews for all types of media.
Press launches and press conferences	Announcing new products, changes or improvements, brochure or advertising campaign launches, annual report publications.
Photography	Studio and location photographic shoots, maintaining photographic library, photo calls.
Lobbying and persuading	Regulatory bodies and government at local, national and international level, e.g. over abolition of duty-free, tourist taxes, visa controls, unfavourable policies or laws. Sometimes manoeuvring against competitors, sometimes in collaboration for the greater good of the industry.
Event management	Staged events around which a story of media interest is woven, award events based on employee motivation schemes or environmental programmes, celebrations such as millennium or jubilee, personality appearances, stage-managed product launches.
Product visits	Open days for general public, familiarization trips for distributors, product visits for journalists.
Exhibitions and programmes	Planning and running exhibitions, attending trade fairs and conferences
Corporate identity	Including corporate graphic identity from business cards to on-site signage, logo design.
Sponsorship trade fairs	Producing packages to attract potential sponsors plus formation of own sponsorship programme.
Product placement	Getting the organization or destination into films, television and video footage
Crisis management	Development of possible crisis scenarios and relevant skills training. Handling negative events as they occur.

be seen to behave responsibly towards the natural and social environment. As 'ethics and social responsibility have traditionally been the bastion of public relations' (Smith and Taylor, 2004: 361), PR is expected to continue its growth in importance.

In common with all other forms of marketing communications, successful PR needs a planned and budgeted programme incorporating objectives and publics to be targeted, activities to be carried out and research and evaluation to assess performance against the objectives set. The remainder of this chapter briefly reviews these processes.

PR activities

The PR activities included as part of PR programmes are noted in Table 16.2. Some are more suited to corporate PR than they are to marketing, but many of these tools are flexible and can be adapted. The spectrum of options is wide-ranging, and each may be considered a specialization in its own right. Indeed some, for example, exhibitions and sponsorship, are treated separately from PR in large organizations. Three of the activities of particular relevance in travel and tourism are pulled out of Table 16.3 for further comments as follows.

TABLE 16.3 Potential negative events requiring crisis management in travel and tourism

Product defects	Outdated lifts in older hotels, brochure inaccuracies.
Product disaster	Aircraft crash, ferry or cruise ship sinkings, hotel building collapse.
Industrial action	Strikes in airlines or hospitality industry, picket lines.
Service delivery system breakdown	Failure of computer reservation system, aircraft fault to remedy.
Takeovers and corporate raids	Hostile bids for an organization.
Customer/employee accidents	Injury or death. Vehicle collisions and crashes, death from natural causes in old age, drink or recreational drug-related injuries and deaths.
Crime against tourists	Pick pockets, vandalism, car theft, muggings, knife attacks, danger of paedophilia in attractions targeted at children.
Collapse of supplier	Airline or tour operator bankruptcy.
Environmental pollution incidents	Fuel spillage, algal blooms, beach and bathing water pollution from sewage.
Health scares	Food poisoning, water contamination, outbreaks of viruses, epidemics.
Tourist/employee kidnapping	Taken hostage for political or financial reasons.
Terrorism and threat of terrorism	Shooting of tourists, bombs in aircraft or hijacking incidents, product sabotage, also threats of terrorism and sabotage. Tourism seen as a good way of gaining publicity for a cause, making tourism vulnerable to terrorism.
Conflict or war	International and civil conflict, armed protest, riots, military coups.
Severe weather	Droughts, heat waves, lack of snow fall for skiing holidays, flooding, storms, hurricanes and cyclones.
Natural disasters	Earthquakes, volcanic eruptions, hurricanes, landslides, avalanches, tsunamis, fires.

- *Media relations* are still the backbone of PR activity. Media relations are about obtaining non-paid-for media coverage, and activity includes writing press releases, feature articles, scripts, preparing press packs, obtaining interviews, holding press conferences and photo calls, and creating an up-to-date database of media contacts. Media relations requires day-to-day maintenance for smooth operation. Through regular contact with journalists who specialize in travel or cover the local catchment area of the organization, good relations can build up trust and make it easier to get an organization's messages across when it matters.

  Today, corporate websites can be the first place that journalists and researchers go to obtain information about an organization; hence, well-maintained media pages are an important PR tool. As explained in Chapter 15, professional journalists and reviewers are now facing growing competition from amateur self-appointed critics who can reach a wide audience through blogs and message boards. The work of PR now includes monitoring and responding to the Internet coverage of the company's activities, and proactively using the web to generate positive stories.

- *Crisis management* is especially important in tourism organizations. Given the inseparability of production and consumption and product perishability, the vulnerability of the industry to external events is considerable. The potential for damage to corporate image and reputation incurred by negative incidents requires skill training and professional management to be in place to deal with events that are bound to occur at some time. Problems are exacerbated if customers are in unfamiliar environments. Table 16.3 illustrates the extensive range of negative events that could befall any tourism organization or destination at any time. Some are controllable to an extent, for example, those relating to product quality. But most are uncontrollable and even unpredictable. In such circumstances, it is important to keep the media and the public informed, to reassure those involved that action is being taken and to avoid recriminations over who is to be blamed.

Recovery time from any negative event will vary with incident severity, crisis management handling and the strength of the tourism brand concerned. PR professionals plan activity for at least 12 months after a major incident, and journalists often revisit a particular incident to see what changes have been made 1 year later.

- *Product placement* is another form of PR and part of a $100 million industry where particular products are 'placed' in films and documentaries. There are no rate cards for this activity; deals are negotiated on a fee and/or promotion basis, and there are product placement agencies that specialize in this field. Just as fast cars can be 'placed' in James Bond films, so can airlines, restaurants, hotels, car rental agencies and destinations. Apparent endorsement by a film's star will be more influential than a simple shot of a background logo. Destination tourism officers encourage filming in their locations as successful television or film productions can boost visitor numbers at a fraction of the cost of an advertising campaign. VisitBritain has a special unit set up to help film producers choose locations and obtain the necessary permissions and cooperation to film there.

  The wild scenery seen in the *Lord of the Rings* trilogy served to raise awareness and interest in New Zealand as a tourism destination. Three recent films featuring Scotland, namely *Braveheart, Rob Roy* and *Loch Ness*, are estimated to have generated £7–15 million additional visitor spending in the Scottish economy (Morgan and Pritchard, 2000).

  Major sporting events are another form of product placement in a destination context. Both Barcelona and Sydney, and most recently, China, used the Olympic Games very effectively to reposition themselves as tourist

MINI CASE 16.1: FILM TOURISM AND AN EXAMPLE OF A PRESS RELEASE

The royal film premiere of *The Other Boleyn Girl* (19 February 2007), attended by Their Royal Highnesses The Prince of Wales and The Duchess of Cornwall, is the latest example of the role of film in drawing attention to Britain's historic destinations and attractions. Starring Scarlett Johansson as the eponymous Mary Boleyn, Natalie Portman as her sister Anne and Eric Bana as King Henry VIII, the film is an engrossing tale of intrigue, romance and betrayal set against the backdrop of a defining moment in Britain's history.

Great Chalfield Manor and Lacock Abbey in Wiltshire, Derbyshire's Haddon Hall and Ockwell Manor in London all doubled for interior and exterior scenes of the Boleyn country home. Kent's Dover Castle, Knole House and Penshurst Place also appear in the film as Whitehall Palace and the Tower of London. Berkshire's Dorney Court, North Lees Hall in Derbyshire and St Bart's Church, London, are also used as locations in the film.

VisitBritain, the national tourist office for Britain, expects *The Other Boleyn Girl* to boost tourism because of the locations that appear on screen and the film's resonance with Britain's royal heritage. Research shows that on average, 60% of potential visitors would be very likely to visit places associated with Britain's royal family or monarchy. The top five royal attractions in the country alone account for millions of visits each year.

A recent survey asked 25 000 people around the world which British icon would best communicate that they were in Britain if they sent it on a postcard: 11% selected an image of the Queen, making her the third most popular choice. Her image was most popular with the Czechs, Russians, Chinese, Polish, Indians and Hungarians.

Tom Wright, Chief Executive of VisitBritain and co-chairman of the forthcoming British Tourism Week, says: 'Our royal family – past and present – retains an enduring popularity around the world and the Queen's image is strongly associated with Britain, particularly among visitors who may not have much familiarity with our destinations. As the greatest potential for tourism growth is coming from newer markets in Eastern Europe, Russia, China and India, global interest in our royal heritage can only help us compete with rival destinations in the future.'

Film tourism or 'set-jetting' is an increasingly popular holiday option. With 40% of potential visitors "very likely" to visit places from films or TV, the industry expects the appearance of British locations to help encourage many more visitors and increase Britain's appeal as a set-jetter's paradise.

Stephen Dowd, chief executive of inbound tourism trade body UKinbound and co-chairman of British Tourism Week, said: 'The stunning locations featured in this film make our country look particularly inviting. Set-jetting is a great way of marketing a destination and Britain's popularity as a location for many of the biggest films has helped us capitalise on this "screen magic". Showcasing destinations through film helps maintain the popularity of our beautiful landscapes and countryside, centuries of history and royal heritage, iconic characters, actors, actresses and literary greats.'

VisitBritain Press Release March 2008

destinations. The role of marketing communications is to exploit the potential of the opportunity with press releases, feature articles, media interviews, websites and so on.

Link article available at www.routledge.com/9780750686938

(1) Connell, J., Meyer, D., 2008. Balamory revisited: an evaluation of the screen tourism destination–tourist nexus. Tourism Management (in press).

Table 16.2 indicates the breadth and depth of activity involved in professional PR programmes. Even a small tourism organization with a small budget will find a well-planned 'do-it-yourself' PR programme beneficial in achieving communication objectives, and often more effective than a low-cost attempt to influence target audiences using media advertising. Only large organizations are likely to employ a PR agency.

Measuring the results of PR

As in all marketing activities, evaluation of PR results should be against the objectives set for the programme. Measuring the outcomes of PR is not an exact science, but usually includes:

- Media content analysis using word counts or, more popularly, column centimetres of media coverage obtained. Column centimetres can be converted to currency equivalents by calculating how much the same space would have cost if purchased at rate card prices for advertising purposes. Key word counts monitor the number of times the organization's name or brands are mentioned.
- A more qualitative approach to media content analysis can assess whether comments were favourable, neutral or unfavourable, note the inclusion of photographs and headlines, and the position of the material on the page (top, middle, bottom, which column, etc.), as well as the type of page itself (editorial, front cover, inside back cover, left, right of page, etc.).
- For larger PR campaigns, attitude or awareness market research studies carried out before and after the programme can be used to monitor any changes in consumer and other publics' perceptions of an organization.

Most large businesses use a press-cutting bureau to carry out a continuous media content analysis. In addition to their control function, press cuttings can also provide material for product endorsement to be used in direct marketing print, exhibition stands, press releases and websites.

Sponsorship

Definition

Sponsorship is a business relationship between a provider of funds, resources or services and an individual, event or organisation, which offers in return rights and association that may be used for commercial advantage.
Sleight, 1989

Sponsorship can be closely related to advertising in that it involves paying for display space in order to communicate to a selected target audience a message about the brand through its association with the event. While the sponsorship itself may only give the right to display the brand name and logo, for example, on clothing, vehicles or buildings, it is usually integrated with advertising and sales promotion campaigns to expand and enhance the message. Expenditure on sponsorship of sport, broadcasting and the arts has grown rapidly in recent years for a number of reasons linked to the fragmentation of traditional media:

- it is seen in a context where competitors are excluded
- it can reach audiences difficult to reach through other media
- it creates favourable brand associations with exciting and prestigious events
- it appeals across linguistic and cultural barriers

Meenaghan, 1998

For this reason, it is increasingly seen as a strategic tool of marketing communications and branding (Amis et al., 1997).

In recent years, both Thomas Cook and Thomsons have sponsored Premiership football clubs. Thomson has paid £4 million for a 4-year shirt sponsorship deal with Tottenham Hotspur.

However, as sponsorship can also be designed to create goodwill among a wide range of publics, for example, by sponsoring community or cultural events, it is often regarded as a PR activity. It can also be used as an opportunity for corporate hospitality and entertaining as part of the sales and key account management function, or for promotional merchandising and sampling.

Sales promotion

Definition

The Institute of Sales Promotion defines it as 'a range of tactical marketing techniques designed within a strategic marketing framework to add value to a product or service in order to achieve specific sales or marketing objectives'.

Sales promotion and merchandising are techniques primarily designed to stimulate consumer purchasing and dealer and sales-force effectiveness in the short term through temporary incentives and displays. It extends beyond consumers to distribution networks and the sales force. Much of sales promotion in practice takes place at points of sale, and the term *merchandising* is often used specifically to mean sales promotion at the point of sale.

Sales promotions come in two basic types. They can offer a reduction in price, or they can include something extra in the 'package' at the normal price. Price-based promotions are easy to understand and have an immediate appeal; hence, it will probably have a greater impact on sales. On the other hand, a price reduction is easy for a competitor to copy, and hence risks provoking a price war. Price cuts can devalue the image of the product, low price being popularly equated with low quality as in the phrase 'cheap and nasty'. There is also the risk already mentioned of customers coming to expect the lower price, making it difficult to increase it again (Morgan, 1996). Added-value packages avoid these dangers, and if used imaginatively, can help to attract attention to the product and reinforce the brand image.

Traditionally, such techniques have been known as 'below-the-line' marketing, distinguishing them from 'above-the-line' advertising. However, sales promotions in the sense of short-term incentives or discounts are often communicated through media advertising as well as through direct marketing and point of sale displays.

Exhibitions and trade shows are sometimes grouped with sales promotion or with PR. However, in view of their importance in tourism marketing, these will be considered separately in the next chapter.

CHAPTER SUMMARY

- In a multimedia world of competing marketing messages, IMC strategies aim to take the best possible advantage of each fleeting opportunity by making sure that each time customers encounter an organization, they get the same clear, coherent and compelling message about the brand. This means the integration of marketing objectives and messages across the range of promotional tools and communication channels.
- The main stages in marketing communication planning involve objective setting, target audience identification, selection of promotional tools, creative and media planning, budget agreement and measurement.
- The principles of communication planning – targeting clear and creative messages to a well-defined audience – apply equally on and offline. The traditional media still have an important role to play, particularly in creating awareness and brand image among those who are not yet actively seeking information.
- What is now vital in the Internet era is that both online and offline communications are coordinated as part of an integrated strategy.

QUESTIONS TO CONSIDER

1. Choose a recent example of media advertising for a tourism organization. Identify both the online and offline dimensions.
2. Analyse its communication objectives and target audience.
3. How is the message 'coded' in words and images in order to appeal and be understood by that audience?
4. How would you use the other marketing communication tools to complement and enhance the message of the campaign?

REFERENCES AND FURTHER READING

Amis, J., Pant, N. and Slack, T. (1997). Achieving a sustainable competitive advantage – a resource based view of sports sponsorship, *Journal of Sports Management*, **11**, pp. 80–96.

Connell, J. and Meyer, D. (2008). Balamory revisited: an evaluation of the screen tourism destination–tourist nexus. *Tourism Management* (In Press).

Ehrenberg, A. (1997). Justifying our Advertising Budgets. In *Admap* 32: 3. pp. 20–24.

Gross, M. (1992). *The Direct Marketer's Idea Book*. New York: AMACOM.

Kotler, P. and Armstong, G. (1999). *Principles of Marketing. Chapter 15* (8th edition). Prentice-Hall.

Masterman, G. and Wood, E.H. (2006). *Innovative Marketing Communications Strategies for the Events Industry*. Oxford: Elsevier Butterworth–Heinemann.

Meenaghan, T. (1998). Current developments and future directions in sponsorship, *International Journal of Advertising*, **17**, pp. 3–28.

Morgan, N. and Pritchard, A. (2000). *Marketing Communications: An Integrated Approach*. Butterworth–Heinemann.

Pickton, D. and Broderick, A. (2008). *Integrated Marketing Communications* (3rd edition). FT Prentice Hall.

Pike, S. (2008). *Destination Marketing: An Integrated Marketing Communication Approach*. Oxford: Elsevier.

Schramm, W. (1955). *The Process and Effects of Mass Communications*. University of Illinois Press.

Sleight, S. (1989). *Sponsorship – What It Is and How To Use It*. McGraw Hill.

Smith, P.R. and Taylor, J. (2004). *Marketing Communications* (4th edition). Kogan Page.

Strong, E.K. (1925). *The Psychology of Selling and Advertising*. McGraw Hill.

GLOSSARY OF ADVERTISING AND PR TERMS IN COMMON USE

Audience	Often used generically to describe readers, viewers, listeners exposed to all forms of media, including websites. 'Target audience' describes the segments identified for communication purposes.
Copy	The words included in an advertisement, normally having three components: a 'headline' to attract attention; 'body copy' to convey information; 'strap line' to conclude or sign off.
Coverage	The proportion of the target audience that is reached by the advertisement.
CPT	'Cost per thousand' of the target group to whom any advertisement is exposed. Cost per thousand is a basic cost figure used in buying media space. As it suggests, it refers to the average cost of reaching 1000 of the target audience, and is useful for comparison across different media types and vehicles.
Creative execution	The choice of appealing themes, ideas, pictures, situations, symbols and words chosen to communicate the desired message.
Direct	Advertising from which the intended audience response is a direct contact with the response producer by telephone, letter, coupon or Internet, without going through a distribution channel, such as a travel agent.
Editorial matter	The content of the media, other than advertising, controlled by editorial policies.
Fees and commission	Traditionally, advertising agencies earned their income through commission paid on purchase of media space. Today, payment structures vary, using fee-based activities and/or results achieved alongside commission-based payments.
Frequency	The number of times an advertisement is placed or inserted in a specific time period. A 'burst' strategy concentrates on the advertisements in a short period of time, and a 'drip' strategy shows advertisements steadily over a longer period of time.
Insertion	One appearance of an advertisement. Media buyers usually purchase a series of insertions rather than a single insertion.
Media	Newspapers, television, radio and all other mass circulation means of communicating either paid or unpaid messages to people. Advertising media are those that sell space to advertisers as a commercial transaction. Websites and the Internet are part of modern media.
Media vehicle	Individual media titles, for example, *The Times*, *Newsweek*, *Vogue*, and so on.
OTS	'Opportunities to see' or opportunities by the target audience to see any particular advertisement. It is a function of coverage and frequency (coverage × frequency).
Position	The place where the advertisement is shown, for example, front cover, inside front/back cover, left/right pages, top/bottom, and so on. Media costs vary with the quality of position.
Proposition	The single-minded clear message of an advertisement, usually focused on the reason to purchase the product, that is, the key benefit.
Rate cards	The published prices for advertising space produced by the media vehicle concerned. Agencies receive discounts on the published prices, which was part of the commission-based system.
Share of voice	Compares an organization's advertising spend to the total market spend on advertising. In the United Kingdom, domestic tourism and inbound tourism have a small share of voice compared with outbound tourism.
USP	'Unique selling proposition' – a particular product or organization characteristic that distinguishes it from competitors and is a main reason to buy.

A romantic break hotel room - "Although brochures remain a crucial part of the marketing communications mix, there is an increasing need for more segmented approaches to brochure design; the romantic 'honeymooners' segment of significant appeal to island destinations and cruise lines among others"

Courtesy of Blake Ashwell, Bournemouth University

CHAPTER 17

Brochures, print and other non-electronic information

We are going to stop racking brochures altogether. It's such a chore, and waste is a big issue. The majority of customers have already booked on Teletext and just come in to pick up a brochure to see what they have booked.

Geoff Dykes, Peregrination Travel Manchester in *Travel Weekly*, August 2005

Known in the United States as *collateral materials*, print and its modern website equivalents represent the third distinctive group of marketing communications to be planned in marketing campaigns, in addition to advertising and PR, sales promotion and merchandising.

While all producers of consumer products use advertising and PR, sales promotion, merchandising and personal selling, few producers of physical goods use print to anything like the extent found in tourism. The design, distribution and large-volume use of printed items has been and remains a major distinguishing feature of travel and tourism marketing. It is strange, therefore, that very little attention is given to it in most tourism marketing books, and virtually none in more general books on marketing.

The previous edition of this book quoted industry predictions that the Internet and interactive digital TV would destroy brochures by 2010. While this prediction was unduly alarmist, the future of marketing print is still uncertain in view of the continuing search for waste reduction, cost savings, consumer demand for continuous access to information 24 hours a day, and the need to adapt to the more fluid pricing and tactical discounting regime of the early twenty-first century. Nevertheless, the fundamental customer need for information will not change in the next decade. The question is, how that information will be delivered in future.

After studying this chapter, you should be able to understand:

- Why printed information materials are still such an important part of marketing communications in travel and tourism and their role in conjunction with Internet developments.

- The different types of printed materials used and their multiple roles in marketing travel and tourism.
- The process involved in producing effective print, both 'in-house', and through external agencies.
- The options for achieving cost-effective distribution to targeted users.
- How to evaluate the marketing results of expenditure on printed information provision.

AN INDICATION OF THE CURRENT USE OF PRINTED MATERIALS AND WEBSITES FOR UK MARKET HOLIDAY CHOICES

A recent online survey of more than 2000 people conducted by consultancy firm *Logan Tod* suggests only 22% of consumers look to the trade for advice, with 70% preferring to put their faith in family and friends and 47% turning to online review sites. While the survey found that 40% of respondents had not visited a travel agency in the last 2 years, tour operators' brochures remain in demand with 46% stating they would visit an agency to pick them up even if they were booking online. The main reason respondents gave for booking online was that it was easier and quicker. More than 76% of respondents said they use the Internet to research destinations and 66% to book flights and accommodation. The research found that people also use the Internet because of the ability to find better prices online, and because websites are open 24 hours a day.

Source: *Travel Weekly*, 23 August 2007.

This evidence seems to bear out our opinion in the previous edition of this book that ICTwould not entirely remove the marketing role of collateral material for most tourism businesses. Printed materials and electronic information, as we said, are mutually reinforcing.

PRINT PRODUCTION – COST AND WASTAGE ON A HEROIC SCALE

Around the developed world, travel and tourism firms are producing billions of printed items paid for out of marketing budgets. The environmental cost in CO_2 emissions as trees are destroyed for paper-making, the costs of road haulage and the cost of waste disposal are all vast. In the United Kingdom alone, there are estimated to be over 150 000 organizations and establishments wholly or partially concerned with aspects of tourism. Nearly all of these are generating pieces of printed information, ranging from the millions of brochures distributed by large tour operators, down to farmhouses distributing a few dozen leaflets for their prospective customers. Britain has over 750 tourist information centres and some 5000 retail travel outlets.

At a conference in 2003, Jeremy Ellis of TUI estimated that the top four vertically integrated UK tour operators produce about 150 publications per year, between one and five editions per publication, up to 800 pages per edition with print runs up to 3 million copies. As late as 2005, one distribution contractor was distributing 150 million brochures a year, weighing some 20000 tonnes, to UK travel agency outlets. Chapter 16 noted the filters that work to prevent much marketing communication from influencing the targeted customer. In the case of printed items, it is obvious that much of the material does not even reach the first stage of 'opportunity to see', and the level of wastage is widely acknowledged to be prodigious. Surveys in the United States have estimated that fewer than six out of every 10 agents even opened all the brochure packs they received and much of the total is simply dumped. A study carried out for the European Travel Commission confirmed the same massive wastage of printed materials produced by national tourist organizations.

In the United Kingdom, the leading tour operators distributing through travel agents use a very approximate conversion rate of between 4 and 15 brochures per person booking a holiday in their main summer programmes, while smaller operators would have to produce comparatively more per customer booking achieved. Developments in print technology and international outsourcing policies have tended to keep the cost of production down compared with other marketing costs. Even so, the cost of a large summer brochure of 200 or more pages (some run to over 500 pages), assuming over a million were produced, averaged out at around £2.00 per brochure in 2006 prices. Industry estimates put print and distribution costs at between £1 and £6 per copy depending on the number of pages and the print run.

Taking a typical example, the print cost of a booking for two persons, assuming 10 brochures are needed at £2.00 each could be £20.00 or £10.00 per person. At 2008 prices, a typical seven-night package to a Mediterranean resort might cost around £600 per person (published price), and tour operators would consider it a normal year if they achieved an average of 3% gross profit on that price = £18.00 Allowing for brochure distribution costs and production costs (but not retail commission), it is obvious that print and distribution cost alone could be the equivalent of over half the gross operating profit on a tour package. In a bad year, the print and distribution costs will far exceed profit per holiday sold. What is clear is that the cost of print as a proportion of marketing expenditure is a major 'up front' cost item to be paid for out of the tour operator's earnings. (In 2005, First Choice sales director Martin Froggatt said brochure production and distribution cost the group £16 million in a year when pretax profits were £115 million.)

It seems reasonable to conclude on this evidence that at least half and often much more of the cost of marketing print is wasted. The importance of achieving even marginal improvements in the effectiveness of brochures and thus reducing such wastage, is an obvious target for marketing management evaluation. The massive attraction of e-commerce on the Internet in this context is clear on the base of cost alone. To reduce the cost and waste, many companies are introducing 'content management systems', which store all the data and images needed for print to provide a single source of up-to-date content for both brochures and web pages. This streamlines and reduces production costs and enables brochures to be created and distributed online. Travel agencies or customers can download and print the specific information they are interested in (at their own expense) rather than take away a preprinted brochure with tens or hundreds of irrelevant pages.

DEFINING INFORMATION MATERIALS

Information materials are part of marketing communications. They may be defined as comprising any form of printed or electronic information materials, paid for out of marketing budgets and designed to create awareness among existing and prospective customers, stimulate interest in and demand for specified products, and/or facilitate their purchase, use and enjoyment.

This definition covers not only the familiar promotional use of information, but also an important 'facilitation' use covering the ways in which many tourism businesses assist customers to decide between and to purchase particular products, and achieve full benefit and enjoyment from using them. Leaflets provided as part of the admission cost to visitor attractions, to inform and 'orientate' visitors to the experience they will receive, are one illustration of print designed to facilitate use and enjoyment.

While travel and tourism is a market of obvious interest to a wide range of commercial publishers, the aforementioned definition includes only information that is part of a communications mix intended to achieve marketing objectives. Excluded from the definition, therefore, are all commercial publications, such as directories, maps, guidebooks, timetables and CDs that are sold through bookshops and other outlets, and for which the object of production is to achieve profit for the publisher through the cover price, and/or advertising revenue. While maps, for example, may be elements of promotional print for tourist boards, the criterion for inclusion in the definition is whether or not their production is geared to marketing objectives. Occasionally, printed items within the definition may also be sold at a cover price. But if so, it is always seen as a contribution towards marketing costs and not a main reason for production. In the United Kingdom, it is normal for the production and distribution costs of some destination management organization brochures at regional and local level to be fully covered by advertising revenue received from businesses buying advertising space. Some tourist boards achieve a surplus on their brochure production costs but, since the surplus is typically set against marketing budgets, such brochures are included within the definition.

The bulk of all information materials are aimed at consumers, but they are also produced to achieve promotional and facilitation objectives targeted at a distribution network. Trade directories and promotional materials, plus their modern B2B website equivalents, are important elements in a marketing budget that uses intermediaries to reach customers and provide booking access.

TYPES OF PRINTED MATERIAL USED IN MARKETING TRAVEL AND TOURISM

From the previous discussion, it will be obvious that the range of printed information materials is immense. The following lists summarize typical items used in practice to influence individual consumers.

Promotional print

- Tour operators' brochures.
- Hotel, holiday centre, caravan park, campsite, and other accommodation brochures.
- Conference centre brochures.
- Specific product brochures (e.g. activity holidays, theatre weekends).
- Attraction leaflets (theme parks, museums, amusement parks).
- Car-rental brochures.
- Sales promotion leaflets (specific incentive offers).
- Posters/show cards for window and other displays in distribution networks.
- Tourist office brochures (general and product-specific).
- Printed letters/inserts for direct mail.

Facilitation and information print

- Orientation leaflets/guides (attractions).
- Maps (mostly provided free out of marketing budgets).
- 'In-house' guides and magazines (accommodation and transport).
- Menus/tent cards/show cards/folders, used 'in-house'.
- Hotel group (and equivalent) directories.
- 'What's on' leaflets (such as those provided out of destination marketing budgets).
- Timetables produced by transport operators.

THE MARKETING ROLE OF INFORMATION MATERIALS AND THEIR MULTIPLE PURPOSES

Drawing on reasons first outlined in Chapter 3, it may be useful to restate briefly the characteristics of travel and tourism products that underlie the need for information materials and explain their importance in conducting marketing campaigns. We wish to stress that these characteristics and the discussion of multiple purposes that follow apply equally to printed and electronically provided information (especially if the latter can be selectively downloaded). A little reflection will show how important these roles are in modern marketing.

- Products are produced and consumed on producers' own premises and cannot be inspected and assessed directly at points of sale away from the place of production. There are no physical stocks of tourist products as there are for manufactured goods. *Information materials are used as product substitutes.*

- Advertising and other forms of promotion mainly serve to create awareness and interest in the product. To convert that interest into a purchase, further information is often needed. *Information materials may be used to respond to enquiries generated by advertising campaigns or to trigger recall of advertising messages at the point of sale.*
- While service production and consumption are simultaneous, the production process is often separated by weeks or months from the act of purchase. Inevitably, many products are ideas and expectations only at the point of sale. *Information materials provide reassurance and a tangible focus for expectations.*
- Especially where infrequently purchased expensive products, such as holidays, are concerned, most customers seek full information and consider several options before making choices. Retailers of holidays are well aware that every minute spent answering questions costs money. *There is a powerful incentive to distribute information materials that reduce customer contact time.*
- There are many marketing reasons for communicating with customers during the production/consumption process, partly to 'facilitate' the experience and inform, and partly to generate a greater level of 'in-house' expenditure. *Information materials serve both facilitation and sales promotion and merchandising roles.*

The multiple purposes

It is obvious from the definition and the range of items included that information materials perform a wide range of functions in travel and tourism. Printed information performs all the roles; electronic media perform most of them. They are summarized in the following list and explained later:

- Creating awareness.
- Promotional - messages/symbols/branding and positioning.
- Promotional - display/merchandising.
- Promotional - incentives/special offers.
- Product substitute role.
- Access/purchasing mechanism.
- 'Proof' of purchase/reassurance.
- Facilitation of product use and information.
- Providing education.

Creating awareness

Some prospective first-time customers will become aware of products through advertising, PR and through the Internet (see Chapter 16). Many others in travel and tourism will gain initial awareness through marketing print first seen in a hotel, at an airport, in a travel agency or passed on by friends. As we said in Chapter 16, the effect of advertising is mainly to create awareness of the brand. This awareness may be recalled only when triggered by the sight of the brochure on display. The battle for awareness is fierce and continuous, and the design appearance of all marketing items is a matter of immense importance. The role of front-cover designs for print can be compared with the role of the packaging of products in a supermarket designed to attract the attention of people passing along the aisles.

Promotion

Brochures, such as those provided by tour operators, are designed to stimulate customers and motivate them to buy. They identify needs, demonstrate in pictures and words the image, positioning and branding of products and organizations, and carry the key messages, closely coordinated with the other communication tools. In this role, they act in the same way as advertising. They also perform a vital display function in the racks of distribution outlets, such as retail travel agents, where they serve in lieu of physical products. In the typical self-service shops run by most travel and tourism retailers, the display role and the customer appeal of brochure covers and contents are vital to marketing success. Supplementary brochures and purpose-designed leaflets are also typically used to communicate and promote special offers and the other sales promotion incentives discussed in Chapter 16.

Websites perform the same promotional role in a different medium. The multimedia options and the ability to change prices continuously as market circumstances alter, give greater flexibility and visual advantages to 'e-brochures' that printed items lack. On the other hand, the feel, the smell and the sheer tangibility of a well-produced brochure are not easily replaced or replicated on most home computers.

Access/purchasing mechanism/marketing research

Many product brochures contain booking forms to facilitate purchase, and these contain the basis of the contract to provide services. Some of these forms may be over-stamped and filled in by travel agents, but all are designed to specify the purchase details. What is primarily designed as a purchasing mechanism, however, is increasingly also used for marketing research purposes. Booking form information can be transferred electronically into databases and used by businesses as a source of valuable customer profile data, such as area of origin, party size and type. The addresses can be analysed by ACORN methods to provide a detailed profile of typical buyers. Websites perform the same role. Whether booking facilities are direct online, or via e-mail or call centres, websites are an access/purchasing mechanism providing simultaneous data capture and analysis.

Product substitute role

Above all, for travel and tourism operators whose business depends on bookings or decisions made away from the place of production, brochures perform a tangible product-substitute role, the marketing importance of which is impossible to overemphasize. The brochure *is* the product at the point of purchase, especially for first-time customers. It confirms the branding message and company values, establishes expectations of quality, value for money, product image and status that must be matched when the product is delivered. Theoretically, the Internet can match much of this role, certainly for lower-cost items and for heavily branded products, such as an overnight in a budget hotel or a low-cost flight. But a question remains as to the speed at which the majority of purchasers will use e-brochures for more expensive and first-time purchases. Some clearly will. But will it be 10%, 25% or over 50% within a decade? Marketing managers have a major task in test marketing their investment in electronic access modes and evaluating customer response. The shift from print to electronic information is inevitable, but it will vary from business to business and there are no industry 'norms'.

Proof of purchase/reassurance

Traditional brochures also act as a substitute for the product in the period between purchase and consumption, which in the case of vacations may extend to several months. It becomes a document to be read several times as a reminder, to stimulate expectations and to show to friends and relatives. It helps to reduce any post-purchase anxiety through reassurance. In Europe, under the terms of the 1993 EC Package Travel Directive, the contents of brochures are covered by precise regulations setting minimum standards. Dissatisfied customers are given rights to claim compensation and failure to provide required information may be a criminal offence for operators. Electronic media can deliver proof of purchase, but its effectiveness in the role of product substitute for high-expense items is open to question.

Facilitation of product use and information

Once customers arrive on a tourism organization's premises or at a destination, it is normal for them to be provided with a wide range of printed materials. Some may be found in rooms (hotels) or seat backs (airlines), at information desks (attractions), on tables (restaurants and bars) or in visitor centres. The literature is designed to explain and promote what is available:

- To promote awareness and use of ancillary services/products.
- To assist customers to get the most value out of their purchase and enhance satisfaction.
- To feature special offers (sales promotion).
- To provide basic information which may be useful.
- To influence customer behaviour and encourage them to spend.

Producers can and do train their staff to communicate some of these options, but staff are usually busy and may not have time to cover the full range of choices. Television screens, videos and interactive options in hotel rooms can also provide some of this information, but printed items remain the main way to provide user-friendly messages to all travellers in exactly the same way. The fact that customers are increasingly 'co-producers in the service delivery process' (see Chapters 7 and 8) provides a further role for information that is intended to help them do this as well as to influence and guide their behaviour.

Carefully designed print can do much to create a sense of welcome from an establishment to its customers. It can communicate corporate values and the message that an organization understands and cares about customer needs and interests. An illustration is the choice that visitor attractions have, either to provide a simple admission ticket or a leaflet of welcome and user advice. The orientation process at Disneyland and other US theme parks uses print to guide and support the enjoyment of visitors in ways that are still exceptions in much of Europe.

Providing education

This is not education in any formal instruction sense but a targeted information process of making people more aware of the products they use and the places they visit. Print can enhance and deepen the experience by helping visitors discover and learn more. The impact of tourism, for example, on the social, cultural as well as physical environment is already an important issue in destinations, such as national parks, in developed and developing countries. Hence, printed information can also be used to promote the ideas of sustainability in a local context and guide people towards choices of more responsible behaviour towards the local environment and culture. Tourism businesses have a vested interest in their locations and a powerful motivation to create customer awareness and provide 'orientation' and understanding of local destination issues. It is in their long-run interest to help create and sustain an attractive and healthy environment, recognizing that destination capacity may depend more on *how* customers use a destination than on the number of visitors.

Education is not confined solely to leisure tourism. Many hotel chains around the world have developed sophisticated programmes to contribute to the environment, and they need to tell all their customers, many of whom are on business. Of course, the word 'education' will not be found in marketing print or on tourism websites. However, it is education, and education is a communication business. The professional skills of marketing managers already have an important educational role for the future, and printed communications will be its primary focus where it matters most – on tourism business premises, in transit and in consumers' homes.

Educating visitors in this way also demonstrates that an organization is behaving responsibly, and hence, enhance its corporate image. Corporate social responsibility is now on the agenda of most large companies for a mixture of altruistic and commercial reasons.

Link article available at www.routledge.com/9780750686938

(1) Chiou, W.B., Wan, C.S., Lee, H.Y., 2008. Virtual experience vs. brochures in the advertisement of scenic spots: How cognitive preferences and order effects influence advertising effects on consumers. Tourism Management 29(1), 146–150.

STAGES IN PRODUCING EFFECTIVE INFORMATION MATERIAL

The seven stages noted in the following list are presented in a logical decision sequence judged relevant to all managers responsible for producing printed or electronic information materials for marketing purposes. Although the distribution of printed materials has special considerations (see later in the chapter), the other stages are similar to those used for designing any form of marketing communication. For larger organizations, they are based on marketing research. Planning the provision of information is normally carried out as one of the elements in the campaign plan, and it draws on data used for planning marketing strategy and objectives. The budget required for print production is best calculated by the 'objective and task' methods outlined in Chapter 12.

1. *Determining the size, profile and needs of the target audience.* Information about target customers is derived through market segmentation and the marketing planning process, and print volume is based on the quantified objectives in the marketing plan. The target profile for advertising (media selection), sales promotion and for print production will normally be identical. Electronic media that is linked to booking systems and e-mails generate its own profile data as prospective customers respond – one of its primary advantages for marketing organizations.
2. *Marketing strategy, branding and positioning.* Here also advertising, print and websites are likely to be planned together, with coordinated messages, images and positioning. If print is the larger part of the budget, it may take the leading role in expressing product images. It will certainly take a leading role in communicating specific brand and product messages to the target audience.
3. *Paper quality, choice of colours, density of copy, graphics*, and the style and density of photographs are varied in practice to match chosen images to selected target audiences. Up-market target groups respond better to heavier-quality paper, lower density per page, pastel colours and thematic photographs. Down-market target groups are more influenced by bold colours, direct and straightforward copy, and are not put off by greater density per page. Website and multimedia design decisions are similar in principle having regard to the possibilities of the new medium rather than print.
4. *Specifying brochure/website objectives*. The essential task is to clarify and state concisely what the brochure or website is expected to achieve in the campaign, especially in terms of the specific products it covers. A list of specific messages, rank ordered according to perceived customer priorities, should be drawn up within the context of the agreed marketing objectives. These statements will be crucial in briefing designers.
5. *Deciding the method of distribution*. The distribution of print to its intended recipients is perhaps the most vital of all the seven stages, because communication can only work if sufficient numbers of prospective customers receive it. The cost of distribution per unit of print may easily exceed the unit cost of its production, and most producers in travel and tourism will have to choose between several distribution options. This vital decision is discussed later in this chapter. For websites on the Internet, of course, the medium is distribution, information, promotion and booking access all in one.
6. *Creative execution*. As for advertising, the way in which product concepts and branding images are presented in print and websites will strongly influence the way in which consumers receive and respond to messages. For printed items, the appearance and appeal of the front cover, especially of items to be displayed

in self-service racks, will be crucial in establishing eye contact and initial visual interest – in comparison with many other brochures aiming to appeal to much the same customers. Without the initial appeal, a leaflet or brochure is unlikely to be picked up and looked through. As Maas noted 'the cover of a brochure is just like the headline of a print advertisement: four out of five people never get beyond it. For these readers, you must get your selling message across on that page (or waste 80% of your money)' (Maas, 1980: 23). That applies equally to the visual appeal and user-friendliness of websites, especially the opening page.

While creative execution will usually be the business of designers (see later), marketing managers must accept full responsibility for the designer's brief and any marketing research associated with it.

7. *Timing*. Most travel and tourism print is required to be available for distribution at specific times of the year when customers are making their travel decisions. Print production and advertising normally require carefully coordinated phasing. As it usually takes several weeks from an initial brief to final production of print, it is vital that print requirements are carefully programmed and that agreed timings are adhered to. If photographs are required, they have to be taken at the right time of the year. Many hotels and visitor attractions have started to plan their brochures in September for production in January, only to find that the key photographs they need should have been taken in July.

   While this may seem obvious, experience demonstrates repeatedly that the bulk of all print is commissioned too late; that most brochure work is rushed, often involving mistakes and penalties of cost; and that important deadlines are missed with consequent loss of revenue. Marketing managers have only limited influence over creative execution, but they should exercise total control over timing. The scope for marginal improvements in better timing alone may have a considerable impact on revenue. This is one of the ways in marketing to achieve marginal revenue gains and marginal budget savings at the same time.

   Yet, one of the advantages of websites is the ease with which they can be changed, modified and updated online at any time and with minimum cost. For tour operators in a 'fluid pricing' market context, website flexibility is an attractive option for notifying price changes compared with costly reprints and distribution of brochure pages.

USING AGENCIES TO PRODUCE INFORMATION MATERIALS

In large organizations, the creative aspects of print and electronic media design may be handled within the organization itself and through advertising and other specialist agencies. Where print production runs are involved, the business is usually outsourced to firms specializing in such services.

Smaller businesses are more likely to outsource both the creative and production processes, obtaining quotes from two or three specialist firms, many of which have access to designers, photographers and copywriters. It is interesting to note that, provided they are computer literate and have some basic training, very small businesses employing fewer than five people are now able to design and create much of their own print. They can also design their own small websites for as little as, say, $300.

Specialist firms will normally undertake whatever aspects of the total information design and production process clients specify. Most will be willing to provide professional and technical assistance with all or most of the following decisions.

Courtesy of Blake Ashwell.

Creative execution of the client's product concepts

- Most effective structure, layout, content and size of brochure or website.
- Design theme, and image presentation, especially of the front cover/first page.
- Use of colours and 'atmosphere' – and multimedia options for websites.
- Artwork and use of photographs/video clips (with due allowance for the delays these may cause in downloading on some household PCs).
- Captions, graphics, copy and choice of typefaces.

For print production and distribution

- Choice of paper weight (affects production and postal costs and indicates quality).
- Packing (bulk and individual copies).
- Distribution.

To get good work from any agency, especially to get the best assistance in aspects of design and layout, it is essential for the client to supply a detailed written brief. The brief should refer to all the stages noted in the previous section, the marketing objectives, branding and the budget available. Distribution considerations (see later in this chapter) must be clearly explained, as they will influence the creative execution, especially for relatively heavy printed items.

In practice, many smaller organizations fail to produce adequate briefs for agencies, and worse, they change their minds after the initial design, layout and artwork have been produced. Although websites are a much more forgiving and flexible medium than print, design changes are certain to add to cost, cause delays and produce a less-than-satisfactory result. Where external agencies are used, the process of agreeing print production usually calls for detailed liaison at the following points:

- Agreement and interpretation of initial design brief, production schedule and costs.
- Preliminary ('rough') artwork sketches, headlines, format and content, colours and typeface.
- Photography (if necessary), finished artwork and copy.
- Printer's proofs for correction.

DISTRIBUTING INFORMATION TO TARGET AUDIENCES

It is easy to focus all attention on the layout, photographs, images and copy. In practice, the most important design consideration for any information is how it will reach its intended target audience. If the answer is direct mail, there is an immediate design concern to minimize the cost of envelopes and postage, which frequently exceed the print design and production costs. If the intention is to distribute through travel agencies or tourist information centres, the size of their standard display spaces will tend to dictate brochure size and page layout.

The distribution options for getting printed items into prospective buyers' hands were always very wide even before the advent of the Internet. Where brochures or leaflets are displayed and given out 'on site', the distribution process and costs can be fully controlled by the producer. Where a larger company, such as an airline, hotel group or car-rental company, controls multi-site outlets, literature distribution at those sites is also easily controlled and costed.

For distribution away from owned premises, there are at least 10 main options for getting print into the hands of prospective buyers. These are summarized as follows:

- Advertisements carrying coupons to be completed by those requiring information.
- Cards or other inserts into press and magazine media, which are an alternative form of media space.
- Direct mail to loyalty club members and other previous customers, using own databases and names and addresses bought for the purpose from a list broker.
- Direct distribution on a door-to-door basis in targeted residential areas.
- Distribution via retail travel agencies.
- Distribution via tourist information centres and public libraries.

- Distribution via relevant third parties. For example, American Express, and many clubs and societies will, for a fee, include printed leaflets with their regular mailings to members, alternatively, via hotel reception desks and similar relevant outlets (suitable for attractions, entertainments, car rental).
- Collaborative distribution via marketing consortia and trade associations (this is a variation of distribution via multi-site operation under one owner).
- Distribution via websites that offer e-mail addresses or call centre numbers as the means to access printed materials or provide pages that can be downloaded at home.

Exhibitions play an important part in tourism marketing, and are a major outlet for brochures and leaflets at shows targeting the trade, the general public or segments interested in specific activities or destinations. The unique advantage of an exhibition as a promotional medium is that it has a self-selecting audience. Everyone at a holiday exhibition or a camping and caravan or boating exhibition is actively interested in what is on display. It is then just a question of attracting them to your stand. In tourism, there are national and international circuits of exhibitions which can keep a resort or major attraction's marketing team busy all winter handing out brochures, loading and unloading vans, and running up bills for food and accommodation. As exhibitions are a form of promotional medium, the same principles of media selection discussed in Chapter 16 apply. An organization should examine the costs, the coverage obtained and the context in which their stand will be seen. The results of attending the exhibition should be carefully monitored both in terms of the initial contacts made and the business that resulted (Morgan, 1996).

Beyond these common choices, there will usually be many other places, such as airports, railway station concourses, bus station waiting rooms, supermarkets and petrol/gas stations, at which relevant opportunities to distribute information may occur. The scope is very wide indeed. Specialist companies exist to provide distribution services for particular sectors, for example, from tour operators to travel agents or from visitor attractions to local hotels, campsites, pubs and cafes.

EVALUATING THE RESULTS OF INFORMATION DISTRIBUTION

Assessing the cost-effectiveness of producing and distributing information will be hard to separate with any precision from the combined effects of online and offline advertising, PR, sales promotion and merchandising. Bookings and sales revenues result from the marketing mix as a whole. Through marketing research, however, it is possible to reach some conclusions, and studies may be carried out:

- To choose between the customer appeal of alternative cover designs and content, using evidence of qualitative discussions with target groups of potential customers (see Chapter 9).
- To measure the results of 'split-runs', in which two different brochure formats are distributed to matched samples of target recipients, and the volume of bookings compared. Using direct mail to distribute print makes this a relatively easy option for many producers.

- To measure customer recall, use and evaluation of brochures through *ad hoc* telephone or postal surveys of brochure recipients identified, for example, from completed coupons included in advertisements.
- To measure customer recall, use and evaluation of brochures in brief surveys conducted, for example, at reception desks when customers arrive on a producer's premises or site.

In every case where printed materials are part of the marketing mix, it is common sense to identify all items with code numbers or letters, which can identify:

- Through what media the print was requested.
- By what distribution methods print reached the customer (assuming more than one method).

Provided that consumer responses are analysed by the codes assigned, the use of printed materials and the associated distribution methods normally provide many opportunities for innovation and testing responses. Use of websites can be measured directly, unequivocally and at low cost by recording the number of customers that open a site and explore its pages as well as by the use of e-commerce, e-mail or call centre numbers/references unique to the Internet. As we have noted elsewhere, the Internet is an excellent low-cost tool for marketing innovation and experimentation, and this is an important part of its attraction in services marketing.

ELECTRONIC ALTERNATIVES TO PRINT

The promotional and access roles of large parts of what traditionally was print information are now being provided mainly by electronic media. This is especially the case for simple and regular transactions, such as hotel, rail or flight bookings. As we saw in Chapters 13 and 14, the developments in ICT now enable visitor information to be transmitted electronically in ways that are not only cheaper than print but offer a richer content. The latest trend in travel and tourism websites is for 'aggregated content' – text, pictures, video clips and sounds – provided not only by the company and its affiliates but by destination-management organizations and by visitors themselves through Web2.0 sites like Tripadvisor, WAYN or YouTube. The technology exists to transmit this not only to the home computer before a visit but also to send selected information about the immediate locality via mobile phone or the car's satellite navigation system at any time during the visit. How far these 'geo-located' services will replace the facilitation role of the brochure and the leaflet remains to be seen.

Importantly, the physical value and qualities of attractively produced print; the ability to touch it, hold it and show it to others; its appeal to humanity down the centuries; and its ability to inspire images and dreams, appear to be a vital part of the experience of travel and tourism. The death of books had been confidently predicted for over 40 years, but more books than ever are being produced and sold, and there is a powerful human attachment to the simplicity, reliability, user-friendliness and great convenience of portable print. The authors do not believe that print is likely to be replaced by electronic communications in the near future.

Electronic information has both a powerful leading *and* complementary role to play, however, and clearly can be used effectively to reduce costs by substantially reducing the existing levels of wastage in retail outlets and in the traditional methods for direct response marketing.

Link article available at www.routledge.com/9780750686938

(1) Seabra, C., Abrantes, J.L., Lages, L.P., 2007. The impact of using non-media information sources on the future use of mass media information sources: the mediating role of expectations fulfillment. Tourism Management, 28 (6), 1541–1554.

CHAPTER SUMMARY

Travel and tourism are information-rich industries. From the initial idea of a visit, through all the stages of decision, booking, payment and anticipation through to arrival and the experience, the process is one of information provision.

This chapter identifies the vital part that information materials play in marketing travel and tourism products within the context of communications paid for out of marketing budgets.

- It notes the massive volume and wastage of printed items traditionally produced in travel and tourism, especially in tour operating, and the important range of functions they perform, distinguishing between promotion and facilitation.
- The different purposes for which information is used in marketing are discussed, and the seven main stages in producing effective information are explained with reference to the roles of specialist agencies available to assist in design, production and distribution.
- The chapter emphasizes a particular need for organizations to analyse the problems of securing effective distribution for printed materials to the targeted audience, and notes the choices available to tourism businesses, recently enormously facilitated by direct customer access to the Internet. The *objective and task* method of budgeting for information provision requirements (introduced in Chapter 12) is recommended, because it makes it easier in practice for managers to measure the results of their expenditure.
- In summary, it is interesting to reflect that, at least for commercial businesses in the travel and tourism industry, the information they distribute physically in print or virtually via the Internet, embodies and communicates all aspects of the marketing mix to the extent that they:
  - State and physically represent the product in consumer terms, and communicate a company's chosen positioning and branding.
  - State the price and other details as the basis of a legally enforceable contract.
  - Are a principal medium of communication.
  - Are part of the distribution process that represents 'place' for customers.
  - Facilitate the customer experience and sense of enjoyment and value for money.
  - Facilitate the relationship that businesses seek to develop with their repeat customers.

- Given the nature of service products in general, and travel and tourism products in particular, the communication of information is often the most important (and expensive) single element within coordinated marketing campaigns. Growing use of the Internet offers significant opportunities for cost savings in traditional print budgets, but the Internet and printed communications still perform complementary rather than alternative roles for the great majority of consumers.

QUESTIONS TO CONSIDER

- Select a current travel brochure or visitor attraction leaflet; identify which of the multiple purposes of information materials outlined in this chapter it is designed to provide; and evaluate how effectively it fulfils them.
- Discuss the strengths and weaknesses of this printed brochure or leaflet in comparison with alternative means of communicating the same messages online.
- On the basis of this analysis, discuss the extent to which the role of printed materials in travel and tourism marketing is likely to diminish in the next 10 years.

REFERENCES AND FURTHER READING

Chiou, W.B., Wan, C.S. and Lee, H.Y. (2008). Virtual experience vs. brochures in the advertisement of scenic spots: how cognitive preferences and order effects influence advertising effects on consumers, *Tourism Management*, **29**(1), pp. 146–150.

Decrop, A. (2007). The influence of message format on the effectiveness of print advertisements for tourism destinations, *International Journal of Advertising*, **26**(4), pp. 505–525.

Feng, R. and Morrisson, A.M. (2007). Quality and value network marketing travel clubs, *Annals of Tourism Research*, **34**(3), pp. 588–609.

Hannam, K. (2005). Discourse analysis in tourism research, *Tourism Recreation Research*, **30**(2), pp. 23–30.

Laesser, C. (2007). There is a market for destination information brochures but is there a future?, *Tourism Review*, **62**(3/4), pp. 27–31.

Maas, J. (1980). Better brochures for the money, *Cornell Hotel and Restaurant Administration Quarterly*, **20**(4).

Morgan, M. (1996). *Promotional Literature. Chapter 19. Marketing for Leisure and Tourism*. Prentice Hall.

Molina, A. (2006). Tourism brochures, usefulness and image, *Annals of Tourism Research*, **33**(4), pp. 1036–1056.

Seabra, C., Abrantes, J.L. and Lages, L.P. (2007). The impact of using non-media information sources on the future use of mass media information sources: the mediating role of expectations fulfillment, *Tourism Management*, **28**(6), pp. 1541–1554.

Applying Marketing in the Main Sectors of Travel and Tourism

Part Five considers the way that marketing operates in each of the following sectors of travel and tourism:

- Destinations
- Accommodation
- Passenger Transport
- Visitor Attractions
- Inclusive tours and product packages

Each sector is very different from the others but the marketing principles are the same. Each chapter looks at the characteristics of organizations and businesses in the sector and examines the main influences that determine the marketing response. The chapters explain what marketing means in strategic and tactical terms and outline in each case the implications of the Internet and e-marketing developments that have shifted traditional marketing approaches since the late 1990s.

A resort in the Maldives - "One of the principal challenges facing many destinations is the need to differentiate themselves from competition with many of them offering very similar product offerings"

CHAPTER 18

Marketing tourism destinations

"Increasingly, therefore, Destination Management Organisations (DMOs) use ICT in order to facilitate the tourist experience before, during and after the visit, as well as for coordinating all partners involved in the production and delivery of tourism"

Buhalis (2006).

This chapter is about the marketing role of national, regional and local tourism organizations. Formerly referred to as National Tourism Administrations (NTAs) or Regional or Local Tourist Boards (RTBs and LTBs), such organizations are more frequently referred to as Destination Marketing Organizations (DMOs) or Destination Marketing Partnerships (DMPs) depending upon their degree of geographic scope, the number and diversity of stakeholders included and their marketing span of influence. For the most part, the latter two terms tend to be used interchangeably although a DMO is increasingly becoming the accepted generic term for such organizations, with NTAs or NTOs (National Tourism Organizations) more specifically referring to the marketing of countries as tourist destinations.

The majority of NTAs/NTOs are not producers or operators. They generally do not sell products directly to visitors and they are not directly responsible for the quality of services delivered, although most aim to influence it. In developed countries they are typically responsible for only a small proportion, however important it may be, of all the travel and tourism marketing programmes carried out on behalf of their country. Although the principles and practice of a DMO approach to marketing of countries are essentially the same as those adopted by regional, state or local tourism offices, the scale and reach of marketing operations is obviously different as are the budgets and broader resources set aside to meet the marketing strategies set.

The chapter begins with a definition of NTOs/DMOs and the scale of their marketing operations. The factors influencing NTO marketing are summarized and the nature of marketing strategy is discussed, distinguishing between what NTOs can achieve by spending their budgets mainly on promotion and what they can achieve through various forms of *facilitation*. Facilitation means providing assistance to the component sectors of the travel and tourism industry within a country and in other countries from which visitors are drawn. Because the marketing process for a DMO is different from that for providers of accommodation, transport or attractions, the process is outlined in some detail. The term *facilitation* is explained in general and with specific reference to the expanding influence of the Internet in destination marketing.

After studying this chapter you should be able to understand:

- The concepts and characteristics of NTOs/DMOs and some key international dimensions of destination marketing.
- Why DMOs have influence in the market place but, generally, very little actual control over the tourism fortunes of a destination.
- The main marketing roles of DMOs and the marketing processes they use in practice.
- The difference between marketing and promotion and marketing facilitation at the destination level.
- The importance for destinations of positioning, branding, images and concepts.

NTOS/DMOS DEFINED: SOME INTERNATIONAL DIMENSIONS OF DESTINATION MARKETING

As defined by Buhalis (2000: 75), a destination represents an 'amalgam of tourism products, offering an integrated experience to consumers'. Within this context, a DMO can be defined as 'any organization, at any level, which is responsible for the marketing of an identifiable destination' (Pike, 2004: 14), while the term NTO is used specifically to designate the 'entity with overall responsibility for marketing a country as a tourism destination' Pike (2004: 14). With approximately 200 NTOs in existence around the world, all of different sizes and organizational patterns, supporting altogether some 1000 foreign branch offices, around two-thirds of the world's tourism offices are estimated to be government ministries or departments and the other third are separate legal entities. Nearly all of them are engaged in one or more aspects of destination promotion although relatively few are practising the systematic approach to marketing developed in this book. Most of the promotional effort organized by these NTOs is aimed at international markets but in recent years many have also been spending considerable sums on the promotion of domestic tourism by residents within their own countries. Larger branch networks, such as those supported by Britain, France or Greece, comprise over *30* offices in the main countries from which they draw their visitors. Most developing countries can afford to maintain only a very few offices in key markets.

In practice, DMO marketing budgets are not aimed at all tourism but targeted at specific market segments. In a recent evaluation of NTO marketing activities, the UNWTO (2003) identified data on marketing budget sizes and their relation to international visitor numbers. Based on the results of a survey sent to 168 NTOs around the world, with a response rate of 33%, the results were analysed according to three marketing budget categories: up to €1 million, €1–€10 million and over €10 million. Destinations in the 'low spend' category included a mix of island states, small South American and former East European countries while those with a 'medium spend' were represented by a mix of larger South American, larger former Eastern European countries and smaller players from western developed countries. Finally, countries with a 'high spend' primarily included countries from the OECD and major players in the world tourism arena. With regard to their actual marketing spend as a percentage of international tourism receipts, the average budget allocated to marketing stands at 0.003%. Hence, irrespective of the size of the destination (vis-à-vis international visitor numbers) the values attached to marketing budgets are all very small when compared to the overall impact such a low spend has in the marketplace.

In common with many other sectors of the expanding travel and tourism industry, the development of professionalism in marketing around the world is still relatively recent in DMOs. It appears certain to become more important over the next decade as markets mature, technology challenges multiply, competition between countries for shares of markets increases and governments put ever greater pressure on the agencies they fund to set targets and demonstrate value for money. On the broad evidence of the data above, notwithstanding the lack of precision in the available statistics, it is reasonable to expect that the application of systematic marketing techniques by NTOs could make a major contribution to cost-effectiveness measured in dollars spent per targeted tourist arrival.

NTO AND DMO MARKETING HAS INFLUENCE, BUT LIMITED CONTROL

The influence of the marketing activity undertaken by DMOs differs from commercial marketing: first, because much of the travel between developed countries is for business and other non-leisure purposes, such as visits to friends and relatives, and these segments are not significantly influenced by the promotional expenditure of a DMO. Secondly, especially for developed destinations, it is obvious that a large proportion of leisure visits would continue to be made without DMO expenditure because they are influenced by previous visits, recommendations of friends and, of course, the private sector marketing efforts of the tourism industry as a whole.

Ideally, all national, regional, state and local authorities would like their DMOs to prove that for every 1000 dollars spent on marketing there is a response that can be measured in the number of visits and expenditure achieved over a given period of time. If such proof were possible, the relevant authorities would be able accurately to allocate larger or smaller budgets to tourism according to their policies for growth, maintenance or other desired priorities. For all destinations, however, apart from the size of their marketing budgets and the quality of the marketing activities in which DMOs engage, there are three main underlying factors outside their control that are continuously at work in determining the actual volume and expenditure of tourism generated between markets of origin and countries, regions, states or municipalities of destination. These factors, discussed separately below, distort the measurement of expenditure and response in all destinations:

1. Expenditure on marketing is only one of the influences that determine tourism volumes and expenditure to any destination.
2. The marketing effort of DMOs is only a part of the total tourism and travel trade marketing effort made on behalf of a destination.
3. Very few DMOs sell products to prospective visitors directly. Even where they take responsibility for operating, say, hotels or transport, these activities are typically only a part of the total product supply.

Marketing is only one of the influences

Chapters 4 and 5 set out the economic, social and behavioural factors at work in societies that collectively determine the volume and types of travel and tourism generated by any particular country. These so-called 'determinants and motivations' of tourism include disposable income per capita, amount of leisure time available, personal mobility, availability of transport systems, the price of travel and exchange rates. The importance of understanding the external business environment as the basis for marketing strategy has been stressed throughout this book and needs no further emphasis here.

It follows that NTO marketing must aim to understand and respond to these external factors but it cannot influence and change them directly. For example, Britain historically has derived about a quarter of its international tourism revenue from US travellers who were its most important market. But neither the British government nor Visit Britain (VB) has any influence over the level of US incomes, the international value of the dollar or the state of the US economy. Nor can they predict acts of terrorism as evident back in September, 2001, or the banking collapse of 2008 but these are the factors that ultimately drive US international tourism. Effective NTO marketing begins with an understanding of the determinants influencing its main markets; it aims to work with the opportunities created by favourable events and to limit the impact of unfavourable ones, such as 9/11. For example, when the Asian Tsunami of 2004 hit the shores of Thailand, Sri Lanka, the Maldives, Andaman & Nicobar Islands, India and Indonesia, the tourism marketing efforts of many of the countries and islands involved were simply overwhelmed by events from which they are continuing to recover today. This point in no way denies the value of destination marketing, but does set it in the wider context of national and international events over which NTOs have no control or influence.

MINI CASE 18.1: TOURISM MARKET RECOVERY IN THE MALDIVES

Although disasters, be they man made or natural, are not new to tourism, the Tsunami that hit many countries in an around the Indian Ocean in December 2004 had a devastating impact on a number of major destinations. In addition to resort destinations in Sri Lanka, Thailand, India and even Eastern Africa, the Maldives was one such destination damaged. But the country has used the Tsunami as a catalyst for a raft of market recovery strategies designed to bring visitors back. With tourism contributing approximately 30% of its GDP, about 40% of local taxation revenues and overall foreign exchange earnings of US$149 million in 2003, tourism in the Maldives represents a significant economic sector which for the most part is dependent on six key markets, namely, Italy, UK, Germany, Japan, France and Switzerland. As with Bali beforehand the disaster resulted in a severe downturn in bookings and arrivals and significant operating losses and substantial costs of repair. Although no two disasters are same, it is now relatively commonplace for destinations in such situations to initiate highly sensitive marketing campaigns, focus attention on domestic and near-foreign markets, work in collaboration with the broader visitor economy and focus on restoring overall yield and positive images in the longer term.

For the Maldives, 19 of the 87 resorts around the country closed immediately after the Tsunami with 13 re-opening after a relatively short period of time. The strategy adopted by the Maldives Tourism promotion Board (MTPB) was aimed at achieving short, medium and long-term benefits. In the first instance, efforts were made to slow down and then stop cancellations and correct media representations about the perceived severity of damage to the Maldives, something that involved significant work with travel intermediaries and charter airlines. US$1.5 million was provided by the MTPB to fund a range of initiatives to stop cancellations while there was an expressed desire to avoid the temptation to offer discounts too soon. This was deemed particularly important as the hasty levying of discounts can not only reduce immediate returns but impact negatively on the longer-term reputation of the destination. In addition, the more general need for communication messages to express sympathy and solidarity was aimed at rebuilding confidence both with customers and prospective visitors, with there being a very distinct need to counter the constant comparison in the international media with other destinations that for the most part were more severely affected. Although with a longer-time horizon, the MTPB also started to develop strategies designed to reduce reliance on travel intermediaries, through increased participation at trade shows and exhibitions around the world. In addition a deliberate focus was adopted for new markets such as China, India and Russia to reduce dependency on current markets. All of the above strategies were considered to be a collective success in that by the end of 2005, occupancy levels had reached pre-Tsunami levels.

Source: Based on Carlsen and Hughes (2007).

NTO marketing is only part of the total marketing expenditure for a country

For most developed countries judgement suggests that an NTO's expenditure on marketing to international visitors is seldom more than around 10% of the total marketing expenditure. It follows that, if the bulk of all tourism marketing expenditure is not controlled by an NTO but by independent third parties, it is impossible for a national organization either to claim all the credit or to be blamed for failure in the fluctuations in visitor arrivals occurring over any given period of time. For countries where tour operators dominate the marketing process, the NTO influence is likely to be especially weak.

Limited influence over the supply of products

In developed tourist destination countries there are thousands of commercial firms and hundreds of public sector organizations engaged in providing and marketing international tourism products and services. Of these, only a small minority has any formal relationship with an NTO through membership of state, regional or area DMOs. Thus a large number of businesses generate a very wide range of tourism products, most of which are beyond the marketing influence of an NTO with regard to volume, design, price and promotion decisions.

SUMMARIZING THE MARKETING ROLE OF NTOS

One may conclude from this consideration of the three external factors that the marketing effort of an NTO, measured against international tourism flows to a destination, will always be:

- Partial or even marginal in terms of the range of segments it covers and the products it influences.
- Submerged to a large extent in the greater impact of the determinants and motivations affecting markets of origin.
- Outweighed by the marketing effort of private sector partner interests in tourism.

Paradoxically, the NTOs of developing tourist destination countries have a far greater *potential* influence over their countries' tourism. They are better placed to evaluate the success of their marketing efforts. In practice, however, they mostly have very restricted budgets, lack the professional management skills to exploit their advantages and are often dominated by powerful tour operator influences.

These conclusions are not intended to imply that NTO marketing expenditure is inevitably ineffective or wasted. They do mean that most NTOs are not in direct control of the tourism products they promote or the results that are achieved as measured in annual visitor numbers and expenditure to or within a country. It is therefore helpful to explain the role of NTO marketing from a perspective of targeted margins and influence rather than control, a very different perspective from that used to explain commercial practice.

On the other hand, NTOs have an influence over tourism marketing that extends well beyond the small proportion of tourism for which they can claim direct influence. The influencing role is, of course, a two-way or partnership process. There are many different models and they have to be tailored to suit different countries. In the UK the influence comes through collaboration between Visit Britain (for international marketing), other tourist boards and commercial partners.

In other developed countries, such as Canada and Australia, powerful public/private sector organizations have been formed to act as lobbies and provide a forum within which NTOs and the travel and tourism industry collaborate.

Link article available at www.routledge.com/9780750686938

(1) Reid, L.J., Smith, S.L.J., McCloskey, 2008. The effectiveness of regional marketing alliances: A case study of the Atlantic Canada Tourism Partnership 2000-2006. Tourism Management 29 (3), 581–593.

DESTINATION PROMOTION ROLE FOR NTOS OR MARKETING FACILITATION?

From the previous discussion it can be concluded that there are two levels to consider in marketing a country as a destination. The first level, concerned with the destination as a whole, is the primary focus of what NTOs do. The second level covers the marketing activity of the mainly private sector operators promoting their individual products. In the first level of marketing, NTOs have to choose between two alternative strategies. One of these is reaching prospective visitors via expenditure on a promotional mix intended to achieve destination awareness and influence prospective customers' attitudes and purchasing behaviour; the other is concerned with exercising a facilitating influence over the tourism industry. The following two sections deal with each strategy in turn.

A promotional strategy

A promotional strategy means devising and implementing promotional and integrated communications programmes, and targeting potential visitors segments with branding, images and key messages. The objectives are typically to make customers aware, motivate their interest, encourage them to surf the Internet, send for product brochures, call direct or go to travel agents in their area.

The decision to invest the greater part of their budgets in promoting destination awareness and images appears to be an obvious and convincing strategy which remains a strategic choice for many key destinations including Egypt, Turkey and Australia. Following the logic of the strategy, the bulk of NTO marketing expenditure and its organizational structure should reflect promotional campaign priorities and be invested in advertising, publicity and promotional materials. In selecting this strategy, however, it has to be assumed that the budget an NTO has to spend is large enough in practice to implement effectively the promotional campaigns its market segmentation studies identify as necessary. To be effective, such campaigns must be of sufficient weight and impact to reach and motivate the necessary numbers of potential buyers who are aware of and predisposed to the destination. But if budgets are not adequate for the task, expenditure on an image-creating strategy may in practice be largely a waste of money – on perfectly logical and desirable objectives that cannot be achieved.

Most NTO budgets for marketing purposes are well under 1% of tourism expenditure in their destinations. This, and the fact that most NTOs cannot influence more than around 10% of all prospective visitors, leads one to question how effective many NTO marketing campaigns are in practice.

Link article available at www.routledge.com/9780750686938

(2) Fyall, A., Callod, C., Edwards, B., 2003. Relationship marketing: The challenge for destinations. Annals of Tourism Research 30 (3), 644–659.

A facilitation strategy

Fortunately there is an alternative strategy, relevant to all DMOs. This is the strategy of *marketing facilitation*, as it is defined in this chapter. Facilitation creates marketing collaboration and networking bridges between a DMO and individual operators in the travel and tourism industry, and between the 'umbrella' campaigns and industry marketing expenditure. The case for marketing facilitation is based on five considerations that are commonly found around the world:

1. That national, regional, state and local governments have policy objectives for wishing to promote tourism. Typically these are now expressed in economic, social and environmental terms that can be interpreted and defined as marketing goals.
2. That budgets granted to DMOs will usually be much less than adequate to undertake all the marketing tasks identified, so that selection of priorities is always required.
3. That the destination possesses a range of tourist areas, products and segments, some growing and some declining, to which it attaches differing priorities and which have different marketing implications for achieving policy objectives.
4. That DMO goals cannot be achieved without private sector support, collaboration and contributions to the cost of campaigns.
5. Although most DMOs can reach no more than 10% of visitors through promotional campaigns, they can aim to reach virtually 100% through one or more forms of facilitation.

These are powerful considerations. The most cost-effective marketing role for a DMO lies in focusing on the contributions that it can best make. These are:

- Research to establish and communicate to its industry partners, promotional priorities for targeted markets and segments. Defining destination images and branding are part of this process.
- Liaising with and influencing private sector partners to achieve the priorities.
- Co-ordinating elements of tourism products (such as tourist information and destination Web sites) not provided by the private sector.
- Providing investment and marketing support for new or growth products relevant to policy goals.

- Creating marketing facilities and co-operative campaigns accessible especially for the thousands of small businesses that would otherwise be unable to participate in marketing on a national or international scale.
- Providing advice and leadership based on its information sources, including intranets to support collaborating businesses.

These marketing processes, co-ordinated often with a planning and regulatory role, amount to a *facilitation strategy* that has important implications for DMO marketing organization and personnel. Such a strategy requires extensive co-operation and joint decision-making with private sector partners. It also requires a substantial commitment to market research and intelligence, and to performance evaluation. Facilitation decisions bring into sharp focus the very difficult task, which all DMOs face, of allocating less than adequate budgets between competing marketing priorities.

The strategy a DMO adopts in practice should vary according to the stage of development the destination has reached. Where destinations are largely unknown in the markets they seek to promote, where existing tourism flows are small and where the tourism industry within the destination is mainly weak and fragmented, the DMO will have no choice but to take the leading role in putting its destination on the map. It will have to play a major role in promoting its destination's products. Even in these circumstances the available budgets will normally not be adequate to engage effectively in image campaigns in several markets and the marketing support of suppliers to the tourism industry, such as hotels and intermediaries, will be essential for success.

For better known, well-established country destinations such as Spain, Australia, the UK and the USA, where the tourism industry has forged its own international links, it should increasingly be possible for the NTO to commit more of its expenditure to the strategy of support and facilitation, more on image definition and branding and web site development and less on buying media space for general image advertising.

DESTINATION POSITIONING THEMES, BRANDING, IMAGES AND CONCEPTS

Whatever the main thrust of strategy, be it promotion or facilitation, DMOs always have a vital function to perform for their destinations in choosing the single-minded communication propositions (messages and symbols) that serve to identify and position or 'brand' their countries in the minds of prospective visitors, and differentiate them from all others.

Amazing Thailand and *Incredible India* represent significant campaigns by Thailand and India, respectively, designed to brand and identify their destinations with unique propositions. To be successful in practice such propositions must be:

- Based on genuine product values and attributes that can be delivered and experienced and that visitors recognize as authentic, not fake.
- Readily understood by customers at the point of purchase.
- Involve at least the leading players in the commercial sector.
- Incorporated into the promotional efforts of a country's regions and resorts.

- Sustained over several years if they are to overcome the communication inertia and barriers referred to in Chapter 16.
- Systematically exploited in a co-ordinated range of sales-promotion and customer-servicing techniques designed to reach visitors on arrival at the destination as well as prospective visitors in countries of origin.

Developing successful images and implementing them effectively require detailed consumer research and creative flair in relation to a destination's intrinsic attractiveness to visitors. This is usually a role that only a DMO can fulfil, and only a DMO can take on the task of communicating the chosen positioning to the tourism industry. But it does not follow that DMOs should have to spend the bulk of their own scarce resources in promoting the image to the general public in markets of origin.

It will often be possible for DMOs to develop co-operative promotional efforts arising directly out of the facilitation and positioning strategy. They can use the processes of collaboration to draw on the financial support of the tourism industry to mount any advertising and publicity campaigns judged necessary to support or enhance the destination image. Working within a strategy of facilitation, a DMO will often play a tactical role with its PR campaigns, e.g. to correct the short-run effects of negative attitudes in markets of origin arising from news stories about prices or personal security.

Table 18.1 lists some recent examples of destination branding and values communicated.

TABLE 18.1 Destination brand core values

Destination	Brand Identity	Core Brand Values
Australia	Brand Australia	Youthful, energetic, optimistic, stylish, unpretentious, genuine, open, fun
New Zealand	New Pacific Freedom	Contemporary and sophisticated, innovative, creative, spirited and free
Western Australia	Brand Western Australia	Fresh, natural, free, spirited
Wales	In Wales you will find a passion for life – Hwyl	Lyrical, sincere, confident, inviting, down to earth, warm
Rotorua	Feel the spirit Manaakitanga	Cultural diversity, stunning natural environment, awe-inspiring earth forces, sense of adventure, people, progressive community

THE MARKETING ROLE FOR NTOS: THE PROCESS

Figure 18.1 illustrates the marketing process for NTOs (on the left of the diagram), side by side with the same process for individual businesses in the travel and tourism industry (on the right). The figure reveals both the similarities in marketing and the important differences that exist. Readers may wish to refer back to Fig. 2.1 in Chapter 2 with which Fig. 18.1 is fully compatible. The main difference occurs at the budget-decision stage where NTOs have the choice of apportioning funds between the two routes shown as direct control of the promotional mix on the left and marketing facilitation in the middle of the diagram. Facilitation forms the important bridge between NTO and the component sectors of the industry, while the promotion strategy reflects the more traditional approach to destination marketing.

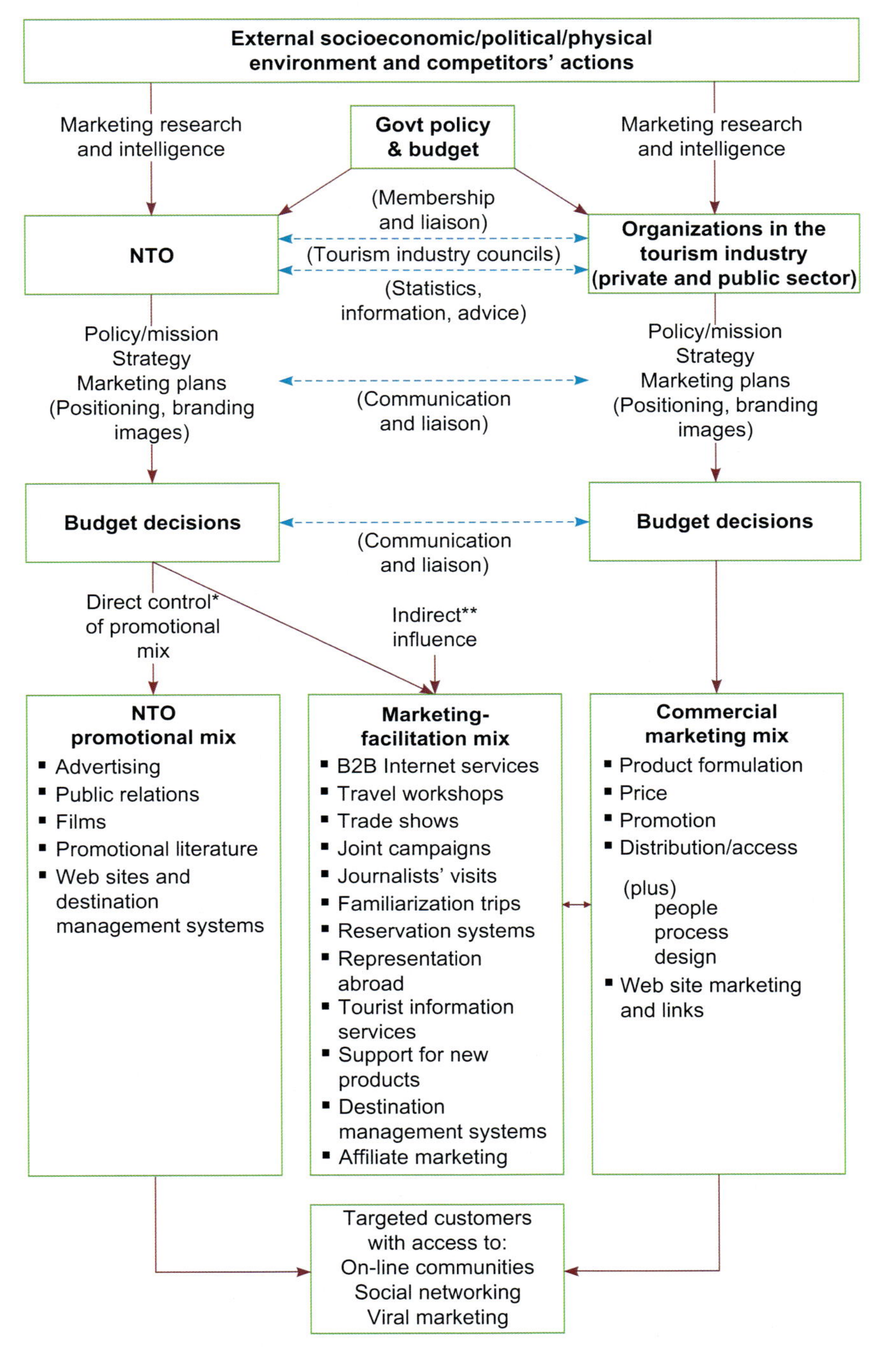

FIGURE 18.1 The destination marketing process for NTOs

The important liaison and co-ordination linkages between NTO and private sector partners are shown in the diagram at the policy level, at the budget decision level (industry financial participation in NTO expenditure and vice versa) and between marketing facilitation and the individual marketing decisions of businesses in the tourism industry. Each of the main stages in Fig. 18.1 is discussed briefly below, followed by a more detailed explanation of the less familiar methods of marketing facilitation.

Researching the external business environment

As in all marketing, the process begins with researching current and potential customers and the external environment. Only a few larger operators, such as airlines and hotel chains, will have the resources to undertake their own large-scale marketing research, especially into international markets. National tourism organizations have a unique role to play, therefore, in gathering and communicating market analysis and trend data, not only for their own marketing purposes but also for the tourism industry as a whole. Most NTOs publish research facts, but few appear to perform the task in a way that is easily accessible and understandable to the majority of smaller businesses. Provision of usable market information is the most important single basis for effective facilitation. Failure to communicate data effectively means that the most potentially valuable method of influencing the decisions of suppliers is lost.

Government policy and tourism strategy

Where governments provide the bulk of an NTO's funding, marketing objectives are naturally required to serve government policy. Most governments do not normally go into tourism marketing objectives in any detail, but lay down the broader strategic goals that NTOs are expected to pursue. These goals, in principle, are much the same all over the world, requiring that tourism revenue should generate employment and foreign exchange earnings in accordance with national economic policy and environmental objectives. Government policies relevant to tourism marketing strategy may be summarized as:

- To generate increased tourism revenue.
- To channel demand by season and by area of the country.
- To protect consumers' interests and enhance the quality of the product and the destination environment.
- To secure more sustainable development in the travel and tourism sector.

The first two of these policies tend to be common to most countries. The second two, discussed later under facilitation, are less well developed.

The representation of the private sector and other organizations in various committees and boards of many NTOs is also a common feature of NTO operations. It is intended to create a productive dialogue between the main organizations in the travel and tourism industry and the direction of government and NTO policy. Marketing strategy is an important aspect of this dialogue and the liaison stages are noted in Fig. 18.1.

MINI CASE 18.2: THE DEVOLUTION OF TOURISM IN ENGLAND

Although the outbreak of Foot and Mouth Disease (FMD) in spring 2001 in the UK and the tragic events of 9/11 in New York were landmark events in shaping tourism in England, political devolution represented an even greater influence when the strategic responsibility for regional tourism was devolved by Government to England's nine Regional Development Agencies (RDAs) responsible for the funding, delivery, management and responsibility for economic performance across all the sectors in their regions. Since 2003, the RDAs have become an integral element of the delivery of domestic tourism and are today in the process of either developing or implementing their regional sustainable tourism strategies. Interestingly, there is no explicit agenda or co-ordination for regional tourism strategy and the regional delivery of tourism being adopted by the RDAs. It is thus possible that each of the region's designated DMOs will be different in scale, scope and level of maturity in that each will reflect their own regional or sub-regional agenda. This applies particularly to the areas of activity that each of the DMOs decides to take on board, their level and source(s) of funding, and their overall engagement with the wider regional agenda.

In a study conducted by Fyall et al. (2007) a number of generic findings were identified with regard to the emergence and development of destination management arrangements in England. First it was recognized that each destination operates in a unique wider environmental and political context and thus no blueprint DMO structure exists for the generic management of destinations and many destinations continue to face considerable pressure on both capital and revenue budgets. In addition, it was found that large capital funds are more likely to be available when tourism is more closely allied to wider regeneration programmes. In view of both internal and external pressures, many DMOs are adopting a more explicit commercial focus while many of the arrangements which are being set up appear to work less well in mature destinations. Where new arrangements were advocated, considerable trust is required from the sector at large to engage more fully while key stakeholders are an essential ingredient for wider destination success. For many destinations a period of evolutionary change was deemed to be more preferable while a positive and genuine approach to partnership working is necessary among all components of the destination as is the ability to continually reinvent within a constant cycle of change. Despite much talk and possible desire for greater involvement in, leadership of, and financial contribution to DMOs by the private sector, local authorities remain essential players in maintaining the impartiality of new destination management arrangements. A holistic view of the management of local destinations, which only DMOs working with local authorities as key players in the visitor economy can provide, is considered paramount for the future successful management of destinations.

Source: Based on Fyall et al. (2007).

Courtesy of Adrain Cox.

Marketing planning

As noted earlier, the limitations of a DMO's budget focus attention on selecting priorities and turning these into strategies and specific targets for products and segments – to be achieved through facilitation and/or promotional campaigns. The marketing planning process for an NTO is no different in principle from any other marketing organization; the techniques are the same. Unfortunately, however, long experience confirms that the travel and tourism industry in most countries is still notorious for the paucity of its research information base compared with what is commonly available for most other manufacturing and service industries. It is a criticism of most NTOs that they have been willing to spend millions of dollars on advertising campaigns and representation at international trade fairs, while expenditure on basic marketing research into visitor interests, behaviour and attitudes, necessary to achieve the most effective use of the money, has been very limited.

Marketing objectives and targets

The most important output of the marketing planning process for a DMO is identification of market/product strategies to match market trends and the product

Product types (destination) ↓ / Market areas (visitor origin) →	*Country A* *Segments 1, 2 and 3*	*Country B* *Segments 4 and 5*	*Country C* *Segment 6*	*Country D* *Segments 7 and 8*	Other market areas/ segments → *Segments 9+*
Resort-based holidays	volume: value: impact	volume: value: impact	volume: value: impact	volume: value: impact	volume: value: impact
Touring holidays by car					
City short break holidays					
Business and conferences					
Other products ↓					

Notes:

1 A developed destination country with domestic tourism and visits from several countries of origin may identify and target as many as fifty or more relevant segments.

2 The products in the matrix are those identified by marketing research, or by analysis of supply. A developed destination country may easily identify over twenty-five principal products that it seeks to promote or facilitate, allowing for area and seasonal variations.

3 Where research is available, it will obviously be used to complete the cells of the matrix; where it is not, the matrix model may still be useful as a tool for summarizing managers' judgements. The process of completing the model may also serve to identify aspects of products and markets requiring new,or additional market research.

FIGURE 18.2 A market/product matrix model for NTO/DMO marketing planning

resource base and the selection of specific, broadly quantified targets for allocating marketing budgets. Figure 18.2 sets out in a format that can be adapted for use in any destination, a simplified model of a market/product planning matrix comprising a number of cells, each of which represents the volume and value of target segments and products.

Deciding which segments and products should be included in the matrix is determined by marketing analysis and planning in collaboration with commercial organizations in travel and tourism. Research (and judgement) is used to estimate the volume and revenue figures to be inserted. The matrix may be used for historic data or as a framework for forecasting. With appropriate supporting statements, a simple model of this type may also play a useful part in summarizing strategy and communicating it to the tourism industry.

Budget decisions

Politicians decide the amount of money that NTOs receive. Whatever the budget, marketing tasks must relate to objectives and the cost of undertaking specified tasks should act as a primary constraint on the choice of objectives. Exactly the same principles apply to DMOs in apportioning budgets between promotional and/or facilitation tasks. Very few countries, however, have successfully developed a systematic method of relating the size of budget required for the achievement of specific objectives. Precedent (what was done last year) and broad comparisons with other precedent-based budgets for public expenditure are still the general rule in budget allocation for NTOs, adjusted – more or less – by annual levels of inflation in a country's economy. Research-based specification of tasks is the only logical basis for budget allocation and for the newer public sector disciplines of targeting, performance monitoring and evaluation.

Internet developments

Clearly, one of the primary concerns when setting budgets is the amount to be allocated to web sites and related ICT developments. As discussed in Chapter 14, the Internet has revolutionized the way in which consumers are able to plan, purchase and 'experience' destinations. For many destinations, Internet-based marketing activity is now an integral component of the work of DMOs – not only for communicating with customers but for the coordination of all components of the destination 'product'. For example, Visitlondon via visitlondon.com is one of many thousands of destinations around the world that provides information and accepts bookings as well as uses the web as a platform to promote policies, shares destination-specific trend and forecasts information. The web can also be used as a vehicle to increase visitor spend via merchandising and to build relationships with customers once they have departed. All of this is possible via the use of increasingly sophisticated Destination Management Systems (DMSs), as evidenced in Chapter 13 and the New Zealand Case Study in Part Six, with more and more destinations taking advantage of database marketing techniques in order to identify and target profitable market niches and e-mail prospective visitors. Increasingly DMSs are being employed by national and regional tourism bodies to underpin the management of DMOs, as well as for the coordination of local suppliers at the destination level. They are also integral to the future success of tourism small businesses that lack the capital and expertise to undertake a comprehensive marketing strategy and who more often than not rely on destination authorities and intermediaries for the wider promotion and coordination of their products.

One particular benefit of the new technologies available to destinations is in their ability to assist users to search and select individual tourism products so that visitors are now able to create their own 'personalised' destination experience. Destination Management Systems are the interfaces between destination tourism enterprises and the outside world. In some instances, such as Australia for example, DMSs have been used for integrating the entire supply at the destination. With the first launch of a web site back in 1996, the focus of the Australian Tourism Commission (ATC) was on promoting the tourist resource in its entirety. The ATC's consumer web site targeted the international travel market and provided international visitors with ready access to information that was designed to 'motivate' them to select Australia as their chosen destination. Based on a dynamic platform, branded and specifically targeted multilingual content was sought to drive conversion form broad interest to actual bookings.

MARKETING FACILITATION STRATEGIES FOR AN NTO

Because marketing facilitation is so important we outline below 12 of the most important facilitation processes used by NTOs around the world.

Flow of research data and marketing intelligence

By providing a regular, user-friendly flow of research data to large and small businesses in the tourism industry, through the analysis of statistics, short reports on market trends and help with research enquiries, an NTO may make valuable inputs to the marketing planning processes of individual businesses in all sectors. Co-operative and syndicated research surveys also provide cost-effective ways in which an NTO can stimulate the flow of relevant data. The regular distribution of research summaries is a practical way of developing contacts with the industry and exercising influence over marketing strategy at the same time. The development of B2B web sites and intranets for this purpose is now the logical and most cost-effective way to provide access. For example, the Finnish Tourism Board (FTB) 'infostructure' provides an excellent example of ICT usage for strategic purposes by the public sector as it has developed integrated systems to support its operations. The FTB aims for all its information to be accessible via the Internet for its employees (intranet), partners (extranet) and the general public (Internet). The wider system includes three individual systems, namely the: *Market Information System* which offers a data management and distribution system for use internally within the organization and its offices internationally; *RELIS*, the Research, Library and Information Service, which provides the backbone of the national travel research and product documentation that connects the travel industry to research and education organizations; and *PROMIS*, the national database of Finnish travel products and services available for public use.

Representation in markets of origin

By establishing a network of offices in foreign countries generating the bulk of its international visitor flows, an NTO can create and maintain vital travel trade contacts while acting also as a point of information and distribution for the destination's range of tourism products. The network of offices may also generate flows of vital marketing intelligence to be fed into the NTO's information system and used in marketing planning. In theory it is now possible to replace much of the 'representation' role of NTOs by web sites via the operation of a 'virtual tourist office' but in practice much will depend on individual functions and the acceptance by actual users that destination 'customer service' operators may be located outside the markets of origin. To date, although the fully 'virtual' DMO does not exist, the scope for utilizing the Internet for many of the traditional information, contact and distribution functions is clearly an attractive and cost saving route to develop to the extent that many DMOs have already begun to 'downsize' and 'outsource' their offices using the technology available.

Organization of workshops and trade shows

For over five decades NTOs have been making arrangements whereby groups of suppliers of tourist products may meet with groups of prospective buyers, such as tour operators, travel agents and other travel organizers, at relatively low cost. Either in the market of origin or at the destination, individual hoteliers, attractions, suppliers of conference facilities or businesses offering youth products can make contact and discuss business in one or two days of intensive meetings. By selecting the theme of workshops, such as self-catering, coach tours or attractions, issuing the invitations and possibly subsidizing the costs of accommodation and travel, an NTO can make a powerful contribution to its objectives. It may, of course, use the workshops as an opportunity to gain marketing intelligence as well as to convey information and other messages designed to promote its aims. There will always be needs for 'pressing the flesh' in personal meetings but much of what occurs at workshops and trade shows can now be done more easily, quickly and more cost-effectively using dedicated web sites, video-conferencing and e-mail. Destinations can also increasingly use virtual environments such as Second Life and Flash demonstrations to explain the destination. See for example http://www.tourisme-montreal.org/ which uses Flash Technology to demonstrate the destination to potential visitors.

Familiarization trips

By arranging for parties of selected foreign travel agents, journalists and tour operators to visit the destination and sample the products available, NTOs can influence the effectiveness with which the travel trade in markets of origin acts in support of the destination and its products. Such trips are part of the sales-promotion process discussed in Chapter 16; they are also a method of improving the advice and information available to customers at key retail outlets and gaining better display space at points of sale. The trips also serve an important PR role and offer many opportunities for communicating key messages to influential people in distribution and media channels. Although web sites cannot replace the actual experience they can back up such trips with much improved multimedia information and extend the reach to a second tier of those who cannot gain a place on the trips available as can they demonstrate the 'experience' and assist the planning of trips.

Travel trade manuals

With a wide variety of products provided by hundreds of businesses in many destinations, it is impossible for all foreign travel agents and tour operators to be serviced individually by an NTO. Traditionally NTOs produce one or more printed trade manuals, which serve as references and guides for use by the travel trade. A conference users' manual, for example, lists the details of all conference facilities, probably classified by area, particular facilities available, prices – including commission available – and how to make bookings. A different trade manual would be required for activity holidays and so on. For smaller businesses such manuals provide lines of access to foreign markets at low cost. Multimedia information on B2B web sites and intranets can now replace traditional manuals and provide much better and more up-to-date information as well as direct on line contact. There are also developments in consumer-to-consumer (C2C) and Web 2.0 technologies that enable and encourage consumers to engage with each other and actively avoid the traditional channels and modes of influence. The Tripadvisor Forum is an ideal example of this.

Support with literature production and distribution

Most NTOs sell advertising space in the range of printed brochures that they promote and distribute internationally as they now sell space on their respective web sites. In the case of printed brochures, the object is to provide cost-effective advertising and distribution opportunities, especially for smaller businesses, and many brochures produce a surplus of revenue over costs. National tourism organizations may also offer direct-mail distribution services for tourist industry printed material or produce *brochure shells* for use by small businesses. These are normally full-colour leaflets containing themed photography and areas of blank space that may be overprinted by a businesses logo and product messages. Low cost desktop publishing software for leaflets and small brochures now offer a better alternative to many small businesses. Although the Internet has taken over much of this activity, in many destinations that appeal to relatively traditional, and often older people, print media remains an important channel for marketing communications and is often used to follow up web site enquiries.

Participation in joint marketing schemes or ventures

Joint schemes or joint ventures are specific marketing projects that an NTO may be willing to support on a joint participation basis of, say, $100 for every $300 contributed by a partner(s). Participation in such schemes normally requires formal application procedures and criteria are applied, e.g. whether or not the products concerned are likely to proceed without some financial support for their marketing or whether they contribute to stated national marketing objectives. Equally important, participants in an adopted scheme may draw on the professional expertise of an NTO's marketing department and the other facilities available for production of print, overseas representation, research advice and so on.

By managing the criteria for selection an NTO can use joint schemes to influence operators in the tourism industry along lines indicated in its strategic planning process. By monitoring the performance of such schemes it also develops its research knowledge of particular products, segments and markets. Dedicated B2B web sites, developed in conjunction with DMSs and related customer databases are now part of the communication process and also the primary means of delivering the expertise and linking a business to other DMO facilities.

Information and reservation systems

Using CRS technology linked to a DMS, NTOs can assist small businesses in their tourism industry to distribute their product offers and achieve bookings. Such systems were traditionally very limited in reach, managed by costly telephones and faxes and were often designed to facilitate commissionable bookings by travel agents. Today, multi-channel tourism distribution strategies are essential in order to reach different market segments and visitors who are at different stages of the customer buying experience (Buhalis, 2003). Tiscover is an appropriate example here in that it provides eTourism solutions to DMOs and tourism businesses throughout Europe and Southern Africa. With its headquarters in Austria, with wholly-owned subsidiaries in Germany, Italy and the United Kingdom, Tiscover is a key market player globally and has over 2000 DMO clients world wide (Karcher and Alford, 2008). The three key elements to the Tiscover offer are: DMS solutions, web solutions and eMarketing activity. In addition its multi-channel distribution strategy enables DMOs and accommodation businesses to reach channels that are otherwise unavailable (see Fig. 18.3).

www.tiscover.com

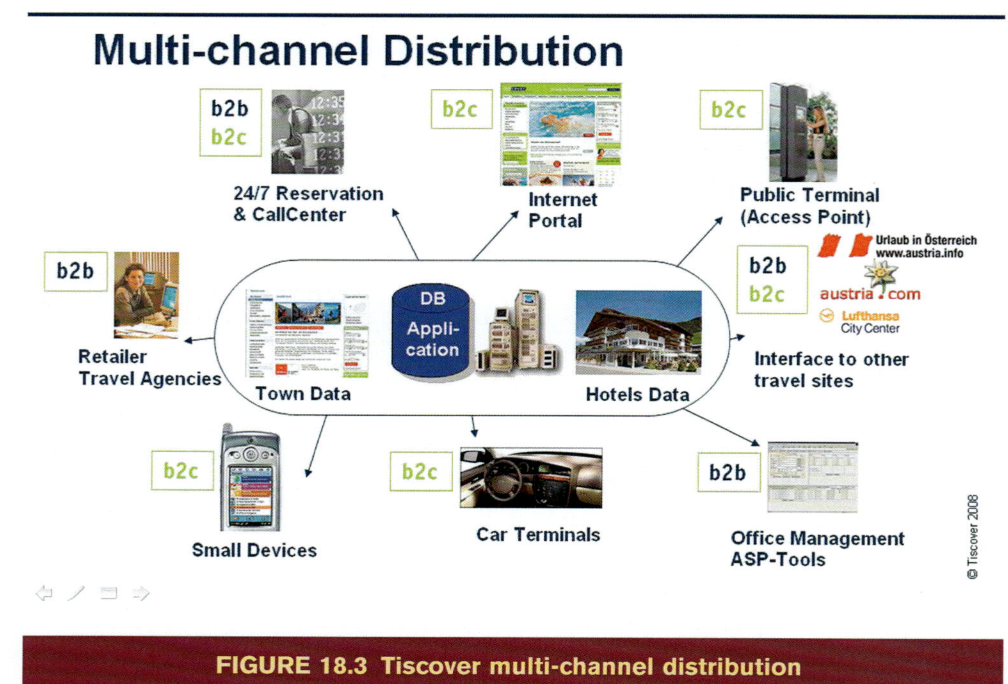

FIGURE 18.3 Tiscover multi-channel distribution

Support for new products

Related to joint marketing schemes, selective proactive marketing support, using criteria established through marketing planning, can be targeted by NTOs to assist innovative new products to emerge and establish themselves in their markets in the initial two to three years after their launch. Smaller businesses are usually unable to afford the start-up costs of national and international marketing; they need access to some form of 'pump priming' as this form of support is often called. It is a well-established technique by which NTOs may contribute to their long-term policy goals. This form of assistance overlaps with the investment and development support programmes that many NTOs also operate, increasingly using marketing orientated criteria. Market access for new products via a DMS database and gateway provide the lowest cost means for implementing this form of marketing support while destination information services and map systems can help guide visitors to the product location.

Trade consortia

Another interesting illustration of the facilitation role for NTOs exists in the support they may offer to private sector consortia of small businesses, formed for the purposes of more efficient marketing. Aided by NTO marketing expertise and some funding support for promotional activities, groups of hire-boat owners, museums, caravan parks, hotels and other facilities may be assisted. As with joint marketing schemes and support for new products, a B2B Web site offers the most cost-effective means of communication for members and a DMO Web site offers the most cost-effective means for communication and distribution to visitors.

Consumer assistance and protection

Marketing for service products always reflects concern for customer satisfaction with the service delivery. For DMOs this task includes information services provided to enable visitors to become aware of and gain access to the full range of available products, about which many would otherwise have no knowledge. By creating and subsidizing a network of visitor information centers in destination areas an NTO can extend its influence and communicate messages direct to a far wider 'audience' of its visitors than it can hope to reach with available budgets through promotional efforts in countries of origin. An NTO may not influence more than say one in ten visitors at most in their country of origin but it may reach two out of three at visitor centres. By their choice of emphasis in the information provided, NTOs can exert considerable promotional influence over visitor movement in destinations and their expenditure patterns. Market research indicates that many visitors to tourism destinations, especially foreign and first-time visitors are open to suggestion and persuasion from all sources of information, especially those having the official endorsement and authority of an NTO and its regional bodies.

Associated with this concern for customer satisfaction are forms of consumer protection, such as the requirement that tourism prices should be clearly notified and the operation of tourism complaint procedures, supplemented in some countries with tourism police. Finally, there is a growing concern in many countries to protect and enhance the quality of tourism products through schemes of quality assurance, such as classification and grading of accommodation and recognition of environmental good practice. Not normally considered a part of NTO marketing, such schemes make no sense unless they are firmly marketing-led and designed around the identified needs of the customers an NTO seeks to promote.

A typical example is *Qualmark New Zealand Limited*, New Zealand tourism's official quality agency. It was established by the Tourist Board, now Tourism New Zealand, and the New Zealand Automobile Association back in 1994 to provide a classification and grading system for the country's hotel, motel and holiday park accommodation (www.qualmark.co.nz). It is now integral to the New Zealand tourism strategy in helping to achieve the industry's goal to enhance the country's reputation as a world-class visitor destination. Usually negotiated with private sector partners, once quality standards have been agreed, DMOs may limit inclusion in their brochures and display in tourism information centres to operators who comply. In this context facilitation becomes a quality control tool for marketing purposes. Here, too, the roles already defined for DMSs and DMO Web sites can be adapted to recognize and support the quality control process and communication to customers.

General advisory services for the industry

Although the provision of advice to businesses is traditionally a time-consuming process that could never reach more than a fraction of the tourism industry, access to information can make a very important contribution to the marketing decisions of suppliers with limited market contacts and budgets too small to commit more than a minimum sum to market research. There are many ways in which expensive person-to-person advice can be extended. An NTO may, for example, organize seminars and conferences on marketing topics and disseminate the contributions as widely as possible through its publications. The development of interactive B2B web sites offers the most cost-effective means of providing advice, with appropriate back up systems for dealing with more detailed enquires and for charging for the services provided. Provision of marketing research data via dedicated Web sites is just one of the ways that advisory services are being streamlined and improved.

CHAPTER SUMMARY

This chapter:

- Explains the scope and extent of NTO marketing in which the principles are the same around the world.
- Discusses three principal reasons why NTOs or DMOs, especially in developed destination countries, are not likely to achieve more than an important but marginal influence over total tourism volume and expenditure.
- Outlines two levels of destination marketing, distinguishing between the role of NTOs and the suppliers of particular products. The strategic choices facing NTOs in deciding how best to deploy their limited budgets are discussed in some detail.
- Outlines the stages in the marketing process for NTOs, paying particular attention to the facilitation strategy. Facilitation is defined as the unique marketing role for an NTO – unique in the sense that if the NTO does not fulfil it, it is unlikely that obviously important tasks will be undertaken at all. Twelve facilitation tasks are described; they serve to co-ordinate the tourism industry as a whole, recognizing and strengthening industry linkages in the products that destinations provide, and devising themes and images to integrate promotional efforts. By its nature, facilitation is task orientated and, in terms of securing value for money from promotional expenditure, it is usually easier to prove success through this strategy than through expenditure on image campaigns. The links between marketing and product formulation that emerge naturally through the facilitation process help to ensure that tourism development in a country is market led.

The principles set out in this chapter are broadly applicable to regional and sub-regional DMOs, which have much the same co-ordinating role and strategic choices in using their resources as NTOs do. Regional and sub-regional DMOs work mainly on domestic tourism and deal with smaller, mainly local operators, but they are in many ways microcosms of their larger national organizations. They are equally able to use and benefit from the use of the latest Internet technology. In particular they can profit from the destination management databases that provide the ideal Internet platform for small businesses.

QUESTIONS TO CONSIDER

1. To what extent are NTOs still valid in the Internet-age?
2. How may the responsibilities and roles of NTOs vary between country destinations in the developing and developed world?
3. Although NTOs and regional tourism bodies have been around for decades, many new DMOs are being established around the world. What are some of the reasons underpinning this growth?

4. Under what circumstances might the private sector take the lead role in DMOs at national, regional, state or local level?
5. Identify and discuss some of the challenges of bringing public and private sector organizations together within a regional DMO.

REFERENCES AND FURTHER READING

Beirman, D. (2003). *Restoring tourism destinations in crisis: a strategic marketing approach*. Oxford: CABI Publishing.

Bennett, O. (1999). Destination marketing into the next century, *Journal of Vacation Marketing*, **6**(1), pp. 48–54.

Buhalis, D. (2000). Marketing the competitive destination of the future, *Tourism Management*, **21**(1), pp. 97–116.

Buhalis, D. (2003). *eTourism: information technology for strategic tourism management*. London: Pearson.

Buhalis, D. (2006). eTourism: encyclopedia of digital government, Vol. II. USA: Idea Group Publishing.

Carlsen, J.C. and Hughes, M. (2007). Tourism market recovery in the Maldives after the 2004 Indian Ocean Tsunami, *Journal of Travel & Tourism Marketing*, **23**(2/3/4), pp. 139–149.

Davidson, R. and Maitland, R. (1997). *Tourism destinations*. London: Hodder & Stoughton.

Fyall, A., Callod, C. and Edwards, B. (2003). Relationship marketing: the challenge for destinations, *Annals of Tourism Research*, **30**(3), pp. 644–659.

Fyall, A., Fletcher, J. and Spyriadis, A. (September 2007). Diversity, devolution and disorder: the management of destinations in England. *Advances in Tourism Marketing Conference, Destination and Event Marketing: Managing Networks, Valencia, Spain, 10–12*.

Fyall, A., Garrod, B. and Tosun, C. (2006). Destination marketing: a framework for future research. In: *Progress in tourism marketing* (Ed. by Kozak, M., Andreu, L.). Oxford: Elsevier. pp. 75–86

Karcher, K. and Alford, P. (2008). Tiscover. In: *eTourism case studies* (Ed. by Egger, R., Buhalis, D.). Oxford: Butterworth-Heinemann.

King, J. (2002). Destination marketing organisations: connecting the experience rather than promoting the place, *Journal of Vacation Marketing*, **8**(2), pp. 105–108.

Morgan, N., Pritchard, A. and Pride, R. (eds) (2002). Destination branding: creating the unique destination proposition. Oxford: Butterworth Heinemann.

Pike, S. (2004). *Destination marketing organisations*. Oxford: Elsevier.

Reid, L.J., Smith, S.L.J. and McCloskey (2008). The effectiveness of regional marketing alliances: a case study of the Atlantic Canada Tourism Partnership 2000–2006, *Tourism Management*, **29**(3), pp. 581–593.

Ritchie, J.R.B. and Crouch, G.I. (2003). *The competitive destination: a sustainable tourism perspective*. Oxford: CABI.

Sheldon, P. (1993). Destination information systems, *Annals of Tourism Research*, **20**(4), pp. 633–649.

UNWTO (2003). *Evaluating NTO marketing activities*. Madrid: United Nations World Tourism Organization.

Vanhove, N. (2006). A comparative analysis of competition models for tourism destinations. In: *Progress in tourism marketing* (Ed. by Kozak, M., Andreu, L.). Oxford: Elsevier, pp. 101–114

Jungle Hotel, Madagascar Rainforest - "For many visitors, the accommodation unit itself represents the core appeal to a destination with the increasing need for the search for more 'authentic' experiences an opportunity for many emerging destinations"

CHAPTER 19

Marketing accommodation

"Simplicity is the key to future hotel success"

Chris Blackwell, Island Outpost Hotels (2008).

With the obvious exception of same-day visits from home, all other forms of tourism involve overnight accommodation. Accommodation is, therefore, one of the five integral components of the travel and tourism product defined in Chapter 7. The many different forms of accommodation and the ways in which they are marketed have a massive influence on visitor choices, behaviour and the types of product they buy.

As with transport, the early development of accommodation for travellers was not concerned with leisure but with the needs of commerce and industry and the administration of countries and empires. The development of accommodation for travellers has always been inextricably associated with the growing and changing needs of transport systems. Inns and taverns and, later, the forerunners of modern hotels were located logically in cities and ports and along the routes that linked them, for much the same reasons that many modern hotels are located along motorways and at airports.

Chapter 20 notes that transport systems are still vitally concerned with non-tourism services, such as journeys to work and the carriage of goods. Accommodation services also have important dimensions unconnected with travel and tourism, such as institutional and welfare provisions in sectors as diverse as schools, prisons, hospitals, the armed services and the care of the elderly. In all these other areas of hospitality the influence of marketing is being felt but this chapter is, of course, only concerned with tourism products. Thus, when considering the meaning of marketing for the accommodation sector, it must be recognized that tourism contributes only part of total turnover. Many hotels, depending obviously on their locations, also provide food, drinks and meeting facilities for residents in their surrounding local communities.

Most national and international hotel groups are still orientated primarily to the needs of business travellers and the expenditure they generate. In the last half of a century, however, in the sunshine resorts of the USA, Europe and the Pacific area, thousands of resort hotels have been built specifically to cater the needs of the leisure market. Similar developments in timeshare resorts also owe their origins to leisure travel. In all such cases developments have exploited the market potential made possible by increasing disposable income in developed countries and modern transport systems. Over the last decade the same development process has been taking place in India and China for exactly the same reasons.

After studying this chapter you should be able to understand:

- The constituent parts of the serviced and non-serviced sectors of accommodation and their role in the tourism product.
- Accommodation products as service 'experiences' and the business characteristics common to all forms of commercial accommodation operations.
- The range of marketing tasks utilized by accommodation suppliers and the implications for the size of marketing budgets in the sector where actual expenditure on marketing is very much greater than the received wisdom in the sector.

DEFINING TOURIST ACCOMMODATION

For the purposes of this chapter, tourist accommodation is deemed to include all establishments offering overnight accommodation on a commercial or 'quasi-commercial' basis to all categories of visitor. The definition does not cover the use of privately-owned accommodation for weekends and holidays, such as second homes, caravans, chalets, boats and wholly-owned apartments in condominiums – unless they are commercially rented through a marketing agency.

'Quasi-commercial' refers to the many tourist accommodation products outside the commercial sector, for which a charge is made to contribute to costs (even if a subsidy is involved). Examples are the British Youth Hostels Association (YHA), a membership organization that traditionally provided a national network of hostels in the UK, mostly for young people willing to use inexpensive and sometimes shared accommodation. The YHA is a non-profit-making body but, in the context of its corporate objectives, it operates increasingly on commercial principles to secure the revenue needed for strategic refurbishment and development programmes that are taking it into market sectors no longer targeted only at youth and low cost. Other forms of quasi-commercial accommodation products may be found in colleges and universities, many of which now market their accommodation capacity for conferences and for holiday at times when students are not in residence. Such operations are increasingly required not only to cover their direct operating costs but also to make a contribution towards the overhead costs of the providing institution.

Serviced and non-serviced accommodation

An important distinction in accommodation for visitors is the split between serviced and non-serviced types. Serviced means that staffs are available on the premises to provide some services such as cleaning, meals and bars and room service. The availability of such services, even if they are not in fact used, is included in the price charged. Non-serviced means that the sleeping accommodation is provided furnished on a rental basis, normally for a unit comprising several beds, such as a cottage, an apartment or caravan. While services for the provision of meals, bars and shops may be available on site on a separate commercial basis, as in a holiday village, they are not included in the price charged for the accommodation.

The serviced sector ranges from first-class and luxury hotels providing full service on a twenty-four hours a day basis at relatively high cost, all the way down to homely bed and breakfast establishments, which may only operate informally for a few weeks in the year. The non-serviced sector, which is known in Britain under the unattractive label of 'self-catering accommodation', comprises a wide range of different units, including villas, apartments, chalets, cottages and caravans. These units are rented on a fully furnished and equipped basis but with no personal services included in the published price. Some of these new units, e.g. in converted historic buildings, may be furnished with antiques and may cost more per person night than four-star serviced accommodation. The bulk of self-catering units, however, still cater for a budget-priced market and the cost per person night is very much less than could be obtained in the serviced sector.

There are so many variations of serviced and non-serviced accommodation products that the distinction is often blurred in practice, although it remains useful for the purposes of analysis and discussion of marketing implications. Styles and types of accommodation also vary according to the traditions of different countries. The accommodation in many holiday villages and timeshare resorts is marketed as 'self-catering' units, for example, but within the village resort there are often extensive provisions of bars, restaurants, coffee shops and a wide range of other services available for purchase, although not paid for in the initial holiday price. In these circumstances the real difference between serviced and non-serviced accommodation appears increasingly irrelevant. In the customer's perception and from a marketing standpoint, however, the difference is clear. The endeavour by accommodation interests and tour operators to keep down published holiday prices explains much of the growth in non-serviced tourist accommodation in recent years.

Using the serviced/non-serviced split, discussed above, the types of accommodation referred to in this chapter are summarized in Fig. 19.1. The boxes in the diagram divide each of the two accommodation sectors by destination and by routes because this fundamentally influences the nature of the accommodation

Sector / Market segment	*Serviced sector*		*Non-serviced sector (self-catering)*	
	At Destinations	On Routes	At Destination	On Routes
Business and other non-leisure	City/town hotels (Monday–Friday) Budget hotels Resort hotels for conferences, exhibitions Educational establishments	Budget hotels Motels Inns Airport hotels	Apartments	Not applicable
Leisure and holiday	Resort hotels Guesthouse/pensions Farmhouses City/town hotels (Friday–Sunday) Budget hotels Some educational establishments	Budget hotels Motels Bed and breakfast Inns	Apart hotels Condominia/timeshare Holiday villages Holiday centres/camps Caravan/chalet parks Gîtes Cottages Villas Apartments/flats Some motels	Touring pitches for caravans, tents, recreation vehicles YHA Some motels

FIGURE 19.1 Principal serviced and non-serviced types of accommodation used in tourism, by market-segment

products that are offered and the type of marketing required. It further distinguishes segments of users for business and other non-leisure purposes. Non-leisure purposes include stays away from home on family business such as school visits, funerals and weddings, or stays in an area while seeking a new house or apartment, and so on.

The role of accommodation in the overall tourism product

For business and other non-leisure visits, it is obvious that accommodation is not normally a part of the trip motivation or part of the destination's attraction. Rooms, serviced or other wise, provide a necessary facility that makes it possible, convenient and comfortable to engage in the primary reason for the travel. In marketing terms, locational convenience, high standards of comfort and efficiency and value for money are, therefore, the primary features or core product to be communicated. Within their price band, the extent to which the primary elements are perceived to be delivered is the basis for customer choice. Accommodation plays an important but functional role.

For holiday and leisure purposes, however, accommodation plays a very different role in the tourism product. While a destination's attractions are likely to remain the dominant motivation for most visitors, destination choices are also influenced by perceptions and expectations of the accommodation available. Sometimes, as with repeat trips to stay at the same hotel or caravan park, the image and quality of the accommodation may be strong enough to make it a primary rather than a secondary aspect of destination choice. More often, though, especially for packaged tours, the destination's appeal is the more important element in motivation and choice of destination.

Leisure visitors are also likely to spend many hours of a stay in their accommodation, especially if the weather is poor. Serviced or non-serviced, their trip and destination enjoyment will be highly geared to perceived value provided and satisfaction experienced with the bedrooms, bathrooms, food and beverage outlets and any other rooms and facilities such as swimming pools and health clubs that may be provided. This holds good in relative terms for tented pitches in camping sites as well as for bedrooms in five-star resort hotels.

In other words, for leisure purposes, accommodation is integrally related to the attractions of a destination as well as being part of the facilities. While transport in the twenty-first century has lost its former appeal as part of the attractions of a visit, it appears probable that accommodation is moving in the opposite direction and enhancing its appeal. Current marketing trends to shorter stays suggest that destination and accommodation marketing are likely to come even closer together in a logical partnership of mutual interests; something that is in evidence every weekend across the UK where destinations and hotel chains are constantly offering co-branded promotional campaigns to boost occupancy which, in turn, increases overall yield for the destination.

THE ACCOMMODATION PRODUCT AS A SERVICE EXPERIENCE

It is worth restating that accommodation products of all types are perceived by customers as 'experiences'. The experience is organized and orchestrated to meet the identified needs and benefits sought by customer segments, as described in

Chapters 7 and 8, and it comprises a series of service operations. For larger organizations, these operations correspond with operating departments, of which the most important are:

- *Booking services* – handling enquiries and bookings, including Internet, telephone, mail and reservation systems.
- *Reception/checkout services* – registering arrivals and departures, checking bookings and allocating rooms, possibly associated with support services, such as baggage handling – includes invoicing and settling accounts.
- *Rooms/site services* – delivering rooms or self-catering units cleaned, checked and ready to occupy.
- *Food and beverage* – (if provided) including restaurants, bars and coffee shops.
- *Other services* – (if provided) including room service, shops, leisure, entertainment and health facilities, secretarial, dry-cleaning and all other services.

As noted in Chapters 7 and 8, product experiences are complex. They are influenced by physical elements (such as buildings and provision of food and drink), sensual benefits (experienced through sight, sound, touch and smell, and conveyed by the quality of buildings and their furnishings) and psychological benefits experienced as mental states of well-being, status and satisfaction (as evidenced in Fig. 19.2).

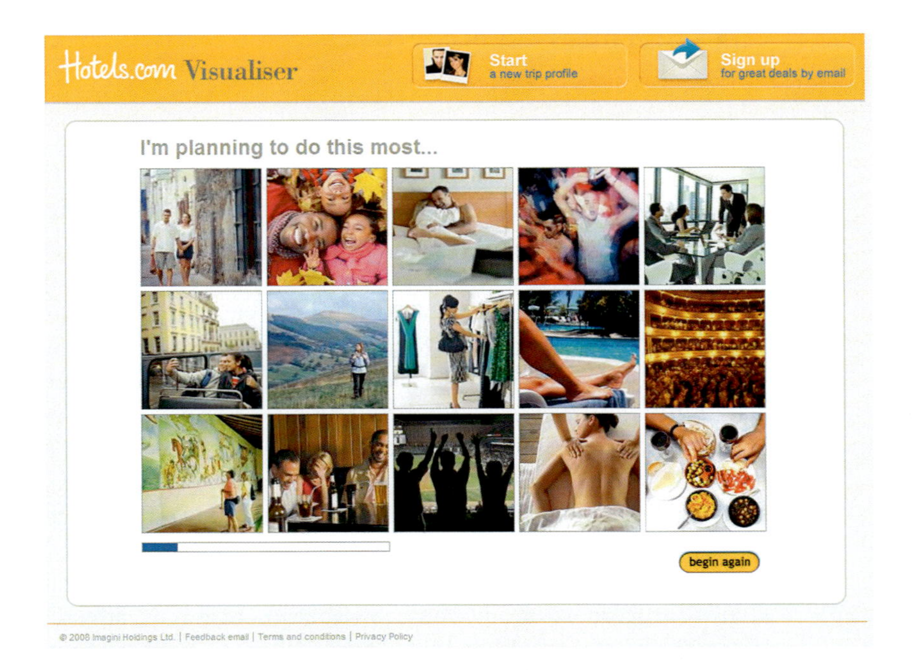

FIGURE 19.2 Source: www.hotels.com: Visualiser website.

For many hotels, it is very much the 'experience' that is being sold. This is evident by the launch of Visualiser in 2008 by Hotels.com that enables consumers to select hotels according to the experience and type of trip they seek. For resort visitors, the perceived benefits of the accommodation product are likely to be closely associated with the benefits associated with the destination's attractions. In other words, a successful destination may provide a 'halo' effect that supports the available accommodation, while an unattractive destination experience will have the opposite effect.

In Chapter 7 a weekend break in a hotel is used to illustrate recommended product formulation methods for tourism, organized around an analysis of target customer segment's needs and benefits sought. The basic components of core formal and augmented products were described, and the roles of process, people and physical evidence or design are covered in Chapter 8. They are not repeated here although they are especially relevant to this chapter.

THE NATURE OF THE ACCOMMODATION BUSINESS

This section focuses on five particular characteristics of any accommodation business, serviced or non-serviced, which strongly influence the way in which marketing is conducted at the strategic and tactical level. Of particular relevance are:

- Choice of location.
- Existence of peaks and troughs in demand.
- Influence of room sales on profits.
- Focus on 'bookers', not occupancy levels.
- High fixed costs of operation.

Location

Location tends to dominate all accommodation operations. It initially determines the customer mix the business can achieve and, therefore, the overall direction of marketing strategy and tactics. Location is also a major influence on the profitability of an operation. Where feasibility studies are undertaken to investigate the value of alternative sites prior to investment in new facilities, the inherent demand potential for each location under investigation is always the primary consideration. Of course, once an accommodation unit is established, location of operations becomes fixed for the lifetime of the asset. Whereas airlines and tour operators can move their operations around the world to serve alternative destinations in response to changes in demand; hotels and holiday villages are an immovable fixture. They have to use skills in marketing to overcome any difficulties that may emerge after the initial location is determined.

Many of the problems faced in accommodation marketing are in fact difficulties stemming from external environment shifts that have affected the market potential of the locations in which they are established. Greater commitment to sales and marketing is the only short-run option for tackling impact on location of unforeseen shifts in the external business environment. Marketing cannot cure all problems, of course, and in some circumstances accommodation businesses have no choice but to operate at a loss for as long as their resources allow or until the market expands. The only alternative is to sell properties, which in a buyer's market, usually means a massive capital loss. Forced sales are a common phenomenon in the accommodation industry, especially smaller businesses with limited financial resources. Less obviously, the type and architectural style of accommodation buildings influence the places in which they are located. In vacation destinations certainly, the physical appearance of hotels, apartments and other accommodation buildings becomes part of the image as well as part of the physical environment of a destination.

Courtesy of Crispin Farbrother.

Business peaks and troughs

By weeks in the year and days in the week, nearly all forms of accommodation are vulnerable to highly variable demand patterns, just as transport operators are. The patterns reflect the nature of the market demand a location sustains. Thus hotels in many towns and cities in northern Europe can normally expect high occupancy from business travellers form Mondays to Thursdays, and the peak of their occupancy in the autumn and spring. Their business trade falls at weekends and in the July–August period. Most self-catering units by the seaside in Northern Europe can anticipate full demand for a period of little over 16 weeks, and many still close completely for around five months of the year. The existence of peaks and troughs in demand is certainly not unique to accommodation businesses but it is a common characteristic to which marketing managers are required to respond.

Marketing efforts cannot reverse the natural locational rhythms of demand but product development and campaigns can be targeted around both existing and new segments to lessen the impact and to generate increased business at the margin.

Profit is driven by room-night sales

Although the sales of room-nights, especially in the serviced hotels sector, seldom contribute more than around 50% of total sales revenue, the average contribution of room sales to profitability is very much greater. Accordingly, the main focus and effort of accommodation marketing has to be on room-night sales. In practice, because nine out of ten people typically make reservations in advance as distinct from impulse purchases by walking in off the street, this means targeting bookings that are made ahead of the customer's arrival. The focus on accommodation sales and on advance booking is even more important for self-catering businesses. Obviously the level of room occupancy achieved directly affects the sale of food and beverages and other services, and effective merchandising to customers once they are 'in-house' is a logical marketing approach to increase total turnover. The key industry measure is on room revenue per available room which is commonly referred to as REVPAR.

Targeting bookers, not room or bed occupancy

There is a common misunderstanding that accommodation marketing focuses primarily on room or bed occupancy. The preoccupation with occupancy is certainly understandable for reasons already discussed, but marketing targets cannot sensibly be expressed as occupancy levels. Occupancy levels are a *result* of marketing effort; they are at best a retrospective statistical measure of marketing success or failure. Marketing targets are always prospective customers and, to use an unattractive but useful word, not just customers but 'bookers'.

A 'booker' is a customer or an agent of the customer, who makes a reservation for one or more persons, for one or more nights, in any form of accommodation. Thus, a person making a family booking for two rooms over seven nights for four people (fourteen room-nights and twenty-eight bednights), is a proper target for marketing strategy and tactics. A secretary who makes regular hotel reservations for one or more members of a company may never see a hotel or meet its staff, but he or she is a 'booker'. The secretary of a national association, responsible for organizing an annual conference for members, may be seeking several hundred room-nights in more than one hotel and is also a booker, and so on –certainly a buyer worth the most careful attention.

In the holiday parks sector of accommodation, offering caravans and chalets for holiday rent, marketing is traditionally considered in terms of 'unit sales' or 'unit rentals'. These terms are no more than trade jargon and accountants' data. The marketing task in this sector, as in the others, is to identify, persuade, sell to and satisfy targeted groups of those who make the bookings.

High fixed costs of operation

The marketing implications for service businesses operating with high fixed costs and low variable costs are discussed in several parts of this book and require little further comment here. Suffice it to note that, once the fixed costs of operation have been covered at the break-even level of occupancy, the marginal costs of filling an additional, otherwise empty room are negligible in all sectors of accommodation. Beyond the breakeven level the contribution to gross profit of additional room sales is very high, especially for self-catering operations, where the marginal costs are even lower than in the serviced sector.

Because the marginal cost of supplying an additional product is low, accommodation suppliers are very often tempted to reduce prices in an attempt to achieve sales, especially last minute sales before unsold capacity is lost forever. The higher the proportion of fixed costs to total costs, the wider the range of price discretion. But there is a counter argument as the confident strategy of easyJet reveals. Their circumstances are not the norm for services marketing, but their commitment is to reduce the price of advance sales and increase prices as the service delivery time approaches.

STRATEGIC MARKETING TASKS FOR ACCOMMODATION BUSINESSES

There are six main elements in the strategic marketing response the accommodation suppliers make to their external business environment and the operational characteristics noted in the first part of the chapter. These are:

- Evaluating strategic opportunities for growth.
- Planning the most profitable business mix of segments, products and price ranges having regard to yield rather than volume.
- Deciding the position, brand or image each accommodation unit (or chain of units) should occupy.
- Internet marketing.
- Encouraging and rewarding frequent users (relationship marketing).
- Developing marketing integration between units in common ownership (chains) or units in individual ownership (voluntary cooperatives).

Evaluating strategic opportunities for growth

In an age of global expansion and development, and the opportunities created by information and communications technology, marketing management plays a vital and growing role in identifying strategic market opportunities. The remarkable development of budget hotels in the UK, building on models earlier developed in the USA and mainland Europe, is one of the more dramatic illustrations of strategic marketing in the accommodation sector.

Strategic growth through mergers, alliances, acquisitions, and other deals with third parties that optimize the value that can be delivered to (and extracted from) existing and targeted groups of customers, is another form of strategic opportunity based on market evaluations as outlined in Chapters 10 and 11.

Link article available at www.routledge.com/9780750686938

(1) Baloglu, S., Pekcan, Y.A., 2006. The website design and Internet site marketing practices of upscale and luxury hotels in Turkey. Tourism Management 27 (1), 171–176.

Planning the business mix

In the context of the demand potential inherent in each location the basic strategic decision for accommodation businesses is to determine the optimum or most profitable mix of segments, for whose needs specific products may be created and promoted. For example, a city centre hotel will obviously target clients travelling for business and meeting purposes, a resort will draw a higher proportion of leisure visitors, and so on. Table 19.1 provides a fairly typical illustration of a customer mix that has important implications for the conduct of marketing.

TABLE 19.1 A typical market/product mix for an urban coastal hotel

Customer mix	% of room sales (per annum)	Volume of room sales (per annum)	Tariff type
1. Business (individuals)	20	5695	Rack rate
2. Business (corporate clients)	30	8540	Corporate rate
3. Vacation (individuals)	10	2847	Weekly inclusive rate
4. Coach tour clients	10	2848	Inclusive group rate
5. Holiday breaks[a]	15	4270	Inclusive price
6. Holiday breaks[b]	15	4270	Wholesale rate
Totals	100	28,470	

Notes: Coastal hotel located near to a business center generating visitors for conferences and general commercial purposes as well as holiday visitors.
Hundred and twenty twin rooms, with 65% annual room occupancy = 28,470 room-nights' capacity over a year (120×365×65%).
Rack rate £150 (twin/double) per room night, including breakfast; £100, single occupancy.

[a] Marketed directly by the hotel to customers.

[b] Rooms allocated to tour operators, and packages marketed by the operator.

Table 19.1 is based on a notional coastal resort hotel within a large urban location that supports a significant element of business visits within its chosen mix of segments. The hotel has two basic customer types (business and leisure), which can be split into six primary segments, each representing a strategic marketing choice and requiring separate marketing campaigns. For convenience of illustration, the business/leisure ratio in Table 19.1 is 50:50. But it could vary from, say, 70:30 to 30:70, according to the strategy the hotel's owners choose, based on their judgement of marketing potential and what they seek to achieve for the hotel in its location. The optimum customer mix for most businesses will usually comprise several segments, targeted to maximize achievable revenue yield and as far as possible minimize the effects of seasonality and other normal business fluctuations.

While the serviced sector may appear to have more scope to plan a coordinated customer mix, exactly the same principle operates for self-catering operators in the non-serviced sector. For example, holiday-park owners who market units such as caravans and chalets for holiday lets, may plan a segmentation strategy that separately targets adults aged over 50 travelling in pairs, from families with children of school age who are largely tied to school holiday periods. They can differentiate between visitors who purchase traditional one or two weeks' stays, and others who are interested in weekends and shorter stays. In each case the segments will be seeking different experiences and may not mix easily.

Devising the optimum mix for any accommodation business usually requires some form of marketing research or at the least an analysis of a customer database or guest-registration records to analyse the volume and revenue of current customers in each location and estimate the potential. Very few operators in the commercial accommodation sector cannot achieve at least a four-way customer split, or business mix, as the basis for a more efficient marketing strategy.

Deciding the position, brand or image

Relevant always to selected target segments, the next and obviously related strategic consideration for accommodation suppliers is to determine the 'position' each unit or group of units should aim to occupy in the minds of its customers. Increasingly, where competitors offer closely similar products to the same group of customers at very similar prices, it becomes necessary for operators to differentiate and brand their products with particular values and identities that can be communicated and understood. Identities, known in marketing jargon as 'positions', are perceptions in the minds of customers. They may be based on specific associations with a company name, such as Four Seasons or Hilton International, or on the strengths of a building and its location. They may be based on management design decisions about the specifics of products on offer, the quality of the staff and service provided, the design and quality of rooms and furnishings, or any combination of these characteristics.

Link article available at www.routledge.com/9780750686938

(2) Medina-Muñoz, D., García-Falcón, J.M., 2000. Successful relationships between hotels and agencies. Annals of Tourism Research 27 (3), 737–762.

Internet marketing

A number of recent trends are beginning to shape the future impact of the Internet on hotel marketing. These include Web 2.0, paid search marketing, eCRM (on-line customer relationship marketing), web analytics and ROI tracking among others. One of the key tasks when operating an Internet-based strategy is the need to distinguish between 'lookers' and 'bookers'. Hence, an eCRM strategy is crucial in determining who these visitors, 'bookers' or 'lookers' are and what their future patterns of behavioural intentions may be. In reality, very few hoteliers truly know who the bulk of their customers are. There is, however, no longer an excuse as the electronic tools and management information systems exist for far more proactive strategies to be set in place. This in turn can lead to a successful retention strategy and the development and continuation of Consumer Generated Media (CGM) such as blogs, discussion boards, review and social networking sites. The need for a suitable strategy to deal with CGM is increasingly becoming a necessity, be it a defensive, corporate sponsored or advertising-driven approach to counter the power of consumer-generated content. For defensive strategies, blogs can be hugely beneficial in word-of-mouth customer property reviews and peer-to-peer recommendations. Blogs can also be useful as interactive communication tools and as a general marketing tool across the hospitality industry more broadly.

In common with other sectors of the visitor economy most accommodation businesses are shifting to direct marketing on-line. Not only has the Internet become the preferred channel to plan and book accommodation in many markets, it has also become the cheapest form of distribution. It is estimated that in the USA, 60% of online bookings will be direct from consumers with the remaining 40% going via a third party (this will change to 65% and 35% by 2010). Because high-speed Internet access is now the norm in so many markets, better imagery and higher display resolution will reinforce web sites as the essential 24/7 marketing media for accommodation providers. With the ability to track and analyze on-line marketing campaigns, web analysis is now a necessary part of marketing evaluation (http://www.hotelmarketing.com, 2007).

Encouraging and rewarding frequent customers

The fourth element in strategic marketing responses for accommodation suppliers is to find ways to encourage and reward their regular or 'loyal' customers. The process is greatly facilitated by the sophistication of customer databases and techniques for data-mining, as well as the ability to use web sites to identify customers' profiles. Some of these reward schemes offer credit facilities in addition to the normal range of benefits, such as rapid check-in and check-out, and upgrades of rooms if availability allows. Some also offer awards through which frequent travellers can earn points for each stay, leading to attractive benefits according to the number of points collected over a given period.

Regular customers represent an important strategic marketing asset for any accommodation business, not only in terms of their own decisions but because they provide a very cost-effective route through which it is possible to reach their friends and others like them, using carefully designed and targeted direct marketing. Customer loyalty strategies in this context are an essential consideration for all accommodation businesses.

While the strategic objective of targeting and rewarding repeat visitors is very clear, not all the reward schemes currently in use are immediately or fully successful. In part this is because they are difficult and often expensive to administer, and partly because they may also serve, unintentionally, to reduce the average room rate to some customers who were prepared to pay a higher price.

Integrating marketing across several units

The sixth strategic consideration reflects a growing dimension in accommodation marketing that is relevant to the other five elements and focuses on the level of co-ordination that individual units can achieve in marketing their products. The strategic advantages of marketing coordination lie in economies of scale and may be summarized as:

Distribution	Referrals of business between units, central reservations services and call centres. Web site presence and linkages with other sites. Better access to retail distribution networks.
Promotion	Corporate positioning and branding. Joint advertising and PR opportunities. Use of professional marketing and sales teams. Access to group brochures and leaflets. Group representation at trade fairs and shows.

Product and pricing	Design and harmonization of products and group quality assurance schemes designed to build up customer satisfaction. Use of yield management programmes to develop and promote price options. Group loyalty schemes for frequent users. Access to group market research.

Obviously, co-ordination is most easily secured through ownership and mergers and is part of the process whereby large, multi-unit accommodation chains have grown over the last 20 years and expanded the scale of their operations. However, modern ICT greatly facilitates the formation and management of strategic alliances and a range of franchising and leasing operations. As a result, branded multi-unit chains are now found in all parts of the world. Many of the chains are global and international in their scope, and there was no indication that this level of growth had reached its limits in 2008. Current economic crisis conditions are likely to favour further integration.

Collaborative alliances of smaller independent businesses, of which one of the best known is the international Best Western chain, provide a competitive response route for individually owned hotels. The search for the marketing advantages of Internet facilitated co-operation is spreading into the small businesses sector of both serviced and non-serviced units. The marketing of gîtes in France and holiday cottages in the UK are examples.

MINI CASE 19.1: SMALL LUXURY HOTELS OF THE WORLD

Small Luxury Hotels of the World (SLH) represents one of the most successful hotel consortium's of its type with more than 400 of the world's finest independently-owned quality hotels being marketed together to benefit from the ease of booking and familiarity of an international group yet managing to retain and promote the unique character, individuality and independence of each of its member properties. Beginning life over 15 years ago as a result of a merger between Prestige Hotels Europe and Small Luxury Hotels & Resorts of North America, SLH now has an extensive global presence and forms one of the most luxurious and exclusive hotel and resort groups around the world. With all the financial, operational and marketing benefits accruing from its consortium approach to business, the luxury status of SLH in the market is reflected not only in its quality of hotels and resorts but also by its extensive list of partner organisation and brands. These include American Express, which has a long-standing partnership having developed the enormously successful Platinum and Centurion card programmes, complete with devoted SLH Platinum and Centurion directories, Audi, Elemis the award-winning luxury spa and skincare brand, the Financial Times, HSBC Premier – the world's largest financial group in terms of market capitalization, Morgan Stanley and Porsche. With the support of its partners, the consortium's activities are designed to provide similar economies of scale to those achieved by the larger international hotel chains, while celebrating the individuality and independence of each of its member properties.

A more recent means of consortium differentiation is SLH's development of special consumer 'experiences' via the development of an extensive range of personalized packages that guarantee that 'something little extra'. Whether it be through their active, gastronomic, spa or cultural 'experiences', SLH has set out to deliver 'ultimate experiences' to targeted customers. In addition, SLH now recognize that their pursuit of excellence does not need to be at the expense of the environment or the community in which a hotel operates. Through its 'Caring Luxury' initiative, SLH encourages its hotels to adopt responsible environmental, economic and social practices, which at the same time provide enriching and rewarding experiences for hotel guests. By practising Caring Luxury, SLH properties help to maximize the positive effects of tourism, such as creating jobs and benefiting small businesses, enhancing guests' awareness of local culture and traditions and identifying ways to conserve and protect local surroundings.

Source: Based on Fyall and Garrod (2005) and www.slh.com.

TACTICAL MARKETING

Strategic decisions are designed to establish a profitable mix of bookings and room occupancy through the production and distribution of appropriately priced, distinctive products that match the needs of identified customer segments. In other words, for accommodation operators in all sectors, three of the traditional four Ps of the marketing mix are strategic decisions, and even the fourth, promotion, must be planned within boundaries set by the positioning strategy.

Tactically, as for passenger transport marketing, the main contribution of marketing is to secure additional marginal sales from targeted buyers at times when rooms are predictably likely to be operating at less than optimum occupancy, as in normal seasonal variations. Its other contribution is to cope with the sudden and often dramatic losses of anticipated business that happen all too often as a result of unpredictable economic or political events.

Occasionally, in certain destinations at certain times, room occupancies in hotels may exceed 80% on an annual basis. At this level, most hotels are full for most of the time and the owners enjoy a rise in prices and profitability. Such circumstances are not the norm, however, and usually are not achieved by marketing alone but by a combination of favourable circumstances in the external business environment. It is more common for accommodation businesses to operate somewhere between 55 and 65% of room occupancy over the months in which they are open for business. In extremes, as in the aftermath of 9/11 in New York, they may drop to 40% or less.

As in other sectors of travel and tourism, reflecting the highly perishable nature of the products, marketing managers are required to manage demand by stimulating additional bookings on a daily and weekly basis. The high fixed costs and low variable costs of operating accommodation give extensive scope for providing short-term incentives to buyers. Tactical marketing for accommodation businesses requires choosing from the range of sales promotion tools discussed in some detail in Chapter 16.

Specifically, sales promotion tactics for accommodation businesses include:

1. Tactical short-term use of the Internet to achieve better communication of promotional offers.
2. Short-term price discounting used especially to sell unsold capacity in unanticipated circumstances. Sales promotions, adding temporary value to products in order to attract targeted customer segments, are often used to attract business at times of predicted seasonal troughs in demand.
3. Partnership deals with complementary partners such as transport operators to achieve mutual objectives.
4. Sales promotions, often using commission incentives, designed to motivate a retail distribution system (where applicable) and achieve added influence at points of sale, including improved display for brochures.
5. Sales promotions, invariably using deep price discounts, designed to motivate and conclude deals with third parties such as tour operators, coach tour operators and other agents making bulk contracts for the supply of accommodation. (This form of selling capacity may have strategic as well as tactical implications.)
6. Use of a sales force (where applicable) to generate additional sales, both from the range of normal buyers and from others targeted for short-run sales initiatives.

While the use of these tactical techniques is clearly sales orientated, their efficient use depends on the detailed knowledge marketing managers have of the profile, needs and probable behaviour of target segments in responding to promotional incentives. As with transport, the accommodation sector is frequently subject to unpredictable external factors and it is always necessary for businesses to allocate contingency funds for use in influencing short-run demand.

THE SIZE OF ACCOMMODATION MARKETING BUDGETS: CHALLENGING RECEIVED WISDOM

With an understanding of the nature and size of the task of implementing strategy and tactics in accommodation marketing, it is appropriate to consider some implications for the size of budgets. The cost of achieving marketing objectives is usually a relatively high proportion of sales revenue in the accommodation sector and the budget allocation is rightly seen as a high-risk decision.

A systematic procedure for allocating money to marketing campaigns in order to achieve planned volume and revenue targets is set out in Chapter 12; the principles in that chapter apply fully to all sectors of commercial accommodation. But this section sets out to challenge what continues to be a widespread belief in the industry in a norm, or rule of thumb, that it is appropriate to spend between 2 and 5% of total sales revenue on 'marketing'.

In fact, although this may be a contentious statement, the real proportion of sales revenue devoted to marketing by most successful organizations in the accommodation business is probably ten times higher. Properly calculated, and based on the view of marketing expressed in this book, the real average proportion of sales revenue devoted to marketing activities by accommodation businesses of all types is probably over 20% in most countries. The case for this statement is justified as follows:

1. In analyzing the annual accounts of an accommodation business, room sales revenue should always be calculated in two ways. First, the sum of *actual* receipts over 12 months from accommodation sales should be calculated (this figure, divided by the number of room-nights sold, provides the *average* room rate achieved over a year). Second, room sales revenue should be calculated as the sum of *target* sales revenue that would have resulted if rooms were sold at the intended published rates over the year (with due allowance for pre-planned group rates for targeted segments such as corporate business travellers, conference visitors and special tariffs for weekend business.
2. In practice, in most years, the planned or target rates will only be achieved for a proportion – say 75% of room nights and the remaining 25% will require deep discounts, for example in negotiating special deals with tour operators or business agencies that will require a better rate than originally planned to deliver business. The point is that these additional discounts are only offered in tactical terms to secure business that would otherwise be lost. This is in practice a real marketing cost.
3. Marketing expenditure should then be calculated as the sum of the costs of all the decisions businesses make to secure the business they actually achieve over the year (not just the expenditure on advertising and sales promotion). This total expenditure should be expressed as a percentage of room-sales revenue and total sales revenue achieved over a year or a planned campaign period.

In practice, hotels around the world continue to produce their accounts according to the agreed conventions in the US originated Uniform System of Hotel Accounts. As a result of an accounting, not a marketing derived process, highly valuable marketing insights are lost. It is recommended that the full costs of marketing can be gained only if separate calculations are undertaken by marketing managers for their own purposes.

In an ideal world a hotel with an excellent product range and a good location will set its rack rates, corporate rates and other group rates for the year ahead. It will complete the trading period without unpredicted events preventing it from achieving the targeted mix of bookings that best matches its capacity. No one in this ideal position accepts group bookings at extra discount if they are confident of filling their rooms with planned rates that raises their yield towards the theoretical maximum. No one offers special rates for leisure-break business if they can fill their rooms at higher rates.

In the real world, of course, hotels and other accommodation businesses must pay their contracted fixed costs out of daily cash flow while contemplating unsold rooms and beds and consequent loss of potential revenue. In these circumstances most discounts from their rack rates and other planned rates in order to manipulate short-run demand. Putting the point bluntly, they reduce prices in order to 'buy' business from whatever sources they can find at whatever price they think is better than the alternative of lost sales. The high fixed cost of accommodation operations makes business at almost any price appear worthwhile in the short run. Of course, over time, price discounting may be counter-productive because it damages the brand positioning and upsets regular customers' goodwill. But businesses in serious cash-flow crises may not have a long run and they will aim to survive by any possible means.

The foregoing explanation is designed to make the point that marketing expenditure should always be calculated as the full cost of all the expenditure actually incurred in achieving their annual turnover. Marketing costs therefore include expenditure defined in the Uniform System of Accounts for Hotels, on:

- Advertising, PR, and other media.
- Sales promotion and merchandising print.
- Production and distribution of information (including direct mail).
- Marketing research.
- Consortia fees (marketing proportion only) or group marketing levy imposed by chains.
- Staff costs, expenses and share of overheads for all undertaking the above work.

It should (but does not under the uniform system) include the full costs incurred in:

- Negotiating with, servicing and paying commission to travel agents, tour operators and other wholesalers, credit card companies and any other eMediaries who receive commission on bookings.
- Negotiating and agreeing discounts for tour operators, coach tour companies and any other group sales.
- Negotiating discounts to secure other forms of group business, such as conferences or airlines.
- Share of costs of central reservation systems and links with GDSs – the vital tools of efficient marketing operations, which must be organized around marketing requirements.
- Investment in web sites and connectivity with call centres and CRSs.

It has to be stressed that the bulk of all the marketing costs of securing business otherwise judged to be at risk or lost, are not in practice included as marketing costs in the Uniform System of Accounts for Hotels; they are allocated elsewhere. This is not a criticism of the uniform system, because it was not conceived around marketing principles but to facilitate industry comparisons using standard definitions for accountants.

The uniform system does the hotel industry no service by perpetuating the myth that marketing costs are of the order of 2–3% of room sales revenue. If an accommodation supplier wishes to understand costs and revenues and make his marketing more efficient, he must count all the costs noted above.

To summarize, almost every accommodation business will in most years operate at average achieved room rates below its planned target. The difference between actual and planned reflects the composition of its segment/product mix and the level of discounting and commission required to achieve business over a defined trading period in each segment. Measured over time and between different hotels in a group, the size of the gap between planned and actual revenue provides a valid measure of a hotel's marketing efficiency. Whichever way the marketing budget is calculated, it is obvious that the true cost of marketing will be substantially greater than the meaningless industry 'norm' of 2–5% usually quoted.

CHAPTER SUMMARY

This chapter:

- Explains and illustrates the characteristics of operations and marketing practice that are common to all sectors of serviced and non-serviced accommodation. It is not restricted to a particular sector or only to large operators in the industry. As with transport, some aspects of marketing are peculiar to individual sectors but the common aspects are more important than the differences. The principles outlined are broadly relevant to all sectors of serviced and non-serviced accommodation defined at the outset.
- Stresses the growing importance of linkages between the accommodation sector and other sectors in the tourism industry for marketing in the future. Other important marketing linkages are currently occurring within different accommodation sectors, such as those found in accommodation consortia formed by serviced and non-serviced operators. Individual producers, especially those owning small units, see consortia as a logical route to achieve branding and the economies of scale in marketing that are vital to successful competition against the growing power of the large chains. The development of destination marketing systems with access to online marketing and booking is another collaborative route for smaller businesses with clear potential for growth.
- Reviews the full costs of marketing accommodation and challenges the conventional wisdom concerning the cost of marketing that continues to inhibit recognition in the industry of the importance of marketing.

QUESTIONS TO CONSIDER

1) Using examples, consider how location determines the marketing strategies adopted by accommodation providers?
2) Compare and contrast three ways in which budget hotel accommodation is marketed differently to traditional four-star and five-star hotels.
3) For a hotel of your choice, how may some of the characteristics of yield management help determine the prices set?
4) Think of three reasons why a higher percentage of the market has traditionally used the Internet more frequently to book airline tickets than hotel accommodation?

5) Outline the benefits and drawbacks of a Frequent Guest Programme (FGP) for an international hotel chain of your choice.
6) In the face of increasing competition from the large scale branded sector, is consortia membership the only marketing solution available to independently owned, mid-market hotels?

REFERENCES AND FURTHER READING

Emmer, R.M., Tauck, C., Wilkinson, S. and Moore, R.G. (2003). Marketing hotels using Global Distribution Systems, *The Cornell Hotel and Restaurant Administration Quarterly*, **44**(5/6), pp. 94–104.

Fyall, A. and Garrod, B. (2005). *Tourism Marketing: A comparative approach*, channel view publications.

http://www.hospitalitynet.org/news/4032088.search?query=maximising+revpar (accessed 24 September 2008).

http://www.hotelmarketing.com/index.php/content/article/070824 (accessed 24 September 2008).

Israeli, A.A. and Reichel, A. (2003). Hospitality crisis management practices: the Israeli case, *International Journal of Hospitality Management*, **22**(4), pp. 353–372.

Karamustafa, K. (2000). Marketing-channel relationships: Turkey's resort purveyors' interactions with international tour operators, *The Cornell Hotel and Restaurant Administration Quarterly*, **41**(4), pp. 21–31.

Kim, W.G. and Cha, Y. (2002). Antecedents and consequences of relationship quality in hotel industry, *International Journal of Hospitality Management*, **21**(4), pp. 321–338.

O'Connor, P. and Piccoli, G. (2003). Marketing hotels using global distribution systems revisited, *The Cornell Hotel and Restaurant Administration Quarterly*, **44**(5), pp. 105–114.

Shoemaker, S. and Lewis, R.C. (1999). Customer loyalty: the future of hospitality marketing, *International Journal of Hospitality Management*, **18**(4), pp. 345–370.

Woods, R.H. (2001). Important issues for a growing timeshare industry, *The Cornell Hotel and Restaurant Administration Quarterly*, **42**(1), pp. 71–81.

A white cruise ship in the Baltic sea glides into Stockholm harbour - "Cruising remains one of the industry's key growth sectors with demand for all types of cruise vacations growing exponentially".

CHAPTER 20

Marketing passenger transport

'Airline alliances have proved to be a major feature of international airlines' responses to the need to change their ways of operating in an industry which is still heavily governed by regulatory constraints'

(Morley, 2003: 48)

The forms of transport available at any period of time and the ways in which they are marketed have a direct, functional influence on the costs and patterns of tourism flows and on the types of product that travellers purchase.

Historically, transport design and development reflect the need to move goods and mail, the need to administer countries and empires, the need to move armies and military equipment, the development of new weapons of war and the need to facilitate the movement of people efficiently in the conduct of business and in their daily lives. Even now, many public transport systems are primarily geared to business, administrative and social requirements, and draw the bulk of their revenue from non-leisure related traffic. In the latter part of the twentieth century, however, transport operators developed their systems increasingly to service leisure and recreation travel. The shift reflected market opportunities to develop into new and growing markets and to utilize surplus capacity, both overall and especially at times of otherwise slack demand. For some, such as charter airlines, expanding leisure markets provided the reasons for the companies' formation and very existence, for other companies such as budget airlines and cruise ships which emerged from the passenger liner industry, expanding leisure markets provided opportunities to create new products and methods of doing business, overturning traditional industry structures.

After studying this chapter you should be able to understand:

- The nature of transport systems and their products and should be able to identify the powerfully binding constraints that exist on their marketing decisions.
- Why the sector's marketing costs are generally much higher as a proportion of revenue earned than those in other sectors.
- The powerful combination of pressures in the business environment and from marketing costs that explain the strategic and tactical marketing challenges for passenger transport operators.

THE NATURE OF TRANSPORT SYSTEMS

Table 20.1 summarizes the wide range of modern transport systems, the marketing of which affects all tourism destinations to some extent. Most destinations are simultaneously influenced by several of these systems. Although this chapter does not deal with private transport, it is included in Table 20.1 because in many countries it is the principal form of competition for public transport to which marketing managers have to respond. For domestic tourism and for much of international tourism in Europe, private cars remain the most popular form of transportation by far.

TABLE 20.1 Principal passenger transport systems used in travel and tourism (with acknowledgement to Derek Robbins)

Air transport	**Long-haul scheduled airlines** operate strongly branded scheduled services around the world carrying business, VFR, leisure and holiday travellers. Product differentiation is achieved by separate cabins for first, business and economy class and it extends to check-in and lounge facilities at terminals. Segmentation is reflected in an extensive range of promotional fares, especially for economy class, with consolidated fares widely available through specialist agencies and the Internet. Over the past decade, long-haul airlines operating with a comparatively high cost base have faced growing competition from charter airlines on profitable leisure routes such as UK–Australia and N. Europe to the Caribbean.
	Medium/short-haul scheduled airlines operate networks mostly within and between developed countries but they also perform a vital role in developing countries in which alternative modes of transport may not be viable. They operate as long-haul carriers do with product differentiation, segmentation, strong branding and promotional fares, and they are often part of the same companies. Medium/short-haul carriers on popular routes have faced strongly growing competition under deregulation from rivals with lower cost bases, such as budget airlines and charter airlines in Europe.
	Charter airlines primarily operate short/medium-haul routes for leisure/holiday travellers. Developed in the 1960s and 1970s for inclusive tour holiday companies (with which most are integrated and often branded), charter airlines dominated most short-haul leisure routes in Europe in 2000. The shift to deregulation of air transport regulation in the 1990s and the growing popularity of short city breaks made it possible for charter airlines to operate scheduled services, develop 'seat-only' sales and extend their operations onto popular long-haul routes. Charter airlines face strong and rapidly growing competition from budget airlines in the twenty-first century in the markets for inter-city leisure and business travel segments.
	Budget or 'no frills' airlines developed in a deregulated air transport regime to provide short/medium inter-city services in the USA in the 1980s, mostly using leased airplanes and secondary rather than primary (high cost) airports. Strongly branded and copied in Europe in the 1990s from the successful model of Southwest Airlines, budget airlines mostly fly cherry picked popular city routes using secondary airports to keep costs down. Avoiding product differentiation and segmentation; providing no additional services; using direct marketing via the Internet and providing no commission for agencies, budget airlines compete aggressively on price for all purposes of travel. They provide competition for scheduled and charter airlines.
Sea transport	**Ferries**, initially mostly developed by railway companies, now operate strongly branded scheduled services on short sea routes that serve as extensions of the road network. By 2000, most are roll-on, roll-off ships designed to carry a balance of cars and their passengers for all purposes, and freight. Seasonality of traffic flows sustains an extensive range of promotional fares to promote use. Most ferries have developed strong marketing links with other businesses to increase their traffic. On highly popular routes where the revenue flows justify it, ferries may face fixed link competition from tunnels (Channel Tunnel between England and France) and bridges (Sweden and Denmark).

	Cruise ships, at one time (early 1980s) thought to be a dying industry, strongly branded cruise ships acting as floating inclusive resorts, have had a remarkable resurgence in the 1990s to become one of the fastest growing sectors of the global holiday industry. Although still only a small segment of the inclusive tour market, the newer ships being built are bigger than the former transatlantic liners of the 1930s and have become a popular alternative to traditional package tours in the USA and Europe. Twenty-first century cruising is facilitated by low-cost flight access (fly-cruise deals) to ports such as Miami and Barcelona.
Rail	**Scheduled rail services** (excluding commuter trains) mostly operate on short-haul city routes for journeys of up to around four hours' duration although fast trains in Europe cover longer journeys and provide competition for air and road traffic. Trains serve all purposes of travel although holidays are now only a small part of the mix and business related revenue is targeted as a vital segment. Product differentiation and segmentation by class of travel is reinforced through a wide range of promotional fares to combat seasonality and draw in traffic at less popular times and days of the week. Rail marketing is becoming more sophisticated in the UK following privatization (mid 1990s) and traffic congestion encourages rail travel for all purposes.
Bus and coach	**Bus services** (excluding local and commuter buses) divide into scheduled express services providing inter-city competition for rail for non-business users, coach tours and excursions, and private hire. Buses play a significant role in the budget price end of the inclusive tour market and excursions for segments such as schools and the over 60s. They can provide support services such as couriers and a social ambience that niche markets' value. Buses also link places that rail may not serve and perform key services such as transfers for other forms of transport by air and sea. Private hire for groups, clubs and associations is an important part of modern tourism and may increase as traffic congestion difficulties impede the use of private transport.
Private transport	At the start of the twenty-first century, cars are the dominant form of transport in developed countries for most domestic tourism, leisure day visits and recreational purposes. In Continental Europe cars are also the preferred mode of travel for tourism between countries. The sheer convenience, flexibility, relevance to modern lifestyles and what often appears to be the low marginal cost of using a car, especially for two or more people, provides private transport with massive competitive advantages. Since the 1990s, however, internationally growing environmental concerns with traffic congestion at destinations, pollution and global warming are likely to tilt the currently favorable regulatory framework against cars. A combination of subsidy, regulation, taxation and promotion is expected to achieve a move towards public transport in the twenty-first century. Car rental at destinations, supporting the use of public transport for the main journey, is likely to grow in popularity.

At first sight it is easy to suppose that each of the forms of transport is so different in kind that comparison and the development of common principles for marketing are impossible. In fact all the systems share some common characteristics, which have important implications for marketing practice. As Burkart and Medlik expressed over 25 years ago: 'A transport system can be analysed in three parts: the track, the vehicle, and the terminal' (Burkart and Medlik, 1981: 111) (see note 4).

- Tracks: controlled air routes/corridors, sea routes, canals, permanent ways (railways), roads, trunk routes and motorways.
- Vehicles: aircraft, ships, trains, buses and coaches, private vehicles.
- Terminals: airports, seaports, stations, garages, and off-street parking.

In considering the external threats and opportunities in the transport marketing business environment that influence marketing managers' decisions, one should note that the three basic elements outlined above are typically owned and controlled by different parties. For example, in the case of air transport, the vehicles are owned and operated by airlines (which in turn may be privately owned or run by state-owned corporations); the routes are effectively owned by governments that allocate and regulate the use of air space, for example, although control may be outsourced to agencies that include private sector funding such as National Air Traffic Services (NATS) in the United Kingdom; and the terminals are owned for the most part by national, regional or local governments and their appointed agencies although some major airports are owned by private companies. At the terminals too, there is a mix of private and public ownership. Ownership and control of sea ferries and buses are similarly divided. In most of Europe, the tracks, vehicles and terminals of rail transport are still in state ownership although not in the UK where ownership was privatized and also separated over a decade ago. For a fuller analysis of rail privatization in the UK see Kain (1998).

Without permission to fly to specific airports, or with permission to fly but only for a specified capacity of certain types of product (such as scheduled rather than charter flights), airlines do not enjoy full scope for responding to the market forces they perceive. Similarly, if the external agencies controlling the routes or the terminal facilities cannot cope with the added volume, marketing decisions to develop new routes or products have a very restricted meaning. Marketing constraints arose over a decade ago through airport congestion in much of Europe and America, and because public sector air traffic control systems have not been developed fast enough to cope with increases in demand.

In private transport, individuals own the vehicles but the routes they use are typically developed, owned and controlled by government and its agencies. On some routes and in some cities, tolls are applied to control use and generate income. At tourism destinations the bulk of the terminal or public parking facilities available for private transport is often provided by local government or otherwise controlled through parking regulations and planning controls. Government policies are increasingly in place in many countries to try to shift tourism from private to public transport systems.

In other words, passenger-marketing strategies have to take account of changes and interactions between the capacity, routes and terminals of both public and private transport. They have to reflect a changing pattern of public and private sector ownership. Such strategies are usually a key element also in the external business environment of all other destination businesses in the tourism industry.

In summarizing the common characteristics of transport systems influencing marketing decisions, it should be noted that:

- All passenger transport systems operate through more or less closely controlled and regulated vehicle movements along controlled networks which link points of origin and destination. When capacity is approached or exceeded, the regulatory role becomes predominant.
- All passenger transport systems display typical characteristics of peaks and troughs in demand, whether by month, week, day or hour.
- The operation of all passenger transport systems requires continuous attention to the utilization of available capacity, whether of vehicles, the routes or terminals given the uneven patterns of demand.
- Most transport systems need massive investment in infrastructure, vehicles, track and control systems. This in turn requires efficient marketing both to justify and to pay back the expenditure.

- Most systems move freight as well as passengers and freight requirements may take precedence.
- Most transport systems are only partly concerned with leisure travel.
- All transport systems contribute to global warming and put pressure on the physical environment, especially that of host communities at popular destinations.

SUPPLY INCREASINGLY LEADS DEMAND FOR TRANSPORT PRODUCTS

In most industries, supply is led by demand. Historically, transport services have generally developed in response to demand arising from economic growth and rising incomes. But, especially in leisure travel, the availability of affordable supply clearly facilitates and generates demand. New roads are acknowledged to generate additional traffic (DOT, 1994), as evidenced by the opening of the M25 orbital motorway around London and the very dramatic growth of passenger numbers carried by budget airlines since the late 1990s on a much expanded route network, reflects the fact that many passengers are newly generated rather than attracted from more expensive rival airlines. Much of modern tourism for leisure purposes can be persuaded through effective marketing, pricing and promotion to switch its choices to alternative destinations. There is in Britain, for example, a huge potential demand for holidays in the USA. Whenever the dollar/pound exchange rate has been favourable to the British, the traffic has surged and vice versa. The greatest obstacle to growth is the cost of travel across the Atlantic and the sheer range of promotional fares on the route proves the point; none more so than after the tragic events of 9/11 when British bargain-hunters flooded to the USA on the back of heavily-discounted air tickets.

When the cost of transport is significantly reduced through new economies of scale, or through some technological, cost-saving breakthrough as achieved by the budget airlines, demand is led by the supply of cheaper transport. In 2008, however, the rising cost of fuel and the precarious economic climate have resulted in a significant rise in transport operating costs at the same time that many prospective buyers have had to re-think their travel plans. This combination produced a fall in demand and contributed to the collapse of the British tour operator XL, airlines such as Zoom and the precarious state of Alitalia. It also explains the need for substantial discount-based promotions by low-cost carriers to encourage people to fly. One airline bucking the trend is Southwest Airlines in the United States. Amid the widespread chaos Gary Kelly, Chief Executive, had the foresight to set in place a series of complex financial hedges to offset rising fuel costs, an initiative that is now delivering financial gains of around $2 billion. So, while other airlines struggle to cope with massive increase in the cost of fuel, Southwest has been able to plan for the near future at least with a relatively stable cost base and so take a lead over many of its competitors in the market.

The powerful leading effect of supply of transport in international tourism markets is especially obvious in the case of islands, such as those in the Pacific area, where the development of new routes acts almost like a tap for new demand. The important point in travel and tourism is that supply and demand is essentially interactive. It is an interaction that can be exploited to good effect by transport marketing managers. That said, the high costs of fuel are beginning to impact quite significantly on prices and the market's affordability and willingness to travel to long-haul locations.

A STRICTLY FUNCTIONAL ROLE FOR TRANSPORT IN THE TOURIST PRODUCT

Although a core part of all tourism products, modern transport is a declining motivation or attraction of a destination visit. There are some exceptions to this, such as steam railways, the Orient Express or cruise ships, although the latter are better understood as floating hotels or resorts than as forms of transport.

Link article available at www.routledge.com/9780750686938

(1) Weaver, A., 2005. The Mcdonaldization thesis and cruise tourism. Annals of Tourism Research 32 (2), 346–366.

The role of transport in leisure travel was not always so functional. In the pioneering days of both public and private transport, journeys of all kinds, especially those by air and sea, could be presented as exciting, glamorous and romantic. In those circumstances the journey was an adventure and an important part of travel motivation. By the 1980s, however, except possibly for children and first-time travellers by air and sea, the journey had lost most if not all of its earlier magic. Experienced travellers, especially those on business trips, increasingly see the journey element as a necessary but unpleasant part of the trip to be endured, not enjoyed.

Journeys by public transport have to be paid for not only in money terms but also in the stress and strain of heavily congested access routes, queuing in crowded terminals, delays, missed connections, harassed staff and risk to personal safety. With private transport, the strain of driving along congested trunk routes and not finding convenient parking space at the destination has removed most of what was once the glamour of the open road. Although the recent opening of Terminal 5 at London Heathrow (designed to handle 35 million passengers a year at capacity) is set to reduce the congestion and frustration of passengers departing and arriving at the airport, and in particular for those transferring flights; recent industrial disputes and problems with baggage carousels suggest that hassle-free travel is more of a utopian ideal than expected reality. It is thus no surprise that marketing for business travel focuses rather more on alleviating the misery than on selling the pleasures.

THE NATURE OF THE TRANSPORT PRODUCT

For charter airlines, cruise ships and most long-distance coach tours, the transport element is usually no more than one component within the overall tourism product, the marketing of which is not normally the responsibility of transport operators. Indeed, the physical transport element may be subcontracted or 'outsourced'. By contrast, although they may also provide linkages with accommodation and destination interests for their customers, scheduled transport operators have full responsibility to design and market specific products based on their vehicles, networks and services.

As defined in Chapter 7, any specific service product offered to customers represents a combination or *bundle* of components available at a specified price. The main components in the passenger transport bundle are:

- Service availability and convenience (reflecting routes offered, schedules and capacity).

- Cost in comparison with competitors (either other operators of the same mode of transport or a rival mode of transport such as between express coach and rail) on the same routes.
- The design and performance of the vehicle (comfort and speed).
- Comfort, seating, ambience and any service offered during the journey.
- Passenger handling at terminals.
- Convenience of booking and ticketing arrangements.
- Contact with staff and their roles in contact with customers.
- Image and positioning of each operator.

Viewed from the customer's standpoint, the core products offered by operators of the same mode of transport, such as airlines or sea ferries, tend to be remarkably undifferentiated in comparison with the products offered in other sectors of the tourism industry. Perceived 'sameness' of product is an obvious problem for marketing managers and it is interesting to note the reasons for it. In what was traditionally a closely regulated transport environment, a combination of formal and informal agreements between governments, other regulatory bodies and other transport operators, served to produce virtual uniformity in the basic components of the formal product (see Chapter 7). In the case of international air transport until the 1980s almost every aspect of the product was covered by agreements, from price down to the smallest detail of in-flight services. The products were commonly offered in identical aircraft with the same cabin layouts.

Even in the more liberal or deregulated transport climate of the new century, the use of the same type of equipment, shared terminals and fierce price competition still produced virtual uniformity in the core product. As a result, most airline marketing focused on product augmentation, corporate images and the quality of service provided by staff. Apart from obvious distinctions between first-class, business-class and economy-class products, the traditional approach to marketing airline products was rather sterile and unimaginative. Seats on transport are just commodities in the eyes of most consumers. This discussion of 'sameness' can be linked to the Internet's impact in creating downward pressure on prices, leading to the 'recommoditization' of services as outlined in Chapter 13, and the alternative approaches offered by the experience marketing concept. It also opens up the extent to which airlines are collaborating in the form of membership of global airline alliances, such as Star Alliance in Case 20.2, as a means of achieving differentiation in the marketplace. The example of Easyjet's Affiliate Network in Chapter 14 where airlines, and other businesses, seek to gain differentiation on the strength of their 'connections' – often in a diagonal sense – also resonates as does the mini-case of Opodo introduced in Chapter 15.

THE DOMINANCE OVER MARKETING OF THE EXTERNAL BUSINESS ENVIRONMENT

Before identifying the strategic and tactical marketing tasks in passenger transport it is first necessary to appreciate the extent to which marketing is constrained by factors in the external and operational environment. Part One of the book illustrates how the business environment dominates tourism-marketing decisions generally.

Passenger transport marketing responds to seven specific external factors over most of which the operators have only very limited control and not much influence. These factors are listed and three of them are briefly discussed below:

- Vehicle technology (major innovations).
- Information and communications technology.
- Regulatory framework.
- Price of fuel.
- Economic growth or decline (national and international economy).
- Exchange-rate fluctuations.
- Environmental issues.

Vehicle technology

It is competition among manufacturers such as Boeing and Airbus that develops the capabilities of vehicles in terms of their size, seat capacity, speed, range, fuel efficiency, noise and passenger comfort. Such developments affect the potential seat/mile costs achievable and thus the profitability of operations. They also influence customer choice, especially as to which destinations can be reached within acceptable time and cost constraints.

While the implications of developing vehicle technology for tourism markets are most obviously seen in public transport, the extension of car ownership and the increasing comfort, reliability and efficiency of motor vehicles, is equally vital to the market growth of many forms of tourism. Most short weekend breaks, self-catering accommodation and day visits to attractions are primarily dependent on car travel.

Courtesy of Dimitrios Buhalis.

Information and communications technology

Information and communications technology developments, covered in Part Four of the book, have made it possible for passenger transport operators to deal efficiently with the increasing volume of business. Led by airlines, the processes for dealing with enquiries, reservations, cancellations, ticketing, invoicing and options on routes and fares are now handled seamlessly by web-based systems. These processes also generate a wealth of research data on the characteristics of customers of great value in the marketing planning process. Information and communications technology developments are also transforming the distribution process for travel and tourism generally, driving down costs and prices and greatly facilitating last minute sales. Many of the developments have been led by transport operators in search of greater cost-efficiency in the conduct of routine operations and, equally important, in the conduct and control of their marketing operations. New strategic marketing linkages between product elements are greatly facilitated by the creation of interactive online Internet networks, connecting the reservation systems of transport operators with those of hotels, car rental organizations and destination marketing organizations. It has also almost reached the stage where major airlines such as British Airways are beginning to migrate to their 'web identity' rather than their traditional 'corporate' identity; in this case BA.com rather than British Airways. Although common in the low-cost airline sector, this is a relatively new trend in the traditional 'flag carrier' sector where the desire to drive customers to web sites to facilitate online bookings and increasingly 'check-in' services is not only serving as a major means of differentiation but also as a means of reducing costs and the need for high-cost, and sometimes unreliable, labour. Even in the case of charter carriers where seat purchases are normally part of a 'package' (as discussed in Chapter 22), the trend towards selling some capacity on a 'seats only' basis has also served as a catalyst for this new 'web identity' trend. Notwithstanding, this in itself was insufficient to save XL.com in the face of severe external environmental pressures. The following case study on Flybe introduces the speed of entry and overall impact low-cost airlines have had on the market and the benefits they derive from being internet-driven businesses.

MINI-CASE 20.1 – FLYBE.COM

With its origins going back almost 30 years (when originally a full service carrier), Flybe is one of the 'low-cost' airlines that have transformed air travel in the UK and Europe. Along with its forebears, Ryanair of Ireland and Easyjet of the UK, Flybe is the antithesis of the high fares, business-traveller and high-cost model of airlines that dominated the regulated skies of the UK up until the mid-1990s. With their flag-carrier status and hub-and-spoke networks, traditional carriers such as British Airways and British Midland, now BMI, held virtual duopoly on domestic routes and short-haul flights to the major European cities. Following the business model of Southwest Airlines in the USA, Flybe set out as a low-cost airline, using low-cost airports and high-daily utilization of its aircraft. With a low, simple-to-understand and transparent fare structure, point-to-point travel with no interlining, direct web-based booking systems that empowered control to the consumer and limited, if any, on-flight service and meals, Flybe followed its forebears onto the marketplace, adopting the low-cost business model in 2002 and holding one key unique selling proposition over its rivals. Rather than focusing its operations in London airports, Flybe set out to be a regional low-cost airline which would achieve a £10–£15 premium above the prices set by so-called hard-core low-cost airlines by providing convenient 'local' departure points.

Through a combination of an aggressive 'retail' approach to marketing, transparent pricing and a low-cost base, Flybe grew dramatically, both through organic growth and through acquisition. In March 2007 it acquired BA Connect, the short-haul network of services from regional airports operated by BA, demonstrating just how dominant budget airlines have become in the short-haul sector. Flybe (2007) flies approximately 7.5 million passengers on 157 routes in 12 countries from 23 UK airports and 32 European airports, earning approximately £500 million per annum. The move to a more aggressive approach to marketing was almost as significant as the low-cost business model itself in that a continuous supply of full-page offers with a strong advertising style, an active PR programme and strong community outreach programme in target markets (including the sponsorship of local football clubs such as Birmingham City, Norwich City, Southampton and Exeter City) have resonated strongly in that Flybe is now the fourth most spontaneously-recalled UK aviation brand.

With major bases at Birmingham, Southampton, Belfast, Channel Islands, Edinburgh and Glasgow, Flybe now flys out of more UK airports than any other airline. It also continues to be a market leader in differentiating its range of passenger services. Today, it is the only low-cost airline to offer a business service, Flybe Economy Plus, and operates what is widely regarded as the most generous Frequent Flyer Programme in the UK. It was also the first carrier of its kind to offer online check-in and the first to offer pre-assigned seating for those pre-booking their seats. It also accepts and acknowledges the problems of global warming and the contribution made by airlines. In this context it works with PURE, a carbon-offset provider, in seeking to meet the UK Government's Code of Best Practice for carbon offsetting.

To conclude, over the past five years Flybe has migrated from a Business-to-Business (B2B) to a Business-to-Consumer (B2C) company. It lives by the Internet, is obsessed with low costs rather than low prices and is driven by marketers with retail rather than an airline orientation to aggressive consumer marketing campaigns.

Source: Based on www.flybe.com.

Environmental issues

There are five main areas of environmental concern for transport operators. They are:

- Noise.
- Emissions.
- Use of energy.
- Congestion.
- Waste production and disposal.

Up to the 1990s these issues had only minor implications for the conduct of marketing. But they were all subjects for later growing regulatory control and these regulations seem certain to affect future costs and the types of transport products that can be marketed. Car journeys are being actively discouraged in Europe and short-haul journeys by air are likely to be discouraged in favour of rail travel. Not all these issues are new, however, and airlines in particular have been active for over two decades, at least in reducing the noise impact around airports and increasing fuel efficiency.

Aircrafts are subject to noise certification standards established by the International Civil Aviation Organization (ICAO). Emissions of carbon dioxide – produced by all forms of transportation using fossil fuels – are critical as carbon dioxide is the principal global warming gas. However, aviation was specifically excluded from the provision of the Kyoto protocol and as such remains unregulated, although there are strong pressures to incorporate it into the EU emission trading scheme in the future. Aircraft emissions of carbon dioxide are estimated at around 3.5% of global warming, and are small in comparison with those of motor vehicles, although large measured in emissions per passenger kilometre carried. Whilst the aviation share seems small and concerns over its carbon emissions disproportionate, it is the rate of growth which creates concern for the future. The industry has grown five-fold in the UK over the last 30 years (DfT, 2003) and based on projected forecasts could contribute around 15–20% of global carbon emissions by 2050. Although aircraft manufacturers such as Boeing (Dreamliner) and Airbus (A380) are making significant technological advances to reduce emissions, total emissions from aviation will continue to rise due to this growth at a time when the UK government is committed to reduce carbon emissions by 60% over 1990 figures by 2050. Not surprisingly the very high costs of fuel are now driving more innovative engineering solutions. Virgin Atlantic, in co-operation with engine manufacturers has already operated a flight from London to Brussels with a mixture of biofuels and kerosene and although the technical data is still being evaluated, early indications are that the biofuels can significantly reduce emissions.

Congestion of transport systems, e.g. at airports, on motorways and in cities, is a major contributor to environmental costs, as it leads to delays, extra fuel usage and increased emissions. In Europe the range of air traffic control systems (ATCs) combined with airport capacity is an important cause of congestion, although Eurocontrol has seen improved co-ordination and compatibility in recent years.

Responding to the 1992 'Earth Summit' at Rio de Janeiro, most leading airlines set up environmental departments and introduced environmental management programmes. British Airways is a leader in this field and aims to integrate environmental considerations into all the airline's normal business practices. Bearing in mind that they are one of the principal determinants of future international leisure travel, however, there is little evidence that airlines as a sector yet recognize the importance to them of sustaining the quality of the natural and built environment of the destinations they fly to. It is perhaps ironic that, as the traditional regulation of routes, capacity and prices is being lifted from transport operators, new forms of regulation for environmental purposes are being introduced. They appear certain to influence future marketing.

Other external factors

External economic factors generally are discussed in Part One of this book. Economic growth or recession and the changing price of oil obviously have a major influence on the market volume carried by transport operators for business and leisure purposes, with the latter especially price elastic.

TWO OPERATIONAL CONSTRAINTS ON PUBLIC TRANSPORT MARKETING

This section focuses on two important constraints that arise from the nature of operating a passenger-transport system.

Capital investment and fixed costs

A principal characteristic of most modern passenger transport operations is the high level of capital investment and fixed costs that are required in terms of purchasing and maintaining vehicles and equipment, setting up and maintaining route networks, funding modern reservation and other marketing systems and employing staff. The level of investment is especially high for international airlines, with modern long-haul 'jumbo jets' (Boeing 747 – 8) costing up to $300 million each at 2007 prices. But, relative to the size of their revenues, heavy capital investment applies equally to shipping lines, railway systems and to bus and coach operations. In each case expensive new equipment, often associated with increased seating capacity per vehicle, is usually justified on the grounds that through more efficient operation it will lower the operating cost per passenger seat/mile and thus permit potentially lower fares to be charged, or more profit to be made at the existing prices. A vital proviso in this argument is that the potentially lower costs can only produce real savings, if enough of the seats on offer are sold.

A related dominant characteristic acting as a constraint on marketing decisions is that the committed costs, or 'fixed' costs, of operating any service are high and the variable costs are low for most modes of transport. This is less true for airlines as, strictly speaking, fuel costs and landing charges are variable costs since they are not incurred if a flight does not take place and the recent increase in the price of oil has taken fuel alone up to around 50% of operating costs. In practical terms, however, once the decision is taken to fly a particular route at a particular time and the service is marketed, all the main costs become effectively 'fixed' and they have to be paid regardless of the number of seats sold. In the current difficult operating environment airlines are increasing to reduce their capacity and their costs in the off-peak season by 'mothballing' planes. Ryanair decided to mothball 20 planes over the off peak winter season of 2008–2009 (The Times 4 June 2008). While full aircraft use more fuel than empty ones, the difference measured on a per seat/mile basis is very small. From a marketing standpoint, it concentrates the mind to recognize that any seat sales achieved after the decision is made to operate a service, and that may be weeks before it is performed, represent over 90% revenue contribution. Up to the break-even load factor this contribution covers fixed costs and, once the break-even load factor is reached, it represents gross profit.

Load factor, yield management and fleet utilization

Because of the investment and high fixed cost implications of passenger transport operations, there are three key measures of operational efficiency that are especially relevant to marketing managers. The most critical measures for marketing are seat occupancy and yield. Seat occupancy is also known technically as the load factor. Yield is a revenue calculation defined as load factor × *average* seat price paid, and seat occupancy and yield are obviously related. For example, a load factor of 55% for a flight in which half the passengers were paying business fares, and the others full economy fare, would yield very much more revenue than a load factor of 60% if only a quarter of the passengers were paying business fares and the others were travelling on heavily discounted promotional fares. Yield may be divided by kilometres flown to provide a comparative measure across different routes.

The third key measure is fleet utilization. As in any form of production based on expensive plant, the more intensively a piece of equipment is used, the better the performance in terms of revenue achieved against the fixed costs incurred. If, for example, an expensive aircraft (on long-haul routes) can be kept in the air and flying with more than a break-even load of passengers, for an average of some 16 hours in every 24 around the year (with allowance for routine inspections and servicing), it can obviously generate more revenue to cover its fixed costs than the same aircraft flying for an average of only 12 hours a day. Utilization is partly a function of efficient maintenance and scheduling the network to achieve the shortest possible turnaround of vehicles; but it is much more a function of generating sufficient demand to justify keeping the vehicles moving. Ferries, trains, buses and even short-haul aircraft typically have a more limited utilization profile over 24 hours than long-haul aircraft.

The role of marketing in passenger transport is not confined solely in achieving higher load factors and increased yield and utilization at the margin. Nevertheless, the imperative need to maintain the level of seat occupancy on each service performed, while achieving high utilization rates throughout the year, dominates all passenger transport marketing. Typically, for scheduled airlines, average load factors and yield exceed the break-even level by little more than two percentage points and in poor years carriers fail to cover their operating costs.

DEFINING THE MARKETING TASK FOR PASSENGER TRANSPORT OPERATORS

The marketing process set out in Chapter 2 (Fig. 2.1) is as applicable to transport operators as to any other producer of consumer products. The marketing tasks in passenger transport derive logically from the characteristics of operations and the strength of the internal and external environment in which they are conducted, as noted above. The main tasks are summarized below under the headings of strategic and tactical marketing, which apply to all forms of public transport operators, whether by rail, road, air, or sea.

It is not easy to get a precise understanding of the level of expenditure on marketing by transport operators. The full marketing cost includes not just advertising and sales promotion but the major investment in providing CRS systems, securing distribution channels and paying commissions. The evidence suggests that the real cost of achieving an average booking for traditional scheduled airlines on international routes is still around 25–30% of sales revenue. It is interesting to compare that with the net profit generated by international airlines expressed as a percentage of sales revenue.

Scheduled airlines have the highest pro rata marketing costs, which help in part to explain the success of both charter and budget airlines whose costs are lower. But competition between forms of passenger transport ensures that the full costs of marketing are normally of the order of 20% or more of sales revenue if the full costs of marketing and overheads, including price discounting from published fares to fill empty seats, are allowed for.

Strategic marketing

The strategic marketing task, explained in Chapter 10 has five main elements:

- Forecasting demand.
- Finding ways to reduce marketing costs.
- Building corporate product and brand strengths.
- Relationship marketing.
- Strategic linkages.

Forecasting demand

Through extensive use of marketing-research techniques and continuous passenger monitoring, all passenger transport operators develop marketing information systems to provide forecasts of market potential. Continuously reviewed, these are the basis on which future operational networks, schedules and the associated investment can be planned. Because fleet leasing or purchases along with other investment needs are geared to revenue forecasts (volume of customers × the average seat kilometre prices they will pay), the ability of marketing managers to provide realistic inputs to demand forecasting is crucial to the profitable development of any transport business. Estimates of traffic flows have to be built up route-by-route, separately for each main market segment. In practice, while forecasting models are normally the responsibility of transport economists and statisticians, the quality of the marketing research inputs relating to segments, products, customer satisfaction and willingness to pay, is a vital contribution.

Inevitably, estimates of future traffic flows will always be surrounded by risk because of the unpredictable nature of the business environment. But the better the operator's knowledge of customer profile and behaviour, the better the chance of reducing the risk.

Finding ways to reduce operating costs through more effective marketing

As noted above, transport operators' marketing costs are high, at around 20–30% of the seat price. Traditionally costs include travel agent commission, commission on credit card usage, GDS costs and the associated heavy investment in computer facilities to service booking systems. It is the analysis of these costs and finding ways of forcing them down which has driven much of the strategic marketing in the sector for the past decade.

The combination of using secondary (low-cost) airports, cherry-picking high volume linear routes, controlling operation cost (no frills) and cutting distribution costs by shifting to Internet based booking systems, has proved a highly successful formula in an era of congested hub airports and rising demand. It effectively halves the operating costs faced by major scheduled carriers. In a very few years Ryanair, Easyjet and Flybe in the UK (see Case Study 20.1) and others around the world such as Air Asia in Malaysia have demonstrated their value to target markets.

Building corporate product and brand strengths

The third element in marketing strategy lies in the way in which operators seek to gain competitive edge over the competitors in the continuous struggle for market share. In an increasingly deregulated market environment, strategy focuses on identifying operators' strengths from a customer standpoint. These strengths may be developed into the product offer, for example, by designing segment specific product 'benefits' for business users, such as business lounges, 'free' drinks, express check-ins, larger reclining seats and limousine services. All of these are forms of product enhancement in ways that alleviate the actual pain of the transport experience – for those that can afford it.

Also parts of strategy are the corporate images, branding and 'positioning' that are built into the customer appeal of products and communicated through advertising and websites to targeted segments. At the highly sensitive margin of business either side of the break-even load factor, assuming they have a choice between more than one operator, uncommitted potential customers may have their choice influenced by positive or negative images of different companies. Recognition of the power of such images explains the considerable commitment of operators to both corporate and product advertising. Interestingly, the budget airlines seem able through their modern approaches to appeal as much or more to customers through 'personality' as the scheduled airlines do spending far more per capita on advertising.

Relationship marketing

The fourth common element in strategic marketing lies in the effort all operators now tend to put into creating and retaining regular, repeat buyers of their services. Mostly business travellers, a small number of frequent users, typically provide a very high proportion of total revenue. For example, 20% of customers could easily generate 75% of all revenue on some routes because of the fares they pay and the frequency with which they travel. Such customers are identified in great detail in modern customer databases. They justify careful cultivation and it is logical to create schemes that reward and incentivize such people. Most leading scheduled airlines make arrangements with 'in-house' travel agents located in the offices of their major corporate clients.

Traditional season tickets have been available for many years on rail and road commuter routes, but competition between airlines is generating new forms of frequent flyer loyalty programmes that are likely to develop further as the databases of transport operators become more sophisticated and able to target individuals.

Link article available at www.routledge.com/9780750686938

(2) Yang, J. Y. and Liu, A., 2003. Frequent Flyer Program: a case study of China airline's marketing initiative—Dynasty Flyer Program. Tourism Management 24 (5), 587–595.

Strategic linkages and alliances

The fifth element in marketing strategy has two aspects. The first aspect lies in the formation of strategic links and alliances between international airlines in the post-regulatory era of the market liberalization that has been one of the most striking transport marketing developments of the last decade. It seems set to continue. Such alliances make it possible to exploit and facilitate global computerization and reservation system linkages, service customers through code-sharing and develop dominant marketing positions. They provide a means to integrate marketing and operations to achieve vital marginal increments in seat occupancy and yield, and gain a competitive edge over rivals in the fiercely competitive marketplace.

Alliances offer a form of 'virtual' corporate consolidation without the full cross-border mergers that most governments have refused thus far to countenance. They provide a way around the regulation of routes imposed by the patchwork quilt of bilateral treaties that still govern international airline operations. The leading major alliances are Star Alliance (including Lufthansa, United, Air Canada, BMI and SIA), One World (including American Airlines, British Airways, Qantas and Canadian Airlines and Iberia) and Sky Team (including Delta Airlines and Air France-KLM). The alliances are fluid and change continuously for the reasons noted above. Since Europe followed America's internal liberalization in the mid-1990s there have been more than 40 deals between the USA and countries in Europe, Asia and South America to get around government controls on routes and fares.

A second aspect of linkages is the way in which some transport operators shift their focus outwards, away from the performance of their traditional roles as operators of vehicles, routes and terminals, towards linkages with other elements of the overall travel and tourism product. In other words, the extent to which providers of transport seek strategic marketing links with destination interests and with the distribution networks of other travel products. The scope for these links is already wide and immensely facilitated by Internet accessibility. It ranges from relatively limited links with car rental operators, accommodation providers and attractions, all the way up to full integration with marketing organizations such as tour operators or wholesalers. From the earliest days of railways, links with hotels were seen as necessary for the efficient development of transport businesses. Closer linkages between transport and the other elements of the product, especially with destination interests, appear probable in the future.

MINI-CASE 20.2 – STAR ALLIANCE

Over a decade ago, Oum and Park (1997) identified six major reasons for alliance formation in the global airline industry, namely that consumers tend to prefer airlines serving a large number of cities that facilitate 'seamless' travel; traffic feed between partners helps to increase load factors and achieve economies of density; alliance members can reduce unit costs by taking advantage of economies of scale, increased traffic density and economies of scope; frequency, schedule convenience and convenience of connecting are seen by customers as major features of quality; an alliance can offer far more variety of itinerary and routing choices; and, that members can take advantage of alliance-wide CRSs through the practice of code-sharing.

In response to the above and wider global forces for change, Air Canada, Lufthansa, SAS, Thai Airways International and United Airlines launched Star Alliance in 1997, the first global airline alliance of its kind in the world. The initial vision 'To be the leading global airline alliance for the high value international traveler' stands true today with the alliance spanning 16,000 daily flights serving 855 destinations in 155 countries. The global reach of the alliance will expand further when Air China, Turkish Airlines and Shanghai Airlines join the network and increase the number of daily flights among the alliance partners to 17,600. As things stand, Star Alliance is the leading alliance in terms of 'available seat kilometres', 'revenue passenger kilometres', 'global passenger shares' and 'operating revenue shares'. Made up of 17 quality airlines, Star Alliance offers a comprehensive global network of routes, a range of products and services commensurate with its leading position and a wide range of frequent flyer travel benefits.

The flexibility of its Frequent Flyer Programme (FFP) is one of the considered strengths of the Star Alliance in that participants in any member programmes are able to accumulate and redeem miles or points on any other member airline. These then in turn contribute towards their 'tier' status (Gold, Silver and Bronze) while passengers also have access to priority travel benefits, Redemption Availability & Sell (RAS) options and an online upgrade redemption option across the network. Paperless ticketing, which can be used across the entire network is estimated to reduce costs by €3 per ticket. In addition, the alliance offers 11 global fare and discount products which include 'Round the World Fares', 'Circle Fares', 'Airpasses' and 'Conventions plus' as well as a corporate travel product, 'Corporate Plus' which offers a much easier, transparent and seamless global corporate accounts system.

To keep abreast of its competitors, Star Alliance is continuing to examine very closely the way business is to be conducted in the future, how technological and digital developments change the way business is done and how the alliance can accommodate such changes and proactively meet with the increasing needs, wants and expectations of business travellers in particular. There is also a need to anticipate how changing patterns of passenger behaviour is likely to impact on the future design of aircraft and airports, while the need to be aware of an sensitive to the wider needs of the environment will need to be heeded.

Source: Based on Fyall and Garrod (2005), Oum and Park (1997) and www.staralliance.com.

TACTICAL MARKETING

In generating demand for unsold seats and achieving additional hours of profitable utilization for expensive vehicles, the contribution of tactical marketing is to mould demand within the already established constraints and to cope with unforeseen fluctuations in demand. Using the wide range of integrated promotional tools set out in Chapter 16, the object is to manipulate customer behaviour to buy more of the available supply of 'perishable' service products than would occur without such expenditure. This section notes four of the main dimensions:

- Marketing the margin.
- Segment specific promotions.
- Tactical pricing and yield management.
- Managing crises.

Marketing the margin

Overall, especially around the break-even level of seat occupancy, the focus of tactical marketing decisions is to secure on a daily basis the vital marginal increment in customer purchases that makes a major difference to profit or loss in the high fixed cost operations of passenger transport systems. Of course some routes on some days at some times of the year are likely to be fully booked. But for the bulk of any transport operator's planned services, extra demand at the margin is a vital contribution to annual profitability. Scheduled operators face much greater problems of this sort than the budget airlines, which carefully 'cherry pick' growth routes calculated to produce the best seat occupancy.

Segment specific promotions

The success of promotion is directly related to the knowledge that marketing managers achieve of the profile, needs and the probable behaviour of the customer segments with which they deal. Chapter 14 stressed that commitment to knowing the customer is a necessary prerequisite for the planning and execution of all forms of effective promotion. The more the promotion is segment and product specific, the greater the need for a detailed understanding of target customers. Data-mining of customer databases provides the necessary market analysis and, in addition to loyalty schemes for regular buyers, most transport operators can develop specific offers, often with third parties such as organizers of events, sports fixtures and festivals that appeal to the targeted group but do not dilute forecast revenue.

Tactical pricing and yield management

For transport operators, most tactical pricing is also segment specific. For example, railways usually do not reduce the fares paid by commuters because their services are overcrowded at commuter times. Similarly they do not reduce the fares paid by first-class travellers because most of them are travelling on business and their demand is proven to be relatively inelastic to changes in price. On the other hand, operators have every incentive to use price, with or without a special product offer, to promote use of the network outside peak periods. A common response is to devise segment-specific fares with conditions designed to prevent the 'dilution of revenue' as it is known, if passengers switch from higher fares they otherwise would have paid.

The whole concept of segment-specific fares, often accompanied with the presentation of services as 'special products', is found internationally under a multitude of different names. Advanced Purchase Excursion Fares (APEX), which are widely used in Europe and North America, are obvious examples of segment-specific fares and products. They usually depend on advance booking, minimum lengths of stay at a destination and restricted times of travel to reduce the revenue dilution. The object is to generate the marginal revenue on specific journeys that yield management programmes indicate would otherwise be performed with empty seats. Where it is possible to provide group fares for pre-booked parties, operators will invariably allow a very significant price reduction; in this context groups are just another illustration of segment-specific promotional activity.

An interesting combination of marketing strategy and tactics is used by EasyJet to promote advance booking. Their cheapest fares are bookable well in advance of the service to encourage early reservations that facilitate planning. As the time of the flight approaches the cost rises. Many other operators in tourism still operate on the reverse principle and reduce price as the date of service approaches. EasyJet succeed because their routes are carefully selected and so far they have not had to handle a major crisis of falling demand.

Managing crises

Reflecting the many unpredictable variations in the external business environment, there is always a strong element of contingency and crisis planning in marketing tactics for transport operators. Each year brings its own examples. Crisis conditions may require massive promotional response, far in excess of any planned budget. The tactics are employed, however, as the only known way to combat unexpected trading losses and to invest in a rapid return to normal trading conditions. How airlines grapple with the 2008/9 fuel price rises and the international financial and economic crisis, which are certain to force many into massive losses, remains to be seen. The only management tools they have are the ones noted in this chapter.

CHAPTER SUMMARY

This chapter:

- Stresses the functional links between the development and capacity of transport operations and the demand for travel and tourism products. Although transport is only one of the five elements of the overall product and performs an enabling, rather than a motivating role, accessibility is a fundamental condition for the development and growth of any destination, especially for international travel.
- Explains the extent to which transport marketing is constrained by constantly changing factors in the external business environment and by the pressures of operational constraints while emphasis is given to the continuous preoccupation with achieving revenue above the break-even level.
- Discussed the contrast between the overall tourism products that ultimately determine travel flows and the specific transport products that are the focus of transport marketing campaigns.
- Stresses the route to product augmentation through a detailed and carefully researched knowledge of consumer segments.

Throughout, although this chapter tends to use airline examples, it seeks to define and illuminate the characteristics of marketing strategy and tactics practised in all forms of transport rather than focusing on the specifics of the particular modes. Undoubtedly there are aspects of marketing which are particular to individual forms of transport but they are derived from the general principles outlined here and they do not alter the conclusions drawn.

The chapter does not deal specifically with charter airlines because these are referred to later in Chapter 22. In practice most charter airlines adopt a form of industrial marketing in which they negotiate their routes, products and capacity, with a relatively small number of major clients. Major charter operators are now owned or linked financially with tour operating companies and usually they do not market their products directly to individual customers. In these circumstances charter airlines provide a vital operational function for tour operators, but it is the latter that takes on the responsibility for marketing to the public.

QUESTIONS TO CONSIDER

1. To what extent are technological breakthroughs in the transport sector driving changing patterns of visitor behaviour in a market of your choice?
2. Compare and contrast the benefits and drawbacks of low-cost air travel compared to train travel in the UK.
3. Critically examine the impact of the increasing price of fuel for an island destination of your choice dependent on long-haul air travel.
4. What marketing strategies and tactics can be used to increase the load factor on flights across the Atlantic for an airline of your choice?
5. Compare and contrast the benefits and drawbacks of two or more Frequent Flyer Programmes (FFPs) for international airlines of your choice?

6. How may the gradual migration towards strategic alliances actually hinder the strategic marketing decisions being taken by individual airlines?

REFERENCES AND FURTHER READING

Burkart, A.J. and Medlik, S. (1981). *Tourism: Past, Present and Future* (2nd edn). Oxford: Butterworth Heinemann.

Department of Transport DOT (1994). *The Standing Advisory Committee on Trunk Road Assessment, Trunk Roads and the Generation of Traffic*. London: HMSO.

Department for Transport DfT (2003). *The Future of Air Transport*. London: The Stationary Office.

Doganis, Rigas (2006). *The Airline Business in the 21st Century* (2nd edn). London: Routledge.

Dowling, R. and Vasudavan, V. (2000). Cruising in the new millennium, *Tourism Recreation Research*, **25**(3), pp. 17–27.

Duval, D.T. (2004). *Tourism and Transport: Modes, Networks and Flows*. Clevedon: Channel View Publications.

Dwyer, L. and Forsyth, P. (1998). Economic significance of cruise tourism, *Annals of Tourism Research*, **25**, pp. 393–415.

Environmental Audit Committee (2006). *Reducing Carbon Emissions from Transport, Ninth Report – Session 2005–06*. London: Stationary Office.

Fyall, A. and Garrod, B. (2005). *Tourism marketing: A collaboative Approach*. Clevedon: Channel View Publications.

Hanlon, P. (1999). *Global Airlines: Competition in a Transnational Industry*. (2nd edn). Oxford: Butterworth-Heinemann.

Hanlon, J.P. (2006). *Global Airlines: Competition in a Transnational Industry* (3rd edn). Oxford: Butterworth-Heinemann.

Kain, P. (1998) The reform of rail transport in Great Britain, Journal of Transport Economics and Policy, 32, Part 2 pp. 247–266.

Lumsdon, L. and Page, S. (2004). *Tourism and Transport: Issues and Agenda for the New Millennium*. Oxford: Elsevier Butterworth Heinemann.

Morley, C. (2003). Impacts of international airline alliances on tourism, *Tourism Economics*, **9**(1), pp. 31–51.

Oum, T.H. and Park, J.H. (1997). Airline alliances: current status, policy issues and future directions, *Journal of Air transport Management*, **3**(3), pp. 133–144.

Page, S. (2005). *Transport and Tourism: Global Perspectives*. Harlow: Prentice Hall.

Scantelbury, M.G. (2007). Cruise ship tourism, *Annals of Tourism Research*, **34**(3), pp. 817–818.

Weaver, A. (2005). The Mcdonaldization thesis and cruise tourism, *Annals of Tourism Research*, **32**(2), pp. 346–366.

Wood, R. (2000). Caribbean cruise tourism: globalization at sea, *Annals of Tourism Research*, **27**(2), pp. 345–370.

Yang, J.Y. and Liu, A. (2003). Frequent flyer program: a case study of China airline's marketing initiative—dynasty flyer program, *Tourism Management*, **24**(5), pp. 587–595.

A view down the River Thames at night, taking in the Houses Of Parliament (including Big Ben) and the London Eye - "Investment in attractions continues apace with destinations of all shapes and sizes seeking to maintain and possibly enhance their attractiveness to visitors

CHAPTER 21

Marketing visitor attractions

'The best form of marketing is word of mouth and the best ambassadors are your visitors'

Tim Smit, The Eden Project (2008: xv)

Visitor attractions that command the attention of media and politicians in most countries are the large national museums and galleries in capital cities, and commercial operators such as the Disney Corporation and Universal Studios in the USA and Legoland at Windsor in the UK. All of these draw over one million visits a year, and the largest over 10 million. But, as with the other sectors of the tourism industry, attractions are increasingly polarized between a few large attractions and thousands of small and micro-sized enterprises. Most managed visitor attractions in the UK and in many other countries receive less than 30,000 visits per annum and generate less than £100,000 earned revenue. Most are based on a single location. Many are owned and managed within the public sector or by trusts and most are not operated as businesses for profit.

This chapter aims to show that the principles of marketing are fully applicable, even in a sector of the tourism industry not generally distinguished by a customer-orientated culture or by its business management skills. It focuses on *managed attractions* based on a wide range of natural, cultural or built resources that, either naturally or after development, have the power to draw or motivate visitors to their locations. The term 'visitor attractions' rather than 'tourist attractions' is used, partly to reflect industry practice and partly because many attractions are visited as much by the residents of an area as by tourists.

After studying this chapter you should be able to understand:

- The main changes in developed societies that are accelerating the growth in supply of attractions, increasing competition and necessitating the adoption of management and marketing techniques.
- The definition of 'managed attractions' and how to categorize the types and characteristics of attraction to which systematic marketing techniques are increasingly applied.

- The nature of the product that attractions offer, the customer segments on which they typically draw and the marketing management approaches applied to attractions.
- Be familiar with the growing need for developing better linkages between attractions and with the publics and other users they serve.

TRADITIONAL AND MODERN CONCEPTS OF ATTRACTIONS MANAGEMENT AND MARKETING

Visitor attractions play an essential role in tourism as 'elements within the destination's environment that largely determine consumers' choices and influence prospective buyers' motivation' (Chapter 1). In fact, as much of transport and accommodation services are increasingly globally branded and marketed, and product options are standardized, visitor attractions have a particularly important role to play in both representing and delivering the experience of the particular sense of *place* that provides the basis for competition between destinations. Many natural, cultural and built attractions are created specifically to conserve and celebrate the unique characteristics of places and the local features and character that make them worth a visit.

Traditionally, many visitor attractions did not need to practice marketing. They were slow adopters, sometimes because they were operating with public sector subsidies and were not expected to charge for admission, and sometimes because their owners, trustees and managers were imbued with vision and passion for the resources they were responsible for, making them inward looking (or product orientated) rather than outward looking to customer requirements. Until the last decade, with the exception of the largest attractions, the ideas of marketing management had not reached the majority of the sector.

In recent years, however, the global growth of travel and tourism and the impact of unrestricted public access to natural, cultural and built resources in their unmanaged state have led to growing recognition of the need for *visitor management*. The overused cliché that 'visitors tend to destroy the very things they travel to see' has its applications in most popular destinations and underlies the growing use of visitor management techniques, especially marketing.

Many visitor attractions are located in environmentally sensitive areas, especially those of a heritage nature. In some places the promotion of public access may be secondary to the principal requirement to conserve a resource for its own intrinsic value. There are cases, for example, sustaining wetlands for the sake of the wildlife, where the objective is to inhibit rather than provide for visitor use and where environmental objectives will take precedence. Allowing for this important caveat, the admission of visitors – especially the revenue they generate to contribute to environmental objectives – is generally a key element in resource conservation schemes. What is new is a growing awareness and sense of urgency that environmental resources generally have a finite capacity in places attractive for tourism, and that visitor management techniques along with resource management techniques must be improved.

Link article available at www.routledge.com/9780750686938

(1) Garrod, B., Fyall, A., 2000. Managing heritage tourism. Annals of Tourism Research 27 (3), 682–708.

Within the range of visitor management techniques available to attractions, marketing is increasingly seen as fundamental to success. It is recognized as the best way to generate revenue to contribute to the costs of operation and maintenance of the resource base, develop and sustain satisfying products, create value for money and influence the volume and seasonality patterns of site visits. But it can only be practised effectively when focused on sites or areas that are enclosed or have controlled access. Large museums and commercial attractions are the obvious examples but the principle of controlling access for management purposes applies also to parts of national parks, country parks, lakes and heritage coastal areas.

What principally distinguishes the present from the past is the polarization between large and small attractions in the public and private sector, the remarkable growth of supply in provision of all forms of attractions, competition for visitors' time and money and the reduction of annual subsidies by the public sector. These changes increasingly require the exercise of more sophisticated management techniques that may be used simultaneously to protect the resource, to enhance the visitor experience, to promote a site and to generate revenue for it in a competitive market.

The concept of applying systematic modern business management techniques at visitor attractions as diverse as museums and national parks is still not yet fully accepted in all countries. The idea of charging for access to the primary assets of national heritage is even less widely accepted, although charging is now common in most new purpose-designed attractions.

MODERN MANAGEMENT UNDERPINS THE DEVELOPMENT OF NEW ATTRACTIONS

As the developed world has shifted into the post-industrial era, the role in society of arts, heritage, culture, hospitality and entertainment takes on greater economic importance and the visitor economy as outlined in Chapter 1 makes an integral contribution as a growth market within the modern economy of most destinations.

This role is fully recognized commercially and is driving massive investment in new retail-based facilities that are marketed as day visitor attractions. Typically comprising a themed mix of entertainment and hospitality as well as retail, these are located close to motorway access within easy reach of city centres. Originating in the USA and Canada as enclosed shopping mall developments, they crossed the Atlantic to Northern Europe in the mid- to late-1990s. The largest of these in the UK (of which there are around eight major players) are attracting over 30 million visits a year each, year round, up to 24 hours a day. The new attractions are managed and marketed with the best professional teams and are designed to appeal to modern consumers with their one-stop, undercover facilities for all age groups. Their potential competitive impact on traditional visitor attractions can be gauged by the fact that some 2500 museums generate just over 70 million visits a year between them. It is not only retail-based attractions that are new on the scene, however, as numerous innovative leisure, sporting and entertainment events and new venues compete head on for day visitors spend with more traditional attractions such as castles, art galleries and museums. With the intensity of competition from attractions that span football stadia such as Old Trafford in Manchester, UK, and industrial and corporate attractions such as Niketown in the USA and Guiness's 'Storehouse' in Dublin, Ireland, there are real fears for the viability and survival of many traditional small attractions.

At the same time, however, 'major new players in the industry are responding strongly to changing market demands with the development of an exciting new genre of attractions' (Stevens, 2000: 354). These undoubtedly will need alternative types of management and organizational structures if they are to work.

MINI-CASE 21.1: MARKETING MANCHESTER UNITED

It is not obvious that Old Trafford, the home of Manchester United Football Club, represents an example of a visitor attraction. However, with over 200,000 annual visitors to the Museum and Stadium Tour it is a significant attraction for both domestic and international visitors alike. With Air Asia (based in Kuala Lumpur, Malaysia) and Tourism Malaysia, two of Manchester United's main sponsors, the appeal of the club and its 'visitor attraction' is truly international with many thousands more visiting the stadium 'virtually' on-line. Located in the North Stand at Old Trafford, visitors can immerse themselves in the history of the 'world's most famous club' and see at first hand the club's magnificent trophy room. With prices varying from £3 for pupils and teachers to £10 for adult entry to both the museum and tour of the stadium the attraction not only serves as an income generator in its own right but as a further catalyst for visits to the club's megastore, hospitality provision and conference and exhibition facilities.

Open all-year round, it is recommended that visitors pre-book tours to avoid disappointment. For school visits, especially during half-term, a number of special activities and events are organized to meet the needs of a demanding market with numerous novelty sessions and competitions keeping everyone interested. For a slightly different audience, the Munich Air Disaster of 1958 where 11 players and club officials lost their lives in a plane crash is currently being commemorated via a special exhibition at the stadium. Logistically, tours do not take place on match days or the day before home European games while tours finish at 12 noon the day before an early kick off. With extensive corporate hospitality, its own TV station, mobile phones, and insurance products, Manchester United is clearly far more than a football club. In essence, it is an experiential product enjoyed by thousands in the UK and overseas with its visitor attraction just one component of an organization with an annual turnover running into hundreds of millions.

Source: www.manutd.com.

Associated with the development of management and marketing is a growing understanding of the ways in which visitor attractions can be developed out of resources and structures not originally thought to be of any interest to visitors, or where none existed previously. Early examples are the construction of Disney World and EPCOT in Florida, which began with the purchase of some 27,400 acres in the mid-1960s of low-lying swamp and agricultural land of no obvious attraction except to mosquitoes. More recent examples of creative development of attractions can be seen in the redevelopment of former industrial cities such as Manchester, Birmingham and Liverpool in the UK, using cultural and heritage visitor attractions as a lead sector in economic regeneration. The modern art gallery movement, epitomized by the Guggenheim at Bilbao (Spain) and the Tate Modern in London, has extended over much of Europe in the last few years.

Interestingly, it is noteworthy in England that over half of all the visitor attractions available at the beginning of the new century had been developed in the previous two decades. New attractions, typically more dependent on admission income rather than public sector subsidies for their survival, tend to be more user orientated in their ethos from the outset, in contrast with more traditional sites. They are also mostly larger and employ professional managers.

Courtesy of Bournemouth University marketing department.

THE CHARACTERISTICS OF MANAGED VISITOR ATTRACTIONS

Managed visitor attractions as discussed in this chapter may now be defined as: *designated permanent resources that are controlled and managed for their own sake and for the enjoyment, entertainment and education of the visiting public*.

Designated means that the resource has been formally committed to the types of use and activity outlined in the definition. Designation may be either a commercial decision within the normal statutory planning regulations that apply to land and structures, a decision by a public sector body acting on behalf of community interests, or the decision of a trust acting on behalf of trust objectives and stakeholders. In all cases effective management requires that the boundaries of a resource or site must be clearly specified – even for wilderness areas such as the upper slopes of mountains – and normally attractions are enclosed or controlled to reduce or prevent public access except at established points of admission.

Permanent is used to exclude from the definition the marketing of festivals, carnivals, pageants, temporary entertainments, concerts, travelling fairs and shows, and any other form of visitor attractions not based on a fixed site or building. Temporary attractions ranging from international sports events to village fairs have their own different forms of marketing, which are not discussed in this chapter. Many permanent sites are, however, used as the venue for such temporary attractions, promoted as part of an annual programme of events designed to promote multiple uses and draw in different audiences.

Within the definition it will be obvious that there is a wide range of different types of attraction. To illustrate the range, 10 different categories of permanent managed attractions are listed in Table 21.1. The marketing principles outlined in this chapter will be found applicable to all of them. The definition is not restricted to attractions that have an admission price, although the attractions listed in Table 21.1 mostly do

TABLE 21.1 Ten main types of managed attractions open to the public

1. Ancient monuments	Typically protected and preserved sites such as fortifications, burial mounds and buildings dating up to the end of the Roman Empire
2. Historic buildings	Castles, houses, palaces, cathedrals, churches, town centres, villages, commonly termed heritage sites
3. Designated areas, parks and gardens	National parks, country parks, long-distance paths, gardens (excluding urban recreation spaces), including sites of particular scenic and resource quality
4. Theme parks	Mostly engineered as artefacts, such as Disney World, but may be associated with historic sites such as Colonial Williamsburg in the USA, or with Gardens as at Alton Towers in Britain
5. Wildlife attractions	Zoos, aquaria, aviaries, wildfowl parks, game parks and safaris, farms open to visitors
6. Museums	The range is enormous; it includes subject-specific museums, such as science and science centres, transport, farms and ships; site-specific museums, such as Colonial Williamsburg (USA) or IronbridgeGorge (Great Britain); or area-based museums, with either national, regional or local collections
7. Art galleries	Most traditional galleries with collections built up over many decades. Includes the new wave of modem art galleries in striking new buildings
8. Industrial archaeology sites	Mostly sites and structures identified with specific industrial and manufacturing processes, such as mining, textiles, railways, docks or canals, and mostly relevant to the period post-1750
9. Themed retail sites	Mostly former commercial premises, such as covered market halls, commodity exchanges or warehouses, used as speciality retail shopping malls, often themed. Includes modern, purpose-built, multi-purpose sites
10. Amusement and leisure parks	Parks constructed primarily for 'white knuckle' rides, such as roller coasters, log flumes, dodgem cars and associated stalls and amusements

charge and the trend is in this direction rather than for free provision. The charge for using the attraction may be made at a ticket office, barrier or a car park, or for the use of parts of the site; it may be obligatory or operated on a voluntary basis. Prices may be intended to cover the full cost of operating an attraction, to cover its current (not capital) expenditure or simply to make some contribution to costs that are otherwise funded by a grant from another source.

POLARITY BETWEEN SMALL AND LARGE ATTRACTIONS

In all countries the visitor attractions shown in Table 21.1 are mostly small in terms of the number of visitors and the revenue they receive. Their lack of marketing knowledge and their small marketing budgets limit what they can achieve in practice to improve their revenue performance. In the terms introduced in Chapter 2, most visitor attractions do not have an outward-looking, proactive corporate culture to guide their decisions and many are still in the cottage industry stage.

Historically, most small attractions were formed and are directed by dedicated enthusiasts and scholars. These enthusiasts have generally always been short of funds and have had to overcome great difficulties in defeating the forces of inertia to establish their sites and the collections that attract people to visit. As a result, many attractions are located in buildings and sites that are barely adequate for the purpose and have only limited facilities for display and interpretation to the general public. At the same time, the management structure of individuals, trusts, local-authority recreation departments and government agencies that control many attractions is not noted for its marketing expertise.

In the UK there are approximately 6000 attractions open to the public for which actual or estimated visitor numbers are recorded. Of these under 10% attract more than 200,000 visits a year and just a handful making an admission charge exceeded a million visits, of which the majority were in or near London, drawing on the large number of overseas visitors. The majority of attractions record less than 50,000 visits a year and at that level they cannot afford to employ professional marketing managers although marketing is clearly vital to all of them. For attractions in general, 2005 visit figures in England showed little change in visitor admissions, with an average sector decrease of −0.5%, following a slight increase in 2004 of 1% (Richards and Wilkes, 2008: 39). The trend for visits to migrate away from the smaller attractions continued with attractions with fewer than 20,000 visits reporting a 2% decline, following two years of lower growth compared with larger competitor attractions (VisitBritain, 2006). The principal author's experience suggests that attractions achieving less than around 250,000 visits per annum are unlikely to be able to generate the revenue needed to operate competitively in marketing terms. Even then they will not generate sufficient revenue to cover all their operating costs *and* a surplus for capital renewals and refurbishment.

Knowledge of the sector suggests that the typical manager of an attraction with less than 100,000 visits is responsible for one site location only, has very limited links with other attractions, has had no formal management and marketing training and has a marketing budget of under £10,000 per annum. Such a manager is very likely to be a dedicated and knowledgeable enthusiast in the attraction's specialism but has to be more concerned with the daily problems of caring for and managing his operations and with financial survival than with expansion and development through marketing initiatives. Through public sector subsidies, grants from national agencies, bequests and the actions of hundreds of thousands of volunteers, smaller attractions continue to perform a vital role in destinations. But for many, survival and development lies in collaboration with others and finding synergy partners to support their operations and marketing programmes.

While collaboration, branding and joint marketing of individually owned businesses are common in accommodation and transport, there are only a few multiples established in the attractions field. The National Trust in the UK, the largest non-government conservation organization in Europe, is an interesting exception. Its massive property portfolio includes 700 miles of coastline in England, Wales and Northern Ireland, 617,500 acres of countryside, moorland, beaches and coastline, 19 castles, 166 fine houses, 47 industrial monuments, 49 churches and chapels, 35 pubs and inns and 150 gardens. Some 200 of these properties attract more than 10,000 visits each a year. With over 50 million people visiting the Trust's open air properties in 2004 and 3.4 million individual members today, the National Trust is a remarkable example of an organization that manages and markets individual attractions under a unified brand image and under central and regional management control. There are some much smaller equivalents and branded voluntary groupings are a logical development in the marketing of attractions, both for promotion and distribution purposes and to communicate to customers their commitments to product quality.

At the other end of the spectrum there are the large branded players, with purpose designed and built attractions such as Disney World, Disney Land and the other major operators in the USA, Disneyland Paris, Legoland, De Efteling, Port Aventura, Madame Tussauds and Alton Towers in Europe. All of these exceed one million visits a year and the largest have more than 10 million. Although many national museums achieve more than a million visits, many do not charge for admission and in the UK all of them receive annual government subsidies of several million pounds each. Judgement suggests a million visits is the bare minimum at which most visitor attractions are likely to approach commercial viability and even then they will need a very favourable site location to succeed.

THE ATTRACTIONS PRODUCT: MARKETING THE EXPERIENCE

As noted in the introduction, most visitor attractions provide or contribute to an important part of the reason for travel. Many heritage attractions are part of the local character and specialities of *place* that lie at the core of the overall travel and tourism product. Some owe their original existence to celebrating and communicating local history (natural, built, economic and social) and their attractiveness to visitors depends on the intrinsic quality of their resources or collections.

Because the product for many attractions, for example, museums and galleries, is first a function of the resource and only second a function of marketing strategy, it is appropriate to consider first the nature of attractions products and the basic segments or audiences they draw on.

Important as the resource is for most attractions, it is not the resource or collection that is the product; it is the *visitor experience* that the resources provide. The attractions product cannot be effectively marketed unless this key point is understood. Theme parks, for example, develop their whole product offering around the experience provided. Attractions based on the natural environment also need to communicate and facilitate access to their resource 'products' interpreted as visitor experiences.

The range of experiences provided by attractions is very wide and in each case reflects the resource that the site provides and its interaction with the interests and personality of each visitor. It ranges from aesthetic pleasure and interest, as in gardens, through 'white-knuckle' thrills and excitement of amusement parks, fantasy as at some of the Tussauds exhibitions, to learning, awareness and self-development associated with many museum and art gallery displays and interpretation.

Link article available at www.routledge.com/9780750686938

(1) Connell, J., 2004. The purest of human pleasures: The characteristics and motivations of garden visitors in Great Britain. Tourism Management 25 (2), 229–247.

In practice what a particular experience provides to visitors can usually be established only through consumer research among key market segments, not through management guesswork. But at all managed sites, the experience provided is a matter of continuous concern with design and product formulation, which can be influenced or controlled by management decisions.

The product components

The visitor experience at managed attractions begins with anticipation. It may be stimulated by effective promotion, especially printed materials and web sites, and by personal recommendation. It begins in earnest with the first signage on the approach to the entrance to the site. From the moment of arrival, well-exemplified by the sense of scale and quality conveyed by Disney World's astonishing motorway-style entrance route and the row of parking direction booths spread across the traffic lanes, every aspect of the experience visitors undergo is potentially under direct management control. To some extent this is also true of transport and accommodation operations but more so for attractions because the purpose of being on site is not usually functional but to derive satisfaction in an awareness and enjoyment of the experience. In some historic buildings and sites the degree of management control may be limited by planning and policy restrictions, but the essential components of the product are internationally the same and may be summarized as follows:

- Quality of the advertising material, promotional literature and web site information, which establishes a 'promise' and influences initial expectations of a visit.
- Effectiveness and appeal of signage that guides first-time visitors to a site/building.
- First visual impression of the appearance of a site and the interest it arouses in prospective visitors – related to a pre-visit expectation.
- Efficiency of car/coach-parking arrangements and ease of access to the entrance.

- Physical appearance, ambience and motivating appeal of the entrance to an attraction.
- Appearance, friendliness and effectiveness of staff in the reception/payment area where most visitors make first contact, and elsewhere on site.
- Efficiency of receiving visitors at the entrance or in a reception area including processes of ticketing, information provision and initial orientation at the point of sale/admission.
- Effectiveness of visitor circulation patterns around the site/building, managed through the logical layout of the resource elements, paths, signposting, leaflets and personal guides.
- Displays, presentation and interpretation of the main elements of the resource, including any audio-visual materials, interactive opportunities and any event or activity provided.
- Location, layout and quality of any subsidiary attractions on the site.
- Location, layout and quality of facilities such as toilets, cafés and shops.
- Facilities to assist visitors with disabilities to have access and enjoy the experiences available.

A useful first stage in the marketing process for attractions is to deconstruct, audit and assess these product elements, both separately and within the overall experience, as part of a 'bundle' or package of components (see also Chapter 7). All parts of the 'package' may be varied by management decisions; some will be strengths and some, weaknesses. Since one of the prime objects of attractions management is to motivate visitors, the processes they adopt for monitoring customer satisfaction and value for money with the product components (see Chapters 11 and 12) will be crucial to success.

MARKET SEGMENTS FOR VISITOR ATTRACTIONS

Experience with researching attractions both in Britain and in other countries indicates that market segmentation is always the practical basis for marketing orientation. Interestingly, in varying proportions, all attractions tend to draw their customers from the same basic range of segments. Differences between sites in the proportions of segments attracted are likely to be explained either by the size and motivating pull of the attraction and its particular features or by locational factors such as proximity to holiday destinations.

For most attractions the influence of locational factors (proximity to main markets) will be at least as strong as the 'pull' of the resource base. The reason is that, apart from specialist visitors with knowledge of the subjects covered by the resource, most first-time visitors to any attraction will have little or no knowledge of the resource when they decide to make a visit. For example, visitors to parks and gardens may well include a few botanists with a deep knowledge of plants and horticulture but they will be a very small proportion of all visitors. Railway museums will draw a few engineers but there will not be many of them and most attractions have to appeal to generalists rather than specialists.

Internationally known attractions, such as Disneyland Paris in France or Shakespeare's birthplace in Stratford-on-Avon, are strong enough and sufficiently well-known to break through the normal locational limitations that govern visitor flows but they are the exception, not the rule.

Practical segmentation of the visiting public begins with user types and only then proceeds to the demographic and other segmentation factors, which are covered in Chapter 6. Within most developed countries in Europe, the following seven segments will normally apply:

1. Local residents living within approximately half an hour's drive from the attraction's location.
2. Regional residents making day visits away from home and drawn, depending on the motivating power of the site, from a distance of up to two hours' driving or more in the case of sites of national significance.
3. Visitors staying with friends and relatives within about an hour's drive from the site.
4. Visitors on holiday staying in hotels, caravan parks and other forms of commercial accommodation within about an hour's drive from the site.
5. Group visits, usually arranged in association with coach companies or organized by direct-marketing contact between groups and the attractions' management.
6. School visits and other educational groups.
7. Corporate and other users of facilities such as conference and seminar rooms, and uses of buildings for receptions, weddings and other functions.

Table 21.2 provides a practical illustration of a segmentation model developed by the principal author for a large heritage attraction just outside London and easily accessible by train. The characteristics of each segment were derived by market research and became the basis for devising marketing strategy and marketing campaigns, and for forecasting and evaluating the results achieved.

Because of the nature of attractions, their fixed locations, spare capacity on most days and the need to draw in as many visitors as possible, it is always logical to target campaigns on selected segments but it is very rarely practical to approach the marketing task by concentrating only on one or two of the possible segments. Where attractions charge for admission, the need to generate revenue will make it even more important to appeal to as many visitor groups as possible.

For the accommodation and transport sectors of travel and tourism, selecting segments is always an essential first step in product design and adaptation. Segmentation for attractions, however, is more important for targeting promotion and distribution than it is for product formulation. For example, if it appears for a particular attraction that holiday visitors will be especially important in its visitor mix, the implication is not so much to design the product for holiday visitors but to focus most promotional and distribution efforts on them. The marketing approach to local residents will be quite different from that aimed at tourists but the product experience they enjoy is essentially the same for most.

Such product flexibility as exists comes mainly from organizing the components and interpretation to meet the needs of particular user groups. Marketing attractions

TABLE 21.2 A segmentation planning model for a large visitor attraction, approximately 10 miles from London

Visitor characteristics	Core location/categories for promotion	First time/ repeat visitors	Transport used for visit	Timing (months)	Current visitor numbers	5-year target numbers
a. Residents in local area and day visitors	Approx. 3- to 5-mile radius of site	90% Repeat	60–65% Car	Year round but mostly weekends except July/ Augusts	12% 66,000	10%, 85,000
b. Residents of Greater London, Home Counties, S. East – day visitors (excluding a.)	1 h travel time of site (effectively 25-mile radius)	55–60% Repeat	55–60% Car	Mostly weekends and July/August	30% 165,000	27% 230,000
c. UK tourists staying with friends/relatives (VFR)	1 h travel time of site (effectively 25-mile radius)	60% First time	50–55%, Car	Mostly March–June, September–December	8% 44,000	6% 52,000
d. Overseas tourists staying with friends/ relatives (VFR)	1 h travel time of site (effectively 25-mile radius)	65% First time	55–60%, Car	Mostly April–October	12% 66,000	14% 120,000
e. UK tourists to London (not VFR)	Central London, mostly on short breaks in hotels	70% First time	80% Public transport	Mostly February–May, September–November	3% 16,500	2.5% 23,000
f. Overseas tourists to London (not VFR)	Central London mostly on one week visits staying in hotels	85% First time	90% Coach	Mostly April–October	19% 104,000	20% 170,000
g. Overseas tourists in groups (additional to d. and f.)	Central London mostly on one week visits staying in hotels	85% First time	90% Coach	Mostly February–May, September–November	9% 49,500	12% 105,000
h. British visitors in groups (day visitor groups and staying visitors groups) (additional to c. and e.)	1 h travel time of site (effectively 25-mile radius) Central London mostly on short breaks in hotels	75% First time	90% Coach	Mostly February–May, September–November	3% 17,000	4% 35,000
i. School/educational parties	5-mile radius of site 1 hr travel time of site (effectively 25-mile radius)	90% Repeat (i.e. same schools)	80% Coach	September–December and April–May	4% 22,000	3.5% 30,000
				Totals	550,000	850,000

to corporate users for function and meetings, for example, is not based on the 'product' marketed to the visiting public and it obviously depends on the quality of the facilities available for such purposes. Where such use is feasible, it adds a potential stream of non-seasonal revenue, often outside normal public visiting hours and may also provide valuable integrating links with a local community.

MARKETING STRATEGY FOR ATTRACTIONS

Commencing from a basic appreciation of products and segments noted above, the primary task for marketing managers is to monitor and interpret the factors in the changing external environment that influence strategy. Four main issues are:

1. *Actions of competitors.* As more places look to the visitor economy to generate employment lost from primary and manufacturing industry, competition in the same market catchment area for the same visitor segments seems certain to increase over the next decade. Much of the new competition will be purpose-designed or adapted to attract and satisfy visitors. Some of it will be subsidized by government and its agencies. In this more competitive environment some older attractions are likely to disappear or have to merge with others, no longer able to attract sufficient customers or adequate funding from other sources to cover their operating expenses and fund the refurbishment needed to remain competitive.
2. *Customer sophistication.* For attractions, as for other service industries, visitors' expectations and their perceptions of satisfaction and value for money are in a continual state of change and development. 'Yesterday' products' quickly lose their appeal if suppliers fail to keep pace with current requirements. All successful attractions pursue a product quality strategy of continual enhancement while increasing visitors' perceived value for money – the best measure of being competitive. The leading edge rapidly becomes the standard against which others are judged.
3. *ICT developments.* Information and communications technology is changing traditional approaches to market research, promotion and distribution as explained in Part Four. Other hardware and software technology has also opened up opportunities that many attractions can utilize in the display and interpretation of their resource base, including lighting, sound, film, lasers, virtual technologies, and new materials such as carbon fibre, Kevlar and fibre optics. For some attractions, such as museums and galleries, digital technology creates income earning possibilities through the communication of objects to audiences away from the sites in which they are located.
4. *More sustainable approaches to managing resources.* In common with all tourism enterprises in the twenty-first century visitor attractions have to respond to global needs to review and develop more sustainable practice. Areas for action lie in their consumption of energy and water, use of chemicals, production and disposal of waste and integration with local community partners for supplies. More importantly, because so many visitor attractions are part of or directly associated with the conservation of built and natural environment resources at destinations, many of them are able to play a much

wider role in communicating sustainable issues to the visiting public. The Eden Project in Cornwall, England is one such leading 'edutainment' attraction that has brought environmental and ecological sustainability to the fore. Table 21.3 (adapted from Middleton and Hawkins, 1998: 169) summarizes the potential role of attractions in sustainability, from a marketing perspective. Looking ahead, the effective performance of this role in destination sustainability may give some attractions an added justification for the continuance of operational subsidies.

TABLE 21.3 Sustainability: a marketing perspective for resource-based visitor attractions

By the nature of their operations resource-based visitor attractions are key players in sustainable development from a marketing perspective. Their marketing decisions strongly influence and in some cases directly control:

- The specific customers targeted for promotion and distribution (from among those staying at a destination and others within easy day-travelling distance).
- Overall design and quality of the experience which the attraction provides.
- The most direct 'hands on' experience of environmental resources accessible to most visitors.
- Communication of information explaining and interpreting the nature of the attraction/resource and its significance.
- The specific presentation of objects, stories and themes, and all the forms of display provided for visitors.
- Opportunities for visitors and residents to meet on equal terms; qualified local guides and interpreters can perform a key role in this process.
- Prices at which visitors are admitted including any promotional and discounted offers.
- Product offers put together with other destination partners such as accommodation and local public transport operators.
- Evaluation of customer profiles and satisfaction through customer research.
- Customer profiles held on databases for analysis and future marketing.
- Marketing objective, visitor volume targets, budgets and programmes.

This combination of influences, all of them part of the modern process of marketing for visitor attractions, is especially important where the attraction being managed is a core part of the environmental quality and appeal of a destination, for example, a castle, a cathedral, a museum or a national park. Non-commercial attractions such as museums have a special role to play because of the authority and extra credibility often attached to their communications.

Strategic marketing plans

Responding to the external factors, the strategic task for attractions revolves around the process of refining the segmentation of the total market (as noted in Table 21.2) and targeting the potential volume of demand from each group. Segmentation is the base for:

- Marketing research and monitoring the nature of the experiences that the resource base is capable of sustaining for each of the main groups in the audience market.
- Product formulation and augmentation to enhance customer satisfaction through development and improved presentation, display and information techniques.

- Pricing and forecasting revenue flows that directly affect both capital and operating revenue decisions.
- Developing effective targeted campaigns for promotion and distribution.
- Evaluating the seasonality and sustainable implications of different groups.
- Analysing the options to develop new segments; new user groups may also identify new uses, such as opening museums in the evenings for functions and receptions.

For image and promotional purposes, it will usually be necessary to identify one principal underlying theme, idea and image, which encapsulates and communicates the experiences the attraction offers. The theme will be based on the resource the attraction exists to serve and it may develop from the research required to appreciate visitors' perceptions of the experience. The chosen theme and image will be the basis for positioning the attraction and the benefits it offers, in all marketing communications.

Strategy may often require the search for effective promotional and distribution linkages and alliances between the attraction and other sites of the same type, or of different types in the same location. Such links, supported by intranets and B2B web sites, may be achieved with the support of tourist boards, or directly between co-operating attractions.

OPERATING CONSTRAINTS ON MARKETING

There are three main operating constraints that influence the marketing of attractions.

The first reflects the familiar concern with the implications of high fixed costs and low variable costs of operation. This affects many attractions even more than it affects transport and accommodation suppliers because of the second main constraint of seasonality. The combination of high fixed costs and seasonality acts as a powerful constraint to which marketing has to respond. A seasonal attraction may experience maximum demand on only about 20 days in the year, which may generate up to a quarter of the year's admissions. For example, a busy summer day at an attraction drawing some half a million visitors a year in a seasonal location will see over 7500 visitors through the turnstiles. By contrast, a day in February may produce only 150 people. Yet, if the quality of the visitor experience is to be maintained, the fixed costs of operating in February are much the same as in July. Any savings in the numbers of part-time staff are offset by the increased costs of heating and lighting. Closure may not be an option if it leads to staff losses and other costs.

Obviously, on a simple pro-rata basis, attractions may operate at a loss in February and at other times of the year, so the role of marketing is to influence demand to generate marginal extra admission income outside the limited number of peak days and maximize throughput on the main revenue earning days. Seasonality also forces the evaluation of alternative audiences such as schools and a range of corporate users that are not geared to normal seasonal patterns.

MINI-CASE 21.2: MANAGING SEASONALITY

Seasonality, reflecting the peaks and troughs of visitor demand, creates a number of significant operational challenges for many visitor attractions. Demand factors are, however, not alone in contributing to seasonality. For example, external factors, such as weather and school vacation patterns, supply-side factors, such as traffic congestion, car parking and public transport access are all challenges faced by attractions in managing and minimizing the negative impacts of uneven flows. Seasonality thus represents a major challenge for many attractions in that it impacts directly on the overall spread of visitor numbers and revenue. Despite this, many attractions continue to rely on season-specific market sectors. Goulding (2008) highlights the fact that approximately 40% of attractions in Scotland still operate for less than nine months of the year.

Although seasonality is viewed as a necessity by some natural attractions as a means for attraction 'recovery' from both social (general wear and tear) and ecological damage, for the majority of attractions it is a challenge to be managed. The choice is either to accept seasonal flows as a '*fait accompli*' and devote more effort to the management of visitors in peak periods or attempt to shift demand within existing peak periods and optimize the 'low season'. More proactive tactical responses can be implemented via product extensions (which may include the staging of ad hoc events) and pricing initiatives that aim to promote the off peaks. A more strategic approach is to devise market diversification strategies, something that a number of whisky distilleries do in Scotland, for example, by hosting corporate events and hospitality. Such a strategy may require the need for investment in facilities, interpretation and services and the adoption of a yield management approach utilized to good effect in accommodation and transport. If there is a history of working together, attractions may come together to broaden the appeal of the destination more widely in the form of a 'joint pass' or the 'collective themeing' of attractions. Evidence also exists of a number of consortia or trade association approaches to countering seasonality.

Public sector responses to seasonality may include fiscal incentives, incentives for the labour force, changing the structure and staggering school vacations, business support services geared to assist seasonal extension and the public provision of wet-weather facilities. Similarly, albeit more broadly, the public sector can contribute to environmental regeneration improving the attractiveness of 'place' and to off-season community events that may stimulate visits to local attractions.

Source: Based on Goulding (2008)

A third constraint affecting many attractions is the extent to which repeat visits to any one site in any one year are usually a minority of all visits. Some attractions have the kind of resource that encourages repeat visits, but many in popular tourist destinations are designed for one visit only. With the competition now facing most attractions, reviewing the product experience and finding new ways to encourage repeat visits as well as first-time visits is therefore a primary concern for most attractions.

This fact also helps to explain why successful large attractions find it necessary to spend 10% or more of their admission revenue on promotion and distribution.

Unlike profitable businesses in other sectors of travel and tourism, it appears to be characteristic and normal for most smaller visitor attractions to survive from year to year on a financial knife-edge. Rising costs of operation tend to overtake any rise in available sources of revenue. Certainly this is true of those in the heritage sector, many of which exist to achieve non-profit-related goals. Costs rise at least in line with inflation and the potential demands of the resource for optimum conservation and refurbishment are usually far in excess of available income. Times of economic recession reduce income from visitors and play havoc with budget forecasts. With high fixed costs committed in advance, a 10% downturn in earned revenue over a year can usually be tackled only by severe cost-cutting for the year following. It is, however, all too easy for attractions to cut costs (including marketing budgets) to the extent that the visit experience becomes tired and worn, and further falls in revenue result as customers turn elsewhere.

THE SIZE OF THE MARKETING BUDGET

Experience suggests that allocating around 10% of admissions revenue for marketing purposes is a realistic guideline for most visitor attractions. There may well be a convincing argument for spending more than this, however, especially to promote awareness of new facilities and on seasonal sales promotion efforts if the evidence achieved through visitor research indicates that the promotional efforts are paying off in admission revenue.

The objective and task approaches to budgeting, outlined in Chapter 12, are particularly appropriate for visitor attractions and the segmentation model set out in Table 21.2 provides an appropriate structure for budget allocation and monitoring.

DEVELOPING NEW MARKETING AND MANAGEMENT LINKAGES

Given the average small size of attractions, they are typically likely to have only one or at most two people with management responsibility. They have to provide all the management skills needed to compete in a more sophisticated visitor market against the major operators with their large management teams. In common with developments in other sectors of the tourism economy, the only logical response to small scale is to join with others to share the management skills that cannot be achieved individually. Such a response has strategic and tactical dimensions but it is not easy for small operators, and the process typically needs a catalyst organization, such as a destination management organization or professional body, to lead the process.

Evidence suggests that all proactive attractions, and most if not all new developments, are seeking a future based on forging business synergy links and collaboration with partners. On the one hand these are intended to help them secure audiences and revenue, and on the other hand to provide mutual management support systems. Based on extensive research into UK museums, and clear evidence of some of the new linkages being developed, it was recommended that all museums should undertake a formal strategic audit of their existing and potential links with other organizations, working to national and regional guidelines (Middleton, 1998). The options include:

- Collocation with partner organizations, especially for new attractions and those faced with closure.
- Development of catering and related facilities to act as stand alone revenue earning entities rather than just a facility for the visiting public.
- Links with universities and other colleges of further and higher education in the co-production of courses and education for life.
- Links with local businesses for the provision of meeting spaces, functions and training seminars.
- Promotional links with other attractions that are not competing directly for the same audiences and users.
- Links with other attractions to share management expertise.
- Links with other companies, especially for museums and galleries, which may be interested to market aspects of their collections using the new digital communication technology.

Many attractions can benefit from a systematic review of public and corporate uses of their facilities and many have developed 'friends' and similar volunteer groups to support their objectives. Cathedrals in popular destinations in the UK, for example, apart from the normal congregations for worship, appeal mostly to first-time visitors. But their prime locations in the centre of cities and towns can also support a combination of events such as concerts and the development of high-quality catering facilities. Such provision can develop and sustain a substantial level of repeat visits (and revenue contribution) from a resident community. They are not just revenue-earning opportunities, they are also ways to integrate visitor facilities functionally within their communities and provide local experiences of place.

Another aspect of this search for linkages may lie in the arrangements for promotion and distribution that can be made with transport and accommodation interests seeking to provide extra interest and motivation in their own product offers. An obvious link is with coach tour operators but hotels offering weekend breaks may be interested to feature admission to attractions as part of an inclusive price. In this context attractions become a part of the augmentation of an accommodation product, which in turn serves as a form of distribution channel for the attraction. Looking ahead, developing networking between different groups of public and corporate users of their facilities is likely to be a key requirement for the survival and prosperity of smaller attractions.

CHAPTER SUMMARY

This chapter

- Stresses the important role of attractions as one of the core elements in the overall tourism product that motivates leisure travellers. It identifies the common characteristics that influence the way that attractions are marketed. Ten categories of managed attractions are noted, all of which are controlled and managed, sometimes to protect and conserve precious heritage resources but mostly to provide access, enjoyment, entertainment and education for the visiting public.
- Outlines the inherent divide between larger and smaller attractions. Larger attractions usually charge for admission and increasingly are professionally managed and marketed. Very few are commercial. Traditional heritage and theme park attractions are facing major new competition from retail-based complexes that are a purpose-designed mix of themed hospitality, leisure and entertainment as well as retail – marketed as leisure day out experiences. The great majority of all attractions, however, are still remarkably small in visitor numbers and revenue. Few were purpose-built for modern tourism and they are inherently product or resource orientated. Most are stand alone operations and have low levels of visitor management and marketing skills. The 'corporate culture' and the profile of this latter group, many of which are subsidized and provide their facilities 'free' or at low admission charges, are obviously not conducive for the development and application of the systematic marketing procedures recommended in this book. For reasons discussed, however, the pressures of competition and the need to generate revenue are forcing changes in professional management throughout the sector.
- Introduces the reader to the definition of products as 'experiences' and suggests that the use of research to deconstruct and assess the components of the experience for product formulation is important to successful marketing.
- Explains that the strategic marketing tasks for attractions reflect the high fixed costs of operation, the seasonality of visitor flows that many experience and the constant need to motivate first-time visits and, so far as possible, sustain repeat visits. Marketing strategy focuses on segmentation, product formulation and positioning, and the need to ensure that the benefits offered by the attraction are clearly understood by targeted prospective visitors.
- Argues that in their essential need for marketing, managed attractions are not different in principle from most other travel and tourism producers. The small scale of most of them puts a particular emphasis on reviewing their traditional stand-alone operations for the visiting public and developing collaborative linkages for management and operational purposes. The relentless pressure on costs of operation and opportunities for more effective mutual collaboration are expected to change the agenda for many attractions in the twenty-first century.

QUESTIONS TO CONSIDER

1. What do you consider to be the principal benefits and drawbacks of charging for admission to a country's national monuments, museums and galleries?
2. What management and marketing strategies can be adopted to minimize the negative impacts of seasonality for an attraction of your choice?
3. How significant is attraction 'size', in terms of visitor numbers, in determining the management and marketing strategies adopted?
4. What 'innovative' Internet-based strategies can be adopted for marketing attractions to two distinct market segments to an attraction of your choice?

REFERENCES AND FURTHER READING

Buhalis, D., Owen, R. and Pletinckx, D. (2006). Information communication technology applications for World Heritage Site management, pp. 127. In: *Managing World Heritage Sites* (Ed. by Leask, A., Fyall, A.). Oxford: Elsevier Butterworth Heinemann.

Connell, J. (2004). The *purest of human pleasures:* the characteristics and motivations of garden visitors in Great Britain, *Tourism Management*, **25**(2), pp. 229–247.

Fyall, A., Garrod, B., Leask, A. and Wanhill, S. (2008). *Managing Visitor Attractions: New Directions* (2nd edn). Elsevier Butterworth Heinemann.

Fyall, A., Leask, A. and Garrod, B. (2001). Scottish visitor attractions: a collaborative future? *International Journal of Tourism Research*, **3**, pp. 211–228.

Garrod, B. and Fyall, A. (2000). Managing heritage tourism, *Annals of Tourism Research*, **27**(3), pp. 682–708.

Goulding, P. (2008). Managing temporal variation in attractions. In: *Managing Visitor Attractions: New Directions* (Ed. by Fyall, A., Garrod, B., Leask, A., Wanhill, S.), pp. 197–216 (2nd edn). Oxford: Elsevier Butterworth Heinemann.

Keynote (2005). *European Tourist Attractions Market Assessment 2005*. Keynote Publications.

Managing World Heritage Sites (Ed. by Leask, A., Fyall, A.). Elsevier Butterworth Heinemann.

Middleton, V.T.C. (1998). *New Visions for Museums in 21st Century*. AIM.

Middleton, V.T.C. and Hawkins, R. (1998). *Sustainable Tourism: A Marketing Perspective*. Oxford: Butterworth Heinemann.

Richards, S. and Wilkes, K. (2008). *Attraction failure and success*. In *Managing Visitor Attractions: New Directions* (2nd edn) (Ed. by A. Fyall et al.) pp. 39–58. Elsevier Butterworth-Heinemann.

Stevens, T. (2000). The future of visitor attractions, *Travel and Tourism Analyst*, **1**, pp. 61–85.

Timothy, D.J. and Boyd, S.W. (2003). *Heritage Tourism*. Prentice Hall.

Dog sledding vacations - "Despite so many forces for change across the world, the 'package holiday' still retains its appeal for much of the mass market. The means by which it is 'packaged' and 'distributed', however, continue to change with developments in eTourism driving the future marketing of this most traditional of tourism products"

CHAPTER 22

Marketing inclusive tours and product packages

"Ultimately, ICT tools reinvent the packaging of tourism to a much more individual-focused activity, offering great opportunities for principals and intermediaries and enhancing the total quality of the final product (fitness to purpose). Electronic tourism distribution channels dictate the choice of product as the difference between products becomes secondary to the easiness of getting an entire transaction completed"

Buhalis and Law (2008)

This chapter focuses on the commercial operators that assemble the components of tourism products and market them as *packages* to the final consumer. A package is essentially a selected combination of individual elements of the travel and tourism product, marketed under a particular product or brand label and sold at an inclusive price. Most such products are aimed at leisure and holiday markets although business incentive travel and many conferences are packaged in similar ways.

International tour operators, such as Touristic Union International (TUI) and Thomas Cook take millions of customers abroad every year and are the best-known and most obvious illustrations of modern tour operation. But independent tour operators are by no means the only businesses marketing travel packages and, increasingly, such packages are part of the marketing armoury of the leading branded suppliers of accommodation, transport, cruise ships and other businesses that were traditionally involved in providing only one of the total product components.

After studying this chapter you should be able to understand:

- The main definitions that present a broad view of the types of packages available in travel and tourism.
- The role of tour operators in the overall travel and tourism product and the nature of the tour-operating business that determines marketing responses.
- How to assess the marketing role of tour operators and the implications for strategy and tactics.
- The role of the Internet in shifting the strategic business environment in which tour operators work.

Courtesy of Dimitrios Buhalis.

DEFINING INCLUSIVE TOUR AND PRODUCT PACKAGES

In Chapter 7, the overall tourism product was identified as a package and defined in terms of five main components, comprising destination attractions, destination facilities and services, accessibility of the destination (including transport), images, brands and perceptions, and price to the customer. This chapter takes a deliberately broad view of packages comprising three distinctive types of business model:

- The first type always includes transport as well as accommodation in the package and acts primarily as an independent contractor doing deals with other businesses on a contractual basis. These contractors are the traditional tour operators that put together programmes for sale months in advance of product delivery. The largest of them now have global links and are structurally integrated with airlines and retail chains under the same ownership. Tour operators are also known as wholesalers in some countries but the tour operator label is more common in Europe. Smaller contractors include inbound travel agents and the many niche operators providing packages for every type of sport, recreation and leisure activity.
- The second type always includes accommodation in the package but may not include transport. This group of packages is put together by hotels and other accommodation and the larger visitor attractions that find it profitable to develop and market their own packages both directly to the consumer and indirectly through travel intermediaries. For many in this group, packages are a form of sales promotion designed to combat the effects of high fixed costs and seasonality. In the transport sector some airlines and sea ferries develop and operate their own packages for the same reason.

- The third type is a hybrid that emerged as a direct result of recent advances in ICT, the disenchantment of many consumers with undifferentiated mass marketing and their demand for products that meet their own specification. As outlined in Chapter 14 an increasing number of new options for creating customized travel packages are now available to these consumers. They can have dynamic or modular packages put together for them by travel agents; they can assemble their own package from airline affiliate networks (see Chapter 14) or through a wide choice of new on-line travel e-mediaries shown in Table 15.2 in Chapter 15.

  So many commercial and non-commercial organizations in the travel and tourism industry are now marketing packages that it is important to be as precise as possible in definitions. There are two main considerations in this, reflecting:

- The nature of the package provided for sale and the business relationship between operator and owners of the main product components.
- The dominant method of distribution to customers.

The nature of the product and the business relationships involved

Product packages are:

Quality assured, repeatable offers comprising two or more elements of transport, accommodation, food, destination attractions, other facilities and related services (such as travel insurance). Product packages are marketed to the general public, described in print or electronic media, and offered for sale to prospective customers at a published, inclusive price, in which the costs of the product components cannot be separately identified.

The definition *excludes* special packages put together for a closed group of users. For example, many conference products in hotels have standard elements and are often referred to as packages. But they are generally put together to meet the needs of specified members of particular organizations and are 'one-off' packages specially adapted for each group purchaser. While important, such packages are not marketed according to the principles outlined in this chapter.

The terms 'quality assured' and 'repeatable' no longer imply mass production of a limited range of identical product types. It means that products offered for sale will be delivered in a consistent or quality-assured way, with quality judged by targeted customers (through market research). In practice, quality assured means operating product control processes to ensure the delivery of product consistency of a standard that matches or exceeds the needs and expectations of consumer segments.

As part of a European Community approach to securing and enforcing customer protection, including requirements for financial arrangements to compensate clients in the event of claims, the EC Package Holiday Directive was drawn up for implementation in all EC countries from 1993. It states:

"Package means the pre-arranged combination of not fewer than two of the following when sold or offered for sale at an inclusive price and when the service covers a period of more than 24 h or includes overnight accommodation: transport, accommodation, other tourist services not ancillary to transport or accommodation and accounting for a significant proportion of the package." (EC Directive)

To summarize, packages may be standardized or bespoke, 'manufactured' by contractors or assembled by accommodation and other tourism businesses providing part of the total offer. In every case the packages that operators assemble are drawn from the five basic elements of the overall tourism product, plus whatever added value of their own operations is built in, such as price guarantees, convenience, accessibility to the customer, image and branding, high standards and sense of security in dealing with a reputable company.

The business relationship is either one of contractual arrangements by independent firms in which the identity of the component elements is normally subsumed within the operator's brand, or contractual arrangements between one component collaborating with targeted partners to produce packages that are branded and marketed under the name of the leading component. Branded hotel packages, for example, are in the latter category, of which many are in domestic rather than international travel. There are probably as many packages now in the second category as in the first.

Distribution method to customers

The second consideration relates to the form of marketing now used to sell packages. All organizations' marketing packages have the basic choice between a strategy based on direct marketing or marketing through third party distribution-networks (Buhalis and Laws, 2001). The development of the Internet and e-commerce has rapidly shifted the traditional distribution patterns used for inclusive tours and packages, and opened the route to strategies that are partly direct and partly through retail intermediaries. As introduced in Chapter 15, Information and Communications Technology (ICT) is fundamentally changing the process of searching, finding and comparing the options available in ways that were not practical before the late 1990s. Increasing numbers of travellers are empowered by on-line information and booking systems to seek their own personal booking efficiencies, with web sites being central to their decision making and shopping behaviour. At the same time, these systems are being offered by a whole range of new entrants to the travel market, including not only new travel intermediaries like Expedia or Tripadvisor but also other companies such as internet service providers, news media and social network sites (see Table 15.2). All these provide competition to the traditional tour operators. As a result, choice and control of distribution channels generally and electronic distribution in particular have now become the dominant strategic issues in packaging, as is further discussed later in the chapter.

The functional role of inclusive tours and packages

Around the world, firms providing international tours and product packages would not have survived and grown as they have unless the services they provided were firmly rooted in the needs of both buyers and sellers. Price and convenience are the dominant characteristics but it is possible to identify six main reasons that explain the international significance of packaging:

- Delivering price advantages that most customers are usually unable to achieve for themselves although this could in certain situations be debated.
- The need for safety and security in remote and unfamiliar destinations and the willingness to pay a premium for expert advice and a support network if it is needed.
- Providing convenience and both psychological and financial security in a 'single purchase' transaction that facilitates and simplifies an otherwise complex process of choice and booking, especially for travel abroad.
- Providing product quality assurance in a branded context and 'guaranteeing' delivery of the promise.
- Backing up the quality assurance promise with legal liability for delivery and obligation to compensate if the contract is not delivered.
- Overcoming the inherent inefficiencies in the supply and demand for leisure travel and tourism, especially for international travel.

The price advantage of prepared packages was always a major strength in the market place because, in a market notorious for its price elasticity, prices charged to individuals attempting to put together for themselves the components of their chosen packages have always been relatively high. This is because individuals cannot obtain the volume discounts available to any large buyer in competitive conditions and (although the Internet is now changing the traditional business models) they are unlikely to gain access to the B2B yield management programmes of different component producers which often provide the best available deals. Delivering low prices was, therefore, a primary basis for competition in major consumer markets and many observers see this as the tour operator's most important function in the travel and tourism industry. On the other hand if customers make their own arrangements direct via the Internet, tour operator overheads and marketing costs do not have to be covered so theoretically prices should be less. Pricing methods have changed for packages with organizations adopting calendar pricing to match demand with supply, something that started with airlines and is now also common for hotels and other forms of accommodation.

Secondly, from a customer's point of view, attempting to define options and choose the elements of an overall product separately, especially for the first time in an unknown destination, is often a very hit and miss and time-consuming process. It is fraught with the risk of making an expensive mistake as well as experiencing a personal sense of failure if things go wrong. For travel abroad, with its added complications of language, currency and distance from home, the problems and inconvenience for inexperienced travellers acting on their own account may be too daunting and too time-consuming, even if the cost is not a problem.

Thirdly, through their contracting procedures, specification of the product in brochures and on web sites, the strategic use of branding and use of representatives at destinations as well as through close monitoring of customer satisfaction, tour operators can sustain and develop the product quality standards needed to reassure many buyers at the point of sale.

Fourthly, modern competition increasingly focuses on product quality promises and, through the EC Package Travel Directive in European countries and through self-regulatory mechanisms; operators must accept legal liability for the products they offer. Consumers can expect virtual guarantees of acceptable product delivery and the right to redress if they have a reasonable complaint.

Finally, with a few exceptions at certain periods and in certain locations, the matching of tourism demand with supply is a remarkably inefficient process for most businesses supplying to travel and tourism, especially in leisure markets. On the supply side, many producers of accommodation and attractions typically operate in a single fixed location, aiming to attract infrequent buyers, many of them buying for the first time and on a once-only basis. Moreover, prospective buyers are usually drawn from a very wide catchment area. For example, over the space of three months in the summer, a hotel in Scotland may draw its customers from up to six overseas countries and up to half the regions in the UK. A resort hotel in Greece or Turkey may draw most of its customers from only four or five countries, yet their addresses may be geographically spread across half the landmass of Europe and the Middle East.

Effective marketing on a national and international basis needed to secure exposure and promotion of their product offers to target customers is still not an option for most independent hoteliers and other small businesses. While advertising in national tourist office guides is as sensible for the Greek and Turkish hotelier as for the one in Scotland, it is seldom a certain or sufficient process to secure the sale of otherwise unsold capacity on a daily basis.

Such businesses have no choice but to look to other sources to supply business they are not able to achieve through their own direct marketing efforts. In this regard many of the marketing strategies advanced in Chapters 14 and 15 are relevant here with many of the new 'gateways' identified in Table 15.2 are crucial in setting the agenda for future web-based bookings.

To summarize, the core value of inclusive tours and product packages is to provide a well-honed marketing mechanism that simultaneously solves producers' needs to sell their capacity and customers' needs for convenience and security at advantageous, affordable prices. At a profit to the companies that do it, packaging solves the natural inefficiency that is inherent in matching demand and supply in most leisure sectors of travel and tourism. That vital role explains its importance in the industry and, notwithstanding growing consumer interest in independent travel, it will be new forms of customized and dynamic packages – a far cry from the mass-market commodity products of the 1970s – that will provide it. There appear to be no reasons why the six functional roles in marketing noted in this section will diminish significantly in importance over the next decade despite the continuing exponential growth of the Internet. For example, the fact that the Internet enables tour operators to embed videos, maps and media-rich material into their marketing efforts has helped to reduce the intangibility of the 'product' and increase the overall appeal of their offers.

THE PROCESS OF CONSTRUCTING AN INCLUSIVE TOUR PROGRAMME

All engaged in marketing packages assemble product elements into what are known as *programmes*. A programme is held on a database (see Chapter 13) and communicated in brochures and through web sites, which usually contain a range of product choices in several destinations. To explain how programmes are constructed, this section focuses on air-inclusive tours as the most developed sector of packaging, but the principles are the same in constructing any programme.

A tour operator offering international tours by air has a choice of using bulk fare rates on scheduled and other airlines or bulk fares available from their own airline. The cost per seat naturally varies according to volume bought and whether the operator charters the whole flight or only a number of seats. All the largest international tour operators now have their own subsidiary airlines to transport the bulk of their programmes and are thus able to secure the lowest possible seat cost available.

A large air international tour programme out of the UK uses up to 20 airports of departure, up to a hundred resorts and cities in a dozen or more countries, and a range of products based on accommodation types from luxury hotels through villas to simple self-catering apartments. Putting a large programme such as this together depends on translating estimates of market demand into production capacity, and matching aircraft seats with beds in batches that add up to full aeroplanes flying between pairs of airports. The skill lies in matching estimated demand with contracted supply, to achieve optimum aircraft utilization, optimum average load factors for flights and maximum occupancy of contracted beds.

The process of putting a programme together is shown in Fig. 22.1. The diagram reflects the initial planning dialogue, common in all types of marketing, between marketing research and forecasting, corporate strategy and marketing implementation. The hardest decision in programme planning always focuses on what volume of products will be offered in the year ahead. Planning may start 18 months before the first customers travel, and product volume has to be turned into numbers of seats and beds in order to see how flight schedules and bed capacity in resorts can best be matched. This process identifies capacity objectives for the staff that negotiate for beds and seats. Optimizing the best match between flight schedules and blocks of beds to achieve the most cost-efficient utilization of aircraft and hotels is, of course, a computer software process and the finalized programmes become inventory systems and communication tools. It is an interactive process, strongly affected by the hotel prices being contracted.

With a draft programme worked out to meet projected demand, the next stage is to draft the all-important price and departure panels, which will appear in brochures and on web sites, stating the price of each inclusive tour product according to the date of departure and number of nights. Normally included on each product page of the brochure below the description of the accommodation, price and departure panels are increasingly produced separately in loose-leaf format to facilitate tactical price changes without reprinting the whole brochure. Up to this stage there is ample room for change in all aspects of the programme, and there are numerous feedback loops in the process, although not all are shown in Fig. 22.1, to avoid clutter. Product prices and capacity are not in practice finalized until the last possible moment, about 10 weeks before the brochure is distributed and customer purchases begin. Even then, as noted later under 'tactics', both may have to be changed more than once after publication.

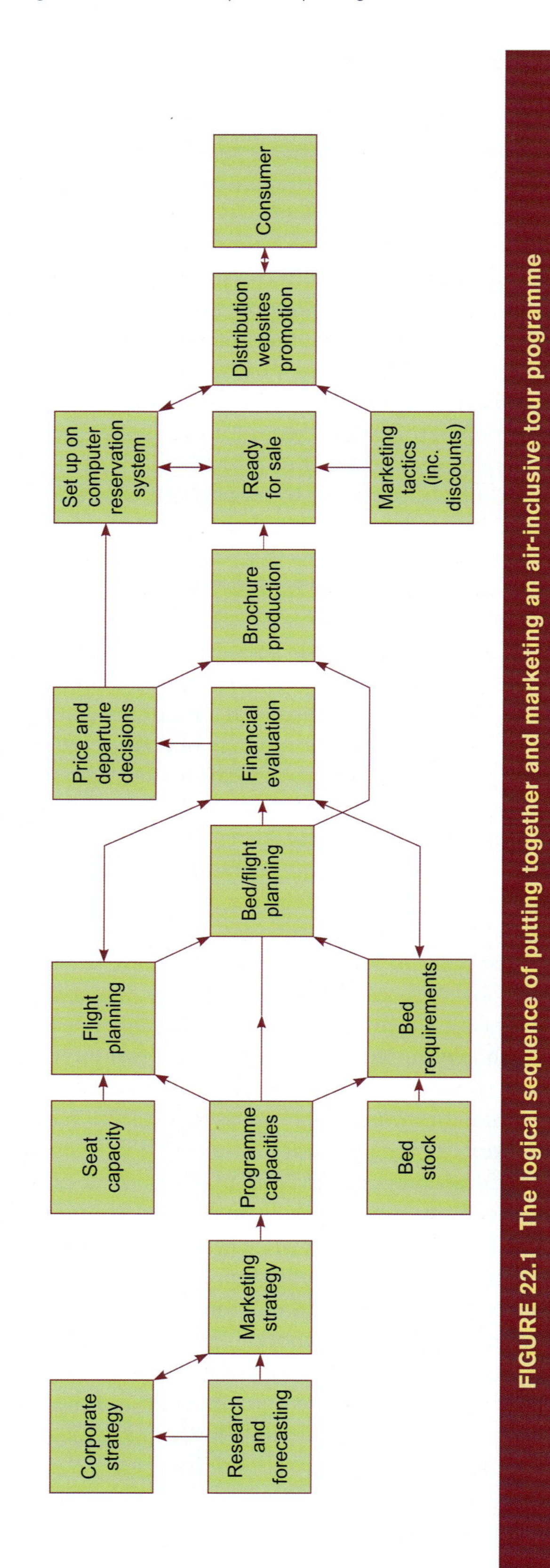

FIGURE 22.1 The logical sequence of putting together and marketing an air-inclusive tour programme

Up until just over a decade ago, most customers would book months ahead of product delivery and the January/February booking period for summer holidays is still the most important time. The consumer trend in all countries to ever-later booking upsets the old certainties, however, and a combination of fluid pricing and repackaging of programmes to meet shifts in last minute demand is not easy for tour operators to handle. The use of the Internet facilitates the process and provides another reason for greater use of the Internet for distribution and promotion. In particular, it is crucial for tour operators proactively to incorporate ICT into their efforts to improve service quality as this now plays a key role in enabling them to package their products 'dynamically' and so differentiate and specialize their products and services to the extent that one-to-one packages are already possible in some cases. For this reason web sites are identified as the core of the promotion and distribution process with direct access to (and from) consumers.

STRATEGIC ISSUES FOR CONTRACTING TOUR OPERATORS

Although this book is concerned with marketing issues rather than overall strategic business decisions, it is nevertheless overall business strategy linked to modern marketing capability that is driving international developments in tour operating. In the UK and Northern Europe, the traditional independent tour-operating models based on firms operating within national boundaries have been overtaken by the processes of globalization. Past decades saw significant developments in horizontal and vertical integration whereby major operators purchased or merged with airlines and retail agencies, and merged with rival operators adding brands within an overall corporate envelope as the opportunity occurred. The purchase of airlines and travel agency chains gave a measure of control and cost containment in the dominant transport and distribution channels although at a cost in future flexibility that may become a major issue in the future.

Recent years have witnessed a remarkable worldwide expansion of takeovers, buy-ups and mergers reflecting business response to a combination of factors noted below:

- Need to match competitors and grow to maintain shares of market – made possible for large players by funding investment through market capitalization on leading stock markets.
- Opportunities and threats provided by information and communications technology, especially the improved knowledge derived from customer databases and the greater efficiency with which large organizations can now be managed.
- Ever greater pressure on costs to maintain price competition, especially distribution and transport costs, and the perceived options of larger size to achieve economies of scale and secure efficient control of sales through retail outlets.
- Need for existing large players to continue to grow – if only to avoid being taken over by competitors – and recognition that such growth in mature markets means expansion into other countries, usually through the purchase of, or mergers with, relevant companies.

- Need to respond to growing customer sophistication and expectations of service excellence.
- Need to respond to the opportunities provided by international branding and developing customer loyalty.

Marketing strategy for tour operators

For tour operators, as for other producers in the travel and tourism industry, it is appropriate to divide the discussion of the marketing task between strategic and tactical considerations. In practice, as any reading of the travel trade press will confirm, the nature of tour operation and the relatively long lead time between planning, promotion and final delivery generates a seemingly continuous atmosphere of 'boom and bust'. This hothouse environment puts great emphasis on the short-run tactics required to survive in a fiercely competitive marketplace. The strategic dimensions are nevertheless vital and become more so as the main generating markets in developed countries reach maturity and international rather than national competition intensifies for the reasons noted above.

Five elements are noted in this section:

- Interpreting the strength and direction of change in the external environment.
- Strategic decisions on volume and pricing.
- Choice of product/customer portfolio.
- Positioning and image.
- Choice and maintenance of distribution systems/preferred marketing method.

The external environment

External influences are especially powerful in their implications for tour operation, reflecting the 'non-essential' character of most leisure products (consumer decisions are easily changed and postponed), fierce competition and the international nature of much of the business. Although lead times are shortening, the susceptibility of operators to changes in the external environment is of course heightened by the advance planning needs. Specifically the demand for inclusive tours demonstrates large annual fluctuations triggered by:

- *Economic events*, such as growth and decline in the economic cycle affecting consumers' real income and confidence, and the impact of international exchange-rate movements on prices. Such events can rapidly and unexpectedly reach crisis proportions as in 2008.
- *Political events and disasters*, as in Kenya, and earthquakes in Turkey.
- *Information and communications technology*, for reasons explained in Part Four.
- *Sustainable development requirements* stemming from changing political and business agendas, and important shifts in consumer attitudes.

Strategic decisions on volume and pricing

For hotels, visitor attractions and transport operators, annual decisions on capacity and price levels tend to be essentially tactical implementing previous strategic judgements and fixed investment in buildings and equipment. Not so for tour operators. A combination of the lead times in programme planning, the unpredictable external business environment and the flexibility options of contracting additional capacity, means that annual decisions on volume and price are strategic rather than tactical issues. Volume and price are of course closely related because of the influences on pricing policy of what the market will bear at any point in time.

In recent years in the UK, massive discounting has been part of the marketing strategy to move the available stock and gain or defend market share. If the initial guesstimates of capacity and pricing are proved wrong by events and overcapacity results, then the whole of marketing tactics revolve around attempts to retrieve the situation in the face of fierce competition. It takes strong entrepreneurial flair and very strong nerves to hold to decisions or change them boldly as events occur. Figure 12.1 (Chapter 12) provides ample evidence of the narrowness of the margins at stake in the crucial volume and price decisions.

Product/market portfolios

The third strategic consideration for operators is concerned with the content and balance of the product portfolio, as represented in their programmes. The volume and price aspects noted earlier are not independent variables but reflect the chosen product portfolio's mix of destinations, accommodation types and range of other elements included in the product, such as excursions. Relative prices of destinations also drive portfolio choices. Where profit or loss is balanced on just a few marginal percentage points above break-even load factors, it becomes vital to offer the range of products judged to be most in demand.

Segmentation of tour operator products continues today facilitated by the growing use of data mining and it is reflected in the way in which brochures, still the main marketing tool for many operators, are put together. There is a strategic balance to be struck between the need for separate brochures to appeal to different market segments, and an equally powerful need to reduce the number of brochures because of the cost and limitations of rack space in retail outlets. There is an uneasy balance at present in which segmentation often occurs within the brochure, but this is not necessarily a cost-effective or consumer-appealing procedure, and strategic changes may be expected in the next few years. Well-designed web sites can offer greater flexibility and efficiency. For example, there exist many creative means by which the web is used to appeal to different market segments. In a study conducted by Cotte et al. (2006), it was found that 'utilitarian-consumption' correlates highly with 'information search' and 'online shopping behaviour' in that such behaviour is rationally task-directed rather than directed by the nature of the experience itself. In contrast, 'pleasure-oriented' consumers tend to enjoy interacting with the web to play web-based games, e-mail or simply chat. By breaking down the profiles of such groups there exists tremendous scope for e-aware marketers. As an example, Lastminute.com collects suitable information to personalize their weekly newsletter sent to consumers and also identifies what parts of the newsletter are accessed by consumers in order to personalize their offerings even further.

Link article available at www.routledge.com/9780750686938

(1) Buhalis, D. and Law, R. (2008). Progress in information technology and tourism management: 20 years on and 10 years after the Internet – The state of eTourism research. *Tourism Management* 29, 609–623.

Positioning, branding and image

Historically, reflecting the strong demand that low prices stimulated in a highly price-elastic market, competition between leading tour operators tended to focus primarily on price and on product portfolios. The names of the companies were always important but image and positioning, although not ignored, very clearly took second place to price competition. As markets mature, however, the focus of competition is finally switching to branding and images. The larger the operators grow, the more they depend on repeat customers and have to switch the competitive focus to communicating brand values reflected in product quality and value for money. Airlines and hotel chains have moved in this direction over the past decade and tour operators are following exactly the same path for the same business reasons. Strong branding is also recognized as essential for effective direct marketing on the Internet and all the main players are now developing their options including cruise ship operators as is evident in Mini-case 22.1 below.

MINI CASE 22.1: ROYAL CARIBBEAN – THE ULTIMATE HOLIDAY EXPERIENCE

With an annual turnover in $ billions and a combined fleet of over 30 ships, Royal Caribbean International (RCI) is the second largest cruise company in the world. With over 30 years of experience of cruising around the Caribbean, Mediterranean, Alaska and Hawaii, RCI has recently pursued a strategy of brand repositioning where it has set out to broaden its segmentation by focusing on the offer of a modern and contemporary experience. With its centre of operations firmly established in Miami, Florida, cruising until recently has been a product heavily biased toward the US market. The UK represents one of the world's fastest growing markets with potential for further development. In essence, cruise lines are offering 'packaged' products like any other tour operator, the only difference being that the resorts are floating rather than static. Their appeal is considerable, however, with a cashless on board environment, a highly flexible and varied product offering multiple destinations and variety of organized excursions, are for the most part 'all inclusive' and considered safe. This said, historically demand for cruises has been held back due to perceptions that it was only for older, retirement markets, expensive and boring.

With a deliberate attempt to reduce the age of first-time cruise passengers, RCI has actively sought to position itself as a new, younger, fresher cruise experience advocating informality, an appetite for life, friendliness, freedom and an innovative approach to the entire holiday experience. With innovative on-board activities (such as ice skating, rock climbing and miniature golf), a 3–1 guest to staff ratio, tailored family programmes, excellent health and fitness suites in addition to the more traditional entertainment package focused around casinos, theatres, nightclubs and bars, RCI has sought to position itself as 'The Ultimate Holiday Experience'. With significant creative treatment attached to its print media and TV campaigns, RCI has reduced the focus of advertising on its ships and instead given attention to on board activities, its younger and more adventure-seeking customers, and in the case of its TV campaigns in particular, a highly content-dense approach to advertising. With young families often now adorning the front pages of its brochures, the company has more a feel of Club Med than any of its cruising rivals. There are slight changes when considering repeat business in that the ships take a slightly higher profile in mail campaigns while its primary Loyalty publication, Crown & Anchor, is slightly more conventional in that it features stronger images of destinations rather than the energetic activities available on board. This is reflected also on RCI's web site with immediate segmentation between those who have ever cruised before, those who have cruised before but are new to RCI and those recipients of Crown & Anchor who have cruised with RCI before.

Although the current economic climate represents a cause for concern for all tour and cruise operators, the quite radical and innovative approach adopted by Royal Caribbean International represents a concerted attempt to both reduce the age of first-time cruisers and break through the traditional stereotypes of cruising.

Source: Based on author experience and www.royalcaribbean.com

Choice of distribution options

As discussed in detail in Part Four of the book, providing convenient product access for customers and its implications for costs, flexibility in pricing, promotion and last-minute sales is a primary strategic issue in tourism marketing. For tour operators the traditional cost of retail distribution is by for the largest item of their total operational budget. They have every reason to assess and pursue alternative options in the search for cost efficiency. Apart from the basic variable costs of commission paid on sales, there are heavy, essentially fixed costs incurred in distribution, including the printing and distribution of brochures, investment in information and communications technology to develop and maintain computer links with retail outlets and via the Internet and call centres, regular sales promotion and merchandising efforts to retail outlets to maintain display space and educationals.

The scope for creating completely new distribution channel outlets by linking strategically with the customer databases of large retailers, banks and credit card companies will further continue to undermine the share of sales handled through traditional retail travel outlets.

TACTICAL MARKETING

As noted in the previous section, strategic decisions determine the product/market portfolio, the product branding and positioning, the capacity of the programme to be offered, the price range in the brochures and the structure of the distribution system to be used. In other words, for tour operators, all the four main Ps are essentially strategic decisions and the principal role for marketing tactics is to secure a continuous flow of bookings for the programme from the day it is offered for sale. The flow of bookings is of course related to the target load factors for seats and beds and the rate at which bookings and deposits are achieved also determines the weekly cash flow required to meet fixed costs and contractual obligations to the component suppliers.

Because of the lead times in getting a programme from initial planning to the point of sale, and especially because competitors' prices and the capacity of their programmes cannot be known in advance, it is almost inevitable that every year operators will find themselves with too much or too little capacity in relation to the available demand. Most years they will also be forced into bursts of discounting to achieve their monthly share targets. This is not incompetence; it is the nature of the business described earlier in the chapter. If sales are slow (see Fig. 22.3) demand will have to be stimulated through sales promotion techniques including price discounting.

Figures 22.2 and 22.3 are simple illustrations of the key point that tactical responses are a function of the rate at which bookings are achieved over the selling period for each programme. Any programme that has been in the market for a year or more will have established a sales pattern, which can be represented as a graph with percentage load factor on the vertical axis, and weeks during which the product is on sale on the horizontal axis. For new products, the pattern will have to be

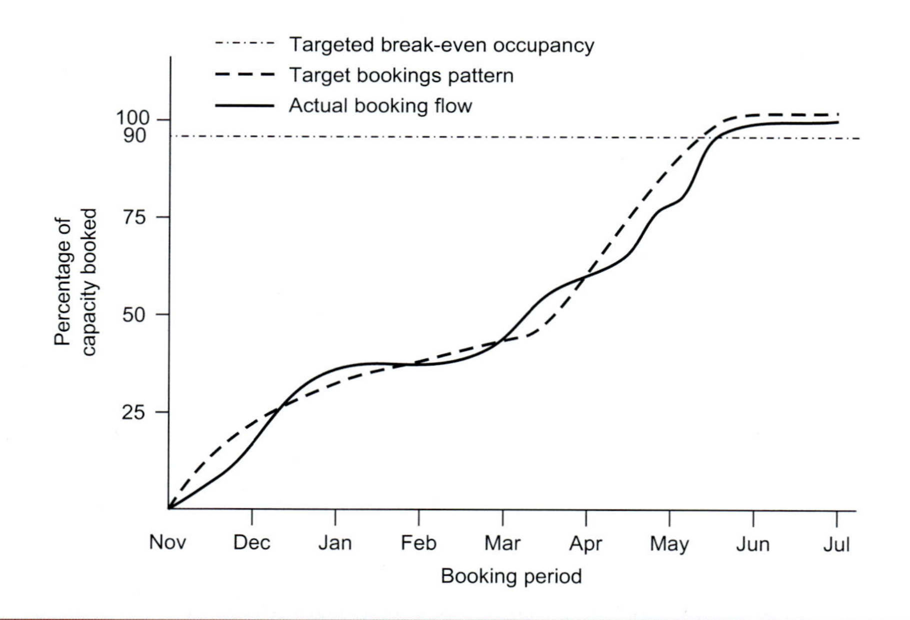

FIGURE 22.2 Targeted vs actual bookings achieved in a normal year for a tour operator

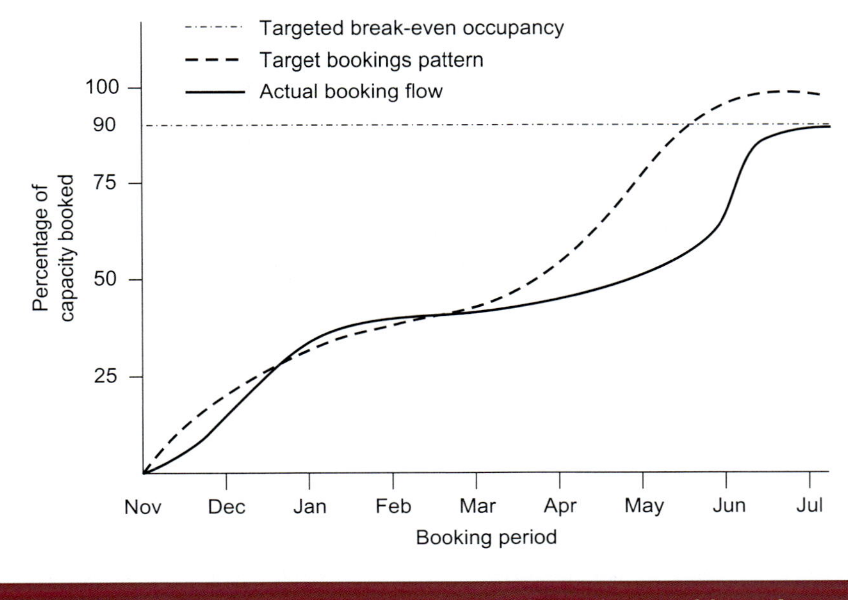

FIGURE 22.3 Targeted vs actual bookings achieved in a problematic year for a tour operator

estimated by marketing managers drawing on previous experience with comparable products. With modern computer technology linked to reservation systems, it is easy to monitor actual bookings against target on a daily basis.

If bookings for a summer product follow the predicted 'normal' sales pattern, the operator's strategy is working as planned, and tactical promotional intervention will be minimal with no need to commit contingency funds. Some last minute intervention may still be necessary in the four weeks before departure, but otherwise Fig. 22.2 represents the implementation of a successful strategy in a good year. If bookings move significantly ahead of prediction and are sustained at a high level over some weeks, provided that the market indications remain favourable, the tactical response will be to look for additional product capacity.

If, as in Fig. 22.3, bookings for a summer product fall significantly below the targeted level during March and April, decisive, aggressive tactical action becomes essential to reach the targeted break-even occupancy level represented in the figure at around the 90% load factor level. For every booking below the 90% level, the operator loses money; for every booking above it up to maximum occupancy, a significant addition to profit is generated. The incentive to engage in active tactical promotion will be obvious.

Although modern revenue yield programmes help the decision process, it is still very much a matter of judgement as to when any additional promotional activity should be committed. Assuming that operators' prices and products are broadly competitive, if one operator identifies a bookings problem ahead in the trend noted in Fig. 22.3, it is probable that all operators in the same product field will see the same problem at about the same time. They will all have to react, but how quickly and by how much will be closely guarded commercial secrets, reflecting their view of the influences at work in the external environment.

For tour operators, discounting has always been the first and most powerful tool but other choices for tactical promotion are:

- Increased advertising weight, especially through web sites and daily newspaper offers.
- Sales promotion aimed at consumers, such as competitions, free children's places (assuming these are not part of the original product) and special discounts for bookings received by a certain date.
- Sales promotion aimed at retailers offering 'last minute' bookings.
- Calls to action via the Internet (see below).

In Fig. 22.3 the tactical action taken in mid-April is shown to push the rate of bookings back up towards target, although only to the break-even level. Traditionally, if tactical effort did not succeed in stimulating demand, the operator would have no choice but to consolidate its programmes by cancelling some departures. Consolidation is increasingly not an option for large companies that depend on the reputation of their brands for quality of delivery and reliability, while consumer protection legislation acts to further reduce this option.

Until the mid-1990s, Operators' direct computer links with retailers were the main route for notifying and selling last minute discounted offers. The merchandising power of a national retailer distribution system to secure last minute sales, often in the days before departure, has been perhaps the retailers' most powerful advantage to operators. Until the advent of e-commerce on the Internet, no other form of marketing in the industry worked as fast and cost-effectively as the combined operator and retailer promotion focused on price. Over the past decade, however, there has been an explosion of travel web sites dedicated to last minute sales, including cyber auctions, which appear likely to achieve the same result at less cost and will therefore grow in popularity. Leading operators will, obviously, develop and use their own sites for this purpose and tactical marketing will take on new dimensions as a result.

CHAPTER SUMMARY

This chapter:

- Sets out a deliberately broad view of marketing inclusive tours and product packages. It notes that, as accommodation businesses, transport companies and the larger managed attractions grow in size and international reach, they are increasingly likely to assemble and market their own packages to improve utilization of their high fixed cost assets and gain cost advantages in marketing.
- Notes that all packages are intended to solve the natural inefficiencies inherent in matching demand and supply, especially in the leisure sector of tourism. All are designed to optimize customer convenience and choice and intended to optimize utilization rates for available capacity that would not otherwise be sold.
- Stresses the strategic strengths and advantages of packaging in the travel and tourism industry. These advantages are likely to become more significant over

the next decade, especially as the major tourism markets mature and the emphasis of competition shifts from price to product customization, branding, quality and better access.

- Highlights that in marketing terms the four Ps for marketing inclusive tours are essentially strategic decisions although the day-to-day pressure on marketing managers to sell their programmes is enormous and puts great emphasis on the tactical sales management of demand.

Overall, a tour operator's brochure and associated web site and eMarketing necessarily put on display all an operator knows about the aspirations and needs of his targeted customers. What is presented, therefore, represents the state of the art of marketing as operators understand it at any point in time. Few other 'manufacturers' have to wear their marketing knowledge quite so obviously 'on their sleeves', as tour operators must.

QUESTIONS TO CONSIDER

1. Is the demise of the traditional 'package' holiday overstated or is there in fact evidence to suggest that new, more individual and contemporary approaches to 'packaging' are more appropriate in the demanding conditions of the new century?
2. Identify three benefits and drawbacks of 'all inclusive' packages to a destination of your choice.
3. Provide examples on how has the Internet impacted on the way in which the industry now 'packages' its product?
4. Identify three factors underpinning last-minute purchases in certain markets and what, if anything, can the industry do to counter this trend?
5. How important is branding in the price-sensitive 'commoditized' market of consumer leisure travel?
6. Select a brochure from a leading tour operator and 'deconstruct' it to identify what it says about segmentation, customer life style and their aspirations.

REFERENCES AND FURTHER READING

Buhalis, D. and Laws, E. (2001). *Tourism Distribution Channels: Patterns, Practices and Challenges*. London: Thomson.

Buhalis, D. and Law, R. (2008). Progress in tourism management: twenty years on and 10 years after the internet: the state of eTourism research, *Tourism Management*, **29**(4), pp. 609–623.

Buhalis, D. and Licata, M.C. (2002). The future of eTourism intermediaries, *Tourism Management*, **23**(3), pp. 207–220.

Buhalis, D. and O'Connor, P. (2005). Information communication technology – revolutionising tourism, *Tourism Recreation Research*, **30**(3), pp. 7–16.

Cotte, J., Chowdhurry, T.G., Ratneshwar, S. and Ricci, L.M. (2006). Pleasure or utility? Time planning style and Web usage behaviors, *Journal of Interactive Marketing*, **20**(1), pp. 45–57.

Kim, D.J., Kim, W.J. and Han, J.S. (2007). A perceptual mapping of online travel agencies and preference attributes, *Tourism Management*, **28**(2), pp. 591–603.

Prideaux, B., King, B., Dwyer, L. and Hobson, P. (2006). The hidden costs of cheap group tours – a case study of business practices in Australia, *Advances in Hospitality and Leisure*, **2**, pp. 51–71.

Wu, S., Wei, P.L. and Chen, J.H. (2008). Influential factors and relational structure of Internet banner advertising in the tourism industry, *Tourism Management*, **29**(2), pp. 221–236.

Case Studies of Marketing Practice in Travel and Tourism

This section contains five case studies:

- *New Zealand:* The use of integrated marketing communications through a destination management system and an award-winning web site.
- *YOTEL:* A new globally relevant business model providing a radically different accommodation offer to airline passengers at airports around the world.
- *Travelodge:* The rapidly expanding business model for budget hotels and its strategy for expansion in Spain.
- *Agra:* Management and marketing for India's iconic World Heritage Site.
- *Alistair Sawday Guides:* A collaborative, entrepreneurial travel guide and e-marketing business model for small accommodation businesses.

These cases illustrate in practice the key messages contained in this book. In their different ways:

1. Each of them reflects strategic planning and innovative thinking that has marketing at its core. Tourism New Zealand, Yotel, Travelodge and Sawday also reflect new business models for their sectors.
2. Each of them is based for its success on the marketing power of the Internet, e-marketing and customer databases. Sawday, New Zealand and Yotel are the most customer centric in the ways outlined in this book. But marketing research, customer awareness and recognition of the absolute importance of delivering the experiences customers want is the focus for all these cases.
3. Each of them reflects branding and positioning based on core values and targeting at customers.
4. India, Sawday and New Zealand reflect collaborative marketing.
5. Relationship marketing and repeat business focus are reflected in Travelodge, Yotel and Sawday.
6. Sustainability is reflected most strongly as a core value in the Sawday case and for New Zealand but the thinking is reflected also in Yotel and Travelodge.

CASE 1

Integrated marketing communications through a destination management system – New Zealand

The web site aims to 'put the power in the hands of the consumer' and give the potential visitor 'the ability to see our country in a way that is meaningful to them'.

(New Zealand website 2007)

Tourism New Zealand's web site www.newzealand.com was launched on July 1, 1999 as part of its global marketing campaign, *100% Pure New Zealand*. It aims to provide potential visitors to New Zealand with a single gateway to everything the destination and its tourist sector has to offer.

BACKGROUND

New Zealand is a small country of four million inhabitants, a long-haul flight from all the major tourist-generating markets of the world. Visitor numbers have grown from 1.5 million in 1999 to 2.5 million in 2008. Australia is the largest market with 38% share, followed by UK (12%), USA (9%), China (5%) and Japan (4.5%). Combined, these markets provided 69.2% of international visitors to New Zealand for the year ended March 2008. Just under half (49%) of visitors arrive for a holiday, followed by visiting friends and relatives (29%), business (11%) and other (11%). The average length of stay is 20.5 days (International Visitor Arrival Survey, YE March 2008).

Tourism is important for New Zealand's economic growth. It currently contributes an annual total of some $18.6 billion to the economy – 9% of New Zealand's gross domestic product. It is also an important source of employment. One in every ten New Zealanders works in the visitor economy and tourism is New Zealand's largest export sector. International visitors contribute $8.3 billion to the economy each year, which accounts for 19.2% of export earnings. Unlike other export sectors, which make products and sell them overseas, tourism brings its customers to New Zealand. The product is New Zealand itself – the people, the places, the food, the wine and the experiences (Tourism New Zealand Strategy for 2015, published 2007).

100% PURE NEW ZEALAND

In 1999, TNZ launched its new destination brand, *100% Pure New Zealand*, to communicate a single, concise brand position to the world. The campaign was applied across all communication media, with the integration of print, television and Internet with events and international media ensuring that the New Zealand brand was built using a consistent theme and strategy. The campaign focuses on images of New Zealand's landscape, scenic beauty, exhilarating outdoor activities and authentic Maori culture. Its power and flexibility has enabled it to be used continuously for 10 years, during which New Zealand has become the tenth strongest national brand in the world according to Simon Anholt's GMI Nation Brand Index (www.nationalbrandindex.com).

THE WEB SITE

The web site has two prime objectives:

- To encourage overseas visitors to the country.
- To connect potential visitors with tourism businesses in New Zealand.

Through www.newzealand.com, potential visitors are able to learn about the diversity of what New Zealand has to offer and how their visit can become a fantastic experience. The web site is a showcase for all that New Zealand has to offer.

It provides an easily available fulfilment mechanism for media advertising campaigns, with the home page tailored to match the current adverts and put visitors in touch with relevant package holiday offers or flights. However, it is also designed to enable independent travellers to customize their own New Zealand holiday.

The web site has different home pages depending on visitors' country of residence. For example, American users are informed how to plan their 'vacation' and 'be here by morning' (stressing the relatively short 12 h overnight flight). British people can plan their 'holiday' with suggestions for walking tours and visiting gardens. The special offers and packages are tailored to each market.

THE DATABASE – A NATIONAL DESTINATION MANAGEMENT SYSTEM (DMS)

The heart of the web site is the database of tourism services operators, both those based in New Zealand and those abroad who offer tourism packages or services to the country. Any tourism-related business can be listed, subject to vetting, by filling in a simple form. This means that even the smallest bed and breakfast address or specialist activity provider can gain a web presence with access to an audience of long-haul visitors. Because participating businesses complete the form and are able to update the information at a later date, they have control over how their attraction or service is presented.

As part of its determination to maintain, drive up and communicate product quality standards, Tourism New Zealand operates a Qualmark assured business scheme for its producer organizations. The scheme is independently assessed against a set of agreed national quality standards that include environment sustainability assessments. It is comprehensive, providing grading for seven different types of accommodation, for example.

A separate page is given to each unique attraction or service – defined as 'the sort of thing a visitor could show up and do' – so larger businesses could have a page for each attraction they offer. The page carries the TNZ style and 100% Pure New Zealand branding so each business benefits from association with the global marketing campaign. The only stipulation is that the business must have contact details so that visitors to the website can get in touch with them directly. The site also allows the business to set up a link to their own website if they have one.

The listing is free because one of TNZ's prime objectives is to connect potential visitors with tourism businesses in New Zealand.

EXPERIENCE-BASED MARKETING

This case illustrates the emphasis put in this book on the growing desire of customers to achieve the experiences that make best sense to them as individuals. On this web site, visitors can search for activities not solely by geographical location but also by the nature of the experience they can potentially have when coming to New Zealand. This means that visitors can find out about New Zealand based on their emotional needs as a traveller. This is important as research shows that activities are the key driver of visitor satisfaction:

- Activities contribute 74% to visitor satisfaction while accommodation and transport contribute 26%.
- The more activities that visitors undertake, the more satisfied they will be.
- Cultural activities are better if they're interactive, such as visiting a marae to learn about traditional Maori life.
- Many long-haul travellers love to learn, and these learning experiences provide them with stories to take home to their friends and family.
- Visitors to New Zealand don't want to be 'one of the crowd'. Activities that involve only a few people feel more special and meaningful. Tour groups are kept small.

To communicate the New Zealand experience the site carries feature articles of special interest, for example UK television personality Ben Fogle on adventure activities in New Zealand, an interactive journey through the Lord of the Rings locations that became Middle Earth and video clips of former New Zealand All Blacks rugby captain Tana Umaga talking about the game. Rugby fans can sign up as members of 'The Front Row Rugby Club' and are encouraged to recommend the club to their friends.

INTERACTIVE MARKETING: PUTTING THE CUSTOMER IN CONTROL

As noted in the quote at the head of this case study, the web site aims to 'put the power in the hands of the consumer' and give the potential visitor 'the ability to see our country in a way that is meaningful to them'.

As the site has developed, additional features have been added to help and guide independent travellers devise their own customized itineraries. To make it easier to plan motoring holidays, the site has 'catalogued the most popular driving routes in the country', with scenic highlights, local activities and accommodation. Driving distances and travelling times are indicated. Travellers can plan the route and use the links to book the accommodation before leaving home. Different routes are highlighted according to the season or to cater for special events like the 2005 British Lions rugby tour.

In recent years, a Travel Planner feature has been added, which allows visitors to click on a button to 'bookmark' places or attractions they are interested in, and then view the results on a map. The Travel Planner offers route recommendations and public transport option between the chosen locations. By registering with the website, they can save their Travel Plan and return to it later. By including their e-mail addresses those who register provide valuable research about prospective customers. The collection of places and activities can be used to assemble and then narrow down options, arrange them on a calendar and print them out to take on the visit.

The visitor can either book the elements of their chosen plan directly using links from the web site or send the

Courtesy of Tourism New Zealand

whole plan to an approved Travel Partner to make the bookings for them. The site also links to local Information Centres.

USER GENERATED CONTENT

The website has a 'Your Words' section where anyone can submit a blog of their NZ travels for review and possible inclusion as a link from www.newzealand.com. While most of these blogs allow users to add comments, the main TNZ site itself does not have a discussion board open to the public to post comments or questions at this time.

EVALUATION

Since its launch the website has won two Webby awards for on-line achievement and innovations. These are awarded by the International Academy of Digital Arts and Sciences. Websites are nominated and voted on by their membership, which for the 2006 award included musician David Bowie, businesswoman Anita Roddick and The Simpsons' creator Matt Groening.

More importantly perhaps, over 400,000 users visit the site every month. While it is impossible to isolate the effect of particular elements of the campaign from external factors, such as the publicity from the film series Lord of the Rings, the growth of tourism to New Zealand has been impressive. Overall tourism expenditure increased by an average of 6.9% per year between 1999 and 2004 with international expenditure increasing at 8.5% per year compared with domestic spending at 5.8% per year. From Britain, visits to New Zealand grew at an average annual rate of 13% between 2002 and 2006, compared to a rate of 4% overall for British visits abroad and 4.5% to Australia (UK Travel Trends 2007).

SUMMARY

100% Pure New Zealand is an example of a long-term investment in destination branding which has formed the basis for the country's integrated marketing communication strategies for 10 years. The web site www.newzealand.com has provided an effective means of converting the interest created by the National Tourist Office's global media campaigns into business for hundreds of tourism businesses through the country. By offering a free web presence under the national brand, it has created a comprehensive database of suppliers in the NZ visitor economy, which then allows individuals or travel organizations to create itineraries and travel packages to suit their own needs and interests.

This 'destination management system' has been used to present ideas for holidays based not on locations or regions but on the experiences and activities the visitors can have in the country. New Zealand is presented as a country offering unique and memorable experiences in an unspoilt and spectacular environment. The success of this competitive strategy may be seen as evidence in support of Pine and Gilmore's theory that we now live increasingly in what they call an *Experience Economy*, especially for higher value services and products (Pine and Gilmore, 1999).

The case also illustrates how the Internet enables independent travellers to plan and book customized travel packages without the aid of traditional intermediaries. The web site provides an alternative to the travel agent as the 'one-stop-shop' for information and bookings of every element of the holiday, while the national brand and quality assurance scheme provide the reassurance that used to be supplied by dealing face-to-face with the high-street agent. The Internet operation combines B2B as well as B2C operations and its use provides a continuing flow of information on prospective visitors' interests.

It could be argued that New Zealand is not a typical destination. New Zealand is a small country with a visitor economy composed mainly of small businesses. It is generally perceived as a safe English-speaking country with a reliable transport infrastructure and a low level of corruption. Because of the long-haul air flight, most visitors stay for longer (average 20 days) and want to see as much of the country as possible on what is often seen as a once-in-a-lifetime visit. These factors undoubtedly fuel the demand for independent travel and increase the attractiveness of a comprehensive destination management system. However, the underlying lessons apply anywhere – the effectiveness of a strong brand, collaborative partnerships between NTO and businesses, an integrated marketing communications campaign, a strategy based on unique experiences and a comprehensive and user-friendly website.

Sources

The material for this case study was obtained from the following New Zealand websites:

www.newzealand.com consumer website, corporate website and travel trade website

New Zealand Ministry of Tourism Research Website
http://www.tourismresearch.govt.nz/

Thanks are due to Tourism New Zealand for checking and up-dating the content of the case study.

CASE 2

YOTEL: an innovative, design led new business model for airport based accommodation

I expect YOTEL to be in the world's top ten hotel brands in the next ten years...a top end product at below expectation price

Simon Woodroffe, Founder of YO! Everything

BACKGROUND

YOTEL is boldly claimed by its founders to be 'a revolutionary new hotel concept...creating a stir in the hotel industry.' The concept and its execution demonstrate all the style of entrepreneurial initiatives that have driven so many leading developments in travel and tourism over the last 100 years. The original idea was conceived in 2002 when Simon Woodroffe, already interested in the Japanese sleeper capsule hotels concept, was upgraded to a first class sleeper cabin on a flight to the Middle East. He made the key connection between high-class design features of first class air travel and the concept of compact cabins built into a relatively small space. The concept would simultaneously deliver economies of scale within a minimum volume of space and a striking, convenient and appealing consumer experience at a relatively very competitive price.

Creative entrepreneurs with the vision, courage and knowledge to put their concepts into place dominate the history of tourism. The stories of Sidney de Hahn, Forte, Laker and Vladimir Raitz (see Middleton 2007) are typical twentieth century illustrations of how visionaries can break the traditional mould of markets. Woodroffe may be on track to achieve the same impact albeit in twenty-first century style and at a speed of development appropriate to a globalized industry that was unknown to the earlier pioneers.

Gerard Greene, a former hotel analyst and executive with Hyatt and Marriott hotels, now CEO of YOTEL read about the concept in the trade press. He wrote to Simon in 2003 saying 'I want to work with you on your concept.' The two struck a deal in 2004 and the first lease on space was agreed for Gatwick in 2006 with the first YOTEL being opened at Gatwick Airport in summer 2007. Drawing on the experience of YO! Sushi restaurants that he created in 1997 and his associated YO! branded ventures, Greene and Woodroffe decided to translate the language of luxury airline travel into the Japanese capsule hotel concepts for implementation at airport locations.

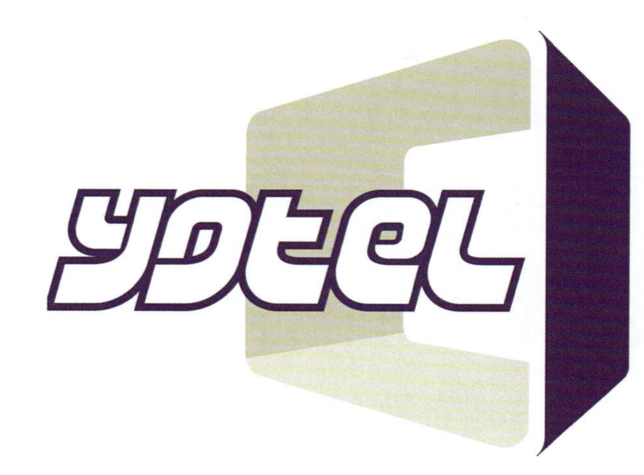

Courtesy of Yotel Limited.

THE STRATEGY

The strategy is elegant in its simplicity. Modern airports are mostly the venue for highly disagreeable, high-tension experiences for many people. First and Club Class lounges certainly help those who can afford them to endure the scheduled transfer waits, flight cancellation and unexpected delays but after an hour or so even that experience loses its initial appeal. With millions of people travelling daily on a 24/7 basis, the opportunity for just a few to purchase a personal space to relax, do business in private, shower or sleep while waiting is highly attractive. Simple sleeping cabins have been available in some airports for many years but, thus far, have always been targeted as a basic functional utility rather than an attractive experience that can compete with rooms in an up-market airport hotel.

The strategy was to provide an attractive high-quality personal accommodation experience for 'captive' markets at airports using the best of modern design flair, achieving economies of scale and minimum marketing costs. It creates a win–win formula that will generate year round high occupancy rates and profitable cost/ revenue outputs while providing excellent value for money. If the formula succeeds, the ability to reproduce it around the world is obvious and attractive to investors.

THE PRODUCT

The basic requirement for a YOTEL is a relatively small volume of space within airports that can accommodate a purpose built structure containing cabins in rows. The first at Gatwick has 46 cabins. Airport space obviously comes at a premium price per square metre but most have under-occupied areas and the footprint of a YOTEL is small. Because it has no requirement for space for parking or grounds or access roads and the cabins are much smaller than standard hotel rooms, footprint is much smaller than for a normal hotel with 46 bedrooms. All the basic utilities for heating, lighting, water and lavatory provision are already immediately available in airports.

The original idea was turned into a prototype by an airline designer working with first class airlines. The cabins are built in rows within a construction frame. They have internal windows so they are suitable for locating anywhere in typical airport buildings or even underground. If the installation space permits, the cabins could be built off-site as modules ready to crane in and plug in to prepared spaces.

There are two designs: Standard and Premium. Both are *en-suite* but the Premium cabins have large double beds that turn into sofas when not needed for sleeping. Standard cabins can also sleep two albeit on smaller beds. The focus is on high-quality design that involves adjustable mood lighting, climate control, attractive surface materials and luxury linen. All cabins are sound-proofed and have work stations, connections for WiFi and Internet and a 'techno-wall' that provides access to a wide rang of TV and audio channels, films and audio entertainment including a juke box with 5000 disks to choose from.

The product experience and customer feedback

The brand is an 'innovative radical design led experience for all. Cocooning its customers into a secure, calm haven for relaxation, entertainment, sleep and rejuvenation.' Every aspect of the customer experience of the product has clearly been thought through to reflect the brand values. 'The brand positioning and brand values define our personality and should be used to influence the way we look, speak and do things.' The key to the cabins is that they are designed to offer inspirational luxury at affordable prices. They have the signature YO! Formula of innovation and entertainment combined in this case with luxury fittings. 'It is all about thinking outside the box', says CEO Gerard Greene. 'We aim to create visually and mentally stimulating experiences by creating a value-for-money yet high design, hip product that travellers desire. YOTEL aims to be the iPOD of the hotel industry.'

Greene also comments 'the majority of hotels around the world are either poorly designed, badly managed or ridiculously expensive.' Especially in the context of airports and surrounding areas, many experienced business travellers will agree with that. Achieving an attractive price (see below) is also a part of the product experience.

Customer feedback on the brand experience is achieved by e-mail derived either from booking processes or though a form completed in the cabins. In the first 12 months 88% of customers were rating aspects of their experience at 8, 9 or 10 out of 10 with 97% saying that they would recommend a friend. A combination of visits by operations management staff and mystery shoppers helps to keep the standards up and a software programme is able to send text messages to management so that immediate action can be taken if customer feedback reveals specific problems such as lack of cleanliness or poor food. There is an indication that the level of external noise outside the cabins can sometimes be intrusive but this has not affected the overall ratings noted above.

Courtesy of Yotel Limited.

DEVELOPMENT AND FINANCING

There is clearly a significant up-front investment in building blocks of cabins. The seed finance for the project was provided by Simon, Gerard and some personal friends to get the project off the ground but a financial agreement arrangement was made in 2006 with Kuwait based IFA Hotels and Resorts. International Financial Advisors have a market capitalization of over $US 1 billion, have developed hotel interests in several countries and have global expansion ambitions. YOTEL is not competing with IFA Hotels and Resorts so with access to their international customers, the YOTEL investment provides a logical synergy for IFA with their other accommodation interests.

THE MARKET

The users are typically likely to be solo or traveller couples, accustomed to using four star or higher rated hotels. What they need at airports is a convenient, stress-free, minimum hassle experience with luxurious comfort in personal space for an overnight or shorter period of hours. They need it for functional purposes such as doing business for which privacy is needed over the Internet or phone and/or for relaxing before, after or between flights, with access to 24 h room service for food and beverages.

With millions of passengers on the move for business and other purposes daily, 24/7, users will define themselves by their needs and ability to pay. The issue for marketing is creating awareness, especially initially. The customers effectively define themselves by being where the YOTEL facilities are located.

Early indications are that the market divides roughly equally between business and non-business customers. Leisure travellers taking advantage of cheap budget airline flights timed to leave or arrive late at night or in the early hours of the morning are also attracted to the offer of a few hours rest at either end of a flight.

Pricing

Pricing is organized and adjusted on line to optimize yield so it will vary by times of the day, week and so on. 2008 prices in the London Airports were quoted to start from £25 per 4 h to £56 per overnight for Standard Cabins and £40 and £82 for premium cabins. The equivalent price for a four-star room near the airport is more likely to be £150 plus the added time, hassle and cost of getting out of the airport and to and from the airport to the hotel. A typical four-star hotel room is most unlikely to provide more room facilities than the cabins and certainly not the visually and mentally stimulating user experience that is offered by YOTEL.

Distribution, Sales Promotion and Advertising

www.Yotel.com is described by the Company as 'the hub of everything.' The whole concept could not work without the Internet and a user-friendly website. It defines and describes the product, identifies availability and price and provides instant on-line access to cabins. The site depicts the cabins visually with 360 degree camera views available. New software had to be designed to cope with the multiple bookings on an hourly as distinct from the industry standard overnight basis and cabins can be booked ahead or (if available) on the spur of a moment when a flight is unexpectedly delayed or cancelled. For the number of units involved in 2008 an expensive advertising budget could not be cost productive although feeding out news stories as the brand develops are of interest to the media and to in-flight magazines of airlines.

For YOTEL, the website combines the brand awareness, product, price, promotion and distribution – in real time. Awareness was created initially by media attractive PR stories of an innovative new product, followed up by investing in ways in which YOTEL can be readily and quickly accessed by search engines relevant to airport accommodation. The latter will pay off 24/7, which advertising will not.

Cost efficiency of operations

YOTELs are staffed by cabin crew, drawing on the airline terminology. There are typically two at any time in the galley, which provides 24 h access to food and drinks and these staff can also meet and assist customers if they seek help. One of these members is typically a senior crew with a role to supervise as needed. Two other crew members provide cleaning services around-the-clock. For pre-bookers, check in and out are automated at the entrance door of the YOTEL by a key pad accepting pre-issued reservation numbers and issuing magnetic key cards for the cabin doors. There is no need for any direct communication with staff unless customers seek it.

Rooms are available in blocks of four or more hours and in airport conditions can theoretically be used by three or four customers in every 24 h. In fact, allowing for such multiple use, early indications are that cabins are already achieving occupancy rates that range from around 120 to 140% and recent press reports have indicated it may be higher at some times.

Many customers are likely to be repeat visitors once the number of YOTELs is expanded around the world and, provided satisfaction levels are high, the market can become self-perpetuating.

Sustainability

By the nature of its concept, its small footprint, low energy costs (the cabins are already situated in environmentally controlled airport spaces), with immediate access to utilities, YOTELs are already more sustainable than conventionally built hotels even of the budget variety. EVAC vacuum drainage for sanitation minimizes water usage and LED lighting reduces electricity consumption. Work is already in hand to utilize recyclable materials in the construction of new units.

SUCCESS TO DATE

With deals in process for more YOTELs to be built around the airports of the world and a new design of an economy cabin, the business model looks exciting at the time of going to print in mid-2008. No-one can know the future but the sheer volume of travellers at airports with needs that match the provision of YOTEL cabins exceeds by hundreds of times than the capacity likely to be built under any realistic scenario of the next five years. The quality of the customer experience is enhanced by a clear value-for-money price and the business model should be more economic-crisis proof than others in the hotel industry and growth seems assured. No doubt competitors will emerge once profitability is proven but the leader with a clear brand will be well-positioned to dominate market share.

ACKNOWLEDGEMENT

The information used in this case was kindly supplied by Gerard Greene (CEO) and Jo Berrington, Marketing Director of YOTEL whose support and permission to use the material is very gratefully acknowledged.

CASE 3

Marketing world heritage – the Taj Mahal, India issues, challenges and opportunities

WORLD HERITAGE AND TOURISM

There are currently 812 sites throughout the world that are inscribed on UNESCO's World Heritage List (WHL). Of these, 628 are cultural sites, 160 are natural sites while 24 are mixed. Spread widely among 137 different countries, they include internationally known icon sites such as Uluru in Australia, Stonehenge in the UK and the Taj Mahal in India. The motivations for listing such sites vary considerably. Traditionally, the more common motivation for inscription involved a mix of conservation, preservation and protection. More recently, however, motivations include nation building, identity and an attraction towards the economic benefits to be gained from tourism at sites that gain increasing prominence. Although the Taj Mahal was not inscribed on the WHL for the purpose of developing tourism, the majority of World Heritage Sites are likely to have to deal with tourism related issues and the likelihood of changing patterns of visitation (Fyall and Rakic, 2006). In essence, inscription on the WHL 'not only confers recognition in terms of conservation, but also raises a site's profile and stimulates tourism demand' Bandarin (2005: v).

Although the above is true for many World Heritage Sites, the assumption that inscription on the WHL automatically results in increased visitor numbers oversimplifies the nature of visitor trends at World Heritage Sites. For example, differences in visitor numbers and behaviour exist between those sites that are easily accessible in urban locations, such as the city of Edinburgh in the UK, as compared to more difficult sites to access in rural or peripheral locations, such as Uluru in Australia. Ultimately, heritage and tourism are mutually dependent in that 'operators and destinations can use them to add value to their products and local services which, in turn, generates greater income from tourists while the heritage sites achieve higher revenues and profile that help when seeking assistance/funding for preservation from authorities' (Fyall and Rakic, 2006: 162). In the context of this case study, however, and in addition to the fact that both conservation and tourism activity need to be managed in a more holistic manner at such sites, one can accept fully how the use of such 'iconic' sites can be deemed indispensable to the marketing of destinations.

Marketing World Heritage Sites

World Heritage Sites are very often the icon images used to market destinations both domestically and internationally. The Taj Mahal in Agra, India is a most suitable example in that it is often used in destination 'image making'. In addition, such images represent powerful and evocative symbols of a country's identity and serve to 'sell' sites, regions and nations to the world. Being endorsed with the UNESCO logo, for example, not only represents a mark of 'quality' to visitors but also it helps to bring the attraction to the attention of a far bigger, and more often than not, less specialized market. In reality, their success as suggested in the previous section, is not always down to the fact that they are featured on the WHL, more that they are marketed well, suitably located or *'en route'* to other sites and attractions.

When marketing World Heritage Sites a number of issues need to be considered. The first relates to the type, scale and reach of the particular market(s). For example:

- is the attraction part of the wider tourism 'system'?
- is it located at a distance from the main visitor resorts and tourist routes?
- is its location a particularly sensitive site that requires the adoption of visitor capacity limits?
- to what extent is the market 'passive' or 'serious' in the degree to which they engage and interact with the site?

This last issue has important implications for the ways in which interpretation and education strategies are developed.

When considering how a site is to be branded, decisions concerning positioning and destination image are relevant as is the extent to which a site is central to the 'selling' of the destination experience. While the UNESCO logo offers an additional mark of quality, authenticity and indicates a 'must-see' site or destination there is also the temptation to 'oversell.' Overselling can create such a high level of expectation that visitors will ultimately end up disappointed. One of the outcomes of excessive levels of visitation may be the need to 'de-market' some sites; de-marketing being when actions are designed to discourage visitors, at least at some times and on some days. Although perhaps understandable, this is politically a sensitive issue in that World Heritage Sites are widely regarded as "must-see" attractions and as ones that mankind is perfectly entitled to see.

TOURISM IN AGRA AND THE TAJ MAHAL

In the context explained above, this case study examines some of the issues surrounding the marketing of the Taj Mahal in India and the extent to which such a site is used as an iconic image of India to the world.

Located 210 km from New Delhi, the capital of India, the Taj Mahal is an immense mausoleum of white marble, which was built in Agra between 1631 and 1648 by order of the Mughal emperor Shah Jahan in memory of his favourite wife. Agra is an ancient city on the bank of the Yamuna River located in Uttar Pradesh. It achieved prominence as the capital of the Mughal sovereigns from 1526 to 1658 and remains a major tourist destination because of its many splendid buildings, most noticeably the Taj Mahal. However, also in close proximity are the Agra Fort and Fatehpur Sikri, all three of which have UNESCO WHS status and are managed and maintained by the Indian Government.

It is thus no surprise that Agra is home to three luxury hotels, four deluxe hotels, seven standard, 13 budget and four government-managed hotels. More broadly, Uttar Pradesh plays an important role in the history of ancient India and Hinduism that goes back 3000 years. Uttar Pradesh was the capital of India since ancient kings and the Mughal Empire up to the present day. While Delhi used to be in Uttar Pradesh, it is now a separate state, New Delhi, with Lucknow the new capital city. With over 166 million inhabitants, Uttar Pradesh is the most populous state in India and is also the most populous sub-national entity in the world. Uttar Pradesh attracts a large number of both national and international visitors although most visits are to Agra itself, for obvious reasons, and to the holy cities. The state also hosts a religious gathering called 'Kumbha Mela' every 12 years where over 10 million Hindus congregate – the largest gathering of humans in the world for a single purpose. One of the challenges for those marketing the Taj Mahal specifically and Agra and Uttar Pradesh more broadly is the fact that most visits to the Taj Mahal are merely part of a more extensive itinerary so a stay may in many instances only be for a few hours.

One of the key challenges for those responsible for managing and marketing the Taj Mahal is not in fact the problems caused by significant visitor numbers but the widespread pollution that, according to Bill Clinton 'has managed to do what 350 years of war, invasions and natural disasters have failed to do. It has begun to mar the magnificent walls of the Taj Mahal'. If travelling from New Delhi, as is common for the majority of international visitors, the bland journey combined with the close proximity of many industrial and chemical installations churning out levels of pollution so close to such an iconic site is clearly not consistent with one's expectations of one of the world's most treasured sites. A number of commentators suggest that environmental pollution is eating away at the site causing serious and long-standing harm to India's prized tourist asset. This is, unfortunately, not a problem confined to the Taj Mahal of course. Venice in Italy is also experiencing as much environmental damage from nearby industrial pollution as it is from its volume of visitors. Despite the laudable intentions and ambitions of sustainable tourism development, the ability and political influence necessary to change the behaviour of some of the world's major industrial polluters remain a considerable challenge for many countries.

Pollution aside, although both the Agra Fort and Fatehpur Sikri are significant tourist sites it is the Taj Mahal that represents the jewel of Muslim art in India. It is one of the universally admired masterpieces of the world's heritage and by far and away remains the most identifiable image to be associated with India. In 2003, the former US President Bill Clinton stated that the world is divided between those that have seen the Taj and those who have not. It was also identified by the National Geographic Traveller as one of two 'must-see' spots in India (Kerala being the other) in the list of 50 such places across the world, a fact also advertised by the Department

TABLE 1 Foreign Exchange Earnings from Tourism (Indian Rupees 10 million)

	India's earnings	%	UP's earnings	UP's share in India (%)
2000	14,238	9.9	2847.60	20
2001	14,344	0.7	2868.80	20
2002	14,195	--1.0	2839.00	20
2003	16,429	15.7	3285.80	20
2004	21,603	–	4320.60	20

Source: Tourist Statistical Book 2004. Department of Tourism, Uttar Pradesh.

TABLE 2 Visits to the Taj Mahal

	2003	2004	2005	2006
Domestic visitors	16,03,942	18,47,955	18,85,286	20,48,120
International visitors	2,50,716	3,64,997	5,93,637	4,91,351

Source: Archaeological Survey of India (2007).

of Tourism. It is thus not surprising that the Indian Government markets Agra and the Taj Mahal to the rest of the world as 'sophisticated', 'luxurious' and a 'man-made paradise on Earth'.

In recent years it is interesting to note that while domestic visits have risen by over 27%, visits by international tourists to the Taj Mahal have almost doubled. Much of this can be attributed to the *Incredible India* marketing campaign launched by the Indian Government back in 2002.

Incredible India

Before 2002, India had not fully grasped the benefits to be achieved from a unified approach to destination marketing. When compared to Thailand, Malaysia and Singapore, India was attracting far fewer international visitors. Its marketing efforts lacked organization and many of its prized heritage assets, such as the Taj Mahal, were omitted completely from marketing activity. Toward the end of 2002, however, and at considerable cost, the first *Incredible India* campaign was launched with the communication objective 'to project India as a unique opportunity for physical invigoration, mental rejuvenation, cultural enrichment and spiritual elevation'. The *Incredible India* campaign represented the first time that India Tourism mounted a concerted, focused and centralized effort to increase what until then was an abysmal tourist inflow given the size of the country and its remarkable wealth of culture, heritage and natural attractions. Over 100 different images were incorporated across 12 themes with 13 million hits to the web site being recorded in the first month of the online campaign going live. The multi-million dollar campaign is widely regarded as being highly successful overseas and instrumental in increasing the number of tourists to India. Re-launched in 2005, www.incredibleindia.org is now widely recognized as a showcase of the very best that India has to offer and records anything up to 25 million page views per month. The campaign is not exclusively online though, extensive print, TV, radio and 'Youtube' coverage are also part of the package. With visitor arrivals going up by 25% between 2004 and 2005 and foreign exchange earnings increasing by an estimated massive 35%, there can be little doubt as to the overall success of the campaign in raising the level of awareness and interest in India as a premier international tourist destination.

Although the *Incredible India* campaign was, and remains, an India-wide campaign the use of the Taj Mahal in many of its images and the consequent rise in international visitors to Agra cannot be overlooked. The two are inextricably interlinked and serve to strengthen each other. For the Taj Mahal in particular, however, there remain a number of marketing issues that need to be considered as the campaign develops further and more and more international visitors are attracted to its doors.

MARKETING THE TAJ MAHAL: FUTURE ISSUES AND CHALLENGES

As with most World Heritage Sites, the biggest challenge for the future is the extent to which a balance can be found between conserving and protecting heritage on the one hand and at the same time continuing to attract and then manage increasing numbers of visitors. With tourism likely to play a more significant role in the process of inscription onto the WHL, there is going to be an even greater need among all parties to maintain a balance between conservation and tourism in the years ahead. There is also the issue of the likely impact on number of visitors, visitor types and patterns of behaviour generated by the continued promotion of iconic World Heritage Sites as core destination marketing images. This is particularly noteworthy in the context of India and the desire by the NTO to tap into more niche tourism markets.

One of the recognized weaknesses to date of the UNESCO WHL is the vacuum of effective visitor management at many of those sites listed. Although one can quite easily make the point that this is not the purpose of the WHL, in reality the pragmatic interpretation of events is that sites will be popular with visitors and hence their effective management ought thus to be a primary concern for those charged with their conservation and preservation. As introduced in Chapter 21, to what extent should sites on the WHL actually become fully 'managed' attractions? This may work well for cultural sites such as the Taj Mahal but the majority of natural sites would struggle to adopt such a stance. The commercial exploitation of attractions, the use of ICT at attractions and the increasing professionalism of the management of attractions generally are likely to impact on the future management of World Heritage Sites while the ability to understand and then deliver the 'visitor experience' is crucial to their ability to meet and exceed the high expectations of visitors. As is the case for many attractions and sites that do not feature on the WHL, World Heritage Sites also tend to suffer from high fixed costs and low variable costs of operation; they have to deal with seasonality, have limited budgets available for marketing and, perhaps most significantly, out of necessity need to collaborate and develop links with numerous partner and stakeholder bodies.

Notwithstanding, although the NTO approach adopted in the case of the Taj Mahal is entirely logical, it will have an impact on the quality and quantity of visitors. One may also question the extent to which images of the Taj Mahal are in fact consistent with the future strategies to develop alternative tourism products in India? If visitor numbers continue to grow, then much will have to be done to maintain what just about remains a unique atmosphere and ambiance at the Taj Mahal and surrounding sites. Although India has a number of other sites that appear on the WHL, including two others in Agra alone, there may be a time when so many sites are listed that the WHL itself loses its propensity to offer sites, and countries, a differential advantage. A slightly different point may be that with other sites listed across India, is there in fact justification for a themed World Heritage Site trail across India?

Perhaps the most pressing issue is the potential overexposure of the Taj Mahal in marketing collateral originating from India and overuse of the UNESCO logo. Although this may have been the case in the past, the huge number of images and products now used in the *Incredible India* campaign are such that this is unlikely to be a problem for the Taj Mahal in the near future. Finally, whether trying to increase, decrease or simply maintain visitor numbers it is always worth remembering that many messages lie outside the control of both the heritage and tourism industries. For example, publications such as *50 Places of a Lifetime* published by National Geographic, *1000 Places to See Before You Die* by Patricia Shultz (2003) and *Unforgettable Things to See Before You Die* by Steven Davey (2004) suggest that iconic sites such as the Taj Mahal will always retain a high profile that, irrespective of the efforts of marketers, will be prominent in the minds of the world.

REFERENCES

Bandarin, F. (2005). In: *The Politics of World Heritage: Negotiating Tourism and Conservatism* (Ed. by Foreword N. Harrison, D., Hitchcock, M.). Clevedon: Channel View Publications.

Fyall, A. and Rakic, T. (2006). The future market for world heritage sites. In: *Managing World Heritage Sites* (Ed. by Leask, A., Fyall, A.), pp. 160–175. Oxford: Elsevier Butterworth Heinemann.

CASE 4

Travelodge budget hotels – strategic development

Low cost and no frills – driven by the Internet. "Budget hotels may lack grand fireplaces, chandeliers and quiet corners for gentlemen to yarn but we are the future….."

Guy Parsons at the BHA Centenary Dinner 2008 in London, UK

The corporate purpose of Travelodge is to make hotels available for everyone in the UK by delivering low cost and maximum value for money accommodation to all customers and providing highly functional, efficient and convenient stop-overs or stay-overs.

This case outlines the growth and development of Travelodge as a leading player in the UK budget hotel sector and its current strategy to develop its business model in the domestic market of Spain.

BACKGROUND TO THE UK BUDGET HOTEL SECTOR

Although the concept of budget accommodation is not new, branded chains of budget hotels have been the fastest growing sector of the UK hotel market over the last 20 years. Travelodge as a low cost, originally motel style concept is the longest established brand name in the sector. It dates back to the USA in 1939 and grew naturally in the post-war decades with many competitors in the American motel market. In mainland Europe the first branded budget chains date from the 1970s with the success of the one- and two-star hotel groups in France, such as Campanile, Ibis and Formula 1. But significant British market growth, reflecting the high cost of land for hotel development in the UK, dates back only to 1985 when there was recognition by the national *Little Chef* roadside restaurant chain that dozens of their sites either had or could purchase inexpensive development land with planning permission for building hotels adjacent to restaurants and petrol/diesel refuelling stations located on main trunk routes (initially not motorways) in all parts of the UK.

The concepts of low-cost formula built hotels, with standardized bathrooms and bedroom furniture and fittings manufactured off site and installed on location, were rapidly developed. *Little Chef* was then part of the Forte Hotel Group that owned Travelodge in the USA at the time and it was a logical development for the company to pioneer the *Travelodge* brand in the UK. The brand introduced a 'no frills' low cost business model based on room rather than per person pricing and quickly came to dominate the UK market as market leader until the 1990s.

From the beginning, the concept of national chains of branded budget hotels in convenient locations adjacent to profitable restaurants providing optional catering found an enthusiastic market response. High annual occupancy rates combined with low building costs, plus low maintenance and staffing costs produced the magic win-win combination of convenient access, low production costs, low prices and excellent value for consumers, with good profitability for operators. The major regeneration of former industrial cities across the UK plus the expansion of the motorway network and regional airports provided other logical locations for budget hotel expansion and the development opportunities soon motivated competitors.

The leading competitor, essentially a 'me too' product at the time, was the Whitbread Group owned Travel Inn formed in 1987. Whitbread also owned chains of restaurants in locations that could support adjacent accommodation units. Taking competitive advantage of the market leader's slower response and its various ownership and management culture changes, the Travel Inn brand was given energetic, aggressive and effective development and marketing and within about a decade had developed market leadership in the budget sector in terms of number of rooms and market share. (Middleton:2001).

Travelodge Turnover 2000–2007 Inclusive

Travelodge UK: Total Sales

2000	2001	2002	2003	2004	2005	2006	2007	2008
£m	£m	£m	£m	£m	£m	£m	£m	£m
110	125	130	133	151	171	201	241	292
Growth	*14%*	*4%*	*3%*	*13%*	*14%*	*17%*	*20%*	*21%*

CONTEXT FOR BUSINESS EXPANSION AND THE COMPETITION

In the late 1980s there were less than 2000 rooms in the branded budget sector in the UK. This grew to around 4000 in 1992 and to 23 000 in 1997 but still only 2.4% of the total hotel market. Just over a decade of remarkable growth later there were estimated to be over 800 branded budget hotels (in total, not just Premier Inn and Travelodge) with some 60 000 bedrooms and ambitions to double the provision again by 2020. In the mid 1990s the USA was estimated to have some 2.4 budget rooms per thousand head of population compared with 0.4 per thousand in the UK. There was ample scope for expansion as the economy developed and the UK population became more affluent and mobile.

Latest available estimates for the UK market indicate some 85 000 budget rooms in 1171 hotels equivalent to 11.7% of total serviced accommodation compared to 33% in the USA and 24% in France. Around 15% of adults are estimated to use a budget hotel for leisure and average some three visits a year each. Business usage of hotels is estimated at 15% of all adults of whom half use budget hotels with an average frequency of 10 visits a year.

The budget hotel market thus divides roughly 60:40 between leisure and business stays and the two markets have seasonal and daily usage patterns that provide synergy rather than direct competition. Importantly, although leisure users have an older profile than business users, at different times of the year and week, some business visitors are also leisure visitors and vice versa. Over 12 months some 6 million stays were made at Travelodges in 2007 providing a massive database of users.

As noted earlier, Travel Inn became the budget sector market leader in the UK by the end of the 1990s. In 2006, after acquiring and absorbing Premier Hotels (a compatible product) Travel Inn re-branded itself firstly Premier Travel Inn and then dropped 'Travel' to become Premier Inn in 2008 with a major promotional campaign and plans for further rapid expansion. As Premier Inn, the leading brand has distanced itself among key customers from Travelodge with which it was sometimes confused.

While Travel Inn was single mindedly consolidating, expanding and changing its image as market leader, Travelodge was undergoing a period of management culture change. In 1996, the Forte hotel business was acquired by Granada. In 2000 the business was merged with the Compass Group who subsequently sold the business on again in 2003 to Venture Capital Company, Permira, The purchase of Travelodge by Permira and the growing competition from Travel/Premier Inn provided the opportunity for a major re-think of the Travelodge Brand and restructuring under a new management team. At that time the brand had some 13 179 rooms in 226 hotels and an estimated market share of the budget sector in 2007 of around 25% compared with Premier Inn's 32%.

TRAVELODGE REPOSITIONING AND MARKETING APPROACH IN THE UK

The business plan that emerged in 2004 was based on a brand repositioning and initial product enhancement investment of some £40 million over a three-year period. That business plan was taken on and strengthened when the Travelodge business was sold again in 2006 to Dubai Investment Capital. As this book goes to Press in mid 2008 a £900 million merger deal had been developed between Travelodge and Premier Inn. In the event, the Whitbread Board called off the deal, which would have created the biggest accommodation chain in the UK with some 60% of the UK budget accommodation market. It seems unlikely that this deal will be revived because of the monopoly it would create in the budget hotel market.

Strategic Objectives – UK market

- The core plan is to grow the brand using the current business model with a £3.5 billion investment strategy at a rate of some 4000 rooms a year with a target of 70 000 rooms by 2020.
- The business model is similar to that of budget airlines. It is a highly focused combination of low cost based on long leasehold rentals of properties,

providing all the essentials at specified and monitored product quality standards, but no frills. Additional services, if available, are charged extra. The model aims to minimize cost and maximize value and convenience for customers with marketing focused on the Internet and the retained customer database.

- The branding reflects the core values of the business model and is applied in the same way to every property with the aim of providing the same quality of experience in every location.

No market is recession proof in the face of an international economic downturn but the existing market shares in the UK and the obvious savings afforded by switching to budget business models suggest that this sector is likely to weather the storms more easily and quickly than higher priced accommodation.

Performance Monitoring

The success of the business model is reflected in annual turnover figures shown in the table above and in room occupancy rates that currently exceed 70% on average rising to over 90% in cities. To assess the all important customer response, continuous performance monitoring of product delivery is based on a Harvard Business Review model indicating that the most effective measure of potential growth for an organization is the propensity for a customer to give a personal recommendation.

Travelodge send a follow-up email to customers 2–3 days after their stay to ask 'How likely is it that you would recommend Travelodge to a friend or colleague?' on a scale of 1–10. 1–6 is considered a negative score, 7 or 8 a neutral score and 9 or 10 as a positive score. The positive scores are then subtracted from negative scores and divided by the total number of responses to give a net percentage of customers' recommendations. These scores are reported for each hotel to give a 'Would You Recommend' score for each hotel, district and region. This becomes a key management tool for rectifying faults and maintaining agreed operational standards. Computers can of course, manage such scores with only the best and worst properties being flagged for management attention.

Internet development

In line with the business model, 87% of bookings in 2007 were achieved via the Website direct (compared with 45% three years earlier) plus 6% telephone enabled by the Website. Less than 1% of bookings came via travel intermediaries. Travelodge is recognized as the No. 2 website in the UK Leisure and Destination sector – as measured by Hit Wise for 2007, and achieved No.1 position in Q1 2008.

Sustainability programme

Recognizing its responsibility as a major business to respond to global warming, Travelodge appointed an Environment Director in 2007. Key targets agreed in 2008 are to:

- Reduce energy consumption by 15% and become carbon neutral by 2015.
- Reduce water consumption in Travelodge by 25% by 2015.

- Not sending any waste to landfill By 2015.
- Operate sustainable sourcing policies
- Invest in our customers, staff and be a benefit to local communities and the wider society.

In addition, Travelodge are evaluating new technology in construction, and hotel design. The company has recently built the world's first recyclable hotel in West London created from shipping containers. The company state "this new design could potentially feature in around a third of our new hotel builds in future years."

STRATEGY TO DEVELOP IN SPAIN

In November 2007 following three successful pilot projects in cities, Travelodge took a major strategic decision to invest Euros 1 billion in 100 hotels in Spain by 2020. The decision reflects confidence in the business model that has developed since 2004 and recognition that major expansion plans are already in place in the UK market up to 2020. Growth into other markets is a logical strategy and the initial target locations are leading cities of Madrid, Barcelona and Valencia, to be followed by airport locations and other cities rather than seaside resorts. In all those locations the Travelodge model offers very competitive prices. Around 20 new hotels are planned to be opened by the end of 2010.

The budget hotel business model is the same as that developed so successfully in the UK; the brand name is the same and the decision reflects the facts that in 2007:

- The Spanish economy has grown strongly over the last decade and created a domestic travel market that is as large as the UK domestic market and judged to be ready to respond to and adopt the budget business model.
- Spain's hotel sector developed rapidly around tourism growth since the 1960s but until 2007 did not have major budget brands. Travelodge is the first major budget brand to launch in the country. It follows other successful budget brand launches in Spain such as IKEA and EasyJet.
- Spanish use of the Internet has developed massively in the last five years to approaching 50% of all adults – not far behind the UK pattern. The circumstances are right for the low cost, no frills Internet marketing approach.
- Approaching two-thirds of regular Travelodge customers in the UK are estimated to be in the market for visits to Spain over the next three years

The hotels will be around 100 rooms each, built (or converted) using the same leasehold model that is used to facilitate the £3.5 billion growth strategy in the UK. Landowners build the hotels and Travelodge takes a 25 year leasehold as the operator.

As this book goes to press, partnership deals with hotel companies in India and China are under consideration. Clearly, development opportunities will be evaluated as they emerge or are researched but the development in Spain is targeted as the main expansion under current plans.

ACKNOWLEDGEMENT

The information used in this case was derived partly from the Travelodge corporate web site but mostly from information kindly supplied by Guy Parsons, Chief Operating Officer for Travelodge, who also read, corrected and much improved the original draft. His support and advice is gratefully acknowledged.

CASE 5

Alistair Sawday guides and website – from books to blogs

At their best, small businesses reflect most of the features and characteristics that are unique to the tourism destinations in which they operate... The sector has vibrancy and originality and can play a vital leading edge role in delivering excellence with personality that big business cannot replicate.

(Middleton; Insights; 1997)

In Chapter 3 of this book and in other parts we have emphasized the polarization in tourism between big international branded organizations with standardized product ranges, and small and micro-businesses that are able to compete on individuality and personality, direct personal communication with customers, and high quality with excellent value for money. Until the late 1990s, apart from a few specialized brochures, most such businesses, however excellent, were limited by an inability to reach markets outside their locality. The advent and the potential of the Internet changed all that. The entrepreneur Alistair Sawday recognized the opportunity and has created the very successful business described in this case.

EARLY DAYS

Alistair Sawday has had a life-long passion for travel. Before his career in publishing high quality travel guides, and more recently his innovative on-line presence, he spent many years leading tour parties all over his beloved France. Driving his approach to life and the values of his business, however, is his life-long passion for the environment. This explains why he stood for the UK Parliament with the Green Party in 1992, and has been vice chairman of the Soil Association (dedicated to organic food principles). Although his business aim is to publish beautiful guidebooks, his much bigger drive is to question who we are as people. This thirst to question life and the environment led to the publication in 2000 of his *Fragile Earth* series closely followed by the books *One Planet Living* and the *Big Earth Book*.

Whether leading guided disaster relief teams in Turkey or working for the VSO in Papua New Guinea, all Sawday's activities to date have been pursued with the same determination, intelligence and exuberance he demonstrates today as an internationally known publisher. His extensive travels perhaps quite naturally led on to his foray into the world of professional travel writing. The launch of his first tour guide in 1994 demonstrated at the outset his entrepreneurial flair and ability to seek out distinct niches in the marketplace. Sawday's first book, a guide on French Bed & Breakfast establishments, rather than simply mirroring other products in the marketplace, instead celebrated homes owned and run by 'people' rather than corporations.

THE SAWDAY BUSINESS CONCEPT

This desire to tap into and contribute to places and properties that are 'special' represents the crux of Alistair's business proposition and approach to living. Although clearly a subjective process, Alistair takes considerable pleasure in finding people and places that 'do their own thing', places that are 'unusual' and follow no trends, places of so-called 'peace and beauty' and people who are kind, interesting and genuine. His commitment to finding only places that he truly likes has built up a large and loyal band of 'owners' and 'readers' who are willing to trust his judgement. This orientation to his business is taken one step further by his determination to only include places and owners that he finds positively 'special' and to avoid at all costs the situation in which it is possible for someone to 'buy' their way into his guides and website. Alistair Sawday is in fact the very essence of the 'brand', the brand proposition exuding 'trust', 'reliability' and that something a little different and 'special'.

Niche marketing and sustainability

Quite deliberately, Sawday has followed a niche marketing strategy where his approach to travel writing – and his website – appeal to discerning, independent travellers seeking transforming experiences. With sales of over a million books to date (covering 20 titles and over 5000 places including England, Europe, Turkey, Morocco and India), it is obvious that he has clearly hit a 'nerve' with his readers. Rather than stay in bland, standardized, ugly concrete hotels that disfigure many of our towns and cities, Sawday goes to great lengths to find places that are 'special' and 'different'. His maxim is that life is simply too short to waste time staying in unpleasant places when a night spent in one of his recommended properties really can be a transforming 'experience'. Importantly, the experience can easily match what is available in four or five star properties – at three star prices.

Sawday is also a committed advocate of 'Slow Travel' and uses this to differentiate his business in accord with the Slow Travel movement and *Go Slow England*. Although the words 'Go Slow' may remind older generations of the dark days of strikes and industrial decay in the mid-to-late 1970s, 'Slow' has taken on new meaning, primarily being inspired by Italy's 'Slow Food' movement. 'Slow' is the antithesis of all things 'Fast' including: food; integrity and authenticity; beauty and pleasure rather than profit; and, people's deepest needs rather than those of large business corporations. After 'Slow Food' came 'Slow Towns' of which the number is growing exponentially. The book *In Praise of Slow* has sold well and is an indication of the considerable numbers of potential Sawday customers in the wider marketplace. Tapping into such a phenomenon, Sawday has recently published his *Go Slow* book while *Go Slow England* is full of his 'special places' selected for the very reason that they offer inspired and inspiring people a 'slow' lifestyle.

Rather than merely representing a marketing stance, however, Sawday's commitment to the broader goals of sustainability runs through his entire business. This encompasses green offices, environmental conditions set on printers and suppliers, support for local economies and more recently a very honest and refreshing approach to carbon offsetting. In 2006, for example, he moved his company into new eco offices. With super-insulation, under floor heating, a wood-pellet boiler, solar panels and a rainwater tank, he has created a working environment benign to the workforce and to the environment. Lighting is low-energy, dark corners are lit by sun pipes and one building is of green oak. Details include the fact that carpet tiles are made from the wool of Herdwick sheep in the Lake District. A number of other decisions have been made, which include:

- Company cars running on gas or recycled cooking oil;
- Kitchen waste composted and other waste recycled;
- Cycling and car-sharing actively encouraged by the company;
- Buying only organic or local food;
- Excluding web links with companies considered unethical; and
- The decision to bank with the ethical Triodos Bank.

ONLINE MARKETING AND RELATIONSHIP BUILDING

Having built a successful business model based on local distinctiveness and sustainability Sawday has in recent years extended it from guidebooks to on-line guides. He now operates a considerable web presence that allows customers to contact the properties listed as well as ordering books online. This offers owners the added benefit of being able to buy a listing on his website at the same time as space in his guidebooks; a subtle approach to cross-selling perhaps. For example, a half-page entry with one colour photograph brings with it a website presence for one year. Costs are determined by the number of rooms with one room costing £490, two rooms £550, three rooms £590, four rooms £675, five rooms £765 and six rooms £830. This combined listing offers several benefits to property owners:

- The guide is consistently one of the best-selling Bed & Breakfast guides in the UK with each edition selling close to 20 000 copies (220 000 copies have been sold since the first British Bed & Breakfast Guide was published in 1996);
- With worldwide distribution by Penguin, Sawday's books are sold throughout the English-speaking world, as well as online through Amazon;
- The *Special Places to Stay* series includes 20 titles and 4500 places to stay worldwide, with only places that are truly liked included, and has built up a large and loyal following of owners and readers who trust his judgement;

- He has pioneered sustainability in publishing and woven it into the fabric of everything the company does; and
- The website received in excess of 1.1 million unique visitors in 2007.

Sawday's web presence is far more than just another website. He has in fact created a travel portal where customers can search the site and then click through to book via the owners' websites or email addresses. The Sawday 'brand' offers what he calls an 'island of reliability' in the unfathomable sea of online accommodation. Sawday states that 'on the unfathomable and all too often un-navigable sea of online accommodation pages, those who have discovered our sites have found them to be islands of reliability'. He claims that the millions of hits the sawdays.co.uk website receives every month is testament to the remarkable success of not only his website but his entire business proposition and philosophy on life. 'With over one million unique visitors to the site per year, visitors saw nearly 8 million entry pages, leading on to a million and three-quarter clicks through to owners' websites. This represents an average of 110 visits and 27 clicks per entry per month. This excellent level of quality "hits" has helped secure significant rankings in search listings so the site is quite often one of the first sites listed when people are searching for places'.

RELATIONSHIP MARKETING

By encouraging customers to pay a subscription to a Travel Club for extra information and benefits, Sawday has also developed a highly effective strategy of relationship marketing. At a minimal cost of £25 customers are able to register to read the full descriptions of all properties. By becoming a member, customers benefit from a far deeper web experience. For example, joining enables a member to:

- Read write-ups in full;
- Make use of the Favourites list to shortlist preferred places;
- Send places you find to your friends and family;
- Send comments back to Sawdays about your stays in the company's special places; and
- Store your contact details so you don't have to fill them in whenever you make an enquiry via the site.

To get these benefits, an annual direct debit payment is required and renewed easily each year so facilitating high levels of retention and customer loyalty. The website also actively encourages user-generated content where members can send comments in online. There is also a very popular 'blog' that Sawday uses to promote himself and, therefore, the brand. Allied to this are blogs on Slow Travel and Climate Change. Quite deliberately, Sawday's blogs are the more relaxed and informal side to the company's online profile where customers are invited to 'come in, relax, and leave a comment or two'. The cult of personality is most evident in Alistair's own blog at alastairsawday.blogspot.com/. Here one is able to read his musings and ruminations on travel, ecological living, sustainability and playing the guitar! There is also a 'Go Slow England' blog at goslowengland.wordpress.com/ where one is able to view sample pages and chat about all things Slow including 'The Hog Blog', written by a Sawday's editor about the joys of pig ownership.

PASSIONATE MAN AND BUSINESS ENTREPRENEUR

Reflecting his own beliefs and core values Alistair Sawday is clearly a passionate believer in the environment, sustainable development and an advocate for quality, slow travel and special places. At the same time he is (or has become) something of a marketing phenomenon. Sawday demonstrates a rare entrepreneurial ability (not unlike Sir Richard Branson perhaps) in that he has been able to combine his own attitude to life with that of his business, which, in turn, has generated a very large and loyal following. Like Branson, Sawday is the brand. His choice of places to visit and places to stay is based on his own subjective judgement while his ability to tap into every contemporary tool available to marketers (both offline and online) to reach out to markets has created a highly effective and integrated approach to marketing. With his use of blogs in particular, Sawday continues to use contemporary platforms to build his brand 'personality' and so maintain his quite unique and 'special' presence in what is a very crowded and dynamic marketplace.

LOOKING AHEAD

The next step in Sawday's plans is the selling of satellite navigation systems and software for mobile phones on the theme of *Special Places: Pubs and Inns of England & Wales*. This product is now available digitally for portable in-car satellite navigation devices, mobile phones or PDAs. Developed with RoadTour it contains 640 full Sawday's reviews with full colour pictures plus an extra 250 'Worth a Visit' recommendations. Available on CD, SD card or as a digital download for Garmin and Windows Mobile phones and PDAs, the product works best with GPS-equipped mobiles, although you can still easily access all the content through the search function without GPS.

SUMMARY

Alistair Sawday's business model appears to be completely in tune with modern, more sophisticated customer needs addressed in this book, and the customer centric approach that we have developed in the chapters. His website portal and the guides fulfil a vital marketing service for small businesses that enables them to compete effectively with international corporations.

The source of this information is Sawday's website, press articles and conference contributions gathered by the authors.

Epilogue: prospects for travel and tourism marketing

(i) Industries don't 'evolve'. Instead, firms eager to overturn the present industry order, challenge 'accepted practice', redraw segment boundaries, set new price-performance expectations and re-invent the product or service concept.

(Hamel and Prahalad, 1994: 303)

(ii) The traditional, firm-centric view of value creation is being challenged by active, connected and informed consumers...No longer does value lie in products and services created by firms and delivered to customers. Increasingly value is being jointly created [co-creation] by the consumer and the company"

Prahalad and Ramaswamy, 2004

A decade apart these two contributions by Prahalad and colleagues at Harvard Business School provide a valuable insight into the changing nature of marketing competition and customer orientation regardless of fluctuations in global economic circumstances. Both are still relevant. Initiative clearly still lies with firms and other organizations eager to overturn the present industry order by developing new business models. But the 1994 view can be interpreted as essentially a top-down management or *firm-centric* view of business competition.

By 2004 the commercial development of the Internet since the mid 1990s had grown from almost zero to embrace some two thirds of the population in many developed countries – and has created some 1.2 billion customers worldwide. At 2008 there are estimated to be some 3 billion mobile phone users for many of whom convenient Internet access will be the next big step in a connected world. All these Internet users are at the sophisticated end of consumer demand and, although it can only be a guess, probably now account for at least 80 per cent of consumer spending on travel and tourism in developed countries. These connected consumers, increasingly using the Internet for their travel purchases are re-writing the traditional marketing approaches of the late 20th century. They are actively seeking to achieve experiences in transactions that meet their personal needs – not passively accepting the products prescribed for them by firms. Value, especially in services, is no longer just designed and delivered by companies in standard formats to buyers; consumers express their own preferences in terms of the product offer. The value and quality of the experience they achieve increasingly depends on the role they play in the transaction process. Hence the concept of co-creation of value identified in the second quotation noted above.

In compiling the 3rd edition of this book in 2000 we were well aware that marketing was on the cusp of a major revolution reflecting the impact of information and communications technology and the advent – then just five years old – of the ability of large businesses to deal directly with their customers – and vice versa. By 2008, the revolution has happened. It is instructive to recollect that the first B2C web sites did not appear until the mid 1990s and even in the fast moving world of marketing the pace of development has been astonishingly fast. For many it's a case of the 'quick and the dead': businesses die if they are too slow to adapt.

2008/9: A NOTE OF CAUTION ABOUT GLOBAL CRISIS CONDITIONS

The third edition of this book appeared at the time of the 9/11 destruction of the twin towers in New York and the burst of the dot.com bubble that seemed at the time to threaten the development of the Internet as well as global stock markets. By co-incidence this edition is written in 2008 in the depths of the global collapse of banking systems and the economic recession fall out of the credit crunch occasioned by the combination of the international impact of the sub-prime mortgage market collapse in the USA and the doubling of oil and other commodity prices in the twelve months to mid 2008. The current circumstances clearly pose the greatest ever threat to the airline industry in particular and long-haul tourism as we now know it. Commentators are describing the current crisis as paralleling the international economic slump following the Wall Street Crash in 1929 with no recovery in sight as we write. On the other hand, while every global crisis in the last quarter of a century has caused some downturns in tourism volume, especially in travel between countries most affected, the international total volume has always bounced back within one to two years and is expected to do so again after the current crisis begins to resolve.

Such crises have repercussions that can easily make predictions written in the heat of current events seem foolish even a year later. Importantly, however, the downturn in commercial trading that is taking place in most if not all sectors of the economy concentrates minds on marketing necessities. Marketing budgets are likely to be cut but the absolute need to gear any business that can survive around a better understanding of customers increases. In buoyant market conditions, growing demand can cover–up weak marketing. Such weaknesses are exposed and magnified in a downturn. As consumer-facing companies grow internationally they have some options to generate growth in parts of the World (such as China, India, Brazil and Russia – the BRIC group of countries) while sustaining downturns for example in North America and Europe. But some crises such as those facing the world economy in 2008/9 have such a massive global impact that few businesses in the private sector can escape the implications. The loss of revenue to the public sector has consequences for actions in that sector too.

The trends outlined in this chapter are selected as having long term impact that will affect the next decade and beyond. We believe they will apply in times of recession as well as growth. The choice of sequence of the points below reflects their significance as we see it. All will affect travel and tourism along with all other sectors of the international economy.

1. 20TH CENTURY ECONOMIC AND POLITICAL POWER OF USA AND EUROPE GIVING WAY TO BRIC COUNTRIES

In retrospect one can see that the 20th century was dominated politically and economically by the USA and Europe and the North American/UK approach to free market economies. Looking ahead for the next decade and beyond, when the global economy recovers from the current economic recession, it is expected that a shift of geo-political power will favour Asia Pacific and Russia and different market systems. The shift toward consumer power noted at the start of this chapter will be played out against a growing but different global market. Growth and development in marketing are also predicted for North America and Europe but these are mature markets and are not expected to produce much annual growth. The BRIC countries in particular are predicted to produce massive growth. They will do so by virtue of their sheer population size and the speed of growth of their middle-income groups. Businesses that supply those markets and feed off their economic development will dominate the global tourism markets of the next quarter century.

As China has demonstrated this century, different political systems obviously alter the business environment in which firms operate but they do not change the fundamentals of marketing. The shift of manufacturing to Asia Pacific carries with it marketing ideas and practices. Given the stage of their development it is likely that the more traditional business-centric views of marketing and even production and sales orientation will continue to be the dominant approach in the developing world markets for the immediate future. But the same shift toward consumer influence will apply over time as consumers gain experience and rise up the income scale.

2. MORE SUSTAINABLE TOURISM – PROGRESS ESSENTIAL

The combination of global population expansion and the rate of economic growth in developing countries in the last decade, building on the existing massive demands of the developed world, has already put immense pressure on the world's scarce fossil fuel and other extracted natural resources. A doubling of oil prices in a year to March 2008 is the most obvious current indicator. Global economic downturn is easing pressure in the short run but it appears certain to return as 'peak oil' is reached. Such growth underlines increasing concerns for climate change resulting from carbon emissions and the need for a global action agenda to deal with it. The influential Stern Report to the UK Government of 2006 concluded that "the scientific evidence is overwhelming: climate change is a serious global threat, and it demands an urgent global response." It also noted that climate change is the greatest and widest-ranging market failure ever seen" and identified the destructive environmental implications if action is not taken on water supplies, farming and fisheries, desertification, biodiversity and especially on the populations of many of the World's poorest nations. It now seems certain that increasing government regulation of all business activities will emerge. Although few believe it will happen, the UK Government has proclaimed a commitment to reduce UK carbon emissions by 80% in 2050.

The world's largest industry is not the world's largest polluter and the witness effect of modern travel and tourism – as well as its contribution to conservation - are part of the process whereby increasing numbers of the populations around the world become directly aware of and concerned about the reality of sustainable issues. Part of the development of marketing experiences and the co-creation of products will certainly involve commitments by suppliers to more sustainable forms of travel and tourism. On the other hand, It has to be recognized that much of travel and tourism, especially aviation and car transport for leisure purposes, is seen by governments politically as non-essential. The temptation to raise carbon taxes, use car taxes and enforce emissions trading to influence prices may well be irresistible to governments desperate to be taking some action in the next decade and travel will may seem to be an easy option. The precedents are already in place.

3. ICT AND CUSTOMER EMPOWERMENT – THE SHIFT OF BALANCE OF POWER FROM BUYER TO SELLER

In reviewing marketing principles for this 4th edition the authors have been repeatedly struck by the fact that, although the principles have been adapted to services rather than goods, much of the basic thinking that underpins the marketing approach to business has not changed significantly in the last quarter of a century. Marketing was developed as a *business-centric* approach to the conduct of exchanges, albeit putting understanding of customers at its core. Business centric is in essence a top down approach to targeted customers whose needs are seen as paramount but who were, under the distribution arrangements available until recently, at the end of the process of product delivery. In the second Prahalad quote at the head of this epilogue marketing is seen to be shifting to a *customer-centric* approach with consumers or users able to take the initiative in buying because of their new-found ability to communicate with suppliers to get what they want – or the way they want it. It is the unique power of the Internet to enable millions of customers to communicate with firms as individuals and become active participants in the buying process rather than receivers, as in the past. Equally significant is the ability of individuals to communicate with other like-minded people and exchange views and ideas about products and anything else that interests them. We believe this shift is the biggest development; indeed a revolution in marketing that is essentially changing the balance of power between businesses and their customers with implications also for not-for-profit organizations and their targeted users. Of all the implications for the future it is the expansion of this *customer-centric* revolution in most sectors of travel and tourism that we believe will have the greatest impact in the next decade. This theme, which draws on Chapters 8 and 14 of this book, would not be significant, however, unless it was happening on a massive global scale.

Evidence of the global scale can be seen by the astonishing progress of Google, which was launched only in 1998 with its first office in a garage in Menlo Park, California. Within 2 years it became the world's largest search engine, introducing a billion page index and servicing some 100 million enquiries a day. Going public in 2004 the site could search 6 billion web items. With *Google Chrome* launched in 2008, the company now offers an Internet browser with which it aims to rival Microsoft's Internet Explorer. The company's corporate mission is "to organize the world's information and make it universally accessible and useful." In the connected future world of PCs, mobile phones and other access points, the scope for browsers and its role in co-creation is already immensely powerful.

These developments open the route to form virtual companies; operate networking alliances; forge links with other suppliers and bring together public and private sector organizations in collaborative marketing. Consumer power is seen in WEB 2.0, viral marketing and blogs, and the issues covered in Chapter 14.

4. EXPERIENTIAL MARKETING AND THE PARADOX OF THE BUDGET PHENOMENON

When drafting for the 3rd edition was already well advanced Pine and Gilmore's book appeared in 1999, too late for full reference at the time. Prahalad and Ramaswamy's book on co-creating unique value with customers appeared in 2004 and effectively pushes the same thinking further to take into account the modern power of the Internet and the connected world. Pine and Gilmore offered a stimulating vision of economic development and progress over the last two centuries, tracing the paradigm shifts from a dominant focus on agrarian production and extractive industries, through the manufacturing era of mass produced goods, and onto the modern era of service based economies. Such services involve the creation and delivery of services delivering benefits and satisfaction to more sophisticated and more demanding 'new' consumers. They argued that beyond efficient services delivery and the focus on product quality is a growing emphasis on service delivery as the staging of experiences that involve and are memorable to growing numbers of 21st century customers. Their mantra, reflected on the book's cover, is *"Work is Theatre & Every Business is a Stage."* The value added by the experience provider is memorable encounters that are personal to each customer because it engages him or her individually as an active participant, not a passive receiver. "Experiences represent an existing but previously unarticulated *genre of economic output*. Recognizing experiences as a distinct economic offering provides the key to future economic growth." (Pine &Gilmore, 1999, page x). In this context, service providers plan strategically to organize their business operations as stagers of experiences and service benefits become memorable sensations. Customers become directly involved with and part of product delivery.

Not developed specifically for travel and tourism, the concepts of marketing experiences and co-production are nevertheless especially relevant to all operators in what we identified as the visitor economy in Chapter 1. For customers seeking value added and judging the products they buy by the quality of the experience they achieve, the experience economy concept offers a fertile way to review marketing and product development and is certainly endorsed by the authors of this book. The concepts of 'every business is a stage' and 'co-creating unique value with customers' can be applied to individual service providers as business organizations, such as hotels, airlines and attractions within the total tourism product. Experiential marketing is a highly relevant approach to all businesses that aim to engage their customers with their brand values and embrace them within improved product quality that will be memorable. In the Case studies in this book, the New Zealand, YOTEL and Sawday case all reflect new approaches to experiential marketing.

It has to be stressed, however, that these are concepts that still apply much more to relatively affluent and sophisticated customers with sufficient disposable income to purchase products that appeal to their self-esteem. It is ideally suited to the top end products of the accommodation and transport sectors. As rapidly developing countries such as China. India and Russia grow their economies, literally hundreds of millions of the world's population are shifting from former subsistence levels of living and achieving what we know in the developed world as middle income or middle class status. Increasingly they will have the aspirations and income to seek out the higher quality of experiences available to them. Tourism and related aspects of the visitor economy are key parts of the provision of those experiences, globally. The quality of the web sites used where Broadband access is available will be central to the ability of average customers to search out what they want, 'test it out' virtually on-line and interact with corporate web sites that facilitate such communication.

Paradoxically, of course, the massive growth around the world of no frills airlines, budget hotels and economy focused fast food restaurants clearly also demonstrate the extent to which a large proportion of any market, not excluding the middle income groups, has and will continue to vote with its wallet for the lowest cost/best value for money option in which aspects of the experience may actually be thoroughly disagreeable but still purchased and if necessary endured for their utility value. To coin a phrase, *never mind the experience, think of the cost saving*. Times of economic crisis cause shifts from premium products to budget options but the longer term expectations of quality of experiences are still dominant and all organizations have to balance the two, often contradictory consumer demands. It can only be done by a deep knowledge of the customer or user.

Over 30 years ago, Middleton and Medlik identified the tourism product as the "complete experience from the time a visitor leaves home to the time he returns to it" (1972). That was a view of the 'total tourism product' discussed in Chapter 7. If elements of the total experience are to be endured or accepted rather than enjoyed, it places an growing emphasis on the parts of the experience that can best focus on stages or platforms that do provide the memorable experiences that most visitors seek to achieve at the places they visit. We return to this issue later under destination management.

5. GLOBALISATION AND INDUSTRY POLARIZATION

Chapter 3 noted the polarization process that – assisted again by the power of modern ICT - is creating a small number of very large, international and often globally branded corporations while at the same time very small or micro-enterprises continue to dominate numerically the experiences most customers will get at every destination. We used the estimate of 1000 small businesses in travel and tourism for every large one to make the point.

So the supply side in travel and tourism divides between:

(a) Company-centric, top down, efficient but inevitably bland big international corporations – for example (Ryanair and Travelodge in Europe that are dedicated to delivering the lowest possible prices for a purely functional experience by stripping out unnecessary expenses.

(b) Small and micro-businesses at destinations that are newly Internet empowered, quality of experience driven and ideally placed to respond in a customer-centric way to the modern ideas of co-creation of value.

The progress of the Internet in creating effective marketing portals for small businesses has been truly remarkable with thousands of guesthouses and small hotels already achieving over half their business via Internet searches even if many of the bookings still arrive by phone. For such small firms, along with attractions and events of every kind, the Internet is opening up regional, national and international markets for the first time, providing information and easy access to millions of potential customers. The B2B aspects are equally significant in facilitating marketing developments.

Big branded corporations are mostly excellent at delivering the product options they have specified but, unless it's a high value luxury product, they find it increasingly costly and difficult to deal individually with customers. Consumer Centric Marketing and Dynamic Packaging (Chapters 7 and 8) provide routes to customize standardized product offers but with most major large-scale operators, if it's not on the screen you have no options. If you want a budget flight, expect to be processed efficiently and quickly and to pay immediately (with a charge for credit cards). Expect to pay again at various stages of the product delivery for large luggage, food and drink and so on. Don't expect on booking to speak to anyone unless it is an automated, time consuming machine with multiple options that cause many people to fling down the phone with exasperation and rage. If it's a budget airline, don't expect to find anyone to give you help or information at the airport until you get to the front of the queue – and you may then be sent off to find another queue. Predicting growing customer alienation and frustration with automated customer 'service' seems a safe prediction and it is common to all big corporations dealing with the general public and low-budget items.

By contrast, if you browse a small business web site but prefer then to use the phone to see if the experience expectation is matched by a voice, you typically get to speak with the proprietor or a partner who will be able to answer queries and respond to requests. By phone or e-mail it is generally easy and pleasant – and human - to do business with a small business, which has all the other personal and business advantages covered in Chapter 3. This was always true of good small businesses. It is only with the advent of the Internet and portals and links that prospective customers can access what is available and communicate with ease. It is also often possible to leave a review of an experience on a portal site that others can share.

With the growing desire of many customers to participate in the product specification and delivery process and tailor it to their own interests, all this means a bright future for small businesses that deliver attractive experiences and what customers judge to be good quality and value for money but not necessarily low cost. Since there are ample quality assurance schemes for small businesses to join, they can also overcome the principal advantage that branding gives to big corporations by offering a form of risk assurance that the quality will be as stated.

In this book, the Case studies of Alistair Sawday and Travelodge provide a fascinating contrast and insight into the business models and operations of two large branded companies. One brand is dedicated to standardized no frills product delivery and the other to individual small businesses distinguished by the specialness of the experiences they offer. The two have radically different visions and values but both are highly relevant to the 21st century.

6. NEW BUSINESS MODELS – TOURISM BUSINESS REGENERATION

With the benefit of hindsight, some of the most dramatic changes in the history of tourism over the last fifty years or so have been driven by entrepreneurial figures with the vision and determination "to overturn the present industry order, challenge 'accepted practice', redraw segment boundaries, set new price-performance expectations and re-invent the product or service concept "(Hamel and Prahalad:1994). Examples in travel and tourism are Southwest Airlines, Ryanair, Easyjet, Laker Airways, Travelodge, Centerparcs, MacDonald's, Costa Coffee and Starbucks. In the

Case Studies for this book, Yotel and Alistair Sawday are excellent examples of entrepreneurial flair and determination. Each of these reflects a radically different business model in their respective sectors of the economy that overturned traditional product and operational approaches. Bill Gates (Microsoft) and Larry Page and Sergey Brin (Google) have achieved rapid, global impact with their business models.

In every case the new models have reinvented the service concept, changed the traditional product approach, developed the existing market exponentially, changed customer expectations and behaviour, radically altered marketing strategies and ways of communicating with customers. Once established, these new approaches have forced many traditional firms out of the market place, unable to compete. There is perhaps something about travel and tourism, especially the opportunity to start an enterprise on a small scale with low barriers to entry compared with many other services. Once started, modern ICT makes it possible to test and refine a new business model before it grows larger and begins to overturn accepted practice.

The Internet with its virtual opportunities to create, communicate and test product concepts at low cost provides unparalled opportunities for consumer centric entrepreneurs to follow in the process outlined above. We can safely predict bold visionaries are planning new business models as we write and there will be several with global impact in the next decade or so. Some may be stimulated by the business failure of some long established corporations in the global economic crisis of 2008/9.

7. DESTINATION MANAGEMENT ISSUES

In this edition we have stressed the need and new opportunities for the business sector to collaborate both in product formulation, integrated communications and though web sites and linkages. Whether they like it or not, commercial businesses and public sector organizations are also interdependent and inextricably locked in the most important area of tourism development – the quality of the destination and the platform or stage it provides for visitor experiences. Quality as perceived by visitors at any destination is fundamental to long run marketing success.

We believe that while there has been massive reinvention and regeneration of travel and tourism business models in recent decades, the same has not been true of destination management in much of the developed world. Other than a seemingly annual attempt to reduce expenditure on it, destination management in the UK for example has barely shifted in its approach in a quarter of a century. Many former destination management systems operated by local government have been outsourced to regional and sub-regional bodies that – whatever the visions may state - have in practice reduced the concept of destination management to promotion and web sites. Yet effective destination management, controlled or influenced largely by local government and public sector agencies such as tourist boards and national parks, is the only way to take responsibility for what can be defined as *the public realm*. Taking its strategic direction and ultimately funded by central governments in most countries, public realm comprises the provision and quality of public spaces such as parks, gardens and squares, and the look, feel and ambience of townscapes, rural areas and villages - especially the centers that visitors seek out to appreciate a sense of place. In other words, public realm comprises the platform within which core visitor experiences – memorable or disagreeable – take place. Public realm is about the design and regeneration of places respecting their local heritage, culture, architecture and it is the underpinning for a successful visitor economy at any destination. It is also a core contributor to the perceived quality of life of local residents and communities and it is that element of residents rather than visitors that locks the destination management issue into a long-term reality that is inescapable. Residents and visitors have a mutual interest in the quality of the public realm.

Public realm is, therefore, or should be the focus for destination management in all places from rural villages and ski resorts to modern cities. The biggest and most dramatic recent illustration of public sector involvement in public realm was in China for the 2008 Olympics. Where destinations are marketed on images of their high quality natural environment, such as New Zealand, or their architecture and heritage buildings as in much of Europe, the role of the public sector, always vital, requires greater attention.

We stress, in other words, that the quality of the experience achieved by visitors is as at least as much and often more dependent on the role of the public sector as it is on the role of the suppliers of individual components of travel, accommodation and attractions. Where many businesses in the private sector are stripping down the service offer to cut all unnecessary costs and achieve the bare minimum price consistent with the safety of operations, growing emphasis is placed on the public sector partners that control the stage on which the core experiences in the visitor economy take place. In 2008 we do not see much recognition of this reality in political agendas that control public spending.

There is a growing need for better understanding and collaboration between the two sectors at destinations, recognizing their mutual dependence on the visitor economy and the importance of providing quality experiences in competition with other destinations. There is every reason for businesses to participate in the processes of destination management bringing their marketing skills as well as an element of funding to the table. It is a sustainable approach in that it offers clear benefits to local communities.

HARNESSING THE GLOBAL POWER OF MARKETING

To conclude, in strategic terms there are a number of balancing acts or trade-offs to be undertaken in global tourism in the next decade. Seven of them are noted below:

Economic values	balanced against	Environmental values and sustainability of operations
Corporate profit	balanced against	Ethical corporate actions
Business centric	balanced against	Consumer centric
Global corporations (thinking local)	balanced against	Small businesses (thinking global)
Quantity/price driven	balanced against	Quality/value driven
Competition driven	balanced against	Collaboration led, focused on destination management
Short-term values (today's business)	balanced against	Strategic long-term positions (tomorrow's business)

Trade-offs in 21st Century Tourism Management

Marketing, as it is explained in this book, has a principal management role to play in achieving each of the strategic trade-offs noted above. In one dimension, marketing is a co-ordinated set of levers or tools designed to match the supply of products to current and future demand. In that sense it is the most honed and proven set of skills available in free societies that encourage competition. Marketing has a century of development thinking and practice behind it and one can claim that services marketing came of age in the 1990s.

In a broader management context, marketing contributes and aims to embrace the consumer perspective and much of the dynamic energy that makes if possible for successful businesses proactively to innovate and 'overturn the present industry order, challenge "accepted practice" and re-invent the service concept'

Strategically, marketing can be identified as the *lingua franca* of the fascinating, volatile and increasingly global business of the *world's largest industry.* Driven by ICT, which can be harnessed to achieve goals, marketing principles and practice are relevant in all parts of the world. Marketing is *not* a corporate goal. It is an approach to the conduct of business in the public and not-for-profit sectors as well as in the private sector, and a management process to achieve organizational goals.

Tactically, to repeat a quote used in the first edition of this book and still as relevant: *'Excellence is a game of inches, or millimetres. No one act is, per se, clinching. But a thousand things... each done a tiny bit better, do add up to memorable responsiveness and distinction... and loyalty... and slightly higher margins'* (Peters and Austin, 1986: 46).

The quote is a useful reminder that quality of service product delivery is always a combination of multiple actions taken every day by many people. Whatever skills marketing managers may possess, they will achieve little if the operations and other key divisions of an organization are not performing their part. Marketing is not effective unless it is integrated within the management structure of an organization from the boardroom down. It is implicit that service excellence can be defined, targeted, measured and improved. It is the responsibility of marketing to undertake and communicate those tasks within the organization. By linking memorable responsiveness to profit margins, the quotation stresses that excellence is a customer-centric approach to business, having particular regard to repeat custom – and the bottom line.

We believe the future lies partly with private sector willingness to recognize its role and responsibilities in sustainable tourism growth and act accordingly in its own long-run self-interest. It lies equally with the political will of governments at all levels to develop and support private/public sector destination partnerships that can achieve better destination management. Neither party is likely to move willingly in directions they believe will compromise their options, but both will in the end be influenced by the demands and expectations of consumers/voters. The significance of the visitor economy to destinations in economic, social and cultural terms and the emergence of more demanding and more aware customers suggest a more responsible approach to the future of global tourism; it will focus on better destination management that embraces both customer and business interests in joint collaboration with community interests at the destination to achieve their mutual interests in achieving and delivering memorable experiences.

This is a deliberately optimistic view for the next decade, recognizing that marketing knowledge and skills will be at the forefront of developments.

Selected Bibliography

See also specific journal references contained at the end of each chapter and link articles identified in all chapters

Adcock, D., Bradfield, R., Halborg, A. and Ross, C. (1997). *Marketing Principles and Practice*. 3rd edn. Financial Times Management.

Allport, G.W. (1935). In *Handbook of Social Psychology* (C. Murchison, ed.), Clark University Press.

Ansoff, H.I. (1987). *Corporate Strategy*. Revd edn. Penguin.

Baker, M.J. (1996). *Marketing: An Introductory Text*. 6th edn. Macmillan.

Baker, M.J. (2000). *Marketing Strategy and Management*. 3rd edn. Macmillan.

Bartels, R. (1976). *The History of Marketing Thought*. 2nd edn. Grid.

Bateson, J.E.G. (1995). *Managing Services Marketing: Text and Readings*. Dryden Press.

Beirman, D. (2003). *Restoring Tourism Destinations in Crisis: A Strategic Marketing Approach*. CABI Publishing.

Bitner, M.J., Booms, B.H. and Tetrealt, M.S. (1995). 'The service encounter', in J.E.G. Bateson (ed.), *Managing Services Marketing: Text and Readings*. 3rd edn. Dryden Press.

Brassington, F. and Pettit, S. (2003). *Principles of Marketing*. 3rd edn. FT Prentice-Hall.

Buhalis, D. and Law, R. (2003). e-*Tourism: Information Technology for Strategic Tourism Management*. FT Prentice Hall.

Buhalis, D. and Laws, E. (Eds). (2001). *Tourism Distribution Channels: Practices, Issues and Transformations*. Thomson Learning.

Burkart, A.J. and Medlik, S. (1981). *Tourism: Past, Present and Future*. 2nd edn. Heinemann.

Carlzon, J. (1987). *Moments of Truth*. Harper Collins.

Carson, D., Gilmore, A. and Gronhaug., K. (2001). *Qualitative Marketing Research*. Sage.

Chernatony, L.de and McDonald, M.H.B. (1992). *Creating Powerful Brands*. Butterworth-Heinemann.

Chisnall, P.M. (1985). *Marketing: A Behavioural Analysis*. 2nd edn. McGraw-Hill.

Chisnall, P.M. (1994). *Consumer Behaviour*. 3rd edn, McGraw-Hill.

Clark. S. (2000). *The Co-marketing Solution*. McGraw Hill.

Cooper, C., Fletcher, J., Fyall, A., Gilbert, D. and Wanhill, S. (2008). *Tourism Principles and Practice*. 4th edn. FT Prentice Hall.

Crouch, S. and Housden, M. (1996). *Market Research for Managers*. 2nd edn. Butterworth-Heinemann.

Coughlan, A., Anderson, E., Stern, L.W. and El-Ansary, A. (2008). *Marketing Channels*. (7th edn). Pearson Education.

Davidson, J.H. (1975). *Offensive Marketing*. Penguin (New edn. 1987).

Davidson, J.H. (1997). *Even More Offensive Marketing*. Penguin.

Davidson, R. and Maitland, R. (1997). *Tourism Destinations*. Hodder and Stoughton.

De Bono, E. (1977). *Lateral Thinking*. Harmondsworth Penguin.

De Pelsmacker, P., Geuens, M. and van den Bergh, J. (2001). *Marketing Communications*. FT Prentice Hall.

Doganis, R. (2006). *The Airline Business in the 21st Century*. 2nd edn. Routledge.

Doyle, P. (1989). Building successful brands: the strategic options. *Journal of Marketing Management*, 5(1): 77–95.

Economist Intelligence Unit (1992). *The Tourism Industry and the Environment*. Special Report No. 2453, EIU.

Engel, J.F., Blackwell, R.D. and Kollat, D.T. (1978). *Consumer Behaviour*. Dryden Press.

Engel, J.F. and Miniard, P.W. (1992). *Consumer Behaviour*. 7th edn. Dryden International.

Evans, N., Campbell, D. and Stonehouse, G. (2003). *Strategic Management for Travel and Tourism*. Elsevier Butterworth Heinemann.

Financial Times (1998). *Distribution Technology in the Travel Industry*. Financial Times (Retail and Consumer).

Fyall, A. and Garrod, B. (2005). *Tourism Marketing: A Collaborative Approach*. Channel View Publications.

Fyall, A., Garrod, B., Leask, A. and Wanhill, S. (Eds). (2008). *Managing Visitor Attractions: New Directions*. 2nd edn. Elsevier Butterworth Heinemann.

Gabott, M. and Hogg, G. (1997). *Contemporary Services Marketing: A Reader*. Dryden Press.

Gee, C.Y., Choy, D.J.L. and Makens, J.C. (1997). *The Travel Industry*. 3rd edn. Van Nostrand Reinhold.

Godin, S. (1999). *Permission Marketing: Turning Strangers into Friends and Friends into Customers*. Simon and Schuster.

Goeldner, C.R. (2000). *Tourism Principles, Practices, Philosophies*. 8th edn. Wiley.

Gross, M. (1992). *The Direct Marketers Ideas Book*. Amacom.

Grover, R. and Vriens, M. (2006). *The Handbook of Marketing Research*. Sage.

Gunn, C. (1972). *Vacationscape*. University of Texas.

Hamel, G. and Prahalad, C.K. (1994). *Competing for the Future*. Harvard Business School Press.

Hanlon, J.P. (2006). *Global Airlines: Competition in a Transnational Industry*. 3rd edn. Elsevier Butterworth Heinemann.

Hart, N.A. (1995). *The Practice of Advertising*. 4th edn. Butterworth-Heinemann.

Hart, N.A. and Stapleton, J. (1996). *The CIM Marketing Dictionary*. 5th edn. Butterworth-Heinemann.

Heath, E. and Wall, G. (1992). *Marketing Tourism Destinations: A Strategic Planning Approach*. Wiley.

Herzberg, F. (1959). *The Motivation to Work*. John Wiley & Sons.

Hoffman, K.D. and Bateson, J.E.G. (1997). *Essentials of Services Marketing*. Dryden Press.

Hofstede, G. (1980). *Culture's Consequences: International Differences in Work related Values*. Sage.

Holloway, J.C. and Taylor, N. (2006). *The Business of Tourism. 7th edn*. Prentice Hall.

Howard, J.A. (1989). *Consumer Behaviour in Marketing Strategy*. Prentice Hall.

Hussey, D.E. (1979). *Introducing Corporate Planning*. 2nd edn. Pergamon Press.

International Passenger Survey (IPS) (annual) *Travel Trends*. Reports on the International Passenger Survey – a year-round survey of passengers arriving in and departing from the UK, conducted for the UK government. The Stationery Office.

Jobber, D. (2007). *Principles and Practice of Marketing*. *5th* edn. McGraw-Hill.

Keegan, W.K. and Davidson, H. (2005). *Offensive Marketing: Gaining Competitive Advantage*. Elsevier Butterworth Heinemann.

Kotler, P. (1976). *Marketing Management: Analysis, Planning, Implementation and Control*. 3rd edn. Prentice-Hall.

Kotler, P. (1991). *Marketing Management: Analysis, Planning, Implementation and Control*. 7th edn. Prentice-Hall.

Kotler, P. and Armstrong, G. (1999). *Principles of Marketing*. 8th edn. Prentice-Hall.

Kotler, P. (1999). *Kotler on Marketing: How to Create, Win and Dominate Markets*. The Free Press.

Kotler, P., Wong, V., Saunders, J. and Armstrong, G. (2005). *Principles of Marketing*. 4th European edn. Prentice Hall.

Kozak, M. and Andreu, L. (2006). *Progress in Tourism Marketing*. Elsevier Butterworth Heinemann.

Krippendorf, J. (1971). *Marketing et Tourisme*. Lang and Cie.

Krippendorf, J. (1987). *The Holiday Makers*. Heinemann.

Leask, A. and Fyall, A. (Eds). *Managing World Heritage Sites*. Elsevier Butterworth Heinemann.

Leppard, J.W. and McDonald, H.B. (1991). Marketing planning and corporate culture. *Journal of Marketing Management*, **7**(3), July, 213–35.

Levitt, T. (1960). Marketing myopia. *Harvard Business Review*, 38, July/August.

Levitt, T. (1974). Improving sales through product augmentation. In *Analytical Marketing Management* (P. Doyle et al. Eds). P. 10, Harper and Row.

Levitt, T. (1981). Marketing intangible products and product intangibles. *Harvard Business Review*, May/June: 37–44.

Lewis, R.C. Chambers, R.E. and Chacko, H.E. (1995). *Marketing Leadership in Hospitality: Foundations and Practices*. 2nd edn. Van Nostrand Reinhold.

Lovelock, C.H. and Wright, L. (1998). *Principles of Services Marketing and Management*. Prentice-Hall.

Luck, D.J. et al. (1970). *Marketing Research*. 3rd edn. Prentice-Hall.

Lumsdon, L. and Page, S. (2004). *Tourism and Transport Issues and Agenda for the New Millennium*. Elsevier Butterworth Heinemann.

Maslow, A. (1970). *Motivation and Personality*. Harper and Row.

Masterman, G. and Wood, E.H. (2006). *Innovative Marketing Communications Strategies for the Events Industry*. Elsevier Butterworth Heinemann.

McCarthy, E.J. (1981). *Basic Marketing, A Managerial Approach*. 7th edn. Irwin.

McDonald, M. (2007). *Marketing Plans*. 6th edn. Elsevier Butterworth-Heinemann.

McDonald, M. and Woodburn, D. (2007). *Key Account Management: The Definitive Guide*. Elsevier Butterworth Heinemann.

McIntosh, R.W. (1990). *Tourism: Principles, Practices, Philosophies*. Wiley.

Medlik, S. (1999). *The Business of Hotels*. 4th edn. Butterworth-Heinemann.

Middleton, V.T.C. (1983). Product marketing: goods and services compared, *Quarterly Review of Marketing*, **8**(4), July.

Middleton, V.T.C. (1994). The tourism product. In *Tourism Marketing and Management Handbook* (S.F. Witt and L. Moutinho Eds). 2nd edn. Prentice-Hall.

Middleton, V.T.C. (1998). *New Visions for UK Museums in the 21st Century*. Association of Independent Museums.

Middleton, V.T.C. and Hawkins, R. (1998). *Sustainable Tourism: A Marketing Perspective*. Butterworth-Heinemann.

Middleton, V.T.C. (2001). *Marketing in Travel and Tourism*. 3rd edn. Butterworth-Heinemann.

Morgan, M. (1996). *Marketing for Leisure and Tourism*. Prentice Hall.

Morgan, N. and Pritchard, A. (2000). *Marketing Communications: An Integrated Approach*. Butterworth-Heinemann.

Morgan, N., Pritchard, A. and Pride, R. (Eds). (2002). *Destination Branding: Creating the Unique Destination Proposition*. Elsevier Butterworth Heinemann.

Morrison, A.M. (1989). *Hospitality and Travel Marketing*. Delmar.

Nykiel, R.A. (2006). *Handbook of Marketing Research Methodologies for Hospitality and Tourism*. Haworth Hospitality and Tourism Press.

Moutinho. L. (Ed). (2000). *Strategic Management in Tourism*. CABI.

Page, S. (2005). *Transport and Tourism: Global Perspectives*. Prentice Hall.

Pine, B.J. and Gilmore, J.H. (1999). *The Experience Economy: Work is Theatre and every Business a Stage*. Harvard Business School Press.

Page, S. (2005). *Transport and Tourism: Global Perspectives*. Prentice Hall.

Pickton, D. and Broderick, A. (2006). *Integrated Marketing Communications*. 3rd edn. FT Prentice Hall.

Pike, S. (2008). *Destination Marketing: An Integrated Marketing Communications Approach*. Elsevier Butterworth Heinemann.

Poon, A. (1993). *Tourism Technology and Competitive Strategies*. CAB Press.

Porter, M.E. (1980). *Competitive Strategy: Techniques for Analyzing Industries and Competitors*. Collier and Macmillan.

Porter, M.E. (1995). *Competitive Advantage: Creating and Sustaining, Superior Performance*. Free Press.

Prahalad, C.K. and Ramaswamy, V. (2004). *The Future of Competition*. Harvard Business School Press.

Ranchhod, A. and Gurau, C. (2007). *Marketing Strategies: A Contemporary Approach*. 2nd edn. Pearson Education.

Rathmell, J.M. (1974). *Marketing in the Service Sector*. Winthrop.

Rogers, E. (1962). *The Diffusion of Innovations*. Free Press.

Rosenbloom, B. (1999). *Marketing Channels: A Management View*. 6th edn. Dryden Press.

Sasser, W.E., Olsen, P.R. and Wyckoff, D.D. (1978). *Management of Service Operations*. Allyn and Bacon.

Schmitt, B.H. (2003). *Customer Experience Management*. John Wiley and Sons.

Schramm, W. (1955). *The Process and Effects of Mass Communications*. University of Illinois Press.

Seibert, J.C. (1973). *Concepts of Marketing Management*. Harper and Row.

Sharpley, R. (2006). *Travel and Tourism*. Sage Publications.

Shaw, S. (1999). *Air Transport: A Marketing Perspective*. 4th edn. Pitman.

Shaw, S. and Stone, M. (1987). *Database Marketing*. Gower.

Shostack, G.L. (1977). Breaking free from product marketing, *Journal of Marketing*, 41, April.

Shostack, G.L. (1984). Designing services that deliver, *Harvard Business Review* January–February.

Sleight, S. (1989). *Sponsorship: What is it and how to use it*. McGraw Hill.

Smith, S.L.J. (1995). *Tourism Analysis: A Handbook*. 2nd edn. Longman.

Smith, P.R. and Taylor, J. (2004). *Marketing Communications: An Integrated Approach*. 4th edn. Kogan Page.

Smith, V. (1977). *Hosts and Guests: The Anthropology of Tourism*. University of Pennsylvania Press.

Stanton, W.J. (1981). *Fundamentals of Marketing*. 6th edn. McGraw-Hill.

Strong, E.K. (1925). *The Psychology of Selling and Advertising*. McGraw Hill.

Swinglehurst, E. (1982). *Cook's Tours: The Study of Popular Travel*. Blandford Press.

Timothy, D.J. and Boyd, S.W. (2003). *Heritage Tourism*. Prentice Hall.

Toffler, A. (1990). *Power Shift*. Bantam.

Theobold, W. (Ed.) (2005). *Global Tourism: The Next Decade*. 3rd edn. Elsevier Butterworth Heinemann

Witt, S. and Moutinho, L. (Eds). (1994). *Tourism Marketing and Management Handbook*. 2nd edn. Prentice-Hall.

UN World Tourism Organization Business Council (1999). *Marketing Tourism Destinations Online*. WTO.

UN World Tourism Organization (2003). *Evaluating NTO Marketing Activities*. UNWTO.

UN World Tourism Organization (WTO) (2007). *Tourism 20:20 Vision*. UNWTO.

UN World Tourism Organization (2008). *Market Trends*. UNWTO.

Wright, L.T. and Crimp, M. (2000). *The Marketing Research Process*. 5th edn. Financial Times/Prentice-Hall.

Zeithaml, V.A., and Bitner, M.J. (2000). *Services Marketing*. McGraw-Hill.

Index

Accommodation, 363–80
as a service experience, 366–8
definition, 364
serviced and non-serviced accommodation, 364–6
marketing budgets, 377–80
nature of the accommodation business, 368–71
business peaks and troughs, 369
high fixed costs, 370–1
location, 368–9
profit driven by room-night sales, 370
targeting bookers, 370
packages, 428
role in overall tourism product, 365–6
strategic marketing tasks, 371–5
business mix planning, 371–3
deciding the position, brand or image, 373
encouraging/rewarding frequent customers, 374
evaluating strategic opportunities for growth, 371
integrating marketing across units, 374–5
Internet marketing, 373–4
tactical marketing, 376–7
See also Hotels
Accor, 41, 132
ACORN (A Classification of Residential Neighbourhoods), 91, 113
Added value, *See* Value added
Advance bookings, *See* Reservations
Advertising, 296–7, 304–5
agencies, 305
costs, 302–3
definition, 304
expenditure, 296
media planning, 301–2
objectives, 304–5
television, 302
terminology, 305, 315
See also Communication
Affiliate marketing, 263, 289
Agra – and the Taj Mahal; Indian World Heritage site case study, 459–64
World heritage and tourism, 459
Incredible India, 462
Marketing the Taj Mahal, 463–4
Air traffic control (ATC) systems, 393
Air transport, 386, 389
environmental issues, 393–4
See also Airlines; Transport
Airbus, 390, 393
Airlines, 384
Central Reservations Systems, 245–6
corporate strategy, 192–4
costs, 50–1
marketing costs, 396
low-cost airlines, 247
sales variance analysis, 234
strategic linkages and alliances, 398
See also Air transport; Transport
AITO, 253–5
Alistair Sawday travel guides, *See* Sawday, Alistair
Alliances, 375, 398
Alton Towers, 412
Amadeus, 246
Amazon, 253, 263
American Express, 41
American Marketing Association, 23, 28, 40, 304
Angehrn, A., 262
APEX (Advanced Purchase Excursion Fares) fares, 401
Armstrong, G., 101
Ashbridge model, 185–6
Association of Leading Visitor Attractions (ALVA), 167
Attitudes, 65, 87
of consumers, *See* Consumers/customers
of management, 25–7
product/production orientation, 26
sales orientation, 26–7
Attractions, *See* Visitor attractions
Augmented product, 128, 129
See also Value added
Australia, 108–10, 342, 343, 345
Australian Tourism Commission (ATC), 352

Bartels, R., 28, 40
Bateson, J.E.G., 145, 148, 151, 152
Beard, J., 80
Bed-banks, 260
Best Western, 375
Birmingham, 127, 409
Bitner, M.J., 143, 145, 146, 148, 151
Blogs, 267
Blueprints, 151–2
Boeing, 390, 393, 394
Booms, B.H., 143
Boston Consulting Group, 189
Bournemouth, 106, 251
Brand loyalty, 106
See also Loyalty schemes
Branding, 195, 197–200, 483
accommodation, 373
advantages of for travel and tourism, 199–200
co-branding, 132–3
destinations, 345–6
New Zealand case study, 448
package tours, 438
transport product, 397
Brazil, 59, 242
Brey, E., 271
BRIC countries, 479
Brin, Sergey, 484
Brindley Centre, Birmingham, 15
Britain, *See* United Kingdom
British Advertising Association, 296
British Airways, 185, 391
call centres, 245
environmental initiatives, 393
Brochures, 323–4
costs, 319
marketing research, 323
national tourism organization support, 354–5
product substitution role, 323–4

Brochures *(Continued)*
wastage, 318–19
See also Information materials; Printed communications
Budapest, 64
Budget, 214–15
accommodation marketing, 377–80
budgeting methods, 226–31
affordable method, 226
competitive parity method, 226
objective and task method, 226, 229–31
percentage of sales revenue method, 226
destination marketing organizations (DMOs), 338–9, 351–2
marketing campaigns, 225
visitor attraction marketing, 421
See also Costs
Buhalis, D., 248, 253, 338, 427
Bulgaria, 126
Burkart, A.J., 57, 385
Business models, 483–4
Business portfolio analysis, 189–91
Business to business (B2B) transactions, 278
Business to customer (B2C) transactions, 277–8
Business travel market segmentation, 103
Buyer behaviour, 90–1
buyer characteristics influencing decisions, 80–4
needs, desires and motives, 80–1
personal circumstances, 81–2
personality, 81
social and cultural influences, 82–4
data use in marketing, 91–2
decision-making process, 87–90
information processing, 86–7
attitudes, 87
learning, 87
perception, 86–7
market segmentation and, 106–10
model of, 78–9
post-purchase feelings, 89
stimulus and response processes, 78–9
See also Consumers/customers
Call centres, 245
Campaigns, *See* Marketing campaigns
Canada, 342
Cancun, Mexico, 126
Capacity, 49
Carlson, J., 92
Carson, D., 267
Cathay Pacific, 132
Center Parcs, 126, 132, 196, 234–5, 483
Centre of Tourism Research and Technologies of the Balearic Islands, 170–2
Chartered Institute of Marketing, UK, 80
China, 8, 15, 22–3, 59, 60, 61, 242, 479, 481
2008 Olympic Games, 8, 15, 485
Chisnall, P.M., 97, 101
Climate change, 34, 66, 71
Club, 18–30, 199
Club Mediterranée, 133
Co-branding, 132–3
Co-marketing, 132–3
Cognitive dissonance, 87
Cognitive learning, 87
Collateral materials, *See* Brochures; Information materials; Printed communications
Commodities, 198
Communication, 139, 140
internal marketing, 146–7
marketing communications, 79, 296, 297–303
choice of tools, 300
creative planning, 301
measuring campaign results, 303
media costs, 302–3
media planning, 301–2
objectives, 297–300
target audience identification, 300
marketing plan role, 217
media communications, 69–70
See also Advertising; Information and communications technology; Information materials; Integrated marketing communications (IMC); Printed communications; Public relations
Competition:,
competitive strategy, 197
fair competition regulation, 68
five forces of, 188
visitor attractions, 417
Complaints, 148
Complementarity, 52
Computer reservations systems (CRS), 245–6
See also Global distribution systems
Consortia, 356
Consumer centric approach, 130, 131, 139, 153–4, 480, 483
Consumer Generated Media (CGM), 373
Consumers/customers:,
access to for marketing research, 175–6
attitudes of, 65–6, 87
characteristics of, 58–9, 80–4
needs, desires and motives, 80–1
personality, 81
socioeconomic circumstances, 81–2
consumer orientation, 12, 130, 131, 139
consumer research, 164
See also Marketing research
customer databases, *See* Databases
customer value, 139–40
empowerment by ICT, 250–1, 480–1
participation in product creation, 130–2
profiles, 110
databases and, 107–8
protection of, 357
retention of, 374
costs of, 148
See also Loyalty schemes; Relationship marketing
satisfaction of, *See* Customer satisfaction
See also Buyer behaviour; Market segmentation; Visitors
Control, 216–17
marketing control, 233
See also Performance monitoring; Quality control; Regulatory factors
Convenience, 139, 140–1
packages, 431
See also Access
Cookies, 270

Copenhagen, 188
Core product, 128–9
Corporate strategy, 191–4
airline, 192–4
See also Strategy
Corporate values, 185–6
Cost to consumer, 139, 140
Holiday Costs Barometer, 125–6
Costa Coffee, 483
Costs:,
accommodation, 370–1
advertising, 302–3
brochures, 319
customer retention, 148
distribution, 279, 284–5, 286
fixed, *See* Fixed costs
marketing mix and, 142
media, 302–3
operating cost reduction, 397
transport, 396
variable, 50–1, 419
See also Budget; Cost to consumer; Price
Cotte, J., 437
Cova, B., 267
Cracow, 64
Creative planning, 301
information materials, 326–7
Crisis management, 308–9, 401
Critical incidents, 148
Cruise ships, 385, 388
Cultural attractions, 123
Culture, 82
cultural differences, 82–3
Customer Experience Management (CEM), 92
Customer Relationship Management (CRM), 92, 269–70
online (eCRM), 373
See also Relationship marketing
Customer satisfaction:,
researching, 176
role of national tourism organization, 357
variance, 235–6
Customer services, *See* Service delivery; Services
Customer value, 139–40
Customers, *See* Consumers/customers

Darling Harbour, Australia, 15
Data processing, 244
Data protection, 271
Data-mining, 91
Database marketing, 91
Internet and, 269–70
Databases, 107–8
customer profiles and, 107–8
market research and, 108
New Zealand case study, 448–9
Davidson, J.H., 183, 198–9, 218, 221
De Bono, E., 86–7
De Chernatony, L., 198, 199
De Efteling, 412
Decision processes, 24
purchasing decision, 87–90
Dell, 130
Demand, 4–8
accommodation, 369
determinants of, 57–8, 59–60
comparative prices, 61–2
demographic factors, 62–3
economic factors, 60–1
environmental concerns, 71
geographic factors, 63–5
government/regulatory factors, 67–9
information and communications technology, 70
marketing managers' response to, 72–3
media communications, 69–70
personal mobility factors, 66–7
socio-cultural attitudes, 65–6
terrorist actions, 72
domestic tourism, 7–8
forecasting by transport operators, 396
seasonality, 50
supply linkages, 12–13, 60
transport, 387
Demographic factors, 62–3
market segmentation, 110
Design features, 153
Destination Management Issues, 484–5
Destination Management Systems (DMSs), 352
New Zealand case study, 447–52
Destination Marketing Organizations (DMOs), 337
definition, 338–9
destination positioning, 345–6
England, 349–50
facilitation strategy, 344–5
marketing influence, 339–42
See also National tourism organizations (NTOs)
Destinations:,
accessibility, 124
attractions, 99
facilities and services, 124
images and perceptions of, 345–6
management issues, 484–5
management systems, 253
positioning, 345–6
promotional strategy, 343
See also National tourism organizations
Diagnosis, 208–9
Differentiation, 100, 197
Digital Divide, 242
Direct mail, 355
Direct marketing, 276
Internet and, 269–70
strategic choice, 276
Discounted prices, 437
Discrete market segments, 102
Disney Corporation, 41, 132, 148, 150, 405
Disney World, Florida, 126, 140, 408–9, 412, 413
DisneyLand, 325, 412
Disneyland Paris, 84–6, 412, 415
Distribution, 275
branding and, 200
costs, 279, 284–5, 286
evolution of distribution systems, 287–9
disintermediation or reintermediation, 288–9
global distribution systems (GDS), 244, 246
hotels, 284–5
ICT influence, 261
information materials, 326, 329–30
evaluation of, 330–1
location importance, 279–81
marketing triangle, 276–8
packages, 430, 435, 439
principles of, 279
research, 164
strategic choices, 276–9
Distribution channels, 281–7
accommodation marketing, 374
benefits of using intermediaries, 283–4
customer perspective, 283–4
supplier perspective, 283
channel choice criteria, 285–7
costs of using intermediaries, 284–5
definition, 282

Distribution channels
(*Continued*)
management, 289–90
See also Distribution
Diversification, 196
Domestic tourism, 4, 7–8
Dowd, Stephen, 310
Doyle, P., 198
Dynamic packaging, 260, 483

E-businesses, 246–7
E-commerce, 246–7
barriers to growth of, 253
package tours, 430
See also Internet; World Wide Web
E-marketing:,
collaborative, 253–5
direct/database marketing, 269–70
ICT impact on marketing mix, 259–61
See also Websites
Early adopters, 82
EasyJet, 211, 263, 289, 389, 397, 401, 483
eBookers, 211
Economic factors, 13–15
determinants of demand, 60–1
market segmentation, 110
tour operation, 436
Economies of scale, 40
Eden Project, Cornwall, 418
Education, role of information materials, 325
Egypt, 343
Electronic information, 331–2
Ellis, Jeremy, 319
Employees, *See* Staff
England:,
political devolution, 349–50
visitor attractions, 409
See also United Kingdom
Environment, 123
destination environments, 123–4
external business environment analysis, 186–8, 348
tour operation and, 436
Environmental issues, 66, 71
climate change, 34, 66, 71
regulation, 68–9
transport, 67, 393–4
See also Sustainability
EPCOT, Florida, 409
Eurostat, 5
Evaluation, 216–17
marketing campaigns, 231–3
newzealand.com website, 451
See also Performance monitoring
Exchange transactions, 23–4, 29–31
Expedia, 262, 430
Experience economy, 252, 452
Experience marketing, 366–8, 481–2

Facebook, 267–8
Facilitation, 337, 344
of product use, 324–5
See also National tourism organizations
Familiarization trips, 354
Farecast, 260–1
Ferries, 260, 384
See also Transport
Film tourism, 309–10
Finland, 66
Finnish Tourism Board (FTB), 353
Firm centric approach, 130, 131, 480
Fishbein, M., 88
Fixed costs, 50–1
accommodation, 370–1
high fixed costs of service operations, 50–1
transport, 394–5
Fleet utilization, 395
Florida, 63
Flybe, 391–2, 397
Focus groups, 166
Fogle, Ben, 449
Formal product, 128, 129
Forte Hotel Group, 465
Four Ps/Cs, *See* Marketing mix
Four Seasons, 373
France, 338
Friedman, L., 265
Fyall, A., 349

Gabbott, M., 89
Galileo/Worldspan, 246
Galleries, *See* Museums
Gater, C., 92
Gates, Bill, 484
Geodemographic analysis, 91
Geodemographic segmentation, 113–14
Geographic factors, 63–5
market segmentation, 110
Germany, 60
Gilmore, J. H., 80, 125, 481
GIS (Geographical Information System), 113
Glasgow, 127
Global distribution systems (GDS), 244, 246
Globalization, 482–3
Goals and objectives, 194–5
advertising, 304–5
information materials, 321–5, 326
marketing communication campaigns, 297–300
marketing objectives, 213–14
national tourism organization objectives, 350–1
objective setting, 191–4
Godin, S., 271
Goodrich, G., 265
Goods, 46, 47
marketing of, 40
Google, 249, 263–4, 480
Government factors, 67–9
Greece, 338, 432
Greene, Gerard, 454, 455, 456
Guggenheim Museum, Bilbao, 15, 409
Guinness 'Storehouse', Dublin, 407

Hamel, G., 182, 477
Hardware trends, 248
Hawkins, R., 16, 71, 101, 418
Hertz, 41
Herzberg, F., 80
Heterogeneity, 48
Hilton International, 373
Hirschmann, E. C., 89
Hoffman, K.D., 145, 151, 152
Hofstede, G., 82–3
Hogg, G., 89
Holbrook, M. B., 89
Holiday Hypermarket, 131–2
Holiday Inn, 41
Hong Kong, 62
Host community, 144
Hotelopia, 289
Hotels, 98, 363
as a service experience, 368
budget hotels, 371, 465–6
distribution costs, 284–5
Internet marketing, 373–4
marketing budgets, 378–9
marketing communications, 298–300
packages, 428
products, 121, 128–9
See also Accommodation; Travelodge case study; YOTEL case study
Howard, J. A., 88
Hyatt, 454
Hygiene factors, 80

Image, 197–200
accommodation, 373
destination, 345–6
package tours, 438
Inbound tourism, 4
Inclusive tours, *See* Packages
Income, demand relationships, 61
India, 8, 22–3, 61, 111–12, 242, 345, 461, 481
call centres, 245
Incredible India campaign, 462–3
Indirect marketing, 276
Information and communications technology (ICT):,
as determinant of demand, 70
databases, 107–8
definition, 242–3
destination management systems, 253
developments, 33, 40, 241–2, 243–7
electronic alternatives to print, 331–2
future trends, 248–9
hardware trends, 248
netware trends, 249
network trends, 248–9
software trends, 248
impact on marketing mix, 259–61
impact on visitor economy, 251–2
influence on tourism marketing, 250–1
consumer empowerment, 250–1, 480–1
Internet adoption by consumer for travel, 251
See also Internet; World Wide Web
Information materials:,
definition, 320
distribution to target audiences, 326, 329–30
evaluation of, 330–1
electronic information, 331–2
marketing role of, 321–5
multiple purposes of, 321–5
production of, 325–9
agency use, 327–9
See also Brochures; Printed communications
Inkbaran, R., 105
Innovation, 233
researching marketing innovations, 177
Innovators, 82
Inseparability, 47–8
Intangibility, 48
Integrated marketing communications (IMC), 293, 296
definition, 294
principles of, 294–5
promotional mix, 304–13
advertising, 304–5
public relations (PR), 306–11
sales promotion, 312–13
sponsorship, 311–12
See also Communications and Tourism New Zealand case study
Interdependence, 51–2
Intermediaries, 281
benefits of using, 283–4
customer perspective, 283–4
supplier perspective, 283
costs of using, 284–5
See also Travel agents
Internal marketing, 146–7
Internal networks, 245
International Civil Aviation Organization (ICAO), 393
International tourism, 5–7
International visitors, 4, 5
Internet, 69, 70, 140, 154, 275
accommodation marketing, 373–4
adoption of by consumer for travel, 251
barriers to growth of, 263
customer experience management, 265–6
customer service and, 149–50
developments, 241–2, 477
Destination Marketing Organizations and, 352
future trends, 248–9
direct/database marketing and, 269–70
e-businesses, 246–7
intranets, 245
marketing research and, 165
service delivery and, 149–50
small business empowerment, 252
virtual companies, 70
See also Information and communications technology; Websites
Intranets, 245
Iso-Ahola, S, 80
Jackson, M., 105
Japan, 60
Jobber, D., 137, 138, 148, 259, 261
Joint marketing schemes/ventures, 355

Kasriel, T., 78
Kelly, Gary, 387
Kotler, P., 28, 88, 101, 122, 128, 139, 226, 231, 232, 294
Krippendorf, J., 52

Laker Airways, 483
Large-scale operations, 33
service operations, 41–3
Las Vegas, 122, 125
Lastminute.com, 247, 437
Law, R., 427
Learning, 87
Legoland, 405, 412
Leppard, J.W., 208
Levitt, T., 41, 122, 151
Life-cycle analysis, 110
Lifestyle segmentation, 111–12
Little Chef, 465
Liverpool, 409
Load factor, 395
Location, 279–81
accommodation, 368–9
See also Distribution; Place
London, 122, 126, 132, 211
Loyalty schemes, 374

McCarthy, E.J., 138–9
McDonald, M.H.B., 198, 199, 205, 208
McDonald's, 41, 100, 483
Madame Tussauds, 412
Maldives, 340–1
Management:,
attitudes, 25–7
marketing orientation, 25–6
product/production orientation, 26
sales orientation, 26–7
information, 244
visitor attractions, 406–9, 421–2
Manchester, 127, 409
Manchester United, 408
Market analysis, 164
See also Marketing research
Market Research Society (MRS), UK, 173
Market segmentation, 97–8
actionable market segments, 101–2
definition, 101

Market segmentation *(Continued)*
marketing and operations view of, 99–100
multiple segments for producers, 98–9
pricing and, 114
segmentation methods, 103–14
visitor attractions, 414–17
Market share variance, 235
Marketing, 4, 21–3
campaigns, *See* Marketing campaigns
characteristics in travel and tourism, 52–3
co-marketing, 132–3
collaborative, 51–2
communications, 79
database marketing, 91
definition, 27–8
exchange transactions, 23–5, 29–31
goods and services, 40–1
harnessing the global power of, 485–6
ICT influence on tourism marketing, 250–1
objectives, 213–14, 350–1
planning, *See* Marketing plans; Strategy; Tactics
relationship marketing, 89, 91–2
system, 29–1, 142–3
World Heritage Sites, 460
See also Direct marketing; E-marketing
Marketing campaigns, 221–2
budgeting methods, 226–31
definition, 222
menu for, 222–4
performance measurement, 231–6
customer satisfaction variance, 235–6
innovation, experimentation and test marketing, 233–4
market share variance, 235
ratio variance, 236
sales variance, 234–5
Marketing communications, *See* Communication
Marketing control, 233
Marketing facilitation, *See* Facilitation
Marketing mix, 13, 29, 137
cost and revenue considerations, 142
definition, 138
four Ps/Cs, 138–41
ICT impact on, 259–61
in context of marketing system, 142–3
marketing-mix programmes, 215–16
people component, 144–7
physical evidence, 152–3
process of service delivery, 147–52
service blueprinting, 151–2
service delivery perceived as scripts, 150–1
website central role in, 261–9
See also Place; Price; Product; Sales promotion
Marketing planning, 205
alternatives to, 206–7
for strategy versus tactics, 217–18
national tourism organizations, 350
process, 206, 207–17
diagnosis, 208–9
marketing budget, 214–15
marketing objectives and targets, 213–14
marketing-mix programmes, 215–16
monitoring, evaluation and control, 216–17
prognosis, 209
stakeholder analysis, 212
SWOT analysis, 209–12
See also Strategy; Tactics
Marketing plans:,
corporate communication role, 217
significance of, 206
visitor attractions, 418–19
See also Marketing planning
Marketing research, 161
agency commissioning, 173–5
categories of, 163, 164
continuous and ad hoc research, 164–5
customer access, 175–6
customer satisfaction, 176
definition, 162
methods, 168–70
national tourism organizations, 348
occupancy studies, 167–8
omnibus and syndicated surveys, 166–7
primary and secondary research, 166
quantitative and qualitative research, 165–6
researching marketing innovations, 177
Marketing strategy, *See* Strategy
Marketing triangle, 276–8
Marriott, 132, 454
Maslow, A., 80
Mass tourism, 15
Measurability, market segments, 102
Media:,
communications, 69–70
costs, 302–3
media relations, 308
planning, 301–2
Medlik, S., 57, 119, 120, 385, 482
Membership schemes, *See* Loyalty schemes
Mexico, 242
Micro-businesses, 33, 43–6
importance of, 44–5
marketing implications, 45–6
types of, 44
Middleton, V.T.C., 16, 33, 43, 71, 101, 119, 120, 218, 282, 418, 482
Mission, 185–6
Mission statement, 186
Monitoring, 216
See also Performance monitoring
Morgan, M., 87, 301
Morrison, A.M., 52
MOSAIC, 91
Motivations, 58, 80–1
Motivators, 80
Museums, 422
See also Visitor attractions
MySpace, 249
Mystery shoppers, 176

National Air Traffic Services (NATS), 386
National tourism organizations (NTOs), 338
definition, 338–9
destination promotion strategy, 343
facilitation strategies, 344–5, 353–8
marketing influence, 339–43
marketing role, 342–3, 346–52
budget decisions, 351–2
external business environment research, 348

government policy and tourism strategy, 348
Internet developments, 352
marketing objectives and targets, 350–1
marketing planning, 350
National Trust, UK, 412
Needs and wants, 80–1
market segmentation and, 104–6
Netherlands, 66
Netnography, 269
Netware trends, 249
Network trends, 248–9
New Delhi, 461
New York, 126, 127, 132
New Zealand, 309, 357, 481, 485
case study, 447–52
See also Destination Management Systems (DMSs)
Niketown, USA, 407
Non-Governmental Organizations (NGOs), 212
Non-serviced accommodation, 364–6
See also Accommodation
Norway, 66

Objectives, *See* Goals and objectives
Occupancy studies, 167–8
Oil prices, 62
Old Trafford, Manchester, 407, 408
Olympic Games, 309–11
China, 8, 15, 485
Omnibus surveys, 166–7
One World, 398
Online communities, 267
Operant conditioning, 87
Operational plans, 218
Opodo, 288, 389
Opportunities, 211
O'Reilly, T., 266–7
Organization for Economic Co-operation and Development (OECD), 10, 170
Orient Express, 388
Outbound tourism, 4

Packages, 427
definition, 428–9
distribution method, 430, 435, 439
functional role, 431–2
nature of product, 429–30
process of inclusive tour programme construction, 433–5
tactical marketing, 440–2
See also Tour operators
Page, Larry, 484
Paypal, 251
Perception, 86–7
of destination, 124–5
Performance monitoring, 164
marketing campaigns, 231–6
customer satisfaction variance, 235–6
innovation, experimentation and test marketing, 233–4
market share variance, 235
ratio variance, 236
sales variance, 234–5
marketing communication campaigns, 303
Perishability, 48–9
Permira, 467
Permission marketing, 92, 270, 271
Personal mobility factors, 66–7
Personality traits, 81
PESTLE, 187
Physical evidence, 152–3
Pike, S., 338
Pine, J. H., 80, 125, 481
Pipelines, *See* Distribution channels
Place, 138, 139, 140–1, 275
ITC influence, 261
location importance, 279–81
See also Distribution
Planning:,
creative, 301
media, 301–2
See also Strategic planning
Plog, S., 81
Poland, 99
Polarization, 482–3
Port Adventura, 412
Porter, M., 188, 197
Positioning, 195
accommodation, 373
destinations, 345–6
package tours, 438
Post-purchase feelings, 89
Post-service economy, 149
Prague, 64
Prahalad, C.K., 130, 477
Precision marketing, 270
Premier Inn, 467
Price, 138, 139, 140
accommodation, 375
as product component, 125–6
comparative, 61–2
competitive strategy, 197
discounting, 437
ICT influence on, 260–1
market segmentation by, 114
package tours, 431, 437
research, 164
strategic role, 197
transport, 401
Primary data, 166
Printed communications, 317, 318
national tourism organization support, 354–5
production and wastage, 318–20
types of printed material, 320–1
See also Brochures; Information materials
Pritchard, A., 301
Producers, 24
Product, 120, 139–40
accommodation, 375
benefits view of, 122
components of, 120, 122–6, 139
destination accessibility, 124
destination attractions and environment, 123–4
destination facilities and services, 124
images and perception of the destination, 124–5
price to consumer, 125–6
specific product components, 127–30
development, 196
differentiation, 100, 197
facilitation of use, 324
formulation, 119, 138
ICT impact on, 259–60
market growth strategies, 195–7
marketing implications of overall product concept, 126–7
new product support, 355–6
packages, 429–30, 437
positioning, 197
visitor attractions product, 412–14
See also Branding
Product/production orientation, 26
Promotion, 138, 139, 140
accommodation, 374
destination promotion, 343
ICT influence, 261
transport, 400–1
See also Sales promotion
Proof of purchase, 324
Psychographics, 111
market segmentation and, 111–12
Public realm, 52, 484–5

Public relations, 306–11
  activities, 307–11
    crisis management, 308–9
    media relations, 308
    product placement, 309–11
  definition, 306
  measurement of results, 311
  terminology, 315
Purchasing decision, 87–90
See also Buyer behaviour

Qualitative research, 165–6
Quality control, 42
Qualmark New Zealand Limited, 357
Quantitative research, 165–6

Radio Times, 303
Ragheb, M. G., 80
Rail transport, 385
See also Transport
Rathmell, J.M., 46
Ratio variance, 236
Really Simple Syndication (RSS) feeds, 261
Regulatory factors, 67–9
  environmental legislation, 68–9
  fair competition, 68
  transport regulation, 68
Relationship marketing, 89, 91–2, 290
Reservations:,
  computer reservation systems, 245–6
  manual systems, 244
  national tourism organization role, 355
Residents, 4, 485
Resorts, *See* Destinations
Revenue, marketing mix and, 142
Rogers, E., 82
Royal Caribbean, 111, 438–9
Russia, 59, 242, 481
Ryanair, 41, 185, 186, 394, 397, 483

Sabre, 246
St Petersburg, 64
Sales orientation, 26–7
Sales promotion, 138, 312–13
  accommodation, 374
  definition, 312
  information materials, 323
  promotional print, 321
  research, 164
  See also Promotion
Sales variance, 234–5
Same-day visits, 5, 7–8
Sandals, 111, 132, 133
Sawday, Alistair, 471–5, 481, 483, 484
  travel guides case study, 471–5
    sawday business concept, 472
    future directions, 475
    niche marketing and sustainability, 472–3
    online marketing and relationship building, 483–74
    relationship marketing, 474–5
Scenario planning, 187–8
Schmallegger, D., 267
Scotland, 309, 432
Search engine marketing, 263–4
Seasonality, 50
  accommodation, 369
  visitor attractions, 419–20
Secondary data, 166
Segmentation, *See* Market segmentation
Self-catering accommodation, 365
Service delivery process, 147–52
  online service delivery, 149–50
  perceived as scripts, 150–1
  service blueprinting, 151–2
Serviced accommodation, 364–6
See also Accommodation; Hotels
Services, 46, 47
  characteristics of, 46–52
    high fixed costs, 50–1
    inseparability, 47–8
    interdependence of tourism products, 51–2
    perishability, 48–9
    seasonality, 50
  ICT impact on, 251–2
  large-scale service operations, 41–3
  marketing of, 40–1
    quality control, 42
  service recovery, 148–9
  small and medium-sized enterprises, 43–6
    micro-business importance, 43–5
    micro-business types, 44
Sharpley, S., 111
Shopping malls, 407
Shostack, G. L., 151–2
Singapore, 132
Singapore Airlines, 186, 200
Slow travel, 472–3
Small and medium-sized enterprises (SMEs), 43–6
  collaborative alliances, 375
  ICT impact on, 252
  micro-businesses, 33, 43–6
    importance of, 44–5
    marketing implications, 45–6
    types of, 44
Small Luxury Hotels of the World, 375–6
Smith, P.R., 302
Social networking, 249, 267–8
Socio-cultural attitudes, 65–6
Socio-cultural influences, 82–4
Socioeconomic circumstances, 81–2
Software trends, 248
Southwest Airlines, 387, 483
Spain, 63, 345
  Travelodge development strategy, 469
Spam, 270
Sponsorship, 311–12
Staff, 144, 145–6
  internal marketing, 146–7
  service recovery, 148–9
Stakeholder analysis, 212
Standards, 42
Stanton, W.J., 143, 222
Star Alliance, 398, 399–400
Starbucks, 483
Strategic business units (SBUs), 181–2, 189–91
Strategic planning, 181, 217–18
  analysis, 186–91
    business portfolio analysis, 189–91
    external business environment, 186–8
  mission, 185–6
  need for, 182–3
  objective setting, 191–4
  process, 183–5
  See also Marketing planning
Strategy, 31–3, 191–4, 200
  accommodation marketing, *See* Accommodation
  distribution, 276–9
  facilitation strategy, 345
  marketing strategy, 194–7
    competitive strategy, 197
    direct vs indirect marketing, 276
    for product-market growth and development, 195–7
    planning process, 194–5
    product positioning, 197
  timescale, 31–3

tour operators, *See* Tour operators
transport marketing, *See* Transport
visitor attractions, 417–19
strategic marketing plans, 418–19
See also Strategic planning; Tactics
Stratford-on-Avon, 415
Strengths, 209–10
Stride, 270
Sundaram, P., 111
Supply:
demand linkages, 12–13, 60
transport, 387
Sustainability, 34, 66, 71, 479–80
market segments, 102
personal transport and, 67
regulation, 68–9
visitor attractions and, 417–18
See also case studies in the book
Sweden, 66
SwimTrek, 211
SWOT analysis, 209–12
Sydney Opera House, 15
Syndicated surveys, 166–7

Tactics, 31–3, 200, 218
accommodation marketing, 376–7
timescale, 31–3
tour operators, 440–2
transport marketing, *See* Transport
See also Marketing planning
Taj Mahal, 459–64
future issues and challenges, 463–4
tourism, 460–2
Tangible product, 128, 129
Target audience:,
identification of, 300
information materials, 326
Targets, 213–14
Tarlow, P., 57
Tate Modern Gallery, London, 15, 409
Technology, *See* Information and communications technology
Television, 69
advertising rates, 302
future trends, 249–50
Tenders, 174–5
Terrorist attacks, 72
Test marketing, 233–4
Thailand, 345
Theme parks, 412
See also Visitor attractions
Thomas Cook, 132, 186, 188, 189–91, 249, 253, 289, 312, 427
Thomson Holidays, 176, 266, 284, 289, 312
Threats, 212
Tiscover, 355
Tour operators, 98, 281–2, 428
collaborative e-marketing, 253–5
market segments, 104
marketing budget, 226–9
marketing strategy, 436–40
distribution options, 439
external environment, 436
position, branding and image, 438
product/market portfolios, 437
volume and pricing, 437
products, 127
strategic issues, 435–6
tactical marketing, 440–2
tour programme construction, 433–5
See also Packages
Tourism, *See* Travel and tourism
Tourism New Zealand case study, 447–52
100% Pure New Zealand, 448
DMS, 448
Experience based marketing, 449
Interactive marketing, 450
User generated content, 451
Touristic Union International (TUI), 427
Tourists, 5
Trade consortia, 356
Trade manuals, 354
Trade shows, 353–4
Transport, 383
external influences on marketing, 389–94
environmental issues, 393–4
information and communications technology, 391
vehicle technology, 390
functional role, 388
marketing costs, 396
marketing task, 395–8
nature of transport product, 388–9
nature of transport systems, 384–7
operational constraints, 394–5
capital investment and fixed costs, 394–5
load factor, yield management and fleet utilization, 395
operators, 98–9
packages, 428
personal transport access, 66–7
regulation, 68
strategic marketing, 396–8
building corporate product and brand strengths, 397
forecasting demand, 396
reducing operating costs, 397
relationship marketing, 397–8
strategic linkages and alliances, 398
supply and demand, 387
tactical marketing, 400–1
crisis management, 401
marketing the margin, 400
segment specific promotions, 400–1
tactical pricing and yield management, 401
See also Airlines; Ferries; Rail transport
Travel agents, 276, 281–2
See also Intermediaries
Travel and tourism, 3–4
See also Vistor economy
changing prospects, 13–16
definition, 5, 8–9
demand for, *See* Demand
domestic tourism, 5, 7–8
international tourism, 5–7
Travel and tourism industry, 9–11
component sectors of, 9–11
polarization, 482–3
Travel Inn, 466
Travelodge budget hotels case study, 465–70, 483
background, 465–6
competition, 467
context for business expansion, 466–7
marketing approach-UK, 467–9
Internet development, 468
performance monitoring, 468
strategic objectives, 467–8
sustainability programme, 468–9
repositioning, 467
strategy to develop in Spain, 469–70
Travelsupermarket, 262
TripAdvisor, 266, 268, 331, 430
Tsunami 2004 impact, 340–1

TUI (Touristic Union International), 132
Turkey, 105–6, 343, 432
TV Times, 303

Umaga, Tana, 449
UN World Tourism Organization (UNWTO), 5, 7
Uncertainty avoidance, 83
UNESCO World Heritage List (WHL), 459–60, 463–4
Uniform System of Hotel Accounts, 379
United Kingdom (UK), 61, 338, 340, 342, 345
- budget hotels, 466–9
- discounting strategy, 437
- domestic tourism, 8
- geodemographic segmentation, 113–14
- political devolution, 349–50
- transport system, 386
- visitor attractions, 409, 411

United Kingdom Tourism Survey (UKTS), 167
United Nations World Tourism Organization (UNWTO), 7, 10
- definitions, 9

Universal Studios, 405
USA, 60, 63, 125–6, 345, 479
- car ownership, 66–7
- domestic tourism, 7

User-generated content, 247, 266–8
- blogs, 267
- New Zealand, 451
- online communities, 267
- social networking sites, 267–8

Users, 24
Uttar Pradesh, 461

Value added, 129, 199
Variable costs, 50–1, 419
Variance analysis, 234
Vehicle technology, 390
See also Transport
Venice, 126
Viable market segments, 102
Viral marketing, 268, 270
Virgin, 41, 185, 196, 199
Virgin Atlantic, 393
Virtual companies, 70
Vision, 185–6
VisitBritain, 310, 340, 342
Visitor attractions, 99, 123–4, 405
- attractions product, 412–14
  - components of, 413–14
- characteristics of managed attractions, 409–11
- management, 406–9, 421–2
- market segments, 414–17
- marketing, 406–7, 421–2
- marketing budget, 421
- marketing strategy, 417–19
- operating constraints on marketing, 419–21
- polarity between small and large attractions, 411–12
- sustainability issue, 417–18
- visitor experience, 412–14 *See also Specific attractions*

Visitor economy, 5, 10, 11
- ICT impact on, 251–2
  - opportunities for smaller businesses, 252

Visitors, 5, 144, 145
- international, 4, 5
- management of, 406–7
- same-day visitors, 5
- *See also* Consumers/customers

Wales Tourist Board, 260
WAYN, 268, 331
Weaknesses, 210
Web 2.0, 247, 266–9
- marketing through, 269

Web sites, *See* World Wide Web
Websites, 318
- affiliate marketing, 263, 289
- attracting people to, 262–3
- central role in the marketing mix, 261–9
  - uses of website for marketing, 262
- customer experience management, 265–6
- design, 264–5
- package tour marketing, 437
- promotional role, 323
- search engine marketing, 263–4
- *See also* Information materials; Internet

Wikipedia, 267
Wonderful Copenhagen, 188
Woodroffe, Simon, 453–4, 456
Workshops, 353–4
World Heritage Sites, 459–60, 463–4
- marketing, 460

World Tourism Organization (WTO), 7, 10
- definitions, 9

World Travel and Tourism Council, 69
World Wide Web, 246
- Web 2.0, 247, 266–9
- *See also* Internet; Websites

Wright, Tom, 310

XL, 206, 387, 391

Yield management, 395, 401
Yosemite National Park, 67
YOTEL case study, 453–8, 481, 484
- Strategy, 454
- Product and product experience, 455
- development and financing, 456
- The market, pricing and marketing activity, 456–7
- success to date, 458
- sustainability, 458

Youth Hostels Association (YHA), 364
YouTube, 249, 331

Zeithaml, V.A., 145, 146, 148, 151
Zoom, 206, 387